The Civil War Roster of
Davidson County, North Carolina

EDITED BY CHRISTOPHER M. WATFORD
AND FROM McFARLAND

---

*The Civil War in North Carolina, Volume 1:
The Piedmont: Soldiers' and Civilians' Letters and Diaries,
1861–1865* (2003; paperback 2009)

*The Civil War in North Carolina, Volume 2:
The Mountains: Soldiers' and Civilians' Letters and Diaries,
1861–1865* (2003; paperback 2009)

The Civil War Roster of Davidson County, North Carolina

Biographies of 1,996 Men Before, During and After the Conflict

CHRISTOPHER M. WATFORD

McFarland & Company, Inc., Publishers
Jefferson, North Carolina, and London

The present work is a reprint of the illustrated case bound edition of The Civil War Roster of Davidson County, North Carolina: Biographies of 1,996 Men Before, During and After the Conflict, *first published in 2001 by McFarland.*

LIBRARY OF CONGRESS CATALOGUING-IN-PUBLICATION DATA

Watford, Christopher M., 1978–
The Civil War roster of Davidson County, North Carolina :
biographies of 1,996 men before, during and after the conflict /
by Christopher M. Watford.
p.   cm.
Includes bibliographical references and index.

ISBN 978-0-7864-6121-9
softcover : 50# alkaline paper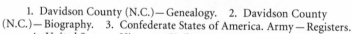

1. Davidson County (N.C.) — Genealogy.   2. Davidson County
(N.C.) — Biography.   3. Confederate States of America. Army — Registers.
4. United States — History — Civil War, 1861–1865 — Registers.
5. North Carolina — History — Civil War, 1861–1865 — Registers.
6. Veterans — North Carolina — Davidson County — Registers.
7. Soldiers — North Carolina — Davidson County — Registers.
8. Veterans — North Carolina — Davidson County — Biography.
9. Soldiers — North Carolina — Davidson County — Biography.   I. Title.

F262.D3 W38   2011   929'.375668 — dc21   01-64078

BRITISH LIBRARY CATALOGUING DATA ARE AVAILABLE

On the cover: John F. Heitman (Duke University Archives)

Manufactured in the United States of America

*McFarland & Company, Inc., Publishers
Box 611, Jefferson, North Carolina 28640
www.mcfarlandpub.com*

Contents

Preface

It was on a cold, rainy, or in other words, typical day in Boone, North Carolina, that I decided to start this project. It has developed into much more than I would ever have thought. From September 1996 to the fall of 1999, I worked steadily on this book. At first my goal was simply to compile a roster of Civil War soldiers from Davidson County, North Carolina. Something told me, however, not to stop with a list of names.

I have always held an interest in the American Civil War, and I decided to construct a "troop book" for my county, collecting all the records of the soldiers on my roster. However, it still did not feel right.

In February 1997, I helped an individual with his genealogy. When he explained that he only wanted to find his Civil War ancestor in order to join a Sons of Confederate Veterans Camp, I was upset. But this is what I needed to show me what was missing in my book project. Too often Civil War historians look at only four years of an individual's life, counting only the times he was present for muster — not the times he helped a neighbor build a home, the times he held his loving wife, the times he rode down a dusty, rutted road to attend church. A Civil War veteran's life was more than four years long.

I wanted to emphasize the humanity along with the name on the muster roll. What happened during the rest of his life? Did he have children? Are there any stories which would otherwise be ignored? I also wanted to provide an accurate interpretation of primary sources for

further study. These men were no different from the soldiers who stormed the beaches of Anzio, went into the fire at Belleau Wood, and stood against insurmountable odds at the Chosin Reservoir. These men were no different from those who returned, either. They were brothers, carpenters, farmers, husbands, clerks, laborers, fathers — citizens in peace, and soldiers in war. Their essence fills the deep reaches of our souls.

Researching this project entailed large amounts of paperwork and a certain methodology which had to be perfected before the project was complete. The first step to the work was a prospective roster. This initial roster included every soldier who had anything whatsoever to do with Davidson County: born, resided, enlisted, or buried there. From this large list, I began to construct master lists. These sheets were contained in five black binders which became my best friends over the next three years.

I organized the names alphabetically and began a look through the 1840, 1850, and 1860 Censuses. If a name was not found in at least two sources, it was eliminated. Then the project continued in full swing. I searched census records, marriage records, land transfers, cemetery records, family file folders, books, journals, and obituaries. Digging through all those records was not an easy task. However, doing the majority of the research in bulk, such as going through the 1870 Census for all five working volumes, helped to speed up the process. Regardless of this advantage, the research was by any reasonable standard slow. The volume of records searched at the Davidson County Public Library was enormous.

One of the chief difficulties in my research was the discovery of inaccuracies in existing sources. Errors were so common that I sometimes felt as if I were going against others in completing this project. While this work will surely contain flaws of its own, I have made it accurate to the best of my knowledge. By establishing a system of cross-checks, I have worked diligently to prevent any major discrepancies from entering the present work.

I have enjoyed every bit of my work, tiring and tedious as it has sometimes been. Working inside the community, I was able to develop good relationships with others who had a common interest. The help I received from the people of the county, whether at the Davidson County Public Library, at home, or at church, was priceless. Thank in no small part to their contributions, I believe this compilation to represent the most complete record possible of the lives of Davidson County's Civil War soldiers.

Acknowledgments

Those who know me are aware of the position this time-consuming project has taken in my life. I have never devoted such effort, time, money, and heart to any project — and that includes my college studies — but I am thankful I had the privilege of performing this task.

The research for this work was not conducted overnight, or without the help and courtesy of librarians at such institutions as the Davidson County Public Library in Lexington, the Forsyth County Public Library, and the Duke University Archives. Also, I am forever indebted to the staff of the Troupe County Archives in LaGrange, Georgia, for shedding light on one of our county's most interesting characters, and to the North Carolina Department of Cultural Resources and State Archives, whose work and publications made this possible.

As the common soldier relied on his commander and friends as well as his inner strength, so did I. I would like to thank those close to me who really helped me during this process: Jeanette Wilson, custodian of the genealogy room at the Lexington Library, whose service was invaluable; Betty Sowers, whose expertise and friendship gave me the boost I needed; Mrs. Bridget Nifong, who contributed much information at the early stages of the process. And Richard Conrad, whose brotherly advice and critique were much appreciated.

I would also like to thank many of the organizations which offered a guiding hand. To the Davidson County Genealogical Society, thank you for your many works which made my job much easier. God bless you! I would also like to thank the historical associations of Forsyth, Rowan, Randolph, and Wilkes counties for helping me track down some of our boys who sought greener fields elsewhere. Thanks also to the Lexington Wildcats Sons of Confederate Veterans Camp 85, the Davidson Guards SCV Camp, as well as to the Thompson-Robbins-Trice Chapter and the Robert E. Lee Chapter of the United Daughters of the Confederacy.

Unfortunately, I cannot list all of the individual contributors to my work; however, many of them do stand out. To Derek Bowers, Grady Beck, and Bud Everhart: your friendly words and assistance have been invaluable. To Doris Everhart, Hattie Snellings, Peggy Freedle, and Virginia Young: your beauty is matched only by your kindness. To Charlotte Charles Landi and James C. Harrison, I offer my gratitude. In addition, I wish to thank the many individuals, such as Brad Hunt, David Goss, and Gary Hall, who told me the stories of their ancestors.

For the many photographs in my work I would like to thank all of my sources, especially Betty Brown, Betty Sowers, and Mike Gordon.

To my comrades in arms, the "Hog Hill Guards" as well as the 4th N.C. State Troops, 30th and 37th N.C. Troops reactivated, I say, many times have we seen the gates of hell swing open, and in more ways than one.

I offer thanks to Tyler Patrick, my best friend and college roommate, as well as Lucas Clawson.

I am deeply grateful to my parents, Jeff and Brenda Watford, and my entire family, for their support; they should be honored to call 24 men listed in this book their ancestors.

Last of all, I acknowledge the men who are featured in this work, who allowed me to intrude into their lives to discover truth, dignity, and understanding more valuable than words can express.

Christopher M. Watford
July 2000

Introduction

The experience of the Davidson County soldier before, during, and after the American Civil War has gone largely uncelebrated. The Davidson County soldier was not a better or worse fighter than his comrades from other counties or states. He was not a soldier who fought for postwar-determined beliefs, and he was not a coward, as his enemy may have wished.

The Davidson soldier was, at his youngest, 14, and at his oldest, 65. At his poorest he was a farmer with four dollars to his name; at his wealthiest, a doctor whose 2000-acre plantation held 287 slaves. The Davidson County soldier volunteered for service on April 23, 1861, and he was taken against his will as late as February 1865. He ranged from a young man intent on impressing a lady by his soldierly exploits in 1861 to a bitter, bruised veteran in 1865. He served in fields as far north as Gettysburg, as far south as Savannah, and as far west as Centralia, Missouri. He was a four-year veteran, and he was listed as a deserter after one week.

The Davidson County soldier was a special man from a special place; however, he was an average part of his state's greater force. The average Davidsonian was a farmer of German descent, 24 years old when conscripted into service. He stood about 5 foot 8 and weighed 150 to 170 pounds. The Davidson soldier was highly literate; eight out of nine could read and write. He owned about $300 in personal property, had no slaves, and found a $50 enlistment bonus was too much to turn down. The Davidson County soldier was likely to be single when serving, and to marry less than five years after the war. Of the 1,996 Davidson County soldiers recorded in this book, 47 served for the Union Army.

The average Davidson County soldier was wounded at either Sharpsburg or Bristoe Station; if captured, he was confined at Point Lookout National Prison. The average Davidson County soldier returned from his term of service and took the oath of allegiance, and wept freely when he returned home.

This project is one of the first of its kind to my knowledge. Each entry includes dates of birth, death, and marriage, the names of the veteran's parents, spouse(s), and children, and the record of his military service. Wherever possible, I have included special stories, letters, pictures, journal entries, articles, and editorial comments. While some editing was done in the interest of length, most entries contain all the information that could be collected.

Each entry traces a soldier's life before the war, his wartime service, and, if he was fortunate, his life after the war. The biographies are meant to be as complete as possible, although the whereabouts of 2,000 men are difficult to know completely. Most of the men whose entries end with "no further records" moved out of the county for unknown destinations between census recordings or other records that are time and place specific. In some cases, the veteran is tracked to another county, then lost. Sometimes there are no records to be found.

In an attempt to bridge the gap between these biographies and the vast history of the American Civil War overall, the text commences with an exploration of the county's role in the war. This historical section offers a background to the biographies as well as a key to understanding elements of the biographies that might otherwise be confusing.

I hope that this work, in some small way, does justice and offers honor to the lives of these men.

Davidson County Before, During and After the War: A Brief History

Antebellum Davidson and the Commencement of Hostilities, 1860–1861

The county of Davidson was organized in 1822 from what was once a part of Rowan County. Upon this division, Lexington was established as the county seat, and the Yadkin River was affixed as the western boundary. The county, taking its name from martyred patriot General William Lee Davidson, had already made a name for itself on the battlefields of the Seven Years' War, the American Revolution, the Cherokee Wars, and the War of 1812.

The geography of the county is both diverse and homogeneous. The soil is mostly composed of Carolina red clay, with underlying beds of slate. Creeks that traverse the land, such as Abbott's, Rich Fork, Tom's, Leonard's, and Swearing, show evidence of relatively young age. Perhaps the best land for agriculture in the county is the fertile flood plain of the Yadkin River. Along the banks of the Yadkin lies the most valuable "bottom land," suitable for most any crop. Two mountains, Three-Hat and High Rock, whose local relief measure greater than 600 feet, are apparent in the Davidson sky. To the

south, the worn peaks of the ancient Uwharrie Mountains roll gently, and upon their slopes, wilderness flourishes, even in modern times.

The people of the county also offered examples of diversity and homogeneity. The 1860 Census lists residents of nine different extractions, immigrants from six foreign countries, including the Ottoman Empire, and settlers originally born in 11 U.S. states, including Maine and Kentucky. However, three quarters of the population could trace its lineage to the Germanic areas of central Europe. The majority of settlers came from the regions of the southern Holy Roman Empire, such as Baden, Hesse, Swiess, Mahren, Bavaria, Alsace, Bohemia, and the Electorate of the Palatine. The mass migration of these people began in the ports of Holland. They arrived in Pennsylvania then moved down the great wagon road to recently opened tracts of land, which had been granted to the lord of Granville in the early half of the eighteenth century. The county was also inhabited by English, Scots, and Irish, who brought their own heritage, language, and Anglicism to the county.

Religion was extremely important to the people of Davidson. Although the Reformed church was dominant in the county on the eve of the war, its influence was not as absolute as it once was. The Baptist and Methodist denominations, which were present in the county as early as 1759 and 1784, respectively, had exploded in church founding and membership in the two decades preceding the conflict to equal the numbers of the Reformed congregations. Therefore, in 1860, the county held three prominent Protestant denominations: Reformed, Baptist, and Methodist. A Presbyterian church was founded in each of the two cities, but only Lexington had an Episcopal church, the church of the southern elite, in 1860.

The county boasted of two incorporated cities, Lexington and Thomasville, and the affluent village of Clemmonsville, which is now part of Forsyth County. Lexington was founded in 1789 and experienced steady growth as the county's center of government, society, and commerce. By 1860, Lexington had 1,543 residents within its limits. Thomasville, originally called Thomas' Depot, was officially founded in 1852 as part of a scheme of Whig J. W. Thomas to capitalize on the growth expected as a result of the construction of the state railroad. Clemmonsville, in the extreme northwest of the county, was the home of nearly 200 residents, including the wealthy Ellis, Moss, Hampton, and Douthit families.

Education was one of the foremost enterprises in the county. Beginning in the 1840s, a move was made to increase the number of common schools. A common school, often one room with students of all ages, was established in each of the townships, and three schools were founded in the areas around each of the cities. The college system of the county was led by Yadkin Institute, which was founded by the Honorable Henry C. Walser and received its charter in 1860. This institute was closely associated with the Methodist church and offered courses in theology, rhetoric, logic, basic medicine, and classical languages. In addition to Yadkin, the close proximity to Braxton Craven's Trinity College offered the privileged sons of the county another option in their education. Female academies were also founded in each of the two cities. Lexington began its female seminary in 1857; Thomasville's equivalent had first opened its doors in 1855. Thomasville's Glen Anna Baptist Female Seminary operated only three weeks at its Randolph Street location before J. W. Thomas bought the school and constructed a new building for it on East Main Street in Thomasville.

Industrially, Lexington was a premier city in the Piedmont. Within the city limits were many mercantile stores, hotels, saddlers, gunsmiths, silversmiths, laundries, and various other enterprises. The city also contained professionals, including attorneys such as James M. Leach and Jesse Hargrave, and physicians such as A. A. Hill, William Lindsay, and R. L. Payne. Financially,

the city was strong, and prominent capitalists, such as Lewis Hanes and John March, founded two banks. Land speculating, trading, and investing in secure mineral rights had great impact on the financial scene in Lexington as well.

Thomasville was conceived for business. The first true industry in the town was a mortuary. The Thomas Store shortly followed, and in three years, two other companies moved to the fledgling city and gave it a boost. The Lines Shoe Factory arrived in 1855, with the Shelly Boot Company following in 1858. These two firms succeeded in the new town, and soon a tobacco warehouse was constructed. Meanwhile, the carpentry business was building under the influence of David S. Westmoreland, Samuel Dorsett, and Willis Whitehart.

Out in the county, the underground riches of the central Carolina slate belt were being tapped in the mining complex of southern central Davidson County. Individual mines named Sechrist, Ida, Tysinger, Conrad Hill, and Silver Hill contributed to the first U.S. gold rush, as well as producing high grades of silver and lead. In 1860, the Silver Hill mining company was the largest employer of free men in the county. In Tyro, the tavern remained the center of friendly conversation, while the Tyro Iron Works, operated by the Thompson family, began to produce items from handheld threshers to cotton gins.

To support these booming industries, the county required a large agricultural base. The majority of the population worked as farmers who grew one crop and sold the excess to provide their income. However, typical of southern agriculture, the plantation dominated. Earlier estimates of the impact of the plantation on the county were completely underestimated. The large plantations, mostly along the Yadkin, held exactly 2,745 slaves in 1860. The largest slaveholder in the county was Peter W. Hairston, an absentee owner whose primary concern was the Cooloomee Plantation in Davie County. The overwhelming majority of people of African descent were slaves, with the exception of 172 free blacks, whose names included Adams, Sears, and Kennedy. From an economic standpoint, slavery was the foremost industry in Davidson County.

The influence of the military on southern culture was apparent in Davidson County. Two prewar militia units were formed in the county during the 1850s. The first such unit was known as the Davidson Guards (later to serve as Company A, 21st N.C. Troops). This unit of 62 men, commanded by James M. Leach, was formed on July 4, 1851. Members of the Davidson Guards drilled according to then-current U.S. Army regulations, but its gatherings were more like community festivals than military camps. The role of this militia would change in the wake of John Brown's raid on Harpers Ferry, Virginia, in 1859. Once a unit to display "soldierly exploits on a mock battlefield," the Davidson Guards had now become defenders of the South after the dreaded general slave revolt predicted by H. R. Hepler. In direct response to John Brown's raid, Thomasville formed its own militia company. The unit of 55 blue-clad troops marched together for the first time on December 17, 1859, under a silk flag made by the students at the Glenn Anna Seminary. The colors resembled the Culpeper Militia flag of Revolutionary War fame and were accepted by the company's commander, William B. Lewis. These units engaged one another in several "battles" in a field south of Thomasville, but their true purpose would become evident on April 12, 1861.

The political climate of the county focused on its three statesmen: Henry C. Walser, James M. Leach, and John W. Thomas, a Democrat and two Whigs, respectively. All three were advocates of the North Carolina Railroad and the improvement of the common schools. Leach, who served as a U.S. Congressman at different times, voted "no" on the inclusion of the Fugitive Slave Act in the Compromise of 1850.

Socially, the family was the most important unit of the community. The majority of farms were one-family farms with both parents and, on average, five children. The mother was the operator and keeper of the home, and she also was expected to be an amateur physician, a teacher, and the spiritual leader of the children. The father was the breadwinner, and he took the male children into the fields or mines with him upon their coming of age. A man was expected to be the spiritual leader of his family, but he was also allowed such diversions as trophy hunting and moderate gambling. Aspirations toward high society were evident in Lexington, as ladies waited for the latest dresses from Europe. In Davidson County, as in the rest of the South, European, especially French, influence was apparent in fashion, dress, and marriage.

The gathering storm began to offer the first drops of its deadly rain on April 12, 1861, when Confederate troops, after taking Fort Moultrie, South Carolina, turned their attention to Fort Sumter. The fall of Sumter sent shock waves throughout the country. Soon, states hoping to compromise and keep tensions at bay were forced to choose sides in the deadly enterprise.

On April 21, 1861, Presbyterian minister Willis Miller announced the news in his sermon and at once called for the Thomasville Rifles to be raised. Two days later, 55 men reported along the tracks at Thomas' Depot. These men boarded a train for Raleigh the same day. In a short time, the Davidson Guards were called into service by former U.S. Congressman Leach. On May 8, 1861, this company, after forming in front of the Davidson County courthouse, boarded a train destined for the capital city. Less than a week later, a company of volunteers known as the Lexington Wildcats mustered at the Lexington train station and departed to their destiny on May 14, 1861. The Thomasville Rifles and the Lexington Wildcats were assigned as Companies B and I of the 4th N.C. Volunteer Infantry, respectively. The Davidson Guards were assigned as Company A of the 11th N.C. Volunteer Infantry.

Soon the blue of the militia was replaced with the well-deserved gray of well-drilled, eager troops. The 4th N.C. Volunteers were assigned to Junius Daniel and were ordered to Suffolk to perform guard duty in the Tidewater area and to protect the recently taken Norfolk Navy Yards. The 11th N.C. Volunteers were assigned to Bonham's Brigade of the Confederate Army of the Potomac, commanded by P. G. T. Beauregard. The 11th N.C. Volunteers were held in reserve during the first battle of Manassas on July 21, 1861.

At home, Davidsonians continued to enlist as 30 volunteers from the southern area of the county traveled to Salisbury, arriving on July 23, 1861. The company formed three days later and was unofficially named the Fisher Light Infantry in honor of the late colonel of the 6th N.C. State Troops, who was killed at Manassas. They soon became Company F of the 7th N.C. State Troops and were assigned duty along the state's coastal plain. On September 19, 1861, another substantial group of men from the northern area of the county traveled to Salem to volunteer for 12 months of service. One of these men, John W. Payne, was elected as a lieutenant in a company which would later become Company G of the 2nd Battalion, N.C. Infantry.

The flood of Davidson men leaving the county to volunteer in other units did not stop. In September an independent company of cavalry formed in Davie County. On October 29, 1861, many of the men from the Midway and Lexington areas crossed the river to volunteer in the Carolina Rangers, which would serve in Wise's Legion for three weeks and would then become Company B of the 10th Virginia Cavalry Regiment.

On November 26, 1861, commissions for the 1861 organization of the militia were issued; a second issue was granted on December 13, 1861; and a final round was granted on February 13, 1862. These men hoped to serve as officers in the militia and remain at home; however, David Smith and George W. Palmer, both field officers in the 1861 militia, would later volunteer for service.

The first eight months of the "one-month" war proved successful for Confederate forces in the field, as well as for the state quartermaster service, whose efficiency and organization proved to be invaluable at such a distressed time. With the resources already committed, Davidson County, and the state, prepared for a long war. Disease initially proved to be the deadliest enemy of Davidsonians in service, taking 18 men.

With the onset of the first winter of the war, troops began to settle into makeshift winter cabins and permanent camps. The 4th and 11th N.C. Volunteers remained at post in Virginia. Men of Company F of the 7th N.C. State Troops were dispatched to the New Bern area, where they would eventually join the brigade of L. B. Branch. The Carolina Rangers patrolled the areas around Perquimans County and Norfolk, Virginia. The 2nd N.C. Battalion received its fateful post at Roanoke Island.

Volunteers and Conscripts: 1862

The new year dawned with somewhat bleak prospects for the county. Davidsonians at home and in the field were left to combat one of the coldest winters ever experienced in the South. For the most part, the impact on families was great, but not profound, as the majority of Davidson soldiers in active service were young men who were not the principal breadwinners of their families. Regardless, the people of the county dealt with loneliness, underemployment, and new outbreaks of pneumonia and typhoid fever. To put future events in perspective, this was not the worst of it.

The winter months saw a quick fall of North Carolina's Tidewater region to the forces of Ambrose Burnside's 9th U.S. Army Corps. In the way of this invading force were the men of the 2nd N.C. Battalion, who were ordered to hold Roanoke Island, the site of two failed attempts at colonization in the late 1500s by Sir Walter Raleigh. The 2nd Battalion was attacked on the morning of February 8, 1862. The battle between the island's defenders and the Union forces lasted until almost night. In the end, the battalion surrendered and was sent to Elizabeth City, North Carolina, in Perquimans County, which had previously fallen to Union forces. On February 21, 1862, the men of the 2nd Battalion, which included 51 soldiers from Davidson County, were paroled and released on the promise not to take up arms for six months. The men abided by this ruling, leaving the battalion inactive until its reorganization in July 1862.

The last gasp of winter and the news of North Carolina's invasion spurred another round of volunteer enlistment. Men from all portions of the county came forward to defend their state and, of course, collected the substantial enlistment bonus. In February and March 1863, hundreds of men volunteered. These men were sent to newly forming units such as the Davidson Artillery, Company A of the 10th N.C. Heavy Artillery Battalion, Companies A and I of the 42nd N.C. Troops, Company K of the 45th NCT, Companies B and H of the 48th NCT, and Company A of the 54th NCT. These units were established, organized, and sent into the field as soon as possible. The urgency became even more apparent when, on March 14, 1862, a Confederate contingent, including the 7th N.C. State Troops, was defeated in the vicinity of New Bern, North Carolina.

Back in Virginia, the volunteer regiments were elevated to state troops and assumed new names; the 4th Volunteers became the 14th NCT and the 11th Volunteers became the 21st NCT. The 14th was assigned to reinforce and help improve the defenses along the Warwick-Yorktown line by General Joe Johnston, once news of the arrival of a massive Union force under General G. B. McClellan was confirmed. The 21st NCT was assigned to the command of Thomas J. "Stonewall" Jackson as part of the new Valley Army.

The men of the 14th were soon welcomed into the struggle on the peninsula formed by the York and James rivers. After nearly ten months of training and guard duty, the 14th NCT was involved in the Confederate victory of Lee's Mill on April 16, 1862. During a lull in the action on both Virginia fronts, the old volunteer units were reorganized, and new officers were elected. The commissioned officers of both companies of the 14th were replaced with more qualified soldiers, while a similar shake-up occurred in the 21st NCT.

By April 15, 1862, the first Conscript Act was passed into law by the Confederate Congress. The act provided that all men between the ages 18 and 35 were eligible for service if conscripted. Many of Davidson County's wealthier citizens were still able to avoid service, since the act also stated that craftsmen, millers, and others who contributed to wartime production were exempt. In addition, even if a citizen were conscripted, he could find a willing man and pay him to take his place.

The 21st NCT was placed in the brigade of Isaac Trimble and performed valorous duty on the battlefields of the Shenandoah. As part of Stonewall Jackson's "foot cavalry," the 21st shared in victories at McDowell, Cross Keys, Port Republic, and Front Royal. On May 25, the Valley Army and the 21st NCT won an important victory, liberating the crucial valley city of Winchester. This victory was at a great cost. The Davidson Guards lost its captain, Jacob C. Hedgecock, along with 16 of its best soldiers.

With the Union forces of General Banks checked and defeated by Stonewall Jackson, the pressure on Richmond resumed. Confederate forces began to evacuate the prepared defenses and retreated along their supply lines to Richmond. Fighting as the rear guard of Colston's Brigade, the 14th NCT fought valiantly around the historic city, which had served as Virginia's colonial capital. One of the tolls of the action on May 5, 1862, was a 15-year-old member of the 14th named Richard Penry. A resolution was passed back home in the county to honor his sacrifice.

Twenty-five days later, the Union Army was less than 25 miles from Richmond. Political pressure forced General Joseph E. Johnston to attack an isolated part of McClellan's force in the Seven Pines area. The 14th was engaged once again, suffering minor losses, but on May 30, 1862, the commander of the eastern Confederate forces, Johnston, fell wounded. Jefferson Davis replaced Johnston with his close advisor, Robert E. Lee who, upon assuming command, began to prepare the Army of Northern Virginia for an offensive move which would expel the Union from the peninsula. New rounds of conscription were ordered, troops were sent up, and new brigade alignments took place. The 14th, which had been part of Colston's Brigade, was now assigned to the command of G. B. Anderson, along with the 2nd NCST, 4th NCST, and 30th NCT.

On June 25, 1862, began the Seven Days, a series of battles fought around Richmond. The 48th NCT fought at King's School House, losing at least 43 men from Davidson County. The unit performed well in its first engagement, despite being outnumbered seven to one. The 7th, 14th, and 21st went on to fight at Mechanicsville, Gaines' Mill, Frayser's Farm, and Malvern Hill. At Malvern Hill, Virginia, on July 1, 1862, it was decided that this would be the decisive blow to defeat McClellan. However, uncoordinated attacks by three columns left confusion in the ranks, and the overwhelming fire power of the Union artillery forced the Confederate advance to halt. Several days later, McClellan withdrew his army unmolested by attack.

Lee's goal to expel the Army of the Potomac from Richmond was achieved, but not without price. North Carolina forces suffered 5,000 losses, including 154 men who called Davidson County home. However, the Confederate forces had won, and, by the beginning of August 1862, conscripts began replenishing the ranks of the 7th, 14th, 15th, and 48th N.C. regiments, as well as adding members to Company A of the 54th NCT and Company B of the 57th NCT. On August 9, the 7th NCST (Branch's Brigade) and the 21st NCT (Trimble's Brigade) of Jackson's corps resumed the offensive at Cheat Mountain; they returned to the Manassas area on August 27, 1862.

The men of Jackson's Second Corps made a courageous stand on the next day. These units included the 21st NCT and the 7th NCST, which took up defensive positions along an unfinished railroad bed. During the hard fighting, the supply of ammunition was exhausted, and the men began to hurl rocks at the advancing enemy. The Union commander, General John Pope, believed that he had isolated Jackson's corps, and he planned to destroy it when the battle resumed the next day. However, Lee brought up the remainder of his army under General James Longstreet. When Longstreet's corps attacked, Pope's army was quickly forced to withdraw, and it began a rapid retreat to the safety of Washington. More conscription in the county occurred on September 10, 1862. This latest large round placed 27 men into the 61st NCT.

Lee, flushed with success, invaded the North, hoping to win a decisive victory which would either force the Union to negotiate or encourage British intervention. The Confederate column crossed the Potomac River on September 4, 1862, and passed through the Maryland countryside. On September 13 and 14, the Union Army engaged Confederate forces at Crampton's Pass and Fox's Gap, where the 15th NCT and the 14th NCT of Garland's Brigade and Anderson's Brigade, respectively, were serving. The 14th suffered only lightly, but of the 15th NCT, nearly 20 Davidson men were wounded or captured in the fight. On September 15, 1862, the federal depot at Harpers Ferry fell to Jackson's corps. Upon collecting supplies, he immediately sent two of his three divisions across the Shepherdstown Pike to assist Lee.

On September 17, 1862, Lee needed all the help he could get. The action near Sharpsburg, Maryland, opened on the Confederate left where Jackson's two divisions stood poised in front of a cornfield. Joseph Hooker's corps opened the attack, and a vicious battle ensued. Engaged in the fighting were the men of the 21st NCT. Despite a spirited resistance, Jackson's forces began to defend their positions around the West Woods. The Dunkard Church became the next scene of Davidson sacrifice. The 48th NCT, as a part of Manning's makeshift brigade, deployed in the vicinity of the small white building with the order to charge. Once they cleared the tree line behind the church, seven Federal regiments appeared before them. The 48th advanced but ran into problems when it had to break into two to get around the church. When the unit tried to reform, it was broken apart by vicious Federal fire. The right wing of the regiment, which included Companies B, H, and K, was hit extremely hard and endured great losses. However, the remainder of the force, spurred on by Major Huske, successfully checked the Federal advance before falling back to the safety of the woods. The 48th NCT had 483 men killed or wounded, including 112 from Davidson County.

Toward the Confederate center, in a sunken wagon

road, stood the men of the 14th NCT of Anderson's Brigade, which had fought at South Mountain two days prior. Two large Federal divisions bore down upon D. H. Hill's force, which included Rodes' Alabama Brigade. For over three hours, the Confederates fought off countless Union assaults, before confusion erupted into tragedy. With mistaken orders, Rodes' Alabamians began to fall back, taking a number of reinforcements with them. With a huge gap visible, the Federals began to pour lead into the road. What was once a perfect defensive position turned into a death trap. The two Tarheel brigades found themselves awash in a sea of blue and fighting for their lives. At the end of this phase of the battle, the Union had captured the sunken road, as well as the colors of the 14th NCT. The survivors reformed with the division of R. H. Anderson and tried to regain their ranks. In the end, the majority of Companies B and I was destroyed, and over half of the 14th Regiment was lost.

Later in the day, the Union again attempted to break the Confederate line. This attack was made against Cobb's Georgia Brigade, which, at the time, included the 15th NCT. The men of Cobb's Brigade held off desperate Union assaults and successfully defended a stone bridge until the line was finally broken. The situation was now desperate for the Confederates. Their flank was collapsing, and Union reinforcements began rushing in. However, the timely arrival of A. P. Hill's division saved the Confederate right from complete and utter collapse. The 7th NCST was present in this force, but it was the last unit to take the field, being in reserve along with the rest of its brigade. With the horrible day over, 70 Davidsonians were left dead where they fell. Along with the dead were at least 275 wounded and around 30 captured, a saddening total of nearly 400 losses from one county alone.

The battle of Sharpsburg was the deadliest single day in American history; however, there was no rest for the Army of Northern Virginia. Within two days the Confederates successfully fell back into the safety of Virginia. By December, the Confederate forces were once again pressed, this time at Fredericksburg, Virginia.

On December 13, 1862, the battle of Fredericksburg unfolded. Action developed first on the Confederate right, where Jackson was positioned. The 21st, 54th and 57th NCT were present. In their first battle, the 54th NCT and the 57th NCT, then in Law's Brigade, made a "simply glorious" counter charge on Prospect Hill, forcing the Union to concentrate its attacks on a stone wall near the crest of Marye's Heights. Two Davidson units helped to defend the stone wall and the Confederate left: the 15th NCT and the 48th NCT. The 48th NCT once again lost nearly half its number. After the smoke cleared, 14 different Yankee attacks had not broken the Confederate line. These attacks resulted in over 12,000 Union casualties and 2,000 Confederate casualties.

As the year drew to a close, winter quarters were established, and commanders and men began to assess the year's gains and losses. From a Davidson County standpoint, the year had seen hard-won victories in the Seven Days, Second Manassas, and Fredericksburg battles. However, it had also seen defeat at Roanoke Island and sheer destruction at Sharpsburg. Of 1,000 men in service, over 400 were lost in action to wounds and to disease in this year alone. For the Davidson units in the Army of Northern Virginia, the winter would bring a welcome and well-deserved rest.

Outside of the Army of Northern Virginia, other units, such as Companies A and I of the 42nd NCT, continued performing their various assignments. The two companies of cavalry offered faithful service, while the militia units back home began to deal with a more serious issue.

The year 1862 was harsh in the county. Over 1,000 of the county's best men had been conscripted into service. Women were left alone in their households. Young boys and older men were busy trying to make a living. By December 1862, the banks were insolvent. A peace movement rally was held at Kennedy's School House, which was quickly broken up by the 65th N.C. Militia. In addition, the two units of militia were plagued by internal conflict, as well as by a situation in the county which foretold much bigger problems in the future.

Even with Confederate victories in the fields of Virginia, the reality of war was that, regardless of victory or defeat, the county would sustain considerable losses in both the human sense and the economic sense. Although the war was far from over, 1863 offered a new hope for victory.

The Universe of Battle: 1863

The first of January came and went as just another day. The first two years of the war had, overall, gone well for Confederate forces in the East. Davidson County troops rested, and their brigades were realigned. The 14th NCT remained, with the 2nd, 4th, and 30th NCT, in a brigade now commanded by Stephen D. Ramseur. The 15th NCT was transferred to the brigade of John R. Cooke, joining the 48th NCT. The brigade of Robert F. Hoke would contain three Davidson units: the 21st NCT, the 54th NCT, and the 57th NCT, along with the 6th NCST. The 10th Virginia Cavalry was assigned to William H. F. Lee's cavalry, and the independent cavalry was assigned to a Georgia battalion formed in Craven County.

The only two units not in the Army of Northern Virginia were the 42nd NCT, recently assigned to a post at Weldon, North Carolina, and Battery A of the 10th N.C. Heavy Artillery, which was assigned to garrison duty in Brunswick County.

At home, the more than 35 men from Company A of the 54th NCT had been serving as lead miners back in the county since October 1862. The militia had its hands full as monthly reports from the state's adjutant general named deserters to be arrested. The output of the family farms was nearly destroyed. The plantations' economic contribution became less significant as time wore on. In March 1863, 100 slaves were transferred from the county for manual labor in Halifax County. This detail was escorted by Colonel Joseph Crouse of the 65th NCM and did not return until May 27, 1863.

The third April of the war saw the brigades of Cooke and Ransom at home in North Carolina. On April 9, the 48th NCT took part in the destruction of the Federal gunboat *George Washington* at Charleston, North Carolina. Back in North Carolina, men of the 15th NCT and the 49th NCT were attacked at Sandy Ridge on April 20. The majority of the captives were held for only two months.

May would bring about the greatest Confederate victory in the East, although the battle of Chancellorsville, May 1–3, still did not predict a certain future. The majority of action in the battle centered around Jackson's flanking march. Jackson took his Second Corps, containing the 7th, 14th, 21st, and 57th NCT, down a plank road, emerging on the extreme Union right. Joseph Hooker, Union commander, believed Jackson to be retreating, not maneuvering to appear en masse on his flank.

The flank attack surged forward, sweeping the woods of both deer and Federal troops. The attack was pressed by Jackson, sending the divisions of both D. H. Hill and A. P. Hill charging forward. The men of the 14th NCT advanced on the right of Ramseur's brigade, clearing the woods of the 150th Pennsylvania and holding off two Federal counterattacks before falling back to Hazel Grove to replenish their cartridge boxes. The 7th advanced with the rest of its brigade while two of the units of Hoke's Brigade in Richard S. Ewell's division pushed their opponents back.

In the aftermath of the battle, Jackson, the brilliant commander of all Davidson County infantry units, fell to a friendly shot. Jackson, refusing to identify himself to a Confederate picket, was shot in the arm on the rainy evening of the third. His arm was successfully amputated, but he died of pneumonia on May 6, 1863. With such a victory, Lee had the freedom to advance once again into the North, inviting foreign intervention, clearing Virginia

of the enemy, and trying to draw Union forces away from the beleaguered defenders of Vicksburg, Mississippi.

With the onset of June came an escalation of both temperature and the war. Lee decided to take his army into Pennsylvania. Preparations were made to draw up additional troops for the campaign. The brigades of Cooke and Ransom, containing the 15th, 48th, and 49th, were ordered to the Richmond area to defend the city if it were attacked by Union forces while the main body of the army was away.

Without Jackson, the army was reorganized into three corps. The 14th and the rest of Ramseur's Brigade (Rodes' division) and the men of Hoke's Brigade (Jubal Early's division) were members of Lieutenant General Ewell's Second Corps. The 7th NCT of Lane's Brigade (Pender's division) was part of the Third Corps, commanded by Lieutenant General Ambrose P. Hill.

With Richmond guarded, Lee advanced across central Virginia and once again into the Shenandoah Valley. After a brief skirmish at Berryville, Virginia, which the 14th NCT retook after a brief fight, the army was free to cross the Potomac River. The 14th was the first unit to cross back into Maryland. After a long, dusty, and hot march over the roads of Maryland and southern Pennsylvania, the two armies drew close at a small town called Gettysburg.

The battle, originally started between Heth's division and the Union cavalry under John Buford, began to build as units started pouring in from both sides. The 7th NCST of Pender's division as well as the lead elements of Early's division struck from the northeast of the town. The 14th NCT was to be held in reserve while the rest of Rodes' division attacked. However, General Ramseur ordered his brigade to swing forward from its rear position and attack the Federal line. The ensuing attack shattered the Union troops, who had taken position behind a small stone fence. The 14th NCT followed up its success and moved into the town along with two other Davidson units, the 2nd N.C. Battalion and the 45th NCT, both of Grimes' Brigade.

The first of July ended with a large amount of Confederate success; however, the Union still held the high ground. The 14th NCT was posted inside the town and would not see action again, nor would the 2nd N.C. Battalion, which sustained heavy losses, or the 45th NCT. While for these units rest was the order, the night of July 2 saw both the 21st NCT and the 57th NCT engaged in a failed attack on Union positions on Culp's Hill. The third of July would see the worst disaster ever suffered by the Army of Northern Virginia: Pickett's Charge.

The only Davidson unit to participate in the charge was the 7th NCST. The 7th waited along with its brigade while an artillery duel raged over the ground between two low ridges. Once the artillery ceased, the men were ordered forward. They advanced into long-range artillery, then into short-range artillery, and then into the mouths of Federal muskets. The 7th continued to advance as its ranks evaporated and was able to make it to the Union lines before being destroyed by on-rushing Federal reinforcements. The great gamble was a failure. The 7th NCST along with its brigade sustained heavy losses. Yet, the fight was not over as men of Company B of the 10th Virginia Cavalry were engaged in a massive cavalry fight. While the 10th Virginia as a regiment had only three men killed overall, the engagement at the east ridge added insult to injury.

On the 4th of July, the Confederates began to retreat through southern Pennsylvania and central Maryland, continually harassed by Union cavalry. The end of the Gettysburg campaign came at Falling Waters on July 14, 1863, when the 7th NCST was engaged in a rearguard battle. With that engagement, the Confederates returned to the safety of Virginia. While the campaign helped to free the hard-pressed state of Virginia from war for over 30 days, it was obviously a substantial defeat.

In July 1863, a new unit was formed in Davidson County. With the state's creation of "a guard for home defense," the Davidson County Home Guard was born. The 14th Battalion N.C. Home Guard was composed of five companies and was commanded by former Lexington Wildcat Jesse Hargrave. The first assignments of the Home Guard were similar to that of the militia, which continued to exist alongside the new force. The immediate concerns of the Home Guard for 1863 included guarding the Silver Hill mine and the bridges, as well as maintaining details, enforcing the law, and arresting deserters.

Much farther south, the 61st NCT of Clingman's Brigade was assigned to defend the besieged city of Charleston, South Carolina. On July 16, 1863, the 61st NCT was held in reserve while Strong's Federal Brigade, which included the now-famous 54th Massachusetts, attacked the Confederate stronghold of Fort Wagner. The attack was repulsed by Confederate forces, with the 61st NCT ready to advance as reinforcements. The 61st would remain with Clingman's Brigade at Charleston for the remainder of the year.

As the colorful leaves of northern Virginia began to fall, Lee was determined not to give up. The general decided to strike back at Bristoe Station. On October 14, 1863, the 15th and 48th NCT was a part of the battle of Bristoe Station. Cooke's Brigade, along with Pettigrew's old brigade, advanced against a railroad line occupied by two Federal divisions. The attack failed and was saved only by the orderly retreat of McRae. The 48th was hit hard once again, losing a large percentage of its men to injury and capture. In November and December 1863, the 21st, 54th, and 57th NCT participated in the unsuccessful Mine Run campaign.

Perhaps encouraged by their success at Bristoe Station, the Federals decided to cross the Rappahannock River. The 54th and 57th NCT were posted at Rappahannock Station on the evening of November 7, 1863. The garrison was overwhelmed in the night by a much larger Federal force. Overall, the surprise attack at Rappahannock Station netted the Union over 2,000 prisoners, including the whole of Company A of the 54th NCT and all but eight of Company B of the 57th NCT. The rest of November saw the retirement of the armies into winter camp. The Army of Northern Virginia had suffered greatly in the past six months and began to recover at its quarters in Culpeper County, Virginia.

Elsewhere, the 42nd NCT of Martin's Brigade was engaged in securing and defending eastern North Carolina from further Federal incursions. The 10th N.C. Heavy Artillery was still performing garrison duty at a variety of posts, including Fort Caswell and Battery Anderson. Conscripts of Davidson County arrived at Camp Holmes and were sent to their respective units by the end of the year.

Into the Maelstrom: 1864

It was the second winter of the war and the men of the Army of Northern Virginia were recovering from the last fall's battles. At home, insurgents led by Davidson County native William Owens had taken to the Uwharrie Mountains. What began as an act of peaceful Quaker protest had become a harbor for deserters and those wishing to avoid conscription. Before long, these "outliers" were well equipped and, thanks to overzealous militia action, belligerent.

In late January 1864, a new campaign under the command of General George Pickett was launched, ostensibly to free Union-occupied eastern North Carolina. While this was the spiritual goal, the real objective was to defend the Weldon rail line and to retake the cities of Kinston, Washington, Plymouth, and New Bern. For this campaign Davidson County was represented by the 21st NCT, 54th NCT, 57th NCT (Hoke's Brigade), 61st NCT (Clingman's Brigade), and 42nd NCT (Martin's Brigade). The first battle in this campaign was fought at Bachelor's Bridge on February 2, 1864. The men of Hoke's Brigade occupied Federal forces while the men of the 42nd NCT charged across the creek and succeeded in taking two blockhouses and compelling a Federal withdrawal.

Winter weather forced a break in the campaign. On March 8, 1864, the 42nd NCT stopped to rest in Tarboro, North Carolina. On March 24, 1864, Hoke's Brigade was defeated in a huge snowball fight with Corse's Brigade. Although fun and games provided a break in the monotony, with the onset of spring, Plymouth became an objective.

The small army under the command of Robert F. Hoke included the 21st NCT and the 61st NCT. On April 20, 1864, Hoke's forces stormed the Federal entrenchments and defeated the Union garrison under General Dan Wessells. Not included in this attack were the 54th NCT and the 57th NCT, which were left at Kinston to secure the town. Hoke's great victory earned him a promotion to major general. His brigade, which contained the 21st, 54th, and 57th NCT, was taken over by General Lewis. After the fall of Plymouth, Hoke set his eyes on Washington, North Carolina, which he had learned was being evacuated. Four days later, all the units of Lewis' brigade set out for the city. Washington was liberated by these forces on April 25, 1864.

The campaign was going well. Only one, very large objective remained: New Bern. Pickett's command began to advance in the direction of Craven County. On May 4, 1864, Lewis captured Pollocksville, and Pickett made plans to lay siege to New Bern. However, confused orders led to a failure to disrupt Federal communications and transportation, and orders to return to the Army of Northern Virginia ended the campaign. On May 8, 1864, all units were transported to the Richmond-Petersburg area by rail.

With a new overall commander, U. S. Grant, the Union Army began to press Lee's army hard and often. The two armies were engaged in the vicinity of Chancellorsville on May 5–6, 1864. In this battle, known as the Wilderness, the 2nd Battalion and the 45th NCT (Daniel's Brigade), the 14th NCT (Ramseur's Brigade), and the 15th and 48th NCT of Cooke's Brigade were all engaged. All three brigades were in different divisions, but they nevertheless saw extensive action from 11 A.M. through the next day. The ground was so heavily wooded that maneuvering was nearly impossible, and the danger of fire became a reality. The ensuing flames consumed much of the Wilderness, catching wounded soldiers in its grip and causing hurried withdrawals and panic. The battle of the Wilderness lasted for two days. Although Lee had inflicted great losses upon his new adversary, his army suffered substantial losses as well. Once again, a large number of Davidsonians were among the casualties.

Despite the successful defense of the Wilderness, Lee was compelled to retreat to the prepared entrenchments defending the area around Spotsylvania Court House.

Federal probing attacks attempted to assess the strengths of the troops in the Confederate works. Grant chose to attack a salient in the line that was known as the "Mule Shoe" on May 12, 1864. The Federal assault hit at daybreak and quickly overwhelmed the defenders of the first line of trenches. Soon a flood of Confederates began retreating in disorder for the safety of other trenches. Lee, fearing the further advance of the Union force, found it absolutely necessary to retake the Mule Shoe.

Ramseur's Brigade, which contained a thousand men at most, including the 14th NCT, ran headlong into a maelstrom of fire. The brigade charged out of the Confederate works and straight into the Mule Shoe, retaking it at muzzle point. The 14th NCT occupied the center of Ramseur's line and along with the rest of its brigade began the task of holding off heavy and spirited counterattacks by the enemy. At 2 P.M. a terrible thunderstorm began, leaving the men of Ramseur's Brigade to deal not only with the enemy but with a torrential downpour. A Georgia brigade finally arrived to secure another portion of the salient. However, the day's work was not done for the 14th NCT. When the line to the right of the Georgians began to falter, Colonel Bennett of the 14th NCT led his regiment in a rush against the weakened line. The men of the 14th secured the salient with a vicious charge and "cold steel." With the day coming to a close, the men of Ramseur's Brigade had accomplished a truly incredible action, which would earn them the sincere thanks of General Robert E. Lee. It would also earn their leader a promotion to major general. Other units performed great service as well. The men of the 2nd Battalion and the 45th NCT had fought bravely, trying to relieve the pressure from the Mule Shoe, despite the death of their commander, Junius Daniel.

Four days later, the forces from the North Carolina campaigns under Pickett were engaged in heavy fighting at Drewery's Bluff. The men of the 21st NCT, 42nd NCT, 54th NCT, 57th NCT, and 61st NCT were all involved in fighting against the forces of Benjamin Butler. The battles of the Bermuda Hundred campaign resulted in the bottling up of Butler by May 20, 1864, rendering his force unable to move against Richmond as Grant had hoped.

Minor battles kept occurring. The 14th was thrown back into the fight, while the 15th NCT and the 48th NCT were engaged in defending the North Anna River bridge on May 22, 1864. Yet that was not the end of Grant's move south. The Confederate and Union forces would clash again, this time at Cold Harbor. The battle of Cold Harbor lasted three days, but July 3, 1864, was the most significant. Defending the heights behind impressive fortifications and well-placed artillery stood the Confederate forces, which included the 15th NCT, 21st NCT, 42nd

NCT, 48th NCT, 54th NCT, 57th NCT, and 61st NCT. The Union's major assaults were bloodily repulsed, resulting in a successful defense of Cold Harbor and the deaths of 6,000 Federals in less than 20 minutes.

Despite fierce action in both Virginia and Tennessee, the 10th Heavy Artillery Battalion continued in its garrison assignments. On June 1, 1864, it was assigned to Fort Anderson, where the soldiers acted as quarantine agents and pickets. The battalion would perform guard duty on several railheads, as well as inspect any blockade runners coming into port at Wilmington.

It still saw heated action in the service of Stuart's cavalry. Riding as scouts and acting as flanking guards, the cavalry played a key role in the Spotsylvania and North Anna campaigns. Although in early May, the 10th Virginia Cavalry had lost its gallant major general at the battle of Yellow Tavern; The Carolina Rangers were now commanded by Brigadier General Chambliss.

Davidson County was the scene of another round of enlistments. With the reserve system in place, young men around the age of 17 began enlisting in what became Company C of the 1st Junior Reserve Battalion. These Davidson teenagers volunteered to serve out of the state and performed lackluster duty in southeastern Virginia until they were combined with two other battalions to form the 70th Regiment NCT, or the 1st Junior Reserve Regiment, under Hoke's command in North Carolina.

To the west, Lynchburg, Virginia, was in danger of falling to the forces of Union General David Hunter. A force was dispatched under the command of Major General Jubal Early to defend the city and to advance up the Shenandoah. Early's Valley Army was assembled at Lynchburg on June 17, 1864. The Davidson County units in the offensive included the 2nd N.C. Battalion, 14th NCT, 21st NCT, 45th NCT, 54th NCT, and 57th NCT.

The small army advanced at a rapid pace up the same valley in the same fashion as Jackson's division had two years earlier. The Confederates liberated town after town until the Yankees were pushed completely out of the Shenandoah, and Early was poised to invade the North. Once again, the Potomac River gave way to the southern soldier. Early's army advanced through Maryland and even ransomed the Pennsylvania border town of Cashtown. The campaign continued, and the Valley Army marched through the streets of Frederick, Maryland, by June 8, 1864.

Washington, D.C., was in danger. Union forces under General Lew Wallace met the Valley Army along the Monocany River on July 9, 1864. Ramseur's division was occupied by Federal militia and dismounted cavalry along the Confederate center and left. General John B. Gordon's division made a successful attack on Wallace's force of dismounted cavalry, sending them back to the defenses of Washington. Not involved in the action were the 21st NCT, 54th NCT, and 57th NCT of Lewis' Brigade, which were left at Frederick. By the morning of July 11, 1864, a Confederate force was camped at Silver Springs, Maryland. The Confederates reported hearing the church bells of the Federal capital before, on July 12, 1864, Early ordered a withdrawal into Virginia.

Disheartening as it was, it was never the intent to take Washington. Back in Virginia, the Army of Northern Virginia was posted in the defensive works around Petersburg and Richmond. On August 25, 1864, the 15th NCT and the 48th NCT participated in the Third Corps' victory at Reams' Station, Virginia. The Confederate forces, composed primarily of North Carolinians, attacked and defeated the battle-hardened Union veterans of General Hancock's Second Corps. With that attack, the siege of Petersburg began. Defending the city in August 1864 were the 15th NCT, 42nd NCT, 48th NCT, and 61st NCT.

The two armies began to settle into massive entrenchments and fortifications. Small battles and skirmishes would be fought throughout the siege. The 42nd NCT was transferred out of the Petersburg line to New Market Heights in order to guard holdings in the Fort Harrison area. In September, the 61st NCT and the rest of Clingman's Brigade was assigned to the Military Department of North Carolina, South Carolina, and Georgia under Lafayette McLaws.

While the monotony of siege warfare had become the way of life in the cold, muddy ditches of Petersburg, a renewed Union offensive began in the Shenandoah Valley. After the Washington raid, an army under Union General Phil Sheridan was assembled in the vicinity of Winchester. This army included an infantry corps and a large force of cavalry.

Sheridan's valley campaign began in earnest on September 19, 1864. The third battle of Winchester, or Opequon, foreshadowed the usefulness of Sheridan's large cavalry contingent. All the Davidson units of Early's command were present and performed bravely until the command for retreat was given. The 14th NCT acted as a rear guard for the retreat, but Company B had eight of its 16 men captured, along with Major Joseph Lambeth.

Sheridan followed up his victory by attacking Early at Fisher's Hill. On September 22, 1864, Early had placed his force on top of Fisher's Hill. The Confederates defended the heights well until the weight of the Union assault caused the line to give way. The battle could have gone much differently, if orders had been conveyed more promptly. However, the result was a near stampede off the hill and to safety nearly two miles away.

The Confederate forces under Early rallied and reformed once again. "Old Jubilee" decided to strike the Yankees as they slept in the early morning of October 19, 1864. The Confederates crossed Cedar Creek at dawn and launched a surprise attack against encamped Federal infantry and cavalry. With the Yankees in full retreat, some men began to help themselves to Union equipment and, more important, food. Despite great success, the attack was slowed, and by 4 P.M., a Federal counterattack had begun.

Cavalry led by General George A. Custer successfully attacked the tired Confederates. Custer was able to drive Gordon and Ramseur back across Cedar Creek, and Ramseur, the former commander of a brigade that included the 14th NCT, was mortally wounded. His division, which included the 2nd Battalion, 14th NCT, and 45th NCT, rallied and fought desperately before it was forced to retreat. Pegram's division, which contained the three regiments of Lewis' Brigade, drew a line to the west of Middleburg. Action was light against this front. However, when Gordon and Ramseur fell back, Pegram, along with the 21st NCT, 54th NCT, and 57th NCT, was compelled to retreat as well. The battle of Cedar Creek, a Confederate defeat, ended in the early evening of October 19, 1864. But Early, whose plan had nearly worked to perfection, had stalled the Union advance down the valley.

Early's troops remained in the vicinity of New Market for the fall of 1864. A substantial part of the harvest of the Shenandoah found its way into Virginia, but Sheridan's flames had claimed the rest. This campaign had covered nearly 300 miles and had taken the Confederates to the gates of Washington and back through the valley in defeat. However, in review, Early had done well. He had certainly performed much better than Lee could have hoped. The campaign came to an end when Early was ordered back to Petersburg in December. His force, along with men from Davidson, arrived in the trenches on December 11, 1864, ending the last of the valley campaigns.

December 1864 found other Davidson County units thrown into action. Two new units were formed within the county by December: Hill's Senior Reserves and Moss' Senior Reserves. These two companies were organized by A. A. Hill and Adolphus Moss, respectively, and were entirely composed of older men, the youngest being 45. The Carolina Rangers were performing duty with Lee's cavalry. The 61st was ordered to Wilmington to defend one of the South's most vital ports. On December 2, 1864, the 10th Heavy Artillery Battalion arrived in the western defenses of Savannah, Georgia, to man the heavy gun emplacements.

William T. Sherman's army advanced on the city, with Slocum's wing in the lead. Orders came from Hardee to abandon the lines and evacuate Savannah on December 20, 1864. As the gunners of the 10th Artillery Battalion were preparing to depart, they were attacked. On December 21, 1864, the unit passed through Savannah with the rest of Hardee's corps; it had lost half its men.

The 14th Battalion of the N.C. Home Guard was completing a year of active service, a year that had opened with the Home Guard trying one of its own, Lieutenant Thomas H. Daniels. The specific charges were not reported. July 1864 had been a month of guard details along the North Carolina Railroad. On August 18, 1864, the battalion had been ordered to Asheboro, Randolph County, to restore security and arrest deserters. The 14th Battalion was then placed under the supervision of General Collet Leventhorpe. The English Home Guard general's policies were harsh. A deserter, or "outlier's," family would be detained. The only way the family could get out of the Asheboro stockade was to have the wanted man turn himself in to the Home Guard.

The exact role of the Davidson Home Guard in Leventhorpe's campaign is unknown. However, the 14th Battalion, along with the 53rd Battalion (Alexander County), was ordered away from Leventhorpe's command on November 20, 1864. The battalion would rest for a short time until it was ordered to Salisbury, North Carolina, under A. A. Harbin on December 7, 1864.

Men of Company A of the 42nd NCT, under the command of J. H. Koontz, arrived at Battery Anderson, part of the fortifications defending Wilmington, by December 15. Christmas, the day of peace and reflection was broken by a Union attack. The company held strong until the weight of the Federal attackers and a shortage of supplies compelled Captain Koontz to surrender his command of 88 men.

The year was drawing to a close, and the Union grip had begun to tighten. The Army of Northern Virginia lay freezing in the trenches around Petersburg, and the forces in the Department of North Carolina were attempting to keep the port of Wilmington out of Union hands. While the year was not as numerically devastating as 1862, 1864 did see 40 percent of Davidson's active soldiers dead, wounded, or captured.

The Long Walk Home: 1865–1870

The fourth January of the war opened with little relief or comfort for Confederate citizens and soldiers. The people and their army were nearly out of every resource and found themselves struggling to survive against the greatest odds. At home, Company F of the 7th

NCST was trying to restore order in Montgomery County. The 76th NCT (6th N.C. Senior Reserves) was organized, incorporating the two senior reserve companies, and placed under the command of Colonel Adolphus Moss of Clemmonsville. Davidsonians hoped for the best, but wishful thinking could not change the long casualty lists, disease, inflation, and the horror stories of Sherman's march through Georgia.

On January 13, 1865, a second major operation was launched against Fort Fisher by the Federal Army and Navy. Davidson County had three units present: Battery A of the 10th N.C. Heavy Artillery, Company C of the 61st NCT, and Company C of the 1st Junior Reserves. The 42nd NCT was left to guard the city of Wilmington. The attack on Fort Fisher began. The 61st NCT and the 1st Junior Reserves, both part of Hoke's command, succeeded in taking the works thrown up by Union General Terry after landing to the north of the defensive complex. Hoke's 6,000 men might have been able to pin the Union troops between the ocean and Fort Fisher; however, under the command of General Braxton Bragg, no further counterattacks were made. The 10th Heavy Artillery manned the heavy guns in the vicinity of "the Mound," dueling with the Federal flotilla bombarding the fort. The defenders gave way, and Fisher fell on January 15, 1865.

With the fall of Wilmington, the last port and hope of the Confederacy was gone. The Confederate nation was blockaded from the rest of the world and cut into four parts. However, the Confederate army survived. The remnants of the 10th Heavy Artillery were converted to infantry service and, along with the men of Hoke's division, found themselves in Hardee's corps of the Army of Tennessee.

In Virginia, the siege of Petersburg continued, although there had been little activity since October 1864, when the Carolina Rangers had fought along the Vaughn Road. On February 1, 1865, there was a heavy snowstorm. The next day saw the battle of Hatcher's Run. The Davidson units under Cooke and Lewis were both present at this fight. The ground held by the 48th NCT was full of undergrowth and tangles, making advance and retreat dangerous enterprises. A dismounted cavalry attack was nearly broken by men of the 21st NCT, 54th NCT, and 57th NCT before additional Union troops were brought into the fight. Once again, the armies fell back to the safety of their entrenchments.

Joseph E. Johnston, now commanding the Army of Tennessee, was faced with a huge problem. By March 10, 1865, Sherman's army was in possession of Fayetteville and was continuing its advance north. Sherman advanced his army in wings; this time, Slocum was in the lead. Johnston resolved to attack Slocum and stall Sherman's entire advance. Utilizing a tactic reminiscent of the Revolutionary War, Johnston was able to engage Slocum and inflict losses before retreating. The battle of Averasborough, North Carolina, on March 16, 1865, included the 10th N.C. Heavy Artillery fighting as infantry.

With a morale-boosting victory at Averasborough, Johnston decided to strike at the isolated wing again. On March 19, 1865, Confederate attacks produced initial success but were broken by Federal reinforcements and counterattacks. On March 21, Marsh's Federal division attempted to attack Johnston's rear. A spirited Confederate defense repelled Marsh, but Johnston had suffered heavy and unaffordable casualties. During the battle, the 10th N.C. Heavy Artillery suffered heavy casualties, and the 1st Junior Reserves redeemed themselves for less-than-gallant conduct at Fort Fisher. The men of the 61st NCT and 42nd NCT were present along with their respective commands. After the defeat, Johnston withdrew, hoping to prepare for a defense of Raleigh.

The war came to the front door of Davidson County. After the battles of the Carolinas campaign, both Confederate and Federal soldiers began arriving in trains at the railroad town of Thomasville. Makeshift hospitals were created out of the Lambeth tobacco warehouse and the yard of the Thomasville Methodist Church. Nearly 2,000 men received medical attention from Confederate surgeons, practicing physicians, and women of the county. The hospital helped to save countless lives; however, over 40 men died while in the town. Over 30 men from both sides and four unknowns were interred in the Thomasville City Cemetery.

Lee was obviously aware of the defeat at Bentonville. The commander of the Army of Northern Virginia decided to strike at the Union stronghold of Fort Stedman, instead of waiting for the eventual assault. Pioneers with axes and three groups of 100 men with unloaded rifles opened the battle of Fort Stedman on March 25, 1865. The pioneers broke through the entrenchments, and the three groups of shock troops attacked. Engaged in the fighting were Grimes' Brigade, which included the 2nd Battalion and the 45th NCT (which actually entered the fort). Also engaged were the 21st NCT, 54th NCT, and 57th NCT, which took batteries 10 and 11 before running into fierce opposition at Fort Haskell and battery 9. The fire from battery 9 compelled Lewis' Brigade to retreat, and soon a Federal counterattack threw the Confederates back into their own lines. Lewis' Brigade lost 271 killed, wounded, or missing, with Grimes losing a comparable number. With Fort Stedman firmly in Union hands, March 1865 drew to a close.

About a week after the defeat at Fort Stedman, men of the 49th NCT under Ransom were stationed along with the rest of Pickett's command at the crucial railroad junction of Five Forks. On April 1, 1865, General Sheridan attacked the Confederates with Custer's cavalry and the Sixth Corps of the Army of the Potomac. After a furious fight, the Union forces proved to be too much, carrying the day and sending Pickett's men rearward.

With a crucial rail line lost, Lee was soon compelled to make plans to evacuate Petersburg and Richmond. On April 2, 1865, the dreaded decisive breakthrough occurred. Grant's army began to storm the trenches and earthworks before them. Ambrose Powell Hill's corps attempted to fight off the breakthrough and provide a rear guard for the Confederate retreat, an action that would result in his death. Engaged in this fighting were the 15th NCT and the 48th NCT of Cooke's Brigade.

Lee began his retreat to Appomattox, where supplies supposedly awaited him, losing Richmond on April 3, 1865. Lee's army was in full retreat and subject to the harassment of Federal cavalry. Fierce rearguard engagements were fought at Farmville and Sayler's Creek before the army arrived at Appomattox Court House on April 8, 1865.

At Appomattox, the great army was cornered. The 10th Virginia Cavalry was ordered to attempt a breakout from the Union encirclement. The Carolina Rangers rode hard but could not escape. The regiment's flag was saved from capture by Sergeant H. R. Berrier of Davidson County. Elsewhere on the field, troops under General Bryan Grimes were preparing for a Federal attack. The 14th NCT fired the last shots of the Army of Northern Virginia at advancing Federal cavalry shortly before the flag of truce passed between the lines. On the afternoon of April 9, 1865, the Army of Northern Virginia, Robert E. Lee commanding, surrendered to Lieutenant General Ulysses S. Grant. Included in the surrender were the 2nd N.C. Battalion, 14th NCT, 15th NCT, 21st NCT, 45th NCT, 48th NCT, 54th NCT, and 57th NCT, all with substantial complements of Davidsonians in their ranks.

Back in North Carolina, the war was still on. The 14th N.C. Home Guard Battalion had been reported on duty in Rowan County in January 1865. In April, the 3rd Home Guard, third class, was organized and given to Colonel Jesse Hargrave. The Home Guard began to serve its military purpose as Federal cavalry rode through the state. Yankee General Stoneman had raided the western North Carolina counties of Watauga, Allegheny, Wilkes, and Yadkin and had captured the city of Salisbury on April 10, 1865. With the fall of Salisbury, the next logical target was the city of Lexington and the Silver Hill mining operation. Units of the 14th N.C. Home Guard, the 3rd Home Guard, third class, and the Rowan County Home Guard prepared to defend an earthen fort overlooking the Yadkin River.

On April 13, 1865, Stoneman sent the 12th Michigan Cavalry, 15th Pennsylvania Cavalry, and a force of 200 volunteers to take York Hill. After a day-long battle, the defenders of Fort York had repelled two close assaults and withstood fire from a battery of horse artillery sent up during the hottest part of the fight. Stoneman's force was defeated, but the railroad bridge was severed on the Rowan side, cutting off Davidson County.

With news of Stoneman's raid and Lee's surrender of the Army of Northern Virginia, Johnston knew it was close to the end. On April 18, Johnston opened up negotiations with General Sherman in what is now Durham County, North Carolina. The plans were finalized, and Johnston surrendered all Confederate forces in North Carolina as well as the Army of Tennessee. Included in the surrender were the men of the 10th N.C. Heavy Artillery, 7th NCST, 42nd NCT, a detachment of Company B of the 48th NCT, 61st NCT, 70th NCT (Junior Reserves), and 76th NCT (Senior Reserves). On April 26, 1865, the surrender was finalized, leaving the men to find their way home. The forces of the Army of Tennessee disbanded in early May 1865. Hoke's division disbanded at Center Church in Randolph County, and the remainder of the county's men returned home.

With the two major Confederate armies defeated, the war was over. However, the paperwork still remained. Men began to return home with their paroles from Lee's surrender at Appomattox, while others reported to Greensboro, North Carolina, to take the oath of allegiance. By July 1865, northern prisons had paroled their captives and sent them home. The men made their way back any way they could. Even with their own to worry about, Davidsonians opened their arms to Confederate soldiers who were making their own way home. Davidson County, specifically the town of Thomasville, was a favorite stop for boys returning to the deep southern states of Georgia, Alabama, and Mississippi.

September 1865 saw the return of the last Confederate soldiers. Families were reunited with relatives who had nearly become physically unrecognizable. A great reunion was held at many of the county's homes but only after a shave and a hot bath to kill the lice. Although the structures of the county had remained in good shape, they were shells awaiting workers and customers. While the war mostly spared the county, the world these men returned home to was very different. An atmosphere of disillusionment prevailed. Familiar sights were treasured, but they were viewed in a different light. This was home, but was it reality? Things had changed, leading some men to migrate west, in search of a better life and cheap land.

However, the overwhelming majority of Davidsonians remained at home.

Davidson County would be placed under the occupation of the 12th Michigan Cavalry during the early days of Reconstruction. While few accounts detail the interactions between this unit and the inhabitants of the county, when the Davidson County courthouse caught fire in November 1865, officers and men of the 12th Michigan carried records and vital documents to safety. Then the Union soldiers went back into the building and contained the fire. Later stories of the courthouse fire would imply that the fire was set and burned the entire structure. In reality, only minor smoke damage occurred throughout the building.

In the five years immediately following the end of hostilities, the Davidsonians began to put things back on track and lay the foundation for the future of the county. The majority of men who had gone to war were unmarried at the time. Of the men who returned, 60 percent of them would be married prior to 1870. These new families prompted a construction boom, providing job opportunities and a larger tax base. The towns of the county offered little for a single man, but Lexington soon became the prime area of relocation for freedmen and their families. The small farms of the county were restaffed, and their crops became more diversified, protecting them from the seasonal price fluctuations. Former tracts of plantation land were opened to sharecropping, which involved Davidsonians both black and white. The factories, mercantile stores, service industries, mills, and transportation were rebuilt and reconstituted even though widespread industrialization of the county would not come until the 1900s. New, diversified manufacturing sectors, such as tobacco and furniture, emerged.

While the residents of Davidson County suffered greatly during the American Civil War, Davidsonians also possessed the fortitude and courage necessary to begin rebuilding their lives. The old axiom "It is much easier to destroy than create" was a lesson learned by the county's people. While lives and families were being rebuilt, it was apparent that the world around the county was changing. Volumes can be written on the South's war records, recovery, and progress, but only a society's respect can pay proper tribute to those who suffered and survived.

The Roster

1. Adams, Benjamin

14th Battalion, N.C. Home Guard

Ben Adams, or "Old Uncle Ben" as the Watford children called him, was born in December 1818. Ben was born as a slave to the Adams family of Old Rowan, later Davidson County. Ben worked for N.C. Congressman Henderson Adams until his emancipation on May 10, 1856. One year later, he married Sarah. Their first child, John, was born in 1858. The couple would go on to have four more children, all boys: William (1859), Alexander (1861), and Simon and Abram (1865). Ben served with his neighbor, S. C. Watford, in the militia and later in the Home Guard. Watford described Ben in his diary: "He was a fine black man with a large frame." After his limited service, Ben returned to farming and became fairly successful. By the 1880 Census, Ben was a widower living with his son John. Ben also had a job watching S. C. Watford's three boys, John Raymond, Ed, and Jesse, while S. C. was away on business in Lexington. By 1900, he had no family living with him in the Conrad Hill township area of Light. He died in 1905 at the age of 86. The four Watford men built him a homemade coffin, put it in their mule cart, and drove the body to Pilgrim Reform (UCC) to be buried in the "colored section" of the cemetery. Roy Watford remembers his uncle talking about Ben's kindness and sense of humor. Ben's service was limited due to the type of unit he was in; however, he is one of at least four African Americans from Davidson County to serve in the Confederate cause.

2. Adams, John Franklin

Private, Carolina Rangers
Company B, 10th Virginia Cavalry
Regiment

John was born in 1840 to the Honorable Henderson Adams and his wife, Rebecca. John helped to manage his father's farm while Henderson was away in Raleigh, and he also attended Yadkin Institute for a year. He volunteered for service in Davie County on October 29, 1861. He was reported on detail until August 1863 and accounted present through August 1864. Company records indicate that he "lost cartridge box 6/23/64, No horse since 7/24/64, Issued clothing 9 & 1 12/64." At the end of the war, he was paroled at Greensboro, North Carolina, on May 5, 1865. He then came home and married Sarah Ann in January 1867. John and Sarah would have two children: Celestia (1867) and Robert Lee (1869). John held many jobs, including being one of the more prominent grocers in Lexington until his death on March 14, 1922, in the city of Raleigh. He is buried in Raleigh's Oakwood Cemetery.

3. Adams, Robert Quick

Private, Company I, 42nd Regiment
N.C. Troops

Robert was born in 1824 to Emanuel Adams (a native of Northampton, Virginia) and Lucy Falkner of Silver Hill township. On June 26, 1852, at the age of 28, he married Emily Younts. Robert and Emily would have two children: Nathaniel (1854) and John (1857), before Robert volunteered on March 8, 1862, at the age of 37, to serve in Company I of the 42nd North Carolina. He was present at Petersburg and Fort Fisher. The last company records list him as present as of August 1864. After the war, he returned home and started his life over again. In 1880, he was employed as a mine superintendent for the copper and silver mines. He also acquired and operated one of the four sawmills in the Hannersville area in 1884. In 1900, Robert Q. Adams passed away at his home. He is buried at Clarksbury Methodist Church.

4. Allred, Clemmons M.

Private, Thomasville Rifles
Company B, 14th Regiment N.C. Troops
(4th N.C. Volunteers)

Clemmons was born in 1838. In 1860, Clemmons was residing with Sam Craven, a master carpenter in the new town of Thomasville, and he worked as a carpenter until he volunteered on April 23, 1861. He was mustered in as a corporal and was promoted to sergeant when the regiment was reorganized on April 27, 1862. On March 1, 1863, he was reduced in rank to private. Clemmons was reported present in the company until wounded at Chancellorsville, Virginia, on May 3, 1863. He was reported absent, wounded, through October of that year. In November, he was detailed to serve as a division provost guard and was reported absent on detail through August 1864. He was returned to duty sometime after and was paroled at Appomattox Court House on April 9, 1865. No further records.

5. Allred, William

Private, Thomasville Rifles
Company B, 14th Regiment N.C. Troops
(4th N.C. Volunteers)

William worked as a carpenter in Thomasville. He volunteered for service on April 23, 1861, was mustered in as a private, and served until he was wounded at Sharpsburg, Maryland, on September 17, 1862. William slowly recovered from his wounds and rejoined the company in January 1863. He was reported absent without leave from July 30 until November 6, 1863. William returned to duty on November 7, 1863, and was reported present through August 1864. No further records.

6. Anderson, Jesse A.

Private, Thomasville Rifles
Company B, 14th Regiment N.C. Troops
(4th N.C. Volunteers)

Jesse was born in 1838 to John and Cynthia Pope Anderson. Jesse was the only son of the house and had two older sisters, Amanda and Jane. He moved out of the house and was apprenticed to Sam Craven, master carpenter. Jesse volunteered for service on April 23, 1861. He received a wound in his left arm at Sharpsburg, Maryland, on September 17, 1862. Jesse recovered and returned to duty in January 1863. He was hospital-ized with a gunshot wound (possibly from Chancellorsville, Virginia) on May 22, 1863. Jesse returned to duty the following day and served until he was captured at Gettysburg, Pennsylvania, between July 1 and July 3, 1863. More than likely, Jesse was disabled at the time of his capture. He died in Federal custody on July 10, 1863, at Gettysburg. Cause of death was not reported.

7. Andrews, David W.

Captain, 65th N.C. Militia Regiment
(1861 organization)

David was born on May 26, 1824. He worked as a farmer and on September 30, 1845, married Delilah C. Fine. Their life together would give them six children: Madison (1848), Euphonia (1850), Adley (1852), Thomas (1856), Matilda (1857), and Franklin (1859). David was commissioned on November 25, 1861. He probably served in the Home Guard upon its creation. David lived in the Conrad Hill township until his death on February 8, 1892. He is buried at Pleasant Hill United Methodist Church.

8. Ausband, Simpson Pruitt

Private, Holtsburg Guards
Company A, 54th Regiment N.C. Troops

Simpson was born on January 4, 1842, to Yarbrough and Nancy Pruitt Ausband. Simpson worked as a miner prior to being conscripted into service on November 11, 1862. He was present or accounted for until detailed to serve as a lead miner in Davidson County on August 3, 1864. Simpson survived the war. He had enlisted under the name of Pruitt, the name of his mother's first husband. He kept the name until 1870, when he became listed as Ausband. Apparently, Simpson found out that Yarbrough Ausband was his true father and, as a result, he changed his last name. He was married to Julia Sullivan and lived in Allegheny County for a time. Simpson died on May 7, 1919. He is buried in the Lexington City Cemetery.

9. Ayer, Henry W.

Second Lieutenant, Thomasville Rifles
Company B, 14th Regiment N.C.
Troops (4th N.C. Volunteers)

Henry was born in 1835. He worked as a clerk for the Conrad Hill mining company until he volunteered at age 26 on April 23, 1861. Henry was mustered in as a first sergeant, and on May 26, 1861, he was appointed to the post of second lieutenant. Henry was present or accounted for until April 26, 1862, when he was defeated for reelection when the regiment reorganized for the war. No further records.

10. Babcock, Edward Warren

Private, Thomasville Rifles
Company B, 14th Regiment N.C. Troops
(4th N.C. Volunteers)

Edward was born in the state of Maine in 1837. He came to the town of Thomasville and worked as a bootmaker in the Lines Shoe Factory prior to volunteering on April 27, 1861. He was mustered in as a private and served in that capacity until he was promoted to sergeant in March or April 1863. He was wounded in the thigh at the battle of Chancellorsville, Virginia, May 1–5, 1863. Edward recovered from his wound, rejoined the company in December, and was promoted to first sergeant in April 1864. For unknown reasons he was reduced in rank to private on August 1, 1864. He reportedly survived the war. No further records.

11. Badgett, Cicero Lowe

Second Lieutenant, Company C, 70th
Regiment N.C. Troops (1st N.C.
Junior Reserves)

Cicero was born on April 20, 1847, to William Harris and Elizabeth Badgett of Emmons. Cicero was a farmer prior to enlisting in the Junior Reserves on May 24, 1864, when he was elected second lieutenant. After the war, he married Martha Jane Adderton on November 21, 1867. Cicero and Martha would have five children: Eugenia (1870), James (1875), Stephen (1878), William (1881), and Samuel (1884). He became one of the best house carpenters in southern Davidson County. Cicero was the last living officer of the A. A. Hill Camp, United Confederate Veterans. He died on January 11, 1937, and he is buried at Clear Springs Baptist Church.

12. Bailey, James W.

Private, Company B, 57th Regiment
N.C. Troops

James was born in 1831 to Elkins and Elizabeth Bailey. James worked alongside his father and older brother, William, on his family's farm near the Yadkin River. He enlisted in Rowan County on July 4, 1862, and was reported present until he was sent to a Richmond, Virginia, hospital on December 4, 1862, with "icterus." James was furloughed on January 5, 1863. He returned to duty in March 1864, but he was sent to the hospital again on August 27, 1864, with "chronic diarrhea." While in the hospital, he was arrested for desertion and court-martialed on December 8, 1864, he was reported under arrest through February 1865. He was sent to the hospital again with "chronic diarrhea" on March 4, 1865. James recovered and returned to duty on March 27, 1865. He received a parole at Salisbury, North Carolina, on May 22, 1865. No further records.

13. Bailey, Thomas A.

*Private, Company B, 42nd Regiment
  N.C. Troops
Howard's Company, N.C. Prison
  Guards, Salisbury*

Thomas was born in Halifax, Virginia, on September 20, 1821. He moved to Wake County, North Carolina, where he met his wife, Calista, around 1845. They moved to Davidson County shortly before 1850, when Thomas was working as a schoolteacher. Their son Samuel was

born in 1852 and within the next eight years three girls were born: Margaret, Caroline, and Virginia. Thomas was 41 years old when he was conscripted into service on July 24, 1862, in Rowan County. Thomas was transferred to Captain Howard's Prison Guards on May 1, 1863, and served there until the end of the war. During his tenure as a guard, he and his wife had another son, James (1864). After the war, in 1869, his last son, William, was born. Thomas died on June 9, 1884, at the age of 62. He is buried at Bethany United Church of Christ.

14. Bailey, William Harrison

*Private, Company B, 57th Regiment
  N.C. Troops*

William was born in 1843, the youngest child of Elkins and Elizabeth Bailey. He worked as a farmer until he enlisted in Rowan County on July 4, 1862. He was reported sick for most of the period between September 18, 1862, and June 4, 1863, with "reubola, orchitis, and typhoid fever." William returned to duty on August 19, 1863. On November 7, 1863, he was captured at Rappahannock Station, Virginia, and was sent to Washington, D.C. He was confined at Point Lookout, Maryland, until he was paroled on February 24, 1865, and transferred to Aiken's Landing, Virginia, for exchange. He was declared exchanged on March 3, 1865. William returned home to the fam-

ily farm, and, in 1867, he and Margaret Young were married by the Reverend William Turner. William and Margaret would have three children: Ben (1869), James (1870), and Florence (1875). No further records.

15. Baker, David

*Private, Thomasville Rifles
Company B, 14th Regiment N.C. Troops
  (4th N.C. Volunteers)*

David worked as a carpenter in Thomasville prior to volunteering for service on April 23, 1861. He served at Williamsburg and during the Seven Days campaign before he became ill and was sent home on furlough. David died in November 1862 of an unknown disease. He is not buried in the county.

16. Baker, Phillip

*Private, Thomasville Rifles
Company B, 14th Regiment N.C. Troops
  (4th N.C. Volunteers)*

Phillip was born in 1836. He volunteered for service in Davidson County on April 27, 1861. Phillip was reported present until he was wounded and captured at Sharpsburg, Maryland, on September 17, 1862. He was confined at Fort McHenry, Maryland, until paroled and transferred to Aiken's Landing, Virginia, for exchange on October 19, 1862. Phillip was declared exchanged on November 10, 1862, and returned to service in September 1863. He was placed on light duty at Gordonsville, Virginia, on December 13, 1863. Phillip served in this capacity for four months until he was retired to the invalid corps on April 27, 1864. He returned home and was paroled at Greensboro, North Carolina, on April 28, 1865. He apparently returned to Guilford County prior to 1870. No further records.

17. Baker, Rufus

*Private, Thomasville Rifles
Company B, 14th Regiment N.C. Troops
  (4th N.C. Volunteers)*

Rufus was born in 1841 and resided in Davidson County with his brothers, working as a farmer prior to volunteering on April 27, 1861. He survived the war and was paroled at Lynchburg, Virginia, in April 1865. Most of his service was spent absent on detail. No further records.

Home of Jackson Hill carpenter and community leader Cicero Badgett (Touart, ***Building the Backcountry***).

18. Baker, William

Private, Thomasville Rifles
Company B, 14th Regiment N.C. Troops
(4th N.C. Volunteers)

William was a resident of Davidson County and worked as a farmer before the beginning of the war. Three of his brothers enlisted on April 27, 1861, leaving him alone to tend the farm. Several months later, he traveled to Camp Bee, Virginia, and volunteered for service on September 10, 1861. William was reported present until he was wounded in the left arm and hip at Spotsylvania Court House, Virginia, on May 12, 1864. William was reported absent, wounded, through August 1864, when he was captured. He was released at Washington, D.C., on April 10, 1865, after taking the oath of allegiance. No further records.

19. Ball, Franklin

Private, Company H, 48th Regiment N.C. Troops

Franklin was born in 1842 to Lexington coachmakers William and Margaret Ball. He worked with his father, learning the family trade, until he was conscripted into service at Petersburg, Virginia, on August 8, 1862. Franklin was reported present until wounded in the left hand at Wilderness, Virginia, on May 5 or 6, 1864. Franklin was granted a furlough to return home on May 25, 1864. Upon his return to service, Franklin was detailed as a teamster until December 31, 1864. He was paroled at Appomattox Court House, Virginia, on April 9, 1865. No further records.

20. Ball, Harrison

Private, Company H, 48th Regiment N.C. Troops

Harrison was born in 1840 to William and Margaret Ball. He was conscripted into service with his brother Franklin at Petersburg, Virginia, on August 8, 1862. During the fighting in the vicinity of the West Woods, Harrison was wounded and taken prisoner at Sharpsburg, Maryland, on September 17, 1862. Harrison was paroled and returned to service prior to October 4, 1862. He was reported absent, sick, until June 1863 and was listed as a deserter on September 23, 1863; he rejoined the company on an unspecified date. He was hospitalized with "phtsis pulmonalis" in Richmond, Virginia, and received a 60-day furlough on April 27, 1864. After Harrison returned, he was once again hospitalized, this time with "chronic bronchitis," on November 1, 1864. He was captured at Petersburg, Virginia, and confined at Washington, D.C., until an unspecified date. He was released after taking the oath of allegiance. Harrison returned home and took his skill elsewhere prior to 1870. No further records.

21. Ball, Henry

Private, Lexington Wildcats
Company I, 14th Regiment N.C. Troops
(4th N.C. Volunteers)

Henry was born in 1841 to William and Margaret Ball. He worked as a coach-maker and as a laborer for A. C. Hege. He volunteered on May 14, 1861. Henry served for two months before he lost his fight with disease on July 28, 1861, at Camp Ellis, Virginia. His body was sent back to his parents in Lexington. He is buried in the Lexington City Cemetery.

22. Barnes, Alexander

Private, Lexington Wildcats
Company I, 14th Regiment N.C. Troops
(4th N.C. Volunteers)

Alexander was born on July 10, 1835, to Alexander and Dorothy Hill Barnes. Alex worked as a farmer, and, prior to 1861, he married Delphine Wyatt. He left his wife and home to volunteer on May 14, 1861. Alex was reported present until he was captured at South Mountain, Maryland, on September 15, 1862. He was confined at Fort Delaware, Delaware, until October 2, 1862, when he was transferred to Aiken's Landing, Virginia, for exchange. Alex was declared exchanged on November 10, 1862, and rejoined the company in May 1863. He was wounded in the right cheek at Chancellorsville, Virginia, on May 3, 1863. Alex recovered from his wounds and returned to the company in July 1863. He was taken prisoner at Fisher's Hill, Virginia, on September 22, 1864, was confined at Point Lookout, Maryland, and was held until June 24, 1865, when he was released after taking the oath of allegiance. Alex returned home to the Boone township where he and Delphine would have eight children: Martha (1866), Mary Jane (1867), Lewis (1869–71), Samuel D. (1873), Charlie (1874), John H. (1875), Ida (1878), and Richard (1880). After his return on September 15, 1865, Alex bought land south of Churchland. There, he took care of his family and set aside land for a cemetery. Alex died on May 23, 1913. He is buried at Pine Primitive Baptist Church.

23. Barnes, Charles Adolphus

Private, Company C, 70th Regiment N.C. Troops (1st N.C. Junior Reserves)

Charles was born on January 11, 1847, to John and Margaret Ratts Barnes. He worked as a farmer until he enlisted in the Junior Reserves on May 24, 1864. After the war, Charles returned home and married Joan Kindley on June 25, 1869. Charles and Joan would have eight children: John (1871), Mary E. (1874), Lillie Etta (1877), Cora (1879), Florence Lee (1881), Sarah L. (1882), Gracie Bell (1886), and Frances (1889). Charles' first home, known as the "Old Jim Barnhart Place," was in the Boone township. In 1912, he and his wife moved to Churchland, where they built a two-story house. Charles' wife, Joan, continued her involvement in the temperance movement until Charles' death on September 6, 1935. He is buried in the Barnes Cemetery at Churchland.

24. Barnes, Elias

Private, Holtsburg Guards
Company A, 54th Regiment N.C. Troops

Eli was born in 1833 to Alexander and Dorothy Hill Barnes. Eli worked on his family's farm until he enlisted on May 1, 1862. Eli was reported present until he was hospitalized with the "mumps" from November 9 until December 3, 1862. He was wounded ten days later at the battle of Fredericksburg, Virginia, on December 13, 1862. He was reported absent, wounded, until he returned to service in June 1863. Eli was shot and captured at Cedar Creek, Virginia, on October 19, 1864. Federal authorities confined him at Point Lookout, Maryland, where he died of disease on November 26, 1864. He is buried in the Point Lookout National Cemetery.

25. Barnes, Hiram Lindsey

Private, Holtsburg Guards
Company A, 54th Regiment N.C. Troops

Charles and Alice Joan Kindley Barnes ca. 1880 (Mary Jo Shoaf, *The Heritage of Davidson County*).

wounded in the shoulder at Cedar Creek, Virginia. He was removed from the field and sent to a hospital in Charlottesville, Virginia. Hiram received another wounded furlough on November 5, 1864. He returned on an unspecified date and served until he was paroled at Appomattox Court House, Virginia, on April 9, 1865. Hiram committed suicide shortly after his return.

26. Barnes, John

Private, Company F, 76th Regiment N.C. Troops (6th N.C. Senior Reserves)

John Barnes joined his two sons in service in January 1864 (Angela C. Pickett, *The Heritage of Davidson County*).

John was born on November 3, 1816, to Richard and Fannie Johnston Barnes in Rowan (Davidson) County. In 1839, John's father died and left him a 160-acre tract of the family farm. John married Margaret Ratts in 1840 and built a two-story house on the land. John and Margaret would have seven children: Sarah (1842), Hiram L. (1844), Charles A. (1847), John T. (1849), Lewis (1851), William (1854), and James, who died in 1862 at the age of four. With two sons already serving in the war, John enlisted in Hill's Senior Reserves in May 1864. He served as a private in Company F of the 6th N.C. Senior Reserves when it was organized in January 1865 and saw limited action. After his time in service, he made a successful living on his farm. He and Henry Clement each donated two acres of land for Churchland Missionary Baptist. John died on September 19, 1892, leaving no will. His estate remained

Hiram was born on April 4, 1844, to John and Margaret Ratts Barnes. He worked as a farmer prior to volunteering for service on March 4, 1862. Hiram was reported present until he was wounded at Cold Harbor, Virginia, around June 3, 1864. He was sent to Richmond, Virginia, and was granted a 60-day furlough on June 26, 1864. Hiram returned to duty prior to October 19, 1864, when he was

Family home of the Bealls, built in 1800 and renovated in 1848 (Angela C. Pickett, *The Heritage of Davidson County*).

James F. Beall, depicted as a major (Clark, *Histories of the Several Regiments*).

unsettled until October 24, 1893. He is buried in the Barnes Cemetery at Churchland.

27. Barnes, Richard L.

*Private, Chatam Light Infantry
Company G, 48th Regiment N.C. Troops*

Richard was born in 1835. He was apprenticed to Joshua Wallen, with whom he lived. Richard married Mary in 1858. Richard and Mary would have one child, Sarah (1859), before Richard was conscripted into service on August 14, 1862. He was wounded at Sharpsburg, Maryland, on September 17, 1862. He was reported present on April 1, 1864. Richard did not return home. No further records.

28. Barneycastle, Alves

*Private, Confederate Guards
Company K, 48th Regiment N.C. Troops*

Alves was born in 1844 and was raised on a modest plantation on the Davidson-Forsyth line. Alves enlisted on March 26, 1862, as a substitute. He served as a private until he was wounded at Sharpsburg, Maryland, on September 17, 1862. Alves succumbed to his wounds and died in the hands of the enemy at Frederick, Maryland, on September 25, 1862.

29. Barnhart, Charles A.

Private, Company D, 48th Regiment N.C. Troops

Charles was born in 1831 and was a single farmer living in Davidson County in 1860. He was conscripted into service on August 8, 1862. He was wounded at Sharpsburg, Maryland, on September 17, 1862. Charles recovered and returned to duty on an unspecified date. He died of "chronic diarrhea" at Lynchburg, Virginia, on January 15, 1864.

30. Beall, James Franklin

*Major, Davidson Guards
21st Regiment N.C. Troops (11th N.C. Volunteers)*

James was born on September 1, 1837, to Dr. Burgess and Elizabeth Beall. He lived with his family and was a medical student before volunteering on May 14, 1861. James was mustered in with the rank of sergeant, and on July 8, 1861, he was elected second lieutenant. With the promotion of Captain James Madison Leach to major, Beall was promoted to captain of Company A on May 25, 1862. He served

only one day as captain before he was wounded at Winchester, Virginia. James returned to his post and led the company at Ox Hill, Virginia, where he was wounded once again. He recovered quickly and led his company into the battle of Chancellorsville, Virginia, where on May 3, 1863, he was struck in the leg. Beall rejoined his command prior to October 1864 and was promoted to major on the eve of the battle of Cedar Creek, Virginia, on October 18, 1864. Beall served as major until he was wounded at Fort Stedman, Virginia, on March 25, 1865. This wound was severe enough to send him home. After the war, James returned to the Cotton Grove township, where he married Margaret Cornelia Harper in 1869. James and Margaret would have three children: Franklin (1870), Caroline (1878), and James (1887). James finished his medical training in 1880 and worked as the company doctor for the Silver Hill mining company. His half brother, Thomas, sold the family home, "Beallmont," to him, and James moved his family there. He was a fine country doctor and a progressive farmer. In 1902, he wrote a history of the 21st North Carolina for Clarke's *Regiments* series. James died on December 7, 1907 and is buried at Jersey Baptist Church. His tombstone reads: "Thanks be to God, which giveth us the victory through our lord Jesus Christ."

31. Beall, Robert L.

Captain and Staff Surgeon, 66th N.C. Militia Regiment (1861 Organization)

Robert was born in 1832 to Dr. Burgess and Eleanor Beall. His mother died in 1836. In 1858, Robert completed his medical studies, and in November he married Mary Ellen, the oldest Harper sister. Robert and Mary would have only one child, Lelia, born in 1861. Robert served in the N.C. Militia as a surgeon and probably served in the Home Guard as well. After 1870, he and his wife left Cotton Grove to move to the city of Lenoir in Caldwell County, North Carolina. No further records.

32. Beall, Thomas Burgess

*Captain, Lexington Wildcats
Company I, 14th Regiment N.C. Troops
(4th N.C. Volunteers)*

Thomas was born on August 29, 1835, to Dr. Burgess and Eleanor Beall. Thomas worked as a successful farmer in the Lexington township. Thomas volunteered for service on May 14, 1861, when he was elected as third lieutenant. When the regiment completed its reorganization on April 27, 1862, Thomas was elected captain. He was commended for his bravery and quick thinking as he and six officers manned a cannon and fired it several times in hopes of stopping an advancing brigade from reinforcing the Federal troops occupying the sunken road at Sharpsburg, Maryland, on September 17, 1862. He was reported present and saw to the everyday maintenance of the company until wounded at Cedar Creek, Virginia, on October 19, 1864. His wounds were so severe that his half brother, Major J. F. Beall of the 21st North Carolina, thought he was already dead. Thomas survived the wound and the war and married Bettie Howard of Rowan County. He sold his home to James and lived in Salisbury, North Carolina, until his death in 1909. Thomas was a leader in post–Reconstruction Salisbury as well as a correspondent for *Confederate Veteran* magazine He is buried in the Old Lutheran Cemetery.

33. Bean, Alexander C.

Private, Company B, 48th Regiment N.C. Troops

Alexander was born in 1835, the son of Gideon Bean. He worked as a farmer until being conscripted into service on August 8, 1862. Alexander died of disease at Culpeper Court House, Virginia, on November 16, 1862.

34. Bean, Curby

Private, Company I, 42nd Regiment N.C. Troops

Curby was born in 1837 to Whitlock and Elizabeth Bean. He worked as a farmer until he enlisted on April 26, 1862, in Rowan County. Curby was wounded at an unspecified engagement on June 27, 1862. After the war, he returned home to seek work. He was employed as a copper miner and was living with William Cameron in the Silver Hill township in 1870. No further records.

35. Bean, James Carrick

Private, Company B, 48th Regiment N.C. Troops

James was born in 1830 to Hezekiah and Elizabeth Carrick Bean. He worked as a farmer and, in 1855, married Lovina Doby. John and Lovina would have four children, John (1859), Emaline (1859), Richard (1860), and James (1862), before James was conscripted on August 8, 1862. He was wounded at Sharpsburg, Maryland, on September 17, 1862. On October 1, he was furloughed for 30 days. James was reported absent without leave from March until June 1863. He was arrested and returned in November 1863. His fifth child was born in 1864, while James was in a hospital. He was furloughed from Hospital No. 8 on August 27, 1864. James survived the war and returned to his farm. He and Lovina would have four more children: Madison (1865), Joseph (1871), Moses L. (1875), and Martha Jane (1881). James died on July 19, 1915. He is buried at Lick Creek Baptist Church.

36. Bean, John

Private, Company B, 48th Regiment N.C. Troops

John was born on January 1, 1832. He was married to Nancy Bean prior to 1859, when his first son, Jesse, was born. John and Mary had a daughter, Elizabeth, in June 1862. John enlisted on August 8, 1862, at the age of 30. He served as a private and was reported present through April 1864. He was hospitalized on May 8, 1864, with a gunshot wound in the hand. He survived the war and returned to farming. Two more children, Goldsberry and James, were born in 1866 and 1867, respectively. John died on December 1, 1894, and is buried at Summerville Baptist Church.

37. Bean, Otho C.

Private, Company B, 48th Regiment N.C. Troops

Otho was born in 1830 to Whitlock and Elizabeth Bean. He worked as a farmer and, in 1854, married Rachael. Otho and Rachael would have three children, Harris (1855), Elizabeth (1857), and Benjamin (1859), before Otho was conscripted on August 8, 1862. Records show that he deserted on August 28, 1862, and he returned in June 1863. Otho was sent to the hospital on April 26, 1864. He was reported present through December 1864. No further records.

38. Bean, Peter

Private, Company D, 55th Regiment N.C. Troops

Peter was born in 1833, the son of Gideon Bean of Cleveland County, North Carolina. He worked as a mechanic prior to enlisting on May 24, 1862. He was hospitalized at Petersburg, Virginia, on December 2, 1862. Peter returned to duty and, six months later, was captured at Falling Waters, Maryland, on July 14, 1863. Peter was confined at Point Lookout, Maryland, until March 16, 1864, when he was received at City Point, Virginia, for exchange. He returned to duty in October 1864 and was reported present until he was captured at Sutherland's Station, Virginia, on April 2, 1865. He was confined at Point Lookout, Maryland, until June 24, 1865, when he was released after taking the oath of allegiance. After the war, Peter married Lovina A. Peter, and they had two children: Nellie (1882) and John (1883). Peter died about 1913 and is buried at Holloways Baptist Church.

39. Beck, Alfred

Private, Company B, 48th Regiment N.C. Troops

Alfred was born in 1839 to George and Doretta Beck. He was a farmer prior to volunteering on March 6, 1862. Alfred was killed a few months later at the battle of King's School House, Virginia, on June 25, 1862.

40. Beck, Ambrose

Private, Company H, 48th Regiment N.C. Troops

Ambrose was born on October 12, 1829. He lived in northern Davidson County and worked as a carpenter. Prior to 1844, he married Elizabeth. Ambrose and Elizabeth had nine children, Jacob H. R. (1845), Cynthia (1846), William L. (1847), Jenny (1851), John (1854), Molly (1857), Andrew (1859), Joshua (1860), and Phoebe (1863), before Ambrose was conscripted in 1863. He was reported present until he was captured at Hatcher's Run, Virginia, on April 1, 1865. He was confined at Point Lookout, Maryland, until June 24, 1865, when he was released after taking the oath of allegiance. After the war, he returned home and welcomed his son William home. Ambrose and Elizabeth would have two more children: Ambrose, Jr. (1867), and Alfred (1868). Ambrose lived in the Thomasville township until he passed away on April 10, 1869. He is buried at Emmanuel United Church of Christ.

41. Beck, Daniel

Private, Company D, 48th Regiment N.C. Troops

Daniel was born in 1837 to John and Mary Beck. Daniel worked as a single farmer prior to being conscripted into service on August 8, 1862, for the war. He was reported present until he died of typhoid fever at Farmville, Virginia, on an unreported date.

42. Beck, Daniel

Private, Lexington Wildcats Company I, 14th Regiment N.C. Troops (4th N.C. Volunteers)

Daniel was the son of David and Mary Beck. He worked as a single farmer prior to volunteering for service on May 14, 1861. Daniel was reported present until he was discharged on January 28, 1862, due to "frequent attacks of intermittent fever and partial paralysis of the lower extremities." No further records.

43. Beck, Daniel M.

Private, Company C, 70th Regiment N.C. Troops (1st N.C. Junior Reserves)

Daniel was born about 1847. He worked as a farmer prior to enlisting in the Junior Reserves on May 24, 1864. After the war, he married Christina McDonald on April 7, 1866. No further records.

44. Beck, George D.

Private, Company D, 48th Regiment N.C. Troops

George was born on November 26, 1829. He worked as a farmer, and in 1849 he married Nancy. George and Nancy would have three children, Joseph (1850), Mary (1854), and Stephen (1859), before George was conscripted on August 8, 1862. He deserted three weeks later. He returned to duty on February 8, 1863, and was reported present through August 1, 1864, when he was reported absent without leave. After the war, he and Nancy had three more children: Sarah (1873), Edward (1876), and Ellen (1879). Nancy Beck died around 1885. In 1897, George married Amanda Beck. The two had no children. George died on February 23, 1918. He is buried at New Jerusalem United Church of Christ.

45. Beck, George F.

Private, Company B, 48th Regiment N.C. Troops

George was born in 1828. He was working as a single farmer in Davidson County in 1860. George volunteered on March 7, 1862, and was reported present until he was wounded at King's School House, Virginia, on June 25, 1862. He was sent to a Richmond, Virginia, hospital, where he died two days later of his wounds.

46. Beck, George Washington

Sergeant, Holtsburg Guards Company A, 54th Regiment N.C. Troops

George was born in 1832 to David and Elizabeth Beck. He worked as a farmer and, in 1860, he married Annie. George and Annie would have one child, Eleanor (1861), before George was conscripted into service on July 21, 1862. He was mustered in as a private and was promoted to sergeant on May 16, 1864. George was sent to the hospital the next day with an unspecified complaint. He returned in September 1864 and served until he was paroled at Appomattox Court House, Virginia, on April 9, 1865.

47. Beck, George Washington

Private, Lexington Wildcats Company I, 14th Regiment N.C. Troops (4th N.C. Volunteers)

George was born in 1837 to Christian and Mary Beck. He worked as a farmer and a miner, and, in 1858, he married Anna. George and Anna would have one child, Cicero (1859), before George was conscripted into service on July 16, 1862. He was reported absent without leave from March 1863 to November 26, 1863. George deserted on February 23, 1864. No further records.

48. Beck, Henry B., Jr.

Private, Lexington Wildcats Company I, 14th Regiment N.C. Troops (4th N.C. Volunteers)

Henry was born in 1836 to Henry and Sophia Beck. He worked on his family's farm and, in 1857, he married Phoebe Hedrick. Henry and Phoebe would have two children, Charles (1858) and Sarah (1860), before Henry was conscripted in Wake County on July 26, 1862. Henry was captured around Frederick, Maryland, on September 15, 1862. He was confined at Fort Delaware, Delaware, until October 2, 1862, when he was transferred to Aiken's Landing, Virginia, for exchange. Henry was declared exchanged on November 10, 1862, and rejoined the company in January 1863. He was reported present or accounted for through August 1864. No further records.

49. Beck, J. A.

Private, Company C, 70th Regiment N.C. Troops (1st N.C. Junior Reserves)

Moore's *Roster* indicates this soldier served, but his genealogy is in question. No further records.

50. Beck, Jacob H. R.

Private, Thomasville Rifles Company B, 14th Regiment N.C. Troops (4th N.C. Volunteers)

Jacob was born in 1845 to Ambrose and Elizabeth Beck. He worked as a farmer and a carpenter prior to volunteering for service on July 29, 1861. He deserted on July 1, 1862, and married Martha Shuler on December 28, 1862. Jacob returned to service on February 23, 1863, and served until he was killed by a bayonet at Spotsylvania Court House, Virginia, on May 15, 1864.

51. Beck, Jacob Riley

*Private, Company B, 48th Regiment
N.C. Troops*

Jacob was born on April 6, 1843, to George W. and Doretta Beck. He worked as a farmer until being conscripted on August 8, 1862. He was reported absent, sick, from September 1862 until April 1863. He was reported present until he was wounded in the left eye at Wilderness, Virginia, on May 5, 1864. Jacob lost the use of that eye but returned to service in September 1864. He was last reported present on December 6, 1864. After the war, Jacob married Susan B. Ward, the widow of William S. Ward, on February 10, 1866. Jacob and Susan would have three children who survived infancy: Elizabeth Caroline (1866), Louisa Sarah (1868), and Harvey (1875). Three children died shortly after birth: Roxanna, Mariah, and William. In 1870, he took an African American child named Alfred into his Emmons home. In 1880, Jacob listed James Pierce of Randolph County as a boarder. Jacob lived in the Emmons township until he passed away on October 25, 1916. He is buried at New Jerusalem United Church of Christ.

52. Beck, James Franklin

*Private, Chatam Light Infantry
Company G, 48th Regiment N.C. Troops*

James was born in 1842 to John and Rachael Beck. He worked as a farmer prior to being conscripted on August 14, 1862. James was reported present until March 31, 1865, when he was captured at Hatcher's Run, Virginia. He was confined at Point Lookout, Maryland, until June 25, 1865, when he was released after taking the oath of allegiance. After the war, he returned home and married Elizabeth Carrick on March 9, 1868. The couple had two children: U. S. Grant (1868) and Nellie (1871). Frank worked as a copper miner for most of his life in the Healing Spring township until his death around 1890.

53. Beck, John L.

*Private, Lexington Wildcats
Company I, 14th Regiment N.C. Troops
(4th N.C. Volunteers)*

John was born in 1832 to David and Rebecca Beck. He worked as a miner at Conrad Hill, and, in 1861, he married Matilda. John and Matilda would have five children: Charles (1863), Eliza Jane (1864), Henry J. (1867), William Lindsey (1870), and Thomas (1873). John volunteered on May 14, 1861. He was reported present until he was wounded in action at Malvern Hill, Virginia, on July 1, 1862. He recovered from his wounds, and, on October 30, 1862, John was sent home to serve as a miner on detail. He served as a miner through the end of the war. John continued to work in the mines right up until his death in 1902. He is buried at Beck's United Church of Christ.

54. Beck, Lewis F.

*Corporal, Holtsburg Guards
Company A, 54th Regiment N.C. Troops*

Lewis was born in 1842 to Henry and Sophia Beck. He worked as a farmer prior to volunteering on March 4, 1862. Lewis was promoted to corporal by December 1862 and was reported present until he was captured at Rappahannock Station, Virginia, on November 7, 1863. He was confined at Point Lookout, Maryland, until March 19, 1864, when he was released for exchange. After he was exchanged on May 14, 1864, Lewis rejoined his company near Petersburg, Virginia. In March or April 1865, he was shot "through the back and bowels" and captured. He was sent to a Federal hospital on April 6, 1865. No further records.

55. Beck, Obediah

*Private, Company G, 6th Regiment
N.C. State Troops*

Obed was born in 1829. He worked as a farmer in the Pilgrim area and in 1843 married Mary D. Obed and Mary would have four children, Lousia (1849), Franklin (1852), John (1859), and Cicero (1863), before Obediah was conscripted into service on August 23, 1864. He was paroled as a teamster at Greensboro, North Carolina, on May 10, 1865. After the war, he began blacksmithing in the Silver Hill township, and he and Mary went on to have four more children: William (1866), Sarah (1870), Leah (1880), and Sadie (1888). Obediah died of the flu on January 2, 1900. He is buried at Pilgrim United Church of Christ.

56. Beck, Richard

*Private, Holtsburg Guards
Company A, 54th Regiment N.C. Troops*

Richard was born in 1830 to Henry and Sophia Beck. He was a farmer and, in 1856, he married Fannie Barnes. Richard and Fannie would have one child, James (1857), before Richard volunteered on March 4, 1862. He was given a discharge on July 19, 1862, due to medical reasons. The couple would have five more boys: John (1860), J. C. (1862), William L. (1862), Thomas B. (1865), and Newton F. (1868). No further records.

57. Beck, Travis

*Private, Lexington Wildcats
Company I, 14th Regiment N.C. Troops
(4th N.C. Volunteers)*

Travis was born in 1834 to David and Rebecca Beck. He worked as a carpenter prior to volunteering for service on May 14, 1861. He was mustered in as a private and was promoted to corporal on April 25, 1862. Travis was reported present until he was wounded at Malvern Hill, Virginia, on July 1, 1862. He rejoined the company and was detailed as a miner in Davidson County until the end of the war. Travis was reduced in rank to private on November 1, 1862. After the war, Travis married Elizabeth Cox on October 15, 1865. No further records.

58. Beck, William

*Private, Lexington Wildcats
Company I, 14th Regiment N.C. Troops
(4th N.C. Volunteers)*

William was born in 1834 to Christian and Mary Leonard Beck. He worked as a farmer and, in 1857, he married Margaret Jane Williams. William and Margaret would have three children, Martha (1858), Miranda (1860), and Ellen (1861), before William was conscripted into service in Wake County on July 16, 1862. In October, he fell seriously ill and was discharged because of a deposit in his right lung. Margaret paid a man $100 to travel to Richmond, Virginia, to bring William home, but William was already dead when the man arrived. Margaret married George Hedrick, Sr., in 1875.

59. Beck, William A.

*Private, Company A, Colonel Mallet's
Battalion (Camp Guard)
Company I, 49th Regiment N.C. Troops*

William was born on May 26, 1836, to George and Doretta Beck. He married

Picture of the family of G. W. Beeker, taken in 1900. George is seated in the center (Luther Reeves).

Ann Elizabeth in 1858. William served in Company A of Mallet's Battalion prior to being transferred around August 24, 1864. William was reported sick through October 1864. He served until he was captured at Petersburg, Virginia, on April 3, 1865. William was confined at Hart's Island, New York, until June 17, 1865, when he was released after taking the oath of allegiance. After the war, William returned home to the Conrad Hill township. William and Ann would have one child: Martha (1866). William died on June 10, 1916, and is buried at Holly Grove Lutheran Church.

60. Beck, William Lindsay

*Private, Company C, 70th Regiment
N.C. Troops (1st N.C. Junior
Reserves)*

William was born in 1848 to Ambrose and Elizabeth Beck. He worked as a farmer prior to enlisting in the Junior Reserves on May 24, 1864. After the war,

William returned home to the Thomasville township, where he married Dicey E. in 1872. William and Dicey would have four children: Amanda (1880), Cynthia (1882), Robert (1885), and Mary (1889). William lived his life as an average farmer in the Thomasville township until his death in 1928. He is buried at Emanuel United Church of Christ.

61. Beck, William O.

*Private, Company E, 5th Regiment
N.C. State Troops*

William was born on February 25, 1842, to Henry and Sophia Beck. William worked as a miner prior to volunteering on June 11, 1861. He was reported present until he was captured at Spotsylvania Court House, Virginia, on May 12, 1864, but no Federal records confirm this. He returned home before December 31, 1866, when he married Sarah E. Coates. William and Sarah would have eight children: Sarah (1871), George M. (1873),

William (1875), Willis (1878), Maggie (1881), Jesse (1883), Thomas (1886), and Cynthia (1889). In 1900 the family moved to Churchland and built a new home with an orchard and a garden. William died on February 12, 1917, of the flu. He is buried at Pine Primitive Baptist Church.

62. Beckerdite, Andrew

*Sergeant, Company I, 42nd Regiment
N.C. Troops*

Andrew was born on September 27, 1829, to John and Elizabeth Beckerdite. He worked as a farmer prior to volunteering for service in Rowan County on March 26, 1862. He was promoted to sergeant in May 1863 and was reported present until he deserted to the enemy prior to June 23, 1864. Andrew was first confined at Knoxville, Tennessee, then was transferred to Louisville, Kentucky, where he arrived on June 23, 1864. Andrew was released at Louisville on July 1, 1864, after taking the oath of allegiance. After the war, Andrew returned home and married Frances Eliza in 1868. Andrew and Eliza would have two children: George (1870) and May F. (1873). In 1870, he was living with his older brother, Franklin, who held the post of county commissioner. Andrew died on May 30, 1906. He is buried at Midway United Methodist Church.

63. Beckerdite, David B.

Sergeant, Uwharrie Boys
Company G, 46th Regiment N.C. Troops

David was born in 1838 to John and Elizabeth Beckerdite. Prior to the war, he worked in Randolph County as a schoolteacher. David enlisted on May 14, 1862, and was reported present until he was wounded in the right thigh at Reams Station, Virginia, on August 25, 1864. He was promoted to sergeant the next day for the "extraordinary gallantry he showed under fire" at Reams Station, Virginia, gallantry which would cost him his left leg in late 1864. David was retired from service on January 20, 1865. After the war, he continued to teach in the vicinity of Thomasville until his death on May 30, 1874. He is buried at Salem United Methodist Church.

64. Beeker, George Washington

Private, Company B, 14th Battalion
N.C. Home Guard
Company D, 64th Battalion, Georgia
Cavalry

George was born on October 19, 1840, to Lewis and Lovina Beeker. He worked as a farmer prior to being pressed into Home Guard service in October of 1863. George was reported as serving in the Home Guard as well as at the Navy Yard at Charlotte, North Carolina, before being transferred to the 64th Georgia Battalion, which was a unit composed of two North Carolina companies. He was paroled at Greensboro, North Carolina, on May 6, 1865. After the war, George returned home to the Tyro township and, in 1867, he married Mary Elizabeth Sharpe. George and Mary would have a relatively small family of four children: Charles (1868), Mary (1872), Albert (1875), and Nancy (1878); however, many grandchildren were born in their lifetime. George remained a farmer in the Tyro township until his death on February 14, 1934. He is buried at St. Luke's Lutheran Church.

65. Beeson, Newell W.

Corporal, Company G,
2nd Battalion, N.C.
Infantry

Newell was born in 1846 in the Edgefield district of South Carolina. He was working as a mechanic and farmer for Moses Evans in 1860. Newell was conscripted into service in Wake County on February 6, 1864. He was appointed corporal on December 15, 1864. Newell was reported present until March 1865, when he was admitted to a hospital in Greensboro, North Carolina. After the war, he returned home to the Abbott's Creek township; he moved to Forsyth County after 1880. No further records.

66. Beeson, Richard F.

Private, Company I, 42nd Regiment
N.C. Troops

Richard was born on June 9, 1839. Records indicate he entered service in 1865 and was paroled at Greensboro, North Carolina, on May 10, 1865. He died on December 4, 1925. He is buried at New Mount Vernon United Methodist Church. No further records.

67. Benson, William F.

Corporal, Company A, 42nd Regiment
N.C. Troops

William was born on June 23, 1838, to Susan Benson. He worked as a farmer prior to volunteering on November 26, 1861. As of September 1, 1863, he was promoted to corporal and served in that capacity until he was captured at Battery Anderson, Fort Fisher, North Carolina, on December 25, 1864. He was confined at Point Lookout, Maryland, until June 23, 1865, when he was released after taking the oath of allegiance. Pension records indicate he was wounded on an unspecified date. William married Amanda C. Hedrick on November 11, 1865. William and Amanda would have one child: Betty (1867). Amanda died, and William married Notie E. McCrary on May 18, 1892. William died on June 16, 1921, and is buried at Ebenezer United Methodist Church.

Home of Andrew Berrier, built ca. 1857 (Touart, *Building the Backcountry*).

68. Berrier, Andrew

Private, Cleveland Mountain Boys
Company D, 15th Regiment N.C. Troops
(5th N.C. Volunteers)
2nd Company B, 49th Regiment N.C.
Troops

Andrew was born on August 25, 1835, to Charles and Susannah Shoaf Berrier. He worked as a farmer and a blacksmith, and, on March 14, 1859, he married Sarah A. Waitman. Andrew and Sarah would have two children, Laura (1860) and Louisa (1861), before Andrew was conscripted into service in Wake County on July 15, 1862. He deserted on November 30, 1862. Andrew returned on February 23, 1863, and was transferred to the 49th Regiment. He was reported present until he was captured at Sandy Ridge, North Carolina, on April 20, 1863, and was confined at City Point, Virginia, until May 28, 1863, when he was exchanged. Andrew was arrested and "lodged in the guardhouse" at Weldon, North Carolina, for desertion on December 23, 1863. However, the roll of honor states that he was discharged on October 16, 1863, under the "writ of habeas corpus." After the war, Andrew returned home, and he and his wife had six more children: Robert (1866), Uma (1869), Charles (1870), Winifred (1872), Sarah E. (1875), and Druscilla (1878). Andrew worked as a farmer in the Arcadia township until he died on May 24, 1894. He is buried at Beulah United Church of Christ.

69. Berrier, Felix L.

Private, Company I, 42nd Regiment
N.C. Troops

Felix was born in 1844. In 1860 he was living in the house of Jacob and Catharine Shoaf. Felix volunteered on March 8, 1862. He was present until he was wounded around Petersburg, Virginia, on July 21, 1864. Felix was retired to the Invalid Corps on December 6, 1864. No further records.

70. Berrier, Henry Israel

Captain, 66th Regiment N.C. Militia (1861 organization)

Henry was born on December 18, 1845, to Charles and Susannah Shoaf Berrier. He worked as a farmer and secured a commission in the prewar militia. He served as a captain in the Midway District Company. Records indicate that he may have also served in the 14th N.C. Home Guard. After the war, he married America C. Michael on December 13, 1866. Henry and America would raise four children: Shockley (1869), Edward (1870), Jacob (1874), and Mary S. (1878). Henry worked as a farmer in the Arcadia township until his death on August 5, 1881. He is buried at Shiloh United Methodist Church.

71. Berrier, Henry J.

Private, Carolina Rangers Company B, 10th Virginia Cavalry Regiment

Henry was born on December 5, 1835. He worked as a farmer, and in 1853, he married Sarah. Henry and Sarah would have two children: Joseph (1855) and Julian (1858), before Henry, now a miller, was conscripted on April 8, 1864. He was reported on detail for July and August 1864, looking for a horse. Henry was reported present through January 27, 1865. Company records indicate that he was "issued clothing on 9/30 & 12/31/64." After the war, Henry returned home and worked as a miller, farmer, and machinist in Lexington until his death on November 11, 1907. He is buried in the Lexington City Cemetery.

72. Berrier, Henry Jackson

Sergeant, Thomasville Rifles Company B, 14th Regiment N.C. Troops (4th N.C. Volunteers)

Jackson was born on December 5, 1836, to Jacob and Christina Grimes Berrier. He worked as a farmer until he volunteered on August 15, 1861. Jackson was promoted to sergeant, reduced in rank, then promoted again by April 1864. He was reported present until he was captured at Farmville, Virginia, on April 6, 1865. Jackson was confined at Point Lookout, Maryland, until June 24, 1865, when he was released after taking the oath of allegiance. After the war, he returned home and married Sallie J. Guyer on August 13, 1876. They had one child, Minnie, in 1879. Jackson died on November 14, 1907. He is buried in the Lexington City Cemetery.

73. Berrier, Hiram Randall

Sergeant, Carolina Rangers Company B, 10th Virginia Cavalry Regiment

Hiram was born on August 5, 1839, to Jacob and Catharine Darr Berrier. He worked as a farmer until he volunteered in Davie County on October 29, 1861. He was promoted to sergeant on April 30, 1862, and was sent on a horse detail during September and October 1863. Hiram returned from detail on November 3, 1863, and served until he was wounded and captured on June 25, 1864. His right leg was amputated. The Federal commander, Colonel Pleasant of the 7th Pennsylvania Cavalry, paroled him and sent him home. Federal records state his appearance: "5'6", fair complexion, dark

Orderly sergeant of the Carolina Rangers, Hiram Berrier (Luther Reeves).

hair, gray eyes." He served as company clerk and orderly. In an April 10, 1864, letter, Hiram wrote to John Tussey:

> Camp Near Charlottesville, Virginia, April 10, 1864.
>
> It is believed by all our generals that we will have some of the hardest fighting to do this summer that has ever been done. Old R. E. Lee says he can whip the whole Yankee nation if they will attack him in his fortifications. I think that he has found out that going into Pennsylvania is like the Negro's Opossom [*sic*]: it costs more than it comes to. I talked with some Yankee pickett near Hamelton's Crossing. They say they are going to elect a new President in the United States and it would be a man who was opposed to the war. They said they would vote for no man who was not in favor of stoping [*sic*] the war. I do not think myself the war will last longer than this year.
>
> Good Bye,
>
> H. R. Berrier to John Tussey

After the war, Hiram married Frances E. Sowers in 1866. Hiram and Frances would have five children: Wade Hampton (1867), Jacob (1869), John L. (1871), Sarah (1874), and Samuel T. (1877). After Franny's death, Hiram married Victoria in 1892. This union produced two children: Esther (1894) and Olmstead (1899). Hiram lived in the Lexington township until his death on August 5, 1910. He is buried at Beulah United Church of Christ.

74. Berrier, Lewis

Sergeant, Carolina Rangers Company B, 10th Virginia Cavalry Regiment

Lewis was born on April 11, 1821, to Phillip and Sivela Grimes Berrier. He was a farmer, and, in 1842, he married Susanna Wagner. Lewis and Susanna would have nine children, Mary Elizabeth (1843), Wilmina (1845), Thomas (1848), Adam (1851), David (1852), Phillip (1854), George (1856), William (1859), and Jeffrey (1861), before Lewis volunteered on October 29, 1861. He was mustered in as a private and was promoted to sergeant on April 30, 1862. Lewis was present through January 27, 1865. Susanna died sometime during the hostilities. After the war, Lewis married

Sally Chamberlain on January 21, 1866. This marriage produced Lewis (1869), Charles (1870), Isaac (1880), China (1882), and Andrew (1884). Lewis lived in the Arcadia township until his death on May 18, 1891. He is buried at Shiloh United Methodist Church.

75. Berrier, Thomas Jefferson

Private, Carolina Rangers
Company B, 10th Virginia Cavalry
Regiment

Thomas was born on October 6, 1847, to Lewis and Susanna Wagner Berrier. He worked as a farmer until he enlisted on December 31, 1864. He returned home and married Nancy McGehee on December 27, 1868. They moved to Cana, Virginia. Thomas died on March 16, 1927, in Carroll County, Virginia, and is buried at Mount Zion Cemetery in Piper's Gap, Virginia.

76. Berrier, William A.

First Lieutenant, 65th Regiment N.C.
Militia (1861 organization)

William was born on October 8, 1833, to Henry and Sarah Berrier. He was a farmer in the Lexington township and married Elizabeth in 1854. The couple had nine children: Lucretia (1856), Cicero (1858), Julia (1860), Mary D. (1863), William (1865), Robert (1868), Triphenia (1871), David (1873), and Ida (1878). William was commissioned as a captain in the Lexington District Company. He lived in the Lexington area until his passing on May 3, 1902. He is buried in the Lexington City Cemetery.

77. Biggers, William D.

Corporal, Company B, 4th Regiment
N.C. State Troops

William was born on November 20, 1841, to the Reverend R. H. and Sarah Hedrick Biggers. He worked as a farmer prior to volunteering in Rowan County, at almost age 20, on June 3, 1861. He was mustered in as a private and was promoted to corporal on September 1, 1861. William was wounded in the hip at Seven Pines, Virginia, on May 31, 1862. He was sent to a hospital, where he remained until March 13, 1863, when he was given a medical discharge. He returned home and began work as a clerk in several stores in Lexington. On June 4, 1872, he

married Mary C. Conrad. The two had no children. William died on July 17, 1899. He is buried in the Lexington City Cemetery.

78. Billings, Benjamin Franklin

Private, Davidson Guards
Company A, 21st Regiment N.C. Troops
(11th N.C. Volunteers)

Ben was born in 1840 to Henry and Mary Long Billings. He worked as a farmer prior to enlisting, at age 21, on May 8, 1861. He deserted around September 1, 1861, and he returned to duty sometime shortly after. Ben was given a discharge on the grounds of "imbecility." On October 1, 1873, he married Ellen M. Parks. No further records.

79. Billings, Meredith B.

Corporal, Lexington Wildcats
Company I, 14th Regiment N.C. Troops
(4th N.C. Volunteers)

Meredith was born in 1842 to Henry and Mary Long Billings. He lived in the home of Smith and Eve Cross while working as a miner at the Silver Hill mine. He volunteered on May 14, 1861, and was mustered in as a corporal. He served in that capacity until he was wounded in the arm at Malvern Hill, Virginia, on July 1, 1862. His arm was amputated, but Meredith died of gangrene on July 21, 1862. He is buried in Hollywood Cemetery in Richmond, Virginia.

80. Billings, Roswell A.

Private, Company A, 42nd Regiment
N.C. Troops

Roswell was born on March 25, 1835, to Henry and Mary Long Billings. He worked as a farmer until he enlisted on May 12, 1862. Roswell was present or accounted for until he was captured at Battery Anderson, Fort Fisher, North Carolina, on December 25, 1864. He was confined at Fort Delaware, Delaware, until June 17, 1865, when he was released after taking the oath of allegiance. After the war, he returned to work as a farmer. On January 1, 1878, he married Sarah Shaw, and the two moved to Cotton Grove. Roswell and Sarah would have two children: Lilly Ann (1879) and Robert E. Lee (1891). Roswell died on October 4, 1912, and is buried at Cotton Grove United Methodist Church.

81. Bischer, Godfrey W.

Private, Company F, 7th Regiment
N.C. State Troops

Godfrey was born on December 1, 1818, to Conrad and Marie Bischer, who were German immigrants from the Bavarian Palatine region. He worked as a farmer, and in 1838, he married Lucinda Loftin. In 1839, their first child, William, was born. They would have eight more children before 1860: John (1840), Margaret (1842), Julia (1844), James (1848), Sarah (1849), Franklin (1853), John Milton (1855), and Rebecca (1858). He was 50 years old when he enlisted on February 22, 1862. He was captured at Hanover Court House, Virginia, on May 27, 1862. Godfrey was sent to Fort Monroe, Virginia, and was confined there until exchanged at Aiken's Landing, Virginia, on August 5, 1862. He returned to service and was captured at Gettysburg, Pennsylvania, between July 1 and 5, 1863. He was confined at Fort Mifflin, Pennsylvania, until he arrived at Fort Delaware, Delaware, on November 17, 1863. Godfrey was paroled on October 30, 1864, was transferred to Venus Point, Georgia, and was exchanged on November 15, 1864. He rejoined his company and took the oath of allegiance at Salisbury, North Carolina, on June 3, 1865. After the war, Godfrey returned home to his farm and family. He had a reputation as a hard worker, which led to a story. One Sunday, a preacher caught Godfrey plowing his field. After that, a few people considered him to be a dreadful sinner. Years after his death on September 7, 1897, people in Jackson Hill still used the phrase "Great Godfrey Bischer" to express shock and surprise. He is buried at Siloam United Methodist Church.

82. Black, Amos

Private, Thomasville Rifles
Company B, 14th Regiment N.C. Troops
(4th N.C. Volunteers)

Amos was born in 1839 to Solomon and Catharine Black. He worked as a farmer prior to being conscripted into service in Wake County on July 16, 1862. He was reported present until he died in "the valley of Virginia" on November 22, 1862, of disease.

83. Black, Casper

Private, Company H, 48th Regiment
N.C. Troops

Casper was born in 1832 to Solomon and Elizabeth Black. In 1860, he was working as a hired farmhand for Henry H. Conrad. He volunteered at age 30, on March 5, 1862. Casper was reported present until he was wounded at Globe Tavern, Virginia, on August 21, 1864. He returned to duty until he was hospitalized on March 26, 1865, with "chronic diarrhea." Casper was captured in a hospital in Richmond, Virginia, on April 3, 1865. He died on April 25, 1865, of "consumption."

84. Black, Elijah

Private, 2nd Company C, 2nd Regiment N.C. State Troops

Elijah was born in Davidson County, where he resided prior to being conscripted into service in Wake County on July 8, 1862. He died of disease at Guinea Station, Virginia, on February 17, 1863.

85. Black, Jesse

Private, Company H, 48th Regiment N.C. Troops

Jesse was born in 1841 to Solomon and Elizabeth Black. He worked as a hired farmhand for David and Elizabeth Fouts. Jesse volunteered on March 5, 1862, and died of pneumonia at Petersburg, Virginia, on July 3, 1862.

86. Black, John Wesley

Sergeant, Company I, 42nd Regiment N.C. Troops

John was born on December 24, 1838, to Jacob and Judith A. Black. John worked as an apprentice in his father's blacksmith shop. In 1861, he married Laura Adams. John and Laura would have one child, David (1862), before John volunteered on March 8, 1862, serving as a private until he was promoted to sergeant in September 1864. He served as sergeant until he was captured at Wise's Forks, Virginia, on March 8, 1865. John was confined at Point Lookout, Maryland, until June 23, 1865, when he was released upon taking the oath of allegiance. After the war, John returned home and continued his trades as a farmer and blacksmith. John and his wife would have seven more children: Franklin, Susannah, Robert, James, Walter, Emma, and Margaret. John died on

May 25, 1905. He is buried at Liberty Baptist Church.

87. Black, Samuel

Private, Company C, 76th Regiment N.C. Troops (6th N.C. Senior Reserves)

Samuel was born on February 17, 1817. He lived in the southern division of Davidson County, and, on November 28, 1843, he married Mary Myers. Samuel and Mary would have seven children, Sandy (1845), Sarah E. (1848), Pleasant (1849), Levi (1852), Andrew (1854), John (1856), and Allison (1858), before Samuel began serving in Moss's Reserve Battalion, which became the 6th Regiment N.C. Senior Reserves. He continued to farm after his service was over. Samuel lived in the Conrad Hill township until his death on September 12, 1892. He is buried at Heath Wesleyan Methodist Church.

88. Black, William

Private, Company H, 48th Regiment N.C. Troops

William was born in 1833 to Solomon and Catharine Black. In 1857, William married Melinda Shuler. William and Melinda would have one child, Fidella (1858), before William was conscripted into service in Petersburg, Virginia, on August 8, 1862. He was wounded at Sharpsburg, Maryland, on September 17, 1862. William was hospitalized at Richmond, Virginia, where he died on November 25, 1862, of wounds received and "typhoid pneumonia."

89. Blackburn, Joshua D.

Private, Davidson Guards Company A, 21st Regiment N.C. Troops (11th N.C. Volunteers)

Joshua was born in 1840. He worked as a farmer prior to enlisting, at age 21, on May 8, 1861. He was reported present until killed in action at the battle of Second Manassas, Virginia, on August 28, 1862.

90. Blackburn, William D.

Private, Davidson Guards Company A, 21st Regiment N.C. Troops (11th N.C. Volunteers)

William was born in 1833. He worked as a farmer and was married to Jane

Cameron prior to enlisting on May 8, 1861. He died of dysentery at Front Royal, Virginia, on October 30, 1861.

91. Blair, Arris

Corporal, Company A, 10th Battalion, N.C. Heavy Artillery

Arris was born in 1836 and worked as a shoemaker in the Lines Shoe Factory prior to the war. He volunteered on April 23, 1861, but deserted on September 1, 1861. He returned and enlisted in the 10th N.C. Heavy Artillery on April 26, 1862. Arris was mustered in as a private and was promoted to corporal in October 1862. He served until the end of the war and was paroled at Greensboro, North Carolina, on May 10, 1865. No further records.

92. Blair, James A.

Private, Company A, 10th Battalion, N.C. Heavy Artillery

James was born in 1830. At the age of 30 he was employed as a schoolteacher and was living with Aquilla Jones. He enlisted on April 26, 1862. James died of disease in eastern North Carolina only a few weeks later, on May 18, 1862.

93. Blair, James Madison

Private, Chatam Light Infantry Company G, 48th Regiment N.C. Troops

James was born in 1830. He resided in Thomasville and worked as a shoemaker with his wife, Rebecca Gray. James was conscripted on August 14, 1862, and was reported present until wounded at Hatcher's Run, Virginia, on February 5, 1865. He was captured in a Richmond, Virginia, hospital and was sent to Point Lookout, Maryland, on May 2, 1865. James was released on June 26, 1865, after taking the oath of allegiance. After the war, he returned home and continued to work in the shoe factory. He and his wife had one son, Albert, who was born in 1872. James died in June 1900. He is buried in the Thomasville City Cemetery.

94. Blair, Joseph F.

Private, Company A, 10th Battalion, N.C. Heavy Artillery

Joseph was born in 1835. He was employed as a shoemaker in Thomasville before marrying Maria in 1858. Joseph and Maria would have two children, Wesley (1859) and Lettie (1862), before Joseph was conscripted on April 26, 1862. He saw much action until he was paroled at Greensboro, North Carolina, May 4 or 5, 1865. No further records.

95. Blair, William F.

Private, Chatam Light Infantry
Company G, 48th Regiment N.C. Troops
Company G, 46th Regiment N.C. Troops

William was born in 1838 to A. P. and Elizabeth Blair. He worked in the Lines Shoe Factory prior to being conscripted into service on August 14, 1862. William was reported present until April 1, 1863, when he was reported transferred to Company G, 46th Regiment, in exchange for Private Matthew Troy. With the 46th, he was wounded at Bristoe Station, Virginia (October 13, 1863), at Wilderness, Virginia (May 5, 1864), and at Ream's Station, Virginia (August 24, 1864). No further records.

96. Bodenheimer, Christian

Private, Company F, 76th Regiment
N.C. Troops (6th N.C. Senior
Reserves)

Christian was born on November 16, 1816. He worked as a farmer in the northern district of Davidson County. He married Catharine Tesh in 1848. Christian served in Hill's Senior Reserves, which became the 6th N.C. Senior Reserves in January 1865. Christian passed away of a nonreported cause on February 22, 1865. He is buried at Abbott's Missionary Baptist Church.

97. Bodenheimer, Christian F.

Private, Confederate Guards
Company K, 48th Regiment N.C. Troops

Christian was born on May 30, 1833, to Christian and Temperance Bodenheimer. He worked as a farmer prior to being conscripted on August 8, 1862. He was wounded severely at Sharpsburg, Maryland, on September 17, 1862. Christian was sent home on furlough. While he was home he married Sarah E. Everett on October 25, 1862. He was allowed to stay at home and was dropped from the rolls on January 1, 1864. Christian recovered from his serious wound, and the couple would have six children:

Frances (1867), James (1868), Richard (1870), William (1872), Robert Lee (1875), and Christian (1878). They lived in the Abbott's Creek area for the rest of their lives. Christian passed away on January 14, 1893. He is buried at Abbott's Creek Missionary Baptist Church.

98. Bodenheimer, David Harrison

Private, Company C, 70th Regiment
N.C. Troops (1st N.C. Junior
Reserves)

David was born in 1846 to John and Mary Evans Bodenheimer. He worked as a carpenter prior to enlisting in the Junior Reserves on May 25, 1864. He served with the regiment until the end of the war. After the war, he returned to his trade, and, on December 22, 1870, he married Mary A. Yokely. David and Mary would have four children: Audry (1880), Caroline (1882), Charles (1887), and William (1890). David lived to be one of the county's last ten living Confederate veterans until his death in 1937. He is buried at Abbott's Creek Missionary Baptist Church.

99. Bodenheimer, Isaiah R.

Second Lieutenant, 66th Regiment
N.C. Militia (1861 organization)

Isaiah was born in 1829 to William and Mary Bodenheimer. He worked as a farmer, and, in 1847, he married Anna Teague. Ike and Anna would have six children: William (1848), John (1854), David (1856), Mary (1858), Jacob (1862), and Pinkney (1865). Isaiah was commissioned to serve as a second lieutenant in the Abbott's Creek District Company on November 26, 1861. After the war, he apparently moved to Forsyth County. No further records.

100. Bodenheimer, Jacob B.

Private, Confederate Guards
Company K, 48th Regiment N.C. Troops

Jacob was born in 1841 to Christian and Mary Bodenheimer. He worked as a farmer prior to being conscripted on August 8, 1862. Jacob was reported present until October 6, 1864, when he deserted to the enemy near Poplar Springs Church, Virginia. He was confined at Washington, D.C., on October 10, 1864, and was released on an

unspecified date after taking the oath of allegiance. No further records.

101. Bodenheimer, Joseph P.

Private, Confederate Guards
Company K, 48th Regiment NC Troops

Joseph was born in 1832. He worked as a farmer until he was conscripted on August 8, 1862. He was captured at Sharpsburg, Maryland, on September 17, 1862. Joseph was confined at Ft. Delaware, Delaware, until he died on October 14, 1862, of unreported causes.

102. Bodenheimer, Pleasant N.

Private, Company A, 42nd Regiment
N.C. Troops

Pleasant was born on December 5, 1838. He worked as a farmer prior to his marriage with Margaret in 1861. Pleasant and Margaret would have one child, Eliza (1862), before Pleasant was conscripted on July 29, 1862. He was reported present until he deserted on September 17, 1863. Pleasant returned to duty prior to April 10, 1864. He was reported present until he was captured at Fort Fisher, North Carolina, on December 25, 1864. Pleasant was confined at Point Lookout, Maryland, until May 12, 1865, when he was released after taking the oath of allegiance. He returned from the war and began blacksmithing in the Midway township. He and Margaret would have four more children: William (1865), Charlie (1868), Elizabeth (1873), and Geneva (1874). Pleasant continued his work in the Lexington township until his passing on July 3, 1924. He is buried at Bethlehem United Church of Christ.

103. Bodenheimer, Randall

Private, Davidson Guards
Company A, 21st Regiment N.C.
Troops (11th N.C. Volunteers)

Randall was born in 1823. He worked as a farmer in the northern district of Davidson County. In 1850, John W. Garrison was living with him as a boarder. In 1842, Randall married Jarusha. Randall and Jarusha would have had five children: Susannah (1844), William (1847), Elizabeth Jane (1851), Isaac (1854), and Martha (1859). Randall lived in the Abbott's Creek area until his death in 1899. He is buried at Abbott's Creek Missionary Baptist Church.

104. Bodenheimer, William

Private, Confederate Guards
Company K, 48th Regiment N.C. Troops

William was born in 1846 to Jacob and Elizabeth Bodenheimer. He worked as a farmer prior to being conscripted on February 1, 1864. William was present through October 6, 1864, when he deserted to the enemy near Poplar Springs Church, Virginia. He was confined at Washington, D.C., until he was released on an unspecified date after taking the oath of allegiance. He returned from the war and on December 26, 1867, he married Phoebe Hines. No further records.

105. Bodenheimer, William

Private, Confederate Guards
Company K, 48th Regiment N.C. Troops

William was born in 1842 to William and Mary Bodenheimer. He worked as a farmer and manager of his family's small plantation. William volunteered in Forsyth County on March 8, 1862. He was killed in action at the battle of Fredericksburg, Virginia, on December 13, 1862.

106. Boggs, Arrington G.

Sergeant, Company I, 42nd Regiment
N.C. Troops

Arrington was born on October 12, 1842, to Adam and Sarah Boggs. He worked as a farmer prior to volunteering on March 7, 1862. He was promoted to sergeant by August 1862 and served until he was captured at Wise's Forks, Virginia, on March 10, 1865. Arrington was confined at Point Lookout, Maryland, until May 12, 1865, when he was released after taking the oath of allegiance. After the war, he returned home, and on May 14, 1867, he married Sarah Jane Lee. The couple would have two children: Charles (1872) and Albert (1874). Arrington lived as a small farmer until his death on April 17, 1898. He is buried at Mount Carmel Methodist Church.

107. Bowers, Adam Roswell

First Lieutenant, Company H, 48th
Regiment N.C. Troops

Adam was born in 1839. He worked as a teacher in Thomasville before he married Mariah M. Sink on August 26, 1860. Adam and Mariah would have one child, John (1861), before Adam volunteered on March 13, 1862, and was elected first lieutenant. He was forced to resign due to a serious lung disease. His resignation was accepted on August 5, 1862. Adam operated a dry goods store and taught school for most of his life. He and Mariah would have five more children: Webster (1865), Minnie (1869), Beatrice (1872), Adam R. (1876), and Margaret (1878). In 1880, he was listed as a schoolteacher in the Lexington township. No further records.

108. Bowers, Andrew

Private, Company F, 76th Regiment
N.C. Troops (6th N.C. Senior
Reserves)

Andrew was born on July 13, 1810. He worked as a farmer in the northern district of Davidson County. In 1845, he married Anna Mariah. They would have eight children: Hamilton L. (1847), Nathaniel Gustavas (1849), Margaret K. (1852), Sarah (1855), Annie Parnetha (1858), Hogan (1861), John (1863), and Stimpson (1867). Andrew served with Moss's Reserves, which became Company F of the 6th N.C. Senior Reserves. He worked as a farmer in the North Thomasville township until his death on February 10, 1890. He is buried at Emanuel United Church of Christ.

109. Bowers, Hamilton Lindsey

Private, Company C, 70th Regiment
N.C. Troops (1st N.C. Junior
Reserves)

Hamilton was born in 1847 to Andrew and Anna Mariah Bowers. He worked as a farmer prior to enlisting on May 25, 1864, in the Junior Reserves. After the war, Hamilton married Tryphenia L. Myers on December 2, 1869. The couple had seven children: Pleasant (1870), Andrew L. (1872), David E. (1873), Jarusha (1874), Charles (1876), Jesse (1877), and Curtis (1879). He lived next door to his father in the Thomasville township and continued farming until his death on November 30, 1890. He is buried at Emanuel United Church of Christ.

110. Bowers, Lorenzo W.

Private, Lexington Wildcats
Company I, 14th Regiment N.C. Troops
(4th N.C. Volunteers)

Lorenzo was born in 1843 to Lovina Bowers. He worked as a farmer prior to volunteering on May 14, 1861. He was reported present until captured at Martinsburg, Virginia, on July 23, 1863. Lorenzo was confined at Point Lookout, Maryland, until March 16, 1865, when he was paroled and transferred to Boulware's Wharf, Virginia, where he was received for exchange. No further records.

111. Bowers, William

Private, Lexington Wildcats
Company I, 14th Regiment N.C. Troops
(4th N.C. Volunteers)

William was born on July 14, 1845, to William and Mary Bowers. He worked as a farmer prior to volunteering on May 14, 1861. He served for the duration of the war until he was paroled at Appomattox Court House, Virginia, on April 9, 1865. After the war, he returned to farming and married Frances E. Hepler in 1873. William and Frances had three children: Oscar (1874), Marvin (1881), and Minnie (1886). He was a member of Rich Fork Baptist Church, where he served as the Sunday school superintendent and a deacon for 24 years. William died on May 18, 1909. He is buried at Rich Fork Baptist Church.

112. Bowers, William

Private, Company B, 48th Regiment
N.C. Troops

William was born in 1831 to Absalom "Apps" and Eve Sechrist Bowers. He worked as a farmer and married a young Susannah in 1856. William and Susannah would have three children, James (1857), Catharine D. (1859), and Jacob (1861), before William was conscripted on August 8, 1862. He served as a private until he was captured at Cold Harbor, Virginia, on June 3, 1864. William was confined at Point Lookout, Maryland, until July 12, 1864, when he was transferred to Elmira, New York. He died in a massive train wreck around Sholoa, Pennsylvania, while en route to Elmira, on July 15, 1864.

113. Bowers, William Henry

Private, Company C, 70th Regiment
N.C. Troops (1st N.C. Junior
Reserves)

Henry was born on July 4, 1847, to George and Margaret A. Bowers. He enlisted in the Junior Reserves on May 25, 1864. He served in this capacity until the war's end. On October 25, 1866, he married Adeline Kepley. Henry and Adeline would have eight children: Jacob (1867), Robert E. Lee (1871), Martha (1873), Julie (1875), Henry M. (1877), John (1880), George (1883), and Luther (1886). He was trained as a cancer doctor and lived in the town of Thomasville. He was a leader in the community, and when his father, George, committed suicide, many people came to support him. Henry moved to Holly Grove around 1910 with his wife and two of his sons and lived there until his death on March 21, 1926. Henry is buried at Holly Grove Lutheran Church.

114. Boyles, Matthew W.

Private, Company D, 1st Regiment
N.C. State Troops

Matthew was born on October 26, 1842. He worked as a farmer and married Susan in 1861. He volunteered for service in Rowan County on June 18, 1861. After the war, he served as a traveling minister in Rowan, Davidson, Davie, and Stanly counties until his death on January 15, 1892. He is buried in the Lexington City Cemetery.

115. Bragg, James D.

Private, Davidson Guards
Company A, 21st Regiment N.C.
Troops (11th N.C. Volunteers)

James volunteered on May 8, 1861. He was reported present or accounted for until he was reported absent without leave in January 1863. James was dropped from the rolls as a deserter. No further records.

116. Brassington, Samuel W.

First Lieutenant, Lexington Wildcats
Company I, 14th Regiment N.C. Troops
(4th N.C. Volunteers)

Samuel was born on May 6, 1836. He worked as an agricultural mechanic and married Mary in 1856. Samuel and Mary would have two children, James (1858) and Mary (1860), before Samuel volunteered on May 14, 1861. He was mustered in as a private and later elected as first lieutenant. Samuel resigned his commis-

sion when the regiment was reorganized on April 26, 1862. He returned home to the Yadkin township. He and his wife had six more children: Emma (1865), Sarah (1866), Jane (1867), Ernest (1872), William (1873), and Martha (1876). Samuel died on September 12, 1881. He is buried at Good Hope United Methodist Church.

117. Bratain, Charles A.

Private, Company C, 70th Regiment
N.C. Troops (1st N.C. Junior
Reserves)

Charles was born in 1847 to Ephraim and Rachael Bratain. He helped his father in his blacksmith shop in Tyro until he enlisted on May 25, 1864. Charles served in the 1st Junior Reserves until he died of disease in January 1865.

118. Brewer, Harrison

First Lieutenant, 66th Regiment N.C.
Militia (1861 organization)
14th Battalion, N.C. Home Guard

Harrison was born in 1820. He worked as a farmer, and in 1846, he married Eliza Everhart. Harrison and Eliza would have two children: Sarah Ann (1849) and Ephraim Lee (1853). In 1860, Ransom and Hubbard Essick were living with him as paid hirelings. Harrison served as first lieutenant in the Thomasville District Company from December 13, 1861, and, according to family history, also served in the Home Guard. No further records.

119. Brewer, Joseph H.

Private, Confederate Guards
Company K, 21st Regiment N.C. Troops
(11th N.C. Volunteers)
Company A, 4th Regiment, U.S. Vol-
unteer Infantry

Joseph was born in 1835 and worked as a farmer prior to volunteering on June 11, 1861. He served as a private until captured at Williamsport, Maryland, on July 14, 1863. Joseph was confined at Fort Delaware, Delaware, until transferred to Point Lookout, Maryland, on October 15, 1863. He was released from Point Lookout on October 12, 1863, after joining the U.S. Army. After the war, he returned home to the Thomasville township, where he married Loretta in 1866. Joseph and

Loretta would have two children: Victoria (1868) and Dora Alice (1869). Dora died at the age of two. In 1870, he and his wife took in Eliza, Amos, James, Alvin, Emory, and Lewis Hartman. No further records.

120. Brewer, L. Elias

Private, Company A, 10th Battalion,
N.C. Heavy Artillery

Elias was born on October 7, 1844. He worked as a farmer prior to being conscripted in Wake County on April 3, 1863. Elias was present through September 1864. After the war, he returned home and married Celia before 1870. Elias worked as a farmer and carpenter in the Midway township until his death on October 2, 1895. He is buried at Centenary Methodist Church.

121. Briggs, Enoch

Private, Lexington Wildcats
Company I, 14th Regiment N.C. Troops
(4th N.C. Volunteers)

Enoch was born on March 30, 1827, the son of Henry Briggs. He worked as a farmer, and, in 1847, he married Sarah (Sally). Enoch and Sally would have four children, John (1848), Phoebe (1851), Jane (1853), and Henry (1864), before Enoch was conscripted in late 1864. He was paroled at Greensboro, North Carolina, on May 6, 1865. After the war, he began work as a silver miner in the Silver Hill township. Before 1890, Sally died. He married Lucinda in 1893, and they had two children: Rosa Lee (1893) and Mashey (1896). Enoch died on March 7, 1865. He is buried at Holloways Baptist Church.

122. Bright, William

Private, Company A, Mallet's Battalion
(Camp Guards)
Chatam Light Infantry, Company G,
48th Regiment N.C. Troops

William enlisted in June 1862 in Company A, Mallet's Battalion. He was transferred to Company G, 48th N.C. Regiment, prior to September 1864. William was wounded in the shoulder at Hatcher's Run, Virginia, on February 5, 1865. He was hospitalized in Richmond, Virginia, and was issued a furlough for 60 days on February 11, 1865. No further records.

123. Brindle, Charles A.

*Private, Company H, 48th Regiment
N.C. Troops*

Charles was born in 1834 to John and Mary Brindle. He worked as a farmer, and in 1854, he married Amanda Smith. Charles and Amanda would have two children, Daniel (1857) and Eli W. (1860), before Charles was conscripted in Petersburg, Virginia, on August 8, 1862. He was wounded at Sharpsburg, Maryland, on September 17, 1862, and was reported absent, wounded, through February 1863. Charles returned in March 1863 but deserted on May 10, 1863. After the war, Charles and his wife had four more children: Sarah (1867), Elizabeth Caroline (1869), Pinkney (1874), and Catherine (1877). No further records.

124. Brindle, John

*Private, Company H, 48th Regiment
N.C. Troops*

John was born in 1833 to John and Mary Brindle. He worked as a farmer prior to being conscripted in Petersburg, Virginia, on August 8, 1862. John was reported present until he deserted with his brother, Charles, on May 10, 1863. He returned on September 27, 1864. Charles was reported present until he was captured at Hatcher's Run, Virginia, on April 2, 1865. He was confined at Point Lookout, Maryland, until June 23, 1865, when he was released after taking the oath of allegiance. No further records.

125. Brinkley, Daniel

*Private, Cleveland Mountain Boys
Company D, 15th Regiment N.C. Troops
(5th N.C. Volunteers)
2nd Company B, 49th Regiment N.C.
Troops*

Daniel was born in 1837 to John and Mary Leonard Brinkley. He worked as a farmer, and, in 1857, he married Cornelia Saintsing. Daniel and Cornelia would have two children, Martha (1858) and John (1859), before Daniel was conscripted in Wake County on July 15, 1862. He deserted when his third child, Mary, was born in September 1862. Daniel returned on February 12, 1863, after his company had been transferred to the 49th Regiment. He was present for the duration of the war and was paroled at Greensboro, North Carolina, on May 8,

1865. After the war, Daniel worked as a gunsmith in the Lexington township. He and Cornelia had three more children: Amanda (1865), Annie (1866), and Susan (1868). He died in 1887.

126. Brinkley, Harrison

*Private, Cleveland Mountain Boys
Company D, 15th Regiment N.C. Troops
(5th N.C. Volunteers)
2nd Company B, 49th Regiment N.C.
Troops*

Harrison was born on August 14, 1840, to John and Mary Leonard Brinkley. He worked as a farmer until he was conscripted in Wake County on July 15, 1862. He was reported present until he deserted in December 1862. Harrison rejoined the company after it was transferred to the 49th Regiment on January 9, 1863. He was arrested and "lodged in the guardhouse" at Weldon, North Carolina, on December 23, 1864. Harrison rejoined the company and was paroled at Greensboro, North Carolina, on May 8, 1865. After the war, he married Louisa J. Hinkle on July 19, 1865. Harrison and Louisa would have eight children: David (1865), Alice Lovina (1869), Mary (1872), Ida (1874), Charles (1877), Minnie (1880), John (1883), and Arthur (1885). Harrison died on March 24, 1905. He is buried at Beulah United Church of Christ.

127. Brinkley, Henry

*Corporal, Davidson Guards
Company A, 21st Regiment N.C. Troops
(11th N.C. Volunteers)*

Henry was born in 1840. He worked as a farmer until he volunteered on May 8, 1861. Henry was wounded at Winchester, Virginia, on May 25, 1862, and at Chancellorsville, Virginia, on May 3, 1863. He was reported absent, wounded, through October 1, 1864, when he was promoted to corporal. Henry returned to duty prior to March 1, 1865, and was present until he was paroled at Appomattox Court House, Virginia, on April 9, 1865. After the war, Henry returned to the Lexington township, where he married Mary in 1865. They had two children: William (1866) and Charles (1869). No further records.

128. Brinkley, Henry B.

*Private, Company B, 48th Regiment
N.C. Troops*

Henry was born in 1844. He worked as a carpenter prior to volunteering on March 6, 1862. Henry was wounded in the arm at King's School House, Virginia, on June 25, 1862. His right arm was amputated, and Henry was discharged on July 18, 1862, at age 18. No further records.

129. Brinkley, John Hamilton

*Private, Cleveland Mountain Boys
Company D, 15th Regiment N.C. Troops
(5th N.C. Volunteers)
2nd Company B, 49th Regiment N.C.
Troops*

John was born on July 19, 1838, to John and Mary Leonard Brinkley. He worked as a farmer prior to being conscripted in Wake County on July 15, 1862. John was reported present through April 1, 1864, when he deserted. He was arrested by the Home Guard and was returned to service on August 31, 1864. John was court-martialed on October 22, 1864. After the war, John returned home, and, on September 9, 1870, he married Paulina Leonard. One month later, on October 9, 1870, he passed away.

130. Britt, Frank J.

*Private, Thomasville Rifles
Company B, 14th Regiment N.C. Troops
(4th N.C. Volunteers)*

Frank was born in Maine in 1841. He moved to Thomasville and worked in the Lines Shoe Factory before he volunteered on April 23, 1861. He was mustered in as a sergeant, but was reduced in rank on July 27, 1861. Frank was present or accounted for until he was killed in action at Malvern Hill, Virginia, on July 1, 1862.

131. Brittingham, John W.

*First Sergeant, Lexington Wildcats
Company I, 14th Regiment N.C. Troops
(4th N.C. Volunteers)*

John was born on August 30, 1825, in Columbia, South Carolina. He worked as a brick mason prior to enlisting in the 1st South Carolina Foot during the Mexican War (1846–48). He moved to the Midway area of Davidson County around 1852, and, on June 2, 1856, he married Mary Yarbrough. They had no children. John continued work as a brick mason prior to volunteering on May 14, 1861. John was mustered in as a first sergeant and was present or accounted for until discharged on September 1, 1861, due to disability. In 1880, he and his wife adopted Lugenia Williams, who was 18 at the time. John died on December 31, 1888, and is buried in the Lexington City Cemetery. His stone bears the inscription: "He served in the Mexican War, was a brave soldier, and a good citizen."

132. Broadway, Andrew A.

Sergeant, Company D, 48th Regiment N.C. Troops

Andrew was born on October 29, 1832, to William and Elizabeth O. Broadway. He worked as a farmer, and in 1853, he married Minerva. Andrew and Minerva would have five children, Horace (1854), Mary F. (1854), William (1855), Thomas O. (1857), and John C. (1858), before Andrew was conscripted on August 8, 1862. He served as a private until he was promoted to corporal in December 1863. He was promoted to sergeant by April 1864. Andrew served as sergeant until he was captured at Ream's Station, Virginia, on August 25, 1864. He was confined at Point Lookout, Maryland, until March 17, 1865, when he was sent to Boulware's Wharf, Virginia, for exchange on March 19, 1865. Andrew was exchanged and put in the hospital for "partitis." Andrew was issued a 30-day furlough on March 26, 1865. He was paroled at Salisbury on May 20, 1865. His wife, Minerva, died sometime prior to 1875, when he married Catharine. No children were produced by the second marriage. Andrew lived in the Tyro area until his death on January 17, 1903. He is buried at Pine Primitive Baptist Church.

133. Broadway, David T.

Private, Holtsburg Guards Company A, 54th Regiment N.C. Troops

David was born in 1837 to William and Elizabeth O. Broadway. He resided as a farmer prior to volunteering on March 6, 1862. He was reported present until he was wounded severely in the thigh on May 4, 1863. David was sent to a hospital in Richmond, Virginia, where he recovered. He returned to duty prior to September 1, 1863. He was captured at Drewery's Bluff, Virginia, on May 16, 1864. David was confined at Point Lookout, Maryland, until he was transferred to Elmira, New York, on August 15, 1864. David died on February 6, 1865, of "intussusception of bowel." He is buried in the Elmira National Cemetery.

134. Broadway, David W.

Private, Holtsburg Guards Company A, 54th Regiment N.C. Troops

David W. was born in 1842 to Samuel and Anne Broadway. He worked as a farmer prior to volunteering on March 4, 1862. He was reported present until he was captured at Rappahannock Station, Virginia, on November 7, 1863. David was confined at Point Lookout, Maryland, until he was paroled for exchange on March 9, 1864. He was exchanged at City Point, Virginia, on March 15, 1864, and was returned to duty on an unspecified date. David was present until he was reported missing in action at Stephenson's Depot, Virginia, on July 20, 1864. No further records.

135. Broadway, John W.

Private, Holtsburg Guards Company A, 54th Regiment N.C. Troops 14th Battalion, N.C. Home Guard

John was born in 1819 and was an uncle to both of the Davids in the 54th Regiment. He was never married and worked as a farmer prior to volunteering on March 4, 1862. John was discharged on May 27, 1862, for being over age. Family history states that he also served in the 14th Battalion, N.C. Home Guard. No further records.

136. Broadway, Samuel

Corporal, Company D, 48th Regiment N.C. Troops

Sam was born in 1830 to William and Elizabeth O. Broadway. He worked as a farmer, and in 1857, he married Margaret. Sam and Margaret would have two children, David (1859) and Sarah (1861), before Sam was conscripted on August 8, 1862. He served as a private until he was promoted to corporal in July 1863. Sam was reported present until he died in a Richmond, Virginia, hospital on October 8, 1864, of "diarrhea chronic." The roll of honor states that he was wounded at an unspecified battle.

137. Broadway, William

Private, Company A, 42nd Regiment N.C. Troops

William was born in 1839 to Thomas and Mary Broadway of the Healing Springs township. William worked as a miller, and in early 1862, he married Hannah. William volunteered on March 6, 1862, and his first child, Nancy, was born in December. He was reported present until he deserted in December 1863. He returned prior to August 20, 1864, when he was wounded in action. William was absent, wounded, through October 1864 and was paroled at Greensboro, North Carolina, on May 10, 1865. After the war, he returned to working in his father's milling business in Jackson Hill. He and Hannah would have four more children: Phoebe (1866), George (1868), Mary (1875), and Cicero (1880). William died prior to 1900.

138. Broadway, William Henry

Private, Lexington Wildcats Company I, 14th Regiment N.C. Troops (4th N.C. Volunteers)

William was born on August 7, 1839, to Samuel and Anne Broadway. He lived in the Boone township and worked as a farmer prior to volunteering on May 14, 1861. William was reported present until he was captured on April 3, 1865, at Petersburg, Virginia. He was confined at Hart's Island in New York harbor until June 17, 1865, when he was released after taking the oath of allegiance. After the war, he married Mariah E. Sharpe on August 21, 1867. William and Mariah would have nine children: Lucy (1868), Mary (1869), Giles (1872), John (1874), Columbia (1876), Media (1878), Charles (1880), Dock (1882), and David (1885). William worked in the Boone area until his death on August 18, 1907. He is buried at Pine Primitive Baptist Church.

139. Brooks, Addison Cause

Private, Company B, 57th Regiment N.C. Troops

Addison lived in the Boone township of Davidson County. He married Noma Williams on September 7, 1858. He worked as a farmer prior to enlisting on July 14, 1862, in Rowan County. Addison was wounded in the hand during the battle of Fredericksburg, Virginia, on December 13, 1862. Two of his fingers were amputated. He spent a lot of time in the hospital. Addison deserted in October 1863 but was reported present in a Richmond, Virginia, hospital in November

1863 with "intermittent fever." He was under arrest from November 20, 1863, until September 1, 1864, when he was returned to regular duty. On September 20, 1864, Addison was captured at Newtown, Virginia. He was confined at Point Lookout, Maryland, until he was released on May 14, 1865, after taking the oath of allegiance. No further records.

140. Brooks, Henry M.

Private, Company B, 57th Regiment N.C. Troops

Henry was born on January 5, 1841, to John and Sarah Brooks. He worked as a farmer, and on June 1, 1862, he married Eliza Jane Lomax. Henry enlisted in Rowan County on July 14, 1862. He deserted from his unit at Fredericksburg, Virginia, on December 25, 1862. After the war, he returned home to Jane, and they would have five children: Martha (1866), John (1872), James (1874), Henry (1878), and Lilly (1879). Henry worked as a farmer until his death on September 15, 1916. He is buried at Wesley's Chapel.

141. Brooks, Hocking

Captain, 66th Regiment N.C. Militia (1861 organization)
14th Battalion, N.C. Home Guard

Hocking was born in 1828. He married Susannah in 1856. Hocking and Susannah would have two children: Emma (1858) and Margaret (1862). He was commissioned as a captain in the Reedy Creek District Company on October 1, 1861. He served in the 66th N.C. Militia prior to being declared nonexempt for service in the 14th N.C. Home Guard on March 23, 1864. No further records.

142. Brown, David F.

Private, Company C, 70th Regiment N.C. Troops (1st N.C. Junior Reserves)

David was born in 1846 to Haley and Jane E. Brown. He worked as a farmer prior to enlisting in the Junior Reserves on May 25, 1864. David served as a private until he died of disease at Lynchburg, Virginia, on January 4, 1865.

143. Brown, Isaac N.

Private, Company G, 2nd Battalion, N.C. Infantry

Isaac was born in 1845 to Joseph and Christina Brown. He worked as a shoemaker prior to enlisting in Wake County on February 26, 1864. Isaac served as a private until he was wounded at Winchester, Virginia, on September 19, 1864. He died of his wounds on September 25, 1864.

144. Brown, Jesse

Private, Company A, 10th Battalion, N.C. Heavy Artillery

Jesse was born on July 16, 1844. He worked as a laborer in Thomasville prior to being conscripted in Randolph County on March 28, 1863. Jesse was reported present until he was captured and paroled at Goldsboro, North Carolina, on March 28, 1865. After the war, he returned home and moved to the Friedburg area, where he died on November 28, 1916. He is buried at Friedburg Moravian Church.

145. Brown, Jonathan D.

Private, Davidson Guards Company A, 21st Regiment N.C. Troops (11th N.C. Volunteers)

Jonathan was born in 1831. He was married to Anna prior to volunteering on May 8, 1861. He was reported present until he was wounded at Winchester, Virginia, on May 25, 1862. He died of his wounds on May 29, 1862.

146. Brown, Joseph A. J.

Private, Company G, 2nd Battalion, N.C. Infantry

Joseph was born in 1826. He worked as a farmer in the Abbott's Creek area and, in 1854, he married Esther. Joseph and Esther would have three children, Viola (1856), John (1858), and Richard (1859), before Joseph was conscripted on September 8, 1862. He was reported present until he was wounded at Gettysburg, Pennsylvania, on July 1, 1863. Joseph died of his wounds on July 5, 1863.

147. Brown, Romulus M.

Private, Company G, 2nd Battalion, N.C. Infantry

Romulus was born in 1846. He resided in northern Davidson County prior to enlisting on January 1, 1864. Romulus served as a private until he was wounded and captured at Winchester,

Virginia, on September 19, 1864. He was sent to the U.S. General Hospital in Baltimore, Maryland, on October 19, 1864. He was transferred to Point Lookout, Maryland, on October 25, 1864. Romulus was paroled immediately and sent to Venus Point, Georgia, on October 29, 1864. He rejoined his company and was sent to a Richmond, Virginia, hospital on February 24, 1865. Romulus was furloughed for 60 days on March 21, 1865. No further records.

148. Brown, Seth B.

Private, Davidson Guards Company A, 21st Regiment N.C. Troops (11th N.C. Volunteers)

Seth was born in 1814. He lived in the Lexington area, and he married Letitia in 1838. Seth and Letitia would have six children: Julia (1839), Joseph (1841), John T. (1843), Martha (1845), Esther (1846), and Lenora (1849). Seth worked as a horticulturist prior to enlisting on May 8, 1861. He served as a private until he was discharged on April 16, 1862, because of "diabetes which is making rapid progress." He died at Manassas, Virginia, on April 25, 1862.

149. Brown, William Patrick

Second Lieutenant, 66th Regiment N.C. Militia (1861 Organization)
Private, Company A, 42nd Regiment N.C. Troops

William was born on February 20, 1832, to Clarissa Brown. He worked as a carpenter, and, in 1853, he married Elizabeth. They had one child, John W. (1854). William was commissioned a second lieutenant in the 66th Militia. On May 10, 1862, he enlisted for the war in Rowan County. William was reported present until August 10, 1863, when he was reported on detached duty in the Confederate Ordnance Department. He was on detail through October 1864. William survived the war and worked as a house carpenter in the Tyro township until his death on July 26, 1901. He is buried at Wesley's Chapel.

150. Bruff, Alfred

Private, Company D, 42nd Regiment N.C. Troops

Alfred was born in 1836 to John and Isabella Livengood Bruff. He worked as a farmer prior to volunteering on March 8, 1862. Alfred served with Company D of the 42nd and was reported absent, sick, on February 2, 1863. He was sick for most of his service and was paroled at Greensboro, North Carolina, on May 6, 1865. After the war, he married Sarah Ann Leonard. Alfred and Sarah would have five children: Mary (1866), James Anderson (1869), Julia (1871), Adam (1874), and Emma (1877). He worked in the Lexington township until his death in 1880. He is buried at Beulah United Church of Christ.

151. Bryant, Augustus S.

Private, Company H, 48th Regiment N.C. Troops

Gus was born on April 15, 1837, the son of Jabez Bryant. He worked as a farmer prior to volunteering on March 17, 1862, when he was mustered in as a corporal. He was promoted to first sergeant prior to being wounded at the battle of Sharpsburg, Maryland, on September 17, 1862. Gus was reported absent, wounded, through February 1863. When he returned to duty, he was reduced in rank to private in March 1863. Gus served as a private until he was paroled at Appomattox Court House, Virginia, on April 9, 1865. After the war, he married Martha Sowers; they would not have any children. He lived in the southwest precinct of Thomasville township until his death on June 28, 1907. He is buried at Fair Grove United Methodist Church.

152. Bryant, Corneilius

Private, Lexington Wildcats Company I, 14th Regiment N.C. Troops (4th N.C. Volunteers)

Neil was born in 1839 to John and Sarah Bryant. He worked as a carpenter, and, in 1857, he married Elizabeth. Neil and Elizabeth would have one child, Roetta (1858), before he volunteered on May 14, 1861. He survived every major battle unscathed and served until he was paroled at Appomattox Court House, Virginia, on April 9, 1865. After the war, he and Elizabeth would have six more children: Cynthia (1866), Mary (1868), Emory (1871), Cora (1874), Curtis L. (1876), and Marshall (1877). Neil lived in the Conrad Hill township until his death. He is buried at Heath Wesleyan Methodist Church.

153. Bryant, Kelley

Private, Company D, 48th Regiment N.C. Troops

Kelley was born in 1834 to John and Sarah Bryant. He worked as a farmer, and, in 1858, he married Martha. Kelley and Martha would have one child, Julius (1859), before Kelley was conscripted on August 8, 1862. He served as a private until he was wounded during the battle of Fredericksburg, Virginia, on December 13, 1862. Kelley returned to service in January 1863 and was reported present until he was captured at Hatcher's Run, Virginia, on April 2, 1865. Kelley was confined at Point Lookout, Maryland, until he was released on June 23, 1865, after taking the oath of allegiance. After the war, Kelley and Martha had eight more children: Robert (1866), George (1867), Henry (1869), Charles (1870), James (1873), Andrew (1875), Luther (1876), and David (1877). He lived in the Conrad Hill township and died prior to 1880.

154. Bryant, Thomas

Private, Thomasville Rifles Company B, 14th Regiment N.C. Troops

Thomas was born in 1832 to John and Sarah Bryant. He worked as a farmer prior to enlisting on April 27, 1861. Thomas was wounded and captured at Sharpsburg, Maryland, on September 17, 1862. He died of his wounds while in Federal hands at Frederick, Maryland, on October 19, 1862.

155. Bryant, William McKinzey

Private, Company H, 48th Regiment N.C. Troops

William was born in 1834 to John and Sarah Bryant. He worked as a farmer prior to enlisting on March 12, 1862. He was killed in action at Sharpsburg, Maryland, on September 17, 1862.

156. Buie, Andrew Jackson

Private, Company F, 7th Regiment N.C. State Troops

Andrew was born on February 9, 1842, to William and Euphemia Buie. Andrew worked as a farmer prior to volunteering in Alamance County on August 1, 1861. He was reported present until he was wounded in the shoulder at

Sharpsburg, Maryland, on September 17, 1862. Andrew was absent, wounded, through October 1864. He was paroled at Greensboro, North Carolina, on April 28, 1865. After the war, he returned home and married Mary E. Nance on April 25, 1867. They would live in the Healing Springs township and have five children: Anne (1868), Lafayette (1870), Nettie (1872), Alice (1876), and Jerry (1878). Andrew worked as a farmer until his death on October 3, 1912. He is buried in the Snider Family Cemetery.

157. Buie, Nevin C.

Private, Company B, 48th Regiment N.C. Troops

Nevin was born in 1834 to William and Euphemia Buie. He worked as a farmhand for Richard Bean prior to being conscripted on August 8, 1862. He was reported present until September 1862 when he was "captured in Maryland." Nevin was hospitalized at Frederick, Maryland, on September 22, 1862. He died on an unspecified date of an unknown cause.

158. Buie, Samuel Jefferson

Private, Company I, 42nd Regiment N.C. Troops

Sam was born on August 9, 1845, to William and Euphemia Buie. He worked as a farmer prior to being conscripted on November 20, 1863. He was present until he was paroled at Salisbury, North Carolina, on June 1, 1865. After the war, he returned to farming. By 1870, he was in school, training to become a teacher. In 1880, he married Barbara and was working as a schoolmaster in the Healing Springs township. Sam and Barbara would have six children: Robert Lee (1883), Ida (1886), Mary (1890), Samuel (1893), Francis (1895), and Emma (1898). Sam died on July 9, 1924. He is buried at First Baptist Church in Denton, North Carolina.

159. Bulleboy, Burrell B.

Private, Company A, 42nd Regiment N.C. Troops

Burrell was born in 1838. By 1860, both of his parents had died, and he was living with his two sisters and one brother, while his six cousins lived in the house next door. Burrell worked as a farmer, and, in 1862, he married Anna. Burrell and Anna would have one child, Joseph (1862), before Burrell traveled to Rowan County and volunteered on March 22, 1862. He was reported present until he deserted on August 18, 1863; He returned on November 5, 1863. Burrell deserted again on August 17, 1864, and returned under "general amnesty" on September 20, 1864. He served as a private until he was captured during the battle at Wise's Forks, Virginia, on March 10, 1865. Burrell was confined at Point Lookout, Maryland, until he was released on June 23, 1865, after taking the oath of allegiance. After the war, he and Anna had three more children: William (1865), Charlie (1867), and Unknown (1870). No further records.

160. Burke, Henry

Private, Company H, 48th Regiment N.C. Troops

Henry was born in 1832 to Edward and Mary Burke. He worked as a farmer, and in 1854, he married Susannah Riley. The couple moved to a piece of land given to them by Henry's father, and they had two children: Elizabeth (1855) and John T. (1859). Henry was conscripted in Petersburg, Virginia, on August 8, 1862. He was reported absent without leave from September 8, 1862, to February 1, 1863. Henry was reported present from February 1, 1863, until he was killed in action at Riddell's Shop, Virginia, on June 15, 1864.

161. Burkhart, Hiram

14th Battalion, N.C. Home Guard

Hiram was born on January 19, 1836, to John and Ellen Burkhart. He lived in the Cotton Grove township and worked as a farmer. He was married to Barbara Jane prior to 1860. Hiram served in the 14th N.C. Home Guard and was reported on a salt detail under William Hampton during January 1865. In 1870, Ann Musgrave, the mother of English native George Musgrave, moved into his home. Hiram died on June 3, 1907. He is buried at Lebanon Lutheran Church.

162. Burkhart, James Franklin

Private, Company I, 42nd Regiment N.C. Troops

James was born on December 10, 1842, to John and Ellen Burkhart. He

worked as a farmer prior to volunteering on March 8, 1862. James was wounded in the arm at Burkeville Junction, Virginia, on August 16, 1862. His left arm was successfully amputated. James was discharged due to disability on October 2, 1862. He returned home and lived with his mother and father. On February 2, 1879, he married Cornelia Swing. The couple lived in the Conrad Hill township and had seven children: Robert E. Lee (1879), Bettie (1881), Samuel (1883), Avery (1887), Joel (1891), Roy (1893), and Maudine (1896). James worked as a farmer until his death on February 17, 1920. He is buried at Beck's United Church of Christ.

163. Burkhart, Obediah

Private, Lexington Wildcats Company I, 14th Regiment N.C. Troops (4th N.C. Volunteers)

Obed was born on May 30, 1841, to John and Ellen Burkhart. He worked as a farmer in the Conrad/Silver Hill area prior to volunteering on May 14, 1861. Obed was reported present until he was paroled at Greensboro, North Carolina, on May 3, 1865. He was detailed for most of the war as a field nurse and an ambulance wagon driver. After the war, Obed married Caroline Smith on February 7, 1867. He and Caroline would have five children: Frances (1868), Louisa (1871), Frank (1874), William (1876), and Albert. Obed was a farmer until he took over for Adam Fritts as the steward of the poor. Obed operated the Davidson County Poor House from 1876 to 1881; in 1880, the poor house had 22 people living in it. Obed died on December 3, 1891, and is buried at Holly Grove Lutheran Church.

164. Burrows, William Francis

Private, Confederate Guards Company K, 48th Regiment N.C. Troops

William was born in 1842 to Henry and Elizabeth Burrows. He worked as a farmer prior to being conscripted on August 8, 1862. William died in a Charlottesville, Virginia, hospital on November 16, 1862. The cause of death was not reported.

165. Burton, Brazel W.

Private, Perquimans Beaureguards Company F, 27th Regiment N.C. Troops

Brazel was born in 1840 to William and Elizabeth Burton. He worked as a shoemaker prior to enlisting in Randolph County on December 3, 1863. Brazel died while he was at home on sick furlough on December 4, 1864. He is buried at Pleasant Grove United Methodist Church.

166. Burton, Calvin F.

Private, Company A, 57th Regiment N.C. Troops

Calvin was born on May 12, 1837, to James and Cornelia Burton. He served as a private in Company A, 57th Regiment N.C. Troops. After the war, he married Catharine Grey in 1869. He worked as a small farmer in the Thomasville area until his death on June 29, 1916. He is buried at Prospect United Methodist Church in Randolph County.

167. Burton, James P.

Private, Company A, 42nd Regiment N.C. Troops

James was born in 1842 to William and Elizabeth Burton. He worked as a farmer prior to volunteering on November 26, 1861. He served as a private until he was paroled at Greensboro, North Carolina, on May 9, 1865. No further records.

168. Burton, Jonathan

Private, Company F, 42nd Regiment N.C. Troops

Jonathan was born in 1839 to William and Elizabeth Burton. He worked as a shoemaker prior to being conscripted on August 8, 1862. He served as a private until he was captured at Battery Anderson, Fort Fisher, North Carolina, in January 1865. Jonathan was confined at Point Lookout, Maryland, until June 23, 1865, when he was released after taking the oath of allegiance. After the war, he married Emily Lane in 1866. Jonathan and Emily would have three children: Lemuel (1867), Jane (1868), and Ashbury (1869). Jonathan worked as a bootmaker in the Thomasville area until his death on December 11, 1912. He is buried at Prospect United Methodist Church in Randolph County.

169. Burton, Samuel J.

Private, Company A, 10th Battalion, N.C. Heavy Artillery

Sam was born in 1841 to William and Elizabeth Burton. He worked as a farmer prior to enlisting on April 2, 1862. He deserted from Fort Campbell, Brunswick County, and boarded a Federal gunboat off Wilmington, North Carolina, on February 18, 1864. Sam was confined at Fort Monroe, Virginia, until released on March 14, 1864, after taking the oath of allegiance. He was sent to Philadelphia, Pennsylvania, and never returned home. No further records.

170. Burton, Zadoc

Private, Company A, 10th Battalion, N.C. Heavy Artillery

Zadoc was born in 1840 to James and Cornelia Burton. He worked as a farmer prior to being conscripted on April 16, 1862. Zadoc was reported present until he died of disease at Fort Campbell, Brunswick County, on February 12, 1864.

171. Byerly, Andrew

Private, Lexington Wildcats Company I, 14th Regiment N.C. Troops (4th N.C. Volunteers)

Andrew was born on April 24, 1838, to Michael and Darla Byerly. He worked as a farmer, and, in 1860, he married Elizabeth. Andrew and Elizabeth would have one child, Laura (1861), before Andrew volunteered on May 14, 1861. He served as a private throughout the war without being injured or captured. Andrew was paroled at Greensboro, North Carolina, on May 5, 1865. After the war, he returned to his family in the southwestern part of the Thomasville township. He and Elizabeth would have six more children: Henry (1867), Julia (1869), James (1872), Albert (1877), Luther (1880), and Everett (1884). Andrew was a farmer until his death on December 17, 1926, at the age of 88. He is buried at Emanuel United Church of Christ.

172. Byerly, Elansom

Private, Davidson Guards Company A, 21st Regiment N.C. Troops (11th Regiment N.C. Troops)

Elan was born on January 16, 1833, to George and Sarah Hege Byerly. He worked as a farmer in the Lexington/ Midway area. In 1853, he married his first wife, Susan Parnell. They would have five children before her death in 1863:

Caroline (1855), Phillip (1857), Henry (1858), Joel (1860), and Andrew Jackson (1861). Elan volunteered on May 11, 1861, and was reported present until he was paroled at Appomattox Court House, Virginia, on April 9, 1865. After the war, he married Fannie Davis on May 24, 1866. Fannie and Elan had five children: Jennie (1868), John (1870), Olin S. (1872), Eva (1876), and Alice A. (1879). Elan worked as a farmer until his death on September 28, 1897. He is buried at Beulah United Church of Christ.

173. Byerly, George Lindsey

Private, Carolina Rangers Company B, 10th Virginia Cavalry Regiment

George was born on January 13, 1845, to Francis and Sarah Bailey Byerly. He worked as a farmer prior to volunteering in Davie County on February 2, 1862. He was present through April 1, 1864, detailed as an ambulance driver. On August 8, 1864, he purchased a horse. The last company records indicate he received a clothing ration on December 31, 1864. After the war, he married Elizabeth Deadman on February 12, 1873. George and Elizabeth would have three children: Samuel (1874), George (1875), and Julius (1880). George worked as a farmer in the Lexington township until his death on January 5, 1924. He is buried at Reeds Baptist Church

174. Byerly, George Lindsey

Private, Cleveland Mountain Boys Company D, 15th Regiment N.C. Troops (5th N.C. Volunteers)
2nd Company B, 49th Regiment N.C. Troops

Lindsey was born in 1846 to Simpson and Margaret Byerly. He worked as a farmer prior to being conscripted in Wake County on July 15, 1862. Lindsey was wounded at Crampton's Pass, South Mountain, Maryland, on September 14, 1862. He recovered from his wounds and rejoined the company on January 1, 1863. On January 9, he was transferred to the 49th Regiment. Lindsey was reported present until August 22, 1864, when he was reported in the hospital in Raleigh, North Carolina, with "diarrhea and anasarca." He returned to duty on December 6, 1864, and served until he was paroled at Appomattox Court House,

Virginia, on April 9, 1865. No further records.

175. Byerly, Jacob

Private, Company C, 76th Regiment N.C. Troops (6th N.C. Senior Reserves)

Jacob was born on October 22, 1817. Jacob was a farmer in the Conrad Hill township and was married to Barbara Leonard. Jacob was almost 47 when he enlisted in May 1864 into A. A. Hill's Senior Reserves, which became Company C, 6th N.C. Senior Reserves in January 1865. Jacob and Barbara didn't have any children but adopted Joseph Carter, who was living with them at the time of the 1880 Census. Jacob died on July 29, 1896. He is buried at Holly Grove Lutheran Church.

176. Byerly, Jesse

Private, Carolina Rangers Company B, 10th Virginia Cavalry Regiment

Jesse was born in 1848 to Simpson and Susan Byerly. He worked as a farmer prior to volunteering in Davie County on October 29, 1861. Jesse was reported present through December 31, 1864, when he was issued clothing. After the war, he married Susannah Leonard on October 31, 1867. The couple would have three children: Samuel (1871), Junius (1885), and Jennie (1887). Jesse worked as a farmer in the North Thomasville township until his death in 1903. He is buried at Pilgrim United Church of Christ.

177. Byerly, John F.

Corporal, Davidson Guards Company A, 21st Regiment N.C. Troops (11th N.C. Volunteers)

John was born on May 14, 1839, to William J. and Francis Byerly. He was studying at the Yadkin Institute prior to volunteering on May 8, 1861. John was promoted to corporal by October 1864. He was hospitalized on October 22, 1864, in Charlottesville, Virginia, with a gunshot wound in the left hand and was reported absent, wounded, through the duration of the war. He married Elizabeth J. Hartley on February 22, 1870. They lived in the Yadkin township with their seven children: William (1872), Nora (1874), Georgia (1876), Thomas

(1878), Tullia (1884), Guler (1886), and Maye (1894). Thomas Byerly became a wealthy banker in the Morgan Financial and Commodities House in New York City. John lived in the Yadkin township until his death on March 27, 1912. He is buried at Friendship Methodist Church.

178. Byerly, Obediah

Private, Company I, 42nd Regiment
N.C. Troops

Obed was born in 1843 to Michael and Darla Byerly. He lived in the Conrad Hill township and worked as a farmer prior to enlisting on March 3, 1862. He went through every action with the 42nd North Carolina and came out unharmed. Obed was paroled at Greensboro, North Carolina, on May 5, 1865. He married Mariah Alberson on November 16, 1865. Obediah and Mariah would have five children: Levi (1865), Edward (1870), William (1872), Lindsay (1873), and Martha (1876). He worked as a farmer in the Conrad Hill area until his death in 1926. He is buried at Holly Grove Lutheran Church.

179. Byerly, Peter Wesley

Private, Company H, 48th Regiment
N.C. Troops

Pete was born in 1842 to Peter and Polly Lowman Byerly. He worked as a farmer and married Albertine Koontz on October 3, 1861. He was conscripted into service at Petersburg, Virginia, on August 8, 1862. Peter was captured during the battle of Sharpsburg, Maryland, on September 17, 1862. He died on September 18, 1862, of injuries sustained while attempting to escape from the Federal provost marshal.

180. Byerly, Wesley

Second Lieutenant, 66th Regiment
N.C. Militia (1861 organization)
14th Battalion, N.C. Home Guard

Wesley was born on April 5, 1834, to Francis and Nancy Phillips Byerly. He worked as a farmer and married Melinda Koontz on November 29, 1858. He served as a commissioned second lieutenant in the Reedy Creek District Company. According to some sources, he also served as an enlisted man in the 14th Battalion, N.C. Home Guard. Sometime prior to 1864, Melinda died. On September 5, 1866, Wesley married Sarah Davis. This

Wesley Byerly's home included a log barn, corn crib, meat building, and a wellhouse (Touart, *Building the Backcountry*).

union produced only one child: Andrew (1868). Sarah passed away, and on April 2, 1868, Wesley married Eliza Swicegood. Wesley and Eliza would have six children: Wesley (1874), Lilla (1875), Frances (1877), Victoria (1879), Ida (1882), and Edward (1885). Wesley lived in the Reedy Creek/Yadkin area until his death on November 13, 1929. He is buried at Friendship United Church of Christ.

181. Cameron, James W. R.

Private, Company F, 7th Regiment
N.C. State Troops

James was born in 1837 to John and Rebecca Cameron. He was working as a carpenter's apprentice for William Redwine in 1860. James volunteered in Rowan County on March 19, 1862. He was killed in action at the battle of Malvern Hill, Virginia, on July 1, 1862.

182. Cameron, Reuben

Corporal, Wharton's Rangers
Company K, 63rd Regiment N.C. Troops
(5th N.C. Cavalry)

Reub was born on January 8, 1833, to John and Rebecca Cameron. He worked as a farmer prior to being conscripted in Randolph County on July 16, 1862, when he was mustered in as a corporal. Reuben was present through August 1864. His

wife, Nancy, died in 1863; he remained single until his death on May 21, 1911. He is buried in the Arnold Family Cemetery.

183. Caneday, Simeon

Private, Carolina Rangers
Company B, 10th Virginia Cavalry
*   Regiment*
Company G, 10th Regiment N.C. State
*   Troops (1st N.C. Artillery)*

Simeon was born in 1842. Listed in the 1860 Census as a "black servant," he volunteered in Davie County on October 29, 1861. Simeon was reported present through May 5, 1862, when he was sent on detail to "get a horse." He came back with an old mare, which was killed at Gettysburg, Pennsylvania, on July 3, 1863. Without his horse, Simeon served in the dismounted company until he was paid $550 and transferred to Company G, 10th Regiment N.C. State Troops. He was present through August 1864. He was paroled at Greensboro, North Carolina, on May 5, 1865. He was living alone in 1870. He is buried in an unmarked grave in the "colored section" of Pilgrim United Church of Christ.

184. Carrick, James

Private, Company C, 70th Regiment
N.C. Troops (1st N.C. Junior
*   Reserves)*

James was born on January 23, 1847, to Richard and Patience Carrick. He worked as a farmer prior to enlisting on May 24, 1864, in the Junior Reserves. He served with the Junior Reserves and was paroled at Greensboro, North Carolina, on May 6, 1865. After the war, James married Sarah in 1874. They would have five children: Minnie (1875), Della (1877), George W. (1881), Clay (1883), and Otho (1886). He lived in the Healing Springs township with his family. After Sarah's death in 1891, James married Caroline. The couple had no children. James died on June 4, 1930. His tombstone inscription at Summerville Baptist Church reads: "Although he sleeps, his memory doth live."

185. Carrick, John F.

Private, Davidson Guards
Company A, 21st Regiment N.C. Troops
(11th N.C. Volunteers)

John was born in 1838 to Joseph and Anna Carrick. He worked as a farmer prior to volunteering on May 8, 1861. John was mustered in as a private and was promoted to corporal on August 8, 1861. He was reported present until he was wounded in the battle of Second Manassas, Virginia, on August 28, 1862. John recovered and was promoted to sergeant on January 5, 1863. He deserted on an unspecified date and was reported "in arrest" on September 24, 1864. He returned to duty prior to November 1, 1864, when he was reduced in rank to private. John was captured at Fort Stedman, Virginia, on March 25, 1865. He was confined at Point Lookout, Maryland, until he was released on June 26, 1865, after taking the oath of allegiance. After the war, John returned home to begin a life as a schoolteacher. On March 5, 1867, he married Eliza Marie Feezor. They lived in the Silver Hill township on the east side of Abbott's Creek about a mile south of Young's Mill. He and Eliza had six children: Cora (1868), William (1871), Elizabeth (1875), Thomas (1879), Florina S. (1879), and Wade Hampton (1886). John helped to found and organize Holloways Baptist Church. John died on May 23, 1914. He is buried at Holloways Baptist Church.

186. Carrick, Joseph E.

Private, Company F, 7th Regiment N.C. Troops

Joseph was born in 1837 to Joseph and Anna Carrick. He worked as a farmer prior to volunteering in Rowan County on July 21, 1861. Joseph was killed in action during the battle of Second Manassas, Virginia, on August 29, 1862.

187. Carrick, Otho

Private, Company B, 48th Regiment N.C. Troops

Otho was born in 1836 to Richard and Patience Carrick. He worked as a farmer prior to being conscripted on August 8, 1862. He was wounded and captured at Sharpsburg, Maryland, on September 17, 1862. Otho was confined at Fort McHenry, Maryland, until he was paroled and transferred to Aiken's Landing, Virginia, and was declared exchanged on November 10, 1862. He was granted a 30-day furlough on November 12, 1862. Otho returned to duty in March 1863 and was present until he was hospitalized on April 22, 1864. He returned to duty prior to October 2, 1864, when he was captured at Petersburg, Virginia. Otho was confined at Point Lookout, Maryland, until he was received for exchange at Cox's Wharf, Virginia, on February 15, 1865. He was sent to a Richmond, Virginia, hospital on the same day. He died on February 22, 1865, of "chronic diarrhea."

188. Carrick, William B.

Corporal, Company B, 48th Regiment N.C. Troops

William was born in 1830, and on August 2, 1853, he married Rebecca Skeen. William and Rebecca would have three children, Martha (1854), Sarah (1856), and Joseph A. (1859), before William was conscripted on August 8, 1862. He was mustered in as a private and was promoted to corporal on January 1, 1863. William was reported present until August 20, 1864, when he was wounded in a skirmish along the Weldon Railroad near Peters-

burg. He was hospitalized at Chimbarazoo, Richmond, Virginia, and was furloughed for 30 days on September 10, 1864. William was reported on detail as a hospital guard in Charlotte, North Carolina, from November 3, 1864, through December 1864. No further records.

189. Carroll, Alsy

Private, Company B, 48th Regiment N.C. Troops

Alsy was born in 1844 to Benjamin and Nancy Riley Carroll. He worked as a farmer prior to being conscripted on August 8, 1862. Records state that he was "sent to the rear on the march to Maryland, failed to report." He was dropped from the rolls as a deserter on May 1, 1864. No further records.

190. Carroll, Benjamin Franklin

Private, Company B, 48th Regiment N.C. Troops

Ben was born in 1840 to Benjamin and Nancy Riley Carroll. He worked as a farmer, and, in 1860, he married Mary. Ben and Mary would have one child, Cicero (1862), before Ben was conscripted on August 8, 1862. He was reported present until he was captured during the battle of Cold Harbor, Virginia, on June 3, 1864. Ben was confined at Point Lookout, Maryland, on June 11, 1864, and was transferred to Elmira, New York, on July 12, 1864. He was released on May 13, 1865, after taking the oath of allegiance. After the war, Ben returned home to Healing Springs and saw his second son, John, for the first time. Ben received

Benjamin Carroll built this Emmons township home in the 1870s (Touart, ***Building the Backcountry***).

100 acres of land from his father in 1866, and he built a log home upon it which would stand until 1980. Ben and Mary had eight more children: Betty (1867), Emanuel (1868), Albert (1869), Dora (1870), Roby (1871), Ella (1874), Jane (1877), and Sirona (1878). Ben was a successful farmer and boasted that he had one of the county's first threshing machines. Ben died about 1882 and is buried at Clear Springs Baptist Church.

191. Carroll, Peter

*Private, Company B, 48th Regiment
N.C. Troops*

Peter was born in 1827 to Benjamin and Nancy Riley Carroll. He worked as a farmer, and he married Mary A. Bean in 1848. Peter and Mary would have five children: William (1849), Eliza (1851), Loveless (1852), Stokes (1855), and Julius (1859), before Peter was conscripted on August 8, 1862. He was present for 20 days, until he deserted at Rapidan Station, Virginia, on August 28, 1862. Peter was arrested by the Davidson Home Guard in March 1863 and was reported under arrest in June 1863. He was sent to a Richmond, Virginia, hospital on September 8, 1863, with "parotitis." Peter was then sent to Castle Thunder Prison but escaped from his guard while en route to the regiment on September 23, 1863. He was listed as a deserter through October 1864 and took the oath of allegiance at Salisbury, North Carolina, on June 5, 1865. Immediately afterward, he took his entire family and moved west, stopping for a year in Greene County, Tennessee. No further records.

192. Carroll, Stephen

*Private, Company B, 48th Regiment
N.C. Troops*

Stephen was born in 1830 to Benjamin and Nancy Riley Carroll. He worked as a farmer, and in 1854, he married Sarah Adeline Cameron. Stephen and Sarah would have three children, Nancy (1856), James (1857), and Caroline (1859), before Stephen was conscripted on August 8, 1862. He was reported sick in a Winchester, Virginia, hospital and was given a furlough on December 27, 1862, for 30 days. Stephen was reported absent without leave on January 26, 1863. He returned to duty on June 30, 1863, and was captured at Little River, Virginia, on

Henry Hudson Caudle and Martha Jane Horney Caudle in 1875 (Betty Brown).

May 20, 1864. Peter returned to his company the next day and deserted again. He took the oath of allegiance at Salisbury, North Carolina, on June 7, 1865. After the war, Stephen sold all of his land and moved to Greene County, Tennessee. The Greene County heritage book states that the Carrolls were then "gone for Texas." No further records.

193. Carter, Francis M.

*Private, Company G, 2nd Battalion,
N.C. Infantry*

Francis was born in 1842 to Giles and Sarah Carter. He worked as a farmer prior to volunteering on September 19, 1861. He was captured at Roanoke Island, North Carolina, on February 8, 1862, and was paroled at Elizabeth City, North Carolina, on February 21, 1862. The provisions of the Conscript Law of November 21, 1862, discharged him. Francis returned home and reenlisted on January 1, 1864, with the rank of corporal. On May 19, 1864, he was reduced in rank to private for "misconduct." Francis served as a private until he was captured at Winchester, Virginia, on September 19, 1864, and was confined at Point Lookout, Maryland, until he was transferred to Aiken's Landing, Virginia, on March 15, 1865, for exchange. In 1870, he was living with his three sisters and his nine-year-old nephew in the Abbott's Creek township. No further records.

194. Carter, William C.

*Private, Chatam Light Infantry
Company G, 48th Regiment N.C. Troops*

William was born in 1830 to David and Catharine Carter. He worked as a farmer, and he married Barbara Hepler on February 21, 1855. They had three children: Margaret (1858), Joseph (1860), and Esther (1862). William enlisted on August 8, 1862. William was killed in action during the battle of Fredericksburg, Virginia, on December 13, 1862.

195. Caudle, Henry Hudson

*Private, Company B, 48th Regiment
N.C. Troops*

Henry was born on November 19, 1836, to Elizabeth Caudle. He worked as a coachmaker, and in 1854, he married Martha Jane Horney. They would have three children: Alexander (1856), James (1858), and Lucy (1861). Henry resided in the city of Lexington prior to enlisting before May 1864. There are few records concerning Henry's service except a letter written from Camp Holmes in 1863. He was paroled at Greensboro, North Carolina, on May 1, 1865. One of his wartime recollections was of traveling to Wilmington, North Carolina, and seeing an ironclad ship and a floating battery. After the war, he returned to his coachmaking business and trained his two sons in the trade. Alex worked on the carpentry aspect, while James performed the necessary blacksmith work. Henry became a trustee of the First Methodist Church in Lexington and was a member of the Sunday school for over 40 years Henry and Martha would go on to have five more children: Lettie (1867), Nancy (1869), Henry (1873), Edward (1876), and Charles (1878). Henry continued his work as a carriage maker until 1885 when his son Alexander formally took over the business. Henry died on February 21, 1899. He is buried in the Lexington City Cemetery.

196. Cecil, Charles Lum

Private, Confederate Guards
Company K, 48th Regiment N.C. Troops

Charles was born on July 19, 1845. He resided on a small plantation run by the Bodenheimers of Davidson/Forsyth County prior to enlisting on April 9, 1862. He served for about six months until he provided a substitute to go in his place. Charles was discharged on November 1, 1862. He came home and married Prudence Kennedy. Their only child, Octavia, was born in 1863. Charles enjoyed "exempt" status through the end of the war. He lived in the North Thomasville township until his death of pneumonia on March 12, 1874. He is buried at Pleasant Grove United Methodist Church.

197. Cecil, Charles Wesley

Private, Confederate Guards
Company K, 48th Regiment N.C. Troops

Charles was born in 1830 to Samuel and Elmina Cecil. He worked as a hireling in the Arcadia area and, in 1856, he took a bride named Elizabeth. They would have three children: William (1857), Rebecca (1860), and Ellen (1862). Charles was conscripted on August 8, 1862. He deserted a week later on August 15, 1862. He was reported absent through December 1862. Charles returned and was reported absent, sick, in a hospital from January through April 1864. He returned to service on May 14, 1864, and was reported present until he deserted to the enemy on August 25, 1864. Charles was confined at Washington, D.C., until he was released on an unspecified date after taking the oath of allegiance. After the war, Charles and Elizabeth had four more children: Richard (1865), Mary L. (1869), Carly D. (1873), and Paulina (1876). Charles lived in the North Thomasville township and was reported working as a "ditcher" in 1900. Charles died in 1912. He is buried at Pleasant Grove United Methodist Church.

198. Cecil, Daniel L.

Private, Confederate Guards
Company K, 48th Regiment N.C. Troops

Company C, 76th Regiment N.C. Troops
(6th N.C. Senior Reserves)

Daniel was born in 1824. He lived in northern Davidson county and worked as a farmer. On May 10, 1849, he married Charity Sink. Daniel served in both companies listed, according to the North Carolina pension records. Daniel and Charity had four children: William (1860), Phoebe (1861), Henrietta (1865), and Noah (1872). They were last reported as living in the North Thomasville township through 1880. No further records.

199. Cecil, Isaac A.

Captain, 66th Regiment N.C. Militia
(1861 organization)

Isaac was born in 1825 to Samuel and Henrietta Cecil. Isaac worked as a blacksmith in the Yadkin township. He accepted a commission as a militia officer on November 24, 1861. After his service, he married Elizabeth Cross on January 9, 1869. They would have no children. No further records.

200. Cecil, J. C.

Private, Confederate Guards
Company K, 48th Regiment N.C. Troops

J. C. enlisted on August 8, 1862. He deserted on August 13, 1862, and was dropped from the rolls in October 1863. No further records.

201. Cecil, Riley

Private, Company I, 76th Regiment N.C. Troops (6th N.C. Senior Reserves)

Riley was born on October 18, 1827. He worked as a farmer, and on October 4, 1849, he married Rachael Stone. Riley and Rachael would have four children: Adaliza (1851), John T. (1858), William C. (1861), and Flora (1863). Riley enlisted in Moss's Senior Reserves, which became Company I, 6th N.C. Senior Reserves in January 1865. After his service, Riley continued to work his farm. He died on September 14, 1884. He is buried at Pleasant Grove United Methodist Church.

202. Cecil, Samuel Lafayette

Private, Company K, 21st Regiment N.C. Troops

Sam was born in 1846 to Richard J. and Sevilla Cecil. He worked as an assistant wagonmaker prior to being conscripted in Wake County on November 13, 1863. He served as a private until he was captured at Cedar Creek, Virginia, on October 19, 1864. Sam was confined at Point Lookout, Maryland, until June 10, 1865, when he was released after taking the oath of allegiance. A family history indicates that during the war, he escaped from a Yankee detail by swimming a large stream. When the war was over, he walked by his home to see if anyone would recognize him. After walking back

Lexington carpenter and distinguished soldier Samuel L. Cecil and his wife, Cornelia Burke Cecil (Robert L. Eanes, *The Heritage of Davidson County*).

a second time, his mother finally recognized him. He stripped his clothes off and immediately took a hot bath to kill the lice on his body. Once that was done, "there was rejoicing such as they had never seen before." On January 5, 1871, Sam married Cornelia Burke. He moved from the Mount Olivet area to the city of Lexington and became a house carpenter. Sam and Cornelia had nine children: John (1871), Henry (1874), Fannie (1876), Eliza Clementine (1878), Maggie (1880), Minnie (1883), Sam Grover (1885), Sally Victoria (1887–90), and Susan (1890). Samuel worked as a carpenter in Lexington and built several houses, including one for Richard Davis, which had five rooms with a fireplace in each one; Sam charged him $240. Sam also worked on his brick kiln, sawmill, and farm. He was a member of the First Methodist Church in Lexington, where he sang in the choir. Sam lived on East Center Street until his death on March 6, 1908. He is buried in the Lexington City Cemetery.

203. Cecil, Solomon

First Lieutenant, 66th Regiment N.C. Militia (1861 organization)

Solomon was born on April 28, 1830, to Sarah Cecil. He worked as a farmer in the Northern Davidson district. Solomon married Radie Kennedy on January 4, 1855. Solomon served as a first lieutenant in the 66th Regiment N.C. Militia. He died on October 6, 1897. No further records.

204. Cecil, Thomas S.

Private, Confederate Guards Company K, 48th Regiment N.C. Troops

Thomas was born on August 31, 1835, to Samuel J. and Elmina L. Cecil. He worked as a farmer prior to being conscripted on August 8, 1862. He deserted on August 14, 1862, and was listed as a deserter until January 1864, when he was reported present for duty. Thomas was present until he deserted to the enemy on September 6, 1864. He was confined at Washington, D.C., until he was released on an unspecified date after taking the oath of allegiance. Thomas returned home and worked as a single farmer. In 1893, he married Augusta. They would have no children. Thomas died on November 21, 1905. He is buried at Bethesda United Methodist Church.

205. Cecil, Wilson L.

Captain, 66th Regiment N.C. Militia (1861 organization)

Wilson was born on July 12, 1824. He worked as a farmer and married Lucy James on March 26, 1857. He served as a captain in the 66th Regiment Militia. Lucy and Wilson had only one child, U. S. Grant (1867). Wilson later became a skilled carpenter in the North Thomasville township and was inducted into the Masonic order. Wilson died on March 24, 1901. He is buried at Spring Hill United Methodist Church.

206. Chamberlain, James

Corporal, Company I, 42nd Regiment N.C. Troops

James was born in 1839 to Barnabus and Elizabeth Chamberlain. He worked as a farmer prior to volunteering on March 6, 1862, with the rank of corporal. James died in a Richmond, Virginia, hospital on September 19, 1862, of "acute rheumatism."

207. Chamberlain, William

Private, Company I, 42nd Regiment N.C. Troops

Will was born in 1840 to Barnabus and Elizabeth Chamberlain. He worked as a farmer prior to volunteering on March 4, 1862. He died in a Lynchburg, Virginia, hospital on August 8, 1862, of "pneumonia typhoides."

208. Chappell, William

Private, Lexington Wildcats Company I, 14th Regiment N.C. Troops (4th N.C. Volunteers)

William was born in 1842 and worked as a miner in the Conrad Hill silver mine prior to volunteering on May 8, 1861. He died on March 3, 1862, of "wounds received in a fight." The place of death was not recorded.

209. Charles, Harper E.

Captain, Guilford Dixie Boys Company E, 22nd Regiment N.C. Troops (12th N.C. Volunteers)

Harper was born on June 3, 1834, and was a student prior to volunteering on May 23, 1861; he was elected first lieutenant the same day. He was promoted to captain on June 13, 1862. Harper was killed in action during the battle of Frayser's Farm, Virginia, on June 30, 1862. His stone at Abbott's Creek Missionary Baptist reads: "Harper Charles, Slain in Confederate Service."

210. Charles, Lewis M.

Private, Company C, 70th Regiment N.C. Troops (1st N.C. Junior Reserves)

Lewis was born in 1846 to Jonathan and Hannah Charles. He enlisted on May 24, 1864. No records indicate that he survived the war.

211. Charles, Martin Lee

Private, Company K, 21st Regiment N.C. Troops (11th N.C. Volunteers)

Martin was born on February 11, 1825, to Risdon and Phoebe Idol Charles. He worked as a farmer prior to being conscripted in Wake County on October 22, 1864. He served as a private until he was captured at Hatcher's Run, Virginia, on February 6, 1865. Martin was confined at Point Lookout, Maryland, until he was released on June 24, 1865, after taking the oath of allegiance. After the war, he married Judy Ann Longworth. Martin and Judy had six children: Theodocia, Phoebe, Martin, Julian, Flora, and Edward. Martin died on September 24, 1889. He is buried at New Friendship Baptist Church in Forsyth County.

212. Charles, Nathaniel Leander

Private, Cleveland Mountain Boys 2nd Company B, 49th Regiment N.C. Troops

Nathan was born on January 26, 1843, to Jacob and Charlotte Rominger Charles. He worked as a farmer prior to being conscripted in Wake County on October 22, 1863. Nathan was reported present until he was wounded in action at Globe Tavern, Virginia, on August 21, 1864. After the war, he returned home and married Mary Jane Smith. They lived in the Midway area and raised their four children, William, Cicero, Daisy, and Conrad. Nathaniel died on October 7, 1926. He is buried at St. Delight Primitive Baptist Church.

213. Charles, Rieson W.

Private, Company C, 70th Regiment N.C. Troops (1st N.C. Junior Reserves)

Rieson was born on January 14, 1847, to Risdon and Phoebe Idol Charles. He worked as a farmer prior to enlisting on May 24, 1864. He was paroled at Greensboro, North Carolina, on May 10, 1865. After the war, he married Susan E. Shore on January 29, 1871. Rieson died on December 12, 1911. He is buried at New Friendship Baptist Church in Forsyth County.

214. Charles, Robert Fulton

Private, Cleveland Mountain Boys
Company D, 15th Regiment N.C. Troops
(5th N.C. Volunteers)
2nd Company B, 49th Regiment N.C. Troops

Robert was born on April 6, 1831, to Risdon and Phoebe Idol Charles. He was named after the inventor of the steamboat. Robert married Martha A. Elliot on July 12, 1851. Five children were born before the war: Louisa (1853), Sarah (1854), Phoebe (1856), Frances (1857), and Branson (1862). He lived in the Midway township and worked as a farmer prior to being conscripted on July 15, 1862, in Wake County. He was captured at South Mountain, Maryland, on September 14, 1862. He was confined at Fort Delaware, Delaware, until he was transferred to Aiken's Landing, Virginia, on October 2, 1862, for exchange. Robert was declared exchanged on November 12, 1862. He deserted the same day and rejoined his company on February 28, 1863. He was captured at Sandy Ridge (Lenoir County), North Carolina, on April 20, 1863. He was sent to New Bern, North Carolina, where he was paroled on May 23, 1863, and sent to City Point, Virginia, for exchange. He escaped from the detail and ran away. Robert returned to duty on June 12, 1863. He deserted for the last time on January 24, 1864. Another son, Charles, was born in 1864. Robert received his parole at Greensboro, North Carolina, on May 9, 1865. After the war, Robert and Martha had five more children: Elizabeth (1865), Julia (1866), Hazeltine (1866), Martha (1869), and Joehannah (1871). Robert died on September 18, 1912, and is buried at New Friendship Baptist Church.

215. Charles, Solomon Maholm

Captain, 66th Regiment N.C. Militia
(1861 Organization)

Private, Company F, 6th Regiment N.C. State Troops
Company F, 76th Regiment N.C. Troops (6th N.C. Senior Reserves)

Solomon was born on November 14, 1827, to Risdon and Phoebe Idol Charles. Solomon was a farmer, and on February 5, 1852, he married Cornelia S. Burton. The couple had four children: Lafayette (1851), John B. (1858), Lenora (1861), and Lucy Belle (1863). Solomon was commissioned a captain in the 1861 militia regiment for upper Davidson County. He enlisted in Alamance County in October 1862 into Company F, 6th N.C. State Troops, and was discharged by the provision of the Conscript Law. He enlisted again, into Hill's Senior Reserves, in January 1865 and served in the 6th N.C. Senior Reserves. After the war, Solomon lived in the Tyro area and worked as a farmer until his death on December 29, 1895. He is buried at Yadkin College Methodist Church.

216. Clement, Henry A.

Third Lieutenant, Holtsburg Guards
Company A, 54th Regiment N.C. Troops

Henry was born on September 18, 1835, to Eve Clement. He worked as a farmer, and on October 31, 1854, he married Margaret J. Wilson. Henry and Margaret would have three children, Charles (1856), Mary (1859), and William (1861), before Henry volunteered on March 4, 1862. He was mustered in as a corporal and by October 14, 1862, was appointed third lieutenant. He was hospitalized at Richmond, Virginia, on November 25, 1862. Rejoining his company in time for the battle of Fredericksburg, he was wounded there. Henry was present until he was hospitalized on May 17, 1864, with an unspecified complaint. He returned to duty and then resigned on March 10, 1865. His resignation was accepted on March 21, 1865. After the war, Henry lived in the Clemmonsville area. He and Margaret had four more children: Maggie (1866), John (1868), Godfrey (1873), and Frederick (1879). Henry died on November 9, 1912. He is buried at Smith Grove Baptist Church.

217. Clinard, Alexander Charles, Jr.

Colonel, 66th Regiment N.C. Militia
(1861 Organization)

A. C. was born in 1835 to Alexander C. and Sarah Tise Clinard. He worked as a blacksmith and a large farmer. He married Emily in 1854. A. C. was commissioned as colonel of the 66th Regiment N.C. Militia until 1863. Afterward, he failed to enlist in another unit or in the Home Guard. A. C. and Emily had ten children: Sarah (1855), David (1857), Eliza (1861), Isabel V. (1865), Emma (1866), Julia (1867), John (1869), Malicia (1872), Flora (1876), and Daisy (1879). A. C. lived in the southwest precinct of the Thomasville township until his death in 1922. He is buried at Rich Fork Baptist Church.

218. Clinard, Dempsey B.

Private, Company H, 16th Battalion, N.C. Cavalry

Dempsey was born in 1845. He enlisted on October 1, 1864, in Wake County and was hospitalized at Raleigh, North Carolina, on February 2, 1865, with "chronic diarrhea." He was issued a 60-day furlough on February 20, 1865, and did not return to service. Dempsey went to Greensboro, North Carolina, and received his parole on May 20, 1865. He married Amanda Elizabeth in 1867. They had five children: Joan (1868), George (1870), Alpheus (1871), Dora (1874), and Henry (1879). He lived in the Abbott's Creek township until his death in 1923. He is buried at Abbott's Creek Missionary Baptist Church.

219. Clinard, Francis

Private, Company C, 70th Regiment N.C. Troops (1st N.C. Junior Reserves)

Francis was born in 1847. He enlisted on May 24, 1864, and was paroled at Greensboro, North Carolina, on May 9, 1865. Francis married Martha Chriscoe on May 20, 1867. They had five children: Edgar (1869), Caroline (1873), Dora (1874), Fannie (1877), and Henry (1879). No further records.

220. Clinard, Francis C.

Sergeant, Davidson Guards
Company A, 21st Regiment N.C. Troops (11th N.C. Volunteers)

Francis was born in 1842 to Alexander C. and Sarah Tise Clinard. He volunteered on May 8, 1861, and by November

Phillip Clinard (Richard L. Conrad, *The Heritage of Davidson County*).

1861, he was promoted to sergeant. He was present until wounded in the arm at Winchester, Virginia, on May 25, 1862. Francis recovered, returned to duty, and was present until he was killed while carrying the 21st Regiment's colors during the battle of Plymouth, North Carolina, on April 20, 1864.

221. Clinard, John A.

Private, Company A, 42nd Regiment N.C. Troops
Howard's Company, N.C. Prison Guards, Salisbury

John was born on November 28, 1843, to Andrew and Keziah Spurgeon Clinard. He worked as a farmer prior to enlisting on January 30, 1862. He was transferred to Captain Howard's Company on May 1, 1862, and worked as a prison guard at the Salisbury stockade. He is buried at Abbott's Creek Missionary Baptist Church. No further records.

222. Clinard, John W.

Private, Company A, 10th Battalion, N.C. Heavy Artillery

John was born in 1839 to Andrew and Rachael Clinard. He resided in Thomasville and worked as a shoemaker prior to volunteering on March 8, 1862. He was promoted to corporal on July 1, 1862, but

was reduced in rank in September 1862. John was present or accounted for through April 1864. He was paroled at Greensboro, North Carolina, on May 5, 1865. No further records.

223. Clinard, Phillip

14th Battalion, N.C. Home Guard

Phillip was born on August 27, 1812, to Alexander C. and Sarah Tise Clinard. He married Mary Ensley on October 18, 1836. Phillip and Mary had five children: Randall (1837), Mary (1840), Nancy (1842), Eliza (1847), and William S. (1856). Phillip served in the 14th Battalion Home Guard as of October 4, 1864, when he was reported with a detail at the lead mines, and he may have served in the 3rd Home Guard regiment. Phillip died on August 23, 1882, and is buried at Mount Pleasant United Methodist Church.

224. Clinard, Randall B.

Private, Company K, 15th Regiment N.C. Troops (5th N.C. Volunteers)

Randall was born on November 24, 1837, to Phillip and Mary Ensley Clinard. He worked as a farmer prior to being conscripted in Wake County on July 15, 1862. He was reported present until captured at South Mountain, Maryland, on September 14, 1862. Randall was sent to Fort Delaware, Delaware, and was confined

Samuel Y. Clinard, a Salisbury prison guard, and a soldier in the 42nd Regiment (Richard L. Conrad, *The Heritage of Davidson County*).

there until transferred to Aiken's Landing, Virginia, for exchange on October 2, 1862. He was declared exchanged on November 10, 1862. Randall returned to duty on January 1, 1863, and served until he was captured at Hatcher's Run, Virginia, on April 2, 1865. He was sent to Hart's Island, New York, and was confined there until released on June 17, 1865, after taking the oath of allegiance. After the war, he married Temperence in 1868. They had two children: Elizabeth (1879) and Dora (1880). Randall lived and worked in the southwest precinct of the Thomasville township. He died on February 9, 1909, and is buried at Mount Pleasant United Methodist Church.

225. Clinard, Samuel Yokely

Sergeant, Company A, Gibbs' Battalion, N.C. Prison Guards, Salisbury
Company A, 42nd Regiment N.C. Troops

Samuel was born on December 3, 1839, to Alexander C. and Sarah Tise Clinard. He worked as a farmer prior to enlisting in Rowan County on March 8, 1862. Samuel was mustered in as a sergeant and served in Gibbs' Prison Guards at Salisbury until joining the 42nd Regiment. Family history states that he was at the battle of Cold Harbor, Virginia, on June 3, 1864; he was able to survive by hiding behind an apple tree while the "bullets fell like rain." Samuel was present until paroled at Greensboro, North Carolina, on May 1, 1865. After the war, he married Margaret Hamner in 1865. Their first child, Emily, was born in 1867. Sam and Margaret would have 11 more children: John (1868), Jacob (1870), Flora (1872), Martha (1874), Minnie (1878), Laura (1882), Walter (1884), Cora (1886), Everett (1888), Samuel (1890), and Fred (1893). He lived with his family in the Fair Grove area until moving to High Point, Guilford County, where he helped to start Mechanicsville Baptist Church, which is now Westchester Baptist. Sam died on May 26, 1924. He is buried at Lebanon Methodist Church.

226. Clinard, William

Second Lieutenant, 66th Regiment N.C. Militia (1861 organization)

William was born on August 2, 1822, to Mary K. Clinard. He worked as a farmer in the northern district of Davidson County prior to marrying Mary in 1845. William and Mary had two children: Alpheus (1848) and Julia Ann (1850). William accepted a commission dated November 1, 1861, in the Browntown District Company. William died on September 25, 1875. He is buried at Abbott's Creek Missionary Baptist Church.

227. Clinard, William Henry

Third Lieutenant, Company H, 16th Battalion, N.C. Cavalry

William was born in 1832 to Andrew and Rachael Clinard. He was transferred from Company D, 62nd Battalion, Georgia Cavalry, on July 11, 1864. William served as third lieutenant until he was killed in action along the Weldon Railroad south of Petersburg, Virginia, on September 30, 1864.

228. Clinard, Wilson

Second Lieutenant, 65th Regiment N.C. Militia (1861 organization)

Wilson was born in 1831 to Mary K. Clinard. He married Elizabeth in 1852. They would have six children: Wilson (1855), John (1857), Jane (1858), Emma (1862), Mary (1866), and Lovina (1869). Wilson accepted a commission in the 65th Regiment N.C. Militia. He lived in the Abbott's Creek area. No further records.

229. Clodfelter, Adam

Private, Confederate Guards Company K, 48th Regiment N.C. Troops

Adam was born on May 6, 1829. He married Mary Kindley on November 25, 1851. Adam and Mary would have five children, Loman (1856), William (1858), Ingram (1859), Young (1860), and Rufus (1862), before Adam was conscripted on August 8, 1862. He was wounded in both thighs during the battle of Fredericksburg, Virginia, on December 13, 1862. Adam was reported absent, wounded, through June 1863, and he was present until reported absent without leave from October 1863 through April 1, 1864. He was paroled at Greensboro, North Carolina, on May 6, 1865. After the war, he and Mary had two more children: Letitia (1865) and Sallie (1869). Adam lived in the Lexington township until his death on January 26, 1905. He

William Clinard (226) bought this home and 135 acres near Wallburg in 1858 (Touart, *Building the Backcountry*).

is buried at Bethesda United Methodist Church.

230. Clodfelter, Adam E.

Private, Company A, 42nd Regiment N.C. Troops

Adam was born on December 6, 1834, to Elias and Susannah Clodfelter. He worked as a farmer prior to enlisting in Rowan County on July 29, 1862. Adam was present and detailed as a teamster on May 23, 1863. He was reported present as a teamster through October 1864 and was paroled at Greensboro, North Carolina, on May 8, 1865. After the war, Adam married Christina Beck. Adam and Christina would have two children: Rebecca (1870) and Eva (1872). Adam lived as a farmer in the Conrad Hill township until his death on October 2, 1929. He is buried at Liberty Baptist Church.

231. Clodfelter, Andrew W.

Private, Company G, 38th Regiment N.C. Troops

Andrew was born in 1842 to Phillip and Amelia Clodfelter. He worked as a farmer prior to being conscripted at Camp Holmes, Wake County, on August 14, 1864. He was present until captured at Appomattox River, Virginia, on April 3,

1865. Andrew was confined at Point Lookout, Maryland, until June 24, 1865, when he was released after taking the oath of allegiance. After the war, Andrew married Fatima Beck on March 31, 1870. They would have four children: Lenora (1868), William (1872), Peter A. (1878), and John A. (1880). Andrew lived in the Conrad Hill township until his death on May 30, 1908. He is buried at Holly Grove Lutheran Church.

232. Clodfelter, Andrew Washington

Sergeant, Company H, 48th Regiment N.C. Troops

Andrew was born on August 5, 1835, to George and Catharine Everhart Clodfelter. He worked as a farmer prior to volunteering on March 6, 1862. He served as a private and was wounded during the battle of Sharpsburg, Maryland, on September 17, 1862. Andrew was hospitalized in Wilmington, North Carolina, on February 18, 1863, with typhoid fever; he returned to duty on February 27, 1863. Andrew was promoted to corporal in April 1863 and promoted to sergeant around July 1863. He came home for a furlough and married Rachael Imbler (Embler) on December 27, 1863. Andrew was reported present until he was paroled at Appomattox Court House, Virginia, on April 9, 1865. After the war, he and Rachael would have three children: Mary Jane (1865), Winnifed Analiza (1868), and John (1873). He lived as a farmer in the Conrad Hill township until his death on January 21, 1925. He is buried at Embler's Grove Family Cemetery.

233. Clodfelter, D. E.

Private, Company E, 5th Regiment N.C. Troops

D. E. was born in 1839. He worked as a farmer prior to volunteering on June 29, 1861. He was wounded and captured at Williamsburg, Virginia, on May 5, 1862. D. E. was confined at Fort Monroe, Virginia, until he was exchanged at Aiken's Landing, Virginia, on August 31, 1862. After an unknown period of time in a Richmond, Virginia, hospital, he rejoined the company on October 23, 1863. D. E. was reported present until he was captured at Spotsylvania Court House, Virginia, on May 12, 1864. No further records.

234. Clodfelter, Daniel A.

First Lieutenant, 66th Regiment N.C. Militia (1861 organization)

Daniel was born in 1839 to Henry and Barbara Clodfelter. He married Mary A. Hiatt on September 8, 1860. He accepted a commission in the Midway District Company. No further records.

235. Clodfelter, Daniel A.

Private, Company I, 2nd Regiment N.C. State Troops

Daniel was born on August 27, 1838, to Henry and Barbara Clodfelter. He worked as a farmer prior to being conscripted on August 18, 1862. He was present until captured on October 20, 1864, in Frederick County, Virginia. Daniel was confined at Washington, D.C., in the Old Capital Prison until transferred to Elmira, New York, on February 3, 1865. He was paroled and sent to James River, Virginia, on March 14, 1865, for exchange. Daniel was exchanged on March 21, 1865, and was present until paroled at Greensboro, North Carolina, on May 4, 1865. After the war, Daniel married Elesia in 1876. He and Elesia would have six children: Lula (1881), Cora (1883), Daisy (1885), Oliver (1888), Winnifred (1891),

and Desiree (1893). Daniel worked as a farmer in the Lexington township until his death on July 3, 1918. He is buried at Pilgrim Lutheran Church.

236. Clodfelter, David

Private, Company A, Colonel Mallet's Battalion (Camp Guards)

David was born on August 21, 1843, to Solomon and Leah Clodfelter. He worked as a farmer prior to enlisting on March 3, 1862. He was transferred to Mallet's Battalion. No further records. After the war, he married Eliza Jane in 1873. David and Eliza had four children: Robert (1880), Joseph (1882), Ida (1884), and Frank (1889). David lived in the Lexington township and worked as a farmer until his death on June 12, 1911. He is buried at Bethesda United Methodist Church.

237. Clodfelter, David C.

Private, Lexington Wildcats Company I, 14th Regiment N.C. Troops (4th N.C. Volunteers)

David was born in 1843 to Joseph and Charity Clodfelter. He worked as a farmer prior to being conscripted in Wake County on July 16, 1862. David was reported present until killed in a skirmish near Spotsylvania Court House, Virginia, on May 10, 1864.

238. Clodfelter, George R.

Private, Cleveland Mountain Boys Company D, 15th Regiment N.C. Troops (5th N.C. Volunteers)
2nd Company B, 49th Regiment N.C. Troops

George was born on May 6, 1836, to Joseph and Charity Clodfelter. He lived in the Lexington area prior to being conscripted in Wake County on July 15, 1862. He deserted at Sharpsburg, Maryland, on September 16, 1862, and returned home to marry Mary Jane Sink in late September 1862. George returned to the company on February 12, 1863, after it had been transferred to the 49th Regiment. He was captured at Sandy Ridge, North Carolina, on April 20, 1863, and sent to New Bern, North Carolina. George was paroled on May 28, 1863, at City Point, Virginia. He was declared exchanged but ran away from his detail. His escape did not last long, as he was apprehended and

brought back to camp on June 12, 1863. George deserted again on August 31, 1864, but returned to duty shortly after. He was reported present until he deserted to the enemy on October 13, 1864. George was confined at Washington, D.C., from October 15, 1864, and was released on an unspecified date after taking the oath of allegiance. After the war, he returned home to his wife. They would have seven children: Nancy (1864), Ida (1867), Daniel (1869), Andrew (1871), Elizabeth (1876), William (1879), and Amanda (1882). In 1870, he took a young black man named Lee Ader into his home. George lived and worked as a farmer in the Midway township until his death on March 13, 1907. He is buried at Bethesda United Methodist Church.

239. Clodfelter, Hamilton L.

Private, Company I, 2nd Regiment N.C. State Troops

Ham was born on July 26, 1832, to Henry and Barbara Clodfelter. He worked as a farmer prior to being conscripted on March 10, 1863, in Wake County. Ham was reported present through October 1864. He was paroled at Greensboro, North Carolina, on May 4, 1865. After the war, he married Susanna in 1866. They would have three children: Frank (1876), Charles (1879), and Connie (1881). He worked as a farmer and blacksmith in the Lexington township. Hamilton died on August 28, 1917, shortly before the start of the First World War. He is buried at Pilgrim Lutheran Church.

240. Clodfelter, Hugh W.

Private, Carolina Rangers Company B, 10th Virginia Cavalry Regiment

"Hughey" was born in 1842 to Joseph and Charity Clodfelter. He lived as a farmer prior to volunteering in Davie County on October 29, 1861. He was reported present through June 1863. During May, the 10th Cavalry participated in a grand review of Stuart's Cavalry at Brandy Station. The following is Hugh Clodfelter's account of the event in a letter to John Leonard (spelling as per original):

> We had a sham battle. The cavalry made noble and gallant charges. They

was about five or six hundred ladies out to see us on the review. It was a right smart sight to see. There is about twenty thousand cavalry hear now. We had a general review hear the other day. They was about fifteen thousand men and horses on the field at one time. They was twelve pieces of artilry firing at once.

For a period of a month, Hugh was reported without a horse. He was detailed in July and August 1863. He returned to regular service in September 1863 and was present through December 12, 1864, when he was issued clothing. No further records.

241. Clodfelter, Jacob

Private, Cleveland Mountain Boys Company D, 15th Regiment N.C. Troops (5th N.C. Volunteers)
2nd Company B, 49th Regiment N.C. Troops

Jacob was born in 1831 to George and Christina Clodfelter. He worked as a farmer prior to being conscripted in Wake County on July 15, 1862. Jacob was transferred to the 49th Regiment and captured on April 20, 1863. He was sent to New Bern, North Carolina, paroled, and sent to City Point, Virginia, for exchange. On May 28, 1863, Jacob ran away from a detail but was apprehended on June 12, 1863. He was reported present until captured at Hatcher's Run, Virginia, on March 31, 1865. Jacob was confined at Point Lookout, Maryland, until he was released on June 26, 1865, after taking the oath of allegiance. After the war, he married Polly Lopp. Jacob lived in the Lexington township until his death on November 5, 1900. He is buried at Pilgrim United Church of Christ.

242. Clodfelter, Jacob

Private, Company B, 57th Regiment N.C. Troops

Jacob was born in 1834 to Joseph and Charity Clodfelter. In 1857, he married Mary, and in 1859, they had a son named Edward. Jacob worked as a farmer prior to enlisting in Rowan County on July 4, 1862. Jacob was reported present until he died in a Lynchburg, Virginia, hospital on December 7, 1863, of "tabes mesenteric." He is buried at Ebenezer United Methodist Church.

243. Clodfelter, John

Corporal, Carolina Rangers Company B, 10th Virginia Cavalry Regiment

John was born in 1844 to Jacob and Barbara Clodfelter. He worked as a farmer prior to enlisting on January 25, 1864. He was reported present through August 1864, when he was promoted to corporal and assigned to the color guard. John was killed in action during the 10th Virginia's attempted breakout at Appomattox Court House, Virginia, on April 9, 1865. According to Sergeant H. R. Berrier, John rushed into a creek to save the regiment's battle flag from capture. He had secured the flag and begun to ride away when he received a fatal shot.

244. Clodfelter, John A.

Sergeant, Carolina Rangers Company B, 10th Virginia Cavalry Regiment

John was born on May 5, 1835, to David and Nancy Myers Clodfelter. He worked as a carpenter, and, in 1860, he married Maria Rothrock. John and Maria would have one child, John L. (1861), before John volunteered in Davie County on October 29, 1861, as a corporal. He was promoted to sergeant in January 1863. John went on a horse detail in September and October 1863. He lost the horse on August 22, 1864. He was present until

paroled at Burkittsville Junction, Virginia, on April 17, 1865. After the war, John and Maria had six more children: Sarah (1865), Frances (1866), David (1870), George (1872), William (1874), and Ida (1879). He lived in the Abbott's Creek area and in the northern areas of Davidson County. He worked as a house carpenter until his death on June 27, 1914. He is buried at New Vernon United Methodist Church, Forsyth County.

245. Clodfelter, Joseph

Private, Company C, 70th Regiment N.C. Troops (1st N.C. Junior Reserves)
Private, Carolina Rangers Company B, 10th Virginia Cavalry Regiment

Joseph was born on July 2, 1846, to Andrew and Franey Sink Clodfelter. He worked as a farmer prior to enlisting on May 24, 1864, in the Junior Reserves. When he came of age, he enlisted in the 10th Virginia on August 1, 1864. Joseph was wounded in action in October 1864. He returned to service on an unspecified date and served until paroled at Greensboro, North Carolina, on May 9, 1865. After the war, Joseph returned to farming in the Lexington township, and on July 10, 1870, he married Mary Nifong. Joseph and Mary had four children: John (1878), Clara (1881), Andrew (1883), and Joseph (1890). He worked as a farmer in

John A. Clodfelter inherited this home off of Old Greensboro Road upon his father's death in 1886 (Touart, *Building the Backcountry*).

the Lexington area for most of his life until he moved to High Point, North Carolina. He died on February 22, 1918, and is buried in Oakwood Cemetery, High Point, Guilford County.

246. Clodfelter, Joseph L.

*Private, Company B, 57th Regiment
N.C. Troops*

Joseph was born in 1847 to Joseph and Charity Clodfelter. He worked as a farmer prior to enlisting in Rowan County on July 4, 1862. Joseph was discharged on August 11, 1862, because of disability. On January 6, 1870, he married Malinda B. Hedrick. He died only a year later, in 1871. He is buried at Pilgrim United Church of Christ.

247. Clodfelter, Leason

*Private, Company H, 48th Regiment
N.C. Troops*

Leason was born in 1813. He worked as a farmer and as a wagoner in the northern district of Davidson County. Leason married Mary Kepley in 1834. According to census records, the two never had any children. Leason worked as a farmer prior to enlisting at "Palmer's" on March 11, 1862, as a substitute. He was captured at Frederick, Maryland, on September 12, 1862. Leason was confined at Point Lookout, Maryland, until paroled and transferred to Aiken's Landing, Virginia, for exchange on October 2, 1862. He was declared exchanged on November 10, 1862. Leason returned to duty prior to March 1, 1863, and served until he was discharged on March 21, 1865, because of "chronic rheumatism and old age." No further records.

248. Clodfelter, William B.

*Private, Chatam Light Infantry
Company G, 48th Regiment N.C. Troops*

William was born in 1841. He worked as a farmer prior to being conscripted on August 14, 1862. He was wounded in the hip during the battle of Fredericksburg, Virginia, on December 13, 1862. He died of his wounds at a Fredericksburg field hospital on December 16, 1862.

249. Clodfelter, William C.

*Private, Company E, 5th Regiment N.C.
State Troops*

William was born in 1839. He worked as a farmer prior to enlisting on July 1, 1861. He died in a Danville, Virginia, hospital of an unreported illness in February 1862.

250. Clodfelter, William S.

*Private, Davidson Guards
Company A, 21st Regiment N.C. Troops
(11th N.C. Volunteers)*

William was born in 1841. He lived in the Lexington area and worked as a farmer prior to volunteering on May 8, 1861. He was present until captured at Woodstock, Virginia, on June 2, 1862. William was confined at Fort Delaware, Delaware, until paroled and transferred to Aiken's Landing, Virginia, on August 5, 1862. He returned to duty and was wounded during the battle of Sharpsburg, Maryland, on September 17, 1862. William recovered and was present until reported "in arrest" for desertion in October 1864. He returned to duty in January 1865 and was present through February 1865. No further records.

251. Coggins, James R.

*Private, Company F, 7th Regiment
N.C. State Troops*

James was born in 1844 to John and Nancy Coggins. He worked as a farmer on his parent's land in Jackson Hill prior to enlisting on May 15, 1862, as a substitute for his father. James served as a private until killed in action at the battle of Chancellorsville, Virginia, on May 3, 1863.

252. Coggins, John

*Private, Company F, 7th Regiment
N.C. State Troops*

John was born on June 22, 1823. He lived and worked as a blacksmith in the Jackson Hill area of Davidson County. In 1842, he married Nancy, and in 1844 they welcomed their first child, James. John and Nancy had six more children: Edney Louisa (1845), Sarah (1849), Oliva Ann (1854), John (1855), Burrell (1858), and Jacob (1861). John volunteered on August 10, 1861, at the age of 39. He was present or accounted for until his son volunteered as his substitute, and John was discharged on May 15, 1862. He took the oath of allegiance at Salisbury, North Carolina, on June 10, 1865. John became

ill and died on October 1, 1866. He is buried in the Coggins Family Cemetery.

253. Coggins, Zachary

*Private, Company D, 48th Regiment
N.C. Troops*

Zach was born in 1844 and worked as a farmer prior to being conscripted on August 4, 1862. He was killed in action during the battle of Fredericksburg, Virginia, on December 13, 1862.

254. Cole, Bennett C.

*Private, Company C, 70th Regiment
N.C. Troops (1st N.C. Junior
Reserves)*

Ben was born in 1846 to William and Martha Cole. He worked on his family's farm prior to enlisting on May 24, 1864. He served with the Junior Reserves and was paroled at Greensboro, North Carolina, on May 10, 1865. After his service, he returned home and continued farming. On August 14, 1873, he married Amanda Kearns. Bennett and Amanda would live in the Healing Springs township and would have three children: Lillie (1874), Louisa (1876), and John (1879). Ben died in 1923 and is buried at Lick Creek Baptist Church.

255. Collett, Ezekiel

*Private, Company K, 42nd Regiment
N.C. Troops*

Ezel was born in 1839 to Charles and Ruth Collett. He worked as a farmer prior to being conscripted in Wake County on October 15, 1862. Ezel deserted on December 19, 1862. He returned to duty in July 1863 and was wounded in an unspecified battle with "buffaloes" (Federal irregulars) in eastern North Carolina. Ezel was reported present until captured at Wise's Forks, Virginia, on March 16, 1865. He was sent to Point Lookout, Maryland, and was confined there until released on June 21, 1865, after taking the oath of allegiance. No further records.

256. Collett, Jacob

*Private, Confederate Guards
Company K, 48th Regiment N.C. Troops*

Jacob was born in 1840 to James and Margaret Collett. He worked as a farmer prior to being conscripted on August 8, 1862. Jacob was reported present until he was captured at Bristoe Station, Virginia, on October 14, 1863. He was confined at the Old Capital Prison in Washington, D.C., until he was released on March 14, 1864, after taking the oath of allegiance. Jacob returned home and on November 24, 1865, he married Elizabeth Haines. The couple would have only two children who would survive, Walter (1880) and Gerome (1890). Apparently, Jacob died before 1900. No further records.

257. Collett, John

Private, Confederate Guards
Company K, 48th Regiment N.C. Troops

John was born on April 4, 1835, to James and Margaret Collett. He was working as a farmer in the Abbott's Creek township when he married Sarah in 1860. John and Sarah would have one child, Ladoc (1861), before John was conscripted in Davidson County on August 8, 1862. He was reported present until he deserted at Weldon, North Carolina, on May 5, 1863. John was listed as a deserter until January 1864 when he returned to duty. He was reported present until paroled at Greensboro, North Carolina, on May 8, 1865. After the war, John and Sarah increased the size of their family. Noah had been born in 1864; after John's return, the couple would have five more children: James (1867), Emily (1869), J. E. (1870), Robert (1873), and Fanny (1877). John continued to work as a farmer in Abbott's Creek and enlisted the help of Zen Carr, a freedman from Mississippi, in 1870. John died on June 5, 1898, and is buried at Bethany United Church of Christ.

258. Collett, William J.

Private, Thomasville Rifles
Company B, 14th Regiment N.C. Troops
(4th N.C. Volunteers)

William was born in 1841 to James and Margaret Collett. He worked as a farmer prior to volunteering on April 27, 1861. He was present until he was mortally wounded during a battle at Winchester, Virginia, on September 19, 1864. His date and place of death are not reported.

259. Collett, William M.

Private, Company I, 4th Regiment N.C. State Troops

William was born on December 23, 1844, to Charles and Ruth Collett. He worked as a farmer prior to being conscripted in Wake County on September 19, 1863. He was reported present until wounded at Spotsylvania Court House, Virginia, on May 13, 1864. William returned to duty and deserted to the enemy at Bermuda Hundred, Virginia, on February 22, 1865. He was released from Federal custody on February 24, 1865, after taking the oath of allegiance. After the war, William returned to farming, and he married Louisa Clinard in 1870. They had only one child who survived, James (1888), before Louisa died in 1891. William married Flora Hedrick the next year and lived with her in the Abbott's Creek township until his death on October 19, 1918. He is buried at Shady Grove United Methodist Church.

260. Collins, Alfred N.

Private, Davidson Guards
Company A, 21st Regiment N.C. Troops
(11th N.C. Volunteers)
Private, Company A, 2nd Battalion, N.C. Local Defense Troops
Company G, 2nd Battalion, N.C. Local Defense Troops

Alfred was born in 1832. He lived in the northern district of Davidson County and worked as a farmer, and in 1850, he married Caroline. Alfred and Caroline would have one child, Louise (1851), before Alfred volunteered on May 8, 1861. He served as a private in the 21st North Carolina until he was detailed to serve in Company A, 2nd N.C. Local Defense, from September through December 1863. Alfred returned to the 21st and served until November 1864, when he was detailed to serve in Company G, 2nd N.C. Local Defense. No further records.

261. Conrad, Daniel W.

Sergeant, Company B, 48th Regiment N.C. Troops

Daniel was born in 1841 and worked as a carpenter prior to enlisting on March 3, 1862. He served as a private until July 1863, when he was promoted to corporal. Daniel served as a corporal until promoted to sergeant on October 31, 1864. He was always accounted present until he was paroled at Greensboro, North Carolina, on May 1, 1865. No further records.

262. Conrad, Henry G.

Sergeant, Company B, 48th Regiment N.C. Troops

Henry was born in 1844 to Jacob and Elizabeth Conrad of Guilford County. He resided in Davidson County and worked as a carpenter prior to enlisting on March 4, 1862. Henry was mustered in with the rank of sergeant and was wounded in action during the battle of King's School House, Virginia, on June 25, 1862. Henry died at Richmond, Virginia, on July 15, 1862, of his wounds. He is buried in Hollywood Cemetery in Richmond.

263. Conrad, Henry Hedrick

Second Lieutenant, 65th Regiment N.C. Militia (1861 organization)

Henry was born in 1824 to David and Eve Hedrick Conrad. He began as a farmer but experimented with several occupations at which he became successful. On July 28, 1848, he married Rachael Lohr. Henry and Rachael would have nine children: David T. (1848), Laura (1852), Robert (1854), Mary (1856), Alexander (1860), Flavius (1862), Elizabeth (1865), Charles (1867), and Loretta (1873). At the time of the war, Henry served as a constable in the Thomasville township. He accepted a commission as

Henry Hedrick Conrad (Richard L. Conrad, *The Heritage of Davidson County*).

Rachael Lore Conrad (Richard L. Conrad, *The Heritage of Davidson County*).

a second lieutenant dated November 1861. No records except the commission exist. He served as the postmaster of Jimes, North Carolina (also called Conrad Siding and Lake). He died in 1894 and was buried at Pilgrim United Church of Christ. A handsome monument was erected by his descendants. H. H. Conrad's home in central Davidson County later was purchased by nationally renowned artist Bob Timberlake.

264. Conrad, Hiram Lafayette

Private, Carolina Rangers
Company B, 10th Virginia Cavalry
Regiment

"Big Fayte" was born on November 18, 1840, to Alexander and Catharine Darr Conrad. He worked as a farmer prior to enlisting in Davie County on October 29, 1861. Hiram was reported present through July 1863, when he was sent on a horse detail. He returned to duty in September and was present for the duration of the war. Company records state that he was wounded in action on May 1, 1864, returned to duty on October 1, 1864, and was issued clothing on December 31, 1864. After the war, Hiram married Sallie Hege on February 12, 1866. They had one child, Emory Curran (1867), before Sallie died in 1869. Hiram married Jane Yokely, and they had two children: Mattie (1873) and

Ada (1875). Hiram lived in the Thomasville township and was a gifted tradesman, working as a cabinetmaker, cooper, and blacksmith. He was considered a master in all three trades and served as a foreman for the construction of the Holly Grove Academy. Hiram died on August 8, 1917. He is buried at Pilgrim United Church of Christ.

265. Conrad, James Madison

Private, Lexington Wildcats
Company I, 14th Regiment N.C. Troops
(4th N.C. Volunteers)

James was born on February 16, 1845, to John H. and Mary Ann Darr Conrad. James worked as a farmer prior to being conscripted in November 1863. He served as a private and was paroled at Appomattox Court House, Virginia, on April 9, 1865. After the war, James married Margaret Myers on June 15, 1865. James and Margaret would have 11 children: John (1867), Andrew (1868), T. J. Jackson (1869), Mary (1870), Thomas (1874), Minnie (1877), Madison (1879), Florence (1882), William (1884), Carrie (1886), and Bertha (1890). James worked as a farmer and as a carpenter until his death on December 15, 1914. He is buried at Emanuel United Church of Christ.

266. Conrad, James N.

Sergeant, Company B, 48th Regiment
N.C. Troops

James was born in 1840 to Joseph and Elizabeth Conrad. He worked in his father's trade of carpentry, and, on January 9, 1862, he and Matilda A. Gaddis were married by the Reverend Frontis Johnston, the future chaplain of the 48th North Carolina. James volunteered on March 6, 1862. He was promoted to sergeant on January 1, 1863. James served as sergeant until he was wounded in the leg at Hatcher's Run, Virginia, on February 5, 1865. He was hospitalized in Richmond, Virginia, and was furloughed for 60 days on March 16, 1865. James did not return from his furlough. After the war, he and Matilda had five children: Robert (1865), Maggie (1866), Norman (1868), Burrell (1873), and Catherine (1875). James lived in the Lexington township and, in 1900, was listed as one of three butchers in Lexington. He died on August 8, 1904, and is buried in the Lexington City Cemetery.

267. Conrad, John H.

Private, Company F, 76th Regiment
N.C. Troops (6th N.C. Senior
Reserves)

John was born on June 1, 1815, to John David and Eve Hedrick Conrad. John married Mary Ann Darr in a service at Pilgrim Reformed on December 4, 1839. John and Mary would have six children, Mary Alunda (1842), James M. (1845), Rebecca (1847), Adam H. (1850), George W. (1852), and Charles Lee (1855), before Mary died in 1856. John continued in carpentry and worked as a farmer in the Conrad Hill township. John married Sarah Bowers on June 2, 1857. They had no children. John enlisted in January 1865 in Hill's Senior Reserves, which became the 6th N.C. Senior Reserves. After his service, he returned to farming in the Holly Grove area, where he became instrumental in founding Holly Grove Lutheran Church and the Holly Grove Christian Academy. John owned a reed organ, which he transported to the church and back to his home every Sunday. John died on August 8, 1898, and was supposed to be buried at Pilgrim United Church of Christ, but the wagon carrying his casket broke down, and he was interred in the nearest cemetery, Holly Grove Lutheran.

268. Conrad, Joseph T., Jr.

First Lieutenant, Company A, 42nd
Regiment N.C. Troops

Joseph was born in 1836 to Joseph and Catherine Conrad. He worked as a carpenter prior to volunteering on November 26, 1861. Joseph was mustered in as a first sergeant. He was appointed second lieutenant on March 18, 1862, and was promoted to first lieutenant on November 20, 1862. Joseph served as a lieutenant until he was captured at Fort Fisher, North Carolina, on December 25, 1864. He was sent to Washington, D.C., via Fort Monroe on January 3, 1865. Joseph was transferred to Fort Delaware, Delaware, on February 3, 1865, and was confined there until June 17, 1865, when he was released after taking the oath of allegiance. After the war, he married Emily A. Leonard on January 1, 1866. He and Emily would have four children: Cornelia (1867), Cora (1870), Ernest (1874), and Bertha (1876). Joseph continued to work as a master carpenter in the town of Lexington until his death on August 7, 1899. He is buried in the Lexington City Cemetery.

269. Conrad, Lindsay Lemuel

Private, Cleveland Mountain Boys Company D, 15th Regiment N.C. Troops (5th N.C. Volunteers)
2nd Company B, 49th Regiment N.C. Troops

Lindsay was born on February 18, 1838, to Alexander and Catharine Darr Conrad. He worked as a farmer and a miller, and on November 9, 1860, he married Eliza Berrier. Lindsay and Eliza would have one child, Ida (1862), before Lindsay was conscripted in Wake County on July 15, 1862. He was wounded and captured at South Mountain, Maryland, on September 14, 1862. Lindsay was sent to Fort Delaware, Delaware, where he was confined prior to being transferred to Aiken's Landing, Virginia, for exchange on October 2, 1862. He was declared exchanged on November 10, 1862. Lindsay was transferred to the 49th Regiment N.C. Troops on January 9, 1863. He was reported absent from this company due to an accident on October 28, 1863, when his foot was cut off on the Gaston and Raleigh Railroad. After the war, Lindsay and Eliza would have six more children: Sallie (1865), Henry (1866), Joseph (1869), Walter (1871), Flora (1876), and Winnifred (1879). During the days of Jefferson Davis' attempted escape to Texas, Davis stayed at the home of Lindsay and Eliza Conrad. Lindsay worked in the Thomasville township as a respected miller until his death on April 10, 1923. He is buried at Pilgrim United Church of Christ.

270. Conrad, William J.

Private, Lexington Wildcats Company I, 14th Regiment N.C. Troops (4th N.C. Volunteers)

William was born in 1836 to Jacob and Elizabeth Kepley Conrad. Before 1860, William was a farmer and had been married twice, to Susanna Brindle and Elizabeth Kepley. Elizabeth died during the winter of 1864. William was conscripted in Wake County on July 16, 1862. He was present until he was hospitalized in Richmond, Virginia, on February 27, 1865, with a gunshot wound. William was captured in the hospital and was sent to Newport News, Virginia, on April 23, 1865. He was confined until released on June 30, 1865, after taking the oath of allegiance. After the war, William married Charlotte Mayabb on February 9, 1867. William and Charlotte would have three children: Jacob (1869), John A. (1870), and George A. (1877). William worked as a farmer in the North Thomasville township until his death on May 25, 1909. He is buried at Pilgrim Lutheran Church.

271. Cook, Darling L.

Private, Company B, 48th Regiment N.C. Troops

Darl was born in April 1837 to Jedethan and Chaney Cook. In 1860 he was living in the household of David Smith as a paid farmhand. Darl was conscripted on August 8, 1862. He was reported present until he deserted from camp on December 6, 1862. Darl returned to duty prior to May 1863. He was reported present until he took the oath of allegiance at Salisbury, North Carolina, on June 2, 1865. After the war, he married Julia in 1866. Darling and Julia would have seven children: Frank (1868), Robert (1869), James (1871), L. Custer (1872), Cicero (1878), Della (1879), and James (1883). He and his family lived in the Allegheny township. Darling worked as a farmer until his death on December 26, 1910. He is buried in the Cook Family Cemetery.

272. Cook, Elam

Private, Company C, 70th Regiment N.C. Troops (1st N.C. Junior Reserves)

Elam was born on August 26, 1846, to Jacob and Nancy Cook. He worked as a farmer prior to enlisting in the Junior Reserves on May 24, 1864. He was reported present until paroled at Lynchburg, Virginia, on May 14, 1865. After the war, he married Amanda. Elam died on April 3, 1898. He is buried at Spring Hill United Methodist Church.

273. Cook, George Washington Smith

Private, Company B, 48th Regiment N.C. Troops

George was born in 1856 to Jedethan and Chaney Cook. He worked as a farmer in the Allegheny township, and on No-vember 27, 1856, he married Juda Smith. Two children were born: Sarah (1857) and Jeanette (1861). George was conscripted on August 8, 1862, and was captured at the battle of Sharpsburg, Maryland, on September 17, 1862. George was confined at Fort Delaware, Delaware, until October 2, 1862, when he was transferred to Aiken's Landing, Virginia, for exchange. He was declared exchanged on November 10, 1862. George deserted on December 6, 1862. He rejoined his company on an unspecified date and was sentenced to prison at Salisbury, North Carolina, by a general court-martial in March 1864. While he was in prison, Martha, his third daughter, was born. George escaped during Stoneman's raid through Salisbury, and he returned to take the oath of allegiance on June 7, 1865. After the war, George returned to his farm and started his life over. He and Juda would have five more children: Matilda (1866), Clarinda (1867), William (1869), Alunda (1874), and Mattie (1877). He died on June 29, 1905, and is buried at Chapel Hill United Methodist Church.

274. Cook, James Madison

Private, Cleveland Mountain Boys Company D, 15th Regiment N.C. Troops (5th N.C. Volunteers)
2nd Company B, 49th Regiment N.C. Troops

James was born in 1844 to Jacob and Nancy Cook. James worked as an apprentice wagonmaker prior to being conscripted on July 15, 1862. He was wounded during the battle of Sharpsburg, Maryland, on September 17, 1862. James was reported absent, wounded, through May 11, 1863, when he was discharged due to the seriousness of the wounds he had received at Sharpsburg. He lived in the Allegheny township and died shortly after 1870. No further records.

275. Cooper, Henry A.

Private, Company B, 48th Regiment N.C. Troops

Henry was born in 1839 to William and Martha Yokely Cooper. He worked as a farmer in the Clemmonsville township prior to enlisting at Camp Magnum, Wake County, on April 23, 1862. Henry was reported present in all records through November 30, 1864. In 1860, he married Susan Flemmings and had two children: Sarah (1861) and Frank (1865). No further records.

276. Cooper, John A.

Sergeant Major, 21st Regiment N.C.
  Troops (11th N.C. Volunteers)
Second Lieutenant, Company E, 21st
  Regiment N.C. Troops
Captain, Company B, 1st Battalion
  N.C. Sharpshooters

John was born in 1839 to William W. and Martha Yokely Cooper. John worked as a peddler of religious books and was married to Julia prior to volunteering in Forsyth County on May 24, 1861; he was mustered in as a sergeant major. John was elected second lieutenant on October 19, 1861, and was transferred to Company E of the regiment. He was promoted to first lieutenant and then to captain and transferred to Company B, 1st N.C. Sharpshooters, on April 26, 1862. John served as the company commander until he was appointed as acting assistant adjutant general to Major General R. F. Hoke in January 1864. He was paroled as an aide-de-camp at Greensboro, North Carolina, on May 1, 1865. After the war, he moved to Yadkin County. No further records.

277. Copple, Alphius K.

Private, Oakland Guards
Company D, 34th Regiment N.C. Troops

Alphius was born in 1840 to Jacob and Delilah Copple. He was conscripted in Asheboro, Randolph County, on August 27, 1864, and deserted on September 5, 1864. He escaped to the Uwharrie Hills and remained there until the end of the war. Alphius married Mary Kindley in 1870. They would have three children: Betty (1871), Julie (1873), and Jane (1875). They lived in the Conrad Hill township. No further records.

278. Copple, Joshua

Private, Oakland Guards
Company D, 34th Regiment N.C. Troops

Joshua was born in 1839 to Jacob and Delilah Copple. He worked as a farmer prior to being conscripted in Asheboro, Randolph County, on August 27, 1864. He deserted on September 5, 1864. Joshua married Alvana Lambeth on February 13, 1868. They lived in the Conrad Hill township and would have two chil-

John W. Coppley, one of the prison guards at Salisbury (LTC John R. Coppley, *The Heritage of Davidson County*).

dren: Samuel (1872) and Thomas (1874). Joshua worked as a farmer and served as a deacon of Liberty Church until his death in 1908. He is buried at Liberty Baptist Church.

279. Copple, Solomon Henry

Private, Oakland Guards
Company D, 34th Regiment N.C.
  Troops

Solomon was born on July 24, 1846, to Jacob and Delilah Copple. He worked as a farmer prior to being conscripted in Asheboro, Randolph County, on August 27, 1864. He deserted on September 5, 1864. Solomon married Frances L. Pope on May 30, 1878. They had one child: Kenneth (1879). He worked as a farmer in the Conrad Hill township until his death on December 19, 1922. He is buried at Pleasant Grove United Methodist Church. His stone reads, "Blessed are the pure in heart, for they shall see God."

280. Coppley (Copple), John W.

Private, Allen's Company, Gibbs
  Battalion, N.C. Prison Guards,
  Salisbury

John was born to Jacob and Delilah Copple. He worked as a farmer prior to enlisting in January 1863 into Allen's Company, N.C. Prison Guards. While

enlisting, his company paymaster told him that the correct spelling of his name was "Coppley," and John kept the spelling. John served as a prison guard and spent a brief time in the vicinity of Wilmington, North Carolina, after the company was called up to act as local defense on October 28, 1864. After his term as a guard, he returned to his farm in the Jackson Hill township. He married Anne Mariah Turner in 1870, and the two would have ten children: Ida (1871), Charlie (1874), James (1875), Eli (1877), Mary (1878), Dora (1880), Eddie (1883), A. Fletcher (1886), Emily (1888), and John Frank (1891). In 1893, John moved to Union Church, Rowan County, until his wife's death in 1912. Upon his wife's death, John returned to Davidson County where he lived with his daughter Dora Minnie in the Southmont area until his death on July 20, 1896. He is buried at Trading Ford Baptist Church.

281. Corneilison, Burgess B.

Private, Lexington Wildcats
Company I, 14th Regiment N.C. Troops
  (4th N.C. Volunteers)

Burgess was born in 1842 to Amy Corneilison. He worked as a carpenter prior to enlisting on May 14, 1861. He was reported present until wounded at Petersburg, Virginia, on August 21, 1864. Burgess was retired to the Invalid Corps on November 15, 1864. After the war, he married Mary Richie on August 23, 1866. No further records.

282. Cornish, Andrew C.

Private, Company B, 57th Regiment
  N.C. Troops

Andrew was born in 1836 to Jacob and Ellen Cornish. He worked as a farmer prior to enlisting in Rowan County on July 4, 1862. Andrew was reported absent without leave for a majority of the period before August 1864. Andrew was detailed as a provost guard for September and October 1864. Andrew was reported present until he was captured at Chester Station, Virginia, on April 5, 1865. He was sent to Point Lookout, Maryland, and was confined there until released on June 24, 1865, after taking the oath of allegiance. After the war, Andrew returned to the Clemmonsville township, where he was last reported living in 1890. No further records.

283. Cornish, Jacob

Private, Cleveland Mountain Boys
Company D, 15th Regiment N.C. Troops
  (5th N.C. Volunteers)
2nd Company B, 49th Regiment N.C.
  Troops

Jacob was born in 1832 to Jacob and Ellen Cornish. He worked as a farmer, and in 1852, he married Fanny Miller. Jacob and Fanny would have five children: Clementine (1853), Hamilton (1855), Levi (1857), Allen (1859), and Mary (1861). By 1860 the family was living in the Clemmonsville home of Levi and Isabella Miller. Jacob was conscripted in Wake County on July 15, 1862. He deserted on an unspecified date and was transferred to the 49th North Carolina while still listed as a deserter. Jacob rejoined the company on April 20, 1863, and was captured at Sandy Ridge, Lenoir County. He was sent through New Bern, North Carolina, to City Point, Virginia, where he was received on May 28, 1863, for exchange. Jacob ran away from his detail and was brought back into camp under arrest on June 12, 1863. He was reported present until January 28, 1864, when he deserted at Goldsboro, North Carolina. Jacob returned some time before April 1864 and was present until captured at Fort Stedman, Virginia, on March 25, 1865. He was confined at Point Lookout, Maryland, until he was released on June 24, 1865, after taking the oath of allegiance. After the war, he and Fanny would move into their own house and raise three more children: William and Sarah (1868) and Charlie (1871). No further records.

284. Cox, Ebenezer

Private, Company B, 48th Regiment
  N.C. Troops

Ebenezer was born in 1839 to Rachael Cox. He worked as a farmer and married Elizabeth Owens on July 8, 1860. Two years later, he was conscripted on August 8, 1862. He was wounded and captured at Sharpsburg, Maryland, on September 17, 1862. Ebenezer died shortly thereafter.

285. Cox, Henry C.

Private, Company F, 2nd Battalion,
  N.C. Infantry

Henry was born on February 8, 1829, to John and Barbara Cox. He worked as

a farmer prior to volunteering in Randolph County on November 20, 1861, for one year. He was hospitalized at Wilmington, North Carolina, on February 1, 1862, with typhoid fever. He returned to duty on February 13, 1863, and was killed in action during the battle of Gettysburg, Pennsylvania, on July 1, 1863.

286. Cox, James F.

Private, Company H, 48th Regiment N.C. Troops

James was born in 1835 to John and Barbara Cox. He worked with his father as the overseer of the poor house prior to being conscripted on August 8, 1862. James was wounded in the breast and left arm during the battle of Fredericksburg, Virginia, on December 13, 1862. He was sent to a Richmond, Virginia, hospital and was issued a 60-day furlough on December 28, 1862. James was reported absent on wounded furlough through November 5, 1863. He died at home in Davidson County on January 20, 1864.

287. Cox, John F.

Private, Lexington Wildcats
Company I, 14th Regiment N.C. Troops
  (4th N.C. Volunteers)

John was born in 1843 to John and Barbara Cox. He worked as a farmer prior to volunteering on May 14, 1861. John was reported present until he died of pneumonia at Mount Jackson, Virginia, on November 23, 1862.

288. Cox, William S.

Private, Company K, 61st Regiment
  N.C. Troops
Company A, 40th Regiment N.C. Troops
  (3rd N.C. Artillery)

William was born on June 22, 1833, to William and Sarah Cox. He worked as

Bought in 1885, Andrew C. Cornish remodeled this brick home in the Clemmonsville area (Touart, *Building the Backcountry*).

a farmer prior to being conscripted in Jones County on July 16, 1862. William was transferred to Company A, 3rd Artillery, on May 17, 1863. He was reported present until he died of unreported causes on November 16, 1864. He is buried at Tom's Creek Primitive Baptist Church.

289. Cranford, Elias G.

Private, Company F, 7th Regiment
  N.C. State Troops

Eli was born in 1843 to Bailey and Martha Cranford. He worked as a farmer prior to enlisting on July 16, 1861. Eli was reported present until he was wounded at New Bern, North Carolina, on March 14, 1862. He returned to service in July 1863 and was present or accounted for until wounded in the left arm during the battle of Spotsylvania Court House, Virginia, on May 12, 1864. His left arm was amputated shortly after. Eli was discharged in Raleigh, North Carolina, on March 23, 1865, due to his disability. No further records.

290. Cranford, James D.

Private, Wilmington Light Artillery

Company E, 10th Regiment N.C. State Troops (1st N.C. Artillery)

James was born on April 15, 1834, to Bailey and Martha Cranford. He worked as a farmer prior to enlisting in Wake County on September 12, 1862. He was reported present through August 1864. After the war, he married Martha and moved to Montgomery County. He died on April 20, 1892, and is buried at Lane's Chapel Methodist Church in Montgomery County.

291. Cranford, Joel

Private, Company F, 7th Regiment N.C. State Troops

Joel was born in 1841 to Lorenzo and Elizabeth Cranford. He lived in the Allegheny township prior to volunteering on March 2, 1862. Joel served until he was paroled at Greensboro, North Carolina, on May 1, 1865. After the war, he married Amanda in 1867 and moved to the town of Lexington. Joel and Amanda went on to have six children: Doctor (1869), John (1870), Luella (1871), Dora (1873), Martha (1875), and Minnie (1879). In 1900 Joel was listed as a picker in a cotton mill. No further records.

292. Cranford, Marrick

Private, Company F, Colonel Mallet's Battalion (Camp Guards)

Marrick was born on October 18, 1844. He enlisted in Mallet's Battalion and served until 1864. After the war, he married Sarah, and they would have three children: Caroline (1864), William (1867), and Nesbeth (1869). Marrick worked as a farmer in the Jackson Hill township until his death on February 12, 1908. He is buried at Lane's Chapel Methodist Church, Montgomery County.

293. Cranford, Wilburn

Private, Company F, 7th Regiment N.C. State Troops

Wilburn was born in 1841 to Lorenzo and Elizabeth Cranford. He worked as a farmer prior to volunteering on June 30, 1861. Wilburn was reported present until he was wounded and captured at Gettysburg, Pennsylvania, on July 3, 1863. He was sent to David's Island, New York, and was confined there until transferred to City Point, Virginia, on September 27,

1863 for exchange. He rejoined his company in March 1864 and was present through May 23, 1865, when he was paroled at Salisbury, North Carolina. No further records.

294. Cranford, William

Private, Company F, 7th Regiment N.C. State Troops

William was born on October 15, 1835, to Lorenzo and Elizabeth Cranford. He worked as a farmer prior to enlisting on June 30, 1861. He was mustered in as a private and was promoted to corporal on September 15, 1861. He was reported present until wounded at Frayser's Farm, Virginia, on June 30, 1862. He rejoined the company in November 1862 and served as corporal until he was reduced in rank on May 12, 1864. He was reported present until he took the oath of allegiance and was paroled by May 30, 1865. William was married to Margaret James and lived in the Jackson Hill township until his death on August 18, 1881. He is buried at Salem United Methodist Church.

295. Craven, Albert G.

Private, Company C, 70th Regiment N.C. Troops (1st N.C. Junior Reserves)

Albert was born in 1846 to Orrin and Sarah Craven. He worked as a farmer prior to enlisting on May 24, 1864, in the Junior Reserves. No further records.

296. Craven, Daniel Harrison

Private, Company G, 2nd Battalion, N.C. Infantry

Daniel was born in 1844 to Samuel and Ruth Craven. He worked as a farmer prior to volunteering on September 19, 1861. Daniel was discharged in January 1862. He reenlisted in February 1863 and was wounded and captured at Gettysburg, Pennsylvania, on July 5, 1863. Daniel was sent to David's Island, New York, and was confined there until he was transferred to City Point, Virginia, on September 16, 1863. He was released on an unspecified date and was reported present until captured at Strasburg, Virginia, on October 19, 1864. Daniel was confined at Point Lookout, Maryland, until he was paroled and sent to Cox's Landing, Virginia, on February 13, 1865, for exchange.

He was admitted to a hospital in Richmond, Virginia, and was furloughed for 30 days on March 2, 1865. No further records.

297. Craven, Thomas M.

Private, Company A, 10th Battalion, N.C. Heavy Artillery

Thomas was born in 1841. He worked as a shoemaker prior to enlisting on April 21, 1862. Thomas died of disease at Wrightsville Sound, North Carolina, on September 28, 1862.

298. Craven, William D.

Sergeant, Company G, 2nd Battalion, N.C. Infantry

William was born in 1843 to Orrin and Sarah Craven. He worked as a farmer prior to volunteering on September 19, 1861. William served as a private until he was appointed sergeant on April 30, 1864. He died on July 26, 1864, in a Winchester, Virginia, hospital of "v.s. breast."

299. Craver, Burgess L.

Private, Davidson Guards Company A, 21st Regiment N.C. Troops (11th N.C. Volunteers)

Burgess was born in 1839 to Alexander and Sarah Craver. He worked as a farmer in the Boone township prior to volunteering on May 8, 1861. Burgess died of "enteric fever" in Blantyre Hospital, Richmond, Virginia, on October 4, 1861.

300. Craver, Franklin

Private, Cleveland Mountain Boys Company D, 15th Regiment N.C. Troops (5th N.C. Volunteers)
2nd Company B, 49th Regiment N.C. Troops

Franklin was born in 1831 to William and Susanna Craver. He worked as a farmer, and, in 1857, he married Adaline. Franklin and Adaline would have three children, Joseph (1859), Nancy (1860), and Jesse (1862), before Franklin was conscripted on July 15, 1862. He deserted on August 21, 1862. Franklin rejoined the company on February 15, 1863, after it had been transferred to the 49th North Carolina. He was reported present until he deserted at Rocky Mount, North Carolina, on August 16, 1863. Franklin was caught and "lodged in the guardhouse" at Weldon, North Carolina, on December 23, 1863. He survived the war and returned home to the Lexington township. He continued to work as a farmer. He and Adaline would have four more children: William (1866), Emory (1874), McDouglas (1877), and Lola B. (1879). He died some time after 1880. No further records.

301. Craver, George Nelson

Private, Cleveland Mountain Boys Company D, 15th Regiment N.C. Troops (5th N.C. Volunteers)
2nd Company B, 49th Regiment N.C. Troops

George was born in 1834 to William and Susanna Craver. He worked as a shoemaker, and on June 21, 1858, he married Mahalia Sink. They would have two children, John (1858) and Bathsheba (1860), before George was conscripted and enlisted in Wake County on July 15, 1862. He deserted on August 21, 1862, rejoined the company on February 15, 1863, and was reported present through June 1863. Mahalia's third child, William was born in 1863 when his father was away. George deserted at Rocky Mount, North Carolina, on August 16, 1863. He was apprehended and "lodged in the guardhouse" at Weldon, North Carolina, on December 23, 1863. He returned to duty on an unspecified date and was captured at the battle of Globe Tavern, Virginia, on August 21, 1864. He was confined at Washington, D.C., until released on August 31, 1864, after taking the oath of allegiance. George returned home, and by 1865, he had another son, Joseph N. After the war, he worked as a wagonmaker in the Yadkin and Arcadia townships. No further records.

302. Craver, John Davidson

Private, Oakland Guards Company B, 34th Regiment N.C. Troops

David was born on August 7, 1826. He worked as a farmer in the northern district of Davidson County, and prior to 1850, he married Christina Hinkle. David and Christina would have seven children: Sarah (1850), John (1853), William (1855), Alexander (1857), Henry (1860), Emanuel (1862), and Ransom (1864). David was conscripted into service on September 26, 1864. He was

reported present and was paroled at Appomattox Court House, Virginia, on April 9, 1865. After the war, he returned home to continue with his farming. Christina died prior to 1878, when David married Nancy. David and Nancy would have three children: Charles (1879), Maggie (1880), and Permonia (1883). David lived in the Arcadia area until his death on June 11, 1910. He is buried at Mount Olivet United Methodist Church.

303. Craver, John Nelson

Private, Company B, 57th Regiment N.C. Troops

John was born on July 4, 1834, to Alexander R. and Sarah C. Craver. He worked as a farmer and a wagonmaker prior to enlisting on July 4, 1862. John was reported present through April 1863. He was detailed to serve as a teamster in September 1864 and served in that capacity until February 1865. After the war, he returned home, and prior to 1875, he married Matilda. They would have one child together, Cora (1876). John continued his work as a farmer and lived in the Tyro area until his death on January 19, 1911. He is buried at Reeds Baptist Church.

304. Cridlebaugh, Thomas

Private, Company G, 2nd Battalion, N.C. Infantry

Thomas was born in 1839 to Susannah Cridlebaugh. He was born in Forsyth County and moved to Abbott's Creek prior to 1860 with his sister, Kezia. He worked as a farmer before he enlisted on September 8, 1862. He was reported present until he was wounded and captured on July 3, 1863, during the battle of Gettysburg, Pennsylvania. He was sent to Point Lookout, Maryland, until he was transferred to the U.S. Hospital, Chester, Pennsylvania, on July 25, 1863. He was treated and released for exchange on September 17, 1863. He was exchanged at City Point, Virginia, on September 23, 1863, and was reported absent, home on parole. Thomas returned to duty in January 1864 and was reported present until he was captured at Strasburg, Virginia, on October 19, 1864. He was sent to Point Lookout, Maryland, where he was confined until March 28, 1865, when he was paroled and sent to Aiken's Land-

ing, Virginia, for exchange. Thomas survived the war and prior to 1867, he married Emma. Thomas and Emma would have seven children together: Charles (1868), George W. (1870), William L. (1872), W. V. (1874), Ernest E. (1876), S. L. (1879), and Junius (1882). Thomas worked as a farmer and a carpenter in the Abbott's Creek township until his death on January 6, 1908. He is buried at Abbott's Creek Missionary Baptist Church.

305. Crissman, Allen T.

Private, Company B, 48th Regiment N.C. Troops

Allen was born on November 13, 1831. He worked for William Hamner as a buggymaker in Lexington. He volunteered for service in Lexington on March 17, 1862, and was wounded at King's School House, Virginia, on June 25, 1862. Allen was issued a 60-day furlough on December 17, 1862, came home, and married Hamner's daughter, Dosha, on December 28, 1862. He was reported absent, wounded or sick, through October 1864. He was retired to the Invalid Corps on December 1, 1864. Allen was paroled at Greensboro, North Carolina, on May 5, 1865. After the war, Allen and Dosha had four children: Martha (1867), Colby (1868), Jane (1870), and Allen L. (1874). Allen and his family lived in Lexington, and in 1880 he was working as a machinist. Allen died on June 5, 1890. He is buried in the Lexington City Cemetery.

306. Crook, Calvin J.

Private, Holtsburg Guards Company A, 54th Regiment N.C. Troops

Calvin was born on April 20, 1842, to Allen and Martha Crook. He lived in the Silver Hill area and was working as a miner in 1860. Calvin volunteered on March 4, 1862, and was detailed as a miner in Davidson County on September 10, 1862. He served as a lead miner through October 1864. After the war, Calvin married Evaline prior to 1869. They would have six children: Ephraim (1871), John (1873), George L. (1874), Susan (1876), Mattie (1877), and James (1879). Calvin continued his work as a miner in the Silver Hill area until his death on August 16, 1918. He is buried at Jersey Baptist Church.

307. Cross, Abram

Private, Chatam Light Infantry
Company G, 48th Regiment N.C. Troops

Abram was born on June 15, 1843, to Jonathan and Rebecca Cross. He worked as a farmer in the southern area of Davidson county before enlisting on August 14, 1862. He was wounded in the right thigh and captured during the battle of Sharpsburg, Maryland, on September 17, 1862. He was sent to a hospital in Frederick, Maryland, on October 15, 1862. He was paroled from Fort McHenry, Baltimore, Maryland, on October 17, 1862, sent to Aiken's Landing, Virginia, and declared exchanged on November 10, 1862. He received a 50-day furlough on January 21, 1863. Abram returned prior to June 23, 1863, and was reported present until May 8, 1864, when he was sent to a Richmond, Virginia, hospital with a gunshot wound in the hand. He returned to duty in September 1864 and, by order of a court-martial, he was ordered to forfeit 12 months' pay. He deserted to the enemy on February 22, 1865, and was confined at Washington, D.C., until he was released on an unspecified date after taking the oath of allegiance. After the war, Abram returned home and lived with his mother. Abram married Sarah in 1870, and the two would raise one child, Clara (1882) in the Silver Hill area. Abram died on January 7, 1929. He is buried at Holloways Baptist Church. His tombstone reads: "Thy God has claimed thee as his own."

308. Cross, Alexander

Private, Company B, 48th Regiment
N.C. Troops

Alex was born in 1834 to David and Elizabeth Cross. He worked as a farmer in the southern district of Davidson county, and on February 7, 1856, Alex married Gilly Riley. They would have only one child, William (1857). Alexander was conscripted and enlisted on August 8, 1862. He was reported present until he died at Petersburg, Virginia, on January 22, 1863, of pneumonia.

309. Cross, David Henderson

Sergeant, Company F, 7th Regiment
N.C. Troops

David was born on June 15, 1834, to Jonathan and Rebecca Cross. He lived in the Silver Hill area and worked as a farmer prior to volunteering for service in Rowan County on June 26, 1861. He was mustered in as a private and was reported present until he was wounded in the thigh during the battle of Fredericksburg, Virginia, on December 13, 1862. He rejoined the company in July 1863 and was promoted to corporal on December 1, 1863. He was promoted to sergeant on September 1, 1864, and was reported present through October 1864. David survived the war and returned home to marry Mary Adams in 1866. David and Mary would have six children together: Berry (1868), John (1870), Sarah Jane (1871), Mary (1877), Edward (1886), and Essie (1892). David lived with his family in his Silver Hill home until his death on March 24, 1916. He is buried at Holloways Baptist Church.

310. Cross, George Washington

Private, Chatam Light Infantry
Company G, 48th Regiment N.C. Troops

George was born in 1834 to Smith and Eve Cross. He worked as a farmer prior to being conscripted on August 14, 1862. He was wounded and captured during the battle of Sharpsburg, Maryland, and was confined at Fort Monroe, Virginia, until October 18, 1862, when he was paroled and transferred to Aiken's Landing, Virginia, for exchange. George was declared exchanged on November 10, 1862. He returned to duty in March 1863 and was present until he was wounded in the mouth at the battle of Wilderness, Virginia, on May 6, 1864. He was detailed for light duty at Salisbury, North Carolina, on September 23, 1864, and was transferred there. George rejoined his company prior to April 1, 1865, when he was captured at Hatcher's Run, Virginia. He was confined at Point Lookout, Maryland, until June 26, 1865, when he was released after taking the oath of allegiance. After the war, George married Jane in 1867. The two had only one child together, Robert Lee (1869). It is uncertain when he died but it was probably before 1880. He is buried at Macedonia United Methodist Church.

311. Cross, Moses H.

Second Lieutenant, Thomasville Rifles
Company B, 14th Regiment N.C. Troops
(4th N.C. Volunteers)

Moses was born in 1843 to Charles and Delia Huffman Cross. In 1850, he was apprenticed to William B. Hamner, a local saddler and tanner. He was living as a paid hand of William A. Wager prior to volunteering for service on April 23, 1861. He was mustered in as a private and was promoted to first sergeant on October 5, 1862. Moses was appointed third lieutenant on November 4, 1863, and was promoted to second lieutenant on May 18, 1864. He was reported present and was paroled at Appomattox Court House, Virginia, on April 9, 1865. After the war, Moses married Martha Sowers on July 9, 1865. The services were conducted by Reverend P. A. Long of Pilgrim Reform. Moses and Martha would have three children together: Minnie (1867), William (1870), and Mary (1872). Moses lived with his family in the Lexington township until his death on April 11, 1913. He is buried at Pilgrim United Church of Christ.

312. Cross, Silas

Private, Company B, 48th Regiment
N.C. Troops

Silas was born on February 19, 1837, to David and Elizabeth Cross. He worked as a farmer, and on July 30, 1857, he married Joan Carrick. They would have only one child together, Amanda (1861). Silas was conscripted for service on August 8, 1862. He was wounded in the left hand during the battle of Sharpsburg, Maryland, on September 17, 1862. His left hand was amputated by Surgeon Lindsay. Silas was discharged on March 6, 1863, because of his disability. Joan died before 1864, and Silas married Martha Shepard on July 9, 1865. Silas and Martha did not have any children. Silas lived as a farmer in the Healing Springs area until his death on July 10, 1923. He is buried in the Cross Family Cemetery.

313. Cross, William A.

Private, Company A, 42nd Regiment
N.C. Troops
Company G, 2nd Regiment Confederate
Engineers

William was born in 1833. He worked as a farmer in the southern district of Davidson County and had a wife, Mary, and a daughter, Jane (1862). He volunteered for service in Rowan County on May 1, 1862, and served as a private until he was transferred to the 2nd Regiment Confederate Engineers on October 10, 1864. No further records.

314. Crotts, Amos

Private, Chatam Light Infantry
Company G, 48th Regiment N.C.
Troops
Company D, 48th Regiment N.C.
Troops

Amos was born in 1835 and worked as a carpenter prior to marrying Susannah in 1862. They would have five children: Emeline (1862), James (1864), William (1865), Charles (1872), and John (1874). Amos was conscripted for service on August 14, 1862. He deserted at Rapidan Station, Virginia, on August 25, 1862, and was dropped from the rolls. Amos returned to duty on September 24, 1864, and enlisted in Company D of the same regiment. He was reported present until he deserted to the enemy on March 16, 1865. He was confined at Washington, D.C., until he was released on an unspecified date after taking the oath of allegiance. After the war, Amos lived in both the Emmons and Conrad Hill townships until his death sometime after 1900.

315. Crotts, Andrew C.

Private, Company D, 48th Regiment
N.C. Troops

Andrew was born in 1835. He resided in the Yadkin area of Davidson County and worked as a farmer. He married Elizabeth sometime prior to 1854, when Sarah, their first child, was born. Andrew and Elizabeth welcomed three more children: Emily (1856), Louisa (1860), and Belle (1861), before he was conscripted on August 8, 1862. He deserted on August 29, 1862, and did not return to duty until December 19, 1863. He was reported present through February 24, 1865, when he was admitted to a Richmond, Virginia, hospital with "debilitias and pneumonia." He was captured in the hospital on April 3, 1865, and was confined at Newport News, Virginia, until he was released on June 30, 1865, after taking the oath of allegiance. After the war, he returned home, and he and Elizabeth had two more children: James (1866) and Charles (1868). Andrew worked as a farmer in the Yadkin township until he died sometime around 1890.

316. Crotts, David

Second Lieutenant, 66th Regiment
N.C. Militia (1861 organization)
14th Battalion, N.C. Home Guard

David was born in 1814 to John and Barbara Crotts. He worked as a miller in the Lexington area, and he married Lydia sometime prior to 1852. David and Lydia had two children: Alfred (1853) and Ellen (1857). David was commissioned as a second lieutenant in the 66th Regiment N.C. Militia and served in the 14th Home Guard as well. No further records.

317. Crotts, David

Private, Company F, 18th Regiment
Arkansas Infantry

David was born in 1830 to Michael and Catharine Crotts. He worked as a farmer, and in 1857, he married Elizabeth. Their first two children, Amanda (1857) and Andrew (1859), were born shortly before the couple's move to Arkansas. While in Arkansas, David joined the 18th Arkansas Infantry and fought in the Department of the Trans-Mississippi. After the war, he returned to Davidson County and started a new life in the Conrad Hill township. He and Elizabeth would have two more children: John (1864) and Bessie (1866). In 1900, David was employed as the manager of the county home, where he worked until his death on September 12, 1907. He is buried at Mount Tabor United Church of Christ.

318. Crotts, George

Private, Company D, 48th Regiment
N.C. Troops

George was born in 1841 and lived in Davidson County until he was conscripted on August 8, 1862. He was captured at Sharpsburg, Maryland, on September 17, 1862, and was paroled ten days later. George failed to rejoin his company, was listed as a deserter, and was dropped from the rolls on November 1, 1862. No further records.

319. Crotts, William C.

Private, Company D, 48th Regiment
N.C. Troops

William was born in 1835. He worked as a farmer, and prior to 1854, he married Sarah. William and Sarah would have

three children: David (1855), Edward (1857), and Robert (1859). He was conscripted on August 8, 1862, and was reported present until he died at Winchester, Virginia, on October 15, 1862, of disease.

320. Crouch, Hiram

Private, Confederate Guards
Company K, 48th Regiment N.C. Troops

Hiram was born in 1833. He worked as a farmer, and in 1850 he was living as a paid farmhand in the home of James and Elizabeth Stewart. He married Susan Proctor on March 13, 1854, and they would have three children: Lethia (1855), Mary Ann (1857), and Josephine (1859). Hiram was conscripted on August 8, 1862, and was reported present through February 1863. He was reported absent, sick, from March 1863 until June 1864. He was discharged on October 19, 1864, because of "disease of the lungs." No further records.

321. Crouch, Jacob C.

Private, Cleveland Mountain Boys
Company D, 15th Regiment N.C. Troops
(5th N.C. Volunteers)
2nd Company B, 49th Regiment N.C.
Troops

Jacob was born in 1831 to Cuthbert and Mary Crouch. He worked as a shoemaker prior to being conscripted into service on July 15, 1862. He was present with his company through its transfer and present until he died at Wilson, North Carolina, between February 21 and 23, 1863, of disease.

322. Crouch, James Anderson

Private, Company G, 2nd Battalion,
N.C. Infantry

James was born in 1845 to Richard and Anna Crouch. He was the youngest of ten children and worked in his father's gristmill. James was conscripted on January 1, 1864, and was reported present until he was captured at the battle of Fisher's Hill, Virginia, on September 22, 1864. He was confined at Point Lookout, Maryland, until released on May 13, 1865, after taking the oath of allegiance. No further records. (Although the 1870 Census lists the family of "Richard A. Crauch" in Washington County, Tennessee, a "James" is not among those listed.)

323. Crouch, John Columbus

First Lieutenant, Confederate Guards
Company K, 48th Regiment N.C.
Troops

John was born on December 14, 1842, the brother of Hiram and Kezia Crouch. He worked as a farmer in northern Davidson County prior to being conscripted on August 8, 1862. John was reported present through August 1864. After the war, he returned home and married Catharine in 1868. He and Catharine would have five children: James (1874), Amos (1877), Jacob (1884), Arthur (1887), and Bertha (1890). He was a member of the Friedburg community and lived there until his death on April 19, 1932. He is buried at Friedburg Moravian Church.

324. Crouch, John R.

Private, Beaufort Rifles
Company I, 2nd Regiment N.C. State
Troops

John was born in 1841 and worked as a farmer prior to being conscripted on August 18, 1862. He was wounded during Pickett's charge at Gettysburg, Pennsylvania, on July 3, 1863. He recovered, returned to service, and was captured at Mechanicsville, Virginia, on May 31, 1864. John was confined at Elmira, New York, where he died on October 26, 1864, of "typhoid pneumonia."

325. Crouse, George W.

Private, Company B, 48th Regiment
N.C. Troops

George was born in 1845 to William and Elizabeth Crouse. He worked as a farmer prior to being conscripted on September 8, 1863. He was wounded at the battle of Wilderness, Virginia (May 5–6, 1864), in the back and left arm as he attempted to carry Private Jacob R. Beck, already wounded, to safety. George's wound was so severe that he was retired from service on March 3, 1865, due to "a fracturing of the seventh rib, and a passing through the lung and the seventh dorsal vertebrae." He returned home and lived with his parents in the Silver Hill township. He moved to Lexington in the early 1900s and was listed as a "producer of agricultural implements" in the 1900 Census. George died shortly thereafter.

He is buried at Beck's United Church of Christ.

326. Crouse, John D.

Private, Company I, 42nd Regiment
N.C. Troops

John was born on May 10, 1825, to John and Margaret Crouse. He worked as a farmer, and, on November 8, 1852, he married Susanna Imbler. They would have four children: Jacob (1853), Betsy (1855), Wiley (1857), and John D. (1860). John volunteered for service on March 8, 1862. He was reported present until he was discharged by June 4, 1863, because of "rheumatismus chronic." After the war, he continued farming in the Conrad Hill area until his death on February 13, 1897. He is buried at Embler's Grove (Old Embler's) Cemetery.

327. Crouse, Joseph

Private, Company C, 70th Regiment
N.C. Troops (1st N.C. Junior
Reserves)

Joseph was born in 1847. He enlisted on May 24, 1864, in the 1st N.C. Junior Reserves. Records of the 42nd Regiment indicate that he may have served with that unit as well. No further records.

328. Crouse, Joseph

Colonel, Staff, 66th Regiment N.C.
Militia (1861 organization)

Joseph was born in 1817. He worked as a farmer and, on December 5, 1842, he married Catharine Grimes. Joseph and Catharine would have seven children before her death in 1861: Angeline (1843), Thomas (1845), Timothy (1847), Franklin (1849), Barbara (1854), James (1857), and Robert (1860). In 1862 he married Barbara Taylor, and they had two surviving children: William (1863) and Joseph (1866). Joseph served as the commanding officer of the 65th Militia Regiment with a commission dated November 1861. He lived in the Conrad Hill/Silver Hill area until his death about 1875. No further records.

329. Crouse, Thomas M.

Private, Company B, 48th Regiment
N.C. Troops

Thomas was born in 1845, the son of Joseph and Catharine Grimes Crouse. He

worked as a farmer prior to being conscripted on September 8, 1863. He was reported present through April 1864. He did not survive the war. No further records.

330. Curry, Calvin W.

First Sergeant, Company C, 70th Regi-
ment N.C. Troops (1st N.C. Junior
Reserves)

Calvin was born in 1846 to Smith and Elizabeth Curry. He worked as a farmer prior to enlisting on May 24, 1864. He was mustered in with the rank of 1st Sergeant. No further records.

331. Curry, James S.

Private, Company A, Mallet's Battal-
ion (Camp Guards)
Company H, 48th Regiment N.C.
Troops

James was born on October 11, 1835, to Smith and Elizabeth Curry. He worked as a farmer and married Sarah in 1858. James and Sarah would have three children: William (1859), James (1861), and Martha (1865). James served in Company A of Mallet's Battalion prior to being transferred to the 48th Regiment by June 17, 1864. He was wounded on an unspecified date and was issued a 60-day furlough on December 9, 1864. He was paroled at Greensboro, North Carolina, on May 9, 1865. Sarah died in 1866. Six years later, James married Margaret. They had three children: Mary (1874), Charlie (1876), and Adam (1879). He worked as a farmer in the Conrad Hill township until his death on July 3, 1900. He is buried at Holly Grove Lutheran Church.

332. Cutting, Leander D.

Corporal, Lexington Wildcats
Company I, 14th Regiment N.C. Troops
(4th N.C. Volunteers)

Leander was born in 1844 to John and Elizabeth Cutting. His father was a native of Mississippi. Leander worked as a carpenter prior to volunteering for service on May 14, 1861. He was promoted to corporal on January 1, 1863. He was present until wounded in the left knee and captured at Winchester, Virginia, on September 19, 1864. He was sent to Fort McHenry, Baltimore, Maryland, on December 10, 1864. He was transferred to

Point Lookout, Maryland, on February 20, 1865, for exchange. He was hospitalized at Richmond, Virginia, and was issued a 60-day furlough on March 10, 1865. No further records.

333. Daniel, Henry C.

Private, Company F, 10th Regiment N.C. State Troops (1st N.C. Artillery)

Henry was born on August 26, 1841, to Travis and Mary Daniel. He worked as a farmer prior to being conscripted in 1864. Henry died on January 29, 1865. He is buried at Lick Creek Baptist Church. No further records.

334. Daniel, James H.

Private, Company B, 71st Regiment N.C. Troops (2nd N.C. Junior Reserves)

James was born on August 28, 1845, to Travis and Mary Daniel. James worked as a farmer prior to enlisting in Rowan County on December 7, 1864. He served in the Junior Reserves and was present during the battle of Bentonville, March 19–21, 1865. After the war, he married Mary Lovina Bean in 1870. James and Mary would have three surviving children: Minnie (1873), Zebulon V. (1877), and James (1888). He lived in the Healing Springs township until his death on September 5, 1906. His stone is decorated by the verse from John 11:25.

335. Daniel, Thomas H.

Private, Company I, 76th Regiment N.C. Troops (6th N.C. Senior Reserves)

Thomas was born in 1813 and resided in the southern district of Davidson County. Thomas served as one of the county's first justices of the peace. He married Amanda F. Pope on July 31, 1852. Records indicate that he served in the 5th Georgia, however, there is limited information regarding his service in that unit. Thomas served in Company I of the 6th N.C. Senior Reserves, which was organized in January 1865. After the war, he returned to his Healing Springs home, and in 1880 he allowed his nephew, Jesse Daniel, to move in. Thomas died on February 24, 1897, and is buried at Lick Creek Baptist Church.

336. Daniel, Woodson

Private, Company I, 76th Regiment N.C. Troops (6th N.C. Senior Reserves)

Woodson was born in 1823 and resided in the southern district of Davidson County. He married Eliza Cameron on October 11, 1849. He and Eliza would have ten children: James (1849), Alice (1851), Travis (1853), William (1855), Mary (1857), Elizabeth (1860), Thomas (1861), Nancy (1864), Anne (1866), and Jane (1869). Records indicate that he served in the 5th Georgia, however, there is limited information regarding his service in that unit. Woodson served in Company I of the 6th N.C. Senior Reserves, which was organized in January 1865. After the war, he continued living in the Healing Springs area. Woodson died on September 6, 1903, and is buried at Lick Creek Baptist Church.

337. Darr, Henry C.

Private, Lexington Wildcats Company I, 14th Regiment N.C. Troops (4th N.C. Volunteers)

Henry was born on March 21, 1824, to Malicah and Susannah Darr. He volunteered for service on May 10, 1861. He was present until he was wounded in the fourth finger of the left hand at Spotsylvania Court House, Virginia, on May 21, 1864. Henry was reported absent, wounded, through August 1864. After

the war, Henry married Elizabeth, with whom he had no children. He was listed as a cancer doctor in the 1870 and 1880 censuses. By 1896, he had married Frances and moved to the Boone township. Henry lived there until his death on March 22, 1909. He is buried at Pine Primitive Baptist Church.

338. Darr, Samuel

Private, Randolph Hornets Company M, 22nd Regiment N.C. Troops (12th N.C. Volunteers)

Sam was born on October 6, 1825, to Malicah and Susannah Darr. He worked as a farmer and married Mary prior to 1858. Sam and Mary would have two children, Susan (1859) and Julie Ann (1862), prior to Sam's conscription at Camp Holmes, Raleigh, North Carolina, on March 15, 1864. He was present through October 1864. After the war, Samuel returned to his farm, and he and Mary would have three more children: Jacob (1865), Mary E. (1866), and Samuel L. (1868). Sam lived in the North Thomasville township until his death on March 15, 1896. He is buried at Mount Pleasant United Methodist Church.

339. Darr, Socrates

Private, Company C, 70th Regiment N.C. Troops (1st N.C. Junior Reserves)

Built in 1850 by Justice of the Peace Thomas H. Daniel, this was the home of four generations of the Daniels family (Touart, *Building the Backcountry*).

Socrates was born in 1847 to Henry and Salome Darr. He worked as a farmer prior to enlisting on May 2, 1864, in the Junior Reserves. He survived the war and moved out of the county by 1880. No further records.

340. Darr, Solomon

Private, Company F, 76th Regiment N.C. Troops (6th N.C. Senior Reserves)

Solomon was born on July 10, 1815. He worked as a farmer in the Pilgrim community, and on February 27, 1848, he married Elizabeth Kanoy. Solomon and Elizabeth would have five children: William (1849), Susannah (1853), Laura (1855), Gaseal (1860), and Franny (1864). Solomon served in the 6th Senior Reserves, which was organized in January 1865. After the war, he continued his farming work and attended Laura's graduation from the Glen Anna Female Seminary. Solomon died on February 13, 1885, and is buried at Pilgrim United Church of Christ.

341. Darr, William Andrew

Private, Company B, 48th Regiment N.C. Troops

Andy was born on September 10, 1828, to Andrew and Mary Darr. He worked as a farmer in the Pilgrim area prior to being conscripted on July 24, 1864. He was wounded at Globe Tavern, Virginia, on August 21, 1864. Andy was then detailed and worked as a cook in the commissary department of General J. R. Cooke's Brigade. He was paroled at Appomattox Court House, Virginia, on April 9, 1865. After the war, he returned home and did battle with several northern visitors in "Uncle Andy and the Carpetbagger," a story handed down by his descendants. On February 13, 1873, Andy married Elizabeth Grimes. In addition to her son, Hamilton, and Andy's "adopted" son, Charles Conrad, they had three children: Minnie (1874), Ernest (1877), and William (1879). Andy worked as a farmer in the Lexington township until his death on February 2, 1895. He is buried at Pilgrim United Church of Christ.

342. Davis, Absalom

Private, Company H, 48th Regiment N.C. Troops

Absalom was born in 1841 to John A. and Barbara Weaver Davis. He worked as a farmer prior to being conscripted and enlisting at Petersburg, Virginia, on August 8, 1862. He was wounded in the forehead and eye during the battle of Fredericksburg, Virginia, on December 13, 1862. He was sent to a hospital in Richmond, where he died of his wounds on January 10, 1863.

343. Davis, Allison

Private, Company H, 48th Regiment N.C. Troops

Allison was born in 1827 to Martha Davis. He worked as a hireling and married Camille Phillips on February 13, 1851. He volunteered for service on March 12, 1862. He was wounded in the thigh during the battle of Fredericksburg, Virginia, on December 13, 1862. He died of pneumonia at Petersburg, Virginia, on January 29, 1863. He is buried in the Blanford Cemetery in Petersburg.

344. Davis, Alpheus L.

Private, Company G, 2nd Battalion, N.C. Infantry

Alpheus was born in 1843 to Martha Davis. He worked as a farmer prior to volunteering in Forsyth County on September 23, 1861. Alpheus was captured at Roanoke Island, North Carolina, on February 8, 1862, and was paroled on February 21, 1862. He rejoined his company and was present until he was wounded and captured during Pickett's charge on July 3, 1863, at Gettysburg, Pennsylvania. He was confined at David's Island, New York, until August 23, 1864, when he was paroled for exchange. He rejoined his company and was captured again at Harpers Ferry, [West] Virginia, on July 10, 1864. Alpheus was confined at Old Capital Prison in Washington, D.C., until transferred to Elmira, New York. He died at Elmira on November 26, 1864, of "chronic diarrhea."

345. Davis, Christian C.

Private, Company K, 1st Regiment Arkansas Mounted Rifles Company E, 25th Arkansas Infantry

Christian was born on September 25, 1838, to John A. and Barbara Weaver Davis. He worked as a farmer and was married to Catharine Sowers prior to

moving to Arkansas in late 1860. While there he served in two Arkansas units, the 1st Mounted Rifles and the 25th Infantry. He lived in Arkansas and died on September 22, 1872. He is buried in South Bend, Arkansas.

346. Davis, Edward L.

Private, Company C, 70th Regiment N.C. Troops (1st N.C. Junior Reserves)

Edward was born in 1847 to John A. and Barbara Weaver Davis. He was working as a miller's apprentice in 1860 and enlisted on May 24, 1864, in the Junior Reserves. He survived the war and became a farmer in the Yadkin township. No further records.

347. Davis, Henry C.

Private, Company D, 48th Regiment N.C. Troops

Henry was born in 1835 and worked as a farmer in northern Davidson county. He was conscripted on August 8, 1862. Henry was reported present until he was wounded in action at Bristoe Station, Virginia, on October 14, 1863. He recovered and was reported present until captured at Fort Stedman, Virginia, on March 25, 1865. He was confined at Point Lookout, Maryland, until he was released on June 26, 1865, after taking the oath of allegiance. No further records.

348. Davis, Henry Jackson

Sergeant, Thomasville Rifles Company B, 14th Regiment N.C. Troops (4th N.C. Volunteers)

Henry was born on October 9, 1840, to John A. and Barbara Weaver Davis. He worked as a farmer prior to volunteering for service on May 20, 1861. Henry was promoted to corporal on November 2, 1862, and to sergeant on August 1, 1864. Henry was present until he was captured at either Winchester or Strasburg, Virginia. He was confined at Point Lookout, Maryland, until February 18, 1865, when he was sent to Boulware's Wharf, Virginia, for exchange. He was declared exchanged and was present with a detachment at Camp Lee, Virginia. on February 22, 1865. He survived the war and returned home to marry Amanda Crotts on August 10, 1865. He moved to Auburn, Arkansas, shortly afterward to join his brother Christian. Henry died on December 25, 1872, in Auburn.

349. Davis, Ivey

*Private, Chatam Light Infantry
Company G, 48th Regiment N.C. Troops*

Ivey was born in 1840 to Rebecca Davis. He was conscripted on August 14, 1862, and was reported present through April 1864. No further records.

350. Davis, James W.

*Private, Holtsburg Guards
Company A, 54th Regiment N.C. Troops*

James was born in 1830 to James and Mary Davis. He worked as a farmer prior to volunteering for service on March 4, 1862. He was wounded and captured during the battle of Fredericksburg, Virginia, on December 13, 1862. He was confined at Old Capital Prison, Washington, D.C., and Fort Delaware, Delaware, prior to being received at City Point, Virginia, for exchange. He was exchanged and returned to duty prior to September 1, 1863. He was captured again at Rappahannock Station, Virginia, on November 7, 1863, and was confined at Point Lookout, Maryland, until paroled and received at City Point, Virginia, for exchange on March 15, 1864. He was hospitalized at Richmond, Virginia, where he died on March 24, 1864, of "pneumonia."

351. Davis, Jesse

*Private, Company I, 42nd Regiment
N.C. Troops*

Jesse was born in 1841 to Sarah Davis. He volunteered for service on March 6, 1862, and was reported present until he died at Hamilton, North Carolina, on May 17, 1863. The cause of death was not reported.

352. Davis, John R.

*Private, Company G, 2nd Battalion,
N.C. Infantry*

John was born in 1844 to William and Kezia Davis. He worked as a farmer prior to volunteering for service on September 19, 1861. He was reported present until he was captured during Pickett's charge at Gettysburg, Pennsylvania, on July 3, 1863. John was confined at Fort Delaware, Delaware, until he was paroled and transferred to City Point, Virginia, on July 30, 1863, for exchange. He was exchanged and sent home on unspecified dates. John died at home on August 16, 1863.

353. Davis, Lindsay

*Private, Company I, 42nd Regiment
N.C. Troops*

Lindsay was born in 1844. He worked as a farmer prior to volunteering for service on March 6, 1862. Lindsay served throughout the war and was paroled at Salisbury, North Carolina, on June 1, 1865. After the war, he returned home and married Sally Morris on December 16, 1866. The couple moved out of the county prior to 1870. No further records.

354. Davis, Roby Silas

*Private, Company F, 7th Regiment
N.C. State Troops*

Roby resided in the southern district of Davidson County prior to being conscripted into service on May 1, 1863. He was hospitalized at Charlottesville, Virginia, on July 27, 1863, with a gunshot wound of the foot. He was reported absent, wounded or sick, through October 1864. Roby was captured at a Richmond hospital during the city's fall on April 3, 1865. He was paroled on April 24, 1865. Roby did not return to Davidson County.

355. Davis, Samuel J.

*Third Lieutenant, Company H, 48th
Regiment N.C. Troops*

Samuel was born in 1843. He lived in the Clemmonsville area prior to being conscripted into service at Petersburg, Virginia, on August 8, 1862. Sam was mustered in as a private and was promoted to corporal in October 1863. He was promoted to sergeant on November 1, 1864, and 14 days later he was appointed third lieutenant. Sam served with this rank until he was paroled at Appomattox Court House on April 9, 1865. After the war, he returned home and married Rebecca V. Mulican on August 27, 1867. He and Rebecca would have six children on their farm in Hampton: Oscar (1868), Spencer (1875), Josephine (1878), Alexander (1881), Isabel (1884), and Conrad (1886). Sam lived as a successful farmer in the Hampton

township as late as 1900. No further records.

356. Davis, Thomas D.

*Private, Company B, 48th Regiment
N.C. Troops*

Thomas was born in 1842. He volunteered for service on March 10, 1862, at "Palmer's." He was reported absent without leave on April 15, 1862. No further records.

357. Davis, Thomas Dough

*Private, Company I, 42nd Regiment
N.C. Troops*

Thomas was born in 1843 to John and Sarah Davis. He worked as a farmer prior to volunteering for service on March 18, 1862. He was reported present until he deserted on May 20, 1863. Thomas returned to duty on December 13, 1863, and was reported present through October 1864. After the war, he married Huldy in 1867. Thomas and Huldy would raise five children on their farm in the Healing Springs township: Louisa (1876), Albert (1878), John (1880), William (1883), and Della (1886). Thomas died after 1910. He is buried at Summerville Baptist Church.

358. Davis, Thomas W.

*First Lieutenant, 65th Regiment N.C.
Militia (1861 organization)*

Thomas was born in 1820 to John and Barbara Smith Davis. He worked as a farmer and a miller prior to the outbreak of the war. Thomas was commissioned as a first lieutenant in the Healing Springs District Company on November 25, 1861. After his term of service, he married Elizabeth Smith in 1865, and they would have two children: Franklin (1868) and James (1873). In the 1880 Census, his mother, Barbara, had moved in with the household at the age of 86. No further records.

359. Davis, Travis W.

*Private, Company I, 42nd Regiment
N.C. Troops*

Travis was born in 1834 to John and Sarah Davis. He worked as a farmer and in 1860 married Elizabeth. Two years later, Bennett was born. Travis volunteered for service on March 6, 1862. He was reported present through every major action of the 42nd Regiment through October 1864. After the war, he and Elizabeth had another child, Elwood (1867). Travis lived as a small farmer in the Emmons township until his death on September 4, 1912. He is buried at Summerville Baptist Church. The inscription on his stone reads: "Farewell loved one, thou art gone forever."

360. Davis, William

Private, Company B, 48th Regiment N.C. Troops

William was born in 1838 to Thomas and Elizabeth Smith Davis. He worked as a farmer prior to being conscripted into service on August 8, 1862. William was reported present until he died of pneumonia in a Charlottesville, Virginia, hospital on December 16, 1862.

361. Davis, William

Private, Company H, 48th Regiment N.C. Troops

William was born in 1828. He worked as a farmer in the southern district of Davidson County and was married to Mary. They would have four children: Cicero (1853), Fanny (1855), Roswell (1858), and Delilah (1859). William was conscripted into service on August 8, 1862. He died in a Richmond, Virginia, hospital on September 13, 1862, of pneumonia.

362. Davis, William Thales

Private, Company C, 70th Regiment N.C. Troops (1st N.C. Junior Reserves)

William was born on March 24, 1848, to Henry and Phoebe Jones Farabee Davis. He worked as a farmer prior to enlisting in the Junior Reserves on May 24, 1864. After the war, he returned home, and, on June 4, 1866, he married Mary F. Young. William and Mary built a two-story house in the Boone township, where they raised ten children: Flora and Ella (1869), Obediah (1871), Martha (1873), Emma (1875), Merritt (1877), William (1879), Lenora (1881), Ollin T. (1884), and Laura (1886). William lived a full life in the Boone township until his death from a heart attack on April 8, 1905. He is buried in the Davis-Darr Cemetery in Churchland.

363. Davis, Woodson

Private, Company I, 42nd Regiment N.C. Troops

Woodson was born in 1833. He worked as a farmer prior to volunteering for service on March 6, 1862. He was reported present until he deserted to the enemy on July 20, 1864. Wood was confined at Fort Monroe, Virginia, until he was released on an unspecified date after taking the oath of allegiance. No further records.

364. Davis, Wyatt

Private, Company B, 48th Regiment N.C. Troops

Wyatt was born on September 25, 1840, to Thomas and Elizabeth Davis. He worked as a farmer prior to being conscripted into service on August 8, 1862. Soon after he entered service, Wyatt caught extremely severe cases of intermittent fever and smallpox. He was admitted to a smallpox hospital in Petersburg, Virginia, on February 26, 1863. Wyatt was detailed as a nurse while staying in the hospital, serving from April 21, 1863, until August 1864. He returned to active service in September 1864 and was wounded at Hatcher's Run, Virginia, on February 5, 1865. After the war, he returned home, and, on May 27, 1866, he

N.C. Junior Reserve Private William Thales Davis, in later life (Mary Jo Shoaf, *The Heritage of Davidson County*).

married Nancy Bean. Wyatt and Nancy would raise seven children in their Healing Springs home: Franklin (1867), Linda (1869), Thomas (1871), Daniel (1873), William Ausler (1875), Tory (1877), and Martha (1879). Wyatt lived with his family until his death on April 27, 1919. He is buried at Lick Creek Baptist Church.

365. Delapp, John

Private, Cleveland Mountain Boys Company D, 15th Regiment N.C. Troops (5th N.C. Volunteers)

John was born in 1839 to Amos and Margaret Delapp. He worked as a farmer prior to being conscripted into service in Wake County on July 15, 1862. He was wounded in the shoulder and captured at Crampton's Pass, Maryland, during the battle of South Mountain on September 14, 1862. He died of his wounds in a hospital at Burkittsville, Maryland, on September 28, 1862.

366. Delapp, John S.

Captain, 66th Regiment N.C. Militia (1861 organization)

John was born on March 4, 1834, to Daniel and Phoebe Delapp. He was married to Fanny C. Phillips on June 27, 1857. She died giving birth to his first child, Sallie (1861). When the war broke out, he accepted a commission as captain of the Reedy Creek District Company on October 1, 1861. He resigned his post on March 31, 1865. John married Sarah A. Jarrett on February 15, 1866, and they would have three children: Lawrence (1868), Oliver (1878), and Bertha (1882). In 1870, his mother, Phoebe, came to live with the household in the Yadkin township. John died on January 25, 1917. He is buried at Good Hope United Methodist Church.

367. Delapp, Joseph Franklin

Second Lieutenant, Company H, 48th Regiment N.C. Troops

Joseph was born on March 11, 1837, to John and Margaret Long Delapp. Joseph worked as a tanner and a farmer, and he was married to Anna E. Wagner. He volunteered for service and was elected second lieutenant on March 8, 1862. Joseph resigned his commission on July 28, 1862, because of "having for the past month been subject to a violent disease." He left his unit and eventually moved to Texas. He died on February 15, 1911, in Gainesville, Texas. He is buried at Fairview Cemetery in Gainesville.

368. Delapp, Robert

Private, Confederate Guards
Company K, 48th Regiment N.C. Troops

Robert was born on February 29, 1829, to John and Margaret Long Delapp. He married a tailor, Phoebe Harmon, on December 3, 1853. They would have three children: Franklin (1855), Isabella (1858), and John (1859). Robert was conscripted on August 8, 1862, and served until he deserted at Weldon, North Carolina, on May 5, 1863. He returned for duty on June 30, 1863, and was reported present until he was captured at Hatcher's Run, Virginia, on April 2, 1865. Robert was confined at Hart's Island, New York, until June 19, 1865, when he was released after taking the oath of allegiance. After the war, he moved his family to Missouri. He died in August 1904 and is buried in Higginsville, Missouri.

369. Delapp, Valentine

Private, Cleveland Mountain Boys
Company D, 15th Regiment N.C. Troops
(5th N.C. Volunteers)

Valentine was born in 1832 to Amos and Margaret Delapp. He worked as a farmer, and in 1855 he married Louisa. He and Louisa would have two children: Anna (1856) and Roswell (1858). He was conscripted into service in Wake County on July 15, 1862. Val died at a Lynchburg, Virginia, hospital on October 1, 1862. The cause of death was not reported.

370. Dickens, Benjamin E.

Private, Holtsburg Guards
Company A, 54th Regiment N.C. Troops

Ben was born on July 2, 1836, to Thomas and Hannah Dickens. He worked as a miner, and in 1861 he married Amanda. Ben and Amanda would have five children: Jesse (1861), Elizabeth (1864), John (1866), Thomas (1869), and Mattie (1876). Benjamin volunteered for service on April 22, 1862. He was detailed from the 54th N.C. Regiment on September 10, 1862, to work as a lead miner in the Conrad Hill mine. He served for the rest of the war as a lead miner. Ben lived and worked in the Silver Hill township and was recorded as being a machin-

ist in 1900. He died on January 29, 1920, and is buried at Old Bethany Methodist Church.

371. Dickens, John

Private, Holtsburg Guards
Company A, 54th Regiment N.C. Troops

John was born in 1820. He worked as a miner and lived with Henry and Hannah Workman. He was married in Rowan County to Nancy Workman in 1858. John and Nancy would have six children: Louisa (1861), Margaret (1864), Rueben J. (1865), Thomas (1869), William (1875), and Mary M. (1877). John was 42 years old when he volunteered for service on April 22, 1862. He was detailed from the 54th N.C. Regiment on September 10, 1862, to work as a lead miner in the Conrad Hill mine and served for the rest of the war as a lead miner. John died sometime prior to June 1880. No further records.

372. Disher, Christian

Private, Cleveland Mountain Boys
Company D, 15th Regiment N.C. Troops
(5th N.C. Volunteers)

Christian was born in 1836 to Paul and Catharine Link Disher. He was living with his grandfather, after whom he was named, in 1860. He married Mary Evans on February 23, 1857. Christian was conscripted into service in Wake County on July 15, 1862. He was hospitalized at Richmond, Virginia, on September 16, 1862. He was issued a 30-day furlough on November 7, 1862, and died in Davidson County of "chronic diarrhea" on November 15, 1862. He is buried at Friedburg Moravian Church.

373. Disher, Henry, Jr.

Private, Cleveland Mountain Boys
Company D, 15th Regiment N.C. Troops
(5th N.C. Volunteers)
2nd Company B, 49th Regiment N.C.
Troops
Company H, 48th Regiment N.C. Troops

Henry was born on February 11, 1836, to Paul and Catharine Link Disher. He worked as a farmer and a blacksmith and married Julia Bratain in 1856. Henry and Julia had two children before her death in 1861: Mary (1857) and Hamilton (1859). Henry was conscripted into service in Wake County on July 15, 1862. He

was transferred along with his company to the 49th Regiment on January 9, 1863. He was reported sick from January 9 until September 30, 1863. He obtained a discharge from the 49th Regiment under a writ of habeas corpus. He reenlisted in Company H of the 48th Regiment subsequent to October 31, 1864. Henry was hospitalized on February 18, 1865, with severe rheumatism and was issued a 60-day furlough on March 29, 1865. In 1866, Henry married a second time, to Mary Anne Weaver. Mary died prior to 1870; they had a daughter, Mariah (1868). Henry married Ellen Wilson in 1871. Henry and Ellen would have one child together: Lulia (1877). Henry lived with his family until his death on May 12, 1903. He is buried at Mt. Olivet United Methodist Church.

374. Disher, Levi

Private, Company H, 48th Regiment
N.C. Troops

Levi was born in 1846. He worked as a farmer prior to being conscripted on March 15, 1864. He was wounded at the battle of Wilderness, Virginia, on May 6, 1864. He returned to duty on June 2, 1864, and was reported present through October 1864. Levi deserted to the enemy on March 8, 1865, and was confined at Washington, D.C., until released on an unspecified date after taking the oath of allegiance. After the war, he married Susan Mize. The couple had one child, Levi (1875). After Susan's death, Levi married Susan Link Disher, the widow of his brother David, in 1894. Levi died about 1896.

375. Disher, Thomas Jefferson

Private, Cleveland Mountain Boys
Company D, 15th Regiment N.C. Troops
(5th N.C. Volunteers)
2nd Company B, 49th Regiment N.C.
Troops

Thomas was born on December 3, 1841, to Paul and Elizabeth Disher. In 1860, he was working as a farmer and living in the home of John Hill. Thomas was conscripted in Wake County on July 15, 1862. He was captured at Crampton's Pass during the battle of South Mountain, Maryland, on September 14, 1862. He was confined at Fort Delaware, Delaware, until paroled and transferred to Aiken's Landing, Virginia, for exchange on October 2, 1862. Thomas was declared exchanged on November 10, 1862, and was transferred along with his company to the 49th Regiment. He was captured at Sandy Ridge, Lenoir County, on April 20, 1863. He was paroled at City Point, Virginia, and returned to duty on May 28, 1863. Thomas was wounded in the hand at Drewery's Bluff, Virginia, on May 16, 1864. He returned to duty prior to July 1, 1864, and was reported present until he was captured at Five Forks, Virginia, on April 1, 1865. Thomas was confined at Hart's Island, New York, until June 18, 1865, when he was released after taking the oath of allegiance. After the war, Thomas returned home, and, on December 26, 1866, he married Paulina Weaver. Thomas was baptized as a Moravian and moved his family to Forsyth County, where he helped to found Oak Grove Moravian Church. He died after 1910 and is buried at Oak Grove Moravian Church in Winston-Salem, North Carolina.

376. Dobey, Calvin

Private, Davidson Guards
Company A, 21st Regiment N.C. Troops
(11th N.C. Volunteers)

Calvin was born in 1827 and worked as a miner in the southern district of Davidson County. Calvin volunteered for service on May 8, 1861. He was reported present until he was wounded in the left arm during the battle of Winchester, Virginia, on May 25, 1862. He was discharged on October 25, 1862, due to "atrophy of the left arm." No further records.

377. Dobey, George M.

Private, Company B, 48th Regiment N.C. Troops

George was born in 1840 to Allen and Elizabeth Dobey. He worked as a farmer prior to being conscripted on August 8, 1862. He was reported present through October 1864 and was paroled at Greensboro, North Carolina, on May 11, 1865. He survived the war, and in the 1880 Census he was married to Elizabeth. No further records.

378. Dobey, James C.

Private, Company I, 42nd Regiment N.C. Troops

James was born on January 15, 1844, to Allen and Elizabeth Dobey. He worked

as a farmer prior to being conscripted into service on July 27, 1863. He was reported present through October 1864; pension records indicate he was wounded in 1864. After the war, he returned home, and in 1880, he married Frances Newsom. James and Frances would have two children: Austin (1882) and Minnie (1886). Frances died in 1887. James married Jane in 1893. James lived in the Healing Springs township until his death on July 25, 1916. He is buried at Summerville Baptist Church.

379. Dobey, William

Private, Company B, 48th Regiment N.C. Troops

William was born in 1837 to Allen and Elizabeth Dobey. He worked as a carpenter, and, on August 21, 1861, he married Jane Davis. William was conscripted on August 8, 1862. He deserted at Sharpsburg, Maryland, on September 17, 1862, and did not return until April 30, 1864. He was reported present until he deserted to the enemy on October 9, 1864. William was confined at Washington, D.C., until he was released on an unspecified date after taking the oath of allegiance. No further records.

380. Dodson, Charles Carroll

Chaplain, Staff, 46th Regiment N.C. Troops

Charles was born on June 6, 1832, to George and Lucinda Foster Dodson. He was an ordained minister and was married to Margaret Leach. He was appointed chaplain of the 46th N.C. Regiment on May 31, 1863. He resigned his post on October 31, 1864, because of physical disability. After his service, he moved to Salem and lived there until he died on May 17, 1884. He is buried at the Salem Cemetery in Winston-Salem, North Carolina.

381. Dorsett, James Madison

Private, Company C, 70th Regiment N.C. Troops (1st N.C. Junior Reserves)

James was born in 1846 to Leonard and Katharine Varner Dorsett. He enlisted on May 24, 1864, in the Junior Reserves. After the war, he returned to farming, and in 1877, he married Roxanna. They would have one child, Lewis

(1879), prior to leaving the county in 1882. No further records.

382. Dorsett, Leonard

Private, Company B, 48th Regiment N.C. Troops

Leonard was born in 1820. He worked as a carpenter and a mechanic. On September 26, 1841, he married Katharine Varner. Leonard and Katharine would have two children, both of whom would serve in the Civil War: William Wesley (1841) and James M. (1846). Leonard volunteered at age 42 on March 12, 1862. He was discharged on December 2, 1862, with "pulmonary tuberculosis." No further records.

383. Dorsett, Samuel J.

Private, Company D, 48th Regiment N.C. Troops

Samuel was born on September 15, 1843, to George and Elizabeth Dorsett. He worked as a farmer prior to being conscripted on August 8, 1862. He died in a Gordonsville, Virginia, hospital on November 25, 1862, of "febris typhoides."

384. Dorsett, William

Private, Company B, 48th Regiment N.C. Troops

William was born in 1828. He worked as a farmer in the southern district of Davidson County. He volunteered for service at the age of 34 on March 12, 1862. He was reported present through December 24, 1864. No further records.

385. Dorsett, William Henry

Private, Thomasville Rifles
Company B, 14th Regiment N.C. Troops (4th N.C. Volunteers)

William was born in 1844 to Samuel M. and Athalia Dorsett. He worked as a carpenter prior to volunteering on April 23, 1861. He was reported present, with a brief promotion to sergeant, until he was wounded in the head during the battle of Gettysburg, Pennsylvania, on July 1, 1863. He recovered from his wound and returned to duty on September 1, 1863. William was reported present until he deserted on February 15, 1864. After the war, he returned home to his parents. He married Elizabeth Gray in 1866. William and Elizabeth would have three children who survived: Etha (1878), Reid (1883), and Arnold (1890). No further records.

386. Dorsett, William Wesley

Private, Company D, 48th Regiment N.C. Troops

William was born in 1841 to Leonard and Katharine Varner Dorsett. He worked as a farmer prior to being conscripted on August 8, 1862. He was reported present until he was captured at Hatcher's Run, Virginia, on April 2, 1865. He was confined at Point Lookout, Maryland, until June 26, 1865, when he was released after taking the oath of allegiance. William married Mary Alice Leonard in 1866. William and Mary had three children who survived: Jesse (1866), Samuel (1869), and George (1874). He lived in the Conrad Hill township and is buried at Liberty Baptist Church.

387. Doty, Isaac

Private, Cleveland Mountain Boys Company D, 15th Regiment N.C. Troops (5th N.C. Volunteers)

Isaac was born in 1832 to Michael and Catharine Doty. Isaac worked as a shoemaker prior to being conscripted on July 15, 1862, in Wake County. He was mortally wounded during the battle of Sharpsburg, Maryland, on September 17, 1862.

388. Douthit, Alpha L.

Private, Davidson Guards Company A, 21st Regiment N.C. Troops (11th N.C. Volunteers)

Alpha was born in 1833 to Benton C. and Paulina Douthit. He worked as a clerk in his father's store prior to volunteering on May 8, 1861. He was discharged on December 8, 1861, because of "general debility from his entire want of constitution and many symptoms of phthisis pulmonalis." No further records.

389. Durham, William

Private, Company A, 10th Battalion, N.C. Heavy Artillery

William was born in 1833. He worked as a farmer, and in 1854, he married Laura. William and Laura would have five children: John (1856), Sarah (1858), Hannah (1860), Isaac (1861), and Alexander (1866). William volunteered for service on April 21, 1862. He was reported present until he deserted on August 9, 1863. He was paroled at Greensboro, North Carolina, on May 8, 1865. He lived with his family in the Midway township prior to leaving the county. No further records.

390. Duskin, Lindsay

Private, Company F, 76th Regiment N.C. Troops (6th N.C. Senior Reserves)

Lindsay was born on March 20, 1818. He worked as a carpenter in the northern district of Davidson County and married Elizabeth in 1849. He and Elizabeth would have four children: George (1851), Joseph (1853), Cynthia (1855), and William (1864). Lindsay attained master carpenter status in 1860. Lindsay enlisted in the Senior Reserves upon their organization on January 23, 1865. After his service, Lindsay continued his carpentry work. Elizabeth died on May 20, 1872. Lindsay lived in the town of Thomasville, and in 1880 he was living in the Mock Hotel. In 1899, Lindsay married Susannah Helton. Three years later, on August 8, 1902, he passed away. Lindsay is buried in the Thomasville City Cemetery. He was a member of the Masonic order.

391. Earnhardt, James Pinkney

Private, Rowan Artillery Company D, 10th Regiment N.C. State Troops (1st N.C. Artillery)

James was born on May 6, 1845. He worked as a farmer prior to volunteering in Rowan County on June 15, 1861. He was reported present until he was captured at Amelia Court House, Virginia, on April 5, 1865. James was sent to Point Lookout, Maryland, and was confined there until released on July 11, 1865, after taking the oath of allegiance. After the war, he married Camilla Trexler. James died on September 27, 1915. He is buried in the Lexington City Cemetery.

392. Earnhardt, Richard Travis

Private, Rowan Artillery Company D, 10th Regiment N.C. State Troops (1st N.C. Artillery)

Richard was born on April 23, 1823. He worked as a merchant in Lexington, and, in 1847, he married Lucy Parker. Richard and Lucy would have eight children: Lucy (1848), Mary (1850), John W. (1852), O. A. (1854), Laura (1856), Jane (1858), Maggie (1860), and Charlotte (1863). Richard volunteered in Rowan County on March 15, 1862. He was reported present throughout the war, and was paroled at Appomattox Court House, Virginia, on April 9, 1865. Richard returned home to Lexington and helped his wife start her own business as a milliner. Richard died on April 15, 1879. He is buried in the Lexington City Cemetery.

393. Easter, George Washington

Private, Company H, 48th Regiment N.C. Troops

George was born on February 16, 1837, to Henry and Catharine Easter. He worked as a hireling prior to volunteering at Wagner's on March 1, 1862. He was reported present until he was wounded in action at Globe Tavern, Virginia, on August 21, 1864. After recovering from his wounds, George returned to service and was captured at Hatcher's Run, Virginia, on April 1, 1865. George was sent to Point Lookout, Maryland, where he was confined until June 12, 1865, when he was released after taking the oath of allegiance. George returned home, and family history records that he was married twice, to Elizabeth Miller (August 12, 1869) and to Eliza Huffman. He did not have any children with either one. George died on January 2, 1926. He is buried at Good Hope United Methodist Church.

394. Easter, Henry

Private, Company H, 48th Regiment N.C. Troops

Henry was born on April 11, 1831, to Henry and Catharine Easter. In 1854, Henry married Frances May, who would die two years later. They had a daughter, Faustine. Henry volunteered for service on March 6, 1862. He was reported present throughout the war and was paroled at Appomattox Court House, Virginia, on April 9, 1865. After the war, Henry returned to the Conrad Hill township and married Sarah Sechrist. Henry served as a deacon at Liberty Baptist Church until his death on May 15, 1898. He is buried at Liberty Baptist Church.

395. Easter, Michael

*Private, Southern Rights Infantry
Company I, 27th Regiment N.C. Troops*

Michael was born on May 31, 1827, to Henry and Catharine Easter. He worked as a farmer, and, on December 3, 1848, he married Cynthia Imbler. Michael and Cynthia would have four children, Naomi (1856), America (1859), James (1861), and Florena (1864), before he was conscripted into service in Wake County on April 1, 1864. Michael was reported present until he was sent to the hospital on July 28, 1864. He was reported absent, sick, through February 1865. He survived the war and returned home to the Tyro township, where he and Cynthia would have two more children: Miranda (1878) and Mary (1879). Michael lived in the Tyro area until his death on March 27, 1901, and is buried at Reeds Baptist Church.

396. Eaton, Samuel W.

*Private, Company B, 57th Regiment
N.C. Troops*

Samuel was born in 1842. He worked as a farmer prior to enlisting in Rowan County on July 4, 1862. He was reported present until he was captured at Rappahannock Station, Virginia, on November 7, 1863. Samuel was confined at Point Lookout, Maryland, until he was paroled and transferred to Boulware's Wharf, Virginia, for exchange on February 20, 1865. Samuel survived the war and returned home to marry Lucinda Eddinger. Samuel was a successful farmer and merchant in the Thomasville township and a leader in the original congregation of Rich Fork Baptist Church. He died on May 10, 1915, and is buried at Rich Fork Baptist Church.

397. Ebert, M. L.

*Private, Confederate Guards
Company K, 48th Regiment N.C. Troops*

M. L. was born in 1836. He resided in the northern district of Davidson County prior to being conscripted into service on August 8, 1862. He was wounded in the left arm during the battle of Fredericksburg, Virginia, on December 13, 1862. He was reported absent, wounded, through June 1863. He was retired to the Invalid Corps on April 11, 1864, due to wounds received at Fredericksburg that "pro-duced contraction of the muscles of the left arm & forearm & loss of power in the hand." No further records.

398. Eccles, Francis M.

*First Sergeant, Davidson Guards
Company A, 21st Regiment N.C. Troops
(11th N.C. Volunteers)*

Francis was born in 1842 to Henry M. and Christina Eccles. He worked as a carpenter prior to volunteering on May 8, 1861. He was mustered in as a private and was promoted to first sergeant on May 5, 1863. He was reported present until he was paroled at Appomattox Court House, Virginia, on April 9, 1865. Francis returned home after the war. In 1870, he was living with his uncle Harrison in the Clemmonsville township. No record is found after 1880.

399. Eddinger, Daniel W.

*Private, Company C, 70th Regiment
N.C. Troops (1st N.C. Junior
Reserves)*

Daniel was born on July 10, 1845, to John and Crissila Kennedy Eddinger. Daniel enlisted on May 24, 1864, and served in the 1st N.C. Junior Reserves. After the war, he married Elizabeth Kiser in 1870. Daniel and Elizabeth would have eight children: Phillip (1868), Jane (1869), Marshall (1871), Mary (1876), Sarah (1878), Minnie (1881), Daniel (1888), and Cora (1891). Daniel lived in the southwest Thomasville township until his death on November 11, 1921. He is buried at Rich Fork Baptist Church.

400. Eddinger, David

*Private, Company C, 70th Regiment
N.C. Troops (1st N.C. Junior
Reserves)*

David was born in 1847 to James and Mary Eddinger. David was away in Surry County at school and returned to enlist on May 24, 1864, in the Junior Reserves. He died in service ca. February 1865, and is buried at Pilgrim United Church of Christ.

401. Eddinger, George Washington

*Private, Company B, 48th Regiment
N.C. Troops*

George was born in 1836 to John and Crissila Kennedy Eddinger. He worked as a farmer, and in 1861, he married Mary Ann Clodfelter. George volunteered for service on March 8, 1862, and was wounded in the battle of Sharpsburg, Maryland, on September 17, 1862. He was sent home and died near Thomasville on December 27, 1862, of smallpox. During the war, he was an avid letter writer and expressed his dread over the anticipated battle at Sharpsburg.

402. Eddinger, John R.

*Private, Company B, 48th Regiment
N.C. Troops*

John was born in 1826 to John and Crissila Kennedy Eddinger. He worked as a farmer, and he and his wife, Sarah, had two children: Franklin and Sarah Ann. John volunteered for service on March 8, 1862. He was reported present until he died in Chimbarazoo Hospital, Richmond, Virginia, on September 13, 1864, of typhoid fever. When his sister Nancy Mallard received word that he was sick, she took a cart to Richmond in hopes of bringing him back to heal. Upon arrival, however, she found out he was dead. John was buried at Hollywood Cemetery, Richmond, Virginia. A memorial stone in his honor is at Pilgrim United Church of Christ.

403. Eddinger, Phillip Henry

*Private, Company B, 48th Regiment
N.C. Troops*

Phillip was born in 1838 to John and Crissila Kennedy Eddinger. He worked as a farmer prior to being conscripted on May 16, 1862. He died near Thomasville on November 25, 1862, of smallpox.

404. Eddinger, William Mack

*Private, Company B, 48th Regiment
N.C. Troops*

William, known as "Billy the German," was born on January 18, 1833, to John and Crissila Kennedy Eddinger. He worked as a farmer, and in 1855, he married Mariah Schuler. William and Mariah would have four children, Burgess (1856), Tabitha (1858), Mary (1860), and Crissy (1862), before William volunteered for service on March 6, 1862. He was reported present throughout the war and survived without harm for its duration. During the war, William kept

William Mack "Billy the German" Eddinger (Richard L. Conrad).

in touch with his family through many letters. He was a religious man who was deeply concerned over the salvation of his brother John. After the war, William and Mariah would have four more children: Charles (1866), Webb (1868), William (1871), and David (1873). William lived in the Thomasville township until his death from heart disease on February 9, 1879. He is buried at Pilgrim United Church of Christ.

405. Edwards, John D.

Private, Company F, 44th Regiment N.C. Troops

John was a carpenter in the southern district of Davidson County and was living with Amos Fritts prior to volunteering in Montgomery County on March 1, 1862. He was reported present until he died in a Richmond, Virginia, hospital on June 11, 1864, of disease.

406. Elbertson, John Henry

Private, Company F, 2nd Battalion, N.C. Infantry

John was born in 1845. He volunteered for service in Randolph County on October 20, 1861. He was captured at Roanoke Island on February 8, 1862. John was paroled at Elizabeth City, North Carolina, on February 22, 1862, and was returned to his unit. He was reported present for the duration of the

war and was paroled at Appomattox Court House, Virginia, on April 9, 1865. After the war, John returned home, married Hannah Wheents on June 16, 1867, and took a job as a copper miner. John and Hannah would have two children: John (1868) and Linny (1870). Sadly, Hannah and the two children would all die before 1880. John moved in with a friend, Jesse Koonce. John died in 1900 and is buried at Clarksbury Methodist Church.

407. Eller, George Washington

Private, Carolina Rangers Company B, 10th Virginia Cavalry Regiment

George was born on February 15, 1835, to George and Mary Eller. He worked as a farmer prior to enlisting on August 1, 1864. George was reported present through October 1864, when he was wounded in an unspecified battle. He was admitted to a Raleigh, North Carolina, hospital on November 24, 1864, with "debilitas." He was retired to the Invalid Corps three days later. After the war, George returned home and lived with his mother. At the age of 51, he married Sarah Belle Kinney in 1886. George and Belle would have two children: Odessa (1887) and Charles (1893). George lived in the Midway area until his death on November 3, 1921. He is buried at Midway United Methodist Church.

408. Eller, John A.

Private, Company A, 42nd Regiment N.C. Troops

John was born on December 19, 1830. He worked as a farmer, and, in January 1858, he married Mary Siceloff. John and Mary would have five children: Laura (1858), Bell (1860), Sarah (1861), Mary E. (1862), and Sarah (1863). John was conscripted into service in Rowan County on July 29, 1862. He was assigned to be an ambulance driver in November 1862 and was present in that assignment through October 1864. After the war, John returned home to the Midway area and started his life over. John's property was classified as being in the North Thomasville township in 1880, however, he lived in Midway until his death on September 22, 1929. He is buried at Midway United Methodist Church.

409. Eller, Samuel F.

Private, Cleveland Mountain Boys Company D, 15th Regiment N.C. Troops (5th N.C. Volunteers)
2nd Company B, 49th Regiment N.C. Troops

Samuel was born in 1838 to George and Mary Eller. He worked as a farmer prior to being conscripted into service in Wake County on July 15, 1862. Sam was wounded in the foot during the battle of Fredericksburg, Virginia, on December 13, 1862. He was transferred while listed as absent, wounded, to the 49th Regiment on January 9, 1863. Sam returned to duty in February 1863 and was reported present until he was captured at Drewery's Bluff, Virginia, on May 16, 1864. He was confined at Elmira, New York, until he was released on June 16, 1865, after taking the oath of allegiance. After the war, Samuel returned home, and on August 25, 1870, he married Elizabeth Siceloff. He and Elizabeth would have two children: Mary (1872) and Loulie (1875). Samuel lived in the Midway area until his death in 1922. He is buried at Midway United Methodist Church.

410. Ellington, George B.

Corporal, Thomasville Rifles Company B, 14th Regiment N.C. Troops (4th N.C. Volunteers)

George was born in 1837 to Henry and Elizabeth Ellington. He worked as a carpenter prior to volunteering for service on April 23, 1861. George was reported present until he was wounded in the left side of the mouth while attending to fallen comrades during the battle of Sharpsburg, Maryland, on September 17, 1862. He recovered from his wounds, rejoined the company in January 1863, and was promoted to corporal on March 1, 1863. He was slightly wounded at both Chancellorsville, Virginia, and Gettysburg, Pennsylvania. George was reported present until August 7, 1864, when he was listed as a deserter; however, he was admitted to a hospital for "diarrhea" on the same day. George received a parole at Gordonsville, Virginia, on June 17, 1865. After the war, George returned to Orange County, where he died on October 4, 1911. An interesting story shows George's compassion during the war:

At a field hospital in Gettysburg, after George's wounds had been treated, he was placed next to a wounded Federal soldier whose eyes had been shot out. The Yankee, who wore several gold rings, offered them all to George, if George would shoot him. George refused to kill the man and administered help to him the best he could.—MAST

411. Ellington, James F.

Private, Thomasville Rifles
Company B, 14th Regiment N.C. Troops
(4th N.C. Volunteers)

James was born in 1837 to Henry and Elizabeth Ellington. He worked as a coachmaker prior to volunteering for service in Wake County on May 9, 1861. He was reported present until he was discharged for unrecorded reasons on August 30, 1861. The 1870 Census lists him as living in Orange County, North Carolina. No further records.

412. Elliot, John Brantley

Private, Company A, 42nd Regiment
N.C. Troops

John was born in 1837 to John and Caroline Elliot. He worked as a farmer prior to enlisting on May 5, 1862. He was reported present until he deserted to the enemy on March 15, 1864. John was confined at Baltimore, Maryland, until March 14, 1865, when he was released after taking the oath of allegiance. After a two-week stay in Baltimore, John made his way home. In 1880 he became a teacher and moved to Montgomery County, where he taught in a one-room schoolhouse in the vicinity of Lanes Chapel. John lived the rest of his life in Montgomery County and died there on July 10, 1912. He is buried at Lanes Chapel Methodist Church.

413. Ellis, Anderson Alexander

Lieutenant Colonel, 54th Regiment
N.C. Troops

Anderson was born in 1829. He worked as a planter in the northern district of Davidson County and was the fifth wealthiest man in Davidson County. Anderson married Mary Judith Bailey in 1853. They would have three children: John W. (1854), Frank (1856), and Frederick (1858). Anderson was the cousin of North Carolina Governor John W. Ellis.

He volunteered for service on May 26, 1862, and was elected captain of the Holtsburg Guards the same day. He served as company commander until he was appointed major on September 7, 1862, and transferred to the field and staff of the 54th North Carolina. Anderson was promoted to lieutenant colonel on May 8, 1863, and served with that rank until he was captured at Rappahannock Station, Virginia, on November 7, 1863. He was confined at Old Capital Prison, Washington, D.C., Johnson's Island, Ohio, and Point Lookout, Maryland, until he was paroled and exchanged on April 30, 1864. Anderson returned to his post on June 29, 1864, and was reported present until he was wounded in the left elbow at Winchester, Virginia, on September 19, 1864. He was furloughed from a Staunton, Virginia, hospital on December 3, 1864. He did not return, and his whereabouts became something of a mystery. A. A. Ellis is listed in the Clemmonsville township in the 1880 Census, however, he is not listed in Forsyth County in 1900. No further records.

414. Ellis, John R.

Private, Company H, 48th Regiment
N.C. Troops

John was born in 1835 to Richard and Tabitha Ellis. He worked as a farmer prior to being conscripted into service at Petersburg, Virginia, on August 8, 1862. John was reported present until he was reported absent without leave during March and April 1863. He was arrested in November 1863 and returned to duty on an unspecified date. John was reported present until he was paroled at Appomattox Court House, Virginia, on April 9, 1865. In 1870 he moved to Catawba County with his brother and was one of three founders of Hickory, North Carolina. No further records.

415. Ellis, William H.

Private, Cleveland Mountain Boys
Company D, 15th Regiment N.C. Troops
(5th N.C. Volunteers)
2nd Company B, 49th Regiment N.C.
Troops

William was born in 1835 to Richard and Tabitha Ellis. He worked as a farmer prior to being conscripted into service in Wake County on July 15, 1862. He was

reported present until May 16, 1864, when he was captured at Drewery's Bluff, Virginia. William was confined at Point Lookout, Maryland, and was then transferred to Elmira, New York, on August 16, 1864. He was confined at Elmira until June 16, 1865, when he was released after taking the oath of allegiance. William returned home from the war and convinced his brother, John, to come with him to Catawba County. In 1871, William bought a half share of a dentistry and mercantile business. He was one of three founders of Hickory, North Carolina. No further records.

416. Ensley, Samuel

Private, Company C, 70th Regiment
N.C. Troops (1st N.C. Junior
Reserves)

Samuel was born in 1847 to Anderson and Ellen Ensley. He worked as a farmer prior to enlisting in the Junior Reserves on May 24, 1864. After the war, he married Eliza Livengood on August 30, 1866. Samuel and Eliza would have four children: William (1870), Madison (1872), Wilson (1875), and Ida (1878). In 1880, they were living in the North Thomasville township. No further records.

417. Epps, Bedford

Private, Company C, 70th Regiment
N.C. Troops (1st N.C. Junior
Reserves)

Bedford was born in 1847 to William and Mary Ann Epps. He worked as a farmer prior to enlisting in the Junior Reserves on May 24, 1864. After the war, he and his brother Beverly moved to Arkansas. No further records.

418. Epps, Beverly R.

Corporal, Thomasville Rifles
Company B, 14th Regiment N.C. Troops
(4th N.C. Volunteers)

Beverly was born in 1844 to William and Mary Ann Epps. He worked as a farmer prior to volunteering on April 23, 1861. He was mustered in as a private and was promoted to corporal on August 1, 1864. He was reported present until he was wounded and captured at Winchester, Virginia, on September 19, 1864. After stays in Baltimore, Maryland, Washington, D.C., and Point Lookout,

Maryland, Beverly was paroled and sent to Venus Point, Georgia, for exchange on November 15, 1864. He rejoined his company prior to April 2, 1865, when he was captured at Petersburg, Virginia. Beverly was confined at Hart's Island, New York, until he was released on June 17, 1865, after taking the oath of allegiance. After the war, he and his brother Bedford moved to Arkansas. No further records.

419. Epps, James W.

Corporal, Thomasville Rifles
Company B, 14th Regiment N.C. Troops
(4th N.C. Volunteers)

James was born in 1838 to William and Mary Ann Epps. He was working as a carpenter, as well as being a student, prior to volunteering on April 23, 1861. James was promoted to corporal on April 28, 1862. He died of typhoid fever in a Richmond, Virginia, hospital on June 29, 1862. He is buried in the Hollywood Cemetery in Richmond.

420. Epps, Thomas G.

Private, Thomasville Rifles
Company B, 14th Regiment N.C. Troops
(4th N.C. Volunteers)

Thomas was born in 1842 to William and Mary Ann Epps. He worked as a farmer prior to volunteering on April 23, 1861. He was reported present until he died of typhoid fever at Farmville, Virginia, on July 1, 1862.

421. Essick, David

Private, Company H, 48th Regiment
N.C. Troops

David was born in 1836. He worked as a farmer prior to being conscripted into service at Petersburg, Virginia, on August 8, 1862. He was wounded during the battle of Sharpsburg, Maryland, on September 17, 1862. David recovered from his wounds and returned to service in March 1864. He was reported present until he was captured at Hatcher's Run, Virginia, on March 25, 1865. David was confined at Point Lookout, Maryland, until he was released on June 12, 1865, after taking the oath of allegiance. After the war, David married Sarah Lovina and had one child: Ida (1873). They moved to Forsyth County prior to 1885. No further records.

422. Essick, John

Private, Company H, 48th Regiment
N.C. Troops

John was born on October 12, 1840, to John and Elizabeth Essick. He worked as a miller prior to volunteering at "Wagner's" on March 1, 1862. He was reported present until he was wounded and captured at Hatcher's Run, Virginia, on February 6, 1865. John was sent to Point Lookout, Maryland, and was confined there until June 12, 1865, when he was released after taking the oath of allegiance. After the war, John returned home. On September 18, 1865, he married Amanda Perryman. John and Amanda would have five children: Andrew (1869), Ida E. (1874), Sarah (1877), John DeWitt (1879), and William Avery (1883). In 1870, John bought 27 acres near Pilgrim Church; on this land he raised his family and operated a cotton gin. John lived in the Lexington township until his death on February 26, 1917. He is buried at Pilgrim United Church of Christ.

423. Essick, Joseph

Private, Company A, 42nd Regiment
N.C. Troops

Joseph was born in 1834 to John and Nancy Essick. He worked as a farmer, and, on January 16, 1862, he married Sarah Ann Easter. He enlisted in Rowan County on July 29, 1862. Joseph was reported present until November 23, 1862, when he died in a Weldon, North Carolina, hospital of typhoid fever.

424. Essick, Ransom

Private, Cleveland Mountain Boys
Company D, 15th Regiment N.C. Troops
(5th N.C. Volunteers)
2nd Company B, 49th Regiment N.C.
Troops

Ransom was born in 1836 to John and Nancy Essick. He worked as a farmer prior to being conscripted into service in Wake County on July 15, 1862. He deserted on August 21, 1862, and returned on January 28, 1863, after his company had been transferred to the 49th Regiment. He was captured at Sandy Ridge, Lenoir County, North Carolina, on April 20, 1863, and was sent to New Bern, North Carolina, where he was paroled. Ransom was present for duty in July 1863 and was reported present

through August 21, 1864, when he was captured at Globe Tavern, Virginia. He was released from the Federal provost marshal on an unspecified date. After the war, he returned home and married Margaret Livengood on January 2, 1867. Ransom and Margaret would have four children together: Charles (1868), John (1873), Nancy (1875), and Lola (1877). After Margaret's death, Ransom married Elizabeth Easter Leonard. Ransom lived in the Lexington township until his death on February 16, 1914. He is buried at Beulah United Church of Christ.

425. Essick, Robert C.

Private, Company I, 42nd Regiment
N.C. Troops

Robert was born in 1833. He worked as a farmer prior to volunteering for service on March 8, 1862. He was reported present until he deserted to the enemy on July 20, 1864. Robert was confined at Fort Monroe, Virginia, and was transferred to Fort Delaware, Delaware. He was confined there until May 11, 1865, when he was released after taking the oath of allegiance. After the war, Robert returned home, and, in 1866, he married Amanda. Robert and Amanda had three children: George (1867), Charlie (1869), and Elizabeth (1875). Robert and his family were living in the Tyro township in 1880. No further records.

426. Essick, Theophilus

Private, Company E, 21st Regiment
N.C. Troops (11th N.C. Volunteers)
Company B, 1st Battalion N.C. Sharp-
shooters

Theo was born in 1837. He worked as a blacksmith in the northern district of Davidson County, and, in 1859, he married Anne. Daniel, their first child, was born in 1860. Theo volunteered for service in the 21st Regiment and was transferred to the 1st N.C. Sharpshooters on April 26, 1862. He was detailed as a blacksmith in the Kirkland/Hoke Brigade through December 1864. Theo was paroled at Appomattox Court House, Virginia, on April 9, 1865. After the war, he returned home to the Arcadia township, and he and Anne would have three more children: Jacob (1866), Elizabeth (1868), and Allen (1870). Theo moved his family to Surry County in 1874. No further records.

427. Essick, Thomas

*Private, Cleveland Mountain Boys
Company D, 15th Regiment N.C. Troops
(5th N.C. Volunteers)
2nd Company B, 49th Regiment N.C.
Troops*

Thomas was born in 1835 to Thomas and Rebecca Fry Essick. He worked as a farmer, and in 1859, he married Rachael. Thomas was conscripted into service in Wake County on July 15, 1862. He deserted on August 21, 1862. He returned on February 13, 1863, after his company had been transferred to the 49th Regiment. He and Rachael had their first child, Martha, in 1863. Thomas was reported present until he was captured at Fort Stedman, Virginia, on March 25, 1865. He was confined at Point Lookout, Maryland, until June 12, 1865, when he was released after taking the oath of allegiance. After the war, Thomas returned home to the Lexington township, and he and Rachael would have two more children: Henderson (1866) and Alice (1872). No further records.

428. Essick, William

*Private, Company I, 42nd Regiment
N.C. Troops*

William was born on October 9, 1833, to Cynthia Essick. He worked as a farmer prior to volunteering on March 4, 1862. William was mustered in as a corporal but was reduced in rank to private in March 1863. He was reported present throughout the war. After the war, William married Amanda Bruff on August 5, 1866. William and Amanda would have two children: Martha (1868) and David W. (1875). He lived with his family in the Lexington township until his death on February 1, 1911. He is buried at Center Methodist Church.

429. Essick, William R.

*Private, Company H, 48th Regiment
N.C. Troops*

William was born in 1843 to Jacob and Mary Essick. He worked as a clerk in his father's blacksmith shop prior to being conscripted on August 8, 1862. He was wounded slightly in the head during the battle of Fredericksburg, Virginia, on December 13, 1862. William was hospitalized in Richmond, Virginia, on July 2, 1864, with chronic diarrhea. He returned

to duty and deserted to the enemy on August 31, 1864. He was confined at Washington, D.C., until he was released on an unspecified date after taking the oath of allegiance. After the war, William returned home and married Emeline Markland on April 26, 1866. William and Emeline would raise four children in the Clemmonsville township: Alexander (1867), Jacob (1868), William (1872), and Charles (1878). No further records.

430. Evans, Alexander

*Private, Company B, 48th Regiment
N.C. Troops*

Alex was born on June 6, 1844, to Levi and Elizabeth Evans. He worked as a farmer prior to volunteering on March 6, 1862. He was reported present through October 1864. Alex was paroled at Greensboro, North Carolina, on May 8, 1865. After the war, he married Eliza Tussey on January 3, 1866. Alex and Eliza would have seven children in their home in the Lexington township. Alex died on September 16, 1923. He is buried at Bethesda United Methodist Church.

431. Evans, David D.

*Private, Company C, 70th Regiment
N.C. Troops (1st N.C. Junior
Reserves)*

David was born on January 27, 1847. He worked as a farmer prior to enlisting in the Junior Reserves on May 24, 1864. After the war, he married Sarah in 1886. David and Sarah lived in the Arcadia township and did not have any children. David died on March 14, 1912. He is buried at Center Methodist Church.

432. Evans, Junius R.

*Private, Company A, 42nd Regiment
N.C. Troops*

Junius was born in 1845 to Michael and Eliza Ripple Evans. He worked as a farmer prior to being conscripted into service on July 29, 1862. Junius was reported present until he was captured at Battery Anderson, Fort Fisher, North Carolina, on December 25, 1864. He was confined at Fort Monroe, Virginia, and was sent to Point Lookout, Maryland, on January 2, 1865. He was confined at Point Lookout until June 12, 1865, when he was released after taking the oath of allegiance. After the war, Junius returned

home and married Martha Hietman on September 16, 1866. They would have only one child: Maggie Lillian (1870). Junius died on June 12, 1902. He is buried at Mount Olivet United Methodist Church.

433. Evans, Michael M.

*Corporal, Davidson Guards
Company A, 21st Regiment N.C. Troops
(11th N.C. Volunteers)
Company D, 1st Regiment U.S. Volunteers*

Michael was born in 1841 to Christian and Phoebe Evans. He worked as a farmer prior to volunteering for service on May 8, 1861. He was reported present until he was wounded in the arm and captured at Gettysburg, Pennsylvania, on July 4, 1863. Michael was confined at Point Lookout, Maryland, and released on January 28, 1864, after joining the U.S. Army. He deserted from the U.S. Army, rejoined his Confederate company on October 1, 1864, and was promoted to corporal. He was reported present through February 1865. No further records.

434. Everhart, Adam

*Private, Company H, 48th Regiment
N.C. Troops*

Adam was born in 1833 to Mathias and Margaret Everhart. He married Margaret Freedle in 1854. Adam and Margaret would have two children: Sarah (1855) and Melinda (1859). Adam worked as a farmer prior to volunteering on March 7, 1862. He was reported present for duty until he was hospitalized at Danville, Virginia, on June 19, 1864, with a gunshot wound to the head. Adam was furloughed on June 21, 1864, and was last reported present in October 1864. No further records.

435. Everhart, Ambrose

*Private, Cleveland Mountain Boys
Company D, 15th Regiment N.C. Troops
(5th N.C. Volunteers)
2nd Company B, 49th Regiment N.C.
Troops*

Ambrose was born in 1841 to Valentine and Nancy Michael Everhart. He worked as a farmer prior to being conscripted into service in Wake County on July 15, 1862. Ambrose was wounded in the arm during the battle of Fredericksburg, Virginia, on December 13, 1862. He recovered from his wounds and rejoined his company in January 1863 after it had been transferred to the 49th Regiment. Ambrose died in a Goldsboro, North Carolina, hospital on May 10, 1863, of either disease or the gunshot wound received at Fredericksburg. He is buried in Goldsboro.

436. Everhart, Andrew, Jr.

Private, Company H, 48th Regiment N.C. Troops

Andrew was born in 1841 to Jacob and Mollie Sappenfield Everhart. Andrew married Sophia Shuler on October 17, 1858. Andrew and Sophia would have two children before her death in 1863: Felix (1859) and William (1863). Andrew worked as a farmer prior to being conscripted into service at Petersburg, Virginia, on August 8, 1862. He was reported present until he was discharged on April 13, 1863, because of "nebulous cornea in both eyes." Andrew returned home, and in 1868 he married Lou Alexander. Andrew and Lou would have six children: John (1870), Lottie (1871), Ida Mae (1873), R. E. Lee (1874), Joseph (1876), and Charles (1877). Andrew lived in the Lexington township until his death on March 25, 1901. He is buried at Pilgrim United Church of Christ.

437. Everhart, Andrew, Sr.

Private, Company H, 48th Regiment N.C. Troops

Andrew was born in 1836 to Jacob and Susan Shoaf Everhart. He worked as a blacksmith, and in 1856, he married Mahalia Shuler. Andrew and Mahalia would have three children: Lemuel (1857), Roswell (1859), and Andrew (1860), before Andrew volunteered for service on March 8, 1862. He was discharged on August 15, 1862, because of "rheumatism." After Andrew returned, he and Mahalia would have six more children: Wesley (1862), Sarah (1864), Annie (1866), Susan (1868), Gideon (1871), and Raymond (1877). Andrew lived in the Lexington township until his death in 1898.

438. Everhart, Andrew C.

Private, Company A, 42nd Regiment N.C. Troops

Andrew was born on October 27, 1842, to John and Susan Everhart. He worked as a farmer prior to volunteering on November 26, 1861. He was reported present until he was captured at Battery Anderson, Fort Fisher, North Carolina, on December 25, 1864. He was confined at Point Lookout, Maryland, until June 11, 1865, when he was released after taking the oath of allegiance. After the war, he came home and married Mary Louisa Leonard on August 11, 1872. Andrew and Mary would not have any children. Andrew died on September 11, 1910, leaving his estate to David Kinney Leonard. He is buried at Midway United Methodist Church.

439. Everhart, Britton

Private, Cleveland Mountain Boys Company D, 15th Regiment N.C. Troops (5th N.C. Volunteers)
2nd Company B, 49th Regiment N.C. Troops

Britton was born in November 1829 to John and Sarah Everhart. In 1851, he married Melinda Leonard. He and Melinda would have four children, Pricey (1852), Sarah (1854), William T. (1856), and Ephraim (1860), prior to Britton being conscripted into service in Wake County on July 15, 1862. He was transferred to the 49th Regiment on January 9, 1863. Britton was captured at Sandy Ridge, Lenoir County, on April 20, 1863, and was sent to New Bern, North Carolina, where he was paroled. He was reported present in July 1863 and served until he was captured at Five Forks, Virginia, on April 1, 1865. Britton was confined at Hart's Island, New York, until June 18, 1865, when he was released after taking the oath of allegiance. After the war, he and Melinda would have two more children: Charles Lee (1867) and David (1869). Britton lived in the Lexington township until his death sometime after 1900. He is buried at Beulah United Church of Christ.

440. Everhart, Christian

Private, Cleveland Mountain Boys Company D, 15th Regiment N.C. Troops (5th N.C. Volunteers)
2nd Company B, 49th Regiment N.C. Troops

Christian was born on March 1, 1830, to Michael and Mary Livengood Everhart. He worked as a farmer prior to being conscripted into service in Wake County on July 15, 1862. Christian was wounded at South Mountain, Maryland, on September 14, 1862, and at Fredericksburg, Virginia, on December 13, 1862. He recovered from his wounds and returned to duty in March 1863. He was reported present until he was captured at Five Forks, Virginia, on April 1, 1865. Christian was confined at Hart's Island, New York, until June 18, 1865, when he was released after taking the oath of allegiance. After the war, Christian married Elizabeth Leonard on August 2, 1866. They would have six children together: Frances (1868), Andrew (1871), Ida (1873), R. E. Lee (1874), Jacob (1876), and John (1880). Christian died on January 15, 1895. He is buried at Beulah United Church of Christ.

441. Everhart, Edward Lindsey

Private, Company C, 70th Regiment N.C. Troops (1st N.C. Junior Reserves)

Edward was born in 1846. He worked as a farmer prior to enlisting on May 24, 1864, in the Junior Reserves. After the war, he married Cornelia Leonard on February 15, 1877. No further records.

442. Everhart, Elijah

Private, Company C, 70th Regiment N.C. Troops (1st N.C. Junior Reserves)

Eli was born on November 2, 1846, to George and Elizabeth Michael Everhart. Eli worked as a farmer prior to enlisting in the Junior Reserves on May 24, 1864. After the war, Eli married Martha Sechrist in 1870. She would die four years later giving birth to their son, George. Eli married Margaret Hepler on January 21, 1877. Eli and Margaret would have one child: Andrew (1877). Eli lived in the Lexington township until his death on January 4, 1896. He is buried at Pilgrim United Church of Christ.

443. Everhart, Emanuel

Private, Company K, 15th Regiment N.C. Troops (5th N.C. Volunteers)

Emanuel was born in 1831 to Mathias and Margaret Everhart. He worked as a farmer and married Susannah Beck in 1854. Emanuel and Susannah would have three children: Andrew (1855), Amanda

(1856), and Henrietta (1859). Emanuel was conscripted into service on July 15, 1862, in Wake County. He was reported present until he died at Brandy Station, Virginia, on November 1, 1863, of disease.

444. Everhart, Emanuel

Private, Company C, 70th Regiment
N.C. Troops (1st N.C. Junior
Reserves)
Company I, 42nd Regiment N.C. Troops

Emanuel was born on November 5, 1845, to David and Elizabeth Sappenfield Everhart. He worked as a farmer prior to enlisting in the Junior Reserves on May 24, 1864. Upon turning 18, he was transferred to the 42nd Regiment and was paroled at Greensboro, North Carolina, on May 5, 1865. After the war, Emanuel married Catharine Schuler on March 27, 1866. Emanuel and Catharine would have five children before her death in 1888: William (1866), Thomas (1868), James Erastus (1871), Mary V. (1874), and Emanuel Parker (1876). Emanuel married Sarah Essick on December 6, 1888. They would have two children: Cora (1889) and Rosa Belle (1894). Sarah died in August 1905. Emanuel married Tabitha Craver on September 19, 1906. Emanuel and Tabitha did not have any children. Emanuel died on June 11, 1917. He is buried at Ebenezer United Methodist Church.

445. Everhart, Felix H.

Private, Company A, 57th Regiment
N.C. Troops

Felix was born in January 1842 to John and Susan Hedrick Everhart. He worked as a farmer prior to enlisting in Rowan County on July 4, 1862. He was reported present until he was wounded in the chest during the battle of Chancellorsville, Virginia, on May 3, 1863. When he did not return from his 60-day furlough, he was declared absent without leave from August 17 to December 31, 1863. Felix returned to duty prior to April 30, 1864. After the war, Felix married Margaret Jane in 1868. Felix and Margaret would have six children: Jennette (1869), John (1871), William (1875), Ernest (1880), Etta (1882), and Brantley (1888). Felix lived in the Lexington township until his death in February 1905. He is buried at Pilgrim United Church of Christ.

446. Everhart, Franklin

Private, Company K, 6th Regiment
N.C. State Troops

Franklin was born on July 16, 1821, to Christian and Susan Hiatt Everhart. He was first married to Franey Clinard, who died in 1853. On May 14, 1855, he married Belinda Green. Franklin and Belinda would have three children, Sarah (1857), Florina (1859), and Martha (1860), before Franklin was conscripted into service prior to October 16, 1864. He was captured at Petersburg, Virginia, on April 2, 1865, and was confined at Hart's Island, New York, until June 21, 1865, when he was released after taking the oath of allegiance. After the war, Franklin and Belinda would have three more children: Franklin (1865), Mary (1867), and Joseph (1869). Belinda died in 1881. Franklin married her sister, Barbara Green, on March 22, 1883. They would have no children together. Franklin lived in the Lexington township until his death on April 18, 1900. He is buried at New Mount Vernon Methodist Church.

447. Everhart, Hamilton Wesley

Private, Cleveland Mountain Boys
Company D, 15th Regiment N.C. Troops
(5th N.C. Volunteers)
2nd Company B, 49th Regiment N.C.
Troops

Hamilton was born on January 12, 1837, to Christian and Susan Hiatt Everhart. He worked as a farmer, and in 1860, he married Barbara Brinkley. Their first child, Samuel, was born in 1861. Hamilton was conscripted into service in Wake County on July 15, 1862. He deserted at Hanover Junction, Virginia, and returned to the company on August 31, 1864, after it had been transferred to the 49th Regiment. He deserted to the enemy on November 4, 1864, and was confined at Camp Hamilton, Virginia, until November 14, 1864, when he was released after taking the oath of allegiance. After the war he returned home to his family in the Midway township. Hamilton and Barbara would have six more children: Henry (1865), Laura (1866), Martha (1871), Jennette (1873), Flora (1877), and Effie (1880). Hamilton lived in the Midway area until his death on September 11, 1908. He is buried at Midway United Methodist Church.

448. Everhart, Henry Washington

Corporal, Carolina Rangers
Company B, 10th Virginia Cavalry
Regiment

Henry was born on November 13, 1838, to Valentine and Nancy Michael Everhart. He worked as a carpenter prior to volunteering in Davie County on October 29, 1861. He was promoted to

Built as a log house shortly after his wedding, this Midway home of Hamilton Wesley Everhart underwent continual improvements (Touart, *Building the Backcountry*).

corporal on March 1, 1863. Henry was reported without a horse on August 1, 1864. The last records of the company list him receiving a clothing ration on December 31, 1864. After the war, Henry returned home and married Amanda Hedrick on September 23, 1866. Henry and Amanda would have five children: Marcus (1867), Eliza (1885), Charlotte (1896), Trever (1898), and Nancy (1900). Henry lived in the Lexington township until his death on November 22, 1905. He is buried at Ebenezer United Methodist Church.

449. Everhart, Hiram

Private, Confederate Guards
Company K, 48th Regiment N.C. Troops

Hiram was born in 1833 to John and Sarah Everhart. He worked as a farmer, and in 1861, he married Lucinda Gates. Hiram was conscripted on August 8, 1862. He was reported present until he was wounded in the jaw at Bristoe Station, Virginia, on October 14, 1863. Hiram died in a Gordonsville, Virginia, hospital on October 20, 1863, of a "hemorrhage."

450. Everhart, Jacob

Private, Brunswick Double Quicks
Company C, 30th Regiment N.C. Troops
Company D, 1st Regiment U.S. Volunteers

Jacob was born in 1841 to Jacob and Elizabeth Everhart. He worked as a farmer prior to being conscripted on July 11, 1863. On July 24, 1863, he was captured at Flint Hill, Virginia. Jacob was sent to Point Lookout, Maryland, and was confined there until January 26, 1864, when he was released after taking the oath of allegiance and joining the U.S. Army. No further records.

451. Everhart, Kelin

Second Lieutenant, 65th Regiment
N.C. Militia (1861 organization)

Kelin was born on February 20, 1834, to Michael and Susan Livengood Everhart. Kelin married Sarah Koontz in 1856, and they would have four children: Mary (1857), George (1862), David (1864), and Levi (1867). Kelin accepted a commission dated November 26, 1861, in the Cotton Grove District Company. After his service in the militia, Kelin lived in the Cot-

ton Grove township until his death on March 21, 1915. He is buried at Lebanon Lutheran Church.

452. Everhart, Lewis

Private, Company I, 42nd Regiment
N.C. Troops

Lewis was born in 1844. He worked as a farmer prior to volunteering on February 28, 1862. Lewis was reported present through October 1864 and was paroled at Greensboro, North Carolina, on May 3, 1865. He was living in the Lexington township in 1870, and, by 1880, he had moved out of the county. No further records.

453. Everhart, Lewis

Private, Davidson Guards
Company A, 21st Regiment N.C. Troops

Lewis was born on December 19, 1828, to Jacob and Susannah Shoaf Everhart. He worked as a farmer, and in 1847, he married Catharine Sowers. Lewis and Catharine would have five children together: Franklin (1849), Jacob (1851), Richard (1855), Delphina (1856), and Susan (1857). Lewis volunteered for service on May 8, 1861. He was reported present until the summer of 1862, when he was discharged due to the provisions of the Conscript Law. Catharine died sometime during 1863–64. Lewis married Mary Clementine Shuler on November 26, 1865; they would have no children. In 1870, Lewis and Clementine moved to Stanly County, North Carolina. Clementine died in 1890, and Lewis married a Stanly County woman, Nancy McGee. Lewis lived in Stanly County until his death on September 16, 1910. He is buried in Stanly County.

454. Everhart, Michael

Private, Cleveland Mountain Boys
Company D, 15th Regiment N.C. Troops
(5th N.C. Volunteers)
2nd Company B, 49th Regiment N.C.
Troops

Michael was born on November 30, 1839, to Michael and Susan Livengood Everhart. He worked as a farmer prior to being conscripted in Wake County on July 15, 1862. He was wounded in the hand at Fredericksburg, Virginia, on December 13, 1862. He recovered from his wound and returned to service in

January 1863, after the company had been transferred to the 49th Regiment. Michael was present for service until he was paroled at Appomattox Court House, Virginia, on April 9, 1865. Michael was married to Louisa Jane Leonard and lived in the Lexington township until his death on April 17, 1918. He is buried at Beulah United Church of Christ

455. Everhart, Valentine

Private, Company H, 48th Regiment
N.C. Troops

Valentine was born on November 13, 1814, to Daniel and Barbara Everhart. In 1848, he married Nancy Michael. Valentine and Nancy would have five children: Joseph (1849), Kate (1850), Edmund (1852), Melinda (1855), and Lucinda (1857). He worked as a farmer in the Lexington township prior to volunteering at age 48, on March 7, 1862. Valentine was apparently discharged because of his age. He lived in the Lexington township until his death on March 3, 1892, and is buried at Pilgrim United Church of Christ.

456. Everhart, William

Private, Cleveland Mountain Boys
Company D, 15th Regiment N.C. Troops
(5th N.C. Volunteers)
2nd Company B, 49th Regiment N.C.
Troops

William was born in October 1832 to John and Susan Hiatt Everhart. He married Lucy Brinkley in 1854. William and Lucy would have four children: George (1859), Hazel (1862), W. T. Sherman (1865), and Alexander (1870). William was conscripted into service in Wake County on July 15, 1862. He deserted on October 30, 1862, and returned on February 20, 1864, after the company had been transferred to the 49th Regiment. William was sent to a Charlotte, North Carolina, hospital on May 15, 1864, with "chronic rheumatism." He was furloughed from Charlotte on August 5, 1864, and did not return. William married Eliza Jane Berrier Hill on June 5, 1873. Eliza brought two children from a previous marriage, Martin and Kelion Hill. William and Eliza would have one child together: Andrew Lindsey (1874). William owned 330 acres of land in the vicinity of Old Pilgrim, and he lived on this property until his death on March

28, 1905. He is buried at Midway United Methodist Church.

457. Everhart, William, Jr.

Private, Company I, 42nd Regiment N.C. Troops

William was born in 1842 to Solomon and Polly Burkhart Everhart. William, Jr., was named after his uncle, who would serve in the same company. He worked as a farmer before volunteering for service on February 28, 1862. He was reported present until he died in a Raleigh, North Carolina, hospital on April 5, 1865, of disease. William is buried in Oakwood Cemetery in Raleigh.

458. Everhart, William, Sr.

Private, Company I, 42nd Regiment N.C. Troops

William was born in 1819 to Phillip and Mary Lookabill Everhart. He worked as a farmer and was married to Margaret Sawyer prior to volunteering on March 8, 1862. William deserted on December 18, 1862. He returned to duty and served through October 1864. After the war, he returned home to his family. William died on May 10, 1883. He is buried in a private lot in the vicinity of the Billy Smith Road in Davidson County.

459. Falkner, Benjamin

Private, Thomasville Rifles Company B, 14th Regiment N.C. Troops (4th N.C. Volunteers)

Ben was conscripted into service in Wake County on July 16, 1862. He was reported present until he was captured in the battle of Wilderness, Virginia, on May 6, 1864. Ben was sent to Point Lookout, Maryland, before being transferred to Elmira, New York. He was confined at Elmira until he died on December 6, 1864, of "chronic diarrheoa."

460. Farabee, Burgess L.

Sergeant, Davidson Guards Company A, 21st Regiment N.C. Troops (11th N.C. Volunteers)

Burgess was born on September 17, 1842, the son of Samuel H. Farabee. He worked as a clerk in the Clemmonsville township prior to volunteering on May 8, 1861. Burgess was promoted to sergeant in May 1862 and was wounded in the leg at Winchester, Virginia, on May 25, 1862. His left leg was amputated, and he was sent home, listed as absent, wounded, through February 1865. After the war, Burgess moved to the town of Thomasville where he was employed as the town's tax collector in 1900. Burgess never married and lived in Thomasville until his death on March 20, 1912. He is buried in the Thomasville City Cemetery.

461. Farabee, John A.

Private, Company C, 70th Regiment N.C. Troops (1st N.C. Junior Reserves)

John was born in 1846, the son of Samuel H. Farabee. He was a student before he enlisted in the Junior Reserves on May 24, 1864. After the war, John returned home to the Clemmonsville township and became a schoolteacher in 1870. No further records.

462. Farabee, Joseph Columbus

Private, Carolina Rangers Company B, 10th Virginia Cavalry Regiment

Joseph was born on August 30, 1824, to Joseph and Mary Harvey Farabee. His father died in July 1860, and Joseph bought 447 acres of his land and a gold pocket watch. In 1845, he married Catharine Swicegood. Joseph and Catharine would have eight children: Margaret (1847), Frances (1850), Saluda (1851), John (1853), Charles (1855), Sally (1857), James McDuff (1859), and Columbus (1862). Joseph was conscripted and enlisted in the cavalry on December 19, 1862. He was reported present through October 1863, although he was without a horse in August 1863. Joseph was reported absent, sick, in November and December 1863. Joseph died in a Lynchburg, Virginia, hospital on July 16, 1864, of disease. He is buried in the Lynchburg City Cemetery.

463. Feezor, Henry P.

Private, Davidson Guards Company A, 21st Regiment N.C. Troops (11th N.C. Volunteers) Company A, 42nd Regiment N.C. Troops

Henry was born in 1841 to Jacob and Anna Feezor. He worked as a farmer prior to volunteering on May 8, 1861, and he was mustered in with the rank of corporal. Henry was present until discharged on February 25, 1862, because of "disability." Henry reenlisted into Company A, 42nd Regiment, with the rank of private prior to October 31, 1864. He was captured at Battery Anderson, Fort Fisher, North Carolina, on December 24, 1864. Henry was confined at Point Lookout, Maryland, until June 27, 1865, when he was released after taking the oath of allegiance. After the war, he married Sarah Carrick on January 12, 1868. Henry and Sarah would have nine children: Lucy (1869), Nancy (1870), Mary (1872), Eugenia (1874), John (1876), Essie (1879), Caroline (1880), Florence (1886), and Peter (1888). Henry died after 1900. He is buried at Stoner's Grove Baptist Church.

464. Feezor, Jacob H.

Private, Company A, 57th Regiment N.C. Troops

Jacob was born on March 29, 1832. He worked as a farmer prior to enlisting in Rowan County on July 4, 1862. Jacob was hospitalized with the mumps from September 26 to October 9, 1862. He recovered from his illness and served until he was captured at Hatcher's Run, Virginia, on February 6, 1865. Jacob was confined at Point Lookout, Maryland, until June 27, 1865, when he was released after taking the oath of allegiance. After the war, he returned home and married Sarah H. in 1867. Jacob and Sarah would have four children: Millard (1868), Walter (1870), Nannie (1874), and Macy (1876). Jacob lived in the Tyro township until his death on June 3, 1905. He is buried at Churchland Baptist Church.

465. Ferrell, Emsley L.

Private, Company B, 57th Regiment N.C. Troops

Emsley was born in 1845 to Burton and Polly Ferrell. He worked as a blacksmith prior to enlisting in Rowan County on July 4, 1862. He was reported present until November 7, 1863, when he was captured at Rappahannock Station, Virginia. Emsley was confined at Point Lookout, Maryland, until he was paroled and transferred to City Point, Virginia, for exchange on March 30, 1864. He returned to duty on August 17, 1864, and was wounded at Winchester, Virginia, on September 19, 1864. Emsley was hospitalized at Kernstown, Virginia, until February 28, 1865. After the war, he married Frances in December 1865. Emsley and Frances would have three children: Lindsay (1866), Mary (1867), and Sarah (1873). Emsley died in 1909. He is buried at Pine Hill Methodist Church.

466. Finch, Samuel Jones

Private, Company K, 63rd Regiment N.C. Troops (5th N.C. Cavalry)

Samuel was born on January 28, 1844, to John H. and Martha Harris Finch. He worked as a farmer prior to being conscripted in January 1864. Sam was issued clothing on September 28, 1864, and was reported present until he was captured on the White Oak Road, Dinwiddie, Virginia, on April 1, 1865. He was confined at Point Lookout, Maryland, until June 26, 1865, when he was released after taking the oath of allegiance. After the war, Sam returned home, and, on July 1, 1869, he married Eliza Gilchrist. Samuel and Eliza would have five children: Charles (1870), Patrick D. (1873), John (1875), Duggan (1880), and Walter D. (1883). No further records.

467. Fine, Daniel

Private, Company F, 76th Regiment N.C. Troops (6th N.C. Senior Reserves)

Daniel was born on October 22, 1819. He worked as a farmer in the southern district of Davidson County. Daniel married Mary Kepley in 1843. Daniel and Mary would have eight children: George (1844), Susannah (1846), Lyia (1849), Alexander (1852), Mary (1854), Martha (1856), Alson (1858), and Frances (1860). Daniel enlisted in the 6th N.C. Senior Reserves in January 1865. After his term of service, he returned home to the Conrad Hill township. Daniel died on June 15, 1885. He is buried at Clarksbury Methodist Church.

468. Fine, Gabriel

Private, Company D, 48th Regiment N.C. Troops

Gabriel was born in 1825. He worked as a farmer in the southern district of Davidson County. He married Florina around 1845. Gabriel and Florina would have six children, Rosanne (1848), Andrew (1850), James (1851), Irena (1856),

Gabriel (1857), and Abraham (1862), prior to Gabriel enlisting as a substitute on August 8, 1862. He was wounded slightly at Fredericksburg, Virginia, on December 13, 1862. Gabriel recovered and was present for duty until May 5, 1864, when, "in the act of giving himself up," a Federal soldier shot him in the abdomen. He was confined at Washington, D.C., until July 26, 1864, when he was transferred to Elmira, New York. He was confined at Elmira until October 11, 1864, when he was paroled for exchange and sent to Venus Point, Georgia, on November 15, 1864. After the war, Gabriel returned to his home in the Conrad hill township. He and Florina would have two more children: Cicero (1867) and Jacob (1869). No further records.

469. Fine, George W.

Private, Company C, 61st Regiment N.C. Troops

George was born in 1844 to Daniel and Mary Kepley Fine. He worked as a farmer prior to being conscripted on August 27, 1862. He deserted at Kinston, North Carolina, on December 10, 1862. George was able to hide from the Home Guard and managed not to be returned to service. George married Mary A. Hepler in 1866. George and Mary would have four children: Valena (1868), Doctor (1870), Lindsay (1872), and Frances (1875). George lived in the Conrad Hill township until his death in 1906. He is buried in an unmarked plot at Clarksbury Methodist Church.

470. Fine, Jonathan S.

Private, Company D, 48th Regiment N.C. Troops

Jonathan was born in 1842 to Daniel and Mary Kepley Fine. He worked as a farmer, and in 1860, he married Serena Cameron. Their first child, Thomas, was born in 1862. Jonathan was conscripted into service on August 8, 1862. He was reported present until he was captured at Hatcher's Run, Virginia, on April 2, 1865. He was confined at Point Lookout, Maryland, until June 26, 1865, when he was released after taking the oath of allegiance. After the war, he and Serena would have three more children: Julia (1865), Newton (1867), and Amanda (1869). Serena died in 1886. Three years later, Jonathan married Phoebe. Jonathan

died after 1900. He is buried at Holloways Baptist Church.

471. Fishel, Charles

Private, Company G, 2nd Battalion, N.C. Infantry

Charles was born in 1843 to Daniel and Nancy Fishel. He volunteered in Forsyth County on September 19, 1861. He was captured at Roanoke Island, North Carolina, on February 8, 1862, and was paroled at Elizabeth City, North Carolina, on February 21, 1862. He was reported present until he was wounded and captured at Gettysburg, Pennsylvania, on July 1, 1863. Charles died of his wounds on August 3, 1863, at David's Island, New York.

472. Fishel, Christian Charles

Private, Confederate Guards Company K, 48th Regiment N.C. Troops

C. C. was born in 1843 to William and Mary Fishel. He worked as a farmer prior to being conscripted on August 8, 1862. He deserted on August 15, 1862, and returned to service in June 1863. C.C. was reported present through July 1864. After the war, he married Susan R. in 1867. C. C. and Susan would have three children: Augusta (1868), Elizabeth (1872), and Samuel (1873). No further records.

473. Fishel, David

Private, Company H, 48th Regiment N.C. Troops

David was born in 1834. He worked as a farmer, and in 1858, he married Nancy. David and Nancy would have one child, Ida (1859), before he was conscripted into service at Petersburg, Virginia, on August 8, 1862. He died in a Richmond, Virginia, hospital on December 12, 1862, of pneumonia.

474. Fishel, Ephraim

Private, Company H, 48th Regiment N.C. Troops

Ephraim was born in 1840 to Jacob and Susannah Fishel. He worked as a farmer prior to being conscripted into service on August 8, 1862. He was reported present until December 13, 1862, when he was wounded in the arm at Fredericksburg, Virginia. He recovered from his wound and rejoined his company on

May 18, 1863. He was killed in action during the battle of Cold Harbor, Virginia, on June 3, 1864.

475. Fishel, James M.

Private, Company G, 2nd Battalion, N.C. Infantry

James was born on March 31, 1845, to Daniel and Nancy Fishel. He worked as a farmer prior to being conscripted on June 23, 1863. He was wounded and captured at Gettysburg, Pennsylvania, on July 3, 1863. James was confined at Hart's Island, New York, Harbor, until he was paroled and transferred to City Point, Virginia, for exchange on September 16, 1863. He was reported absent without leave until assigned to hospital duty and retired to the Invalid Corps on May 4, 1864. After the war, he returned to his parent's home in the Freidburg area. In 1877, he married Mary J. Foltz. James and Mary would have five children; however, they either died in childbirth or in early infancy. James died on April 14, 1923. He is buried at Freidburg Moravian Church.

476. Fishel, Sanford J.

Private, Company H, 48th Regiment N.C. Troops

Sanford was born on March 29, 1832. He worked as a farmer, and, in 1853, he married Louisa. Sanford and Louisa would have five children, Mary (1854), Amanda (1856), Emma (1857), Evander (1859), and Julia (1861), before he was conscripted into service on August 8, 1862. He was left in a hospital in Harpers Ferry, where he was captured in late September 1862. Sanford took the oath of allegiance and was allowed to go home in October 1862. After his return, he and Louisa would have three more children: Cora (1864), Reuben (1867), and Columbus (1869). Sanford lived in the Freidburg area until his death on March 23, 1909. He is buried at Freidburg Moravian Church.

477. Fitzgerald, Ira Addison

Second Lieutenant, Holtsburg Guards Company A, 54th Regiment N.C. Troops

Ira was born in 1836 to Ira and Nancy Hayden Fitzgerald. He worked as an overseer prior to volunteering for service on April 1, 1862. He was mustered in with the rank of first sergeant. Ira was then elected second lieutenant on September 27, 1862. He served as an officer until he was wounded in the right leg at Fisher's Hill, Virginia, on September 19, 1864. He was hospitalized at Danville, Virginia, and was furloughed for 30 days on October 6, 1864. He did not return to service. After the war, he married Ellen Houston in 1867. Ira and Ellen would have only one child, Jesse (1869). Ira died in 1901. He is buried in the Fitzgerald-Hayden family cemetery.

478. Fitzgerald, John Burgess

Second Lieutenant, Company B, 57th Regiment N.C. Troops

John was born on February 8, 1835, to Ira and Nancy Hayden Fitzgerald. He worked as a farmer, and in 1858, he married Mary M. John and Mary would have two children, Charlie (1859) and William (1861), before John enlisted in Rowan County on July 4, 1862. He was elected third lieutenant the same day. He was hospitalized at Richmond, Virginia, on October 13, 1862, with "icterus." John was issued a furlough on October 16, 1862. He stayed at home and was dropped from the rolls as "disabled." John and Mary would have ten more children: Thomas (1864), John (1867), Cora (1869), Mary (1870), Margaret (1871), Fletcher (1878), James (1880), Ernest (1881), Nancy (1883), and Sadie (1884). John died on September 11, 1911. He is buried in the Fitzgerald-Hayden Family Cemetery.

479. Floyd, Isham

Private, Company F, 53rd Regiment N.C. Troops

Isham was born in 1830. He married Elizabeth Gordon on September 28, 1860. He worked as a farmer prior to being conscripted on November 19, 1862. He was reported present until he was hospitalized on December 16, 1863, with "reubola." Isham returned on January 12, 1864, and served until June 13, 1864, when he deserted at Lynchburg, Virginia. After his return, Isham and Elizabeth would have three children: Catharine (1864), John (1865), and Joseph (1868). Elizabeth died in 1879. Isham married Bathsheba, and they would have three children: Minnie (1894), George (1894), and Miles (1898). James died after 1900. He is buried at Clarksbury Methodist Church.

480. Floyd, James Roby

Private, Company A, 42nd Regiment N.C. Troops

James was born in 1835 to Bazel and Rachael Floyd. He worked as a farmer, and, in 1859, he married Winnifred. James volunteered on March 1, 1862. He was reported present until he deserted in November 1862. James and Winnie would have seven children: James (1862), David (1863), Caroline (1866), John (1869), Bazel (1872), Henry (1874), and Julius (1877). James lived in the Healing Springs township. No further records.

481. Floyd, John Davidson

Private, Company A, 42nd Regiment N.C. Troops

John was born in 1840 to Bazel and Rachael Floyd. On May 25, 1859, he married Susan Fishel. John volunteered for service on November 21, 1861. He was reported present until he died of typhoid fever in a Weldon, North Carolina, hospital on April 1, 1863.

482. Floyd, Levi

Private, Company H, 48th Regiment N.C. Troops

Levi was born in 1821. He worked as a farmer in the southern district of Davidson County, and in 1856, he married Mary M. Levi and Mary would have only one child together, Althea Louise (1857). Levi was conscripted into service sometime in the summer of 1864 and served until he was paroled at Appomattox Court House, Virginia, on April 9, 1865. After the war, he returned home to the Conrad Hill township, where he lived until his death on July 14, 1894. He is buried at Heath Wesleyan Church.

483. Floyd, William Franklin

Private, Company A, 42nd Regiment N.C. Troops

William was born on September 6, 1836, to Bazel and Rachael Floyd. He married Priscilla Skeen in 1857. William and Priscilla would have three children, Roxanne (1858), Charles (1859), and Thomas (1862), before he was conscripted into service on July 8, 1862. He was reported present until he deserted on August 23, 1863. After the war, he returned home to southern Davidson County. He and Priscilla would have three more children: David (1867), Robert (1871), and Rachael (1873). William died on June 30, 1878. He is buried at Holloways Baptist Church.

484. Folkner, James

Private, Thomasville Rifles
Company B, 14th Regiment N.C. Troops
(4th N.C. Volunteers)

James was born in 1839. He worked as a farmer prior to volunteering on April 23, 1861. He died in a Richmond, Virginia, hospital on June 19, 1862, of typhoid fever.

485. Ford, Francis W.

Private, Davidson Guards
Company A, 21st Regiment N.C. Troops
(11th N.C. Volunteers)

Francis was born in 1840 to Alfred and Susan Ford. He worked as a farmer prior to volunteering on May 8, 1861. Francis was reported present until September 1, 1864, when he was hospitalized at Charlottesville, Virginia, with a gunshot wound. He returned to duty on September 28, 1864, and deserted on October 1, 1864. Francis was apprehended and returned to duty in January 1865. He was reported present until he was paroled at Farmville, Virginia, between April 11 and 21, 1865. Francis returned home to the Lexington township. On May 30, 1868, he married Mary Rutherford. Francis and Mary would have four children: William (1869), Susan (1870), Lee (1872), and Mary (1879). Francis and Mary left the county with their family between 1880 and 1890. No further records.

486. Ford, Thaddeus Constantine

Quartermaster, 65th Regiment N.C.
Militia (1861 organization)

T. C. was born on October 23, 1827, to Daniel and Mary McCrary Ford. T. C. married Caroline McCrary. He served as the deputy sheriff in 1860 and was commissioned quartermaster of the 65th N.C. Militia on November 25, 1861. After the war he continued serving as deputy sheriff until his death on January 3, 1899. After his death, Caroline became a substantial capitalist in Lexington. T. C. was buried in the Lexington City Cemetery.

487. Ford, William Franklin

Private, Company B, 48th Regiment
N.C. Troops

William was born on July 10, 1840, to Alfred and Susan Ford. William volunteered for service on March 4, 1862. He was present throughout the war and returned home to the town of Lexington. In 1870, he began a job managing a textile mill in Salisbury, North Carolina. Later that year, he married Mary Sullivan. William and Mary would have seven children: Susan (1871), William (1872), Adolphus Gustavus (1873), James (1875), Mary Ada (1881), Oscar C. (1883), and Joseph (1885). In 1900, William was listed as the manager of the Lexington Furniture Factory. William lived in the town of Lexington until his death on June 29, 1931. He is buried in the Lexington City Cemetery.

488. Ford, William P.

Second Lieutenant, 65th Regiment
N.C. Militia (1861 organization

William was born in 1837 to Daniel and Nancy McCrary Ford. He worked in the town of Lexington before accepting a commission in the Lexington District Company on November 25, 1861. After his service, he married Ellen Owen on July 25, 1865. William died on November 14, 1866. He is buried in the Lexington City Cemetery.

489. Forshee, George L.

Private, Holtsburg Guards
Company A, 54th Regiment N.C. Troops

George was born in 1837 to Ira and Emeline Forshee. He worked as a miner prior to enlisting on April 22, 1862. He was detailed for duty as a lead miner at the Conrad Hill mine on September 10, 1862. George served as a miner for the duration of the war. After the war, George married Catharine in 1866. George and Catharine would have three children: Thomas (1867), John (1876), and Alice (1879). George died sometime prior to 1900.

490. Forshee, Joseph

Private, Lexington Wildcats
Company I, 14th Regiment N.C. Troops
(4th N.C. Volunteers)

Joseph was born in 1835 to Ira and Emeline Forshee. He worked as a miner

prior to volunteering on May 14, 1861. He was reported present until he was wounded and captured at Gettysburg, Pennsylvania, on July 3, 1863. Joseph was confined at Point Lookout, Maryland, until April 30, 1864, when he was paroled and transferred to City Point, Virginia, for exchange. He was reported absent with a furlough in August 1864. Joseph was paroled at Appomattox Court House, Virginia, on April 9, 1865. After the war, Joseph married Rachael. No further records.

491. Forshee, Stephen Kearney

Private, Lexington Wildcats
Company I, 14th Regiment N.C. Troops
(4th N.C. Volunteers)

Stephen was born in 1839 to Ira and Emeline Forshee, who named him after Colonel Stephen W. Kearney of Mexican War fame. He worked as a miner prior to volunteering on May 14, 1861. Stephen was reported present until he was detailed in Davidson County as a miner on October 30, 1863. He served in this capacity for the duration of the war. Stephen continued his work in the Silver Hill mine, and on January 21, 1869, he married Margaret Beck. Stephen and Margaret would have four children. No further records.

492. Forshee, William

Private, Lexington Wildcats
Company I, 14th Regiment N.C. Troops
(4th N.C. Volunteers)

William was born in 1838 to Ira and Emeline Forshee. He worked as a miner prior to volunteering for service on May 14, 1861. He was reported present for service until he was wounded in the left leg and captured at Spotsylvania Court House, Virginia, on May 12, 1864. William was confined in a Washington, D.C., hospital, where he died on June 17, 1864, of gangrene.

493. Foster, Giles N.

Private, Company A, 10th Battalion
N.C. Heavy Artillery
Company A, 2nd Regiment Confederate
Engineers

Giles was born in 1834. In 1855, Giles married Tabitha, with whom he would have two children: Columbus (1857) and Crissila (1859). He worked as a carpenter prior to enlisting on April 16, 1862. He was promoted to artificer on July 1, 1862, but he was reduced in rank in June 1863. Giles was transferred to the 2nd Regiment Confederate Engineers in August 1863. No further records.

494. Fouts, Absalom

Private, Stanly Marksmen
Company H, 14th Regiment N.C. Troops
(4th N.C. Volunteers)

Ab was born in 1842 to Mary Fouts. He worked as a farmer in the Allegheny township prior to being conscripted into service on July 16, 1862. Ab served throughout the war and survived unscathed. After the war, he married Ellen in 1866. In 1875, Absalom would move to Stanly County, where he and Ellen would raise seven children. No further records.

495. Fouts, Andrew

Private, Cleveland Mountain Boys
Company D, 15th Regiment N.C. Troops
(5th N.C. Volunteers)
2nd Company B, 49th Regiment N.C. Troops

Andrew was born in 1831 to Daniel and Susan Fouts. He worked as a farmer prior to being conscripted into service in Wake County on July 15, 1862. He was transferred to the 49th Regiment on January 9, 1863. Andrew was wounded twice: at Bermuda Hundred, Virginia, on May 20, 1864, and at Petersburg, Virginia, on July 1, 1864. Andrew died of his wounds in a Richmond, Virginia, hospital on September 1, 1864.

496. Fouts, Charles A.

Private, Company H, 48th Regiment N.C. Troops

Charles was born in 1833. He worked as a farmer, and, in 1854, he married Irena. Charles and Irena would have two children, Jane (1855) and Robert (1859), before Charles was conscripted on August 31, 1862. He was wounded and captured at the battle of Sharpsburg, Maryland, on September 17, 1862. Charles died of his wounds in Federal custody on September 20, 1862.

497. Fouts, Erastus

Private, Company C, 70th Regiment N.C. Troops (1st N.C. Junior Reserves)

Erastus was born in 1845 to Daniel and Phoebe Fouts. He worked as a farmer prior to enlisting on May 24, 1864, in the Junior Reserves. After his service, Erastus married Augusta Grimes on September 11, 1869. Erastus and Augusta would have three children while living in the Thomasville township: Caroline (1871), John W. (1873), and Albert (1876). Erastus died on July 7, 1907. He is buried at Emanuel United Church of Christ.

498. Fowler, Charles

Sergeant, Confederate Guards
Company K, 48th Regiment N.C. Troops

Charles was born in 1838 to Patrick and Jemina Yarbrough Fowler. He worked as a farmer prior to being conscripted on August 8, 1862. He was reported present through October 31, 1864, when he was promoted to sergeant. Charles was captured at Hatcher's Run, Virginia, on April 2, 1865. He was confined at Hart's Island, New York, until June 18, 1865, when he was released after taking the oath of allegiance. After the war, he returned home to the North Thomasville township and married Ruth E. Craven on January 17, 1869. Charles moved to Forsyth County sometime after 1870. No further records.

499. Fowler, Thomas

Private, Confederate Guards
Company K, 48th Regiment N.C. Troops

Thomas was born in 1839 to Patrick and Jemina Yarbrough Fowler. He worked as a farmer prior to being conscripted on August 8, 1862. He was wounded in the hand at Sharpsburg, Maryland, on September 17, 1862. Thomas returned to duty on an unspecified date and was reported disabled and on detached service at Charlotte, North Carolina, from January 1864 through October 1864. He was paroled at Charlotte, on May 6, 1865. After the war, he married Louise; the two would not have any children. Thomas lived in the Abbott's Creek township until his death in 1915. He is buried at Calvary United Church of Christ.

500. Fowler, William

Private, Confederate Guards
Company K, 48th Regiment N.C. Troops

William was born in 1841 to Patrick and Jemina Yarbrough Fowler. He was

conscripted on August 8, 1862. He was wounded in the thigh at Sharpsburg, Maryland, on September 17, 1862. William died of his wounds in Shepherdstown, [West] Virginia, on October 7, 1862.

501. Fraley, Munford S.

Private, Company D, Colonel Mallet's Battalion (Camp Guard)
Company F, 7th Regiment N.C. State Troops

Munford enlisted in the summer of 1862 and served as part of Mallet's Battalion. In July 1864, he was transferred to the 7th N.C. Regiment. He was reported present until he was paroled at Greensboro, North Carolina, on May 1, 1865. No further records.

502. Frank, George Washington

Private, Company B, 48th Regiment N.C. Troops

George was born in 1840 to Alexander and Susannah Frank. He worked as a farmer prior to volunteering on March 6, 1862. He died of "apoplexy" in a Richmond, Virginia, hospital on November 13, 1862.

503. Frank, Jesse M.

Private, Company B, 48th Regiment N.C. Troops

Jesse was born on April 17, 1843, to Alexander and Susannah Frank. He worked as a farmer prior to being conscripted on July 30, 1862. Jesse was captured at Frederick, Maryland, on September 12, 1862. He was confined at Fort Delaware, Delaware, until he was paroled and transferred to Aiken's Landing, Virginia, for exchange on October 2, 1862. He was declared exchanged on November 10, 1862. Jesse was reported absent, sick, until March 1863, when he returned to service. He was reported present through October 1864. After the war, Jesse returned home to the Jackson Hill township, and on December 3, 1868, he married Margaret Surratt. Jesse and Margaret would have only one child, Barbara (1869). Jesse died on December 1, 1915. He is buried at Lineberry United Methodist Church.

504. Frank, John Alexander

Private, Davidson Guards
Company A, 21st Regiment N.C. Troops

John was born in 1830 to Susannah Frank. John worked as a farmer prior to being conscripted into service in Wake County on June 6, 1863. He was reported present until he was wounded at Winchester, Virginia, on September 19, 1864. John returned to service in February 1865 and was reported present until he was paroled at Appomattox Court House, Virginia, on April 9, 1865. After the war, he came home to the Emmons township, where he was living with his mother and two sisters in 1870. No further records.

505. Frank, John M.

Second Lieutenant, 65th Regiment N.C. Militia (1861 organization)

John was born in 1836 to Peter and Mary Frank. He worked as a farmer, and, on February 3, 1859, he married Lovina Hedrick. John accepted a commission in the Silver Valley District on December 26, 1861. No further records.

506. Frank, Peter Martin, Jr.

*Private, Bridger's Artillery
Company C, 36th Regiment N.C. Troops (3rd N.C. Artillery)*

Peter was born on March 24, 1837, to Peter and Mary Frank. He married Sarah E. Grimes on May 20, 1858. Peter and Sarah would have three children, Robert (1859), Mary (1861), and Margaret (1864), before Peter was conscripted into service on March 5, 1864. He was reported present until he was captured at Bentonville, North Carolina, on March 19, 1865. He was confined at Point Lookout, Maryland, until June 26, 1865, when he was released after taking the oath of allegiance. After the war, Peter returned to the Cotton Grove township where he and Sarah would have five more children: Ellen (1866), William (1870), Corneilia (1872), Bessie (1873), and Esther (1877). Two other children, Laura and Ada, both died early in infancy. Peter died on March 24, 1908. He is buried at Lebanon Lutheran Church.

507. Frank, Theophilus

Private, Company B, 48th Regiment N.C. Troops

Theo was born on February 24, 1824. He worked as a farmer, and, in 1850, he married Elizabeth. Theo and Elizabeth would have four children, Mary (1851), Andrew (1853), Barbara (1856), and Susanna (1860), before Theo was conscripted on October 16, 1863. He was reported present through October 1864. Theo survived the war and returned home to the Emmons township. Theo died on June 5, 1884, and is buried at New Jerusalem United Church of Christ. His uniform coat and pants, as well as a slouch hat he wore during the war, are on display at the New Market Battlefield Hall of Valor Museum.

508. Freedle, William Franklin

Private, Company K, 15th Regiment N.C. Troops (5th N.C. Volunteers)

William was born on October 10, 1843, to Lewis and Elizabeth Brinkley Freedle. He worked as a farmer prior to being conscripted into service in Wake County on December 15, 1863. William was reported present until he was wounded during the battle of Wilderness, Virginia, on May 5, 1864. He was reported absent, wounded, through October 1864. He was paroled at Greensboro, North Carolina, on May 8, 1865. After the war, he married Catharine Freedle in 1868. William and Catharine would have five children: Elisa (1869), Sarah (1871), Martha (1874), Ellen (1875), and Allen (1878). William lived in the Lexington township until his death on March 17, 1922. He is buried at Beulah United Church of Christ.

509. Fritts, Adam

Private, Company A, 42nd Regiment N.C. Troops

Adam was born on March 11, 1838, to Adam and Sally Leonard Fritts. He worked as a farmer, and, on June 11, 1862, he married Jerusha Cutting. Adam was conscripted into service in Lenoir County, North Carolina, on July 27, 1863. His first child, Lillian, was born in 1864. He was reported present until he was captured at Battery Anderson, Fort Fisher, North Carolina, on December 25, 1864. Adam was confined at Point Lookout, Maryland, until June 27, 1865, when he was released after taking the oath of allegiance. After the war, he returned home to the town of Lexington, where he and Jerusha would have two more children: Ida (1868) and Bessie (1875). Adam lived in Lexington until his death on August 6, 1893. He is buried in the Lexington City Cemetery.

510. Fritts, Adam

Private, Company B, 48th Regiment N.C. Troops

Adam was born in 1830 to Reuben and Polly Billings Fritts. He married Elizabeth Leonard in 1858, and they had one child, John (1860), before Adam volunteered for service on March 6, 1862. He died of typhoid fever at Staunton, Virginia, on November 5, 1862.

511. Fritts, Amos

*Private, Lexington Wildcats
Company I, 14th Regiment N.C. Troops (4th N.C. Volunteers)*

Amos was born on September 8, 1828, to John and Rebecca Younts Fritts. He worked as a farmer, and, on September 10, 1857, he married Mary Stockinger. Amos and Mary would have four children together before her death in 1865: James (1858), George (1859), Laura (1862), and Polly (1865). Amos was conscripted into service in Wake County on July 16, 1862. He was reported present through August 1864. Amos was paroled at Greensboro, North Carolina, on May 5, 1864. After the war and Mary's death, Amos married Pauline Stockinger, Mary's sister, on January 20, 1866. Amos and Pauline would have eight children: William (1866), Margaret (1868), Sarah (1869), Rachael (1873), John (1874), Amos (1877), Leah (1879), and Charles (1881). Amos lived in the Lexington township until his death on March 3, 1885. He is buried at Pilgrim United Church of Christ.

512. Fritts, Andrew Henderson

Private, Company I, 76th Regiment N.C. Troops (6th N.C. Senior Reserves)

Andrew was born on November 17, 1816, to George and Phoebe Byerly Fritts. He married Charity Michael in 1840. Andrew and Charity would have 13 children: Hamilton (1842), Susan (1844), Henry (1846), Mary (1848), Madison (1850), Phillip (1852), George (1852), Mary (1857), America (1860), Charles (1862), Charity (1863), Margaret (1864), and Thomas (1868). Andrew worked as a farmer prior to enlisting in the Senior Reserves in January 1865. After his service he returned to the Lexington township, where he lived until his death on February 3, 1881. He is buried at Beulah United Church of Christ.

513. Fritts, Franklin

Second Lieutenant, 66th Regiment N.C. Militia (1861 organization)

Franklin was born in 1835. He worked as a railroad hand for the North Carolina Railroad prior to accepting a commission in the Farmer's Creek District Company on January 25, 1862. After his service, Franklin married Jane E. Jones on January 17, 1867. In 1880, Franklin was still working for the railroad. Franklin died before 1900. No further records.

514. Fritts, George

First Lieutenant, 66th Regiment N.C. Militia (1861 organization)

George was born in 1825. He worked as a farmer, and, on December 22, 1861, he married Mary Ann Cox. George and Mary would have four children: John (1860), Caroline (1864), Josephine (1872), and George A. (1877). George accepted a commission in the Farmer's Creek District Company on October 1, 1862. George lived in the Lexington township until his death on January 27, 1899. He is buried at Pilgrim United Church of Christ.

515. Fritts, Hamilton C.

Second Lieutenant, 66th Regiment N.C. Militia (1861 organization)

Hamilton was born in 1842 to Andrew H. and Charity Michael Fritts. Hamilton married Martha Gobble on June 22, 1862, and moved to the Tyro area. Hamilton and Martha would have six children: Lilla (1866), Phillip (1869), Alice (1872), Polly (1873), Martha (1876), and Alice (1879). Hamilton accepted a commission in the Cross Roads District Company on November 26, 1861. No further records.

516. Fritts, Henderson

Private, Cleveland Mountain Boys Company D, 15th Regiment N.C. Troops (5th N.C. Volunteers) 2nd Company B, 49th Regiment N.C. Troops

Henderson was born on April 21, 1834, to William and Anna Fritts. He worked as a farmer prior to being conscripted in Wake County on July 15, 1862. Henderson was transferred to the 49th Regiment on January 9, 1863, and was captured at Sandy Ridge, Lenoir County, on April 20, 1863. He was sent to New Bern, North Carolina, and was exchanged on May 28, 1863, at City Point, Virginia. Henderson was reported present until he was captured at Drewery's Bluff, Virginia, on May 16, 1864 . He was confined at Elmira, New York, until he died of unreported causes on August 22, 1864.

517. Fritts, Henry Giles

Private, Company A, 42nd Regiment N.C. Troops

Henry was born on August 27, 1845, to Andrew H. and Charity Michael Fritts. He worked as a farmer prior to being conscripted into service at Danville, Virginia, on October 17, 1863. He was hospitalized on June 4, 1864, with a gunshot wound. Henry returned to service on August 4, 1864, and was reported present until he was captured at Battery Anderson, Fort Fisher, North Carolina, on December 25, 1864. He was confined at Point Lookout, Maryland, until May 12, 1865, when he was released after taking the oath of allegiance. After the war, he married Saluda Farabee on May 2, 1867. They would have four children: Joseph (1868), James (1872), Daisy (1875), and William (1877). Also, in 1870, Henry adopted four orphaned black children: Virginia, Matilda, Rosa, and George Hairston. Henry lived in the Tyro area until his death on April 19, 1875. He is buried at St. Luke's Lutheran Church.

518. Fritts, Hiram W.

Private, Jones Rifle Guards Company G, 2nd Regiment N.C. State Troops

Hiram was born on April 17, 1826. He worked as a farmer prior to being conscripted in December 1864. He was captured at Petersburg, Virginia, on March 25, 1865. Hiram was confined at Point Lookout, Maryland, until he was released on June 26, 1865, after taking the oath of allegiance. Hiram was one of the unfortunate who died of pneumonia before he could reach home. Hiram died on July 18, 1865, aboard a steamer docked at Newport News, Virginia.

519. Fritts, Jesse H.

Private, Company A, 42nd Regiment N.C. Troops

Jesse was born in 1843 to Adam and Phoebe Fritts. Jesse worked as a farmer prior to volunteering on November 26, 1861. He was reported present until he was captured at Battery Anderson, Fort Fisher, North Carolina, on December 25, 1864. Jesse was confined at Fort Delaware, Delaware, until June 19, 1865, when he was released after taking the oath of allegiance. No further records.

520. Fritts, William A.

Private, Company B, 48th Regiment N.C. Troops

William was born on January 12, 1843, to Joseph and Charlotte Reid Fritts. He reportedly wanted to enter the ministry at one point, however, he worked as a farmer before volunteering for service on March 6, 1862. William was wounded at King's School House, Virginia, on June 25, 1862. He was sent home on furlough during which he married Lucretia Bowers on September 25, 1862. He returned to duty prior to May 1, 1863. William was assigned to light duty as an enrolling officer on February 19, 1864. He was reported present until he was wounded at Bristoe Station, Virginia, on October 14, 1864. William was reported as a provost guard in Raleigh, North Carolina, in December 1864. He was paroled at Greensboro, North Carolina, on May 5, 1865. After the war, William and Lucretia would have three children before her death in 1871: Martha (1867), Robert (1869), and Catharine (1871). William married Albertine Grimes in 1873. William and Albertine would have six children: Frances (1874), Adam Luther (1877), Jacob (1879), James (1882), Everett (1891), and Alice (1894). William lived in the Conrad Hill township until his death after 1900. He is buried at Holly Grove Lutheran Church.

521. Fry, Anderson

Private, Davidson Guards Company A, 21st Regiment N.C. Troops

Anderson was born in 1843 to Nathan and Sarah Fry. He worked as a farmer prior to volunteering on May 8, 1861. He was wounded at the battles of Fredericksburg, Virginia, (December 13,

1862) and Chancellorsville, Virginia, (May 3, 1865). Anderson recovered from his wounds and was reported present until he was captured at Sayler's Creek, Virginia, on April 6, 1865. He was confined at Newport News, Virginia, until June 27, 1865, when he was released after taking the oath of allegiance. After the war, he married Mary Howerton on February 23, 1868. No further records.

522. Fry, Franklin

Private, Company K, 31st Regiment N.C. Troops

Franklin was born in 1839 to Salome and Mary Fry. He worked as a farmer prior to being conscripted into service at Camp Holmes, Wake County, on May 20, 1863. Franklin was reported present throughout his term of service and was paroled at Greensboro, North Carolina, on May 5, 1865. After the war, he returned home and accepted at job on the Cotton Grove farm of John Lookabill, with whom he was living in 1870. No further records.

523. Fry, George Washington

Private, Company C, 70th Regiment N.C. Troops (1st N.C. Junior Reserves)

George was born in 1847 to Nathan and Sarah Fry. He worked as a farmer prior to enlisting in the Junior Reserves on May 24, 1864. After the war, he came home, and, on February 25, 1875, he married Nancy M. Hartley. George and Nancy would have two children: Mary (1878) and Daisy (1880). George died on an unspecified date. He is buried in the Ellis-Fry Cemetery.

524. Fry, James T.

Private, Company F, 7th Regiment N.C. State Troops

James was born in 1837 to Nathan and Sarah Fry. He married Sarah in 1858, and they would have two children, John (1859) and Serena (1860), before James volunteered for service on March 11, 1862. Their third child, Laura, was born in 1863. He was reported present through October 1864. For most of that time he was detailed with the ambulance corps as a driver. James was paroled at Greensboro, North Carolina, on May 1, 1865. After the war, James returned home to

Sarah, and they would have three more children: Henry (1865), Sarah (1867), and William (1869). James died sometime before 1880. He is buried in the Ellis-Fry Cemetery.

525. Fry, Peter

Private, Company A, 42nd Regiment N.C. Troops

Peter was born in 1838 to Salome and Mary Fry. He worked as a farmer prior to volunteering in Rowan County on March 6, 1862. He was reported present until he was captured at Battery Anderson, Fort Fisher, North Carolina, on December 25, 1864. He was confined at Point Lookout, Maryland, by way of Fort Monroe, Virginia, until June 27, 1865, when he was released after taking the oath of allegiance. No further records.

526. Fry, William

Private, Davidson Guards Company A, 21st Regiment N.C. Troops

William was born in 1831. He married Mary Ann in 1852. William and Mary Ann would have two children, Julius (1853) and Amanda (1857), before William volunteered on May 8, 1861. He was reported present until he was wounded in the eye during the battle of Second Manassas, Virginia, on August 28, 1862. He was reported absent, wounded, through February 1865. No further records.

527. Fulk, Calvin C.

Private, Confederate Guards Company K, 48th Regiment N.C. Troops

Calvin was born in 1838. He was conscripted into service in Forsyth County on April 10, 1863. He was reported present until he was wounded in the battle of Cold Harbor, Virginia, on June 3, 1864. Calvin was reported absent, wounded, through October 1864. He died on an unspecified date while in service.

528. Fuller, Isham

Private, Company E, 64th Regiment Georgia Infantry

Isham was born on July 10, 1839. He served as a private in the 64th Georgia Infantry and was paroled at Greensboro, North Carolina, on May 8, 1865. After the

war, he married Miranda Arnold. Isham died on January 18, 1921. He is buried at Pleasant Hill United Methodist Church.

529. Fultz, Amos

Private, Cleveland Mountain Boys Company D, 15th Regiment N.C. Troops (5th N.C. Volunteers)
2nd Company B, 49th Regiment N.C. Troops

Amos was born in 1842 to Elijah and Louisa Fultz. Amos worked as a mechanic prior to being conscripted into service in Wake County on July 15, 1862. He was reported present through January 9, 1863, when he was transferred to the 49th Regiment. He was reported present with the 49th until he was captured at Five Forks, Virginia, on April 1, 1865. Amos was confined at Hart's Island, New York, until June 18, 1865, when he was released after taking the oath of allegiance. No further records.

530. Fultz, Francis M.

Private, Cleveland Mountain Boys Company D, 15th Regiment N.C. Troops (5th N.C. Volunteers)
2nd Company B, 49th Regiment N.C. Troops

Francis was born on January 12, 1842, to Theophilus and Melvina Fultz. He worked as a farmer prior to being conscripted into service in Wake County on July 15, 1862. Francis was transferred to the 49th Regiment on January 9, 1863. He was dropped from the rolls when he failed to return from a furlough in September 1863. After the war, Francis became an apprentice to Arcadia thresher maker Joseph Miller. Francis learned the trade, and in 1872, he took up repairing farm machinery as an occupation. On April 9, 1874, he married Lutitia Tesh. Francis and Lutitia would have nine children: Arwell (1875), Lena (1878), David (1880), Ransom (1881), Mary (1882), Lucy (1884), Albert (1887), Ida (1892), and Ethel (1895). Francis lived in the Arcadia township until his death on August 5, 1923. He is buried at Freidburg Moravian Church.

531. Gallimore, Aaron E.

Captain, 65th Regiment N.C. Militia (1861 organization)

Aaron accepted a commission in the Silver Hill District Company on Decem-

Francis and Letitia Fultz would raise nine children in this Arcadia township home (Touart, *Building the Backcountry*).

ber 26, 1861. He resigned on January 9, 1865. No further records.

532. Gallimore, Alfred B.

Private, Company F, 7th Regiment N.C. Troops

Alfred was born on July 15, 1828. He married Delithia in 1853. Alfred and Delithia would have three children, Emsley (1855), Franklin (1857), and Linda (1860), before Alfred was conscripted into service in Wake County on November 26, 1863. Alfred deserted on February 28, 1864, and came home, never returning to service. Alfred farmed in the Emmons township until his death on September 13, 1875. He is buried at Tom's Creek Primitive Baptist Church.

533. Gallimore, Benjamin Franklin

Private, Lexington Wildcats Company I, 14th Regiment N.C. Troops

Benjamin was born in 1840. He worked as a miner before volunteering on May 14, 1861. He was reported present through August 1864. After the war, Ben married Phoebe in 1865. Ben and Phoebe would have two children: Louisa (1866) and John (1868). No further records.

534. Gallimore, Burgess L.

Private, Lexington Wildcats Company I, 14th Regiment N.C. Troops

Burgess was born in 1838. He worked as a farmer, and, on February 9, 1862, he married Phoebe Beck. Burgess was conscripted in Wake County on July 16, 1862. He was reported present until he deserted to the enemy on February 23, 1864. Burgess took the oath of allegiance in an unspecified location and returned home to the Conrad Hill township. Burgess and Phoebe would have three children: Margie (1867), John (1871), and Margaret (1873). No further records.

535. Gallimore, Daniel Wilson

Private, Lexington Wildcats Company I, 14th Regiment N.C. Troops

Daniel was born in 1839. He worked as a miner prior to enlisting on May 14, 1861. He was present throughout the war but was detailed for most of 1863 and 1864 as a teamster. Daniel was paroled at Greensboro, North Carolina, on May 15, 1865. After the war, Daniel married Roanna Palmer. Daniel and Roanna would have three children in the Conrad Hill township, Marcus (1866), John (1867), and Elizabeth (1870), before moving to Randolph County. No further records.

536. Gallimore, Ebenezer

Private, Lexington Wildcats Company I, 14th Regiment N.C. Troops

Ebenezer was born in 1839. He worked as a farmer prior to volunteering on May 14, 1861. He was reported present until he was killed in action at Gettysburg, Pennsylvania, on July 3, 1865.

537. Gallimore, Harmon

Private, Confederate Guards Company K, 48th Regiment N.C. Troops

Harmon was born on July 25, 1846. He volunteered on March 8, 1862. Harmon was reported present throughout the war. After the war, he returned home, and, on December 18, 1868, he married Gilly Cross. Harmon and Gilly would have two children: Ronda (1870) and John (1874). Harmon lived in the Emmons/Cotton Grove area until his death on July 24, 1921. He is buried at Tom's Creek Primitive Baptist Church.

538. Gallimore, James

Private, Lexington Wildcats Company I, 14th Regiment N.C. Troops

James was born in 1820. He worked as a farmer, and, in 1840, he married Rebecca. James and Rebecca would have eight children, Terry (1841), Catharine (1844), Sarah (1846), Delila (1848), Margaret (1854), Sampson (1856), Noah (1859), and John (1861), before James volunteered on May 14, 1861. He was present until discharged on August 14, 1862, because of being over age. James returned to the Emmons township, where he and Rebecca would have two more children: Frances (1865) and William (1869). No further records

539. Gallimore, Jesse

First Lieutenant, Company F, 76th Regiment N.C. Troops (6th N.C. Senior Reserves)

Jesse was born in 1815 and was a compatriot of law in 1842, when he married Sarah. Jesse and Sarah would have four children: Henry (1848), Sandra (1850), Lilly (1855), and Thomas (1857). Jesse accepted a commission in the Senior Reserves upon its inception in 1865. After the war, he returned to the Conrad Hill township prior to moving to Randolph County. Jesse died sometime prior to 1880 and is buried in a private cemetery in Randolph County.

540. Gallimore, Joel C.

*Private, Company C, 70th Regiment
N.C. Troops (1st N.C. Junior
Reserves)*

Joel was born in 1847. He worked as a farmer prior to enlisting in the Junior Reserves on May 24, 1864. After the war, Joel married Isabelle S. May on August 21, 1867. Joel and Isabelle would have two children: Eldora (1868) and Coraella (1869). Isabelle died before 1880. Joel moved his family to Stanly County, where he is found in the 1900 Census. He died in Stanly County.

541. Gallimore, M. C.

*Private, Company D, 48th Regiment
N.C. Troops*

M. C. was born in 1843 and worked as a farmer prior to being conscripted on August 8, 1862. He died of disease at Culpeper Court House, Virginia, on November 5, 1862.

542. Gallimore, Ransom H.

*Private, Company C, 30th Regiment
N.C. Troops*

Ransom was born on May 11, 1826. He worked as a farmer and, in 1846, he married Rebecca. Ransom and Rebecca would have six children: Armon (1847), Margaret (1848), Louisa (1849), Ruth (1851), Martha (1853), and Mariah (1858), before Ransom was conscripted on July 15, 1863. He was captured at Kelly's Ford, Virginia, on November 7, 1863. Ransom was confined at Point Lookout, Maryland, until September 18, 1864, when he was paroled and transferred to City Point, Virginia, for exchange. He was exchanged and hospitalized at Richmond, Virginia, on September 23, 1864. Ransom was issued a 60-day furlough from the hospital on October 4, 1864, from which he did not return to service. After the war, Ransom lived in the Jackson Hill township until his death on March 25, 1884. He is buried at Jackson Creek Baptist Church.

543. Gallimore, William D.

*Private, Company D, 48th Regiment
N.C. Troops*

William was born in 1843. He worked as a farmer prior to being conscripted on August 8, 1862. He died of disease at Winchester, Virginia, on October 5, 1862.

544. Gallimore, William M.

*Private, Company G, 33rd Regiment
N.C. Troops*

William was born in 1817. He worked as a miller before he was conscripted on August 15, 1863. William was reported present until he was wounded at Ream's Station, Virginia, on August 24, 1864. He was reported absent, wounded, throughout the rest of the war. No further records.

545. Gardner, James B.

*Private, Confederate Guards
Company K, 48th Regiment N.C. Troops*

James was born in 1834. He was conscripted on August 8, 1862. James died of unknown causes at Shepherdstown, [West] Virginia, on September 26, 1862.

546. Garner, Lindsey

*Private, Company D, 36th Regiment
N.C. Troops (3rd N.C. Artillery)*

Lindsey was born on August 12, 1821. He worked as a farmer, and in 1843, he married Dolsy Ann Harris. Lindsey and

Lindsay Garner was conscripted at 43, having already lost a son and a nephew (Mozelle Wood, *The Heritage of Davidson County.*)

Dolsy would have five children, William (1845–62), Nancy (1850), Phoebe (1852), Elizabeth (1856), and Turner (1858), before Lindsey was conscripted into service on August 24, 1864. He was reported present until December 21, 1864, when he deserted to the enemy at Hilton Head Island, South Carolina. Lindsey was transferred to the provost marshal general in New York, New York, on January 25, 1865. Lindsey came home to the Emmons township, where he died sometime before 1880. He is buried in the Garner Family Cemetery.

547. Garner, William

*Private, Company B, 48th Regiment
N.C. Troops*

William was born to 1845 to Lindsey and Dolsy Gardner. He worked as a farmer before volunteering on March 6, 1862. He was wounded at King's School House, Virginia, on June 25, 1862. William died of his wounds in Richmond, Virginia, on July 1, 1862.

548. Garner, William H.

*Private, Company I, 42nd Regiment
N.C. Troops*

William was born on April 15, 1849, to John L. and Jeminah Garner. He worked as a farmer prior to volunteering on March 12, 1862. He was present until he deserted on May 27, 1864. After the war, he married Tabitha in 1866. William and Tabitha would have four children: Annie (1867), Nancy (1868), Henry (1869), and Martha (1872). William lived in the Jackson Hill township until his death on May 13, 1920. He is buried at Tom's Creek Primitive Baptist Church.

549. Garrison, John W.

*Private, Confederate Guards
Company K, 48th Regiment N.C. Troops*

John was born on April 29, 1832. He worked as a farmer, and, in 1856, he married Mary. John and Mary would have five children: Charity (1857), Mary (1860), William (1861), Christian (1866), and Sarah (1869). John's service record contains only the information of his conscription on August 8, 1862. John lived in the Abbott's Creek township prior to his death on November 8, 1911. He is buried at Abbott's Creek Primitive Baptist Church.

550. Gattis, Nathan

Private, Lexington Wildcats
Company I, 14th Regiment N.C. Troops
(4th N.C. Volunteers)

Nathan was born in 1842 to Margaret Gattis. He may have been mulatto, a person of mixed white and African blood. He worked as a farmer prior to volunteering on May 14, 1861. He was reported present until he deserted to the enemy on February 23, 1864. No further records.

551. Gentle, Richmond Baxter

Private, Davidson Guards
Company A, 21st Regiment N.C. Troops
(11th N.C. Volunteers)

R. B. was born on April 28, 1846, to Joseph and Sarah Temple Gentle. In 1860, he was living with Michael and Sarah Lanier. Richmond volunteered for service at the age of 17 on January 27, 1864. He served as a courier and was "a fine marksman on the skirmish line." He was reported present until he was paroled at Appomattox Court House, Virginia, on April 9, 1865. R. B., or "Old Boss" as he was later called, came home and married Nancy B. Sowers on February 7, 1867. R. B. and Nancy would have three children: Charles (1867), P. Klein Zwingley (1872), and Bessie (1875). R. B. created two inventions, a device to separate wheat grains according to size and a device for hanging slaughtered hogs. He died on May 11, 1936. He is buried at Reeds Baptist Church. An article dated July 16, 1931, describes R. B.:

> Mr. Gentle is very fond of reading and has worn out three bibles. Because he does not wear glasses, he must have special books with big print. ... Mr. Gentle looks like a man who has a sunny disposition and his mind is keen and alert.

552. Gibbons, Hamilton

Private, Lexington Wildcats
Company I, 14th Regiment N.C. Troops
(4th N.C. Volunteers)

Hamilton was born in 1843 to Peter and Elizabeth Gibbons. He worked as a farmer before volunteering on May 14, 1861. He was present or accounted for until he died of disease at Goldsboro, North Carolina, on October 20, 1862.

553. Gibson, George

First Lieutenant, 65th Regiment N.C.
Militia (1861 organization)

George was born in 1818. In 1840, he married Martha. George and Martha would have seven children: William (1841), Sarah (1843), Mary (1845), Nancy (1847) Roanna (1849), George G. (1855), and James (1858). George accepted a commission in the Lick Creek District Company on December 26, 1861. No further records.

554. Gibson, William A.

Private, Company C, 61st Regiment
N.C. Troops

William was born in 1841 to George and Martha Gibson. William worked as a single farmer and helped to found Sexton's School House in 1861. William was conscripted on August 27, 1862. He was reported present until he was furloughed from a Richmond, Virginia, hospital on October 1, 1864. William did not return to service. After the war, William married Martha Thompson on August 15, 1865. William and Martha would have only one child: Richard H. (1876). William and his family were charter members of Mount Ebal Methodist Church. William died sometime after 1900, and he is buried at Mount Ebal Methodist Church.

555. Gillam, John A.

Private, Company K, 15th Regiment
N.C. Troops (5th N.C. Volunteers)

John was born in 1830. He worked as a farmer in the northern district of Davidson County, and, in 1857, he married Mary. John and Mary would have two children, William (1858) and John (1860), prior to John being conscripted into service on July 15, 1862. He was wounded in the leg and captured at Sharpsburg, Maryland, on September 17, 1862. John was taken to a Federal hospital in Burkittsville, Maryland, where his left leg was amputated. According to a Federal surgeon: "For a few days he seemed to improve under the use of tonics and stimulators but soon got worse & died on Oct. 12, having been delirious for the last week." John died on October 12, 1862.

556. Glover, John A.

Private, Company K, 15th Regiment
N.C. Troops (5th N.C. Volunteers)

John was born in 1843. He worked as a miller before volunteering for service on May 8, 1861. He was reported present until he was killed in action at Winchester, Virginia, on September 19, 1864.

557. Gobble, Alexander

Private, Company K, 15th Regiment
N.C. Troops

Alex was born in 1834. He worked as a farmer in the Tyro area, and, in 1854, he married Susan. Alex and Susan would have four children, Wesley (1855), Cornelia (1857), Martha (1859), and Eliza (1862), before Alex was conscripted into service in Wake County on July 15, 1862. Alex was wounded and captured at Crampton's Pass, Maryland, on September 14, 1862. He was confined at Point Lookout, Maryland, until he was paroled and transferred to Aiken's Landing, Virginia, on October 2, 1862, for exchange. Alex was exchanged on November 10, 1862. Alex returned to service in February 1863 and was reported present through October 1864. After the war, Alex returned home to the Tyro township and was a fairly successful farmer by 1870. No further records.

558. Gobble, Burrell C.

Private, Company A, 42nd Regiment
N.C. Troops

Burrell was born on December 8, 1846, to Godfrey and Sophia Cope Gobble. He worked as a farmer prior to volunteering for service on May 1, 1864, in Washington County, North Carolina. He was reported present until he was captured at Battery Anderson, Fort Fisher, North Carolina, on December 25, 1864. Burrell was confined at Point Lookout, Maryland, until June 17, 1865, when he was released after taking the oath of allegiance. After the war, Burrell married America H. Koontz on April 24, 1867. Burrell and America would have two children: Cora (1868) and Martha (1870). Burrell was listed as "Dr. Gobble" in both the heritage book and a book on the history of Reeds Baptist, however, no record of medical training was found. Burrell lived in the Tyro township until his death on November 8, 1930. He is buried at Reeds Baptist Church.

559. Gobble, David C.

Private, Company A, 42nd Regiment N.C. Troops

David was born in 1843 to Thomas and Susannah Gobble. He worked as a farmer before volunteering in Rowan County on January 22, 1862. He deserted on December 30, 1862, and returned to service in July 1863. He was reported present until he was wounded in an unspecified engagement on July 25, 1864. David was absent, wounded, for the duration of the war. He was paroled at Greensboro, North Carolina, on May 8, 1865. After the war, he married Ellen R. Davis on September 26, 1867. David and Ellen would have two children, Eliza (1868) and Sofia (1871), before the family moved out of the county prior to 1880. No further records.

560. Gobble, Hiram H.

Private, Holtsburg Guards Company A, 54th Regiment N.C. Troops

Hiram was born in 1837 to Richmond and Elizabeth Gobble. He worked as a farmer prior to volunteering for service on March 24, 1862. Shortly before going off to war, he married Irene. Their first child, Uphrenia, was born in 1863. Hiram was hospitalized twice during the war, once in November for a malaria-like intermittent fever and in August 1864 for an unspecified complaint. Hiram was paroled at Appomattox Court House, Virginia, on April 9, 1865. He was one of only eight men from the Holtsburg Guards left to surrender. After the war, Hiram returned to the Boone township, where he and Irene would have two more children: Frances (1867) and Sarah F. (1869). Hiram and his family moved out of the county before 1880. No further records.

561. Gobble, Hubbard A.

Private, Ellis Guards Company C, 15th Regiment N.C. Troops (5th N.C. Volunteers)

Hubbard was born in 1836. He worked as a farmer, and, in 1857, he married Sarah Scott. Hubbard and Sarah would have three children, Frances (1858), Semacean (1860), and Phillip (1862), before Hubbard was conscripted on July 15, 1862. He deserted and was at home between August 28, 1862, and July 31, 1864. Hubbard returned to service and was reported present until he was captured at Hatcher's Run, Virginia, on April 1, 1865. Hubbard was confined at Point Lookout, Maryland, until he died of "acute diarrhea" on June 15, 1865. He is buried in the Point Lookout National Cemetery.

562. Gobble, James M.

Private, Ellis Guards Company C, 15th Regiment N.C. Troops (5th N.C. Volunteers)

James was born in 1844. He worked as a farmer prior to being conscripted into service on July 15, 1862. James was reported present until he was captured at Hatcher's Run, Virginia, on April 1, 1865. He was confined at Point Lookout, Maryland, until June 27, 1865, when he was released after taking the oath of allegiance. After the war, he returned to the Boone township, and on February 22, 1866, he married Sarah Hedrick. James and Sarah would have two children, Mary (1867) and Charles (1870), before moving out of the county prior to 1880. No further records.

563. Gobble, Phillip H.

Private, Holtsburg Guards Company A, 54th Regiment N.C. Troops

Phillip was born in 1840 to Jacob and Jane Gobble. He worked as a farmer prior to volunteering on March 22, 1862. Phillip was hospitalized with the mumps in Richmond, Virginia, on November 9, 1862. He returned to duty on December 10, 1862. Phillip died of "bronchitis acute" in a Richmond, Virginia, hospital on February 14, 1863. He is buried in the Hollywood Cemetery in Richmond.

564. Gobble, Robert Alexander

Private, Holtsburg Guards Company A, 54th Regiment N.C. Troops

Robert was born on August 11, 1835, to Richmond and Elizabeth Gobble. He worked as a farmer prior to volunteering on March 25, 1862. He was reported present until he was captured at Fort Stedman, Virginia, on March 25, 1865. Robert was confined at Point Lookout, Maryland, until June 27, 1865, when he was released after taking the oath of allegiance. After the war, Robert returned to the Boone township, and, on October 10, 1867, he married Sarah Jane Young. Robert and Sarah would have only one child, Mary Anne (1869). Robert lived in the Boone township until his death on April 18, 1904. He is buried at St. Luke's Lutheran Church.

565. Gordon, Alfred Thomas, Jr.

Private, Franklin Guides to Freedom Company K, 44th Regiment N.C. Troops

Alfred was born on January 18, 1844, to Alfred and Mary Gordon. He worked as a farmer prior to being conscripted on September 24, 1864. He deserted to the enemy on December 28, 1864. Alfred was confined at Washington, D.C., until he was released on an unspecified date after taking the oath of allegiance. Alfred returned home, and, on May 13, 1869, he married Jane Lambeth. Alfred and Jane would have six children: Julia (1869), John (1874), Samuel (1876), Edward (1878), Emma (1884), and Mary (1892). Alfred lived in the Conrad Hill township until his death on May 12, 1926. He is buried at Clarksbury Methodist Church.

566. Gordon, David

Private, Captain McCorkle's Reserve Company

David was born in 1835. He worked as a farmer, and, in 1857, he married Elizabeth. David and Elizabeth would have two children: Noah (1858) and Lindsey (1861). Records indicate that David was a part of Captain Matthew McCorkle's Reserves, although the only battalion raised by that officer was a Senior Reserve battalion. David lived in the Conrad Hill township until his death before 1900. He is buried at Clarksbury Methodist Church.

567. Gordon, Joseph E.

Private, Company F, 53rd Regiment N.C. Troops

Joseph was born in 1830 to Esther Gordon. He worked as a farmer prior to being conscripted into service in Randolph County on November 19, 1862. He was reported absent without leave between April 13, 1863, and January 1, 1864. Joseph returned to service and then deserted while on leave in Lynchburg, Virginia, on June 12, 1864. No further records.

568. Gordon, Ransom

Private, Franklin Guides to Freedom
Company K, 44th Regiment N.C.
Troops

Ransom was conscripted into service in Davidson County on September 21, 1864. He was reported present through October 1864. No further records.

569. Gordon, Roswell G.

Private, Bladen Light Infantry
Company B, 18th Regiment N.C. Troops
(8th N.C. Volunteers)

Roswell was born in 1840 to John and Mary Gordon. He married Delilah Imbler (Embler) on November 1, 1863. He was conscripted into service at Camp Holmes, North Carolina, on September 1, 1864. Roswell deserted on October 1, 1864, and came home to his wife. Roswell and Delilah would have seven children: Mary (1866), Tillet (1871), Elwood (1873), Edward (1874), Lenora (1876), Samuel (1878), and Charles (1881). Roswell lived in the Conrad Hill township until his death sometime prior to 1900. He is buried at Clarksbury Methodist Church.

570. Gordy, John

Private, Company H, 15th Regiment
N.C. Troops (5th N.C. Volunteers)

John was born in 1835. He worked as a farmer prior to being conscripted into service in Wake County on July 15, 1862. John was wounded at Sharpsburg, Maryland, on September 17, 1862, and was reported missing. No further records.

571. Goss, Alexander

Private, Company I, 76th Regiment
N.C. Troops (6th N.C. Senior
Reserves)

Alexander was born in 1818 to Frederick and Mary Goss. Alexander worked as a carpenter in the northern district of Davidson County and married Anna in 1846. Alexander and Anna would have two children: Cicero (1847) and George (1853). Alexander enlisted in the Senior Reserves upon their inception in January 1865. After his service, he returned to his trade and moved to Thomasville in 1873. Alexander lived in the town of Thomasville until his death on May 6, 1892. He is buried in the Thomasville City Cemetery.

572. Goss, Cicero

Private, Company C, 70th Regiment
N.C. Troops (1st N.C. Junior
Reserves)

Cicero was born in 1847 to Alexander and Anna Goss. He worked as a carpenter prior to enlisting in the Junior Reserves on May 24, 1864. After his service, Cicero married Susan Owen on August 31, 1873, and moved to the Cotton Grove township. Cicero and Susan would have eight children: Minnie (1875), Grace (1876), Annie (1882), Grover C. (1885), James (1888), Hugh (1890), Roy (1893), and Nathaniel (1896). Cicero worked as a carpenter in the Cotton Grove/Healing Springs area until his death in 1926. He is buried at Lebanon Lutheran Church.

573. Goss, George Washington

Private, Lexington Wildcats
Company I, 14th Regiment N.C. Troops
(4th N.C. Volunteers)

George was born in 1843 to Rachael Goss. He worked as a farmer prior to volunteering on May 28, 1861. He was wounded at Gaines' Mill, Virginia, on June 27, 1862. George recovered from his wounds and rejoined the company in January 1863. He was reported present until he was killed in action during the battle of Spotsylvania Court House, Virginia, on May 12, 1864.

574. Goss, Leonard C.

Private, Lexington Wildcats
Company I, 14th Regiment N.C. Troops
(4th N.C. Volunteers)

Leonard was born in 1845 to Rachael Goss. He worked as a farmer before volunteering for service on June 1, 1863. He was reported present until he was wounded at Spotsylvania Court House, Virginia, on May 12, 1864. Leonard recovered and was paroled at Appomattox Court House, Virginia, on April 9, 1865. No further records.

575. Gray, Alfred

Private, Company G, 2nd Battalion,
N.C. Infantry
Company A, 10th Battalion, N.C. Heavy
Artillery
Company D, 10th Battalion, N.C. Heavy
Artillery

Alfred was born in 1838. He worked as a farmer, and, in 1857, he married Betty Helton. Alfred and Betty would have two children, William (1859) and Francis (1860), before Alfred volunteered for service in September 1861. Alfred was captured at Roanoke Island, North Carolina, on February 8, 1862. When the 2nd N.C. Battalion was reorganized, Alfred enlisted in Company A, 10th N.C. Heavy Artillery on April 3, 1862. He was reported present until he was transferred to Company D of the 10th Battalion on May 23, 1865. After the war, he and Betty would have three more children: Louisa (1863), Arlando (1865), and R. E. Lee (1869). No further records.

576. Gray, Harrison

Private, Company A, 10th Battalion,
N.C. Heavy Artillery
Company D, 10th Battalion, N.C. Heavy
Artillery

Harrison was born in 1844. He worked as a farmer prior to volunteering on April 3, 1862. He was present until May 23, 1863, when he was transferred to Company D of the 10th Battalion. Harrison died sometime prior to February 1865.

577. Gray, John W.

Corporal, Company A, 36th Regiment
N.C. Troops (2nd N.C. Artillery)
2nd Company I, 10th Regiment N.C.
State Troops (1st N.C. Artillery)

John was born on February 8, 1843, to Robert and Mary Jane Gray. John worked as a bricklayer before enlisting on July 8, 1862. He was transferred to the 1st N.C. Artillery in November 1863. John was promoted to corporal in July 1864, and he served until he was paroled at Greensboro, North Carolina, on May 1, 1865. After the war, John returned home to Thomasville and John married Nancy I. Burton on June 9, 1874. John and Nancy would have seven children: Eugene (1875), Roberta (1877), Robert Lee (1880), Jesse (1881), William (1883), Frederick (1889), and Julius (1891). John lived and worked in the town of Thomasville until his death on August 21, 1932. He is buried in the Thomasville City Cemetery.

578. Gray, Samuel

Private, Company G, 2nd Battalion,
N.C. Infantry

Company A, 10th Battalion, N.C. Heavy Artillery

Company D, 10th Battalion, N.C. Heavy Artillery

Samuel was born in 1844. He worked as a farmer before volunteering in Forsyth County on September 19, 1861. He was captured at Roanoke Island, North Carolina, on February 8, 1862. Samuel was paroled and enlisted in the 10th N.C. Heavy Artillery instead of joining his former unit when it was reorganized in April 1862. Samuel was transferred to Company D of the same battalion on May 23, 1863. He was reported present until he was paroled at Greensboro, North Carolina, on May 16, 1865. No further records.

579. Green, Benjamin Franklin

Private, Company C, 70th Regiment N.C. Troops (1st N.C. Junior Reserves)

Ben was born on October 18, 1845, to John and Elizabeth Green. He worked as a farmer prior to enlisting in the Junior Reserves on May 24, 1864. After his service, he returned home to the Abbott's Creek township. On December 16, 1865, he married Phoebe J. Collett. Ben and Phoebe would have six children: Mary (1872), Matthew (1875), Francis (1878), S. E. (1879), Dula (1883), and John (1886). Benjamin lived in the Abbott's Creek township until his death on April 1, 1928. He is buried at Shady Grove United Methodist Church.

580. Green, George Washington

Private, Company D, 48th Regiment N.C. Troops

George was born on February 11, 1828. He married Cynthia Albertine

George and Cynthia Green. George was discharged from service due to "chronic inflammation of the left knee" (Hugh E. Green, *The Heritage of Davidson County*).

Swicegood in 1854. George and Cynthia would have three children, Edward (1856), Thomas (1858), and Corneilia (1860–63), before George was conscripted on August 8, 1862. He was discharged on August 31, 1862, because of "chronic inflammation of the knee joint." Two more children, James (1863) and Columbus (1864), were born before he was paroled at Salisbury, North Carolina, on May 18, 1865. After the war, George and Cynthia would have three more children: William (1866), Flora (1869), and Mildred (1873). George lived in the Boone township until his death on December 26, 1909. He is buried at St. Luke's Lutheran Church.

581. Green, Jesse S. P.

Private, Confederate Guards Company K, 48th Regiment N.C. Troops

Jesse was born in 1828. He worked as a blacksmith prior to being conscripted on August 31, 1862. He died of typhoid fever in a Lynchburg, Virginia, hospital on November 11, 1862.

582. Green, Robert Lafayette

Private, Confederate Guards Company K, 48th Regiment N.C. Troops

Robert was born on May 2, 1830. In 1855, he married Margaret E., with whom he would have four children, Albert (1856), Charles (1858), John (1860), and Vandora (1862), before Robert was conscripted on August 8, 1862. He was wounded at Sharpsburg, Maryland, on September 17, 1862. Robert returned to duty on an unspecified date and was reported present until he was detailed for light duty on March 13, 1865. After the war, Robert came home to the Abbott's Creek township where he and Margaret would have four more children: Perry (1865), Luther (1869), Cynthia (1874), and Laura (1876). Robert died on February 27, 1899. He is buried at Shady Grove United Methodist Church.

583. Green, Shepherd

Private, Cleveland Mountain Boys Company D, 15th Regiment N.C. Troops (5th N.C. Volunteers)

Shepherd was born in 1839, the son of Benjamin Green. He worked as a farmer prior to being conscripted into service in Wake County on July 15, 1862.

He was wounded at Sharpsburg, Maryland, on September 17, 1862. Shepherd died of his wounds in a Winchester, Virginia, hospital on October 4, 1862.

584. Green, Solomon

Private, Confederate Guards Company K, 48th Regiment N.C. Troops

Solomon was born in 1832. He worked as a farmer, and, in 1855, he married Mary Ann. Solomon and Mary would have two children, Louisa (1857) and Elizabeth (1860), before Solomon was conscripted into service on August 8, 1862. He was wounded three times during his service: in the thigh at Sharpsburg, Maryland, (September 17, 1862), by a shell at Bristoe Station, Virginia (October 14, 1863), and at Wilderness, Virginia, (May 5–6, 1864). During this time, he and Mary had two more children: Sarah (1863) and Barbara (1864). He recovered from his wounds each time and was reported present until he was captured at Hatcher's Run, Virginia, on April 2, 1865. Solomon was confined at Hart's Island, New York, until June 19, 1865, when he was released after taking the oath of allegiance. After the war, he and Mary would have one more child: John (1875). No further records.

585. Green, William

Second Lieutenant, 66th Regiment N.C. Militia (1861 organization)

William was born in 1839 to Jesse and Elizabeth Green. He accepted a commission in the Piney Grove District Company on December 13, 1861. After his service, he lived by himself on his farm in the Abbott's Creek township. William died before 1900. He is buried at Smith Grove Baptist Church.

586. Gregson, Burgess

Private, Company A, 10th Battalion, N.C. Heavy Artillery

Burgess was born in 1834. He worked as a shoemaker in the Lines Shoe Factory in Thomasville, and, on January 31, 1862, he married Ruth Burton. Burgess volunteered on March 13, 1862. He was reported present until he was captured at Savannah, Georgia, on December 7, 1864. Burgess was confined at Point Lookout, Maryland, until May 13, 1865, when he was released after taking the oath of allegiance. No further records.

587. Griffith, Zadock

Second Lieutenant, 66th Regiment N.C. Militia (1861 organization)

Zadock was born on March 25, 1821. He worked as a farmer, and, in 1847, he married Emily. Zadock and Emily would have four children: James (1849), Charles (1851), Thomas (1854), and Jennie Bell (1861). Zadock accepted a commission in the Clemmonsville District Company on October 1, 1861. After his service, he continued living in the Clemmonsville area until his death on July 10, 1889. He is buried at Friendship United Methodist Church.

588. Grimes, Hamilton L.

Private, Carolina Rangers Company B, 10th Virginia Cavalry Regiment

Hamilton was born in 1843 to Phillip and Susannah Leonard Grimes. He volunteered for service in Davie County on October 29, 1861. He was reported present through January 27, 1865. Company records state that he was without a horse from July to September 1864. Hamilton survived the war but did not survive the trip home. He died in April 1865 in the vicinity of Danville, Virginia.

589. Grimes, Henry Jackson

Captain, Carolina Rangers Company B, 10th Virginia Cavalry Regiment

Henry was born in 1832 to Henry and Christina Grimes. He worked as a machinist prior to volunteering for service in Davie County on October 29, 1861, when he was elected first lieutenant. He was promoted to captain after W. B. Clement's appointment as major on September 25, 1863. Henry was present throughout the war and was last mentioned in company records on December 31, 1864. After the war, Henry returned to the Lexington township, and, on January 20, 1870, he married Sarah King. Henry and Sarah would have four children: George (1871), Henry (1873), Bertha (1875), and Clyde (1877). Henry operated his own sawmill in the Lexington area from 1870 until his death in July 1886. He is buried in the Lexington City Cemetery.

590. Grimes, Rueben Harrison

Private, Company H, 48th Regiment N.C. Troops

Rueben was born on May 22, 1842, to Peter and Susanna Younts Grimes. He worked as a farmer prior to volunteering on March 4, 1862. Rueben was mustered in as a private, but by December 13, 1862, he had been promoted to corporal. He was wounded in the shoulder at Fredericksburg, Virginia. He was promoted to sergeant in March 1863. Rueben was reduced in rank in October 1864 to private. He was reported present until he was paroled at Appomattox Court House, Virginia, on April 9, 1865. After the war, Rueben returned home to the Conrad Hill township, and, on May 28, 1871, he married Martha Fritts. Rueben and Martha would have only one child: Eva (1872). Rueben died on October 10, 1917. He is buried at Pilgrim United Church of Christ.

591. Grimes, Thomas Franklin

Second Lieutenant, Carolina Rangers Company B, 10th Virginia Cavalry Regiment

Thomas was born in 1843 to Henry and Christina Grimes. He worked as a farmer prior to volunteering in Davie County on October 29, 1861; he was elected second lieutenant the same day. He was reported present until January 1, 1863, when he resigned because of "ill health and suffering from spermaoirheoa for six years." After he returned home, he lived in the Midway township until he moved to Forsyth County sometime after 1871. Thomas married Rebecca Kimbrough and lived in the Waughtown area until his death on April 6, 1885. He is buried in the Kimbrough Family Cemetery in Forsyth County.

592. Grimes, Thomas William Stetson

Corporal, Company C, 70th Regiment N.C. Troops (1st N.C. Junior Reserves)

Thomas was born on April 24, 1847, to Absalom and Catharine Long Grimes. He worked as a farmer prior to enlisting in the Junior Reserves on May 24, 1864. After his service, he returned home to the Thomasville township, and, on November 25, 1869, he married Margaret

Bowers. Thomas and Margaret would have seven children: Hillary (1871), Alice (1873), David A. (1879), Rosco (1884), Walter (1887), William (1890), and McCoy (1893). Thomas lived in the Thomasville township, where he served as a member of the Emanuel UCC consistory, until his death on February 16, 1925. He is buried at Emanuel United Church of Christ.

593. Grimes, William Lindsey

Private, Company H, 48th Regiment N.C. Troops

William was born on April 8, 1846, to Peter and Susanna Younts Grimes. He worked as a farmer prior to enlisting on December 1, 1864. He was reported present until he was paroled at Appomattox Court House, Virginia, on April 9, 1865. After the war, he returned home to the Conrad Hill township, and, on April 1, 1866, he married Sarah Elizabeth Myers. William and Sarah would have only one child: Charles (1868). William died on October 21, 1920. He is buried at Holly Grove Lutheran Church.

594. Grubb, Alexander

Private, Holtsburg Guards Company A, 54th Regiment N.C. Troops

Alex was born in 1846 to John and Catharine Grubb. He worked as a blacksmith prior to being conscripted into service on February 4, 1864. He was reported present until he was wounded in the left arm at New Market, Virginia, on September 24, 1864. Alex lost his left arm below the elbow to the surgeon's saw. He was discharged on January 17, 1865, because of his disability. After the war, he returned to his family's home in the Boone township. On October 30, 1870, he married Jenette Kinder. Alex and Jenette would have four children: Robin (1872), Martha (1874), Cora (1876), and R. E. Lee (1878). No further records.

595. Grubb, Ambrose

Private, Franklin Guides to Freedom Company K, 44th Regiment N.C. Troops

Ambrose was born in 1844. In 1862 he married Mary Mahalia; their first child, Ambrose, was born later that year. He worked as a farmer prior to being conscripted into service on November 29, 1862. Ambrose deserted on January 6,

1863, and returned to service sometime prior to April 30, 1864. He and Mary had their second child, Docky A., in 1864. He was reported present until he was "shot through the left leg below the knee" near Petersburg, Virginia, in September 1864. Ambrose was sent to Richmond, Virginia, and was captured in his hospital bed when the city fell on April 3, 1865. After the war, Ambrose returned to the Conrad Hill township, and, he and Mary would have five more children: Cicero (1867), David (1870), Robert (1878), and Maggie and Allie (1884). Maggie and Allie would marry men named Lambeth and Hill, respectively, and at 105 years old, would become the world's oldest living set of identical twins. Ambrose died on December 23, 1909. He is buried at Clarksbury Methodist Church.

596. Grubb, Andrew

Private, Davidson Guards
Company A, 21st Regiment N.C. Troops
(11th N.C. Volunteers)

Andrew was born in 1841. He worked as a farmer prior to volunteering on May 8, 1861. He was reported present until he was wounded and captured at Chancellorsville, Virginia, on May 3, 1863. Andrew was confined at Washington, D.C., and Fort Delaware, Delaware, until he was paroled and transferred to City Point, Virginia, for exchange on May 23, 1863. Andrew was declared exchanged and was present for duty until he deserted on September 29, 1864. He returned prior to March 1, 1865, and was captured at Fort Stedman, Virginia, on March 25, 1865. Andrew was confined at Point Lookout, Maryland, until June 27, 1865, when he was released after taking the oath of allegiance. After the war, he returned home to the Boone township, and, on April 8, 1875, he married Louisa Barnes. Andrew and Louisa would have two children: William (1876) and Mary (1878). Andrew lived in the Boone township until his death on June 27, 1892. He is buried at St. Luke's Lutheran Church.

597. Grubb, David

Private, Ellis Guards
Company C, 15th Regiment N.C. Troops

David was born in 1844. He worked as a farmer prior to being conscripted into service in Wake County on July 15, 1862. He was captured at Crampton's Pass, Maryland, on September 14, 1862. No further records.

598. Grubb, Henry

Private, Ellis Guards
Company C, 15th Regiment N.C. Troops

Henry was born on August 18, 1835. He worked as a farmer prior to being conscripted into service in Wake County on July 15, 1862. Henry was wounded and captured at Crampton's Pass, South Mountain, Maryland, on September 14, 1862. He was confined at Point Lookout, Maryland, and was reported in a Federal hospital in Philadelphia, Pennsylvania, on January 19, 1863. Henry took the oath of allegiance and arrived home sometime after the official end of hostilities. He married Louisa Snider in 1867. Henry and Louisa would have four children: Maggie (1870), Henry C. (1874), John (1879), and Nota (1882). Henry died on December 6, 1909. He is buried in the Grubb Family Cemetery.

599. Grubb, Henry A.

Private, Holtsburg Guards
Company A, 54th Regiment N.C. Troops

Henry was born in 1833. He worked as a farmer, and, in 1856, he married Melinda Hedrick. Henry and Melinda would have two children, Mary (1857) and Susan (1860), before Henry enlisted on May 14, 1862. He was reported present until he was sent to a Richmond, Virginia, hospital on November 9, 1862, and then transferred to a smallpox hospital in Petersburg, Virginia, where he died of smallpox on December 18, 1862.

600. Grubb, Jackson

Corporal, Davidson Guards
Company A, 21st Regiment N.C. Troops
(11th N.C. Volunteers)

Jackson was born in 1839. He worked as a farmer prior to volunteering on May 8, 1861, when he was mustered in as a corporal. Jack died of typhoid fever at Thoroughfare Gap, Virginia, on September 19, 1861.

601. Grubb, John

Private, Company A, 42nd Regiment N.C. Troops

John was born in 1835. He worked as a farmer, and, on March 2, 1859, he married Mary Kepley. John enlisted sometime prior to December 24, 1864, when he was captured at Battery Anderson, Fort Fisher, North Carolina. John was confined at Point Lookout, Maryland, until he was released on June 27, 1865, after taking the oath of allegiance from a hospital bed. That evening, he died of pneumonia. He is buried at the Point Lookout National Cemetery.

602. Grubb, Michael

Private, Chatam Light Infantry
Company G, 48th Regiment N.C. Troops

Michael was born in 1839 to Peter and Sarah Grubb. He worked as a farmer prior to being conscripted into service on August 14, 1862. He was reported present until he was wounded at Hatcher's Run, Virginia, on February 5, 1865. Michael was sent home on furlough, and on March 3, 1865, he married Susan Essick. Michael returned to service and was captured at Hatcher's Run, Virginia, on April 2, 1865. He was confined at Point Lookout, Maryland, until June 27, 1865, when he was released after taking the oath of allegiance. After the war, Michael returned home to his new wife, and they would raise four children in the Boone township: Mary (1867), James (1868), Henry (1878), and Joseph (1882). No further records.

603. Grubb, Ransom

Private, Cleveland Mountain Boys
Company D, 15th Regiment N.C. Troops
(5th N.C. Volunteers)
2nd Company B, 49th Regiment N.C. Troops

Ransom was born in 1843 to Peter and Sarah Grubb. He worked as a farmer prior to being conscripted into service in Wake County on July 15, 1862. Ransom was wounded at Sharpsburg, Maryland, on September 17, 1862. He recovered from his wounds and was transferred to the 49th Regiment on January 9, 1863. Ransom was reported present through October 1864. After the war, he returned home, and, on October 15, 1868, he married Eliza Easter. Ransom and Eliza would have one child, Cornelia (1869), while living in the town of Lexington. No further records.

604. Grubb, William

*Private, Company H, 48th Regiment
N.C. Troops*

William was born on July 21, 1839, to Peter and Sarah Grubb. He worked as a hireling prior to volunteering at "Wagner's" on March 8, 1862. He was reported present until he was wounded and captured at Hatcher's Run, Virginia, on April 1, 1865. William was confined at Point Lookout, Maryland, until June 27, 1865, when he was released after taking the oath of allegiance. After the war, William returned to the Lexington township. On December 27, 1866, William married Phoebe Essick. William and Phoebe would have seven children: Fostine (1868), Robert Lee (1868), Mary (1870), Noah (1872), Susan (1874), Callie (1876), and William (1879). William lived in the Lexington township until his death on March 11, 1925. He is buried at Bethesda United Methodist Church.

605. Guyer, Andrew C.

*Sergeant, Company A, 10th Battalion,
N.C. Heavy Artillery*

Andrew was born on December 11, 1840, to Joseph and Mary Guyer. He worked as a farmer before enlisting on April 25, 1862. He was mustered in as a private, was promoted to corporal on December 1, 1862, and was promoted to sergeant on April 21, 1864. He was paroled at Greensboro, North Carolina, on May 5, 1865. After the war, Andrew returned home to the Clemmonsville township and was working as a dry goods clerk in 1870. Andrew died on November 11, 1905. He is buried at Bethany United Church of Christ.

606. Guyer, Harper F.

*Private, Thomasville Rifles
Company B, 14th Regiment N.C. Troops*

Harper was born in 1840 to Joseph and Mary Guyer. He worked as a farmer prior to volunteering on April 23, 1861. He was reported present until he was wounded at Malvern Hill, Virginia, on July 1, 1862. Harper died of his wounds at Gaines' Mill, Virginia, later that same day.

607. Hackett, James A.

*Private, Davidson Guards
Company A, 21st Regiment N.C. Troops
(11th N.C. Volunteers)*

James was born in 1823. He worked as a farmer prior to volunteering on May 8, 1861. He was reported present until he was discharged on August 31, 1862, because of being over age. No further records.

608. Hagman, Hamilton D.

*Sergeant, Watauga Marksmen
Company B, 37th Regiment N.C. Troops*

Hamilton was born in 1836 to John and Sarah Hagman. He worked as a farmer prior to volunteering in Watauga County on September 14, 1861, he was appointed corporal the same day. He was promoted to sergeant in February 1863. Hamilton was reported present until he was wounded in the right hip at Chancellorsville, Virginia, on May 3, 1863. He recovered from his wounds and returned to service on September 1, 1863. Hamilton was reported present until he died of unreported causes on June 5, 1864.

609. Haith, John H.

*Private, Davidson Guards
Company A, 21st Regiment N.C. Troops
(11th N.C. Volunteers)*

John was born in 1842, the son of William H. Haith. He worked as a farmer prior to volunteering on May 8, 1861. John was reported present until he deserted on July 26, 1863. No further records.

610. Haith, William

*Private, Davidson Guards
Company A, 21st Regiment N.C. Troops
(11th N.C. Volunteers)*

William was born in 1825. He worked as a ditcher, and, in 1841, he married Mary. William and Mary would have four children, John (1843), Eliza (1845), Samuel (1846), and Rebecca (1850), before William volunteered on May 8, 1861. He was reported present until he was wounded at Winchester, Virginia, on May 25, 1862. William died of his wounds in Charlottesville, Virginia, on August 15, 1862.

611. Haithcock, Solomon

*Private, Confederate Guards
Company K, 48th Regiment N.C. Troops*

Solomon was born in 1840 to Nicholas and Nancy Haithcock. He worked as a farmer prior to being conscripted on August 8, 1862. Solomon was wounded in the side at Bristoe Station, Virginia, (October 14, 1863) and in the right shoulder at Wilderness, Virginia, (May 5, 1864). He was hospitalized until he rejoined his company prior to July 1864. Solomon was reported present until he was captured at Hatcher's Run, Virginia, on March 25, 1865. He was confined at Point Lookout, Maryland, until June 27, 1865, when he was released after taking the oath of allegiance. No further records.

612. Haley, Harrison

*Private, Company B, 48th Regiment
N.C. Troops*

Harrison was born on October 1, 1840, to Charles and Sarah Haley. He married Cornelia prior to 1859. Harrison and Cornelia would have one child, Emma (1860), before Harrison volunteered at Camp Magnum, Raleigh, on April 3, 1862. He was present or accounted for until he was wounded at Hatcher's Run, Virginia, on February 5, 1865. After the war, he returned home to the Clemmonsville township, where he and his wife would have three more children: Mary (1866), Jennie (1866), and Adeline (1869). Harrison lived in the Clemmonsville area until his death on July 24, 1871. He is buried at Mount Pleasant United Methodist Church.

613. Haley, Thomas

*Private, Company C, 70th Regiment
N.C. Troops (1st N.C. Volunteers)*

Thomas was born on July 5, 1846, to William and Edith Haley. He worked as a farmer prior to enlisting in the Junior Reserves on May 24, 1864. After his service he returned home. The 1900 Census lists one daughter, Sibly (1899), in the household. He died on October 1, 1909. He is buried at Good Hope United Methodist Church.

614. Hall, John Alexander

*Private, Perquimans Beaureguards
Company F, 27th Regiment N.C. Troops*

John was born on July 22, 1824. He worked as a farmer and married Mary A. Dorsett prior to 1855. John was conscripted into service in Randolph County on December 3, 1863. He was reported present until he was wounded at Wilderness, Virginia, on May 5, 1864. John recovered from his wounds and returned to service on November 1, 1864. John survived the duration of the war and was paroled at Greensboro, North Carolina, on May 15, 1865. After the war, John returned to his Thomasville township home, which was just a few feet from the Randolph County line. John, who was a member of the Masonic order, died on November 18, 1890. He is buried at Pleasant Hill United Methodist Church.

615. Hall, John Masten

Private, Company A, 42nd Regiment N.C. Troops

John was born in 1820. He worked as a farmer, and, on November 21, 1846, he married Rachael Fouts. John was conscripted into service in Halifax County on March 4, 1863. He was reported present through October 1864 and was hospitalized at Greensboro, North Carolina, on March 11, 1865. No further records.

616. Hall, John Thomas

Private, Trojan Regulators Company F, 44th Regiment N.C. Troops

John was born on January 31, 1840. He married Ettia Elizabeth prior to 1860. John and Ettia would have one child: Eliza Jane (1862), before John was conscripted into service in Montgomery County on October 9, 1862. He was reported present until he was wounded at Wilderness, Virginia, on May 5, 1864. John was paroled at Salisbury, North Carolina, on May 2, 1865. After the war, John returned to the Emmons township where he and Ettia would have another child, Thomas (1869), before moving to Montgomery County after 1880. John lived in Montgomery County until his death on August 10, 1917. He is buried at Lanes Chapel Methodist Church.

617. Hall, M. Mumford

Private, Company C, 70th Regiment N.C. Troops (1st N.C. Junior Reserves)

Mumford was born in 1847. He worked as a farmer prior to enlisting in the Junior Reserves on May 24, 1864. After his service, Mumford returned to the Thomasville township, and, in 1876, he married Temperance. Mumford and Temperance would have three children, Albert (1879), Tura (1882), and Nora (1887), before moving to Randolph County after 1900. No further records.

618. Hall, Robert B.

Private, Company F, 7th Regiment N.C. Troops

Robert was born in 1841 to Daniel and Melinda Hall. He worked as a farmer in the Jackson Hill area before volunteering in Rowan County on March 1, 1862. He was wounded at Ox Hill, Virginia, on September 1, 1862. Robert recovered from his wounds and rejoined the company in May 1863. He was reported present for the duration of the war and was paroled at Greensboro, North Carolina, on May 1, 1865. No further records.

619. Hall, William S.

Private, Stanly Marksmen Company H, 14th Regiment N.C. Troops (4th N.C. Volunteers)

William was born on October 3, 1830. He worked as a farmer in the Allegheny township, and, on May 5, 1860, he married Adeline Burke. William was conscripted into service in Wake County on July 15, 1862. He was reported present until he was wounded at Chancellorsville, Virginia, on May 3, 1863. William recovered from his wounds and returned to service in July 1863. He was reported present until he was paroled at Appomattox Court House, Virginia, on April 9, 1865. After the war, he returned home to Adeline, and the two moved to Montgomery County before 1870. William died on May 10, 1911. He is buried at Lanes Chapel Methodist Church.

620. Hammer, Alvin R.

Private, Company G, 2nd Battalion, N.C. Infantry

Alvin was born in 1846 to Isaac and Melinda Hammer. He worked as a farmer prior to being conscripted on February 8, 1865. He was hospitalized at Richmond, Virginia, on February 24, 1865. Alvin was issued a 60-day furlough on March 16, 1865. After the war, Alvin returned home to Arcadia and married Wilma in 1875. Alvin and Wilma would have one child, Louise (1876), before moving to

Forsyth County prior to 1880. No further records.

621. Hammer, Solomon A.

Private, Company G, 2nd Battalion, N.C. Infantry

Solomon was born in 1842 to Isaac and Melinda Hammer. He worked as a farmer prior to volunteering in Forsyth County on September 19, 1861. Solomon was present until he was captured at Roanoke Island, North Carolina, on February 8, 1862. He was captured another time and was "absent in the hands of the enemy" until April 1865. No further records.

622. Hamner, William B.

Second Lieutenant, Company B, 48th Regiment N.C. Troops

William was born on December 9, 1831, to William H. and Delilah Hamner. He worked as a harness maker in his father's saddlery. On January 7, 1854, he married Jemina Yarbrough. Jemina would bear one child, Robert (1857), before her death in 1858. William volunteered for service on March 9, 1862, and was mustered in as a first sergeant. He was elected second lieutenant on October 20, 1862, and was reported present until he was paroled at Greensboro, North Carolina, on May 1, 1865. After the war, William returned to the Lexington saddlery and continued his work. In 1867, he married Catharine Conrad. William and Catharine would have three children: Mary Ann (1868), Gertrude (1872), and William (1878). William lived in Lexington until his death on June 8, 1917. He is buried in the Lexington City Cemetery.

623. Hampton, William B.

Major, Staff, 66th Regiment N.C. Militia (1861 organization)

William was born on January 16, 1830. He worked as a planter in the Clemmonsville area and accepted a commission as major on November 25, 1861. He served as major in the 66th Regiment N.C. Militia. After his service, he returned home and freed his 25 slaves according to the 13th Amendment. He lived as a bachelor until he married Sarah Jackson in 1882. William and Sarah would have two children: John (1884) and Charlie (1891). William died on March 10, 1911. He is buried at Centenary United Methodist Church.

624. Hanak, William

Private, Davidson Guards
Company A, 21st Regiment N.C. Troops
(11th N.C. Volunteers)

William was born in 1816. He worked as a farmer in the northern district of Davidson County prior to volunteering at age 45 on May 8, 1861. William was present through September 1, 1861. No further records.

625. Hanes, Christian

Private, Company K, 15th Regiment
N.C. Troops (5th N.C. Volunteers)

Christian was born on March 24, 1836, to David and Sarah Fishel Hanes. He worked as a farmer, and, on May 11, 1858, he married Barbara Temple. Christian was conscripted into service on July 15, 1862, and died of disease at Richmond, Virginia, on September 5, 1862. He is buried in the Hollywood Cemetery in Richmond.

626. Hanes, Edwin L.

Private, Confederate Guards
Company K, 48th Regiment N.C.
Troops

Edwin was born in northern Davidson County. He worked as a farmer, and, on June 25, 1852, he married Ruth A. Davis. Edwin was conscripted on August 8, 1862. He was killed in action at Sharpsburg, Maryland, on September 17, 1862.

627. Hanes, John C.

Private, Company C, 70th Regiment
N.C. Troops (1st N.C. Junior
Reserves)

John was born on October 13, 1846, to Solomon and Catharine Hanes. He worked as a farmer prior to enlisting in the Junior Reserves on May 24, 1864. After the war, John returned to the Yadkin township, where on February 20, 1868, he married Nancy Temple. John and Nancy would have five children: Sarah (1869), Dora (1871), Thurston (1879), Seth (1884), and Flora (1888). John lived in the Yadkin township until his death on July 6, 1916. He is buried at Good Hope United Methodist Church.

This home was built in 1879 by former militia major and county magistrate William B. Hampton (Touart, *Building the Backcountry*).

628. Hanes, Jonathan

Private, Davidson Guards
Company A, 21st Regiment N.C. Troops
(11th N.C. Volunteers)

Jonathan was born on February 1, 1833, to David and Sarah Fishel Hanes. He operated a grist mill, and, on June 17, 1857, he married Susanna Leatherman. Jonathan and Susanna would have two children, Tryphenia (1858) and Matthew (1860), before Jonathan volunteered for service on May 8, 1861. He was reported present until he was captured at Petersburg, Virginia, on April 2, 1865. Jonathan was confined at Hart's Island, New York, until June 17, 1865, when he was released after taking the oath of allegiance. After the war, he returned to the Arcadia township. Jonathan and Susanna would have two more children who survived infancy: David (1866) and Laura (1870). Jonathan died on January 4, 1900. He is buried at Mount Olivet United Methodist Church.

629. Hanes, Joseph B.

Second Lieutenant, 66th Regiment
N.C. Militia (1861 organization)

Joseph worked as a farmer prior to accepting a commission in the Reedy Creek District Company on December 26, 1861. No further records.

630. Hanes, Lewis Clark

Quartermaster (Captain), 48th Regiment N.C. Troops

Lewis was born on August 31, 1827. He lived in the town of Lexington and worked as a clerk of court and a notary public. On May 24, 1848, he married Mary C. Eccles. Mary died before 1851. On July 21, 1851, he married Louisa Thompson. Lewis and Louisa would have two children, Charles (1854) and James (1857), before he volunteered on March 21, 1862, and was appointed first lieutenant of Company B, 48th Regiment N.C. Troops. He was promoted to captain and assigned as regimental quartermaster on July 8, 1862. Lewis served as quartermaster until he was assigned to the Quartermaster's Depot in Salisbury, North Carolina, on August 4, 1864. Louisa died in January 1865, and Lewis married Lenora Humphreys on February 21, 1865. Lewis was paroled at Greensboro, North Carolina, on May 3, 1865. After the war, he returned home to Lexington. Lewis and Lenora would have four children: Mary (1866), Lewis (1868), Susan (1872), and Myrtle (1877). Lewis was a substantial investor, a clerk of court, and an agent for his own life and fire insurance company. He lived in Lexington until his death on January 24, 1905. He is buried in the Lexington City Cemetery.

631. Hanes, Phillip

Private, Davidson Guards
Company A, 21st Regiment N.C. Troops
(11th N.C. Volunteers)

Phillip was born in 1837 to Solomon and Catharine Link Hanes. He worked as a farmer and married his second cousin Susanna Hanes on August 20, 1857. Phillip volunteered for service on May 8, 1861. He died of typhoid fever at Danville, Virginia, on July 15, 1861.

632. Haney, Thomas S.

Private, Company A, 10th Battalion,
N.C. Heavy Artillery

Thomas was born in 1837. He married Catharine prior to 1862. Thomas volunteered for service on March 13, 1862, was reported present for the duration of the war, and was paroled at Greensboro, North Carolina, on May 5, 1865. After the war, he returned home to Thomasville, where he and Catharine would have two children: Luella (1865) and John (1867). No further records.

633. Hannah, Emory Columbus

Private, Company C, 70th Regiment
N.C. Troops (1st N.C. Junior
Reserves)

Emory was born in 1847 to Dr. Solomon and Jane Hannah. He worked as a farmer prior to enlisting in the Junior Reserves on May 24, 1864. Emory died at Drewery's Bluff, Virginia, in January 1865.

634. Hannah, Levi Columbus

Private, Montgomery Boys
Company K, 34th Regiment N.C.
Troops

Levi was born on March 5, 1824, to Solomon and Jane Hannah. He worked as a farmer and married Temperance before 1860. Levi was conscripted into service at Camp Holmes, North Carolina, on December 3, 1863. He was reported present until he was wounded in the back at Spotsylvania Court House, Virginia, on May 12, 1864. Levi was reported absent, wounded, through October 1864. After the war, he returned home to the Allegheny township where he died on October 15, 1912. He is buried in the Hannah Family Cemetery in New Hope, Randolph County.

Jesse Hamilton Hargrave, Jr., whose home is pictured above, served as a company commander, colonel of the Home Guard, and one of the county's premier attorneys (Touart, ***Building the Backcountry***).

635. Hardister, Leonard W.

Private, Company K, 5th Regiment
N.C. State Troops

Leonard was born on August 9, 1843. He worked as a farmer prior to being conscripted into service in Wake County on July 15, 1862. Leonard deserted on September 14, 1862, and returned to service in June 1864. He was reported absent, sick, in December 1864 and was paroled at Salisbury, North Carolina, on May 29, 1865. After the war, he returned to the Jackson Hill township where he died on October 27, 1895. He is buried at Pine Hill United Methodist Church.

636. Hargrave, Alexander H.

Private, Company A, 10th Battalion
N.C. Heavy Artillery

Alexander was born on October 22, 1841, to Jesse Hamilton and Elizabeth Lindsey Hargrave. He worked as a small planter prior to volunteering on April 3, 1862. Alexander was reported present through September 1864. After the war, he moved to the Abbott's Creek township where he married Phoebe J. Bodenheimer in 1875. Alexander died on February 3, 1903. He is buried at Abbott's Creek Missionary Baptist Church.

637. Hargrave, Jesse Hamilton, Jr.

Captain, Lexington Wildcats
Company I, 14th Regiment N.C. Troops
(4th N.C. Volunteers)
Lieutenant Colonel, 14th N.C. Home
Guard

Jesse was born on November 17, 1838, to Jesse Hamilton and Elizabeth Lindsey Hargrave. He worked as an attorney, and in 1860, he married Martha Clement. Jesse practiced law until he volunteered for service on May 14, 1861; he was elected captain the same day. Jesse was reported present until April 26, 1862, when he resigned after being defeated for reelection. He returned home and was appointed to the post of lieutenant colonel, commanding the 14th N.C. Home Guard, in October 1863. The majority of the correspondence between Colonel Hargrave and the Home Guard command involved enforcing conscription and organizing two Home Guard units in the county. Jesse was credited with the ongoing production of lead at the Silver Hill mine and with the investigation of arson on railroad bridges in the county. For three weeks in July 1864, Jesse functioned as the commander of all Home Guard forces in the Piedmont and was headquartered at Asheboro, North Carolina, until the arrival of Brigadier

General Collet Leventhorpe. After the war, Jesse and his compatriot J. M. Leach sued the U.S. government to recover the cost of the courthouse, which had been burned inside while it was being used as a barracks by the 12th Michigan Cavalry Regiment. In one of the few acts of concern, the men of the 12th Michigan had come running out of the courthouse with boxes of crucial county records, preserving them for future generations. Jesse did not win the suit. Jesse died on October 20, 1879. He is buried in the Lexington City Cemetery.

638. Hargrave, Jesse Hamilton, Sr.

Colonel, 3rd Regiment N.C. Home Guard, 3rd Class

Jesse was born on November 17, 1816. He worked as an attorney and as a planter before he married Elizabeth Lindsey on October 24, 1843. Jesse and Elizabeth would have seven children: Jesse Hamilton (1838), Alexander (1841), Tullia (1844), John (1846), Ida (1850), Sarah (1857), and Matilda (1858). Jesse was commissioned as commander of the 3rd N.C. Home Guard in Lexington on April 15, 1865. After his service he continued to live in Lexington until his death on October 16, 1869. He is buried in the Lexington City Cemetery.

639. Hargrave, Robert B.

Sergeant, Lexington Wildcats Company I, 14th Regiment N.C. Troops (4th N.C. Volunteers)

Robert was born on October 11, 1841, to Alfred and Susan Owen Hargrave. He was studying at Yadkin Institute before he volunteered on May 14, 1861. Robert was promoted to sergeant on April 25, 1862. He was reported present until he was killed in action at Chancellorsville, Virginia, on May 3, 1863. His body was sent home to his family and he was interred in the Lexington City Cemetery. His stone reads: "Fell at the battle of Chancellorsville, May 3, 1863. Aged 21 yrs. 6 mos. And 22 days. His remains were brought home and buried here May 28, 1863. C. S. A."

640. Hargrave, Samuel

Lieutenant Colonel, 3rd Regiment N.C. Home Guard, 3rd Class

Samuel was born on December 14, 1807. He worked as a planter before receiving a commission with the N.C. Home Guard, 3rd Class, which was organized on the eve of the battle of York Hill on April 15, 1865. He died on August 29, 1865. He is buried in the Lexington City Cemetery.

641. Harley, Jesse

Private, Company B, 48th Regiment N.C. Troops

Jesse was born in 1840. He worked as a farmer prior to being "transferred to" the 42nd Regiment on February 22, 1864. He was reported present until he was hospitalized at Richmond, Virginia, on August 17, 1864. Jesse was furloughed for 60 days on September 8, 1864. He was reported present in October 1864. No further records.

642. Harmon, Charles

Private, Confederate Guards Company K, 48th Regiment N.C. Troops

Charles was born in 1844 to Valentine and Elizabeth Harmon. He worked as a farmer prior to being conscripted into service on August 8, 1862. Charles died of disease at Upperville, Virginia, on October 30, 1862.

643. Harmon, Hamilton Valentine

Corporal, Company G, 2nd Battalion, N.C. Infantry

Hamilton was born in 1834. He worked as a farmer prior to volunteering in Forsyth County on September 19, 1861. Ham was captured at Roanoke Island, North Carolina, on February 8, 1862, and was paroled at Elizabeth City, North Carolina, on February 22, 1862. He was promoted to corporal in January 1863. He was reported present until he was captured at Petersburg, Virginia, on March 25, 1865. Ham was confined aboard the hospital steamer *Hero of the Jersey* before being admitted to the U.S. General Hospital in Baltimore, Maryland, on May 19, 1865, with "gunshot wound in the left temporal region of the face, inverted bone and loss of the left eye." Hamilton was sent to Fort McHenry, Maryland, where he was released on June 9, 1865, after taking the oath of allegiance. After the war, Hamilton returned to the Thomasville township. On January 12, 1871, he mar-

ried Rebecca M. Beard, who had been nursing him. Ham and Rebecca would have two children: Leona (1876) and Numa (1878). Hamilton died on April 1, 1917. He is buried at Midway United Methodist Church.

644. Harmon, James Madison

Private, Confederate Guards Company K, 48th Regiment N.C. Troops

James was born prior to 1832. He worked as a farmer in the northern district of Davidson County, and, on June 5, 1856, he married Phoebe Weaver. He was conscripted on August 8, 1862. James was reported present until he died of "phthisis pulmonalis" in Lynchburg, Virginia, on January 22, 1863.

645. Harris, Arlindo P.

Private, Company A, 66th Regiment N.C. Troops

Arlindo was born in 1845. He worked as a farmer prior to being conscripted into service in Orange County on February 24, 1863. Arlindo was reported present until he was wounded in an unspecified engagement on July 3, 1864. After the war, Arlindo returned home. In 1870, he married Caroline Lambeth. Arlindo and Caroline would have three children: Edgar (1871), Montgomery (1878), and William (1882). Arlindo lived in the Conrad Hill township until his death in 1920. He is buried at Liberty Baptist Church.

646. Harris, Calvin G.

Private, Company A, 10th Battalion, N.C. Heavy Artillery

Calvin was born on December 22, 1845, to William and Caroline Harris. He worked as a farmer prior to being conscripted on January 20, 1864. Calvin was reported present until he was paroled at Center Church, Randolph County, on April 29, 1865. After the war, he returned to the Healing Springs township. On October 13, 1869, he married Ellen Fitzgerald Hayden. Calvin and Ellen would have six children: Essey (1871), Della (1873), Jenny (1875), Charles (1877), William (1882), and Tinkie (1885). Calvin lived in the Healing Springs area until his death on March 7, 1905. He is buried at Macedonia United Methodist Church.

647. Harris, Emsley Lee

*First Lieutenant, Company I, 42nd
Regiment N.C. Troops*

Emsley was born in 1839 to Emsley and Patience Roberts Harris. He worked as a farmer prior to volunteering on March 6, 1862. Emsley was appointed second lieutenant on July 1, 1862, and then first lieutenant on December 23, 1862. Emsley was reported present until he was wounded in the arm at Kinston, North Carolina, in March 1865. After the war, he returned home to the Emmons township, and on January 4, 1866, he married Miranda Williams. Emsley and Miranda would have one child: William (1869). Emsley lived in the Emmons township until he died on December 30, 1910. He is buried at New Jerusalem United Church of Christ.

648. Harris, Frank A.

*Private, Davidson Guards
Company A, 21st Regiment N.C. Troops
(11th N.C. Volunteers)*

Frank was born in 1844 to H. W. and Mahalia Harris. Frank worked as a farmer before he volunteered for service on May 8, 1861, and was mustered in as a sergeant. He was wounded in the left wrist at Fort Stedman, Virginia, on March 25, 1865. Frank was sent to a Richmond, Virginia, hospital and was captured there in the city's fall on April 3, 1865. After the war, he returned home to the Clemmonsville township. Frank married Jane E. Wagner on April 27, 1866. No further records.

649. Harris, George Washington

*Private, Davidson Guards
Company A, 21st Regiment N.C.
Troops (11th N.C. Volunteers)*

George was born in 1823. He worked as a farmer in the southern district of Davidson County, and, on April 14, 1853, he married Elizabeth Kearns. George and Elizabeth would have three children, Martha (1856), Clay (1861), and Robert (1862), before George was conscripted on July 25, 1862. He deserted on February 10, 1864, and returned to duty before September 19, 1864, when he was wounded and captured at Winchester, Virginia. George was confined at Point Lookout, Maryland, until November 15, 1864, when he was paroled and transferred for exchange at Venus Point, Georgia. After the war, he and his family moved to Lexington. George lived in the town of Lexington until his death on August 1, 1898. He is buried in the Lexington City Cemetery.

650. Harris, Gray W.

*Private, General Bragg Guards
Company G, 8th Regiment N.C. State
Troops*

Gray was born on June 11, 1830. He worked as a farmer, and, in 1855, he married Elizabeth. Gray and Elizabeth would have two children, John (1857) and Walter (1860), before Gray volunteered for service in Pitt County on September 9, 1861. He was captured at Roanoke Island, North Carolina, on February 8, 1862, and was exchanged in August 1862. Gray was reported present until he was captured along the Weldon Railroad near Petersburg, Virginia, on February 1, 1865. He was confined at Point Lookout, Maryland, until he was paroled and transferred to Boulware's Wharf, Virginia, on March 16, 1865, for exchange. After the war, Gray returned to his family in the Emmons township. Gray and Elizabeth would have six more children: Thomas (1863), Willis (1868), James (1869), Cornelia (1873), William (1875), and Sally (1880). Gray died on March 10, 1898. He is buried at Fairview United Methodist Church.

651. Harris, Hammet J.

*Captain, Company A, 10th Battalion,
N.C. Heavy Artillery*

Hammet was born on March 8, 1826. He worked as a farmer, and in 1851, he married Harriet Lines from Connecticut. Hammet and Harriet would have four children, Emira (1853), Thomas (1855), Hammet (1856), and William (1860), before Hammet enlisted on April 26, 1862. He was promoted to first lieutenant on July 11, 1862. When the commander of Company A resigned after being charged with conduct unbecoming an officer, Hammet was appointed captain on March 23, 1863. Hammet was reported present until he was hospitalized at Greensboro, North Carolina, in March 1865. He was paroled at Asheboro, North Carolina, on April 29, 1865. After the war, Hammet returned to Thomasville where he and Harriet would have two more children: Robert Lee (1869) and Hattie J. (1870). Hammet worked as a house carpenter until his death on September 30, 1889. He was a member of the Masonic order. He is buried in the Thomasville City Cemetery. His stone reads, "Mason, and a devoted father at rest."

652. Harris, Isham

*First Sergeant, Davidson Guards
Company A, 21st Regiment N.C. Troops
(11th N.C. Volunteers)*

Isham was born in 1838. He worked as a farmer prior to volunteering on May 8, 1861. Isham was promoted to first sergeant on April 26, 1862, and was wounded in the foot at Winchester, Virginia, on May 25, 1862. Isham recovered from his wounds and was reported present until he was killed in action at Hazel River, Virginia, on August 22, 1862.

653. Harris, James Edward

*Sergeant, Company A, 10th Battalion,
N.C. Heavy Artillery*

James was born in 1843 to William and Eveline Finch Harris. He worked as a farmer prior to enlisting on July 1, 1862. James was promoted to sergeant in September 1862. He was reported present until he was wounded and captured at Bentonville, North Carolina, on March 19, 1865. James was confined at David's Island, New York, until May 1865, when he was released after taking the oath of allegiance. After the war, James married Carolyn Reid on October 4, 1865. James lived in the Emmons township until his death in 1908. He is buried at Lick Creek Baptist Church.

654. Harris, Jesse B.

*Private, Lexington Wildcats
Company I, 14th Regiment N.C.
Troops (4th N.C. Volunteers)*

Jesse was born in 1839 to William and Caroline Harris. He worked as a farmer prior to volunteering on May 14, 1861. He was detailed as a miner on October 10, 1862, and served in that capacity for the duration of the war. After the war, Jesse returned to the Cotton Grove township where he married Annie in 1867. Jesse and Annie would have one child, James (1869), before they moved out of the county in 1882. No further records.

655. Harris, L.

Private, Company C, 70th Regiment
N.C. Troops (1st N.C. Volunteers)

L. enlisted in the Junior Reserves on May 24, 1864. No further records.

656. Harris, Samuel

Second Lieutenant, 65th Regiment
N.C. Militia

Sam was born on March 28, 1836, to William and Eveline Finch Harris. He worked as a farmer, and, on April 7, 1858, he married Emily H. Myers. Sam and Emily would have four children: Melankthan (1861), Charles (1863), Patrick (1867), and Maria (1874). Sam accepted a commission in the Thomasville District Company on December 26, 1861. Sam lived in the Thomasville township until his death on February 11, 1904. He is buried at Fair Grove United Methodist Church.

657. Harris, Thomas Jefferson

Private, Company H, 48th Regiment
N.C. Troops

Thomas volunteered on March 6, 1862, and was mustered in as a corporal. He later enlisted illegally in the 59th N.C. under the pretense of "having received a discharge from the 48th Regiment." Thomas was apprehended by his officers and "taken back, where he was reduced in ranks" on August 1, 1863. After this fiasco, Thomas was reported present through December 7, 1864. No further records.

658. Harris, Turner

Private, Company C, 61st Regiment
N.C. Troops

Turner was born on November 1, 1829. He worked as a farmer, and, in 1859, he married Sarah Wood. Turner and Sarah would have one child, Andrew (1860), before Turner was conscripted into service in Wake County on August 27, 1862. He was captured at Kinston, North Carolina, on December 4, 1862. Turner returned to duty on August 23, 1863, and was detailed to serve as a teamster in September 1864. After the war, Turner returned home to Sarah, and their family would include five more children: Turner (1863), Jerome (1865), Julius (1865), Cora (1871), and Elizabeth (1879).

Turner died on August 23, 1906. He is buried at Canaan United Methodist Church.

659. Harris, Wiley N.

Private, Lexington Wildcats
Company I, 14th Regiment N.C.
Troops (4th N.C. Volunteers)

Wiley was born in 1835. He worked as a farmer prior to volunteering on May 26, 1861. Wiley was arrested for desertion on September 24, 1864, but was released and returned to service on March 1, 1865. Wiley was paroled at Appomattox Court House, Virginia, on April 9, 1865. No further records.

660. Harris, William B.

Private, Davidson Guards
Company A, 21st Regiment N.C.
Troops (11th N.C. Volunteers)
Company I, 1st Regiment U.S. Volunteer Infantry

William was born in 1845 to H. W. and Mahalia Harris. He worked as a farmer prior to volunteering on May 8, 1861. He was discharged because he was under age. William married Mary in 1863, and they would have one child, James (1864). William reenlisted on January 27, 1864. William was present until he was captured in the battle of Cold Harbor, Virginia, on June 8, 1864. He was confined at Point Lookout, Maryland, until June 22, 1864, when he was released after joining the U.S. Army. After the war, William and Mary would have two more children while living in the Allegheny township: William (1867) and Dora (1868). William and Mary left the county prior to 1880. No pension was drawn on William's one-year period of service in the Union Army. No further records.

661. Harrison, Harris

Private, Company G, 66th Regiment
N.C. Troops

Harris was born on August 8, 1844, to James and Sarah Harrison. He worked as a farmer prior to being conscripted into service in Lenoir County on September 11, 1862. After the war, Harris married Margaret J. Riley on December 17, 1865. Harris and Margaret would have three children together: John R. (1867), Elizabeth (1870), and Albert (1875). Har-

ris lived in the Emmons township until his death sometime after 1900. He is buried at Tom's Creek Primitive Baptist Church.

662. Harrison, James Chandler

Private, Chatam Light Infantry
Company D, 48th Regiment N.C.
Troops

James was born in 1836 to James and Elizabeth Harrison. He worked as a farmer prior to being conscripted on August 14, 1862. James was reported present until he was wounded at Bristoe Station, Virginia, on October 14, 1863. He recovered from his wounds and rejoined the company in January 1864. James was reported present until he was wounded at Wilderness, Virginia, on May 5, 1864. His wounds were so severe that he was retired to the Invalid Corps on December 27, 1864. After the war, James returned home to the Jackson Hill township and lived with his parents until he was married to Ellen Newsom sometime after 1880. James and Ellen did not have any children of their own, however, they did adopt several orphaned children. James continued his farming and also worked as a schoolteacher part time. James died between 1907 and 1909. He is buried on the Nolen Reid farm, which is located three miles south of Denton, North Carolina.

663. Harrison, John E.

Private, Wilmington Light Artillery
Company E, 10th Regiment N.C. State
Troops (1st N.C. Artillery)

John was born on April 1, 1830, to James and Sarah Harrison. He worked as a farmer prior to being conscripted into service in Wake County on September 9, 1863. John deserted in June 1864. After the war, John married Mary, John and Mary lived in the Jackson Hill township until John died on December 22, 1904. He is buried at Tom's Creek Primitive Baptist Church. His stone reads: "In my father's house are many mansions."

664. Harrison, Joseph A. C.

Private, Company A, 10th Battalion,
N.C. Heavy Artillery

Joseph was born in 1823. He worked as a farmer in the southern district of Davidson County, and, in 1847, he married Elizabeth. Joseph and Elizabeth would have eight children: William (1848), Ben (1850), Nathan (1852), Nancy (1853), Emaline (1857), Moses (1860), Columbus (1861), and Margaret (1867). Joseph was conscripted into service on May 31, 1863, and was reported present through August 1864. Joseph returned home to the Jackson Hill township. No further records.

665. Hart, Henry

Private, Company B, 48th Regiment N.C. Troops

Henry was living by himself in 1860, and he was conscripted into service prior to October 31, 1864. He was paroled at Greensboro, North Carolina, on May 19, 1865. The last records of the Hart family list Henry as married to Cynthia with one child, Isaac, in 1870. No further records.

666. Hartley, Daniel S.

Private, Company K, 15th Regiment N.C. Troops (5th N.C. Volunteers)

Daniel was born in 1836. He operated a mill, and, on November 19, 1859, he married Martha Jane Walser. Daniel and Martha would have one child, John (1861), before Daniel was conscripted into service in Wake County on July 15, 1862. He was captured at Crampton's Pass, Maryland, on September 14, 1862. Daniel was confined at Fort Delaware, Delaware, until October 2, 1862, when he was paroled and transferred to Aiken's Landing, Virginia. Daniel was declared exchanged on November 10, 1862. He was reported present until he was wounded in the left hand on the Weldon Railroad near Petersburg, Virginia, on August 21, 1864. Daniel was reported absent, wounded, and a second child, Dossy, was born in 1864. On March 14, 1865, he was discharged because of his disability from his wounds. After the war, Daniel returned to the Tyro township where he and Martha would have four more children: Perry (1867), Mock (1871), Frances (1874), and Luther (1876). Daniel lived in the Tyro township until his death in 1897. He is buried at St. Luke's Lutheran Church.

667. Hartley, Hiriam Hamilton

Private, Company K, 15th Regiment N.C. Troops (5th N.C. Volunteers)

Beside his family's plantation, this mill (which is now no longer standing) served as the starting point of Hiriam H. Hartley's business career (Edith L. Lumsden, *The Heritage of Davidson County*).

Hiriam was born on September 14, 1839, to John and Elizabeth Swaim Hartley. He worked as a mill owner and a planter at Horseshoe Bend, and, on January 23, 1860, he married Alice Wilson. Hiriam and Alice would have two children, John (1860) and James K. P. (1861), before Hiriam was conscripted in Wake County on July 15, 1862. He was wounded and captured at Crampton's Pass, Maryland, on September 14, 1862. Hiriam was confined at Fort Delaware, Delaware, until October 2, 1862, when he was paroled and transferred to Aiken's Landing, Virginia, for exchange. Hiriam was exchanged on November 10, 1862, and returned to service in January 1863. His third son, Thomas, was born in 1863. Hiriam was reported present for the duration of the war. After the war, Hiriam returned to the Tyro township; he and Alice would have four more children, Daniel (1865), Barton (1868), Alice (1869), and William (1870), before Alice died in 1874. Hiriam married Ellen F. Davis in 1875. Hiriam and Ellen would have six children, Harold (1877), Eugene (1879), Ernest (1881), Jerome (1884), Clarence (1887), and Ellen (1890), before Ellen died in December 1890. Hiriam then married Louise H. Creath, and worked as a miller, and ran a successful farm in the western half of the county. He was a partial owner of the Grimes

Brothers Mill and Moffitt Enterprises, and he served as the first adjutant of the A. A. Hill Camp, United Confederate Veterans. Hiriam was elected to the N.C. House of Representatives for several terms in 1882–86 and again in 1864–1901. Hiriam died on February 24, 1920. He is buried at St. Luke's Lutheran Church.

668. Hartley, James Franklin

Private, Holtsburg Guards Company A, 54th Regiment N.C. Troops

James was born in 1830. He worked as a carpenter and a mechanic, and, on April 28, 1852, he married Margaret McBride. James and Margaret would have two children, John (1853) and Cicero (1857), before James volunteered on March 6, 1862. For much of the time until July 29, 1863, he was transferred to different hospitals for various symptoms of typhoid fever. James was captured at Rappahannock Station, Virginia, on November 7, 1863. He was confined at Point Lookout, Maryland, until he was paroled and transferred to City Point, Virginia, on March 13, 1864, for exchange. He was furloughed for 30 days on March 18, 1864. James was wounded severely in the leg at Winchester, Virginia, on September 19, 1864. He was sent home and was paroled at Salisbury, North Carolina, on May 22,

1865. After the war, James returned to the Tyro township. No further records.

669. Hartley, James K. Polk

Private, Holtsburg Guards
Company A, 54th Regiment N.C. Troops

James was born on April 24, 1840, to James and Elizabeth Swaim Hartley. He worked as a small planter before he volunteered for service on March 6, 1862. James was captured at Rappahannock Station, Virginia, on November 7, 1863. He was confined at Point Lookout, Maryland, until March 15, 1864, when he was paroled and transferred to City Point, Virginia, for exchange. James was declared exchanged and returned to duty on July 20, 1864. He was reported present until he was captured at Stephenson's Depot, Virginia, on July 20, 1864. James was confined at Camp Chase, Ohio, until March 2, 1865, when he was transferred to Boulware's Wharf, Virginia. He arrived on March 11, 1865. After the war, James married Agnes Lanier on October 7, 1868. James and Agnes would have four children: Phillip (1871), Charlie (1881), Hiriam (1883), and J. Early (1888). James worked with his brother, Hiriam, in many of his investments. When the Hartleys sold their mill to the Grimes brothers, James and Hiriam became tobacco manufacturers. By 1900, the Hartley Tobacco Warehouse and Factory had become one of the nation's leading tobacco processors. James lived in Lexington and had another home in the Yadkin College area. James died on August 4, 1921. He is buried at Yadkin College Methodist Church.

670. Hartley, Michael

Private, Company H, 48th Regiment N.C. Troops

Michael was born in 1834 to Nancy Hartley. He worked as a farmer, and, on April 9, 1862, he married Ellen Burke. Michael was conscripted into service at Petersburg, Virginia, on August 8, 1862. He was wounded in the arm at Fredericksburg, Virginia, on December 13, 1862. Michael recovered from his wounds and returned to service on March 1, 1863. Michael was present until he was wounded at Globe Tavern, Virginia, on August 21, 1864. He and Ellen had their first child, Anna, in 1864. He returned to service prior to February 7, 1865, when

he was sent to a hospital in Richmond, Virginia, with a gunshot wound. Michael was furloughed for 60 days on March 24, 1865. After the war, Michael returned to the Midway township where he and Ellen would have one more child, William Henry (1867). Michael died prior to 1880. No further records.

671. Hartley, Thomas Washington

Second Lieutenant, 65th Regiment N.C. Militia (1861 organization)

Thomas was born in 1830. He worked as a farmer, and, on November 26, 1851, he married Sarah Gobble. Thomas and Sarah would have nine children: Maggie (1855), Mattie (1857), Flora (1859), Thomas (1861), Henry (1863), Walter (1865), John (1869), Fanny (1874), and Lena (1878). Thomas accepted a commission in the Reedy Creek District Company on October 1, 1861. Thomas worked as a miller after his term of service. He died on December 27, 1904, and is buried at Friendship Methodist Church.

672. Hartley, William H.

Private, Company E, 42nd Regiment N.C. Troops

William was born in 1843. He worked as a farmer prior to being conscripted into service at Camp French on November 1, 1862. William was reported present until he was wounded and captured at Bentonville, North Carolina, on March 19, 1865. He was confined at Hart's Island, New York, until June 27, 1865, when he was released after taking the oath of allegiance. After the war, William returned to the Clemmonsville township and married Margaret Bowers on January 2, 1867. William and Margaret had one child, Jane (1868), before William moved his family to Yadkin County before 1880. No further records.

673. Hartley, William W.

Private, Lexington Wildcats
Company I, 14th Regiment N.C. Troops (4th N.C. Volunteers)

William was born in 1843. He worked as a farmer prior to volunteering in Northampton County on June 4, 1861. William died of unreported causes at Fort Bee, Virginia, on January 29, 1862.

674. Hartman, John A.

Private, Cleveland Mountain Boys
Company D, 15th Regiment N.C. Troops (5th N.C. Volunteers)
2nd Company B, 49th Regiment N.C. Troops

John was born on June 2, 1843, to Christian and Elizabeth Hartman. He worked as a farmer prior to being conscripted into service in Wake County on July 15, 1862. John was transferred to the 49th Regiment on January 9, 1863. John was reported present until he was captured at Fort Stedman, Virginia, on March 25, 1865. He was confined at Point Lookout, Maryland, until June 27, 1865, when he was released after taking the oath of allegiance. John returned to the Midway township and married Catharine Delapp on August 1, 1869. John and Catharine would have three children: Alexander (1870), Phoebe (1872), and William (1876). John lived in the Midway township until his death on March 16, 1919. He is buried at New Friendship Baptist Church.

675. Harvey, James Estle

Private, Holtsburg Guards
Company A, 54th Regiment N.C. Troops

James was born in 1843 to Thomas and Mary McCarn Harvey. He worked as a miner prior to volunteering on March 6, 1862. James was detailed to work as a lead miner in the Conrad Hill mine on September 10, 1862. James served in this capacity throughout the war and was paroled at Greensboro, North Carolina, on May 6, 1865. After the war, James continued his work in the mines, and, on February 4, 1868, he married Elizabeth Beck. James and Elizabeth would have two children: William (1868) and Elizabeth (1870). The last census record for the family lists them as living in the Silver Hill township in 1870. No further records.

676. Hauser, John W.

Private, Davidson Guards
Company A, 21st Regiment N.C. Troops (11th N.C. Volunteers)

John was born in 1838 to William and Elizabeth Hauser. John worked as a farmer prior to volunteering on May 8, 1861. He was reported present until he was wounded severely at Gettysburg,

Pennsylvania, on July 1, 1863. Jon was reported absent, wounded, through February 1865. No further records.

677. Hayworth, Barnabus

Private, Company A, 42nd Regiment N.C. Troops

Barnabus was born on May 7, 1841, to John and Martha Hayworth. Barnabus worked as a coachmaker's assistant prior to volunteering in Rowan County on March 12, 1862. He died of typhoid fever in Petersburg, Virginia, on October 25, 1862. Barnabus' body was sent home and was interred on November 11, 1862, at Abbott's Creek Missionary Baptist Church.

678. Hayworth, John Franklin

Private, Company E, Colonel Mallet's Battalion (Camp Guard)

John was born in 1830. He worked as a farmer, and, on October 1, 1854, he married Emaline Payne. John and Emaline would have four children, Julius (1855), William (1857), Charles (1859), and Delphina (1862), before John enlisted in Mallet's Battalion. After his service, John returned home to the Abbott's Creek township where he and Emaline would have three more children: Sarah (1865), Reuggen (1867), and Rebecca (1869). John died on March 25, 1902. He is buried at Abbott's Creek Missionary Baptist Church.

679. Hayworth, Sanford S.

Private, North State Boys Company K, 45th Regiment N.C. Troops

Sanford was born on June 17, 1846, to John and Martha Hayworth. He worked as a farmer prior to being conscripted into service in Guilford County on September 1, 1864. Sanford was wounded on April 5, 1865, and was paroled at Appomattox Court House, Virginia, on April 9, 1865. After the war, Sanford returned to the Abbott's Creek township. On April 25, 1866, he married Delphina Davis. Sanford and Delphina would have eight children: Martin (1867), James (1867), Matthew (1869), John (1872), Jane (1874), Addison (1882), David (1887), and Bessie (1889). Sanford lived in the Abbott's Creek area until his death on June 22, 1913. He is buried at Abbott's Creek Primitive Baptist Church.

680. Hayworth, William Andrew

Private, Company G, 2nd Battalion, N.C. Infantry

William was born before 1830. In 1850, William married Cynthia. William and Cynthia would have four children, Martha (1851), Louzena (1856), Caroline (1858), and Daniel (1861), before William was conscripted on July 28, 1864. He was reported absent, wounded, between August and October 31, 1864. William was paroled at Appomattox Court House, Virginia, on April 9, 1865. After the war, William returned home to the Abbott's Creek area where he and Cynthia would have two more children: George (1865) and John (1869). No further records.

681. Healey, John F.

First Lieutenant, Company I, 1st Regiment Confederate Engineers

John was born in Dublin, Ireland, in March 1837. He immigrated to Davidson County in the 1850s to work as an engineer in the Conrad Hill mine. According to his stone, he was a first lieutenant in the 1st Regiment Confederate Engineers. John died on February 25, 1912. He is buried at Lick Creek Baptist Church.

682. Hean, Solomon

Private, Company D, 48th Regiment N.C. Troops

Solomon was born in 1832. He worked as a miner prior to being conscripted into service on August 8, 1862. Solomon was reported present until he was hospitalized with a gunshot wound at Charlottesville, Virginia, on May 7, 1864. He was issued a 60-day furlough on June 8, 1864. Solomon returned to service and was hospitalized at Richmond, Virginia, where he died of dysentery on January 30, 1865. He is buried in the Hollywood Cemetery in Richmond.

683. Hedgecock, Alfred

Private, Davidson Guards Company A, 21st Regiment N.C. Troops (11th N.C. Volunteers)

Alfred was born in 1841 to Barnett and Elizabeth Hedgecock. Alfred worked as a farmer prior to volunteering on May 8, 1861. He was reported present until he was mortally wounded at the battle of Second Manassas on August 28, 1862. Place of burial was not reported.

684. Hedgecock, Jacob C.

Captain, Davidson Guards Company A, 21st Regiment N.C. Troops (11th N.C. Volunteers)

Jacob was born in 1832. He worked as a small planter prior to volunteering on May 8, 1861, when he was mustered in as first lieutenant. When J. M. Leach was appointed major, Jacob was promoted to captain on July 8, 1861. Jacob commanded the Davidson Guards until he "was pierced by a half dozen balls or more" at Winchester, Virginia, on May 25, 1862. It was said of him later: "A braver or truer man was never sent to the field of battle."

685. Hedgecock, William

Private, Company G, 2nd Battalion N.C. Infantry

William was born in 1846 to Barnet and Elizabeth Hedgecock. He worked as a farmer prior to volunteering for service on September 19, 1861. William was reported present until he was killed in action at Gettysburg, Pennsylvania, on July 1, 1863.

686. Hedley, Thornton

Private, Company B, 48th Regiment N.C. Troops

Thornton resided in Davidson County prior to being conscripted into service subsequent to October 31, 1864. He was paroled at Greensboro, North Carolina, on May 6, 1865. No further records.

687. Hedrick, Adam

Private, Company K, 15th Regiment N.C. Troops (5th N.C. Volunteers)

Adam was born on May 24, 1837, to Peter and Rachael Long Hedrick. Adam worked as a farmer, and, on May 5, 1858, he married Mary A. Tussey. Adam and Mary would have one child, Charles (1861), before Adam was conscripted into service in Wake County on July 15, 1862. He was captured at Crampton's Pass, Maryland, on September 14, 1862. Adam was confined at Fort Delaware, Delaware, until October 2, 1862, when he was paroled and transferred to Aiken's Landing, Virginia, for exchange. Adam was exchanged on November 10, 1862, and returned to duty in January 1863. He was reported present until he was captured at Bristoe Station, Virginia, on October 14, 1863. Adam was confined at Point Lookout, Maryland, via Washington, D.C., where he stayed until February 24, 1865, when he was paroled and transferred to Aiken's Landing, Virginia, for exchange. Adam was exchanged and returned to duty on March 31, 1865, only to be captured again the very next day at Hatcher's Run, Virginia, on April 1, 1865. Adam was sent to Point Lookout, Maryland, where he was confined until June 13, 1865, when he was released after taking the oath of allegiance. After the war, Adam returned to the Lexington township where he and Mary would have two more children: Ida (1868) and Halley (1876). Adam died on February 20, 1914. He is buried at Pilgrim Lutheran Church.

688. Hedrick, Adam S.

Corporal, Company B, 48th Regiment N.C. Troops

Adam was born on April 7, 1829. He worked as a farmer, and, on August 3, 1850, he married Ellen M. Ford. Adam and Ellen would only have one child: Druscilla (1851). Adam was conscripted into service on August 8, 1862. He was promoted to corporal and was reported present through October 31, 1864. Adam was paroled at Greensboro, North Carolina, on May 1, 1865. After the war, Adam returned home to the Lexington township, where he continued his farming and was persuaded to serve on the Pilgrim Reform consistory by the Reverend P. A. Long. Adam died on July 15, 1905. He is buried at Pilgrim United Church of Christ.

689. Hedrick, Alfred

Private, Company C, 70th Regiment N.C. Troops (1st N.C. Junior Reserves)

Alfred was born in 1847. He worked as a farmer prior to enlisting in the Junior Reserves on May 24, 1864. After the war, Alfred returned to the Lexington township. He married Louisa Snider on February 22, 1866. Alfred and Louisa would have five children: William (1867), George (1869), Dora (1873), Lula (1875), and Lemuel (1878). No further records.

690. Hedrick, Alfred

Second Lieutenant, 65th Regiment N.C. Militia (1861 organization)

Alfred was born in 1824. He worked as a farmer, and, in 1848, he married Elizabeth Beck. Alfred and Elizabeth would have six children: James (1849), Cicero (1851), Jesse (1853), Susanna (1854), Christina (1858), and Mary (1860). Alfred accepted a commission in the Four Mile Branch District Company on November 25, 1861. No further records.

691. Hedrick, Benjamin Franklin

Private, Company B, 48th Regiment N.C. Troops

Benjamin was born on October 14, 1843, to Benjamin and Mary Swing Hedrick. Ben worked as a farmer prior to volunteering on March 4, 1862. He was wounded in the head at King's School House, Virginia, on June 25, 1862. Ben recovered from his wounds and was reported present until he was paroled at Greensboro, North Carolina, on May 8, 1865. After the war, Ben returned to the Silver Hill township, and, on December 26, 1867, he married Louvina Swing, a second cousin. Ben and Louvina would have four children before her death in 1880: Charles (1869), Thomas (1871), Henry (1873), and James (1876). Benjamin married Amanda Leonard in 1883; they would not have any children. Benjamin lived in the Silver Hill township until his death on July 10, 1931. He is buried at Beck's United Church of Christ.

692. Hedrick, Commodore Decatur

Private, Company D, 16th Missouri Infantry

C. D. was born on July 11, 1829. He worked as a farmer, and, on January 19, 1851, he married Phoebe Briggs. C. D. and Phoebe would have six children: Elizabeth (1852), John (1858), Alben (1860), Alexander (1862), Frank (1864), and Joseph (1869). According to *Broadfoot's Roster of Confederate Soldiers* and a photocopy of a roster for the 16th Missouri, C. D. served in the 16th Missouri, although the exact circumstances of his enlistment in Centrailia, Missouri, are unknown. C. D. returned home to the Silver Hill township and lived there until his death on June 11, 1873. He is buried at Beck's United Church of Christ.

693. Hedrick, Daniel

Private, Company K, 15th Regiment N.C. Troops (5th N.C. Volunteers)

Daniel was born in 1839 to Daniel and Anna Koontz Hedrick. He worked as a farmer, and, on June 1, 1862, he married Albertine Grubb. Daniel was conscripted into service in Wake County on July 15, 1862. He was captured at Crampton's Pass, Maryland, on September 14, 1862. Daniel was confined at Point Lookout, Maryland, until October 2, 1862, when he was paroled and transferred to Aiken's Landing, Virginia, for exchange. Daniel was declared exchanged on November 10, 1862. He was reported present until he died of "variola confluent" in Richmond, Virginia, on February 10, 1863. He is buried in the Hollywood Cemetery in Richmond.

694. Hedrick, David

Private, Company B, 57th Regiment N.C. Troops

David was born in 1843 to John and Christina Hedrick. He worked as a farmer prior to enlisting on July 4, 1862. David was reported present until he was sent to a Liberty, Virginia, hospital on November 8, 1862. He was issued a furlough and returned home, where he died on March 1, 1863. He is buried at Beck's United Church of Christ.

695. Hedrick, David

Private, Company K, 15th Regiment N.C. Troops (5th N.C. Volunteers)

David was born on October 13, 1841, to Daniel and Anna Koontz Hedrick. He worked as a farmer prior to being conscripted into service in Wake County on July 15, 1862. David was captured at Crampton's Pass, Maryland, on September 14, 1862. He was confined at Point Lookout, Maryland, until October 2, 1862, when he was paroled and transferred to Aiken's Landing, Virginia, for exchange. David was declared exchanged on November 10, 1862. He returned to duty in January 1863 and was reported present until he was captured at Hatcher's Run, Virginia, on March 31, 1865. David was confined at Point Lookout, Maryland, until June 27, 1865, when he was released after taking the oath of allegiance. After the war, he returned home and married Alice Hudson on August 15, 1867. David and Alice would have eight children: Frances (1867), Ellen (1872), John (1875), America (1877), Julia (1881), Jesse (1885), David (1888), and J. Early (1895). David died on October 18, 1928. He is buried at Mount Carmel United Methodist Church.

696. Hedrick, George A.

Private, Lexington Wildcats
Company I, 14th Regiment N.C. Troops
(4th N.C. Volunteers)

George was born in 1840 to Benjamin and Mary Swing Hedrick. He worked as a farmer prior to volunteering on May 14, 1861. George was reported present until he was wounded at Spotsylvania Court House, Virginia, on May 12, 1864. George's wounds were so severe that he was retired to the Invalid Corps on October 31, 1864. After the war, George returned to the Silver Hill township where he married Sarah A. Beck on April 9, 1865. George and Sarah would have five children: Thomas (1866), Edward (1869), Elizabeth (1874), George (1876), and Martha Jane (1878). George lived in the Silver Hill township until his death in 1926. He is buried at Beck's United Church of Christ.

697. Hedrick, George Franklin

Private, Company A, 42nd Regiment
N.C. Troops

George was born on August 28, 1841, to John and Phoebe Berrier Hedrick. He worked as a blacksmith prior to being conscripted into service at Petersburg, Virginia, on October 31, 1862. George was reported present until he was captured at Battery Anderson, Fort Fisher, North Carolina, on December 25, 1864. He was confined at Point Lookout, Maryland, until June 13, 1865, when he was released after taking the oath of allegiance. After the war, George married Sarah Sowers on January 16, 1868, and moved to Lexington. George and Sarah would have only one child: Robert Lee (1876). In 1900, George was employed as a labor foreman in the Hartley Tobacco Warehouse. George died on January 21, 1935. He is buried in the Lexington City Cemetery.

698. Hedrick, George M.

Private, Company C, 70th Regiment
N.C. Troops (1st N.C. Junior
Reserves)

George was born in 1846 to John and Sarah Hedrick. He worked as a farmer prior to enlisting in the Junior Reserves on May 24, 1864. George returned home to the Conrad Hill township, and, on May 27, 1869, he married Fanny C. Hanner. George and Fanny would have five children, Emory (1871), Susan (1872), Henry (1873), Louise (1875), and Carol R. (1878), before the family moved out of the county after 1880. No further records.

699. Hedrick, George W.

Sergeant, Company B, 48th Regiment
N.C. Troops

George was born in 1838 to Benjamin and Mary Swing Hedrick. He worked as a farmer prior to volunteering on March 6, 1862. George was mustered in as a sergeant and was reported present until he was wounded at King's School House, Virginia, on June 25, 1862. He died of his wounds on July 22, 1862, in Richmond, Virginia. He is buried at Beck's United Church of Christ.

700. Hedrick, George W.

Private, Carolina Rangers
Company B, 10th Virginia Cavalry
Regiment

George was born on September 22, 1839, to Peter and Mary Bowers Hedrick. He worked as a farmer prior to enlisting in Davie County on October 29, 1861. George was reported present throughout the war, and in July and August 1864, he was reported without a horse. George returned home to the Lexington township where he lived until his death on October 8, 1884. He is buried at Beulah United Church of Christ.

701. Hedrick, Henry

Private, Company K, 15th Regiment
N.C. Troops (5th N.C. Volunteers)

Henry was born on January 25, 1835, to Daniel and Anna Koontz Hedrick. Henry worked as a farmer, and, in 1861, he married Mary Leonard. Henry and Mary would have one child, Eliza (1862), before Henry was conscripted into service in Wake County on July 15, 1862.

Henry was captured at Crampton's Pass, Maryland, on September 14, 1862. He was confined at Point Lookout, Maryland, until October 2, 1862, when he was paroled and transferred to Aiken's Landing, Virginia, for exchange. Henry was declared exchanged on November 10, 1862. He was listed as a deserter until he was discharged because of disability on April 21, 1864. After he returned home with his discharge, Henry and Mary would have another child, David (1865). Henry lived in the Boone township util his death on September 24, 1893. He is buried at Shiloh United Methodist Church.

702. Hedrick, Henry C.

Captain, 65th Regiment N.C. Militia
(1861 organization)

Henry was born on April 6, 1821. He worked as a farmer, and, on January 21, 1847, he married Rachael Kepley. Henry and Rachael would have five children: George (1847), Emily (1851), John H. (1855), Jacob (1858), and Richard (1859). He accepted a commission in the Conrad Hill District Company on November 25, 1861. After his service, he lived in the Conrad Hill area until his death on September 29, 1881. He is buried at Beck's United Church of Christ.

703. Hedrick, Jacob

Private, Company A, Colonel Mallet's
Battalion (Camp Guard)
Company B, 48th Regiment N.C. Troops

Jacob was born on July 16, 1830. He worked as a farmer, and, on March 20, 1858, he married Eliza M. Kepley. Jacob and Eliza would have two children, David (1859) and Abigail (1862), before Jacob enlisted in Mallet's Battalion in the spring of 1862. He was transferred to the 48th Regiment in the early summer of 1864. Jacob was reported present until he was paroled at Greensboro, North Carolina, on May 1, 1865. After the war, Jacob returned to the Silver Hill township where he lived until his death on March 23, 1896. He is buried at Beck's United Church of Christ.

704. Hedrick, Jacob Lindsey

Private, Company C, 70th Regiment
N.C. Troops (1st N.C. Junior
Reserves)

Jacob was born on January 31, 1847, to Benjamin and Mary Swing Hedrick. He worked as a small farmer prior to enlisting in the Junior Reserves on May 24, 1864. After the war, Jacob returned to the Silver Hill township. On October 1, 1874, he married Lundy Jane Leonard. Jacob and Lundy would have three children: Martin (1875), Louisa (1879), and Ida M. (1896). Jacob became a successful farmer in the Silver Hill area where he lived until his death on September 21, 1931. He is buried at Beck's United Church of Christ.

705. Hedrick, Jacob W.

Private, Company B, 48th Regiment
N.C. Troops

Jacob was born in 1842 to Jasper and Mary Hedrick. He worked as a farmer, and, on October 31, 1861, he married Amanda C. Hedrick. Jacob was conscripted on August 8, 1862. He was reported present until he died of "diarrhoea chronic" in Richmond, Virginia, on September 16, 1864.

706. Hedrick, James Franklin

Private, Davidson Guards
Company A, 21st Regiment N.C. Troops
(11th N.C. Volunteers)

James was born in 1846 to Sarah Hedrick. He worked as a farmer prior to enlisting on October 1, 1863. James was reported present until he was wounded at Plymouth, North Carolina, on April 18, 1864. James was hospitalized at Richmond, Virginia, in March 1865, with gunshot wounds of the left and right heels. He was captured in his hospital bed when the city fell on April 3, 1865. James was confined at Newport News, Virginia, until June 30, 1865, when he was released after taking the oath of allegiance. After the war, he returned home, and, on December 26, 1865, he married Sarah Hedrick. James lived in the Emmons township until his death on December 31, 1919. He is buried at New Jerusalem United Church of Christ.

707. Hedrick, Jefferson

Corporal, Company B, 48th Regiment
N.C. Troops

Jefferson was born on November 24, 1842, to Benjamin and Mary Swing Hedrick. He worked as a farmer prior to volunteering on March 4, 1862. Jeff was mustered in as a corporal and on June 25, 1862, he was wounded at King's School House, Virginia. He was hospitalized with chronic diarrhea on January 29, 1864. Jeff returned to duty on March 29, 1864, and was reported present until he was paroled at Appomattox Court House, Virginia. After the war, Jefferson married Eva H. Ward on February 5, 1867. Jefferson and Eva would have two children: Caroline (1868) and Margaret (1871). Jefferson lived in the Sliver Hill area and became a successful farmer as well as a talented woodworker. He died on January 11, 1904, and is buried at Beck's United Church of Christ.

708. Hedrick, John

Private, Company I, 42nd Regiment
N.C. Troops

John was born in 1830. He worked as a farmer prior to volunteering on March 6, 1862. He was reported present until he was hospitalized at Goldsboro, North Carolina, between May 18, 1863, and August 28, 1864. John was issued a 60-day furlough on December 16, 1864. No further records.

709. Hedrick, John Franklin

Corporal, Thomasville Rifles
Company B, 14th Regiment N.C. Troops
(4th N.C. Volunteers)

John was born in 1843 to Jacob and Catharine Hedrick. John was a student prior to volunteering on April 28, 1861. He was promoted to corporal on July 29, 1861. John died of disease at Fort Bee, Virginia, on December 13, 1861.

710. Hedrick, Joseph

Private, Company I, 76th Regiment N.C.
Troops (6th N.C. Senior Reserves)

Joseph was born on March 19, 1816. He worked as a farmer in the southern district of Davidson County, and, on October 4, 1840, he married Catharine Darr. Joseph and Catharine would have three children, Phoebe (1841), Elizabeth (1844), and Sarah (1851), before Joseph enlisted in the Senior Reserves in January 1865. After his service, Joseph continued farming in the Conrad Hill township until his death on June 16, 1871. He is buried at Beck's United Church of Christ.

711. Hedrick, Joseph

Corporal, Company B, 48th Regiment
N.C. Troops

Joseph was born in 1841 to Daniel and Margaret Hedrick. He worked as a farmer and an amateur blacksmith prior to volunteering on March 3, 1862. Joseph was captured while sick in Frederick, Maryland, on September 12, 1862. He was confined at Point Lookout, Maryland, until October 2, 1862, when he was paroled and transferred to Aiken's Landing, Virginia, for exchange. Joseph was declared exchanged on November 10, 1862. Company records state that he "deserted from hospital" in 1864. After the war, Joseph married Elizabeth in 1865. Joseph and Elizabeth would have two children: Cornelia (1866) and Alice (1870). Joseph lived in the Silver Hill township until his death on June 16, 1874. He is buried at Beck's United Church of Christ.

712. Hedrick, Joseph Lafayette

Private, Davidson Guards
Company A, 21st Regiment N.C. Troops
(11th N.C. Volunteers)

Joseph was born about 1847 to Jacob and Mary Hedrick. He worked as a farmer prior to enlisting in Lenoir County on January 27, 1864. Joseph was reported present until he was captured at Fort Stedman, Virginia, on March 25, 1865. He was confined at Point Lookout, Maryland, until June 28, 1865, when he was released after taking the oath of allegiance. After the war, Joseph returned home and married Laura Ann Everhart on February 18, 1868. Joseph and Laura would have three children: James (1869), Emmit (1872), and Bessie (1875). No further records.

713. Hedrick, Michael L.

Private, Lexington Wildcats
Company I, 14th Regiment N.C. Troops
(4th N.C. Volunteers)

Michael was born in 1835 to Captain Jacob and Barbara Hedrick. He was a student under the tutelage of the Reverend P. A. Long of Pilgrim Reform before he was conscripted into service in Wake County on July 15, 1862. Michael was reported present through August 1864. After the war, Michael returned home to the Silver Hill township. In 1865, Michael married Amanda Jane. Michael and Amanda would have seven children: Charles (1865), James (1868), Alice (1871), Emma (1873), Susan (1875), Sarah (1878), and Ellen (1882). Michael was ordained into the German Reform church and served as the pastor for Beck's Reform for a period of time. Michael died on July 8, 1884. He is buried at Beck's United Church of Christ.

714. Hedrick, Moses L.

Private, Company C, 70th Regiment N.C. Troops (1st N.C. Junior Reserves)

Moses was born in 1847, the son of Jesse Hedrick. He worked as a farmer prior to enlisting in the Junior Reserves on May 24, 1864. After the war, he returned home to the Silver Hill township and married Jane in 1874. Moses and Jane would have three children: Matthew (1875), Samuel (1878), and Jane (1880). No further records.

715. Hedrick, Phillip E.

Private, Company B, 48th Regiment N.C. Troops

Phillip was born in 1831. He worked as a farmer in the southern district of Davidson County, and, on October 5, 1851, he married Elizabeth Kepley. Phillip and Elizabeth would have four children, Laura (1857), James (1858), Frances (1859), and Wiley (1860), before Phillip was conscripted on August 8, 1862. He deserted near Kenansville, Duplin County, in January 1863. Phillip returned to duty prior to July 1, 1863. He was reported present through December 6, 1864. After the war, Phillip returned to the Conrad Hill township, and he and Elizabeth would have four more children: Charles (1865), Allison (1867), Henry (1868), and Jacob (1874). Phillip died sometime after 1880. He is buried in an unmarked plot at Hedrick's Grove United Church of Christ.

716. Hedrick, Phillip J.

Captain, 65th Regiment N.C. Militia (1861 organization)

Phillip was born on November 13, 1830, to Captain Jacob and Catharine Hedrick. Phillip accepted a commission in the Silver Valley District Company on December 26, 1861. Phillip married Eliz-

abeth Hedrick, a second cousin, on March 20, 1862. Phillip and Elizabeth would have six children: Brantley (1866), Cicero (1871), Martha (1868), George (1872), Catharine (1874), and Edward (1876). Phillip lived in the Emmons township until his death on June 11, 1909. He is buried at Beck's United Church of Christ.

717. Hedrick, Wiley

First Lieutenant, 65th Regiment N.C. Militia (1861 organization)

Wiley was born on March 27, 1836. He worked as a farmer, and, on March 26, 1858, he married Mary Ann Miller. Wiley and Mary would have six children: Albert (1859), Sarah (1861), Mary (1863), Sophronia (1867), Alice (1869), and Hammet (1871). Wiley accepted a commission in the Four Mile Branch District Company on November 25, 1861. Wiley lived in the Silver Hill township until his death on February 12, 1915. He is buried at New Jerusalem United Church of Christ.

718. Hedrick, William D.

Private, Carolina Rangers Company B, 10th Virginia Cavalry Regiment

William was born on February 1, 1841, to Peter and Mary Bowers Hedrick. He worked as a farmer prior to traveling with his friend Hugh Clodfelter to Davie County to volunteer on October 29, 1861. William was reported present until he was wounded in the shoulder in May 1864. He was admitted to a Richmond, Virginia, hospital on May 19, 1864, and was issued a 60-day furlough in July 1864. While at home, William married Lucretia Leonard on September 12, 1864. William was present to receive pay and a clothing ration on December 31, 1864, and he was paroled at Greensboro, North Carolina, on May 1, 1865. After the war,

William and Lucretia would have three children: John (1867), Robert (1870), and Minnie (1872). William lived in the Lexington township and worked for Mosely and Son, Tobacconists, until his death on August 30, 1884. He is buried at Beulah United Church of Christ.

719. Hedrick, William F.

Private, Company C, 70th Regiment N.C. Troops (1st N.C. Junior Reserves)

William was born in 1847 to Valentine and Elizabeth Hedrick. He worked as a farmer prior to enlisting in the Junior Reserves on May 24, 1864. After the war, William returned to the Silver Hill township, and, on August 10, 1870, he married Linda Surratt. No further records.

720. Hedrick, William M.

Captain, 65th Regiment N.C. Militia (1861 organization)

William was born in 1823 to Jacob and Eve Hedrick. He worked as a farmer, and, on May 4, 1848, he married Mary Black. William and Mary would have four children: Lindsey (1850), Anne (1853), Elinor (1864), and John (1867). William accepted a commission in the Hamby's Creek District Company on December 26, 1861. After his service, William returned to the Thomasville township and continued farming. William lived in the Kendall Mill area until his death on December 7, 1896. He is buried at Emanuel United Church of Christ.

Silver Hill home of Militia Captain Phillip J. Hedrick (photograph by author).

721. Hege, Alexander

Private, Company C, 70th Regiment N.C. Troops (1st N.C. Junior Reserves)

Alex was born in 1847. He worked as a farmer prior to enlisting in the Junior Reserves on May 24, 1864. After the war, Alex returned to the Reedy Creek area where, on April 26, 1872, he married Elizabeth Raker. Alex and Elizabeth would have two children: John (1879) and William (1881). Alex died in 1936. He is buried at Good Hope United Methodist Church.

722. Hege, Alexander J.

Private, Company K, 15th Regiment N.C. Troops (5th N.C. Volunteers)

Alexander was born on February 8, 1835, to Valentine and Leah Disher Hege. On September 19, 1857, he married Nancy Scott. Alexander and Nancy would have three children, Fannie (1859), Mary (1860), and Frank (1862), before Alexander was conscripted into service in Wake County on July 15, 1862. He was reported present until he was wounded in both of his eyes and captured at Sharpsburg, Maryland, on September 17, 1862. Alex was confined at Fort McHenry, Baltimore, Maryland, until October 17, 1862, when he was paroled and transferred to Aiken's Landing, Virginia, for exchange. He was declared exchanged on November 10, 1862. Alexander was reported absent, wounded, through October 1864. It can be surmised that he lost all vision in his left eye where the bullet struck the temporal region, and his right eye experienced corneal trauma; however, he recovered partial use of it in later life. Nearly blind, Alexander returned home to the Yadkin township. Alexander and Nancy would have three more children: Susan (1865), William (1871), and Nancy (1878). Alexander died on September 27, 1920. He is buried at Mount Olivet United Methodist Church.

723. Hege, Christian

Private, Company H, 48th Regiment N.C. Troops

Christian was born in 1830 to Valentine and Leah Disher Hege. Christian worked as a farmer, and, on October 13, 1855, he married Charlotte Hanes. Christian and Charlotte would have two children, Edward (1858) and John (1861), before Christian was conscripted on August 8, 1862. Christian was wounded three times during the war: at Sharpsburg, Maryland (September 17, 1862), at Fredericksburg, Virginia (December 13, 1862), and at Bristoe Station, Virginia (October 14, 1863). Christian recovered from all three of his wounds fairly swiftly and was reported present until he deserted to the enemy on March 25, 1865. He was confined at Washington, D.C., until March 30, 1865, when he was released after taking the oath of allegiance. After the war, Christian returned to the Yadkin township where he was living in 1870. No further records.

724. Hege, Constantine A.

Private, Company H, 48th Regiment N.C. Troops

Constantine was born on March 13, 1843, to Solomon and Catharine Gunther Hege. He was a student prior to being conscripted into service on August 8, 1862. Constantine was reported present until he was captured at Bristoe Station, Virginia, on October 14, 1863. He was confined at Washington, D.C., until March 14, 1865, when he was released after taking the oath of allegiance. After the war, Constantine moved to Forsyth County where he was married twice: to Frances Spaugh and to her sister, Martha. A member of the Moravian faith, Constantine died on July 26, 1914. He is buried in "God's Acre," Salem Moravian Cemetery, Winston-Salem, North Carolina.

725. Hege, Eli

Private, Company H, 15th Regiment N.C. Troops (5th N.C. Volunteers)

Eli was born in 1844 to Thomas and Sarah Link Hege. He worked as a farmer prior to being conscripted into service in Wake County on July 15, 1862. Eli was captured at Crampton's Pass, Maryland, on September 14, 1862. He was confined at Point Lookout, Maryland, until October 2, 1862, when he was paroled and transferred to Aiken's Landing, Virginia, for exchange. Eli was declared exchanged on November 10, 1862. He was reported present until he died prior to May 1, 1863, in Richmond, Virginia. Eli is buried in the Hollywood Cemetery in Richmond.

726. Hege, George W.

Private, Davidson Guards Company A, 21st Regiment N.C. Troops (11th N.C. Volunteers)

George was born on February 14, 1843, to Henry and Elizabeth Grimes Hege. He worked as a farmer prior to volunteering on May 8, 1861. George died of typhoid fever at Thoroughfare Gap, Virginia, on September 23, 1861.

727. Hege, Henry J.

Private, Company C, 70th Regiment N.C. Troops (1st N.C. Junior Reserves)

Henry was born on March 29, 1847, to Valentine and Sarah Michael Hege. He worked as a farmer prior to enlisting in the Junior Reserves on May 24, 1864. After the war, Henry returned to the Tyro township. On December 23, 1879, Henry married Melinda Walser. Henry and Melinda would have three children who would all die within three years. Henry died on January 8, 1895. He is buried at Reeds Baptist Church.

728. Hege, Jacob

Private, Confederate Guards Company K, 48th Regiment N.C. Troops

Jacob was born in 1832 to Jacob and Catharine Weisner Hege. He married Lucinda Spaugh prior to volunteering in Forsyth County on March 21, 1862. Jacob died of typhoid fever at Petersburg, Virginia, on August 25, 1862.

729. Hege, John E.

Private, Company H, 48th Regiment N.C. Troops

John was born in 1841 to Valentine and Leah Disher Hege. He worked as a farmer prior to being conscripted into service at Petersburg, Virginia, on August 8, 1862. John was wounded at Sharpsburg, Maryland, on September 17, 1862. He recovered from his wounds and returned to service until he was sent to a Richmond, Virginia, hospital with "chronic rheumatism" on December 11, 1862. John returned to service on January 1, 1863, and was reported present until he died of disease on December 31, 1863.

730. Hege, Zacharias C.

*Private, Carolina Rangers
Company B, 10th Virginia Cavalry
Regiment*

Zacharias was born on November 6, 1837, to Christian and Anne Vogler Hege. He was conscripted into service on March 5, 1864. Zacharias was reported present until July 1864 when he was hospitalized with an unspecified complaint. He returned by October 31, 1864, when he received pay. Zacharias was present until he was paroled at Appomattox Court House, Virginia, on April 9, 1865. After the war, Zacharias moved to Forsyth County where he married Sarah Lane. Zacharias died on January 9, 1890. He is buried in "God's Acre," Salem Moravian Cemetery, Winston-Salem, North Carolina.

731. Hegler, Charles W.

*Private, Company F, 7th Regiment
N.C. State Troops*

Charles was born in 1842. He worked as a farmer prior to volunteering on July 20, 1861. Charles was reported present until he was captured at Hanover Court House, Virginia, on May 27, 1862. He was confined at Fort Columbus, New York, until August 5, 1862, when he was paroled and transferred to Aiken's Landing, Virginia, for exchange. Charles was declared exchanged and rejoined his company prior to November 1, 1862. Charles was wounded in the right leg and captured at Fredericksburg, Virginia, on December 13, 1862. He was confined in a Washington hospital until February 12, 1863, when he was paroled and transferred to a hospital in Petersburg, Virginia. Charles was transferred to a hospital in Salisbury, North Carolina, in October 1863. Charles died of disease in Salisbury on January 18, 1864. He is buried in the Old Lutheran Cemetery in Salisbury.

732. Heitman, Alfred McCrary

*Captain, Company C, 70th Regiment
N.C. Troops (1st N.C. Junior
Reserves)*

Alfred was born on August 14, 1845, to Henry and Eve McCrary Heitman. Alfred lived with his parents before being commissioned as captain of the Davidson County Junior Reserves on May 24,

1864. After the war, Alfred returned to the town of Lexington and began work as commercial trader. On November 17, 1870, Alfred married Josephine Earnhardt. Alfred and Josephine would have three children in their Poplar Grove home: Bertha (1871), Harvey (1873), and Henry Cameron (1877). Alfred died in 1885. He is buried in the Lexington City Cemetery.

733. Heitman, John Augustus

*Unknown rank, 9th Battalion, N.C.
Home Guard*

John was born on November 11, 1816, to John and Nancy Williams Heitman. He worked as a farmer, and, on March 10, 1840, he married Anna Kinsey. John and Anna would have only two children: Orrin Burgess (1845) and Mary (1848). Records in *Broadfoot* and the *Bradley Home Guard* series confirm that J. Augustus Heitman served in the 9th N.C. Home Guard. The exact nature of his service is unknown. After the war, John continued to live in the Lexington township. John died on March 2, 1893. He is buried at Ebenezer United Methodist Church.

734. Heitman, John Franklin

*Captain, Company H, 48th Regiment
N.C. Troops*

John F. Heitman, commander of Company H, 48th Regiment N.C. Troops, posed for this picture in Richmond, Virginia, in February 1863 (Duke University Archives).

The Reverend John F. Heitman, post war minister, education advocate, and professor and defender of Trinity College (Duke University Archives).

John was born on March 17, 1840, to Henry and Eve McCrary Heitman. He studied for one year at Yadkin College before entering as a sophmore at Trinity College in Randolph County. John was a member of a militia company made up of students (known as the Trinity Guards) prior to volunteering on March 21, 1862, when he was mustered in as 1st Sergeant. John was promoted to 1st Lieutenant on August 6, 1862. He was wounded in the arm at Fredericksburg, Virginia, on December 13, 1862, and was promoted to Captain on February 10, 1863. John lead the company with great skill through all of its campaigns, and, his record mentions he "acted gallantly" at Bristoe Station, Virginia, on October 13, 1863. John sought to make his preparations for the ministry and so he resigned his commission on October 21, 1863. Col. Walkup and Lt. Col. Hill refused his resignation on the grounds that "he can serve his country very materially where he now is, and if his resignation was excepted he would not be exempt from the enrollment under any law." John continued to command the company until he was captured at Sayler's Creek, Virginia, on April 6, 1865. John was confined at Johnson's Island, Ohio, until June 18, 1865, when he was released after taking the oath of allegiance. After the war, John returned to the Davidson County, teaching school in Thomasville area. In 1868, John completed his education at Trinity and took a position as principal of the Kernersville School. John remained in Kernersville for only a year, quitting in 1869 to join the Methodist Episcopal Church, South. Upon his confirmation, John served in Plymouth, Mt. Airy, and Winston-Salem. While at station in Chapel Hill he met and married Emma Carr in 1879. In 1883, Rev. Heitman was elected to serve as a professor of Greek and German at Trinity College. By 1891, when the college was moved to Durham by Guilded Age tycoon, Washington Duke, Rev. Heitman resigned his professorship and his position as chairman of the faculty. John remained in the Trinity area, becoming headmaster of Trinity Preparatory School, still affiliated with the Western

Master cabinetmaker and teacher William A. Heitman (Betty Sowers).

North Carolina Conference. Rev. Heitman watched over the school, and even admitted girls into the male institute. John died in his home on June 15, 1904. He is buried at the Trinity Cemetery, Trinity, North Carolina. Surviving him were his wife, Emeline, and their six children.

735. Heitman, Orrin Burgess

Private, Ranelburg Riflemen
Company B, 13th Regiment N.C. Troops
(3rd N.C. Volunteers)

Orrin was born on March 23, 1845, to John Augustus and Anna Kinsey Heitman. He worked as a farmer, and on January 1, 1863, he married Elizabeth Ripple. Orrin was conscripted into service in Mecklenburg County on March 1, 1863. Orrin was reported present until he was captured at Petersburg, Virginia, on April 1, 1865. He was confined at Point Lookout, Maryland, until June 13, 1865, when he was released after taking the oath of allegiance. After the war, Orrin and Elizabeth would have four children, Phillip (1867), John (1868), Charles (1872), and David (1875), before the family moved to Mississippi after 1880. Orrin died on October 1, 1917, and is buried in Bolton, Mississippi.

736. Heitman, William Augustus

Captain, Company F, 76th Regiment
N.C. Troops (6th N.C. Senior
Reserves)

William was born on May 28, 1837, to Henry and Eve McCrary Heitman. He worked as a skilled cabinetmaker like his father, and, on November 7, 1857, he married Martha Tussey. William and Martha would have three children in their Poplar Grove home in the Ebenezer area: Numa (1860), Mary (1861), and Callie (1864), before William accepted a commission as the captain of the Senior Reserves in January 1865. After the war, he returned to the Lexington township where he and Martha would have five more children: Addie (1865), Wilton (1866), Edgar M. (1867), Robert (1871), and Bessie (1874). William returned to his trade of cabinet making but he also taught and served as a schoolmaster at the Arnold Academy, founded in 1891 William lived in the Lexington township until his death on May 30, 1910. He is buried at Ebenezer United Methodist Church.

737. Helmstetter, Hamilton

Private, Company A, 38th Regiment
N.C. Troops

Hamilton was born on October 10, 1841, to John and Lucy Helmstetter. He worked as a farmer prior to being con-scripted into service at Camp Holmes, Raleigh, on August 14, 1864. He was reported present until he was paroled at Appomattox Court House, Virginia, on April 9, 1865. After the war, Hamilton married America Swicegood on February 18, 1869. Hamilton and America would have two children: John (1870) and Charles (1874). Hamilton lived in the Tyro township until his death on August 27, 1913. He is buried at St. Luke's Lutheran Church.

738. Henderson, John R.

Private, Davidson Guards
Company A, 21st Regiment N.C. Troops
(11th N.C. Volunteers)

John was born in 1843. He worked as farmer prior to volunteering on May 8, 1861. John was wounded in the knee at Winchester, Virginia, on May 25, 1862. He recovered from his wounds and returned to service before March 1, 1863. John was wounded again in the same knee at Chancellorsville, Virginia, on May 3, 1863. John was retired from service on March 2, 1865, due to "anchylosis of the left knee." No further records.

739. Hepler, Alexander J. Grimes

Private, Company C, 7th Regiment
N.C. State Troops

Alex was born on September 14, 1827. He worked as a blacksmith, and, on July 25, 1859, he married Tryphenia E. Conrad. Alex was conscripted into service on August 12, 1864. He was reported present through October 1864. After the war, he returned to the Conrad Hill township. Alex and Tryphenia would only have one child, Joseph (1868), who survived infancy. Alex was elected a deacon in Liberty Baptist Church and continued to work as a blacksmith until his death on October 17, 1897. He is buried at Liberty Baptist Church.

740. Hepler, Benjamin Franklin

Private, Company F, 13th Regiment
N.C. Troops (3rd N.C. Volunteers)

Benjamin was born in 1846 to Claudia Hepler. Benjamin worked as a farmer prior to being conscripted on March 13, 1863. He was wounded at Chancellorsville, Virginia, on May 3, 1863, and recovered from his wounds shortly thereafter. Benjamin was reported present until he was killed in action at Cold Harbor, Virginia, on June 1, 1864.

741. Hepler, David Henderson

*Private, Chatam Light Infantry
Company G, 48th Regiment N.C. Troops*

David was born on March 24, 1845, to John and Darinda Hepler. He worked as a farmer prior to being conscripted into service on January 18, 1864. David was reported present until March 31, 1865, when for lack of food, he and 15 other members of company G deserted to the enemy. David was confined at Washington, D.C., until he was released on April 15, 1865, after taking the oath of allegiance. After the war, David returned home to the Conrad Hill township where he married Louisa J. Lopp on August 6, 1874. David and Lucinda would have ten children: Mary (1876), Lacy E. (1877), Charlie Oscar (1880), Lula (1882), Bessie (1883), Edgar (1885), Ida (1890), Early (1892), Pearl (1897), and Ola (1899). In addition, David and Lucinda lost three children in infancy: Millie, Maude, and Bertha, who are all buried at Liberty Baptist Church. David and his family ran a store, which would remain in the Liberty community after his death on September 5, 1916, and remain in operation until the 1930s. David is buried at Liberty Baptist Church.

742. Hepler, Enoch

*Private, Company E, 53rd Regiment
N.C. Troops*

Enoch was born in 1839 to Peter and Catharine Sechrist Hepler. He worked as farm laborer prior to volunteering for service on March 27, 1862. Enoch died of typhoid fever at Petersburg, Virginia, on August 2, 1862.

743. Hepler, Robert D.

*Unknown rank, Snead's Company, 1st
Battalion, Local Defense Troops*

Robert was born in 1845 to Peter and Catharine Sechrist Hepler. He was reported as serving in Snead's Company of the 1st Battalion. Robert married Catharine Moore in 1866. Robert and Catharine would have ten children: Helena (1867), William (1869), Hattie (1872), Clarendon (1873), David (1875), Claudius (1876), Robert (1878), Alice (1880), J. Early (1884), and Ernest (1886).

Home of Liberty storekeeper David H. Hepler. This home was inherited by his son, Lacy (Touart, ***Building the Backcountry***).

Robert lived in the Thomasville township until his death on April 27, 1914. He is buried at Fair Grove Methodist Church.

744. Hepler, Samuel Jefferson

*First Lieutenant, Thomasville Rifles
Company B, 14th Regiment N.C. Troops
(4th N.C. Volunteers)*

Samuel was born on September 6, 1841, to David and J. E. Hepler. He worked as a farmer prior to volunteering on April 23, 1861. He was mustered in as first sergeant, and he was appointed second lieutenant on April 27, 1862. Samuel was reported present until he was wounded in the left arm at Sharpsburg, Maryland, on September 17, 1862. Samuel was promoted to first lieutenant on October 4, 1862. His left arm was amputated, and he resigned his commission on May 15, 1863, because of his disability. After the war, Samuel returned to the Thomasville township and married Sarah A. Hunt on September 8, 1866. Samuel and Sarah did not have any children. Samuel died on August 25, 1903. He is buried at Fair Grove United Methodist Church.

745. Hepler, Samuel L.

*Private, Chatam Light Infantry
Company G, 48th Regiment N.C. Troops*

Samuel was born on March 2, 1844, to Solomon and Rebecca Hepler. He worked as a farmer prior to being conscripted on August 14, 1862. Samuel was wounded at Sharpsburg, Maryland, on September 17, 1862. He recovered from his wounds and returned to service on an

unspecified date. Samuel was reported present until he was paroled at Greensboro, North Carolina, on May 8, 1865. After the war, Samuel returned home to the Tyro township where he died on January 26, 1868. He is buried at Pleasant Hill United Methodist Church.

746. Hepler, Thomas

*Private, Thomasville Rifles
Company B, 14th Regiment N.C. Troops
(4th N.C. Volunteers)*

Thomas was born in 1832. In 1860, he was working as a carpenter's apprentice to master carpenter Sam Dorsett. Thomas volunteered on April 23, 1861. He was present until he was captured at Winchester, Virginia, on September 19, 1864. Thomas was confined at Point Lookout, Maryland, until March 18, 1865, when he was paroled and transferred to Boulware's Wharf, Virginia. Thomas did not return home. No further records.

747. Hepler, William J.

*Private, Thomasville Rifles
Company B, 14th Regiment N.C. Troops
(4th N.C. Volunteers)*

William was born to David and J. E. Hepler. He worked as a farmer prior to volunteering on July 29, 1861. William was killed in action at Sharpsburg, Maryland, on September 17, 1862.

748. Hiatt (Hyatt), David A.

*Private, Company C, 70th Regiment N.C.
Troops (1st N.C. Junior Reserves)*

David was born on November 7, 1847, to Wiley and Leah Hiatt. David lived with his parents prior to enlisting in the Junior Reserves on May 24, 1864. After the war, David returned to the Midway township where he married Sally Anderson on January 18, 1872. David and Sally would have four children: Charlie (1873), Emmet (1875), Estella (1877), and James (1880). David was reported as working in a foundry in 1880. David died on January 15, 1938. He is buried at Midway United Methodist Church.

749. Hiatt (Hyatt), Frederick

Private, Confederate Guards
Company K, 48th Regiment N.C. Troops

Frederick was born in 1836 to Wiley and Leah Hiatt. He worked as a farmer prior to being conscripted on August 8, 1862. Frederick was wounded in the mouth and face at Fredericksburg, Virginia, on December 13, 1862. He returned to duty in March 1863 and was reported present through August 23, 1864. No further records.

750. Hiatt (Hyatt), John

Private, Confederate Guards
Company K, 48th Regiment N.C. Troops

John was born in 1840 to Wiley and Leah Hiatt. He worked as a farmer prior to being conscripted on August 8, 1862. John was wounded at Fredericksburg, Virginia, on December 13, 1862. He returned to duty on March 1, 1863, and was reported present until he deserted to the enemy on September 27, 1864. John was confined at Washington, D.C., until September 30, 1864, after taking the oath of allegiance. No further records.

751. Hiatt (Hyatt), John Austin

Private, Company K, 15th Regiment
N.C. Troops (5th N.C. Volunteers)

John was born on October 2, 1834, to Willis and Sarah Brinkley Hiatt. He worked as a farmer, and, on August 5, 1854, he married Melinda Hedrick. John and Melinda would have two children, John (1860) and Joseph (1862), before John was conscripted into service in Wake County on July 15, 1862. He was reported present until he was captured at Wilderness, Virginia, on May 5, 1864.

Joseph Hiatt, a member of the Carolina Rangers (Leonard, *Jacob Wagner of "Old" Rowan*).

John was confined at Old Capital Prison, Washington, D.C., until he died of "chronic diarrhea" on August 11, 1864. His body was sent back to North Carolina, and he was interred at Oakwood Cemetery in Raleigh.

Gazelle Ann Wagner at 17 (Leonard, *Jacob Wagner of "Old" Rowan*).

752. Hiatt (Hyatt), Joseph Alfred

Private, Carolina Rangers
Company B, 10th Virginia Cavalry
Regiment

Joseph was born on January 9, 1843, to Willis and Sarah Brinkley Hiatt. He

Photograph of home of Joseph and Gazelle Hiatt, taken about 1880 (Leonard, *Jacob Wagner of "Old" Rowan*).

worked as a farmer prior to being conscripted on March 3, 1863. Joseph was reported present throughout the war, with the exception of serving on a horse detail in July 1864, and was last reported on January 27, 1865, when he received pay. After the war, Joseph married Gazelle Angeline Wagner in 1865. Joseph and Angeline would have nine children: John (1866), Willis (1868), Sarah (1870), Phillip (1873), Mary (1878), George (1882), Carlis Ford (1883), Joe Elkin (1886), and Fannie B. (1890). Joseph worked as a tenant farmer in the Lexington township. Joseph died on November 12, 1913. He is buried at Midway United Methodist Church.

753. Hiatt (Hyatt), Larkin A.

Private, Company D, 47th Regiment N.C. Troops

Larkin was born on March 24, 1844. He worked as a miller's apprentice prior to volunteering on March 26, 1862. Larkin was reported present until he was wounded in the left hand and captured at Gettysburg, Pennsylvania, on July 3, 1863. Larkin was confined in the U.S. Military Hospital in Baltimore, Maryland, until August 23, 1863, when he was paroled and released for exchange at City Point, Virginia. He was discharged on March 17, 1864, because of his disability. After the war, Larkin returned to the Midway area. He married Laura Long on October 4, 1866. Larkin and Laura would have two children: John (1867) and Solomon (1870). Larkin operated his own mill in the Midway township until his death on August 11, 1934. He is buried at Midway United Methodist Church.

754. Hiatt (Hyatt). Wesley

Private, Lexington Wildcats Company I, 14th Regiment N.C. Troops (4th N.C. Volunteers)

Wesley was born in 1839. He worked as a blacksmith's apprentice to B. L. Trexler prior to volunteering on May 14, 1861. He was reported present until he was discharged from active field service on May 25, 1863, and detailed for light duty through August 1864. After the war, Wesley returned home, and, on September 17, 1865, he married Louisa Williams. Wesley and Louisa moved out of the county before 1880. No further records.

755. Hilb, Leopold

Private, Lexington Wildcats Company I, 14th Regiment N.C. Troops (4th N.C. Volunteers)

Leopold was born in Baden-Hesse, Germany, and worked as a peddler prior to volunteering on May 14, 1861. He was reported present until he was discharged because of being an "unnaturalized foreigner" on September 25, 1862. No further records.

756. Hill, Albert Alfred

Lieutenant Colonel, 48th Regiment N.C. Troops

A. A. Hill was born in Iredell County on November 14, 1827, to James A. and Elvira Morrison Hill. He moved to Lexington after receiving his medical training and opened up an office with Dr. W. D. Lindsey in Lexington beside the March Hotel. A. A. volunteered in a newly forming company on February 21, 1862, and was appointed captain the same day. He was promoted to major on October 20, 1862, and was wounded in the right shoulder at Fredericksburg, Virginia, on December 13, 1862. Nearly a year later, he was promoted to lieutenant colonel on December 4, 1863. He was reported present in September 1864 and was with his men until he was paroled at Appomattox Court House, Virginia, on April 9, 1865. After the war, A. A. returned to Lexington and continued his medical practice, and on February 20, 1868, he married Margaret Ellis. A. A. and Margaret would have two children: Frederick (1868) and Albert (1873). A. A. died on October 1, 1888. He is buried in the Lexington City Cemetery. A few years later, the only camp of United Confederate Veterans based in Lexington would bear his name. It was said of him: "He was a good and kind officer. All of his men liked him. He made a very fine appearance and was always with his men."

757. Hill, Hiram

Private, Company K, 15th Regiment N.C. Troops (5th N.C. Volunteers)

Hiram was born in 1833. He worked as a farmer, and, on February 14, 1857, he married Sarah Everhart. Hiram and Sarah would have two children, Ephraim (1859) and John (1862), before Hiram was conscripted into service in Wake County

on July 15, 1862. He was reported present until he was captured at Hatcher's Run, Virginia, on April 2, 1865. Hiram was confined at Hart's Island, New York, until he was released on June 18, 1865, after taking the oath of allegiance. Hiram returned home, and he and Sarah would have four more children: Fannie (1866), Sarah (1868), Cicero (1875), and Robert Lee (1876), before the family moved out of the state in 1880. No further records.

758. Hill, Jackson

Private, Company K, 15th Regiment N.C. Troops (5th N.C. Volunteers)

Jackson was born on August 29, 1842, to William and Sarah Hege Hill. He worked as a farmer prior to being conscripted into service in Wake County on July 15, 1862. Jack was captured at Crampton's Pass, Maryland, on September 14, 1862. He was confined at Point Lookout, Maryland, until October 2, 1862, when he was paroled and transferred to Aiken's Landing, Virginia, for exchange. Jack was declared exchanged on November 10, 1862. He was reported present until he was wounded in the shoulder and back at Wilderness, Virginia, on May 5, 1864. Jack's wounds were so severe that he was retired from service on February 28, 1865. After the war, Jack returned home, and, on March 13, 1867, he married Martha Shoaf. Jack and Martha would have five children: Kelin (1866), William (1870), Roland (1874), Mack (1876), and Lewis (1879). Jackson moved to Texas prior to 1881. He died on April 18, 1888, and is buried in Rogers, Texas.

759. Hill, Jesse

Private, Company K, 21st Regiment N.C. Troops (11th N.C. Volunteers)

Jesse was born on September 11, 1828, to William and Sarah Hege Hill. He worked as a farmer, and, on August 20, 1850, he married Emeline Charlotte Chitty. Jesse and Charlotte would have only one child: Dock (1857). Jesse was conscripted into service on January 1, 1864. He was reported present until he was hospitalized in Richmond, Virginia, on March 27, 1865. Jesse recovered from his illness and was reported present until he was captured at Sayler's Creek, Virginia, on April 6, 1865. Jesse was confined at Newport News, Virginia, until June 27,

1865, when he was released after taking the oath of allegiance. After the war, Jesse returned home to his family in northern Davidson County. He lived in the Arcadia area until his death on January 2, 1882. He is buried at Good Hope United Methodist Church.

Jesse left several letters which were later transcribed and placed in the Lexington library. (Both letters below use the original spelling.) This letter, dated October 21, 1864, describes Jesse's actions when the Federal counterattack pressed the Confederates off the field at Cedar Creek, Virginia:

Camp near New market

... Tha reinforced and giv us the worst whipping we ever had and have run back about 35 miles. I myself run and keep all the tricks that I got. I run about five miles before tha run me twise the river. I had to lay down wet and tha was a big frost that morning and I had no fire and but one blanket. I got a pocket book with 44 dollars of greenback and a nap sack and a blanket and a good oil cloth and a pare of boots and severl other little tricks and a little pocket knife.

This letter, dated June 8, 1864, describes the battle of Cold Harbor, Virginia, on June 3, 1864, and a skirmish some time on June 7, 1864:

State of Va in about 8 miles

Our reg and line exstended on our right for about 3 miles and tha sed we kild six thousand of the yankeys and tha we did not lose more than four houndred in kiled and wouded it is a sete to see the battle field after a fight. It was a right smart fight yesdereday and the bullets has ben comin through a munsk us every day for the 10 days You said you wanted to know when Sam was kild he was kild on the 16th of May.

760. Hill, John

Private, Davidson Guards
Company A, 21st Regiment N.C. Troops
(11th N.C. Volunteers)

John was born in 1822. He worked as a farmer, and, on September 22, 1852, he married Nancy A. Matherly. John and Nancy would have two children, Isaac (1856) and John (1858), before John was conscripted into service in Wake County

on June 6, 1863. He was reported present until wounded in the chest at Cold Harbor, Virginia, on June 1, 1864. John was present in the hospital until company records list him as a deserter on August 8, 1864. John returned home and was living with his family in the Tyro township in 1880. No further records.

761. Hill, Kelin

Private, Company K, 15th Regiment N.C. Troops (5th N.C. Volunteers)

Kelin was born on August 7, 1832, to William and Sarah Hege Hill. He worked as a farmer prior to being conscripted into service in Wake County on July 15, 1862. Kelin was captured at Crampton's Pass, Maryland, on September 14, 1862. He was confined at Point Lookout, Maryland, until October 2, 1862, when he was paroled and transferred to Aiken's Landing, Virginia, for exchange. Kelin was declared exchanged on November 10, 1862. He returned to service in February 1863 and was reported present until he was captured at Hatcher's Run, Virginia, on April 2, 1865. Kelin was confined at Hart's Island, New York, until June 18, 1865, when he was released after taking the oath of allegiance. After the war, Kelin returned home to the Tyro area where he died on December 17, 1867. He is buried at Good Hope United Methodist Church.

762. Hill, Sian

Private, Company G, 46th Regiment N.C. Troops

Sian was born on September 8, 1838. He worked as a farmer, and, in 1860, he married Elizabeth. Sian and Elizabeth would have one child, Louisa (1861), before Sian volunteered on March 12, 1862. He deserted on August 25, 1862, and returned to duty on January 1, 1863. His second child, Eliza, was born in 1863. He was reported present until he was paroled at Appomattox Court House, Virginia, on April 9, 1865. After the war, Sian returned to the Emmons township where he and Elizabeth would have six more children: Roxanna (1869), Calvin (1871), Cora (1873), Harris (1875), James (1877), and Dora (1879). Sian worked as a farmer in the Emmons township until his death on April 10, 1914. He is buried at Tom's Creek Primitive Baptist Church.

763. Hill, Valentine

Private, Company K, 21st Regiment N.C. Troops (11th N.C. Volunteers)
Company A, 4th Regiment U.S. Volunteer Infantry

Valentine was born on November 15, 1825, to William and Sarah Hege Hill. He worked as a farmer, and, on August 14, 1862, he married Delilah Walser. Valentine and Delilah would have one child, Clara (1863), before Valentine was conscripted into service on November 13, 1863. He was reported present until he was captured at Winchester, Virginia, on September 19, 1864. Valentine was confined at Point Lookout, Maryland, until October 12, 1864, when he took the oath of allegiance and joined the U.S. Army. After the war, Valentine returned home to the Tyro area where he and Delilah would have six more children: Sarah (1868), Robert Lee (1870), David (1872), Columbus (1874), Andrew (1876), and Romulus (1878). Valentine lived in the Tyro township until his death on September 25, 1895. He is buried at Good Hope United Methodist Church.

764. Hill, William

Private, Company H, 48th Regiment N.C. Troops

William was born in 1840 to William and Sarah Hege Hill. He worked as a farmer, and, on October 30, 1859, he married Eliza Jane Berrier. William was conscripted into service at Petersburg, Virginia, on August 8, 1862. He was reported present for the duration of the war and was paroled at Appomattox Court House, Virginia, on April 9, 1865. No further records.

765. Hilliard, Benjamin F.

1st Sergeant, Company B, 48th Regiment N.C. Troops

Ben was born in 1835 to Joseph and Susan Hilliard. He worked as a farmer, and, on November 2, 1858, he married Virginia A. Hall. Ben and Virginia would have one child, Sally (1861), before Ben was conscripted on August 8, 1862. He was promoted to first sergeant after "displaying signal courage" at Fredericksburg, Virginia, on December 13, 1862. Ben was reported present throughout the war and was paroled at Greensboro, North Carolina, on May 3, 1865. After the war, Ben and Virginia would have six more children: June (1869), Lenora (1872), Mary (1874), Hester (1875), Benjamin (1876), and Frederick (1879). In 1870, Benjamin adopted four orphaned black children: Eugenia, Jonathan, John, and Jane. He lived in the Lexington township until his death in 1890. He was the first member of the A. A. Hill Camp, United Confederate Veterans, to die.

766. Hilliard, John J.

Private, Trojan Regulators
Company F, 44th Regiment N.C. Troops

John was born in 1839. He worked as a farmer prior to being conscripted on March 1, 1863. John was present until he was hospitalized at Richmond, Virginia, on February 28, 1865. No further records.

767. Hilliard, Samuel Ruffin

Private, Company K, 15th Regiment
N.C. Troops (5th N.C. Volunteers)

Samuel was born in 1841. He worked as a farmer prior to volunteering for service in Nash County on April 24, 1861. He was wounded in the abdomen at Lee's Mill, Virginia, on April 16, 1862. Samuel recovered from his wounds and returned to service in March 1863. Samuel was retired to the Invalid Corps on January 6, 1865. No further records.

768. Hilton, Cyrus

Private, Confederate Guards
Company K, 48th Regiment N.C. Troops

Cyrus was born on June 5, 1843, to John and Martha Hilton. He worked as a farmer prior to enlisting at Camp Magnum, Raleigh, on April 6, 1862. Cyrus was reported present until he was discharged on November 1, 1862, after providing a substitute. After his service, Cyrus returned home, and, on January 2, 1870, he married Jane Clark. Cyrus and Jane would have one child: Mayfield (1870). Cyrus lived in the North Thomasville township until his death on September 25, 1915. He is buried at Zion United Church of Christ.

769. Hilton, Evan

Private, Confederate Guards
Company K, 48th Regiment N.C. Troops

Evan was born in 1833 to John and Martha Hilton. He worked as a farmer prior to enlisting at Camp Magnum, Raleigh, on April 6, 1862. Evan was reported present until he was wounded at King's School House, Virginia, on June 25, 1862. Five days later, on June 30, 1862, Evan died of his wounds.

770. Hilton, Jesse

Private, Confederate Guards
Company K, 48th Regiment N.C. Troops

Jesse was born in 1821 to John and Martha Welborn Hilton. He worked as a farmer in the northern district of Davidson County, and, in 1843, he married Jane Mendenhall. Jesse and Jane would have seven children: Cynthia (1845), John (1847), Martha (1849), Mary (1852), Francis (1854), Nancy (1856), and Roxanne (1858), before Jesse enlisted at Camp Magnum, Raleigh, North Carolina, on April 6, 1862. He died of dysentery in Raleigh on April 30, 1862. Jesse is buried in the Oakwood Cemetery in Raleigh.

771. Hilton, John

Private, Company C, 70th Regiment
N.C. Troops (1st N.C. Junior
Reserves)

John was born in March 1847 to Jesse and Jane Mendenhall Hilton. He worked as a farmer prior to enlisting in the Junior Reserves on May 24, 1864. After the war, John returned home to the Thomasville township. John married Sarah Delphina Morris on February 6, 1868. John and Sarah would have four children: Elzevian (1874), Gaddy (1881), Robert Lee (1883), and Casabane (1886). No further records.

772. Hilton, Lorenzo

Private, Company A, 10th Battalion
N.C. Heavy Artillery

Lorenzo was born on April 27, 1837. He worked as a farmer, and, in 1856, he married Jane Stone. Lorenzo and Jane would have one child, Richard (1860), before Lorenzo was conscripted on March 11, 1863. He was reported present throughout the war, and he was paroled at Greensboro, North Carolina, on May 6, 1865. After the war, Lorenzo returned to the Thomasville township where he and Jane would have four more children: John (1865), Laura (1869), Jacob (1871), and Ally (1873). Lorenzo lived in the Thomasville township until his death on

February 5, 1923. He is buried at Mount Pleasant United Methodist Church.

773. Hilton, Truman

Private, Townsend's Company, Local
Defense

Truman was born on February 4, 1846, to Zebulon and Clarena Hilton. He worked as a farmer and a shoemaker in the northern district of Davidson County. Records indicate that Truman served in Townsend's Company, although the exact nature of his service is unknown. After his service, Truman returned home where he married Mary Gray in 1878. Truman and Mary would have three children: Stella (1879), Clyde (1882), and Maudie (1886). Truman died sometime after 1920. He is buried at Pleasant Grove United Methodist Church.

774. Hines, Elias P.

Second Lieutenant, 66th Regiment
N.C. Militia (1861 organization)

Eli was born in 1834 to Joseph and Joyce Hines. He worked as a farmer, and, on April 16, 1859, he married Margaret H. Clodfelter. Eli accepted a commission in the Piney Grove District Company on January 2, 1862. After his service he returned to the Abbott's Creek area until 1880; he later moved to Guilford County. No further records.

775. Hinkle, Alexander

Private, Company K, 15th Regiment
N.C. Troops (5th N.C. Volunteers)

Alex was born in 1834 to Mathias and Barbara Shoaf Hinkle. He worked as a miller, and, on April 16, 1859, he married Elizabeth Essick. Alex and Elizabeth would have three children: Henry (1859), Pauline (1862), and John (1864). Alex was conscripted into service in Wake County on July 15, 1862. He was reported present until he deserted on August 20, 1862. The census reports the family living in the Lexington township in 1870. No further records.

776. Hinkle, Christian

Private, Company K, 15th Regiment
N.C. Troops (5th N.C. Volunteers)

Christian was born on October 13, 1838, to Mathias and Barbara Shoaf

Christian Hinkle in 1866 (Betty Sowers).

Hinkle. He worked as a miller, and, on December 10, 1859, he married Emaline Shoaf. Christian and Emaline would have two children, Solomon (1861) and Barbara (1862), before Christian was conscripted into service in Wake County on July 15, 1862. He was reported present until he was captured at Hatcher's Run, Virginia, on April 2, 1865. Christian was confined at Hart's Island, New York, until June 18, 1865. After the war, Christian returned to the Lexington township where he and Emaline would have six more children: Alpheus (1866), Susan (1867), Emma (1869), Delphina (1873), Early (1876), and Mary Lee (1877). Christian lived in the Lexington township until his death on November 21, 1883. He is buried at Beulah United Church of Christ.

777. Hinkle, Emanuel

Private, Company K, 15th Regiment N.C. Troops (5th N.C. Volunteers)

Emanuel was born on October 13, 1839, to Mathias and Barbara Shoaf Hinkle. On February 15, 1859, Emanuel married Evaline Everhart. Emanuel and Evaline would have two children before her death in December 1862: Lindsay (1860) and Polly (1862). He worked as a farmer prior to being conscripted into service in Wake County on July 15, 1862. He was reported present until he was discharged on October 5, 1862, because of frequent epileptic seizures. Emanuel returned home and married Sarah Easter on February 26, 1869. Emanuel and Sarah would only have one child: Charlie (1869).

Emanuel lived in the Lexington township until his death on February 4, 1899. He is buried at Beulah United Church of Christ.

778. Hinkle, John A.

Private, Snead's Company, Local Defense

John was born in 1848. He worked as a farmer prior to serving in Snead's Company. After his service he returned to the Lexington township where he married Sarah E. Wagner on July 23, 1865. John and Sarah would have nine children: Zena (1868), Eliza (1870), William (1872), David (1875), Lillian (1876), Ida (1878), Numa (1880), John (1882), and Mary (1885). John lived in the Lexington township until his death on April 15, 1921. He is buried at Bethesda United Methodist Church.

779. Hinkle, Mathais

Private, Company D, 13th Regiment N.C. Troops (3rd N.C. Volunteers)

Mathias was born on January 1, 1825, to Mathias and Barbara Shoaf Hinkle. He worked as a farmer, and, on May 20, 1846, he married Mary Link. Mathias and Mary would have four children, Louisa (1848), David (1850), Henry (1853), and Louvina (1855), before Mathias was conscripted on February 28, 1864. He deserted on April 9, 1864, and returned on October 4, 1864. Mathias was reported present until he was paroled at Greensboro, North Carolina, on May 5, 1865. After the war, Mathias returned home to his family and lived in the Lexington township until his death on January 28, 1888. He is buried at Beulah United Church of Christ.

780. Hinkle, Ransom

Private, Company K, 15th Regiment N.C. Troops (5th N.C. Volunteers)

Ransom was born on October 13, 1839, to Mathias and Barbara Shoaf Hinkle. He worked as a farmer, and, on December 20, 1860, he married Elvina Shoaf. Ransom and Elvina would have one child, Martha (1862), before Ransom was conscripted into service in Wake County on July 15, 1862. He deserted on August 20, 1862. Ransom returned to service on March 9, 1863, and was reported present until he was captured at Hatcher's Run, Virginia, on April 2, 1865. Christian was confined at Hart's Island, New York, until

June 18, 1865. After the war, Ransom returned home to his wife, and they would have six more children: Mary (1865), Jacob (1868), Robert (1871), Lilly (1874), Alice (1876), and Margaret (1878). Elvina died in 1882. Ransom married Paulina Berrier in 1884. Ransom died on April 26, 1889. He is buried beside his first wife at Beulah United Church of Christ.

781. Hix, John H.

Private, Lexington Wildcats Company I, 14th Regiment N.C. Troops (4th N.C. Volunteers)

John was born in 1842 to Henry and Jane Hix. He was a student prior to volunteering on May 14, 1861. He was reported present until he was killed in action at Chancellorsville, Virginia, on May 3, 1863.

782. Hix, Richard D.

Private, Company B, 48th Regiment N.C. Troops

Richard was born in 1843 to Henry and Jane Hix. He worked as a farmer prior to enlisting in Wayne County on May 16, 1862. Richard was reported present throughout the war and was paroled at Statesville, North Carolina, on May 27, 1865. No further records.

783. Hix, Thomas

First Lieutenant, Lexington Wildcats Company I, 14th Regiment N.C. Troops (4th N.C. Volunteers) Company B, 48th Regiment N.C. Troops

Thomas was born in 1839 to Henry and Jane Hix. He was a medical student at Yadkin College before he volunteered for service on May 14, 1861. He was discharged on September 7, 1861, because of disability. Thomas reenlisted on February 22, 1862, and was appointed third lieutenant on March 21, 1862. He was promoted to first Lieutenant on October 20, 1862, and he served in that capacity through October 1864. After the war, he completed his medical training at the state university in Chapel Hill, North Carolina, and began his life in Stanly County. No further records.

784. Hix, William W.

Private, Company H, 40th Regiment N.C. Troops (3rd N.C. Artillery)

Company F, 13th Battalion, N.C. Light Artillery

William was born on August 9, 1839. He worked as a farmer prior to being conscripted into service in Wake County on July 16, 1862. He was reported present with the 3rd N.C. Artillery before being transferred to the 13th Battalion on November 4, 1863. William was reported present or accounted for through December 1864. After the war, William returned to the Emmons township. He moved to the Cotton Grove area around 1880. William lived in the Cotton Grove township until he died on January 8, 1901. He is buried at Jersey Baptist Church.

785. Hodge, Richard

Private, Company A, 46th Regiment N.C. Troops

Richard was born on September 11, 1824. He worked as a farmer, and, on November 18, 1848, he married Sarah Noah. Richard and Sarah would have two children, Martha (1852) and Margaret (1857), before Richard enlisted in Rowan County on April 15, 1862. He was reported present until he was captured at Hatcher's Run, Virginia, on April 1, 1865. Richard was confined at Point Lookout, Maryland, until June 27, 1865, when he was released after taking the oath of allegiance. After the war, Richard returned home and suffered tragedy: by 1874 both of his children were dead. Richard died on December 10, 1892. He is buried in the Reed Family Cemetery.

786. Hoffman, John S.

Private, Company G, 13th Regiment N.C. Troops

John was born on March 8, 1845. He worked as a carpenter prior to being conscripted on March 27, 1864. John was reported present until he was paroled at Appomattox Court House, Virginia, on April 9, 1865. After the war, John returned home and married Jane in 1865. John and Jane would have three children: John (1865), Eliza (1875), and Laura (1877). John lived in the Yadkin township until his death on August 9, 1882. He is buried at Good Hope United Methodist Church.

787. Holder, Henry

Private, Company I, 42nd Regiment N.C. Troops

Henry was born in 1845 to George and Jane Powell Holder. He worked as a farmer prior to volunteering in Rowan County on March 26, 1862. Henry was reported present until he was wounded in the left knee at Bermuda Hundred, Virginia, on May 19, 1864. His left leg was amputated. Henry died of his wounds in Petersburg, Virginia, on July 29, 1864.

788. Holder, William A.

Private, Davidson Guards Company A, 21st Regiment N.C. Troops (11th N.C. Volunteers)

William was born in 1840. He worked as a farmer prior to volunteering on May 8, 1861. William was reported present until he deserted on October 26, 1864. No further records.

789. Holland, John W.

Private, Company C, 70th Regiment N.C. Troops (1st N.C. Junior Reserves)

John was born on June 21, 1848, to William and Susan Holland. John worked as a farmer prior to enlisting in the Junior Reserves on May 24, 1864. After the war, John returned home to the Lexington township, and, on December 5, 1871, he married Sarah Davis. John and Sarah would have three children: Lena (1873), Thomas (1875), and Henry (1878). John lived in the Lexington township until his death on May 16, 1921. He is buried at Centenary United Methodist Church.

790. Holt, Elijah

Private, Company H, 48th Regiment N.C. Troops

Eli was born in 1839 to Richard and Susan Holt. Eli worked as a shoemaker, as well as an overseer on his uncle's plantation prior to volunteering on March 17, 1862. Eli died of typhoid fever in Petersburg, Virginia, on July 17, 1862. He is buried in the Blanford Cemetery in Petersburg.

791. Holt, Eugene Rainey

Second Lieutenant, Colonel Mallet's Battalion (Camp Guard) Company C, 48th Regiment N.C. Troops

Eugene was born on May 10, 1844, to Dr. William R. and Louisa Holt. He was studying for the medical field when he was conscripted on July 6, 1862. He was appointed second lieutenant in Mallet's Battalion on September 28, 1863. Eugene died of unreported causes on April 22, 1865.

792. Holt, Henry

Private, Company H, 48th Regiment N.C. Troops

Henry was born in 1841 to Dr. William R. and Louisa Holt. Henry worked as an overseer on his father's plantation, "Linwood," prior to enlisting on May 8 1862. He was reported present and was detailed as a shoemaker in Danville, Virginia, until September 1864. Henry was captured at Hatcher's Run, Virginia, on April 2, 1865. He was confined at Point Lookout, Maryland, until June 15, 1865, when he was released after taking the oath of allegiance. Henry did not return to North Carolina, and it is presumed that he died on his way home.

793. Holt, William M.

First Lieutenant, Lexington Wildcats Company I, 14th Regiment N.C. Troops

William was born on May 16, 1837, to Dr. William R. and Louisa Holt. William worked as a clerk prior to volunteering for service on May 14, 1861; he was appointed second lieutenant the same day. William was elected first lieutenant and served in that capacity until he died of disease on June 17, 1862. He is buried in the Lexington City Cemetery.

794. Holton, Alson Clark

Private, Company C, 61st Regiment N.C. Troops

Alson lived in the southern district of Davidson County, and, on March 9, 1852, he married Nancy Skeen. Alson and Nancy did not have any children prior to Alson's conscription into service in Wake County on August 27, 1862. He deserted on June 18, 1863, and did not return until he took the oath of allegiance at Salisbury, North Carolina, on May 31, 1865. (His name is mistakenly spelled *Haltom* in volume 13 of *Jordan's Roster*.)

795. Hoover, Franklin

Private, Company C, 70th Regiment N.C. Troops (1st N.C. Junior Reserves)

Frank was born on January 20, 1847, to David and Susan Brindle Hoover. He worked as a farmer prior to enlisting in the Junior Reserves on May 24, 1864. After the war, Frank returned home to the Reedy Creek area. On November 2, 1871, he married Lorraine Link. Frank and Lorraine would have two children: William (1877) and John (1878). Frank lived with his family in the Reedy Creek township until his death on April 11, 1926. He is buried at Good Hope United Methodist Church.

796. Hoover, Pleasant A.

Captain, 66th Regiment N.C. Militia (1861 organization)

Pleasant was born on July 18, 1830, to Charles and Sarah Hoover. Pleasant worked as a carpenter, and, on May 25, 1853, he married Margaret Jane Holmes. Pleasant and Margaret would have seven children: Almeda (1855), Victoria (1860), Anna (1864), David (1865), Charles (1867), Emma (1869), and George (1872). Pleasant accepted a commission in the Hunt's Fork District Company on December 13, 1861. After his service he lived with his family in the Thomasville township. He was a member of the Masonic order. Pleasant died on November 8, 1907. He is buried at Mount Pleasant United Methodist Church.

797. Hopkins, James Humphrey

Private, Company C, 61st Regiment N.C. Troops

James was born on January 23, 1837. He worked as a farmer, and, in 1857, he married Nancy Carrick. James and Nancy would have two children, William (1859) and Eliza (1861), before James was conscripted into service in Wake County on August 27, 1862. He was reported absent, sick, from November 1862 through April 1863. He and Nancy had a third child, John, in 1863. James returned from his sickness in June 1863 and was reported present through April 1864. After the war, James returned home to the Allegheny township where he and Nancy would have one more child, Margaret (1877). James lived in the Allegheny area until his death on September 8, 1899. He is buried at Lanes Chapel Methodist Church.

798. Horn, Corneilius

Private, Lexington Wildcats Company I, 14th Regiment N.C. Troops (4th N.C. Volunteers) Company H, 48th Regiment N.C. Troops

Corneilius was born in 1821. He worked as a farmer in the Lexington area, and, in 1841, he married Perina. Corneilius and Perina would have seven children, Elizabeth (1842), Noah (1844), Lucy (1847), Peter (1848), Delphina (1853), Elijah (1855), and Henry (1857), before Corneilius volunteered for service on May 14, 1861. He and Perina had another child, Rachael, in 1862. He was discharged from the 14th Regiment on August 7, 1862, according to the provisions of the Conscript Law. Corneilius reenlisted on October 14, 1863. He was reported present until he was wounded in the arm at Petersburg, Virginia, on October 1, 1864. He was recommended for retirement on February 10, 1865. Corneilius was paroled at Greensboro, North Carolina, on May 3, 1865. After the war, Corneilius and Perina would have two more children: Eliza (1866) and Mary (1868). No further records.

799. Horn, Noah

Private, Company H, 48th Regiment N.C. Troops

Noah was born in 1844 to Corneilius and Perina Horn. He worked as a farmer prior to volunteering on March 5, 1862. Noah was reported present until he was wounded at King's School House, Virginia, on June 25, 1862. Noah returned to service by January 1863 and was reported present until he was wounded in the right hand at Petersburg, Virginia, on June 15, 1864. Noah lost his third finger as a result of his wound. Noah recovered, and after a brief furlough, he was reported present until he was paroled at Appomattox Court House, Virginia, on April 9, 1865. After the war, Noah returned home and, on September 10, 1867, he married Sarah A. Albertson. Noah and Sarah left the county prior to 1870. No further records.

800. Howerton, Samuel W.

Chaplain, Staff, 15th Regiment N.C. Troops (5th N.C. Volunteers)

Samuel was born in 1834 in Person County. He moved to Davidson County

prior to 1860. He worked as a Methodist minister in the town of Thomasville prior to being appointed chaplain on April 10, 1863. Samuel resigned on October 10, 1864. After his service, Sam continued his ministry and was given the pastorship of Fair Grove Methodist Church. He and his wife, Alice, would have two children: Ella (1862) and Sophronia (1864). Samuel died around 1900. He is possibly buried in an unmarked grave in the vicinity of his wife's stone at Fair Grove United Methodist Church.

801. Hudson, John F.

Private, Company D, 48th Regiment N.C. Troops

John was born in 1814 to Marcus and Rebecca Hudson. He enlisted on August 8, 1862, as a paid substitute. He was reported present throughout the war. John served as a teamster and a blacksmith for most of his term of service. After the war, John married Catharine Weaver on November 21, 1867. John and Catharine would have four children: Ida (1868), David (1870), Allen (1874), and John (1879). No further records.

802. Hudson, Marcus

Private, Company H, 48th Regiment N.C. Troops

Marcus was born in 1825 to Marcus and Rebecca Hudson. He worked as a farmer, and, on December 27, 1847, he married Rebecca Shuler. Marcus and Rebecca would have six children, Catharine (1842), Franklin (1849), Elizabeth (1851), Sarah (1852), Thomas (1856), and John (1859), before Marcus was conscripted into service on October 14, 1863. He was reported present through October 1864, although he was sick for most of that period. Marcus survived the war and moved his family out of the county prior to 1870. No further records.

803. Hudson, Robert C.

Private, Thomasville Rifles Company B, 14th Regiment N.C. Troops (4th N.C. Volunteers)

Robert was born in 1837. He worked as a shoemaker prior to volunteering on April 23, 1861. Robert was reported present until he was captured in a hospital in Richmond, Virginia, during the city's fall on April 3, 1865. He was paroled at

Richmond on April 18, 1865. No further records.

804. Hudson, William G.

*Second Lieutenant, 65th Regiment
N.C. Militia (1861 organization)*

William was born in 1820 to Marcus and Rebecca Hudson. He worked as a painter, and, in 1852, he married Affrie. William and Affrie would have three children: Emily (1853), Elisa (1855), and Margaret (1859). William accepted a commission in the Thomasville District Company on December 26, 1861. No further records.

805. Huff, Barton E.

*Sergeant, Company B, 48th Regiment
N.C. Troops*

Barton was born in 1844 to Daniel and Mary Huff. He worked as a farmer prior to volunteering on March 3, 1862. Barton was promoted to sergeant on January 1, 1863, and was reported present until he was furloughed from Richmond, Virginia, on August 1, 1863. Barton returned to duty prior to March 1864. No further records.

806. Huff, Burgess L.

*Private, Davidson Guards
Company A, 21st Regiment N.C. Troops*

Burgess was born in 1834 to Daniel and Mary Huff. He worked as a farmer prior to volunteering on May 8, 1861. He died of "enteric fever" at Front Royal, Virginia, on October 21, 1861.

807. Huff, Obediah

*Private, Company C, 70th Regiment
N.C. Troops (1st N.C. Junior
Reserves)*

Obed was born in 1848 to Daniel and Mary Huff. He worked as a farmer prior to enlisting in the Junior Reserves on May 24, 1864. After the war, Obed returned home to the Cotton Grove township. In 1880, Obediah was employed as a laborman for the North Carolina Central Railroad. No further records.

808. Huffman, Daniel

*Private, Company H, 48th Regiment
N.C. Troops*

Daniel Huffman's Reedy Creek home dates from around 1840. Daniel is believed to have died while in a Salisbury hospital (Touart, *Building the Backcountry*).

Daniel was born in 1826 to Adam and Catharine Huffman. He worked as a farmer, and, on March 15, 1853, he married Sarah Ann Hicks. Daniel and Sarah would have three children, John (1854), Harrison (1856), and Eliza (1858), before Daniel was conscripted into service on August 8, 1862. He was reported present until he was hospitalized at Richmond, Virginia, on July 29, 1864, with "chronic diarrhea." He was issued a 30-day furlough on August 4, 1864. Daniel was reported in the hospital at Salisbury, North Carolina, on November 1, 1864. No further records.

809. Huffman, James

*Private, Davidson Guards
Company A, 21st Regiment N.C. Troops*

James was born in 1826 to Adam and Catharine Huffman. He worked as a deputy sheriff prior to volunteering on May 8, 1861. James was wounded at Second Manassas, Virginia, on August 28, 1862. He was captured on October 1, 1862, and was sent to City Point, Virginia, until he was exchanged on November 18, 1862. James returned to duty prior to March 1, 1863, and served through February 1865. No further records.

810. Hughes, Jacob S.

*Private, Company B, 48th Regiment
N.C. Troops*

Jacob was born in Davidson County prior to volunteering on March 12, 1862. He died of "fever" at Goldsboro, North Carolina, on June 3, 1862.

811. Hughes, James

*Private, Davidson Guards
Company A, 21st Regiment N.C. Troops*

James was born in 1844 to Phillip and Cora Hughes. He worked as a farmer prior to being conscripted into service on October 1, 1863. James was reported present until he was captured at Winchester, Virginia, on September 14, 1864. He was confined at Point Lookout, Maryland, until January 21, 1865, when he was paroled and transferred to Boulware's Wharf, Virginia, for exchange. After the war, James returned to the Emmons township and married Della Nancy Myers on April 24, 1867. James and Della would have four children: Frances (1877), Lelah (1882), Susan (1885), and Jacob (1889). James died sometime after 1900. It is believed that he may be buried in an unmarked grave at Hughes' Grove Baptist Church.

812. Hughes, John Wilson

*Private, Company K, 38th Regiment
N.C. Troops*

John was born on October 14, 1842, to Samuel and Mary Hughes. He worked as a farmer prior to being conscripted in Wake County on July 1, 1864. John deserted on August 25, 1864, and did not return until he took the oath of allegiance at City Point, Virginia, on February 12, 1865. After the war, John returned home and married Susan on December 24, 1865. John and Susan would have five children: Sarah (1867), William (1869), Julie (1871), Sam (1877), and John (1880). John lived as a small farmer in the Conrad Hill township until his death on May 28, 1915. He is buried at Hughes' Grove Baptist Church.

813. Hughes, Phillip S.

Private, Company B, 48th Regiment N.C. Troops

Phillip was born in 1838. He worked as a farmer prior to volunteering on March 12, 1862. Phillip was killed in action at King's School House, Virginia, on June 25, 1862.

814. Hughes, William

Private, Company A, 70th Regiment N.C. Troops (1st N.C. Junior Reserves)

William was born on July 11, 1846, to Phillip and Cora Hughes. He worked as a farmer prior to enlisting in the Junior Reserves on July 4, 1864. After the war, he returned home where he married Elizabeth Kepley on October 15, 1869. William and Elizabeth would have four children: Susan (1871), Mary (1873), Elias (1877), and Minnie (1885). William lived in the Emmons township until his death on June 10, 1933. He is buried at Pleasant Grove United Methodist Church.

815. Humphreys, John H.

Quartermaster Sergeant, 48th Regiment N.C. Troops

John was born in 1837 to James and Susannah Hargrave Humphreys. John was a student prior to being conscripted on August 8, 1862. He was promoted to quartermaster sergeant and was transferred to the regimental staff in November 1862. He served in that capacity until the end of the war. After the war, John returned home to Lexington, where he married Sarah A. Owen on February 18, 1866. John and Sarah moved to the Boone township where they would have six children: James (1868), Andrew (1872),

Nancy (1874), Gertrude (1876), and Martha and Mary (1880). No further records.

816. Humphreys, Robert H.

Sergeant, Lexington Wildcats Company I, 14th Regiment N.C. Troops (4th N.C. Volunteers)

Robert was born on May 30, 1864, to James and Susannah Hargrave Humphreys. Robert was a student prior to volunteering on May 14, 1861. He was mustered in as a sergeant, however, he was later reduced in rank. Robert was wounded at Sharpsburg, Maryland, when a bullet grazed his head on September 17, 1862. He recovered from his wounds, rejoined the company in March 1863, and was promoted to sergeant. Robert was reported present throughout the war and was paroled at Thomasville, North Carolina, on May 1, 1865. After the war, Robert returned to the town of Lexington where he married Mattie Goss on February 23, 1871. Robert and Mattie would have two children: Victor (1872) and Jessica (1875). Robert owned a mercantile shop in the city and was a shareholder in the Lambeth Tobacco Warehouse in Thomasville. Robert lived in Lexington until his death on January 3, 1894. He is buried in the Lexington City Cemetery.

817. Huneycutt, Ambrose

Private, Company K, 15th Regiment N.C. Troops (5th N.C. Volunteers)

Ambrose was born in 1838. He worked as a farmer prior to being conscripted into service in Wake County on July 15, 1862. Ambrose was wounded in the thigh and captured at Crampton's Pass, Maryland, on September 14, 1862. He died of his wounds in a Federal hospital in Burkittsville, Maryland, on November 21, 1862.

818. Huneycutt, George

Private, Company K, 15th Regiment N.C. Troops (5th N.C. Volunteers)

George was born in 1834. He worked as a farmer, and, on February 25, 1858, he married Tabitha Wisenhunt. George and Tabitha would have one child, Ambrose (1859), before George was conscripted into service in Wake County on July 15, 1862. George was wounded and captured

at Crampton's Pass, Maryland, on September 14, 1862. He was confined at Fort Delaware, Delaware, until October 2, 1862, when he was paroled and transferred to Aiken's Landing, Virginia, for exchange. George was exchanged on November 10, 1862. He returned to the company on March 7, 1863, and was reported present until he was captured at Hatcher's Run, Virginia, on April 2, 1865. George was confined at Hart's Island, New York, until June 18, 1865, when he was released after taking the oath of allegiance. No further records.

819. Hunt, Alston Osborne

Private, Company C, 61st Regiment N.C. Troops

Osborne was born in 1838 to Andrew and Hannah Hunt. He worked as a farmer, and, in 1859, he married Sarah. Osborne and Sarah would have one child, Mary (1861), before Osborne was conscripted into service in Wake County on August 27, 1862. He deserted at Kinston, North Carolina, on December 10, 1862. Osborne returned to service on December 16, 1863, and was reported present until he was hospitalized at Petersburg, Virginia, on January 18, 1864. He contracted hepatitis and was sent to another hospital on March 17, 1864. Osborne was furloughed in October 1864. After the war, Osborne returned home to the Emmons township where he and Sarah would have one more child: Susan (1868). Osborne had a 200-acre farm on which he raised a variety of crops as well as tended an orchard. Osborne died in 1919–20, according to his stone in his private cemetery, the Osborne Hunt Cemetery, which is located off Wright Road on a hill overlooking Hogg Branch.

820. Hunt, Andrew

Private, Company B, 35th Regiment N.C. Troops

Andrew was born on October 19, 1844, to Andrew and Hannah Hunt. Andrew was conscripted on May 1, 1863. He was reported present until he was discharged on October 13, 1863, because of disability. On May 2, 1864, Andrew married Margaret Copple. Andrew and Margaret would have two children: Loney (1886) and Thomas Jonathan (1896). Margaret died sometime in 1897. Andrew married Louisa in 1898; they would

Charles A. Hunt (mounted), a Lexington businessman and Confederate lieutenant, in front of "the Homestead" (Touart, *Building the Backcountry*).

have no children. Andrew lived in the Emmons township until his death on April 24, 1915. He is buried at Clarksbury Methodist Church.

821. Hunt, Charles Andrew

Second Lieutenant, Lexington Wildcats Company I, 14th Regiment N.C. Troops (4th N.C. Volunteers)

Charles was born on October 10, 1843, to Andrew and Elizabeth Hunt. Charles volunteered for service on May 14, 1861, and was appointed sergeant. He was elected third lieutenant on April 27, 1862, and was promoted to first lieutenant on October 1, 1862. Charles served as first lieutenant and was wounded at Chancellorsville, Virginia, on May 3, 1863. Charles recovered from his wounds and was reported present until he was wounded and captured at Winchester, Virginia, on September 19, 1864. He was confined at Fort Delaware, Delaware, until February 27, 1865, when he was transferred to City Point, Virginia, for exchange. Charles was exchanged and was issued a 30-day furlough on March 7, 1865. After the war, Charles returned to Lexington and married Frances Holt on December 23, 1869. Charles inherited "Homestead" from his wife's late father, Dr. William R. Holt. Charles and Frances

would have four children: Louise (1870), Charles A. (1872), Camille (1874), and Lloyd R. (1883). Charles operated a very successful mercantile shop in Lexington known as C. A. Hunt & Co. until he sold it in 1885. Charles used the money from this sale to fund the opening of the Wennoah Cotton Milling Company in 1887. Charles then went in with George Mountcastle to begin the Nokomis Cotton Mill in 1900. The profitable mills operated throughout Charles' life. Charles was a leader in the community, and his wife, Frances, served as the organist for the Episcopal church in Lexington for over 30 years. A story reported in *Confederate Veteran* in 1904 recalls an experience Charles had during the war:

> In the sad days of 1864 a soldier of the 14th North Carolina was wounded near Winchester, Virginia, and was carried to a hastily improvised hospital in the town. As he lay there, a ministering angel by the name of Mrs. Taylor took him into her home and watched over him night and day. Upon his recovery, the soldier gave his benefactress a small gold cross, which he had worn during his service. Mr. C. A. Hunt, distinguished veteran of Lexington, North Carolina, received the cross from which he parted forty years ago.

It was pinned to a silk battle flag, and was sent to him by the son of Mrs. Taylor.

Charles lived in the town of Lexington until he died on February 22, 1925. He is buried in the Lexington City Cemetery.

822. Hunt, Obediah

Private, Lexington Wildcats Company I, 14th Regiment N.C. Troops (4th N.C. Volunteers)

Obed was born in 1840. He worked as a blacksmith prior to volunteering on May 14, 1861. Obed died of diphtheria in Lynchburg, Virginia, on June 28, 1862.

823. Hunt, Phillip Willis

Private, Company K, 63rd Regiment N.C. Troops (5th N.C. Cavalry)

Phillip was born on April 22, 1824. He worked as a farmer, and, in 1859, he married Frances. They had no children. Phillip enlisted in Randolph County on August 23, 1862. He was reported present until he was hospitalized with "chronic diarrhea" on January 13, 1865. Phillip was paroled at Greensboro, North Carolina, on May 16, 1865. After the war, Phillip returned to the Emmons township where he lived until his death on November 15, 1919. He is buried at Pleasant Hill United Methodist Church.

824. Hunt, William Henley

Sergeant, Lexington Wildcats Company I, 14th Regiment N.C. Troops (4th N.C. Volunteers)

William was born April 20, 1841, to Andrew and Elizabeth Hunt. He was a student prior to volunteering on May 28, 1861. William was promoted to sergeant on September 12, 1861, and was reported present until he was wounded in the right leg and captured at Gettysburg, Pennsylvania, on July 5, 1863. He was confined at Fort Delaware, Delaware, until June 19, 1865, when he was released after taking the oath of allegiance. After the war, William returned to Lexington where he married Lettie Conrad on December 19, 1867. William and Lettie would have four children: Jessica (1869), William (1872), Henry (1877), and Walter (1880). William lived in the town of Lexington until his death on March 25, 1886. He is buried in the Lexington City Cemetery.

825. Idol, David H.

Drummer, 2nd Battalion, N.C. Infantry

David was born on December 28, 1829, to Jacob and Martha Idol. He worked as a farmer, and, in 1856, he married Mary. David and Mary would have three children, Adolphus (1857), Emerson (1859), and Jacob (1860), before David was conscripted into service on November 1, 1862 . He was reported present for the duration of the war and acted as chief musician of the battalion from May 1863. After the war, David returned home where he and Mary would have two more children: Alpheus (1863) and Minnie (1868). David lived in the Abbott's Creek area until his death on June 20, 1873. He is buried at Abbott's Creek Primitive Baptist Church.

826. Idol, John Wesley

Second Lieutenant, 66th Regiment N.C. Militia (1861 organization)

John was born in1830 to Jacob and Martha Idol. He worked as a farmer, and, in 1856, he married Elizabeth. John and Elizabeth would have three children: Charles (1857), Julia (1860), and Mary (1861). John accepted a commission in the Browntown District Company on December 13, 1861. John lived in the Abbott's Creek township until his death on October 28, 1916. He is buried at Mount Pleasant United Methodist Church.

827. Imbler (Embler), David

Corporal, Company H, 48th Regiment N.C. Troops

David was born on February 21, 1831, to David and Mary Imbler (Embler). He worked as a farmer, and, on March 12, 1854, he married Didma Sullivan. David was conscripted into service at Petersburg, Virginia, on August 8, 1862. He was promoted to corporal in March 1863. David was reported present until he was paroled at Appomattox Court House, Virginia, on April 9, 1865. David returned home to his farm in the Conrad Hill township where he lived until his death on July 20, 1912. He is buried in the Embler's Grove Family Cemetery.

828. Imbler (Embler), Joseph

Sergeant, Company H, 48th Regiment N.C. Troops

Joseph was born in 1839 to Jacob and Catharine Imbler (Embler). He worked as a farmer prior to volunteering on March 6, 1862. He was promoted to corporal on November 1, 1862, and promoted to sergeant in February 1863. He served as a sergeant until he was killed in action at Petersburg, Virginia, on August 17, 1864.

829. Imbler (Embler), Stephen

Private, Company H, 48th Regiment N.C. Troops

Stephen was born in 1832 to David and Mary Imbler (Embler). He worked as a farmer, and, on March 23, 1852, he married Leatha Floyd. Stephen and Leatha would have three children, Andrew (1855), Martha (1857), and Robert (1860), before Stephen was conscripted into service at Petersburg, Virginia, on August 8, 1862. He was reported present until he was captured at Cold Harbor, Virginia, on June 4, 1864. Stephen was confined at Point Lookout, Maryland, until he was transferred to Elmira, New York, on July 12, 1864. He was confined at Elmira until March 14, 1865, when he was paroled and transferred to Boulware's Wharf, Virginia, for exchange. Stephen was hospitalized at Richmond, Virginia, with "scorbutus" and was issued a 30-day furlough on March 23, 1865. After the war, Stephen returned home to the Conrad Hill township where he and Leatha would have three more children: Schofield (1868), Sarah (1871), and Rueben (1873). Stephen died sometime in late 1904. He is buried in the Embler's Grove Family Cemetery.

830. Ingram, Andrew

Private, Company K, 28th Regiment N.C. Troops

Andrew was born in 1822 to James and Catharine Ingram. He worked as a farmer, and, in 1847, he married Barbara. Andrew and Barbara would have four children, John (1847), Columbus (1851), Tabitha (1853), and Loretta (1859), before Andrew was conscripted into service on November 20, 1863. He was reported present until he died of "abscesses chronic" at Lynchburg, Virginia, on June 1, 1864.

831. Ingram, James

Private, Company I, 42nd Regiment N.C. Troops

James was born in 1832 to James and Catharine Ingram. He worked as a farmer, and, in 1853, he married Amanda N. Sowers. James and Amanda would have two children, Thomas H. (1854) and Burgess (1859), before James enlisted in Rowan County on May 1, 1862. He was reported present until he was captured at Wise's Forks, Virginia, on March 8, 1865. James was confined at Point Lookout, Maryland, until June 28, 1865, when he was released after taking the oath of allegiance. After the war, James returned home to the Conrad Hill township where he and Amanda would have six more children: Lindsay (1864), John (1867), Betty and Ben (1870), Minnie (1871), and Martha (1877). James lived in the Conrad Hill area until his death around 1895. He is buried at Mount Tabor United Church of Christ.

832. Ingram, James William

Private, Lexington Wildcats Company I, 14th Regiment N.C. Troops (4th N.C. Volunteers) Laborer, Confederate Navy Depot, Charlotte

William was born in 1841 to James and Catharine Ingram. He worked as a miner prior to volunteering for service on May 14, 1861. William was reported present until he was transferred to the Confederate Navy on April 5, 1864. No further records.

833. Jackson, Charles H.

Private, Davidson Guards Company A, 21st Regiment N.C. Troops (11th N.C. Volunteers)

Charles was born in 1841. He worked as a farmer, and, in 1862, he married Mary Anne. Charles was conscripted into service on June 6, 1863. He was wounded and captured at Gettysburg, Pennsylvania, between July 2 and 4, 1863. William was confined at Point Lookout, Maryland, until August 1, 1863, when he was paroled and transferred to City Point, Virginia, for exchange. Charles was declared exchanged and then deserted on February 10, 1864. He and Mary Anne had their first child, Cicero, in 1864. He returned to service prior to November 1, 1864, and was reported present until he was paroled at Appomattox Court House, Virginia, on April 9, 1865. After the war, Charles returned to the Emmons township where he and Mary Anne would have two more children: Emma (1866) and Elizabeth (1867). Charles and his family moved out of the county prior to 1880. No further records.

834. Jackson, Joseph J.

Private, Company A, 10th Battalion N.C. Heavy Artillery
Company D, 10th Battalion, N.C. Heavy Artillery

Joseph was born in 1838 to Solomon and Sarah Jackson. He worked as a shoemaker prior to being conscripted into service on March 11, 1863. Joseph was reported present in Company A until he was transferred to Company D of the 10th Battalion. He died of "erysipelas" at Wilmington, North Carolina, on June 27, 1864.

835. Jackson, Thomas J.

Private, Davidson Guards
Company A, 21st Regiment N.C. Troops (11th N.C. Volunteers)

Thomas was born in 1840 to Solomon and Sarah Jackson. He worked as a shoemaker prior to volunteering on May 8, 1861. Thomas was wounded in the head at Winchester, Virginia, on May 25, 1862. He died of his wounds at Winchester on May 29, 1862.

836. Jackson, William J.

Private, Company G, 2nd Battalion N.C. Infantry

William was born in 1841 to Solomon and Sarah Jackson. He worked as a shoemaker prior to volunteering in Forsyth County on September 19, 1861. William was captured at Roanoke Island, North Carolina, on February 8, 1862. He was paroled and returned to service at Elizabeth City, North Carolina, on February 22, 1862. William was reported present until he was wounded at Gettysburg, Pennsylvania, on July 1, 1863. He recovered from his wounds and rejoined his company prior to December 1863. William served for the duration of the war. William returned to Davidson County for a short time, then, as family history goes, "headed west beyond the Mississippi." No further records.

837. James, Andrew Jackson

Private, Company K, 15th Regiment N.C. Troops

Andrew was born in 1834 to Daniel and Elizabeth James. He worked as a farmer, and, in 1853, he married Sarah. Andrew and Sarah would have four children, Louisa (1854), Mary (1856), Jane (1857), and Franklin (1860), before Andrew was conscripted into service in Wake County on July 15, 1862. He was wounded in the shoulder at Fredericksburg, Virginia, on December 13, 1862. While in a Lynchburg, Virginia, hospital, Andrew died of pneumonia on January 16, 1863.

838. James, David

Private, Company H, 48th Regiment N.C. Troops

David was born in 1832 to Daniel and Elizabeth James. He worked as a farmer, and, on May 24, 1853, he married Emaline Hale. David was conscripted into service in Petersburg, Virginia, on July 15, 1862. He was wounded at Sharpsburg, Maryland, on September 17, 1862. David recovered and returned to service on January 11, 1863. He was reported present until he died of disease at Lynchburg, Virginia, on June 22, 1864.

839. James, Jesse

Private, Company H, 48th Regiment N.C. Troops

Jesse was born in 1830 to Daniel and Elizabeth James. He worked as a farmer, and, on June 5, 1858, he married Susan Weaver. Jesse was conscripted into service in Petersburg, Virginia, on August 8, 1862. He was wounded at Fredericksburg, Virginia, on December 13, 1862. William died of his wounds at Richmond, Virginia, on December 20, 1862. He is buried in the Hollywood Cemetery in Richmond.

840. James, John

Private, Confederate Guards
Company K, 48th Regiment N.C. Troops

John was born in 1829. He worked as a planter, and, on November 10, 1850, he married Elizabeth Phillips. John volunteered for service on March 22, 1862. He was reported present until he died of "dyspepsia" in Richmond, Virginia, on October 9, 1863. He is buried in the Hollywood Cemetery in Richmond.

841. James, Theophilus

Private, Company H, 48th Regiment N.C. Troops

Theophilus was born in 1838 to Daniel and Elizabeth James. Theo was conscripted into service in Petersburg, Virginia, on August 8, 1862. He was reported present until he died of dysentery at Gordonsville, Virginia, on March 25, 1864.

842. Jarrett, Addison

Private, Company B, 48th Regiment N.C. Troops

Addison was born in 1843 to Nathaniel and Margaret Jarrett. He worked as a farmer prior to enlisting at Poctaglico, South Carolina, on April 4, 1863. Addison served as a provost guard for Walker's division from April 14, 1864, and was reported present through October 14, 1864. No further records.

843. Jarrett, Alfred

Private, Company B, 48th Regiment N.C. Troops

Alfred was born in 1845 to Nathaniel and Margaret Jarrett. He worked as a farmer prior to enlisting at Gordonsville, Virginia, on September 28, 1863. Alfred was reported present throughout the war and was paroled at Greensboro, North Carolina, on May 15, 1865. No further records.

844. Jarrett, Julius

Private, Company B, 48th Regiment NC Troops

Julius was born in 1845 to Nathaniel and Margaret Jarrett. He worked as a farmer prior to volunteering on March 17, 1862. Julius was reported present until he was wounded at Ream's Station, Virginia, on August 22, 1864. He was issued a 60-day furlough on October 21, 1864. Julius' wounds were so severe that he was retired to the Invalid Corps on January 10, 1865. No further records.

845. Jarrett, William

Private, Company B, 48th Regiment N.C. Troops

William was born on October 10, 1833, to Nathaniel and Margaret Jarrett. He worked as a farmer, and, in 1858, he married Margaret. William and Margaret would have two children, Frances (1859) and James (1862), before William volunteered on March 17, 1862. William was wounded at Fredericksburg, Virginia, on December 13, 1862. He recovered from his wounds and returned to duty on May 10, 1863. William was reported in a hospital in Danville, Virginia, with a gunshot wound on June 15, 1864, however, the place and date of his wound were not mentioned in the records. He was reported present in September 1864 and was accounted for until he was paroled at Greensboro, North Carolina, on May 15, 1865. After the war, he returned home to the Conrad Hill township where he and Margaret would have five more children: Mary (1866), Albert (1867), William (1869), Florina (1871), and Norman (1873). William lived in the Conrad Hill area until his death on October 27, 1923. He is buried at Liberty Baptist Church.

846. Jarvis, Bryant

Private, Company K, 15th Regiment N.C. Troops

Bryant was born in 1829 to William and Sarah Jarvis. He worked as a farmer, and, on September 1, 1848, he married Susan Trondale Waisner. Bryant and Susan would have one child, Bryant (1861), before Bryant was conscripted into service in Wake County on July 15, 1862. He was wounded and captured at Crampton's Pass, Maryland, on September 14, 1862. Bryant was confined at Fort Delaware, Delaware, until October 2, 1862, when he was paroled and transferred to Aiken's Landing, Virginia, for exchange. Bryant was exchanged on November 10, 1862. He returned to the company on January 1, 1863, and was reported present until he was captured at Bristoe Station, Virginia, on October 14, 1863. Bryant was confined at Point Lookout, Maryland, until March 17, 1864, when he died of unreported causes. He is buried in the Point Lookout National Cemetery.

847. Jenkins, David A.

Private, Company G, 66th Regiment N.C. Troops

David was born on January 1, 1820. He worked as a farmer, and, in 1846, he married Mary, who would die in 1864. David and Mary would have two chil-

dren, Louisa (1847) and Eli (1859), before David was conscripted into service on September 22, 1862. After the war, David married Rebecca Shuler on April 29, 1866. David and Rebecca would raise five children in the Lexington township: Enoch (1867), Abram (1869), Edward (1872), Marie (1874), and Samuel (1878). David lived in the Lexington township until his death on March 25, 1907. He is buried at Beulah United Church of Christ.

848. Johnson, Alson Gray

Private, Company C, 61st Regiment N.C. Troops

Alson was born in 1829 to James and Nancy Johnson. He worked as a farmer, and, on August 22, 1854, he married Adeline Elizabeth Fouts. Alson was conscripted into service in Wake County on August 27, 1862. He was reported present until he was captured at Morris Island, South Carolina, on August 26, 1863. Alson was confined at Hilton Head Island, South Carolina, until September 1864, when he was released after taking the oath of allegiance. After the war, he returned home and lived with his wife in the Allegheny township. Alson managed a farm as well as several rental farms and homes. He died on October 7, 1900, and is buried at Clear Springs United Methodist Church.

849. Johnson, Calvin

Private, Company E, 5th Regiment N.C. State Troops

Calvin was born in 1830. He worked as a miner in the Silver Hill township, and in 1850, he married Mary. Calvin and Mary would have four children, Nancy (1851), Lewis (1852), Adaline (1854), and Susan (1857), before Calvin volunteered in Rowan County on June 15, 1861. Calvin deserted at Manassas Junction, Virginia, on July 21, 1861. No further records.

850. Johnson, Chapman

Private, Company H, 48th Regiment N.C. State Troops

Chapman was born in 1845 to Dr. John L. and Elizabeth Johnson. He was employed as a brickmaker prior to enlisting on July 15, 1862, as a substitute. Chapman was reported present until he deserted to the enemy on October 6, 1864. He was confined at Washington, D.C.,

until he was released after taking the oath of allegiance. Chapman left the county prior to 1870. No further records.

851. Johnson, Eli W.

Private, Lexington Wildcats Company I, 14th Regiment N.C. Troops (4th N.C. Volunteers)

Eli was born in 1840. He worked as a farmer prior to volunteering on May 14, 1861. Eli was wounded at Sharpsburg, Maryland, on September 17, 1862. He died of his wounds at a field hospital on September 20, 1862. The roll of honor indicates that Eli was "as gallant a man as ever fought."

852. Johnson, Frontis

Chaplain, 48th Regiment N.C. Troops

Frontis was born in 1837 to Methodist missionaries serving in Constantinople, Turkey, in the domains of the Ottoman Empire. Frontis married Christena while he was serving as an associate minister in Davidson County prior to 1862. Frontis and Christena would have three children: Oliver Platt (1863), William (1865), and Mary (1867). Frontis was appointed chaplain on October 4, 1862, and resigned for unreported reasons on December 12, 1862. After his service, Frontis returned to the Lexington home of Eli and Catharine Penry. Frontis moved his family west before 1880. No further records.

853. Johnson, Green L.

Private, Franklin Guides to Freedom Company K, 44th Regiment N.C. Troops

Green was born in 1831 to Daniel and Elizabeth Leonard Johnson. He worked as a farmer, and, on May 26, 1855, he married Mary Ann Burton. Green was conscripted into service in Johnston County on July 16, 1862. He was reported present until he was listed as a deserter in January 1863. Green returned home and lived in the Thomasville area until his death prior to 1880. He is buried at Spring Hill United Methodist Church.

854. Johnson, James Ivey

Private, Company F, 7th Regiment N.C. State Troops

James was born in 1840 to Harris and Elizabeth Johnson. He worked as a farmer prior to being conscripted into service in Wake County on October 14, 1863. James was reported present until he was hospitalized at Richmond, Virginia, on June 27, 1864, with a gunshot wound. He recovered, returned to service, and was captured at Hatcher's Run, Virginia, on March 25, 1865. James was confined at Point Lookout, Maryland, until June 28, 1865, when he was released after taking the oath of allegiance. After the war, James returned home and married Eliza Daniel on February 13, 1868. James and Eliza left the county prior to 1880. No further records.

855. Johnson, James S.

*Private, Company F, 7th Regiment
    N.C. State Troops*

James was born in 1839 to Allen and Elizabeth Johnson. He worked as a farmer prior to volunteering in Rowan County on July 12, 1861. James was killed during Pickett's charge at Gettysburg, Pennsylvania, on July 3, 1863.

856. Johnson, John H.

*Private, Company B, 48th Regiment
    N.C. Troops*

John was born in 1841 to Allen and Elizabeth Johnson. He worked as a tailor prior to volunteering in Forsyth County on March 8, 1862. John died of typhoid fever in Richmond, Virginia, on November 17, 1863.

857. Johnson, John L.

*Hospital Steward, Company H, 48th
    Regiment N.C. Troops*

John was born in 1812 in Philadelphia, Pennsylvania. John received his medical training in Philadelphia, and, in 1840, he married Elisa. John moved to Davidson County prior to 1850. John and Elisa would have ten children, John (1841), Mary (1843), Chapman (1844), Lewis (1846), Moss (1848), Caroline (1850), Emma (1852), Ash (1854), Lewya (1857), and Sally (1860), before John enlisted on July 15, 1862, as a substitute. He was captured at Sharpsburg, Maryland, on September 17, 1862. John was paroled and rejoined his company five days later. John was appointed hospital steward by March 1, 1863. He served in that capacity until he was paroled at Appomattox Court House, Virginia, on

April 9, 1865. John lived in the Emmons township until his death in 1900. He is buried at Salem United Methodist Church.

858. Johnson, Joseph Y.

*Private, Company C, 17th Tennessee
    Cavalry Regiment.*

Joseph was born on October 13, 1840, to Daniel and Elizabeth Leonard Johnson. He worked as a farmer prior to serving in the 17th Tennessee Cavalry. After the war, Joseph returned to the Thomasville area and married Louenza Gilliam on February 2, 1871. Joseph lived in the Thomasville township until his death on November 8, 1914. He is buried at Spring Hill United Methodist Church.

859. Johnson, Lindsay F.

*Private, Company F, 29th Regiment
    N.C. Troops
Company F, 5th Regiment U.S. Volunteer Infantry*

Lindsay was born in 1844. He worked as a farmer, and, in 1860, he married Louvina Shirley. Lindsay and Shirley would have one child, William (1862), before Lindsay enlisted on an unreported date. He was captured at Jonesboro, Georgia, on September 5, 1864. Lindsay was confined at Camp Douglas, Illionois, until November 1, 1864, when he was released after joining the U.S. Army. After the war, Lindsay returned to the Silver Hill township where he and Shirley would have two more children: Eliza (1866) and Riley (1869). Lindsay lived in the Silver Hill area until his death on June 17, 1914. He is buried in the Workman Cemetery at Cedar Grove Church.

860. Johnson, Peter

*Private, Company F, 53rd Regiment
    N.C. Troops*

Peter was born on May 24, 1846, to Clinton and Sarah Johnson. He worked as a farmer before he volunteered on April 2, 1862. Peter deserted in September 1862 and was absent until he returned on February 28, 1863. Peter deserted to the enemy at Gettysburg, Pennsylvania, on July 3, 1863. He was confined at Fort Delaware, Delaware, until August 1, 1863, when he was released after taking the oath of allegiance. After the war, he was employed as a copper miner, and, on Jan-

uary 7, 1866, he married Jane Clodfelter. Peter and Jane would have three children: Charles (1866), Gerome (1869), and Lucy Ann (1876). Peter lived and worked in the Conrad Hill township until his death on November 30, 1914. He is buried at Liberty Baptist Church.

861. Johnson, Reuben A.

*Private, Holtsburg Guards
Company A, 54th Regiment N.C. Troops*

Reuben was born in 1845 to William and Nancy Johnson. He worked as a farmer prior to enlisting on May 28, 1862, as a substitute for John Mosely. Reuben was reported present until he was hospitalized at Richmond, Virginia, on January 13, 1863. He returned to duty but was hospitalized again on March 19, 1863. Reuben died of "chronic diarrhea" in Richmond, Virginia, on March 24, 1863. He is buried in the Hollywood Cemetery in Richmond.

862. Johnson, Romulus S.

*Private, Company C, 70th Regiment
    N.C. Troops (1st N.C. Junior
    Reserves)
Company B, 48th Regiment N.C. Troops*

Romulus was born on January 29, 1847, to Daniel and Elizabeth Leonard Johnson. He worked as a farmer prior to enlisting in the Junior Reserves on May 24, 1864. He served in the 70th N.C. Troops until he was transferred to the 48th Regiment on an unspecified date. Romulus was paroled at Greensboro, North Carolina, on May 5, 1865. He returned to the Thomasville township and married Linda Elizabeth prior to 1870. Romulus died on December 8, 1917. He is buried at Pleasant Hill United Methodist Church.

863. Johnson, Titus Winborne

*Private, Company B, 48th Regiment
    N.C. Troops*

Titus was born on July 4, 1837, to Allen and Elizabeth Johnson. He worked as a farmer prior to being conscripted on August 8, 1862. Titus was captured at Sharpsburg, Maryland, on September 17, 1862. He was confined at Fort Delaware, Delaware, until October 2, 1862, when he was paroled and transferred to Aiken's Landing, Virginia, for exchange. He was declared exchanged on November 10,

1862. Titus returned to duty and was wounded at Fredericksburg, Virginia, on December 13, 1862. He recovered from his wounds and rejoined his company in March 1863. He was wounded in the right side at Ream's Station, Virginia, on August 25, 1864. Titus was issued a 60-day furlough on December 31, 1864. He took the oath of allegiance at Salisbury, North Carolina, on June 3, 1865. After the war, he returned home to the Jackson Hill township where he lived until his death on April 17, 1913. He is buried at Salem United Methodist Church.

864. Johnson, William

Private, Company H, 48th Regiment N.C. Troops

William was born in 1832 to Clinton and Sarah Johnson. He worked as a hireling prior to volunteering on March 6, 1862. William was reported present until he was captured at Bristoe Station, Virginia, on October 14, 1863. He was confined at Washington, D.C., until December 17, 1863, when he was released after taking the oath of allegiance. No further records.

865. Johnson, William Augustus

Corporal, Davidson Guards Company A, 21st Regiment N.C. Troops (11th N.C. Volunteers)

William was born in 1840 to Wiley and Sarah Elrod Johnson. He worked as a farmer prior to volunteering on May 8, 1861. William was promoted to corporal on April 26, 1862, and served in that capacity until he was paroled at Farmville, Virginia, on April 11, 1865. After the war, William returned home to marry Sarah A. Rominger on November 8, 1865. William and Sarah would have two children: James (1866) and Robert Lee (1868). William and his family moved out of the county prior to 1880. No further records.

866. Johnson, William J.

Private, Holtsburg Guards Company A, 54th Regiment N.C. Troops

William was born in 1818. He worked as a farmer, and in 1838, he married Nancy. William and Nancy would have five children, Ransom (1838), Eliza (1841), Alice (1842), Milton (1844), and George (1853), before William volunteered on March 4, 1862. He was reported present until he died of unreported causes in Richmond, Virginia, on April 2, 1863.

867. Jones, Cyrus P.

Second Lieutenant, Thomasville Rifles Company B, 14th Regiment N.C. Troops (4th N.C. Volunteers)

Cyrus was born in 1842, the son of A. D. Jones. He worked as a shoemaker prior to volunteering on April 23, 1861, when he was appointed corporal. Cyrus was promoted to first sergeant on April 27, 1862, and, on October 4, 1862, he was appointed second lieutenant. Cyrus was wounded at Chancellorsville, Virginia, on May 3, 1863. He recovered from his wounds and was promoted to second lieutenant on November 4, 1863. Cyrus was killed at Spotsylvania Court House, Virginia, on May 12, 1864.

868. Jones, James P.

Private, Company D, 21st Regiment N.C. Troops (11th N.C. Volunteers)

James was born in 1841 to William H. and Julia Jones. James worked as a silver miner prior to volunteering in Forsyth County on July 8, 1862. He was reported present throughout the war and was paroled at Appomattox Court House, Virginia, on April 9, 1865. After the war, James returned to the Lexington township where he married Elizabeth Glover on October 18, 1865. James and Elizabeth would have four children, John (1867), William (1869), Amanda (1876), and James (1879), before the family moved out of the county prior to 1890. No further records.

869. Jones, James W.

Private, Thomasville Rifles Company B, 14th Regiment N.C. Troops (4th N.C. Volunteers)

James was born on August 27, 1837, the son of A. D. Jones. He worked as a machine operator in the Lines Shoe Factory prior to volunteering on April 23, 1861. James was discharged for unreported reasons on September 9, 1861. After his service, James returned to Thomasville where he married Melinda C. Gray on June 24, 1862. James and Linnie would have three children: Edmund (1863), Minnie (1867), and Robert C. (1873). James continued his work in the shoe manufacturing business, and, in 1880 he was employed as a factory superintendent. James lived in the town of Thomasville until his death on February 19, 1894. He is buried in the Thomasville City Cemetery.

870. Jones, Joseph A.

Private, Company A, 10th Battalion, N.C. Heavy Artillery

Joseph was born in 1843 to Thompson and Sarah Jones. He worked as a farmer prior to volunteering on April 2, 1862. He was reported present until he deserted to a Federal gunboat off the coast of Wilmington, North Carolina, on February 4, 1864. Joseph was confined at Fort Monroe, Virginia, until he was released on March 14, 1864, and sent to Philadelphia, Pennsylvania. No further records.

871. Jones, Samuel John

Private, Company G, 2nd Battalion, N.C. Infantry

Samuel was born in 1842. In 1860, he was living in the Abbott's Creek home of James Lane. Samuel worked as a farmer prior to volunteering on September 19, 1861. He was reported present until he was captured at Roanoke Island, North Carolina, on February 8, 1862. Samuel was paroled at Elizabeth City, North Carolina, and returned to service on February 22, 1862. He was reported present until he was discharged on November 21, 1862, under provisions of the Conscript Act. After the war, Samuel returned to the Abbott's Creek township where he married Jane in 1869. Samuel and Jane would have three children: Ida E. (1870), Mary Jane (1873), and Nathaniel A. C. (1879). Samuel and his family left the county sometime prior to 1890. No further records.

872. Jones, Samuel S.

Second Lieutenant, 66th Regiment N.C. Militia (1861 organization)

Samuel was born in 1828 to Wiley and Mary M. Jones. Samuel worked as a teacher, and, on April 20, 1848, he married Agnes Elizabeth Bodenheimer. Samuel and Agnes would have eight children: Maria (1844), Phoebe (1845), James (1847), David (1848), Roseanne (1850), Noah (1853), John (1855), and Oliver

(1864). Samuel accepted a commission in the Clemmonsville District Company on December 25, 1861. Samuel was still teaching school when the Clemmonsville township was ceded to Forsyth County. No further records.

873. Jones, Wesley C.

Second Lieutenant, 66th Regiment N.C. Militia (1861 organization)

Wesley was born in 1834 to Wiley and Mary M. Jones. Wesley worked as a farmer, and, in 1860, he married Mary. Wesley and Mary would have five children: Francis (1862), John (1864), Walter (1867), Fannie (1869), and Minnie (1874). Wesley accepted a commission in the Clemmonsville District Company on December 25, 1861. After his service, Wesley continued his farming in the Clemmonsville district until well after 1880. No further records.

874. Jordan, Alston J.

Corporal, Company A, 10th Battalion, N.C. Heavy Artillery

Alston was born in 1837 to John R. and Mary Jordan. He worked as a farmer prior to being conscripted into service in New Hanover County on November 15, 1862. Alston was promoted to corporal on April 21, 1864. He was reported present through February 1865. No further records.

875. Jordan, John M.

Private, Thomasville Rifles Company B, 14th Regiment N.C. Troops (4th N.C. Volunteers)

John was born on October 11, 1832, to John R. and Mary Jordan. He worked as a farmer, and, on October 7, 1852, he married Esther Stone. John and Esther would have four children, Elvina (1855), Dolphin (1857), Ellen (1859), and Mary T. (1860), before John was conscripted into service in Wake County on July 16, 1862. He was reported present through August 1864. After the war, John returned home where he and Esther would have three more children: John (1865), Emma (1866), and Flora (1872). Esther died in 1875. John married a second time to Mary in 1890. John and Mary would have two children: Martha (1893) and Cramer (1897). John lived in the Thomasville township until his death on October 12,

1915. He is buried at Pine Woods Methodist Church.

876. Kanoy, John A.

Private, Stanly Marksmen Company H, 14th Regiment N.C. Troops (4th N.C. Volunteers)

John was born in 1831. He worked as a farmer prior to being conscripted into service in Wake County on July 16, 1862. John was captured at Sharpsburg, Maryland, on September 17, 1862. He was confined at Fort Delaware, Delaware, until October 2, 1862, when he was paroled and transferred to Aiken's Landing, Virginia, for exchange. John was declared exchanged on November 10, 1862. He returned to duty and was reported present until he was wounded in the thigh at Chancellorsville, Virginia, on May 3, 1863. John died of his wounds at Richmond, Virginia, on June 7, 1863. He is buried in the Hollywood Cemetery in Richmond.

877. Kanoy, John W.

Private, Stanly Marksmen Company H, 14th Regiment N.C. Troops (4th N.C. Volunteers)

John was born in 1841 to David and Sophia Kanoy. He worked as a farmer prior to being conscripted into service in Wake County on July 16, 1862. John was wounded at Sharpsburg, Maryland, on September 17, 1862. He died of his wounds in Maryland on October 1, 1862.

878. Kearnes, J. V.

Private, Uwharrie Boys Company H, 38th Regiment N.C. Troops

J. V. was born on 1843 to Henry Harrison and Susan Dixon Kearnes. He worked as a farmer prior to volunteering on November 4, 1861. J. V. died of disease on August 5, 1862. He is buried at Salem United Methodist Church.

879. Kearnes, Jacob T.

Private, Company C, 70th Regiment N.C. Troops (1st N.C. Junior Reserves)

Jacob was born in 1846. He worked as a farmer prior to enlisting in the Junior Reserves on May 24, 1864. After the war, he returned home to the Emmons township where he married Mary Elizabeth

Kearnes on November 15, 1872. Jacob and Elizabeth moved to Randolph County prior to 1880. No further records.

880. Kearnes, James

Private, Trojan Regulators Company F, 44th Regiment N.C. Troops

James was born on March 12, 1837. He worked as a farmer, and, in 1857, he married Nettie Brewer. James and Nettie would have one child, John (1858), before her death in 1870. James volunteered in Montgomery County on March 1, 1862. He was reported present until he was captured at Sutherland's Station, Virginia, on April 2, 1865. James was confined at Hart's Island, New York, until June 19, 1865, when he was released after taking the oath of allegiance. After the war, James returned to the Jackson Hill township where he married Caroline Morris in 1875. James and Caroline would also have only one child: Arthur (1878). James lived in the Jackson Hill township until his death on March 15, 1937. He is buried at Pine Hill Methodist Church.

881. Kearnes, John A.

Private, Trojan Regulators Company F, 44th Regiment N.C. Troops

John was born on November 11, 1845, the son of S. L. Kearnes. He worked as a farmer prior to volunteering on March 1, 1863. John was reported present until he was captured along the Boydton Plank Road, Virginia, on October 27, 1864. He was confined at Point Lookout, Maryland, until March 30, 1865, when he was paroled and transferred to Boulware's Wharf, Virginia, for exchange. John was paroled at Troy, North Carolina, on May 23, 1865. After the war, he returned to the Jackson Hill township where he married Mary Ann in 1867. John lived in the Jackson Hill area until his death on November 14, 1925. He is buried at Pine Hill Methodist Church.

882. Kearnes, London S.

First Lieutenant, 65th Regiment N.C. Militia (1861 organization)

London was born in 1820. He was married to Susanna prior to accepting a commission in the Rock Spring District Company on November 25, 1861. No further records.

883. Kearnes, Samuel Spencer

Private, Uwharrie Boys
Company H, 38th Regiment N.C. Troops

Samuel was born in 1847. He was conscripted into service at Camp Holmes, Raleigh on October 22, 1864. Samuel was reported present until he was captured at Petersburg, Virginia, on April 3, 1865. He was confined at Point Lookout, Maryland, until June 28, 1865, when he was released after taking the oath of allegiance. After the war, Samuel returned to the Allegheny township where, in 1867, he married Elithue S. They would not have any children, and Elithue would die in 1885. Samuel lived alone on his farm until his death in 1911. He is buried at Salem United Methodist Church.

884. Kearnes, Silas G.

Private, Randolph Rangers
Company G, 46th Regiment N.C. Troops

Silas was born on May 7, 1840. He worked as a farmer prior to being conscripted into service in Wake County on August 16, 1862. Silas was reported present until he was wounded at Wilderness, Virginia, on May 5, 1864. He recovered from his wounds and returned on November 20, 1864. Silas was reported present until he was captured at Hatcher's Run, Virginia, on March 31, 1865. He was confined at Point Lookout, Maryland, until June 28, 1865, when he was released after taking the oath of allegiance. After the war, Silas returned home and married Ruth Ann in 1868. Silas lived in the Allegheny township until his death on December 11, 1878. He is buried at Salem United Methodist Church.

885. Kearnes, William T.

Private, Trojan Regulators
Company F, 44th Regiment N.C. Troops

William was born on June 4, 1827. He worked as an overseer for Casper Smith, and, on February 10, 1858, he married Martha Elliot. William was conscripted into service prior to December 29, 1864, when he received a clothing ration. He was reported present until he was paroled at Appomattox Court House, Virginia, on April 9, 1865. While he was away in service, Martha died, leaving William to return to an empty home. William married Mary Sheets on February 2, 1866. William would live in the Healing Springs township until his death on July 21, 1895. He is buried at Salem United Methodist Church.

886. Keith, John K.

Private, Trojan Regulators
Company F, 44th Regiment N.C. Troops

John was born on April 15, 1834. He worked as a farmer prior to volunteering in Montgomery County on March 1, 1862. John was wounded and captured at Bristoe Station, Virginia, on October 14, 1863. He was confined at Point Lookout, Maryland, until April 17, 1864, when he was paroled and transferred to City Point, Virginia, for exchange. John returned to service prior to October 27, 1864, when he was captured at Boydton Plank Road, Virginia. He was confined at Point Lookout, Maryland, until March 30, 1865, when he was released after taking the oath of allegiance. After the war, he returned to the Allegheny township where he lived until his death on December 25, 1922. He is buried at Lineberry United Methodist Church.

887. Kendall, Hezekiah Addison

Private, Company K, 42nd Regiment N.C. Troops

Addison was born on January 12, 1835, to Nathan and Catharine Kendall. He worked as a farmer just south of Thomasville, and, in 1859, he married Tabitha. Addison and Tabitha would have two children, Irene (1860) and William (1862), before Addison was conscripted in Wake County prior to April 20, 1864. He deserted on July 9, 1864. After the war, Addison returned home to the Thomasville township where he lived until his death on January 15, 1895. He is buried at Fair Grove United Methodist Church.

888. Kennedy, Andrew Jackson

Private, Company A, 10th Battalion, N.C. Heavy Artillery
Company A, 2nd Regiment Confederate Engineers

Andrew was born on April 2, 1829, to John and Sabrina Kennedy. He worked as a carpenter, and, on May 10, 1853, he married Rebecca Morris. Andrew and Rebecca would have four children, Sarah (1854), Henry (1856), Deborah (1859), and John (1862), before he volunteered on March 14, 1862. Andrew was reported present until he was transferred to the 2nd Regiment Confederate Engineers in August 1863. After the war, Andrew returned to Thomasville where he and Rebecca would have three more children: Preston (1866), Samuel (1867), and Robert Lee (1870). Andrew lived in the North Thomasville township until his death on October 2, 1912. He is buried at Pleasant Grove United Methodist Church.

889. Kennedy, Andrew L.

Private, 2nd Company H, 40th Regiment N.C. Troops (3rd N.C. Artillery)

Andrew was born on November 15, 1835, to Burrell and Elizabeth Veach Kennedy. He worked as a carpenter before marrying Mary Kennedy on December 4, 1858. Andrew and Mary would have two children, Amanda (1859) and Lutitia (1863), before Andrew was conscripted sometime prior to May 19, 1865, when he was paroled at Greensboro, North Carolina. After the war, Andrew returned to the North Thomasville township where he and Mary would have four more children: Susan (1866), Betty (1871), Jesse (1878), and Caroline (1883). Andrew died on July 3, 1902. He is buried at Pleasant Grove United Methodist Church.

890. Kennedy, Charles B.

Private, Company A, 10th Battalion, N.C. Heavy Artillery

Charles was born in 1837 to Jacob and Sarah Kennedy. He worked as a farmer prior to volunteering on March 12, 1862. He was reported present until he was captured at Savannah, Georgia, on December 7, 1864. Charles was confined at Point Lookout, Maryland, until he died of chronic diarrhea on April 7, 1865. He is buried in the Point Lookout National Cemetery.

891. Kennedy, Daniel D.

Private, Company I, 76th Regiment N.C. Troops (6th N.C. Senior Reserves)

Daniel was born on February 19, 1821. He worked as a farmer, and, on April 17, 1839, he married Barbara Myers. Daniel and Barbara would have nine children: Isaac (1840), Sarah (1841), Margaret

(1844), Catharine (1846), John W. (1849), Trifena (1852), David (1856), Alfred (1859), and Mary (1864). Daniel served in the Senior Reserves upon their creation in January 1865. Daniel returned from his service and lived in the Thomasville township until his death on July 17, 1869. He is buried at Emanuel United Church of Christ.

892. Kennedy, Emanuel

Private, Company B, 45th Regiment N.C. Troops

Emanuel was born on May 5, 1847, to Burrell and Elizabeth Veach Kennedy. He worked as a farmer prior to volunteering in Guilford County on March 10, 1862. Daniel was captured at Gettysburg, Pennsylvania, when he was left behind to help nurse the wounded. He was confined at David's Island, New York, until September 8, 1863, when he was paroled and transferred to City Point, Virginia, for exchange. Emanuel returned to service and was captured at North Anna, Virginia, on May 24, 1864. He was confined at Elmira, New York, until May 29, 1865, when he was released after taking the oath of allegiance. Emanuel returned home to the Thomasville area where he lived until his death on June 10, 1870. He is buried at Pleasant Grove United Methodist Church.

893. Kennedy, Franklin B.

Second Lieutenant, 66th Regiment N.C. Militia (1861 organization)

Franklin was born on October 12, 1835, to Thomas and Sarah Kennedy. He worked as a farmer, and, on October 16, 1856, he married Mary Ann Hayworth. Franklin and Mary would have three children: Dennis (1857), Sarah (1859), and John T. (1864). Franklin accepted a commission in the Rich Fork District Company on May 22, 1862. Franklin lived in the North Thomasville area until his death on February 18, 1886. He is buried at Mount Pleasant United Methodist Church.

894. Kennedy, James H.

Private, Confederate Guards Company K, 48th Regiment N.C. Troops

James was born in 1832 to Thomas and Sarah Kennedy. He worked as a teacher prior to volunteering in Forsyth County on March 22, 1862. James was reported present until he deserted to the enemy on March 3, 1865. He was confined at Washington, D.C., until he was released on March 5, 1865, after taking the oath of allegiance. After the war, James returned home to the North Thomasville township where he married Cynthia in 1867. James and Cynthia would have five children: William (1868), Robert (1870), Prudence (1874), John (1877), and James L. (1879). James continued his work as a teacher until his death in 1899. He is buried at Pleasant Grove United Methodist Church.

895. Kennedy, John S.

Corporal, Confederate Guards Company K, 48th Regiment N.C. Troops

John was born in 1842 to Burrell and Elizabeth Veach Kennedy. He worked as a farmer prior to volunteering in Forsyth County on March 1, 1862, he was mustered in with the rank of corporal. John was killed at King's School House, Virginia, on June 25, 1862.

896. Kennedy, Joseph B.

Private, Company G, 2nd Battalion, N.C. Infantry

Joseph was born in 1845 to Bryson and Lydia Kennedy. He worked as a farmer prior to enlisting on February 24, 1864. Joseph was reported absent, sick, from May through December 1864, then deserted in January 1865. No further records.

897. Kennedy, Josephus C.

Ordnance Sergeant, 70th Regiment N.C. Troops (1st N.C. Junior Reserves)

Josephus was born on August 6, 1846, to Jacob and Sarah Kennedy. He worked as a farmer prior to enlisting in the Junior Reserves on May 24, 1864, when he was appointed ordnance sergeant. After the war, Josephus returned to the North Thomasville township where he would marry Louretta Sledge in 1869. Josephus and Louretta would have eight children: Arthur (1870), Jacob (1873), Dora (1875), Jessie (1878), John (1883), Rosco (1886), Eugene (1889), and Blanch (1894). Josephus died on May 1, 1906, and is buried at Pine Woods United Methodist Church.

898. Kennedy, Martin

Hospital Steward, Staff, 45th Regiment N.C. Troops

Martin was born in 1836 to John and Sarah Kennedy. He worked as a farmer prior to volunteering in Guilford County on March 10, 1862. He was appointed hospital steward in November 1862. After the war, Martin returned home to the Abbott's Creek township where he married Elvira in 1870. Martin and Elvira would have only one child: Walter (1886). Martin lived in the Abbott's Creek township until his death prior to 1900. He is buried at Pleasant Grove United Methodist Church.

899. Kennedy, Michael Lorenzo

Private, Company E, 5th Regiment N.C. State Troops

Michael was born in 1844 to Elizabeth Kennedy. He worked as a farmer prior to volunteering in Rowan County on June 8, 1861. Michael was wounded at Williamsburg, Virginia, but was then reported present until he deserted on August 15, 1862. He returned on March 26, 1863, and was reported present until he deserted to the enemy on February 26, 1865. Michael was confined at Washington, D.C., until February 28, 1865, when he was released after taking the oath of allegiance. He was furnished transportation to Indianapolis, Indiana. Michael never returned to Davidson County. No further records.

900. Kennedy, William C.

Corporal, Company A, 10th Battalion, N.C. Heavy Artillery

William was born on January 25, 1839, to Elizabeth Kennedy. He worked as a farmer prior to enlisting on April 2, 1862. William was promoted to corporal in September 1862 and was reported present through September 1864. After the war, William returned home to the North Thomasville township where he married Cynthia A. in 1865. William and Cynthia would have four children: Mary (1866), Hattie (1868), Lynden (1870), and Claudia (1873). William lived in the North Thomasville township until his death on November 6, 1899. He is buried at Pleasant Grove United Methodist Church.

901. Kennedy, William J.

Private, Company B, 48th Regiment N.C. Troops

William was born in 1839 to Burrell and Elizabeth Veach Kennedy. He worked as a farmer prior to volunteering on March 4, 1862. William was reported present until he died of a gunshot wound in Richmond, Virginia, on June 24, 1864. The place and date of his wound were not reported.

902. Kepley, Andrew

Private, Lexington Wildcats Company I, 14th Regiment N.C. Troops (4th N.C. Volunteers)

Andrew was born in 1837 to Mathias and Elizabeth Kepley. He worked as a farmer, and, on March 9, 1859, he married Nealy Hedrick. Andrew and Nealy would have one child, Elizabeth D. (1860), before Andrew was conscripted into service on July 16, 1862. Andrew was wounded and captured at Sharpsburg, Maryland, on September 17, 1862. Andrew died of his wounds at a Federal hospital in Shepherdstown, [West] Virginia, on October 7, 1862.

903. Kepley, George

Private, Company C, 61st Regiment N.C. Troops

George was born on April 9, 1826. He worked as a farmer, and, in 1851, he married Isabel. George and Isabel would have one child, William (1852), before George was conscripted on August 27, 1862. He deserted at Kinston, North Carolina, on December 10, 1862. George returned and was imprisoned in Wilmington, North Carolina, in May–June 1863. He was reported in hospitals at Charleston, South Carolina, and Petersburg, Virginia, because of deafness until December 24, 1863, when he was issued a 60-day furlough. George did not return from his furlough. After the war, George returned to the Conrad Hill township until his death on November 29, 1891. He is buried at Holly Grove Lutheran Church.

904. Kepley, James E.

Private, Holtsburg Guards Company A, 54th Regiment N.C. Troops

James was born in 1840 to Daniel and Mary Kepley. James worked as a farmer, and, on December 7, 1860, he married Eliza Cornish. James volunteered on March 3, 1862, and was reported present until he was captured at Rappahannock Station, Virginia, on November 7, 1863. He was confined at Point Lookout, Maryland, until March 15, 1864, when he was transferred to City Point, Virginia, for exchange. James was declared exchanged prior to September 1864. He was reported present until he was paroled at Appomattox Court House, Virginia, on April 9, 1865. After the war, he and Eliza moved to the Yadkin township where they would have four children: Cicero (1866), Lindsay (1869), Martha (1877), and Charles (1879). James and his family moved out of the county prior to 1884. No further records.

905. Kepley, Leonard

Private, Company C, 76th Regiment N.C. Troops (6th N.C. Senior Reserves)

Leonard was born on June 19, 1814. He worked as a farmer in the Three Hat Mountain area of the Conrad Hill township, and, in 1836, he married Elizabeth. Leonard and Elizabeth would have four

Leonard Kepley, ca. 1880, was joined in service by two of his sons (Elizabeth E. Ross, *The Heritage of Davidson County*).

children: Peter A. (1838), Eliza (1840), David (1845), and Bathsheba (1849). Leonard served in Hill's Senior Reserves before the battalion was merged into the 6th N.C. Senior Reserves in January 1865. After his service, Leonard continued farming in the Conrad Hill township. Leonard died on March 2, 1902. He is buried at Holly Grove Lutheran Church.

906. Kepley, Mathias

Private, Lexington Wildcats Company I, 14th Regiment N.C. Troops (4th N.C. Volunteers)

Mathias was born in 1845 to Mathias and Elizabeth Kepley. He worked as a farmer prior to being conscripted into service in Wake County on July 16, 1862. Mathias was reported present until he was killed in action at Sharpsburg, Maryland, on September 17, 1862.

907. Kepley, Peter Austin

Private, Company C, 61st Regiment N.C. Troops

Peter was born on November 7, 1837, to Leonard and Elizabeth Kepley. He worked as a farmer, and, on June 2, 1859, he married Phoebe Swing. Peter and Phoebe would have two children, Matilda (1860) and Eliza (1861),

Peter A. Kepley, shown ca. 1900, was conscripted into the 61st N.C. Troops but deserted after three months (Elizabeth E. Ross, *The Heritage of Davidson County*).

Home of Peter and Phoebe Swing Kepley in the vicinity of Holly Grove (Elizabeth E. Ross, *The Heritage of Davidson County*).

before Peter was conscripted on August 27, 1862. He deserted on December 10, 1862. Peter returned home and avoided arrest until the end of the war. Peter and Phoebe would have nine more children in their Conrad Hill home: Sarah (1863), Martha (1865), Elizabeth (1867), David (1870), Wiley (1871), James O. (1873–91), Robert (1875), Peter (1877), and William (1879). Peter lived in the Conrad Hill township until his death on April 13, 1928. He is buried at Holly Grove Lutheran Church.

908. Kepley, William H.

Private, Company A, 42nd Regiment N.C. Troops

William was born in 1842 to Selena Kepley. He worked as a farmer prior to volunteering on November 26, 1861. William was reported present until he was captured at Battery Anderson, Fort Fisher, North Carolina, on December 24, 1864. He was confined at Point Lookout, Maryland, until May 15, 1865, when he was released after taking the oath of allegiance. After the war, William returned home, and, on March 26, 1867, he married Mahalia Keller. William and Mahalia left the county prior to 1870. Mahalia later filed for a pension, stating falsely that William was wounded at First Manassas, Virginia. No further records.

909. Kesler, Alfred William

Private, Lexington Wildcats Company I, 14th Regiment N.C. Troops (4th N.C. Volunteers)

Alfred was born on September 21, 1837. He worked as an apprentice mechanic prior to volunteering on May 14, 1861. Alfred was reported present until he was captured at Farmville, Virginia, on April 6, 1865. He was confined at Point Lookout, Maryland, until June 28, 1865, when he was released after taking the oath of allegiance. After the war, Alfred returned to the Boone township where he married Missouri Sharpe on August 5, 1865. Alfred and Missouri would have ten children: America (1867), John (1869), Margaret (1870), James (1872), Richard (1874), Mary (1877), Cora (1882), Andrew (1885), Amanda (1887), and Nancy (1892). Alfred lived and worked as a farmer in the Boone township until his death on April 18, 1895. He is buried at Churchland Baptist Church.

910. Kesler, Robert L.

Private, Lexington Wildcats Company I, 14th Regiment N.C. Troops (4th N.C. Volunteers)

Robert was born on December 7, 1827. He worked as a farmer, and, in 1854, he married Delilah Jane. Robert and Delilah would have four children, John (1855), Sarah (1857), Martha (1859), and

Charles (1862), before Robert was conscripted in Wake County on July 16, 1862. He was reported present until he was paroled at Appomattox Court House, Virginia, on April 9, 1865. After the war, Robert returned home to the Boone township where he and Delilah would have two more children: William (1869) and Henry (1871). Robert worked as an agricultural mechanic until his death on February 21, 1875. He is buried at Reeds Baptist Church.

911. Kessley, John H.

Private, Company D, 48th Regiment N.C. Troops

John was born in 1836. He worked as a farmer prior to being conscripted into service on August 8, 1862. John was killed in action at Sharpsburg, Maryland, on September 17, 1862.

912. Killey, Harmon

Surgeon, N.C. Conscript Bureau, Asheboro

Harmon was born in 1829. He worked as a physician and was listed as a surgeon in the Asheboro office of the North Carolina Conscript Bureau by *Moore's Roster*. No further records.

913. Kimel, Daniel

Private, Company C, 30th Regiment N.C. Troops

Daniel was born on September 14, 1844, to Jacob and Nancy Pickle Kimel. He worked as a farmer prior to enlisting at Camp Holmes, Raleigh, on June 20, 1863. Daniel was reported present until he was captured at Farmville, Virginia, on April 6, 1865. He was confined at Newport News, Virginia, until June 27, 1865, when he was released after taking the oath of allegiance. After the war, Daniel returned to Arcadia where he married Mary Rominger on December 17, 1868. Daniel and Mary would have eight children: Jonas (1870), Cicero (1872), John (1873), Catharine (1876), Claudia (1879), Maudie (1884), Nellie (1887), and Thomas (1889). Daniel lived in the Arcadia township until his death on March 11, 1898. He is buried in the Kimel Family Cemetery.

914. Kimel, Noah L.

Private, Company K, 15th Regiment N.C. Troops (5th N.C. Volunteers)

Noah was born on March 27, 1842, to Jacob and Nancy Pickle Kimel. He worked as a farmer prior to being conscripted on July 15, 1862. Noah was discharged because of disability on September 2, 1862. After the war, Noah returned home to the Arcadia area where he married Mary M. Yokely on December 24, 1868. Noah and Mary would not have any children. Noah died on January 27, 1893. He is buried at New Friendship Baptist Church, Forsyth County.

915. Kincey, George

Private, Company H, 48th Regiment N.C. Troops

George was born in 1841. He worked as a hireling in the town of Lexington until he volunteered for service on March 6, 1862. George was reported present until he died of pneumonia at Raleigh, North Carolina, on January 29, 1863.

916. Kindley, James Madison

Private, Company C, 61st Regiment N.C. Troops

James was born in 1842 to Jesse and Susan Kindley. He worked as a farmer prior to being conscripted in Wake County on August 27, 1862. James deserted at Kinston, North Carolina, on December 10, 1862. He returned to service on December 16, 1863, and was placed under arrest. James was returned to duty in January 1864 and deserted again on March 10, 1864. He returned on October 9, 1864, when he was last reported. After the war, James returned to the Conrad Hill township where he married Nancy in 1865. James and Nancy would have seven children: Cicero (1866), Augustus (1868), U. S. Grant (1870), Emma (1872), Annie (1874), William (1876), and Mary Anne (1877). James worked as a farmer until his death in 1896. He is buried at Hughes Grove Baptist Church.

917. Kindley, William R.

First Lieutenant, 65th Regiment N.C. Militia (1861 organization)

William was born on December 14, 1841, to Jesse and Susan Kindley. He worked as a farmer prior to accepting a commission in the Silver Valley District Company on December 26, 1861. After his service, he married Elizabeth Copple on December 21, 1865. William and Eliz-abeth would have six children: Thomas (1866), Frances (1868), Henry (1870), Nerus (1871), Samuel (1883), and Ethel (1890). William died on January 16, 1921. He is buried at Liberty Baptist Church.

918. Kinney, Alexander Roby

Private, Company F, 7th Regiment N.C. State Troops

Alexander was born in 1839 to the Reverend Alfred and Elizabeth Kinney. He worked as a farmer prior to volunteering in Rowan County on July 21, 1861. Alexander was reported present until he died at Carolina City, North Carolina, on January 18, 1862. His body was returned and interred at Lick Creek Baptist Church.

919. Kinney, Alfred Douglas

Private, Company D, 14th Regiment N.C. Troops (4th N.C. Volunteers)

Alfred was born on September 23, 1841, to the Reverend Alfred and Elizabeth Kinney. Alfred worked as a farmer prior to being conscripted into service in Wake County on July 16, 1862. He was reported present until wounded in action at Chancellorsville, Virginia, on May 3, 1863. Alfred recovered from his wounds and rejoined the company in November 1863. He was reported present until he was captured at Bethesda Church, Virginia, on May 30, 1864. Alfred was confined at Elmira, New York, until June 30, 1865, when he was released after taking the oath of allegiance. While imprisoned at Elmira, Alfred and his messmates were able to sneak past the guards and into the food store room. The group was caught, and their punishment was to be stripped of their clothing and marched naked around the prison. After the war, Alfred returned home to the Emmons township where he married Sarah Surratt in 1876. Alfred and Sarah would have six children: Ora (1879), Berry (1882), Numer Roby (1884), Ethel (1889), Alfred Grady (1891), and Jerome (1894). Alfred died on October 18, 1927. He is buried at Lick Creek Baptist Church.

920. Kinney, Daniel F.

First Lieutenant, Company F, 7th Regiment N.C. State Troops

Daniel was born in 1836 to the Reverend Alfred and Elizabeth Kinney. He worked as a farmer prior to volunteering in Rowan County on June 29, 1861. Daniel was appointed bugler on February 15, 1862, and then promoted to Sergeant on November 1, 1862, for "gallant conduct." He was appointed to the post of second lieutenant on March 9, 1863, and promoted to first lieutenant on May 3, 1863. Daniel was captured during Pickett's charge at Gettysburg, Pennsylvania, on July 3, 1863. Daniel was confined at Johnson's Island, Ohio, by way of Fort Delaware, Delaware, until March 22, 1865, when he was paroled and transferred to Cox's Wharf, Virginia, for exchange. He did not return to service after his exchange. After the war, Daniel returned home where he married Jane C. Blackburn on March 3, 1867. Daniel and Jane would have six children: Laura (1869), Essie (1870), Claude (1872), John (1874), Alfred (1876), and Robert (1869). Daniel worked as an agent for the railroad between 1870 and 1880. No further records.

921. Kinney, Ebenezer B.

Private, Company C, 61st Regiment N.C. Troops

Ebenezer was born in 1834. He worked as blacksmith, and, in 1857, he married Hannah Floyd. Ebenezer and Hannah would have two children, William (1858) and David (1861), before Ebenezer was conscripted in Wake County on August 27, 1862. He was reported present until he was "left sick on the road between Goldsboro and Wilmington on January 1, 1863." Apparently, Ebenezer left service and was dropped from the rolls on June 1, 1863. After his return home, Ebenezer and Hannah would have ten more children: Mariah (1864), Romaine (1866), Essie (1870), Eulyss (1877), Bazel (1879), Mentie Rachael, Nivens, Mattie, Dora, and Ada. Ebenezer died on November 2, 1886. He is buried at Holloways Baptist Church.

922. Knouse, Jonas

Private, Company C, 70th Regiment N.C. Troops (1st N.C. Junior Reserves)

Jonas was born on April 27, 1847, to John S. and Charity Knouse. Jonas worked as a farmer prior to enlisting in the Junior Reserves on May 24, 1864. After the war, Jonas returned home to the Arcadia township where he married Paulina Mock on February 14, 1869. Jonas and Paulina would have five children: Laura (1870), Clara (1872), George (1874), Jacob (1879), and Mary (1882). Jonas lived in the Arcadia area until his death on September 13, 1911. He is buried at Mount Olivet United Methodist Church.

923. Knoy, William

Private, Thomasville Rifles
Company B, 14th Regiment N.C. Troops
(4th N.C. Volunteers)

William was born in 1832 to Ellis and Mary Knoy. He worked as a farmer, and, on January 5, 1858, he married Mary Ann Leonard. William was conscripted into service in Wake County on July 16, 1862. He was killed in action at Sharpsburg, Maryland, on September 17, 1862.

924. Koontz (Koonts), Absalom Abraham

Private, Company K, 15th Regiment
N.C. Troops (5th N.C. Volunteers)

"Apps" was born on November 4, 1828, to Jacob and Elizabeth Hege Koontz. He worked as a farmer, and, on August 7, 1850, he married Adeline Gobble. Apps and Adeline would have three children, Margaret (1851), Elmina (1853), and Tazewell (1854), before Apps was conscripted in Wake County on July 15, 1862. He was wounded and captured at Crampton's Pass, Maryland, on September 14, 1862. Apps died of his wounds in Federal hands in the vicinity of Frederick, Maryland, on September 25, 1862.

925. Koontz (Koonts), Alfred Franklin, Sr.

Private, Carolina Rangers
Company B, 10th Virginia Cavalry
Regiment

Alfred was born on June 15, 1827, to John and Mary Strange Koontz. He worked as a farmer, and, on July 27, 1848, he married Mary A. Grubb. Alfred and Mary would have six children, Margaret (1849), William L. (1852), Cornelia (1854), Mary (1856), Addison N. (1858), and Alfred Jr. (1861), before Alfred volunteered in Davie County on October 29, 1861. He died of disease on January 2, 1862. His body was returned and was interred at Wesley's Chapel.

926. Koontz (Koonts), Andrew Jackson

Private, Company G, 7th Regiment
Confederate Cavalry
Company B, 48th Regiment N.C. Troops

Andrew was born in 1835 to David and Susan M. Koontz. He worked as a farmer, and, on January 26, 1859, he married America E. Hedrick. Andrew and America would have one child, Mary Jane (1859), before Andrew enlisted in the 7th Confederate Cavalry. He was transferred to the 48th Regiment on August 8, 1862. Andrew was killed in action at Sharpsburg, Maryland, on September 17, 1862. Records state that Andrew was "shot through the head while bravely advancing on the enemy."

927. Koontz (Koonts), Casper

Private, Company K, 15th Regiment
N.C. Troops (5th N.C. Volunteers)

Casper was born on September 15, 1829, to David and Barbara Hedrick Koontz. He worked as a farmer, and, on March 17, 1853, he married Elizabeth Koontz. Casper and Elizabeth would have four children, Sarah (1854), George W. (1856), David H. (1859), and Phillip (1861), before Casper was conscripted into service in Wake County on July 15, 1862. He was reported present until he died of typhoid fever in Goldsboro, North Carolina, on February 25, 1863. Casper was buried in Goldsboro.

928. Koontz (Koonts), David

Private, Company K, 15th Regiment
N.C. Troops (5th N.C. Volunteers)

David was born on June 13, 1836, to David and Barbara Hedrick Koontz. He worked as a farmer, and, on May 11, 1858, he married Catharine Koontz. David and Catharine would have two children, Jacob (1860) and Mary D. (1862), before David was conscripted in Wake County on July 15, 1862. He was reported present until he deserted on July 31, 1863. David and Catharine's third child, Henry D., was born in 1864. David returned to duty and was reported present until he was captured at Hatcher's Run, Virginia, on April 2, 1865. He was confined at Hart's Island, New York, Harbor, until June 20, 1865, when he was released after taking the oath of allegiance. After the war,

David returned home to his family in the Lexington township. David and Catharine would have three more children: Charles G. (1867), Laura F. (1870), and Albert L. (1874). David lived in the Lexington township until his death on October 9, 1912. He is buried at Beulah United Church of Christ.

929. Koontz (Koonts), Ezekiel

Private, Lexington Wildcats
Company I, 14th Regiment N.C. Troops
(4th N.C. Volunteers)

Ezekiel was born in 1833 to Andrew and Margaret Hedrick Koontz. He worked as a farmer, and, on December 29, 1855, he married Sarah Hedrick. Ezekiel and Sarah would have two children, Martha (1856) and Mary (1859), before Ezekiel was conscripted on July 16, 1862. Ezekiel was listed as missing at Sharpsburg, Maryland, on September 17, 1862. No further records.

930. Koontz (Koonts), George

Private, Company H, 48th Regiment
N.C. Troops

George was born on December 15, 1837, to David and Barbara Hedrick Koontz. He worked as a farmer prior to volunteering at "Wagner's" on March 1, 1862. George died of disease in Liberty, Virginia, on November 30, 1862.

931. Koontz (Koonts), George, Jr.

Private, Company H, 48th Regiment
N.C. Troops

George was born on August 12, 1845, to George and Polly Leonard Koontz. George was conscripted into service on October 13, 1863. He was reported present until he was captured at Hatcher's Run, Virginia, on April 2, 1865. George was confined at Point Lookout, Maryland, until June 28, 1865, when he was released after taking the oath of allegiance. After the war, George returned to the Lexington township where he married Elizabeth Lanning, the widow of William Lanning, on December 6, 1866. George and Elizabeth would have seven children: Martha (1868), John F. (1869), Virginia (1870), Mack W. (1871), Jacob R. (1874), Maggie (1876), and Bonnie Lee (1879). George died on August 22, 1931. He is buried at Beulah United Church of Christ.

Captain Jacob H. Koontz was captured along with his company at Battery Anderson on Christmas Day, 1864 (Clark's Regiments).

932. Koontz, (Koonts) Henry F.

Private, Company A, 42nd Regiment N.C. Troops

Henry was born on December 24, 1845, to Joel and Elizabeth Shoaf Koontz. He worked as a farmer prior to enlisting on March 1, 1864. Henry was reported present until he was captured at Battery Anderson, Fort Fisher, North Carolina, on December 24, 1864. He was confined at Point Lookout, Maryland, via Fort Monroe, Virginia, until June 28, 1865, when he was released after taking the oath of allegiance. After the war, Henry returned home to the Boone township where he married Mary E. Sink on April 25, 1867. Henry and Mary would have eight children: Charles F. (1868), Edward (1870), Etta (1876), Ada (1879), Maude (1881), Loyd P. (1884), Lela (1887), and Pearl (1891). Henry died on December 21, 1919. He is buried at St. Luke's Lutheran Church.

933. Koontz (Koonts), Jacob

Private, Carolina Rangers
Company B, 10th Virginia Cavalry Regiment

Jacob was born on December 26, 1847, to David and Barbara Hedrick Koontz. He was a student prior to volunteering for service in Davie County on November 11, 1862. Jacob was reported present through July 1863, when he was

reported with no horse. Jacob acquired a horse and received a clothing ration on December 31, 1864. After the war, Jacob returned to the Tyro township where he married Phoebe Leonard on March 11, 1869. Jacob and Phoebe would have nine children: Rome (1869), David (1871), Catharine (1872), Jacob (1875), Jasper (1877), Adam (1879), Minnie A. (1881), Ella (1883), and Clay R. (1886). Jacob died on April 28, 1928. He is buried at Beulah United Church of Christ.

934. Koontz (Koonts), Jacob H.

Captain, Company A, 42nd Regiment N.C. Troops

Jacob was born on September 6, 1835, to Andrew and Margaret Hedrick Koontz. He worked as a farmer until he volunteered for service on February 27, 1862, and was appointed first lieutenant. On June 17, 1862, he married Harriet Green. On November 20, 1862, Jacob was promoted to captain of the company. Jacob led the company until he was captured at Battery Anderson, Fort Fisher, North Carolina, on December 24, 1864. As legend goes, Jacob tied a white handkerchief to his sword and surrendered the remnants of the 42nd Regiment. Jacob was confined at Fort Delaware, Delaware, until June 17, 1865, when he was released after taking the oath of allegiance. Records state that he was "a good officer." After the war, Jacob returned home and saw his daughter Hester (1863) for the first time. Jacob and Harriet would have three more children: Ernest (1866) and Gertrude and Eugene C. (1871). Jacob lived in the Tyro area and constructed a home that is revered as a marvel in Davidson County architecture. Jacob died on April 2, 1873. He is buried at St. Luke's Lutheran Church.

935. Koontz (Koonts), Jacob, Jr.

Private, Company A, 42nd Regiment N.C. Troops

Jacob was born in 1823 to Jacob and Elizabeth Hege Koontz. He worked as a farmer, and, in 1844, he married Mittie Ellen Miller. Jacob and Mittie would have six children, Hiram L. (1845), Obediah B. (1848), Eliza Ann (1852), Alexander (1856), Barbara (1858), and Amanda (1860), before Jacob enlisted on an unspecified date. Jacob was reported present until he was paroled at Greensboro,

North Carolina, on May 9, 1865. Jacob died in late May of 1865. He is buried in the vicinity of Reeds Baptist Church.

936. Koontz (Koonts), Jesse S.

First Lieutenant, 66th Regiment N.C. Militia (1861 organization)

Jesse was born on February 6, 1833, to David and Sevele Sowers Koontz. He worked as a farmer, and, on January 18, 1854, he married Lutitia Gobble. Jesse and Lutitia would have four children: Flora J. (1856), Joycie L. (1859), Matrona R. (1862), and Jessie L. (1864). Jesse accepted a commission in the Cross Roads District Company on November 26, 1862. Jesse lived in the Tyro township until his death on January 10, 1865. He is buried at Beulah United Church of Christ.

937. Koontz (Koonts), John H.

Captain, 66th Regiment N.C. Militia (1861 organization)

John was born on April 24, 1837, to Andrew and Margaret Hedrick Koontz. He worked as a farmer, and, on March 15, 1860, he married Jane Elizabeth Craver. John accepted a commission in the Cross Roads District Company on November 26, 1861. After his service, John and Jane would have two children: Webster M. (1867) and Sarah Caroline (1873). In 1871, John bought a 267-acre tract of the Davidson County portion of Peter W. Hairston's "Cooloomee" plantation. John lived in the Tyro township until his death on January 30, 1923. He is buried at Reeds Baptist Church.

938. Koontz (Koonts), John Wesley

Private, Company A, 42nd Regiment N.C. Troops

John was born on May 22, 1824, to John and Mary Strange Koontz. He worked as a farmer, and, on June 28, 1845, he married Susan Sink. John and Susan would have eight children, Mary (1846), Charles L. (1848), Ellen (1850), Sarah (1853), Martha (1855), Harriet (1855), Elizabeth F. (1857), and John S. (1863), before John was conscripted on October 24, 1864. He was reported present until captured at Battery Anderson, Fort Fisher, North Carolina, on December 24, 1864. John was confined at Point

Captain Jacob H. Koontz built this house in 1868. He and his wife would live in the farm's granary until its completion (Touart, *Building the Backcountry*).

Lookout, Maryland, until June 23, 1865, when he was released after taking the oath of allegiance. After the war, John returned home to the Tyro township. John and Susan would have two more children: James (1868) and Walter (1871). John died on February 28, 1893. He is buried at Wesley's Chapel.

939. Koontz, (Koonts) Michael

Second Lieutenant, 65th Regiment N.C. Militia (1861 organization)

Michael was born on August 23, 1820, to David and Sevele Sowers Koontz. He worked as a farmer, and, on January 9, 1843, he married Sophronia "Franey" Shoaf. Michael and Franey would have eight children: Cornelia (1844), Mary (1848), Jesse (1850), David L. (1853), Obediah (1856), Mack M. (1858), John F. (1862), and Charles (1864). Michael accepted a commission in the Ebenezer District Company on October 1, 1861. After the war, Michael was known as an eccentric character. One story in the *Dispatch* told of Michael's arrival in Lexington after a trip to Kansas, where he had bought a coat made from the furs of seven different animals. His home was known as "the sundial house." Each of the posts

on the porch corresponded to a figure on a sundial, so that when the sun struck the post, it cast a shadow that told the time of day. Michael lived in the Lexington township until his death on August 20, 1912. He is buried at Beulah United Church of Christ.

940. Koontz (Koonts), Penn Kelin Zwingley

Private, Company H, 48th Regiment N.C. Troops

Kelin was born in December 13, 1842, to David and Sevele Sowers Koontz. He was named after the founder of the German Reform church. Kelin worked as a farmer prior to being conscripted into service at Petersburg, Virginia, on August 8, 1862. There is some question regarding his service in the 7th Confederate Cavalry Regiment. He was reported present until he was captured at Cold Harbor, Virginia, on June 3, 1864. Kelin was confined at Point Lookout, Maryland, until June 11, 1864, when he was transferred to Elmira, New York. He was confined at Elmira until July 3, 1865, when he was released after taking the oath of allegiance. After the war, Kelin returned home to the Tyro township where he married Eliza Perrell on November 28, 1865. Kelin and Eliza would have one child, C. L. (1868), before moving to Virginia prior to 1880. No further records.

941. Koontz (Koonts), Phillip

Private, Carolina Rangers Company B, 10th Virginia Cavalry Regiment

Phillip was born on September 11, 1826, to Andrew and Magdalene Hedrick Koontz. Phillip worked as a farmer, and,

One of the county's more original and interesting characters, Michael Koontz, ca. 1865 and 1908 (Betty Sowers).

on June 9, 1849, he married Sevele M. Sowers. Phillip and Sevele would have six children, Sylvester (1850), Meshack (1852), Spruce (1854), Mary (1857), Cicero B. (1859), and Andrew J. (1862), before Phillip enlisted on December 19, 1862. He was reported present until he was sent on a horse detail in September–October 1863. Phillip was wounded twice, in May 1864, and at Nance's Shop, Virginia, on June 25, 1864. He was furloughed from a Richmond, Virginia, hospital on August 17, 1864. Phillip returned home where he and Sevele would have one more child before her death in 1865: Virginia (1865). Phillip married Catharine Taylor on August 10, 1865. Phillip and Catharine moved to Lane, Kansas, where they would have seven children: Phillip (1866), Hillary E. (1869), Lula B. (1871), Minnie H. and Henry (1872), Wade Hampton (1875), and Harry C. (1880). Phillip lived in Kansas until his death on November 20, 1889. He is buried in the Lane Quaker Cemetery, Lane, Kansas.

942. Koontz (Koonts), Samuel

Private, Carolina Rangers
Company B, 10th Virginia Cavalry
Regiment

Samuel was born on April 13, 1823, to Andrew and Magdalene Hedrick Koontz. He worked as a farmer, and, on May 6, 1846, he married Louisa Shoaf. Samuel and Louisa would have eight children, Triphenia (1847), Mary A. (1849), Wilson S. (1851), Parthenia (1853), Malinda (1854), Roberta (1856), Andrew J. (1859), and John H. (1862), before Samuel enlisted in Davie County on December 19, 1862. He was listed as absent, without a horse, on July 15, 1864. Samuel was reported present from September 1864 through December 31, 1864, when he was issued a clothing ration. After the war, Samuel and Louisa moved to Davie County, where they would have one more child: Thomas (1866). Samuel lived in Davie County until his death on September 27, 1895. He is buried at Salem Methodist Church.

943. Koontz (Koonts), William

Private, Lexington Wildcats
Company I, 14th Regiment N.C. Troops
(4th N.C. Volunteers)

William was born in 1833. He worked as a carpenter prior to volunteering in

Northampton County on June 4, 1861. William was present until he was reported absent without leave in November 1863. No further records.

944. Koontz (Koonts), William Addison

Private, Holtsburg Guards
Company A, 54th Regiment N.C. Troops

William was born on January 8, 1835, to John and Mary Strange Koontz. He worked as a farmer, and, on January 8, 1852, he married Christina Shoaf. William and Christina would have one child, John (1852), before William volunteered on March 4, 1862. He was hospitalized with hepatitis at Richmond, Virginia, on May 1, 1863. William recovered from his sickness and returned to service on September 1, 1863. He was reported present until he was captured at Rappahannock Station, Virginia, on November 7, 1863. William was confined at Point Lookout, Maryland, until March 15, 1864, when he was transferred to City Point, Virginia, for exchange. William was exchanged and continued to serve until he was paroled at Appomattox Court House, Virginia, on April 9, 1865. After the war, William returned to the Lexington township. He died around 1875.

945. Kritesafeezor, Henry

Private, Confederate Guards
Company K, 48th Regiment N.C. Troops

Henry was born on June 11, 1832, to John and Susannah Kritesafeezor. He worked as a farmer, and, on November 7, 1855, he married Charity Myers. Henry and Charity would have four children, Mary (1856), John (1858), George (1859), and Kate (1862), before Henry was conscripted on August 8, 1862. Henry deserted a week later and did not return until September 30, 1864. Henry was reported present until February 6, 1865, when he deserted to the enemy. He was confined at Washington, D.C., until February 13, 1865, when he was released after taking the oath of allegiance. After the war, Henry returned home to the Clemmonsville township where he and Charity would have five more children: Daniel (1865), William (1866), Henry (1868), Tena (1871), and Cora (1874). Henry lived in the Friedburg area of Clemmonsville until his death on February 29, 1912. He is buried at Friedburg Moravian Church.

946. Lambeth, Benjamin Franklin

Private, Company H, 48th Regiment
N.C. Troops

Benjamin was born in 1840. He worked as a farmer, and, on March 23, 1861, he married Elizabeth Myers. Benjamin volunteered for service on March 3, 1862. He was wounded in the left arm at Fredericksburg, Virginia, on December 13, 1862. Benjamin recovered from his wounds and returned to service in March 1863. Benjamin was reported present until he was paroled at Appomattox Court House, Virginia, on April 9, 1865. No further records.

947. Lambeth, David H.

Private, Company B, 48th Regiment
N.C. Troops
Company K, 27th Regiment N.C. Troops

David was born on August 1, 1845. He worked as a farmer prior to volunteering on March 6, 1862. David was discharged on September 19, 1862, because of "debility from recovering from typhoid fever." David reenlisted into the 27th Regiment at Camp Holmes, Wake County, on April 23, 1863. He was wounded and captured at Bristoe Station, Virginia, on October 14, 1863. David was confined at Point Lookout, Maryland, until April 30, 1864 when he was paroled and transferred to City Point, Virginia, for exchange. Once exchanged, he was reported as absent, wounded, until December 29, 1864, when he was retired to the Invalid Corps. After the war, David returned to Thomasville where he began work as a schoolteacher. On August 23, 1872, David married Augusta. David and Augusta would have four children: Burrell (1874), Albert (1875), Charlie (1876), and Caroline (1880). David lived in Thomasville until his death on August 16, 1927. He is buried in the Thomasville City Cemetery.

948. Lambeth, David Thomas

Third Lieutenant, Thomasville Rifles
Company B, 14th Regiment N.C. Troops
(4th N.C. Volunteers)

David was born at Horseshoe Bend on Reedy Creek on December 19, 1830, to Shadrach and Jane Thomas Lambeth. David worked as a farmer, and, on October 28, 1856, he married Caroline Simmons. David and Caroline would have three children, Frank (1857), Mary (1859), and Jane (1861), before he volunteered on April 23, 1861. David was appointed third lieutenant the same day. He was reported present until May 22, 1861, when he resigned or was discharged from service. David returned home to Thomasville where he and Caroline would have eight more children: Brantley (1863), Eliza (1865), John (1867), Virginia (1872), David, Jr. (1873), Alice (1875), Robert Lee (1878), and Caroline (1881). David lived in Thomasville until his death on July 21, 1899. He is buried in the Thomasville City Cemetery.

949. Lambeth, David Thornton

First Lieutenant, 65th Regiment N.C. Militia (1861 organization)

David was born in 1822. He worked as a farmer, and, in 1846, he married Christina. David and Christina would have five children: Mary A. (1847), Martha (1849), Sarah (1850), Thomas L. (1851), and Susan (1852). David accepted a commission in the Thomasville District Company on December 26, 1861. No further records.

950. Lambeth, Dudley M.

Private, Thomasville Rifles Company B, 14th Regiment N.C. Troops (4th N.C. Volunteers)

Dudley was born in 1840. He worked as a farmer prior to volunteering on May 10, 1861. Dudley was killed in action at Malvern Hill, Virginia, on July 1, 1862.

951. Lambeth, James F.

Private, Company D, 48th Regiment N.C. Troops

James was born in 1839. He worked as a farmer prior to being conscripted on August 8, 1862. James was reported present until captured at Hatcher's Run, Virginia, on April 2, 1865. He was confined at Point Lookout, Maryland, until June 28, 1865, when he was released after taking the oath of allegiance. After the war, James returned to the Thomasville township where, in 1875, he married Amanda Younts. James and Amanda would have four children: Charles (1877), John (1880), Joshua (1882), and Walter (1884). James died sometime after 1900. No further records.

952. Lambeth, John K.

Private, Company H, 48th Regiment N.C. Troops

John was born in 1829. He worked as a farmer, and, on January 6, 1857, he married Mary Gray. John and Mary would have one child, Emsley (1858), before John volunteered on March 31, 1862. He was reported present until wounded at Globe Tavern, Virginia, on August 21, 1864. John recovered from his wounds and was reported present until he was captured at Nottoway, Virginia, on April 5, 1865. He was confined at Point Lookout, Maryland, until June 28, 1865, when he was released after taking the oath of allegiance. No further records.

953. Lambeth, John W. Thomas

Private, Company D, 16th Missouri Infantry
Sergeant, Company H, 48th Regiment N.C. Troops

John was born in 1829 to Silas and Mary Lambeth. John worked as a farmer, and, on October 22, 1848, he married Margaret Kepley. John and Margaret would have six children, Eliza (1851), Robert (1853), Polly (1856), John (1858), Margaret (1860), and Bessie (1861), before John volunteered for service in the 16th Mississippi. He was transferred to the 48th N.C. Regiment on December 29, 1862. John was promoted to sergeant on March 17, 1863, and was captured at Bristoe Station, Virginia, on October 13, 1863. He was confined at Point Lookout, Maryland, via Washington, D.C., until March 4, 1865, when he was received at Boulware's Wharf, Virginia. After the war, John returned to the Thomasville township where he and Margaret would have three more children: Andrew (1865), Emma (1871), and Charlie (1872). John moved to the Holly Grove area where he lived until his death on July 28, 1883. He is buried in the Kepley Family Cemetery.

954. Lambeth, Jones Harrison

Private, Company D, 48th Regiment N.C. Troops

Jones was born in 1839 to Needham and Elizabeth Pope Lambeth. He worked as a farmer prior to volunteering on March 17, 1862. He was later "rejected by the medical surgeons" on an unspecified date. Jones returned home to the

Thomasville area and married Amanda Younts on March 22, 1874. Jones was later married twice more, to Martha Hilton and Julia Murphy. Jones lived in the Thomasville township until his death around 1900. He is buried at Emanuel United Church of Christ.

955. Lambeth, Joseph

Private, Company F, 76th Regiment N.C. Troops (6th N.C. Senior Reserves)

Joseph was born in 1821. He worked as a farmer, and, in 1844, he married Loucretia Kepley. Joseph and Loucretia would have five children: Miranda (1844), Lemuel (1845), Salde (1864), Rowena (1868), and Julia (1870). Joseph enlisted in Hill's Senior Reserves, which became the 6th N.C. Senior Reserves in January 1865. Joseph worked as a small farmer in the Emmons township until his death on August 9, 1897. He is buried in the Lambeth Family Cemetery in the vicinity of Cid, North Carolina.

956. Lambeth, Joseph Harrison

Major, Staff, 14th Regiment N.C. Troops (4th N.C. Volunteers)

Joseph was born in 1840 to Dr. Shadrach and Jane Thomas Lambeth. Joseph worked as a clerk in the town of Thomasville before volunteering as a private on April 23, 1861. Joseph was promoted to third lieutenant on May 26, 1861, and to captain on April 26, 1862. Joseph served as company commander until he was promoted to major and transferred to the field staff on July 5, 1862. Joseph was wounded in the right thigh and captured at Winchester, Virginia, on September 19, 1864. He was hospitalized at Baltimore, Maryland, until he was sent to prison at Point Lookout, Maryland, on an unspecified date. Joseph was confined at Point Lookout until he was released and transferred to Venus Point, Georgia, where he was received for exchange on November 15, 1864. Joseph was paroled at Greensboro, North Carolina, on May 2, 1865. After the war, he returned home to the town of Thomasville where he began several enterprises and married Mary Clarissa Mahala, daughter of J. P. Mahala. Joseph and Mary would have two children: John W. (who would follow in his father's footsteps in the business world) and William Alexander (who would become a member of the faculty at the University of Virginia).

After Mary's death in 1870, Joseph married Virginia Loflin in 1873. Joseph and Virginia would have three children: Virginia (1874), Eugene (1880), and Rosalie (1884). Joseph profited from the sale of a successful tobacco warehouse and created a cigarette factory, along with James A. Leach, in 1868. He also operated Lambeth & Co. in 1870–78. In 1895, Joseph bought controlling interest in the Thomasville Manufacturing Company, which made chairs and cabinetry. Later, in 1897, he and his son John W. Lambeth created Lambeth Furniture, which was the foremost producer of kitchen safes in the South. Joseph retired from his enterprises in 1910 and lived out his days in his home. Joseph passed away on March 10, 1914. He is buried at Fair Grove Methodist Church.

957. Lambeth, Lorenzo D.

Private, Company K, 15th Regiment
N.C. Troops (5th N.C. Volunteers)
Company K, 48th Regiment N.C. Troops

Lorenzo was born on March 3, 1836, to Samuel and Rachael Myers Lambeth. Lorenzo was a student under the Reverend P. A. Long prior to being conscripted into service in Wake County on July 15, 1862. On February 3, 1863, he was transferred to the 48th Regiment. He was reported present until he was wounded in action at Wilderness, Virginia, on May 5, 1864. Lorenzo returned to service prior to July 1864. He was paroled at Appomattox Court House, Virginia, on April 5, 1865. After the war, Lorenzo returned home and married Susan in 1866. Lorenzo and Susan would have three children: Phoebe (1866), Pleasant (1867), and Charles (1868). Lorenzo lived in the Midway township until his death on October 11, 1916. He is buried at Old Vernon Methodist Church.

958. Lambeth, Samuel Jefferson

Private, Company C, 70th Regiment
N.C. Troops (1st N.C. Junior
Reserves)

Samuel was born on April 1, 1846, to Samuel and Rachael Myers Lambeth. He worked as a farmer prior to enlisting in the Junior Reserves on May 24, 1864. After the war, Samuel returned home where he married Barbara Miller on December 22, 1868. Samuel and Barbara would have ten children: John (1871),

Joseph (1873), Lee (1875), Minnie (1876), Arthur (1880), Hattie (1881), Thomas (1884), Franklin (1887), Albert (1891), and Burley (1892). Samuel lived to be the county's last surviving veteran; he died on June 16, 1940. He is buried at Hebron United Church of Christ.

959. Lambeth, William

Private, Company C, 30th Regiment
N.C. Troops

William was born in 1826. He worked as a farmer prior to volunteering. William was promoted to corporal on May 1, 1862, and was wounded at Malvern Hill, Virginia, on July 1, 1862. He was discharged on February 4, 1863, due to disability. William reenlisted into service at Camp Holmes, Raleigh, on July 1, 1863. He served as a private and was reported present through August 1864. After the war, William returned to the Lexington township, where he married Melinda Myers on March 11, 1870. William and Melinda would have two children: Flora (1872) and Everett (1873). William lived in the Lexington area until his death sometime prior to 1900. No further records.

960. Lane, Alexander

Second Lieutenant, 65th Regiment
N.C. Militia (1861 organization)

Alexander was born in 1840 to Sophia Lane. He worked as a farmer prior to accepting a commission in the Lick Creek District Company on December 26, 1861; serving as a second lieutenant. On August 9, 1863, he married Martha Thompson. The couple moved out of the county prior to 1870. No further records.

961. Lanier, Alexander

Private, Davidson Guards
Company A, 21st Regiment N.C. Troops
(11th N.C. Volunteers)
U.S. Army

Alexander was born in 1845 to Lewis and Dovey Lanier. He worked as a farmer prior to being conscripted in Wake County on June 6, 1863. Alexander was reported present until he was captured at Winchester, Virginia, on September 19, 1864. He was confined at Point Lookout, Maryland, until October 17, 1864, when he was released after joining the U.S. Army. The unit to which he was assigned

was not reported. After the war, Alexander returned to the Allegheny township where he married Annie Morris on August 4, 1870. Alexander and Annie would have four children: Elizabeth (1873), John (1874), Minnie (1877), and Roby (1880). No further records.

962. Lanier, Drury G. H.

Private, Davidson Guards
Company A, 21st Regiment N.C. Troops
(11th N.C. Volunteers)

Drury was born on February 4, 1840, to Thomas and Sarah Temple Lanier. He worked as a farmer prior to volunteering on May 8, 1861. Drury was reported present until he died of disease at Lynchburg, Virginia, on July 1, 1864.

963. Lanier, Edward

Private, Company K, 15th Regiment
N.C. Troops (5th N.C. Volunteers)

Edward was born on February 4, 1840, to Thomas and Sarah Temple Lanier. He worked as a farmer, and, on November 21, 1860, he married Martha Alice Walser. Edward and Martha would have one child, Drury G. (1861), before Edward was conscripted in Wake County on July 15, 1862. He was wounded at Crampton's Pass, Maryland, on September 14, 1862. Edward recovered from his wounds and returned to duty on June 23, 1863. He was reported present until he was captured near Petersburg, Virginia, on February 6, 1865. Edward was confined at Point Lookout, Maryland, until June 28, 1865, when he was released after taking the oath of allegiance. After the war, Edward returned home where he and Martha would have four more children: Burl M. (1866), Isabella (1868), Stella (1872), and Sarah (1873). Edward and his family moved to Davie County around 1880. Edward lived in Davie County until his death on August 9, 1902. He is buried at Fulton United Methodist Church.

964. Lanier, Israel

Private, Company E, 5th Regiment
N.C. State Troops

Israel was born in 1839. In 1850, Israel and his sister were living in the home of Alsy Doby. Israel volunteered for service in Rowan County on June 17, 1861. He was wounded at Seven Pines, Virginia, on May 31, 1862, and did not return to service until March 1, 1863. Israel was killed in action at Chancellorsville, Virginia, on May 2, 1863.

965. Lanier, James C.

Second Lieutenant, Company C, 61st Regiment N.C. Troops
Company B, 61st Regiment N.C. Troops

James was born on December 18, 1839, to John and Margaret Lanier. James worked as a mechanic prior to being conscripted on August 27, 1862. James was promoted to corporal on January 16, 1863, and to sergeant on October 13, 1863. He served as a sergeant until he was wounded in action at Drewery's Bluff, Virginia, in May 1864. James returned to duty and was elected second lieutenant on September 4, 1864. James was transferred to Company B of the 61st Regiment, where he served as acting commander from October 1864 until the end of the war. After the war, James returned home where he would marry Nancy Harrison on October 15, 1868. James and Nancy would have 11 children: John R. (1870), Cornelia (1872), Elkannah (1875), Margarel (1878), Stephen (1879), Minnie (1881), Oscar (1883), Bartie (1886), Myrtle (1888), Nellie (1891), and Irvin (1895). James worked as a successful farmer in the Allegheny township until his death on December 10, 1910. He is buried at Tom's Creek Baptist Church.

966. Lanier, Lewis

Private, Company I, 42nd Regiment N.C. Troops

Lewis was born in 1843. He worked as a farmer prior to volunteering on March 7, 1862. Lewis was reported present through November 5, 1864. No further records.

967. Lanier, Phillip

Private, Franklin Guides to Freedom Company K, 44th Regiment N.C. Troops

Phillip was born on August 18, 1845, to William and Elizabeth Riley Lanier. He worked as a farmer prior to being conscripted on November 8, 1863. Phillip was reported present until captured at Petersburg, Virginia, on April 2, 1865. He was confined at Hart's Island, New York, until June 19, 1865, when he was released after taking the oath of allegiance. After the

war, Phillip returned to the Emmons township. Phillip died on August 16, 1937. He is buried at Lick Creek Baptist Church.

968. Lanier, Thomas

Private, Company C, 61st Regiment N.C. Troops

Thomas was born on December 15, 1838, to John and Margaret Lanier. He worked as a farmer, and, on September 25, 1859, he married Nancy A. Cox. Thomas was conscripted into service on August 27, 1862. He was reported present until furloughed on October 7, 1864. The roll of honor indicates that he was wounded around Petersburg, Virginia, in an unspecified engagement. After the war, Thomas returned home to the Emmons township. Thomas and Nancy would have four children: John (1873), Cicero (1875), Margaret (1876), and Jeremiah (1879). Thomas lived in the Allegheny township until his death on March 3, 1888. He is buried in the Lanier Family Cemetery.

969. Lanier, William R.

Private, Lexington Wildcats Company I, 14th Regiment N.C. Troops (4th N.C. Volunteers)

William was born in 1843 to Lewis and Dovey Lanier. He worked as a farmer prior to volunteering at Camp Daniel on September 12, 1861. William was present until he was reported absent without leave from May 25, 1863, until November 20, 1863. William then deserted to the enemy at Bermuda Hundred, Virginia, on January 25, 1865, and took the oath of allegiance on January 27, 1865. After the war, William returned home and married Marinda in 1865. William and Marinda would have two children: Mary (1866) and Charles (1869). No further records.

970. Lanning, George Washington

Private, Company I, 42nd Regiment N.C. Troops

George was born on February 14, 1840, to William and Rachael Wilson Lanning. He worked as a farmer prior to being conscripted on May 4, 1863. George was reported present until he was paroled at Greensboro, North Carolina, on May 8, 1865. After the war, George returned home to the Tyro area. George married

Barbara Temple Hanes, the widow of Christian Hanes, who had died in the war. George and Barbara would have eight children: William P. (1867), Cora Lee (1869), Henry F. (1875), Minnie (1877), Walter (1880), Phillip (1882), Edward (1886), and Alice (1888). George lived in the Tyro area until his death on January 8, 1888. He is buried at Wesley's Chapel.

971. Lanning, John

Private, Company K, 8th Regiment N.C. State Troops

John was born on May 2, 1831, to William and Rachael Wilson Lanning. He worked as a farmer, and, on October 17, 1854, he married Lucy A. Brown. John and Lucy would have two children, Clarilla (1856) and William (1858), before John volunteered for service in Rowan County on August 16, 1861. His term of service lasted only one day as he was "rejected by the mustering officer on August 17, 1861." After the war, John returned home to the Tyro township where he and Lucy would have four more children: James (1865), Martha (1867), Baxter (1872), and John (1873). John lived in the Tyro area until his death on February 17, 1875. He is buried at St. Luke's Lutheran Church.

972. Lanning, Marion

Private, Thomasville Rifles Company B, 14th Regiment N.C. Troops (4th N.C. Volunteers)

Marion was born in 1840 to William and Rachael Wilson Lanning. He worked as a farmer prior to volunteering on August 15, 1861. Marion died of "measles" at Richmond, Virginia, on June 26, 1862.

973. Lanning, Obediah

Private, Company H, 48th Regiment N.C. Troops

Obediah was born in 1843 to Joseph and Rosanna Smith Lanning. He worked as a farmer prior to being conscripted in Wake County on October 18, 1863. Obediah was reported present through April 1864. No further records.

974. Lanning, Robert

Private, Company K, 15th Regiment N.C. Troops (5th N.C. Volunteers)

Robert was born on March 17, 1832, to Joseph and Rosanna Smith Lanning. Robert worked as a farmer prior to being conscripted in Wake County on July 15, 1862. He was reported present until November 20, 1862, when he was discharged because of "phthisis." On August 16, 1866, Robert married Elizabeth Koontz. Robert and Elizabeth would have four children: Mary Alice (1867), Joseph H. (1869), Albert L. (1874), and Elizabeth J. (1877). Robert lived in the Tyro township until his death on December 4, 1895. He is buried at Reeds Baptist Church.

975. Lanning, Thomas F.

Sergeant, Company A, 42nd Regiment N.C. Troops

Thomas was born on May 3, 1837, to William and Rachael Wilson Lanning. He worked as a farmer prior to volunteering on November 26, 1861, when he was mustered in as a corporal. Thomas was promoted to sergeant on May 10, 1862, and was reported present until he was wounded at Bermuda Hundred, Virginia, on May 20, 1864. Thomas recovered from his wounds and was captured at Battery Anderson, Fort Fisher, North Carolina, on December 24, 1864. He was confined at Fort Delaware, Delaware, until June 19, 1865, when he was released after taking the oath of allegiance. After the war, Thomas returned home to the Tyro township where he married Mary Ratts on December 23, 1865. Thomas and Mary would have five children: Eliza C. (1867), Ellen E. (1868), Mary (1870), George (1872), and Margaret (1875). Thomas died on May 2, 1924. He is buried at Wesley's Chapel.

976. Lanning, William

Private, Company K, 15th Regiment N.C. Troops (5th N.C. Volunteers)

William was born on May 25, 1834, to Joseph and Rosanna Smith Lanning. He worked as a farmer, and, on April 17, 1862, he married Elizabeth Koontz. William and Elizabeth would have one child, who died as an infant, before William was conscripted in Wake County on July 15, 1862. William was reported present until he died of disease at Charleston, South Carolina, on April 27, 1863.

977. Lash, John A.

Private, Davidson Guards
Company A, 21st Regiment N.C. Troops (11th N.C. Volunteers)

John was born on January 19, 1843. A Moravian, he worked as a small farmer prior to being conscripted into service in Wake County on October 15, 1864. John was reported present until he was captured at Sayler's Creek, Virginia, on April 6, 1865. He was confined at Newport News, Virginia, until June 27, 1865, when he was released after taking the oath of allegiance. After the war, John returned to the Friedburg community where he would marry Sarah Hill on January 8, 1878. John and Sarah would have two children: Henry (1882) and Belinda (1883). John worked as a farmer until his death on December 16, 1895. He is buried at Friedburg Moravian Church.

978. Lashmit, Franklin

Private, Company K, 21st Regiment N.C. Troops (11th N.C. Volunteers)

Franklin was born on September 16, 1824. He worked as a farmer, and, in 1851, he married Maria. Franklin and Maria would have five children, Thomas (1852), Frances (1853), Ellen (1857), Cornelia (1861), and Mary before Franklin was conscripted on November 13, 1863. He was reported present until May 7, 1864, when he deserted. Franklin returned to duty on October 16, 1864, and was reported present until he was captured at Fort Stedman, Virginia, on March 25, 1865. He was confined at Point Lookout, Maryland, until June 28, 1865, when he was released after taking the oath of allegiance. After the war, Franklin returned to the Arcadia township where he and Maria had two more children: Harry (1867) and William (1870). Franklin was a neighbor and friend of Jesse Hill and is mentioned several times in Hill's letters. Franklin died on July 24, 1874. He is buried at Mount Olivet United Methodist Church.

979. Lashmit, William F.

Private, Company G, 33rd Regiment N.C. Troops

William was born in 1831. He worked as a farmer prior to being conscripted into service in Forsyth County on July 15, 1862. William was reported present until he was

wounded at Chancellorsville, Virginia, on May 3, 1863. He was reported absent, sick, and absent, wounded, until he returned to service in September 1864. William was reported present until he was captured at Petersburg, Virginia, on April 2, 1865. He was confined at Point Lookout, Maryland, until June 28, 1865, when he was released after taking the oath of allegiance. No further records.

980. Lawrence, Edward S.

First Lieutenant, Company F, 76th Regiment N.C. Troops (6th N.C. Senior Reserves)

Edward was born on June 7, 1817. He operated a flour mill, and, in 1858, he married Mary F. Andrews. Edward and Mary would have two children: Nancy (1859) and Thomas W. (1866). Edward enlisted in Moss' Senior Reserves, which became the 6th N.C. Senior Reserves in January 1865. Edward continued to operate his flourmill in the Cotton Grove township until his death on May 27, 1892. He is buried at Pleasant Hill United Methodist Church.

981. Leach, Alexander A.

First Lieutenant, Thomasville Rifles
Company B, 14th Regiment N.C. Troops (4th N.C. Volunteers)

Alexander was born in 1834. He worked as a carpenter prior to volunteering on April 23, 1861, when he was mustered in as a corporal. Alexander was elected to the post of third lieutenant on April 25, 1862, and was promoted to first lieutenant on November 4, 1863. Alexander served as both first lieutenant and company commander from the date of his promotion through April 2, 1865. After the war, Alexander returned home to the Thomasville area. On February 6, 1866, he married Pattie Cornelia Leach. Alexander and Pattie would have five children: Daisy (1869), Eva (1878), James (1880), Charles (1883), and John (1885), before Alexander moved out of the county prior to 1890. No further records.

982. Leach, James Addison

Sergeant, Randolph Rangers
Company G, 46th Regiment N.C. Troops

James was born on September 12, 1839, to James and Margaret Mendenhall Leach. James was a student prior to being

James A. Leach, businessman, politician and representative in post-reconstruction North Carolina (Betty Brown).

conscripted on July 8, 1862. He was mustered in as a private, but on March 27, 1863, he was detailed to serve as regimental sergeant major until April 30, 1863. He was detailed as regimental commissary sergeant on November 7, 1863. James served as commissary sergeant through December 1864. He was reported present until he was paroled at Appomattox Court House, Virginia, on April 9, 1865. After the war, James returned home to the Thomasville area where, on January 12, 1865, he married Lavina Dobson. James and Lavina would have three children, Daisy (1869), Myrtle (1872), and Eva (1878), before Lavina's death. James then married Martha Ann Lewis. They would not have any children together. James was very involved in the community of Thomasville during the post-reconstruction period. James, in partnership with Joseph H. Lambeth, owned several properties in the town, including a shoe factory, a mercantile business, and a tobacco warehouse. In 1866, Leach Tobacco manufactured one of the finest quality machine-rolled cigarettes. James entered politics and was elected mayor of Thomasville for several years in the 1870s and 1880s. He also served as a state representative (1882–86) and a state senator (1888–92). James was a member of the Masonic order until his death on July 27, 1897. He is buried in the Thomasville City Cemetery.

983. Leach, James Madison

Lieutenant Colonel, 21st Regiment N.C. Troops (11th N.C. Volunteers)

James was born on January 17, 1815, near the family home of "Landsdowne," to William and Nancy Brown Leach. James attended the U.S. Military Academy at West Point and graduated in 1838. James was admitted to the American Bar Association in 1842 and began to practice law in the city of Lexington. On January 24, 1846, he married Eliza Montgomery. Leach, a Southern Whig, was elected to Congress in 1859, and he resigned in 1861. James and Eliza would have five children, Mary (1849), Julian (1850), William P. (1852), Madison (1860), and Archibald (1861), before James volunteered for service on May 8, 1861. He was elected as captain the same day and was reported present until he was promoted to lieutenant colonel on July 3, 1861. James resigned from the staff of the 21st North Carolina on December 23, 1861, and became a Confederate States congressman in 1864. James served from 1866 to 1869 as a North Carolina state senator; he fought for improvements in common schools and transportation. James Leach was elected to the United States Congress once again and served two terms between 1871 and 1875. He and Jesse Hargrave sued the U.S. Government to recover the cost of rebuilding the courthouse after it burned while being used as a barracks for the 12th Michigan Cavalry. The two did not win their famous lawsuit. James and his family moved to Randolph County sometime after 1870. James lived in Randolph County until his death on June 1, 1891. He is buried at Hopewell United Methodist Church.

984. Leathco, James Pinckney

Private, Lexington Wildcats
Company I, 14th Regiment N.C. Troops (4th N.C. Volunteers)

James was born in 1838 to Louvina Leathco. He worked as a farmer and was living with Peter Gibson in 1850. James volunteered on May 14, 1861, and was reported present until September 30, 1862, when he was hospitalized at Richmond, Virginia, with a gunshot wound. He returned to service prior to January 1, 1863. James was reported present until he deserted to the enemy on December 5, 1863, and took the oath of alle-

giance in [West] Virginia. No further records.

985. Leatherman, Elias

Private, Company H, 48th Regiment N.C. Troops

Elias was born in 1843 to Daniel and Nancy Leonard Leatherman. Elias worked as a hireling prior to volunteering at "Wagner's" on March 1, 1862. He was reported present until he was wounded in the mouth at Fredericksburg, Virginia, on December 13, 1862. Elias was hospitalized at Richmond, Virginia, until he died of his wounds on December 20, 1862.

986. Leatherman, John

Private, Company H, 48th Regiment N.C. Troops

John was born in 1839 to Daniel and Nancy Leonard Leatherman. He worked as a hireling prior to volunteering on March 25, 1862. John was captured at Frederick, Maryland, prior to September 26, 1862, when he was paroled. John returned to service prior to January 1863 and was reported present until he was wounded in both thighs at Spotsylvania Court House, Virginia, on May 12, 1864. John was sent to Richmond, Virginia, where he was hospitalized on May 18, 1864. John died of his wounds on May 25, 1864.

987. Leatherman, William

Private, Raleigh Rifles
Company K, 14th Regiment N.C. Troops (4th N.C. Volunteers)

William was born on June 12, 1830, to Daniel and Nancy Leonard Leatherman. He worked as a farmer, and, on December 22, 1853, he married Mary Everhart. William and Mary would have three children, Dock (1854), Romulus (1856), and Louisa (1857), before William was conscripted into service in Wake County on June 17, 1863. Their fourth child, John, was born in 1863. William was reported present through August 1864 and was paroled at Greensboro, North Carolina, on May 4, 1865. After the war, William returned to the Boone-Tyro area where he and Mary would have four more children: Britton (1865), Nancy A. (1868), Alice V. (1870), and Triffie (1874). William worked as a farmer until his death on September 3, 1910. He is buried at Shiloh United Methodist Church.

988. Ledford, Preston Lafayette

Corporal, Thomasville Rifles
Company B, 14th Regiment N.C. Troops
(4th N.C. Volunteers)

Preston was born on December 6, 1839, to Henry and Catharine Ledford. His father was a master gunsmith, but Preston chose to enter the field of education and worked as a schoolteacher prior to being conscripted in Wake County on July 15, 1862. He was promoted to corporal on August 1, 1864, and was reported present until he was captured at Jarratt's Station, Virginia, on April 3, 1865. Preston was confined at Hart's Island, New York, until June 17, 1865, when he was released after taking the oath of allegiance. After the war, Preston continued working as a teacher and schoolmaster in the Abbott's Creek township. In 1900, he was listed as a boarder for John Broadway. Preston served as school superintendent in the 1910s. He wrote his book, *My Reminisces of the Civil War*, in 1917. Preston died on May 26, 1922. He is buried at Bethany United Church of Christ. Both Ledford High School and Ledford Middle School were named in his honor.

989. Lee, John W.

Private, Company C, 70th Regiment N.C. Troops (1st N.C. Junior Reserves)

John was born on June 20, 1847, to James and Masan Lee. He worked as a carpenter prior to enlisting in the Junior Reserves on May 24, 1864. After the war, he returned home to the Light area of the Conrad Hill township where he married Sarah in 1872. John and Sarah would have five children: Maude (1873), Annie (1878), John (1881), Ernest (1890), and Harvey (1892). John worked as a carpenter and as a successful farmer and was a member of the Masonic order. After he gave up his carpentry trade, John served as an investor and entrepreneur in Thomasville's fledgling business sector. John served as a county commissioner for over 12 years and on the Davidson County school board for two terms. John lived in the Conrad Hill township until his death on November 26, 1922. He is buried at Fair Grove Methodist Church.

990. Lefler, Daniel

Private, Company H, 48th Regiment N.C. Troops

Daniel was born in 1840 to Aaron and Catharine Lefler. He worked as a farmer in the Allegheny township prior to volunteering in Rowan County on March 19, 1862. Daniel was reported present until he was killed in action at Bristoe Station, Virginia, on October 14, 1863.

991. Leonard, Absalom

Private, Company H, 48th Regiment N.C. Troops

Absalom was born in 1836 to George and Mary Waitman Leonard. He worked as a hireling prior to volunteering on March 12, 1862. Absalom was reported absent without leave from September 19, 1862, through February 11, 1863. He was reported present until he was wounded in the breast at Petersburg, Virginia, on June 15, 1864. Absalom died of his wounds in Richmond, Virginia, on June 16, 1864.

992. Leonard, Alexander, Jr.

Private, Company I, 42nd Regiment N.C. Troops

Alexander was born in 1845 to Alexander and Sivela Hunt Leonard. He worked as a farmer prior to being conscripted on May 4, 1862. Alexander was reported present until he was hospitalized at New Bern, North Carolina, on March 15, 1865, with a gunshot wound in the lung. Alexander died of his wounds on March 18, 1865. He is buried at Cedar Grove Cemetery in New Bern.

993. Leonard, Alexander, Sr.

Private, Company I, 42nd Regiment N.C. Troops

Alexander was born in 1814 to Valentine and Sarah Koontz Leonard. He worked as a farmer, and, in 1838, he married Sivela Hunt. Alexander and Sivela would have four children, George (1839), Valentine (1841), Amanda (1844), and Alexander, Jr. (1845), before Alexander was conscripted on May 4, 1862. He was reported present until discharged on February 20, 1863, because of "a frail constitution, undersized and generally of no service as a soldier." Alexander returned home to the Lexington township. He died

on January 25, 1887, and is buried at Mount Olivet United Methodist Church.

994. Leonard, Alexander L.

Private, Company H, 48th Regiment N.C. Troops

Alexander was born on May 8, 1845, to David and Katharine Livengood Leonard. He worked as a hireling prior to volunteering on March 6, 1862. Alexander was reported present until he was wounded at Bristoe Station, Virginia, on October 14, 1863. Alexander returned to duty prior to March 1864, and he was paroled at Appomattox Court House, Virginia, on April 9, 1865. After the war, Alexander returned home to the Lexington township where, on January 11, 1866, he married Serena Jane Leonard. Alexander and Serena would have six children: Elizabeth (1868), William H. (1870), John (1872), Fannie (1874), Delphina (1876), and Moses Luther (1878). Alexander worked as a farmer until his death on November 15, 1913. He is buried at Beulah United Church of Christ.

995. Leonard, Alfred

Private, Company H, 48th Regiment N.C. Troops

Alfred was born in 1833 to Michael and Nancy Owens Leonard. He worked as a farmer, and, in 1852, he married Sarah Temple. Alfred and Sarah would have four children, Mary (1853), Henry (1857), Martha (1857), and Valentine (1861), before Alfred enlisted on April 24, 1862. He was issued a discharge on October 10, 1862, due to disability from "necrosis or typhoid fever." Alfred returned home to the Lexington township where he and Sarah would have two more children: John (1864) and Michael (1868). Alfred died around 1875. No further records.

996. Leonard, Alvarian

Private, Company D, 42nd Regiment N.C. Troops

Alvarian was born in 1840 to Solomon and Mary Leonard. He worked as a farmer, and, on September 26, 1861, he married Eliza Bruff. Alvarian volunteered for service in Davie County on March 3, 1862. Alvarian was reported present through October 1864 and was paroled at Greensboro, North Carolina, on May 6, 1865. After the war, Alvarian returned home to his wife in the Tyro township. Alvarian and Eliza would have three children: John (1866), Emma (1868), and Robert Lee (1870). Alvarian died on January 17, 1911. He is buried at Reeds Baptist Church.

997. Leonard, Burgess

Private, Davidson Guards
Company A, 21st Regiment N.C. Troops
(11th N.C. Volunteers)

Burgess was born on November 11, 1845, to John and Crissilla Leonard. He worked as a farmer prior to enlisting on October 1, 1863. Burgess was reported present until he was paroled at Appomattox Court House, Virginia, on April 9, 1865. After the war, Burgess moved to the city of Lexington, where, on April 5, 1866, he married Elizabeth Ward. Burgess and Elizabeth would have two children, Robert Lee (1867) and Amanda (1868), before Elizabeth's death in 1872. Burgess married Sarah J. Miller on July 29, 1888. Burgess and Sarah would not have any children. Burgess lived in the Lexington township until his death on November 28, 1916. He is buried in the Lexington City Cemetery.

998. Leonard, Casper

Private, Company H, 48th Regiment
N.C. Troops

Casper was born on December 16, 1839, to George and Mary Waitman Leonard. He worked as a hireling prior to volunteering on March 14, 1862. Casper was reported present until he was captured at Bristoe Station, Virginia, on October 14, 1863. He was confined at Washington, D.C., until October 27, 1863, when he was transferred to Point Lookout, Maryland. Casper was confined at Point Lookout until he was released for exchange on February 24, 1865; he was received on March 4, 1865. After the war, Casper returned home and, on February 14, 1866, he married Susannah Hill Myers. Casper and Susannah would have five children: Jackson (1868), Lucy (1871), Lindsay (1875), Annie (1877), and Celia (1879). Casper lived in the Lexington township until his death on January 4, 1890. He is buried at Beulah United Church of Christ.

999. Leonard, Daniel

Private, Company K, 15th Regiment
N.C. Troops (5th N.C. Volunteers)

Daniel was born in 1820 to John and Eve Leonard. He worked as a farmer, and, on February 5, 1844, Daniel married Phoebe Hinkle. Daniel and Phoebe would have one child, Sophronia (1847), before Phoebe's death in 1848. Daniel married Mary Craver on September 18, 1849. Daniel and Mary would have five children: Martin (1852), Julia A. (1854), Margaret (1856), Daniel (1858), and Emeline (1859), before Mary's death in 1861. Daniel married Elizabeth Easter on April 30, 1863, and was conscripted into service on December 15, 1863. He was reported present until discharged on January 7, 1865, due to "general debility, dropsy, and a gunshot wound of the right leg." After the war, Daniel returned home, and he and Elizabeth would have their only child, Mary Lena, in 1867. No further records.

1000. Leonard, Daniel

Private, Company A, 42nd Regiment
N.C. Troops

Daniel was born on July 4, 1842, to Solomon and Mary Leonard. He worked as a farmer prior to enlisting in Rowan County on May 6, 1862. Daniel was reported present until he was captured at Battery Anderson, Fort Fisher, North Carolina, on December 25, 1864. He was confined at Point Lookout, Maryland, until June 28, 1865, when he was released after taking the oath of allegiance. After the war, Daniel moved to Davie County, where he died on July 15, 1868.

1001. Leonard, David Daniel

Private, Company K, 15th Regiment
N.C. Troops

David was born on November 3, 1839, to David W. and Elizabeth Sink Leonard. He worked as a farmer prior to being conscripted in Wake County on July 15, 1862. David was reported present until he was captured at Petersburg, Virginia, on February 6, 1865. He was confined at Point Lookout, Maryland, until June 28, 1865, when he was released after taking the oath of allegiance. After the war, David returned to the Lexington township where, on April 29, 1866, he married Terrifa Fostine Tussey. David

and Terrifa would have four children: Susanna Nettie (1868), Medora (1870), Callie (1872), and Ida E. (1875). David died on January 3, 1878. He is buried at Pilgrim United Church of Christ.

1002. Leonard, David Sink

Private, Company C, 70th Regiment
N.C. Troops (1st N.C. Junior
Reserves)

David was born on April 6, 1847, to David and Susanna Sink Leonard. He worked as a farmer prior to enlisting in the Junior Reserves on May 24, 1864. After the war, David returned home to the Lexington township, where, on February 17, 1870, he married Martha Wagner. David and Martha would have seven children: Robert E. (1870), Addie (1873), Dora Mae (1876), George (1879), Fred Lee (1882), Samuel (1885), and Duke (1890). David worked as a farmer until his death on May 20, 1926. He is buried at Bethesda United Methodist Church.

1003. Leonard, Emanuel

Private, Company H, 48th Regiment
N.C. Troops

Emanuel was born in 1845 to Jacob and Sarah Leonard. He worked as a farmer prior to enlisting at Orange Court House, Virginia, on January 28, 1864. Emanuel was reported present until he was captured at Hatcher's Run, Virginia, on March 31, 1865. He was confined at Point Lookout, Maryland, until June 28, 1865, when he was released after taking the oath of allegiance. No further records.

1004. Leonard, Felix W.

Private, Cleveland Mountain Boys
Company D, 15th Regiment N.C. Troops
(5th N.C. Volunteers)
2nd Company B, 49th Regiment N.C.
Troops

Felix was born on December 18, 1841, to Daniel and Phoebe Brinkley Leonard. He worked as a farmer prior to being conscripted into service on July 16, 1862. Felix was reported present until January 9, 1863, when he was transferred with his company to the 49th N.C. Regiment. He was reported present until he was captured at Fort Stedman, Virginia, on March 25, 1865. Felix was confined at Point Lookout, Maryland, until June 28, 1865, when he was released after taking

The family of David Sink Leonard, ca. 1890 (Leonard, *Jacob Wagner of "Old" Rowan*).

the oath of allegiance. Felix returned home to the Midway township after the war, and, on November 10, 1867, he married Sarah Everhart. Felix and Sarah would have three children: Mary Louvina (1868), Crissie (1872), and Felix A. Lee (1879). Felix lived as a successful farmer until his death on June 29, 1903. He is buried at Midway United Methodist Church.

1005. Leonard, Franklin

Private, Company C, 70th Regiment N.C. Troops (1st N.C. Junior Reserves)

Franklin was born in 1847 to Jacob and Sarah Leonard. He worked as a farmer prior to enlisting in the Junior Reserves on May 24, 1864. No further records.

1006. Leonard, George Riley

Private, Company H, 48th Regiment N.C. Troops

Riley was born on May 3, 1841, to George and Mary Waitman Leonard.

Riley worked as a farmer, and, on November 17, 1859, he married Catharine Whirlow. Riley and Catharine lived in the Shiloh area of the county, and they would have two children, Mary J. (1860) and Henry Lindsey (1861), before Riley was conscripted into service at Petersburg, Virginia, on August 8, 1862. Riley was wounded in the foot at Sharpsburg, Maryland, on September 17, 1862. He was issued a furlough for 30 days on October 10, 1862, and returned home. Riley returned to service on an unspecified date but was reported present in January 1863. His service records state that, while serving with another company, "at Gettysburg, Pennsylvania, July 1–3, 1863, he was wounded in the breast by a burst shell and left to be dead. After recovering consciousness he crawled on his hands and knees for a good ways and hid behind some rocks until he was rescued." Despite his wounds,

1862 Ambrotype of George Riley Leonard in a nine-button Richmond Shell Jacket (Marie Hinson, *The Heritage of Davidson County*).

Riley returned to service in October 1863, only to be wounded in the left hand and chest two weeks later at Bristoe Station, Virginia, on October 14, 1863. He was sent home on a furlough on November 3, 1863, and returned to duty sometime prior to May 1, 1864. Riley was wounded for a fourth time at the battle of Wilderness, Virginia, on May 5, 1864. The bones in his right foot were fractured, and he was sent home once again. Riley was declared absent without leave when his furlough expired, but he was retired from service on March 25, 1865, due to disability from his wounds. After his service, Riley recovered from his wounds and lived a full life. Riley and Catharine would have six more children: Sarah Elizabeth (1865), George H. (1867), William (1869), Lou Ella (1872), Amanda C. (1874), and Arthur Lee (1881). Riley remained in the Shiloh area, where he was elected county coroner for eight years. Riley was active in the A. A. Hill Camp, United Confederate Veterans, until his death on July 6, 1929. He is buried at Shiloh United Methodist Church.

1007. Leonard, George Washington

Private, Company D, 10th Battalion, N.C. Heavy Artillery

Riley and Catharine Whirlow Leonard in later life (Marie Hinson, *The Heritage of Davidson County*).

George was born in 1826 to Solomon and Polly Leonard. He worked as a farmer, and, in 1847, he married Louisa Freedle. George and Louisa would have seven children, Martha (1849), William A. (1851), Pleasant (1853), Marinda (1856), Mary Elizabeth (1858), Andrew (1860), and Julia C. (1862), before George was conscripted into service in Wake County on February 4, 1864. He was reported present through October 1864. After the war, George returned to the Conrad Hill township where he and Louisa would have three more children: Sarah (1866), George (1871), and Lou Ellen (1875). George would work as a farmer in the Conrad Hill township until his death on May 30, 1900. He is buried at Beck's United Church of Christ.

1008. Leonard, Hamilton Jones

Private, Company C, 70th Regiment N.C. Troops (1st N.C. Junior Reserves)

Hamilton was born on February 8, 1847, to David and Elizabeth Michael Leonard. He worked as a farmer in the household of Levi and Eliza Evans prior to enlisting in the Junior Reserves on May 24, 1864. After the war, Hamilton returned home to the Tyro township, where on September 10, 1868, he married Ellen Young. Hamilton and Ellen would have eight children: Curtis (1869), Mattie (1877), Harper (1879), Mamie (1883), John B. (1884), Elissa V. (1886), Baxter H. (1889), and Robert Lee (1891). Hamilton died on January 6, 1920. He is buried at Shiloh United Methodist Church.

1009. Leonard, Henderson

Private, Company H, 48th Regiment N.C. Troops

Henderson was born on September 22, 1843, to George and Mary Waitman Leonard. He worked as a hireling prior to volunteering for service on March 12, 1862. Henderson was captured at Sharpsburg, Maryland, on September 17, 1862. He was sent to a Federal hospital in Frederick, Maryland, until he recovered and then was sent to Fort McHenry in Baltimore, Maryland. Henderson was confined there until October 17, 1862, when he was paroled and transferred to Aiken's Landing, Virginia, for exchange. He was declared exchanged on November 10, 1862, and returned to duty on an unspecified date. Henderson was reported present until he was captured at Hatcher's Run, Virginia, on April 2, 1865. He was confined at Point Lookout, Maryland, until June 28, 1865, when he was released after taking the oath of allegiance. After the war, Henderson returned home where he would marry Martha Leonard on January 9, 1868. Henderson and Martha would move to Lexington and have seven children: Laura (1870), Julia (1872), Rufus (1874), Phillip R. (1876), Columbus (1877), Numa Allen (1883), and Cora (1887). Henderson's family belonged to the Methodist church in Lexington. Henderson died on February 18, 1912. He is buried in the Lexington City Cemetery.

1010. Leonard, Henry E.

Private, Company B, 48th Regiment N.C. Troops

Henry was born in 1840 to David and Elizabeth Sink Leonard. He worked as a farmer prior to volunteering on March 17, 1862. Henry was reported present until he was sent to a Danville, Virginia, hospital with a gunshot wound of the right wrist on June 16, 1864. In September 1864, Henry was detailed to serve in the Quartermaster's Department of General John R. Cooke's Brigade. After the war, Henry returned home and married Lucy Beard on May 24, 1865. Henry and Lucy moved out of the state prior to 1870. No further records.

1011. Leonard, Henry Newton

Private, Company H, 48th Regiment N.C. Troops

Henry was born on January 18, 1841, to Michael and Nancy Owen Leonard. Henry worked as a hireling prior to volunteering for service at Wagner's on March 1, 1862. He was reported present until August 16, 1864, when he was reported in a Richmond, Virginia, hospital with "chronic diarrhea." Henry returned to duty on October 6, 1864, and was last reported present on November 30, 1864. After the war, Henry returned to the

Shiloh area, where on December 24, 1865, he married Wilhelmina Lanier (widow of Drury H. Lanier). Henry and Wilhelmina would have seven children: Lewis (1866), Ellen (1868), Nancy (1871), James T. (1874), Thaddeus (1879), Burl Bassett (1882), and Caroline (1886). Henry worked as a farmer until his death on March 10, 1892. He is buried at Shiloh United Methodist Church.

1012. Leonard, Hubbard

Private, Company E, 29th Virginia Infantry Regiment

Hubbard was born on December 10, 1840, to Valentine and Catharine Waitman Leonard. He moved to Rockingham County, North Carolina, prior to 1857. He volunteered for service in the 29th Virginia on June 26, 1861. After the war, he moved to Carroll County, Virginia, and married Sarah Vernon. Hubbard died on May 13, 1918, and is buried in Carroll County.

1013. Leonard, Jacob

Private, Company E, 29th Virginia Infantry Regiment

Jacob was born on August 23, 1842, to Valentine and Catharine Waitman Leonard. He moved to Rockingham County, North Carolina, with his brother Hubbard prior to 1857. He volunteered for service in the 29th Virginia on June 26, 1861. After the war, he moved to Carroll County, Virginia, and married Lucinda Jones. Jacob died on May 3, 1919, and is buried in Carroll County.

1014. Leonard, Jacob

Private, Company I, 42nd Regiment N.C. Troops

Jacob was born in 1842. He worked as a farmer prior to enlisting into service sometime prior to being captured at Wise's Forks, Virginia, on March 16, 1865. Jacob was confined at Point Lookout, Maryland, until June 28, 1865, when he was released after taking the oath of allegiance. No further records.

1015. Leonard, Jacob R.

Private, Thomasville Rifles Company B, 14th Regiment N.C. Troops (4th N.C. Volunteers)

Jacob was born in 1838 to Daniel and Catharine Wagner Leonard. Jacob worked as a farmer prior to volunteering for service on April 26, 1861. He was mustered in with the rank of corporal, but he was reduced in rank on June 29, 1861. Jacob was reported present until September 19, 1864, when he was captured at Winchester, Virginia. He was confined at Point Lookout, Maryland, until March 18, 1865, when he was paroled and transferred to Boulware's Wharf, Virginia, for exchange. No records indicate that he was exchanged. No further records.

1016. Leonard, Jesse

Private, Company D, 42nd Regiment N.C. Troops

Jesse was born in 1840 to Jacob and Mary Stockinger Leonard. Jesse worked as a farmer, and on January 26, 1860, he married Christina Younts. He volunteered for service in March 1862 and was reported present until September 7, 1862, when he died of disease in Petersburg, Virginia. He is buried in the mass grave at the Blanford Cemetery in Petersburg.

1017. Leonard, Jesse

Private, Company H, 48th Regiment N.C. Troops

Jesse was born in 1836 to Michael and Nancy Owen Leonard. He worked as a farmer, and, prior to 1860, he married Parthea Martin. Jesse was conscripted into service on August 8, 1862. He was reported present at all engagements until he was killed in action during the battle of Cold Harbor, Virginia, on June 3, 1864.

1018. Leonard, John

Private, Company I, 42nd Regiment N.C. Troops

John was born on an unknown date, and his genealogy could not be determined. John was paroled at Greensboro, North Carolina, on May 6, 1865. No further records.

1019. Leonard, John Adam

Private, Carolina Rangers Company B, 10th Virginia Cavalry Regiment

John was born on December 1, 1842, to David W. and Elizabeth Sink Leonard. He worked as a farmhand prior to enlist-ing in Davie County on October 1, 1863. John was present until he was reported absent, sick, in a Richmond, Virginia, hospital in June 1864. He recovered from his sickness and was reported present until he was discharged on January 27, 1865. John returned home from service and married Amanda Leonard on February 4, 1866. John lived in the Lexington township until his death on November 23, 1918. He is buried at Bethesda United Methodist Church.

1020. Leonard, John Adam

Private, Company B, 48th Regiment N.C. Troops

John was born in 1838 to David and Susanna Sink Leonard. He worked as a farmer, and, on April 18, 1859, he married Amanda Cross. John volunteered for service on March 8, 1862, and was killed in action at Sharpsburg, Maryland, on September 17, 1862. There is a stone in his honor at Bethesda United Methodist Church.

1021. Leonard, John Ross

Private, Company B, 48th Regiment N.C. Troops

John was born in 1847 to Polly Leonard. John worked as a farmer prior to volunteering for service on March 6, 1862. His leg was fractured by a bullet at the battle of King's School House, Virginia, on June 25, 1862. John was sent to Richmond, Virginia, where he died of his wounds a month later, on July 25, 1862. He is buried at Hollywood Cemetery in Richmond.

1022. Leonard, Joseph B.

Private, Company H, 48th Regiment N.C. Troops

Joseph was born on December 5, 1838, to Green and Mary Leonard. Joseph volunteered at "Wagner's" on March 1, 1862. No further information about his service is reported. He married Delphina O. and lived in the North Thomasville area until his death on July 2, 1918. He is buried at Mount Pleasant United Methodist Church.

1023. Leonard, Joseph B.

Second Lieutenant, 66th Regiment N.C. Militia (1861 organization)

Joseph was born in 1835 to David and Susanna Sink Leonard. He worked as a farmer, and in 1856, he married Elizabeth Kanoy. Joseph and Elizabeth would have eight children: W. Clinton (1857), John (1862), Annie E. (1865), Susanna (1868), Mary Jane (1871), Joseph Henderson (1874), Rettie May (1876), and Winnifred (1879). Joseph accepted a commission as second lieutenant in the Ebenezer District Company on November 26, 1861. After the war, Joseph continued to work as a farmer until his death in 1918. He is buried at Pilgrim United Church of Christ.

1024. Leonard, Joseph Bentley

Private, Carolina Rangers
Company B, 10th Virginia Calvary
Regiment

Joseph was born in 1843 to George and Sally Wagner Leonard. He worked as a farmer prior to volunteering in Davie County on October 29, 1861. Joseph was reported present through March 1863. He was dispatched on a horse detail and on detached service through October 1863. Joseph returned to duty in November of that year and was reported present through December 31, 1864, when he drew a clothing ration. Joseph was paroled at Greensboro, North Carolina, on May 9, 1865. Prior to 1870, Joseph married Sarah Shemwell, daughter of Dr. Obediah Shemwell, and moved to Rowan County. He is buried at Trading Ford in Rowan County.

1025. Leonard, Joseph Franklin

Private, Carolina Rangers
Company B, 10th Virginia Calvary
Regiment

Joseph was born on March 21, 1845, to Daniel and Polly Fritts Leonard. He worked as a farmer prior to enlisting in Davie County on March 3, 1863. Joseph was reported present through December 31, 1864, when he drew a clothing ration. After the war, Joseph returned home to the Lexington township where, on August 7, 1866, he married Ellen Clodfelter. Joseph and Ellen would have five children: Mary J. (1869), Cicero R. (1872), Julius Calvin (1874), Sydney H. (1875), and Walter J. (1878). Joseph worked as a farmer and a carpenter until his death on April 9, 1909. He is buried at Pilgrim United Church of Christ.

1026. Leonard, Laffayette

Captain, 66th Regiment N.C. Militia
(1861 organization)

Laffayette was born on August 8, 1828, to Valentine and Susanna Leonard. Laffayette worked as a farmer prior to being commissioned as captain in the Ebenezer District Company on December 13, 1861. He died of unreported causes on April 17, 1862. He is buried at Pilgrim United Church of Christ.

1027. Leonard, Levi

Private, Company I, 35th Regiment
N.C. Troops

Levi was born in 1824 to Solomon and Mary Leonard. He worked as a farmer in the southern district of Davidson County, and, on March 18, 1844, he married Mary A. Grubb. Levi and Mary would have one child, Sarah (1848), before Levi was conscripted into service on April 1, 1863. He was reported present until hospitalized at Charlottesville, Virginia, on May 31, 1864. Levi recovered from his wounds and returned to service on June 13, 1864, and was reported present until captured at Five Forks, Virginia, on April 1, 1865. He was confined at Hart's Island, New York, until May 20, 1865, when he died of "chronic diarrhea."

1028. Leonard, Obediah

Private, Lexington Wildcats
Company I, 14th Regiment N.C. Troops
(4th N.C. Volunteers)

Obediah was born in 1838 to Mathias and Christina Beck Leonard. He worked as a farmer prior to being conscripted on July 16, 1862. Obediah was reported present until September 17, 1862, when he was listed as "missing." He was dropped from the rolls in November 1863.

1029. Leonard, Robert W.

Private, Davidson Guards
Company A, 21st Regiment N.C. Troops
(11th N.C. Volunteers)

Robert was born on an unspecified date and worked as a farmer prior to enlisting on October 1, 1863. Robert was reported present until he was wounded in the left shoulder at Fort Stedman, Virginia, on March 25, 1865. Robert died in a Petersburg, Virginia, hospital on April

26, 1865. He is buried in the Blanford Cemetery in Petersburg.

1030. Leonard, Samuel

Private, Company C, 70th Regiment
N.C. Troops (1st N.C. Junior
Reserves)

Samuel was born in 1847. He worked as a farmer prior to enlisting in the Junior Reserves on May 24, 1864. After the war, Samuel returned to the Lexington township where, on December 13, 1866, he married Susanna Myers. Samuel and Susanna moved out of the county prior to 1880. No further records.

1031. Leonard, Samuel

Private, Company H, 48th Regiment
N.C. Troops

Samuel was born in 1835 to Daniel and Leah Livengood Leonard. He worked as a farmer prior to volunteering for service at "Wagner's" on March 1, 1862. Samuel was reported present until he was wounded in the face at Fredericksburg, Virginia, on December 13, 1862. He recovered from his wounds and returned to duty in March 1863. Samuel spent time in two hospitals with "chronic diarrhea" until he was captured at Hatcher's Run, Virginia, on March 31, 1865. He was confined at Point Lookout, Maryland, until June 28, 1865, when he was released after taking the oath of allegiance. After the war, Samuel returned home and, on March 13, 1866, he married Betsy Sowers Bruff. Samuel and Betsy would have one child: Phillip (1870). Samuel worked as a farmer until his death sometime after 1900. He is buried at Shiloh United Methodist Church.

1032. Leonard, Solomon, Jr.

Private, Company B, 57th Regiment
N.C. Troops

Solomon was born in 1838 to Solomon and Mary Leonard. Solomon worked as a carpenter prior to enlisting in Rowan County on July 4, 1862. He was reported present until he was wounded in the left knee at Chancellorsville, Virginia, on May 4, 1863. Solomon recovered and returned to duty on July 23, 1863, and was reported present until he was captured at Rappahannock Station, Virginia, on November 7, 1863. Solomon was confined at

Point Lookout, Maryland, until he was paroled and received at City Point, Virginia, for exchange on March 16, 1864. He was declared exchanged on March 20, 1864, and was reported present until he was captured at Winchester, Virginia, on September 19, 1864. Solomon was again confined at Point Lookout until March 15, 1865, when he was paroled and transferred to Boulware's Wharf, Virginia. Solomon was exchanged on March 18, 1865, and was sent to a Richmond, Virginia, hospital the next day. After the war, Solomon headed to Arkansas. While there, he married Minerva Ann Goza. Solomon lived in Dallas County, Arkansas, until his death on August 22, 1911. No further records

1033. Leonard, Theophilus

Private, Carolina Rangers
Company B, 10th Virginia Cavalry
*   Regiment*

Theophilus was born in 1836 to Daniel and Leah Livengood Leonard. Pension records indicate that he enlisted in Davie County on October 29, 1861, and served in Company B, 10th Virginia Cavalry. Theophilus died in Davie County prior to 1900. No further records.

1034. Leonard, Valentine

Private, Company K, 15th Regiment
*   N.C. Troops (5th N.C. Volunteers)*

Valentine was born on October 11, 1840, to Alexander and Sivela Hunt Leonard. He worked as a farmer prior to being conscripted into service in Wake County on July 16, 1862. Valentine was reported present until he was discharged on October 5, 1862, because of "epilepsy fits every night." Valentine returned home to the Tyro township where, in 1862, he married Lucy Johnson Leonard, widow of George W. Leonard. Valentine and Lucy would have 13 children: John (1863), Laura C. (1864–1865), Henry W. (1866), Ellen (1868), Charles (1870), Mack Dolan (1872), George V. (1874), Robert L. (1876), Margaret (1878), Lucy Mittie (1880), Julia (1882), Lemma (1884), and Jesse Lee (1888). Valentine worked as a farmer and was a member of Reeds Baptist Church until his death on September 7, 1921. He is buried at Reeds Baptist Church.

1035. Leonard, Valentine

Private, Lexington Wildcats
Company I, 14th Regiment N.C. Troops
*   (4th N.C. Volunteers)*

Valentine was born in 1836 to Michael and Nancy Owen Leonard. He worked as a farmer prior to volunteering for service on May 14, 1861. Valentine died of unreported causes in a Richmond, Virginia, hospital on July 13, 1862.

1036. Leonard, Wiley

Private, Company B, 48th Regiment
*   N.C. Troops*

Wiley was born in 1842 to Polly Leonard. He worked as a hireling prior to volunteering for service on March 6, 1862. Wiley was wounded in the leg at King's School House, Virginia, on June 25, 1862. As a result of his wounds, Wiley lost his right leg to the surgeon's saw and was officially retired from service on August 17, 1864. After his retirement, Wiley returned home to the Silver Hill township. Wiley would live in the area, remaining single, until his death on October 14, 1929. He is buried at Beck's United Church of Christ.

1037. Leonard, William B.

Private, Company B, 48th Regiment
*   N.C. Troops*

William was born in 1843 to Mathias and Christina Beck Leonard. He worked as a farmer until he volunteered for service on March 4, 1862. William was wounded in action at Sharpsburg, Maryland, on September 17, 1862. On the march into South Carolina, William fell sick and was reported present but in sick quarters in February 1863. William died of typhoid fever at Charleston, South Carolina, on March 23, 1863. His body was returned and was interred at Beck's United Church of Christ.

1038. Leonard, William H.

Private, Company H, 48th Regiment
*   N.C. Troops*

William was born in 1844 to Michael and Nancy Owen Leonard. He worked as a farmer prior to being conscripted on February 18, 1863. William was present until he was reported absent in November 1864. While at home, William married Susanna Hanes on November 3,

1864. He returned to service prior to March 6, 1865, when he deserted to the Federal army. William was confined at Washington, D.C., until he was released on an unspecified date after taking the oath of allegiance. After the war, he returned home to the Lexington area where he and Susanna would have three children: Edward (1866), Charley (1868), and Lemmy (1870). Susanna died in 1877, and in 1880, William married Sarah Leonard Bruff, the widow of Alfred Bruff. Sarah would bring with her five children: Mary (1866), James (1868), Julia (1871), Walter (1874), and Emma (1877). No further records.

1039. Leonard, Wint

Private, Thomasville Rifles
Company B, 14th Regiment N.C. Troops
*   (4th N.C. Volunteers)*

Wint was born in 1841 and worked as a farmer prior to volunteering for service in Thomasville on April 23, 1861. Wint was wounded at Sharpsburg, Maryland, on September 17, 1862. Wint was taken to a Federal field hospital and then transferred to Frederick, Maryland, where he died of his wounds on November 15, 1862.

1040. Lewis, George T.

Private, Lexington Wildcats
Company I, 14th Regiment N.C. Troops
*   (4th Regiment N.C. Volunteers)*

George was born in 1833 and was employed as a carpenter, working for John Cutting in Lexington, prior to volunteering for service on May 14, 1861. George died of disease at Camp Ellis, North Carolina, on July 31, 1861.

1041. Lewya, Andrew

Private, Company I, 42nd Regiment
*   N.C. Troops*

Andrew was born in 1815. He resided in the central part of Davidson County, and, on December 10, 1836, he married Sarah Ann Byerly. Andrew and Sarah would have four children: Esther (1839), Wesley (1842), Roswell (1843), and Isaiah (1847). Andrew was employed as a shoemaker prior to being conscripted into service on May 8, 1862. Andrew was reported present until he was paroled at Greensboro, North Carolina, on May 5, 1865. After the war, Andrew returned to the Conrad Hill township; he died sometime before 1880. No further records.

1042. Lewya, Roswell

Private, Company I, 42nd Regiment N.C. Troops

Roswell was born in 1841 to Andrew and Sarah Ann Byerly Lewya. Roswell worked as a farmer prior to being conscripted into service on May 8, 1862. He was reported present until May 3, 1865, when he was paroled at Greensboro, North Carolina. The *Charlotte Western Democrat* of April 4, 1865, reported that he was wounded in a battle "in 1865." After the war, Roswell returned to the Conrad Hill township where, in 1866, he married Sarah. Roswell and Sarah would have six children: Julie (1867), Victor (1869), Eliza (1872), Mary (1873), William (1876), and Robert (1886). The 1900 Census lists Roswell as a "brick moulder" living in the Conrad Hill township. No further records.

1043. Lindsey, Andrew D.

Surgeon, North Carolina Conscription Bureau, Asheboro, N.C.

Andrew was born on November 15, 1814. He lived in the Bethany area and received his medical training prior to 1840, when he married Sarah. Andrew and Sarah would have six children: Juliann (1841), John (1842), Elizabeth (1844), Robert (1847), Mary (1850), and Andrew (1854). Andrew served as a medical official in the North Carolina Conscript Bureau for his service during the conflict. Andrew returned to the Bethany area where he lived out his days as a country doctor and a benefactor of his church. Andrew died on April 3, 1872. He is buried at Bethany United Church of Christ.

1044. Lindsey, John A.

Private, Company C, 70th Regiment N.C. Troops (1st N.C. Junior Reserves)

John was born on January 29, 1846, to James M. and Catharine Lindsey. John worked as a carpenter prior to enlisting in the Junior Reserves on May 24, 1864. After the war, John returned home and continued his work as a farmer. In 1900, he was still listed as single. John died on May 21, 1927. He is buried at Mount Pleasant United Methodist Church.

1045. Lindsey, Robert Wilson

Second Lieutenant, Company C, 70th Regiment N.C. Troops (1st N.C. Junior Reserves)

Robert was born on August 28, 1846, to Dr. Andrew and Sarah Lindsey. Robert worked as a clerk in his father's doctor's office in Lexington prior to volunteering for service as a second lieutenant in the Junior Reserves on May 24, 1864. After the war, Robert returned home and attended Trinity College for one year. Robert died of unreported causes on December 5, 1869. He is buried at Bethany United Church of Christ.

1046. Lindsey, William Dillon

Surgeon, 48th Regiment N.C. Troops

William was born on June 5, 1820, to David and Sarah Lindsey. William completed his medical training in Philadelphia, Pennsylvania, in 1845. The new physician returned home where he opened his medical practice across from the Hargrave home. On October 10, 1846, he married Elizabeth A. Holt, the daughter of W. R. Holt. Elizabeth died in 1848. William married Elizabeth Gray in 1850. William and Elizabeth would only have two children who survived infancy: Arthur (1851) and David (1863). In 1860, Lindsey had a very successful practice as well as substantial real estate holdings totaling over $60,000. In 1857, he had donated the land for the Lexington Episcopal Church, and in the same year, he was appointed to the board of directors of Lexington National Bank. William enlisted on April 10, 1862, and was appointed surgeon on October 14, 1862. He resigned his commission as surgeon on April 3, 1863, because of "the condition of my private affairs." After his resignation, William returned home to take care of his family and his practice, serving as a county commissioner during the last days of the war. William remained a prominent citizen of Lexington and was a benefactor to the Episcopal diocese. William died on January 2, 1870. He is buried in the Lexington City Cemetery. The inscription on his stone reads: "A fine physician."

1047. Lineback, Edward

Musician, Davidson Guards Company A, 21st Regiment N.C. Troops (11th N.C. Volunteers)

Edward was born in 1839. He worked as a farmer in the Friedburg area prior to volunteering for service on May 8, 1861. Edward was mustered in as a private and served in that capacity until he was promoted to bugler on February 28, 1865. Edward was paroled at Appomattox Court House, Virginia, on April 9, 1865. No further records.

1048. Lines, Charles L.

Private, Thomasville Rifles Company B, 14th Regiment N.C. Troops (4th N.C. Volunteers)

Charles was born in Connecticut in 1834 to Charles M. and Anna Coltrane Lines. The family moved to Thomasville, and Charles Sr. and George opened up a shoe factory. Charles was living at the Smiths' boardinghouse in 1860 and working as a supervisor in the factory. He volunteered for service on March 17, 1862, and was wounded at Sharpsburg, Maryland, on September 17, 1862. After he recovered, Charles returned to service in February 1863. He was reported present until wounded in the leg at Gettysburg, Pennsylvania, on July 1, 1863. Charles rejoined the company in September 1863 and was reported present until he was wounded in the right foot and captured at Winchester, Virginia, on September 19, 1864. Charles was hospitalized at several Federal hospitals until he was confined at Point Lookout, Maryland, on October 26, 1864. He was in prison until November 15, 1864, when he was paroled and transferred to Venus Point, Georgia, for exchange. Charles was paroled at Appomattox Court House, Virginia, on April 9, 1865. After the war, Charles continued to manage the shoe factory. One of his biggest tasks was to find labor and material. In 1873, the C. M. & George Lines Co. opened its company store. Charles continued to have a controlling interest in the company until he returned to Connecticut prior to 1885. No further records.

1049. Link, Davidson M.

Private, Company H, 48th Regiment N.C. Troops

Davidson was born in Rowan County in 1819. He worked as a farmer along the Yadkin River, and, in 1845, he married Catharine Myers. Davidson and Catharine would have six children, Catharine (1847), Levi (1851), William (1855), Martha (1858), Mattie (1859), and Valentine (1861), before Davidson enlisted on March 6, 1862. No further records vouch for his service in the 48th Regiment. After the war, he and Catharine would welcome two more children into their Yadkin home: John (1865) and Michael (1868). Davidson continued to work on his farm until his death prior to 1880. No further records.

1050. Link, Samuel

*Private, Thomasville Rifles
Company B, 14th Regiment N.C. Troops
(4th N.C. Volunteers)*

Samuel was born in 1836. He worked as a farmer in western Davidson County until he was conscripted into service on July 15, 1862. Samuel died of unreported causes at Winchester, Virginia, on September 8, 1862.

1051. Link, Thomas A.

*Private, Company C, 70th Regiment
N.C. Troops (N.C. Junior Reserves)*

Thomas was born in January 1847 to William and Sarah Pickett Link. Thomas worked as a miller's apprentice prior to enlisting in the Junior Reserves on May 24, 1864. After the war, Thomas returned home to the Lexington township where, in 1867, he married Eliza Ann Craver. Thomas and Eliza would have two children: Hugh L. (1870) and Mary Jane (1873). Thomas worked both as a farmer and as a part-time miller. He was a member of the A. A. Hill Camp, United Confederate Veterans. Thomas died in 1936. He is buried at Beulah United Church of Christ.

1052. Link, William, III

*Private, Company H, 48th Regiment
N.C. Troops*

William was born on January 3, 1821, to William and Catharine Hege Link. William worked as a farmer and a miller in the Lexington area, and, in 1846, he married Sarah Pickett. William and Sarah would have eight children: Thomas (1847), Mary Elizabeth (1850), Susannah

(1853), Junius Costen (1854), Louranne (1855), Eli D. (1856), Sarah C. (1857), and John L. (1860). William volunteered for service on March 3, 1862, and deserted on August 22, 1862. William was granted amnesty and operated his mill with the permission of the government. William died on July 24, 1874. He is buried at Beulah United Church of Christ.

1053. Livengood, Andrew

*Private, Company F, 5th Missouri
Cavalry*

Andrew was born on April 15, 1840. He worked as a shoemaker's apprentice, and in 1858, he, along with several other Davidson County men, tried their luck in Missouri. While in Missouri, he volunteered for service in the 5th Missouri Cavalry Regiment. In 1867, Andrew returned to Davidson County where he bought land in the Midway community. Andrew worked as a farmer and was a member of Midway Methodist Church and Mount Pleasant Methodist. Andrew died on February 14, 1911. He is buried at Mount Pleasant United Methodist Church.

1054. Livengood, Christian

*Private, Company E, 42nd Regiment
N.C. Troops*

Christian was born in 1835 to Christian and Christina Shoaf Livengood. He worked as a miller, and, on August 10, 1853, he married Susannah Shoaf. Christian and Susannah would have five children, Alcena (1855), Seretta Pauline (1856), Corneila (1858), Benberry Columbus (1860), and Susan (1862), before Christian volunteered for service on March 8, 1862. He was reported present until paroled at Greensboro, North Carolina, on May 9, 1865. After the war, he made the long trip home and was exposed to the elements. He moved to Davie County, but his body had weakened, and he died in 1866. He is buried in Davie County.

1055. Livengood, Elias

*Private, Company H, 48th Regiment
N.C. Troops*

Elias was born in 1832 to Christian and Christina Shoaf Livengood. Elias worked as a farmer, and, on January 10, 1854, he married Eliza Jane Shoaf. Elias

and Eliza would have three children, Henry (1855), Mary Ann (1857), and Amanda (1860), before Elias was conscripted into service on August 8, 1862. He was reported present until May 25, 1864, when he was hospitalized at Richmond, Virginia, with "debility." Elias was returned to duty on August 2, 1864, but was hospitalized once again on November 21, 1864. Elias died in December 1864. He is buried in the Hollywood Cemetery in Richmond.

1056. Livengood, Felix

*Private, Company H, 48th Regiment
N.C. Troops*

Felix was born in 1839 to John and Molly Leonard Livengood. He worked as a farmer prior to enlisting on April 17, 1862. Felix was wounded in the thigh at Fredericksburg, Virginia, on December 13, 1862. Felix recovered from his wounds and rejoined the company on March 1, 1863. Felix was reported present until he was killed in action at Reams' Station, Virginia, on August 25, 1864.

1057. Livengood, Jackson

*Private, Company I, 42nd Regiment
N.C. Troops*

Jackson was born in 1840. He worked as a farmer prior to volunteering on February 28, 1862. Jackson's term of service was short: he passed away of unreported causes on March 28, 1862.

1058. Livengood, John F.

*Private, Company D, 42nd Regiment
N.C. Troops*

John was born in 1845 to John and Molly Leonard Livengood. John volunteered for service in Rowan County on March 18, 1862. He was reported present through October 1864. John returned home to the Tyro area and moved immediately to Mocksville, Davie County, where he was paroled on June 3, 1865. No further records.

1059. Livengood, Samuel Lorenzo

*Private, Company A, 10th Battalion,
N.C. Heavy Artillery*

Sam was born on March 25, 1838, to Lewis and Phoebe Livengood. Sam worked as a shoe cutter, and, in 1860, he married Mary Elizabeth. He and Mary would have one child, Allison (1861), before Sam was conscripted on March 5, 1863. He was reported present until he was paroled at Greensboro, North Carolina, on May 9, 1865. After the war, Samuel returned to the shoemaking business in the North Thomasville township. Sam and Mary would have four more children: Lewis (1865), Franklin (1869), Jacob (1871), and Augusta (1873). Samuel died on March 19, 1886. He is buried at Bethany United Church of Christ.

1060. Livengood, William A.

*Private, Company A, 42nd Regiment
N.C. Troops
Howard's Company, N.C. Prison
Guards, Salisbury Prison*

William was born in 1834 to George and Margaret Livengood. William worked as a farmer, and, in 1856, he married Mary. William and Mary would have two children, James (1859) and Emma (1861), before William volunteered for service in Rowan County on January 20, 1862. He was reported present until May 1, 1862, when he was transferred to Captain Howard's Company, Gibbs' Battalion, at the Salisbury Prison. No further records.

1061. Loflin, Burrell T.

*Private, Franklin Guides to Freedom
Company K, 44th Regiment N.C. Troops*

Burrell was born on June 1, 1841, to John and Louvina Doby Loflin. He worked as a farmer prior to being conscripted into service on November 8, 1863. Burrell was reported present until October 27, 1864, when he was captured at Burgess' Mill, Virginia. He was confined at Point Lookout, Maryland, until June 28, 1865, when he was released after taking the oath of allegiance. After the war, Burrell returned home to the Allegheny township. He married Rebecca Davis on November 8, 1868. Burrell and Rebecca would have no children together. Rebecca died in 1894, and Burrell married Electa Harris in 1897. Burrell died on March 28, 1909. He is buried in the Davis-Loflin Family Cemetery. The inscription on his stone reads: "We will meet again. Peace, perfect peace."

1062. Loflin, Lindsey

*Private, Company D, 42nd Regiment
N.C. Troops*

Lindsey was born in 1843 to Daniel and Margaret Loflin. He worked as a miner prior to volunteering for service in Rowan County on March 18, 1862. Lindsey was reported present until he was discharged on June 18, 1863, because of serious chronic bronchitis. Lindsey died on the trip home.

1063. Loflin, Martin Jonas

*Private, Company I, 42nd Regiment
N.C. Troops*

Martin was born in 1822. Pension records indicate that he served in the 42nd Regiment. On November 1, 1864, he married Margaret J. Goss. Martin and Margaret would have three children: Emily (1865), John (1866), and William (1869). Martin continued farming in the Allegheny township until his death around 1900. He is buried in the Badgett Family Cemetery.

1064. Loflin, Wiley

First Sergeant, Company I, 42nd Regiment N.C. Troops

Wiley was born on December 21, 1837. Wiley worked as a hireling in the Jackson Hill township prior to volunteering for service on February 28, 1862. He was mustered in as a sergeant and was promoted to first sergeant in August 1864. Wiley was reported present until he was captured at Wise's Forks, Virginia, on March 10, 1865. He was confined at Point Lookout, Maryland, until June 28, 1865, when he was released after taking the oath of allegiance. After the war, Wiley returned home, where, on September 2, 1866, he married Sarah E. Harris. Wiley and Sarah would have two children: William (1867) and Mary (1870). Wiley continued his work as a farmer and also served as postmaster until he died on May 15, 1910. He is buried at Canaan United Methodist Church. The inscription on his stone reads: "Friendship may wear a garland. Gold may link a chain. But love can form a clasp unbroken to remain."

1065. Loflin, William N.

*Private, Trojan Regulators
Company F, 44th Regiment N.C. Troops*

William was born in 1831 in the Allegheny township. He was listed as a farmer working by himself in 1860. William was

conscripted into service in Montgomery County on March 3, 1863. He was reported present until captured at Petersburg, Virginia, on April 2, 1865. William was confined at Point Lookout, Maryland, until June 28, 1865, when he was released after taking the oath of allegiance. After the war, William returned home where he resumed farming. In 1880, William moved to the Jackson Hill township, where he died in 1907. He is buried at Jackson Creek Baptist Church.

1066. Loftin, Corneilus

*Private, Company B, 48th Regiment
N.C. Troops*

Corneilus was born in 1828 to John and Sarah Loftin. Corneilus worked as a farmer prior to being conscripted into service on August 8, 1862. He was wounded and captured at Sharpsburg, Maryland, on September 17, 1862. Corneilus was left in the hands of the enemy, where he died on an unreported date.

1067. Loftin, Jeremiah

*Private, Company F, 7th Regiment
N.C. State Troops*

Jeremiah was born in 1845 to Thomas and Margaret Loftin. He worked as a farmer prior to volunteering for service on April 1, 1863. Jeremiah was wounded in the thigh and captured at Gettysburg, Pennsylvania, on July 3, 1863. He was hospitalized at David's Island, New York, until he was transferred to Point Lookout, Maryland, on January 24, 1864. He partially recovered from his wounds, was paroled on March 6, 1864, and was transferred to City Point, Virginia, for exchange. Jeremiah was declared exchanged and sent to light duty at Salisbury, North Carolina, in September 1864. He was paroled at Salisbury on May 2, 1865. After the war, Jeremiah returned to the Jackson Hill township, where in 1876, he married Caroline. Jeremiah and Caroline would have one child, David (1879), prior to moving to Randolph County in 1883. No further records.

1068. Loftin, John James

*Charlotte Ordnance Depot, Confederate
States Navy*

John was born in 1846 to Corneilus and Louvina Loftin. John worked as a farmer and, according to *Moore's Roster*, he served in the Confederate Ordnance Department in Charlotte, North Carolina. After his service, John began to build a life in the Jackson Hill township. In 1875, he married Louvina Jane, and the couple would have four children: Mary (1877), Julia (1880), Minnie (1884), and Robert (1890). No further records.

1069. Loftin, Julius J. C.

First Sergeant, Company F, 7th Regiment N.C. State Troops

Julius was born on December 20, 1840, to C. G. and Priscilla Loftin. Julius worked as a farmer prior to volunteering for service on August 10, 1861. He was mustered in as a private and was reported present until he was wounded at Gaines' Mill, Virginia, on June 27, 1862. Julius rejoined his company in January 1863, and was reported present until he was wounded in the right thigh at Chancellorsville, Virginia, on May 3, 1863. Julius recovered from his wounds in December 1863 and was promoted to sergeant on December 15, 1863. He was promoted to first sergeant on May 12, 1864. Julius was reported present through November 15, 1864. He was paroled at Greensboro, North Carolina, on April 28, 1865. After the war, Julius returned home to the Jackson Hill township where, on December 16, 1867, he married Sarah Russell. Julius and Sarah would have four children: Martha (1869), Carrie (1871), Robert (1874), and Charlie (1877). Julius continued managing his successful farm until his death on January 30, 1926. He is buried in the Thomas Loftin Family Cemetery.

1070. Loftin, Wilborn

Private, Company A, 10th Battalion, N.C. Heavy Artillery

Wilborn was born in 1823 and worked as a farmer in the southern district of Davidson County. In 1854, Wilborn married Mary, with whom he would have three children: Elizabeth (1856), Margaret (1858), and Alexander (1860). Wilborn was conscripted in Davidson County on March 20, 1863. He was reported present until he deserted from service at Savannah, Georgia, on December 21, 1864. Wilborn never returned home, and several scholars on the Loftin family believe he abandoned both the army and his family.

1071. Loftin, William C.

Private, Franklin Guides to Freedom
Company K, 44th Regiment N.C. Troops

William was born in 1836 to John and Louvina Loftin. He was working as a carpenter in 1860, and on January 9, 1862, he married Linea Surratt. No records of William's service are given in *N.C. Troops: A Roster*; however, North Carolina pension records indicate that William did serve in the 44th Regiment. William and Linea would have two children, James (1870) and Nancy (1874), in their Allegheny township home. William continued his carpentry until he died sometime prior to 1900. He is buried at Taylor's Grove Methodist Church in Montgomery County.

This home of William Loftin was built by Cicero Badgett in the 1880s (Touart, ***Building the Backcountry***).

1072. Loftin, William Moses

Private, Company G, 66th Regiment N.C. Troops

William was born on September 11, 1835, to John and Sarah Loftin. William worked as a farmer and also helped his father distill 500 gallons of medicinal brandy for the Confederate Medical Corps prior to being conscripted on September 8, 1862. After the war, William returned home to the Jackson Hill township, where in December 1865, he married Elizabeth Ward. William and Elizabeth would have ten children: Robert (1866), Moses (1867), Howard (1867), Lula (1871), Albert (1873), Robert Hoke (1874), Polly (1878), Stephen Kearney (1882), Dellie (1883), and Zeb Vance (1891). William continued his work as a farmer and also, as some believe, his father's "business" until he passed away on August 3, 1918. He is buried in the Clear Springs Cemetery.

1073. Loman, Franklin

Private, Company H, 48th Regiment N.C. Troops

Franklin was born in 1839 to Mary Phillips, who married John Loman in 1860. He worked as a hireling prior to volunteering for service at "Wagner's" on March 6, 1862. Franklin deserted in September 1862 but returned by January of the next year. He was last reported in the records of the company on December 21, 1864. No further records.

1074. Loman, John

Private, Company H, 48th Regiment N.C. Troops

John was born in Guilford County in 1810. John worked as a farmer in the northern district of Davidson (Old Rowan) County, and, on November 2, 1830, he married Jane Durham. John and Jane would have seven children, Frank (1839), Luvina (1840), Christena (1847), Nancy (1849), John (1852), Lindsay H. (1854), and Henry (1856), before Jane's death in 1857. John married Mary Phillips three years later and was given a stepson, John. John and his stepson enlisted as substitutes on March 6, 1862. John was wounded in action at King's School House, Virginia, on June 25, 1862, and was sent home on furlough until September 1862. John returned to service and was reported present until sent to the hospital between July 31 and September 21, 1863. He was discharged for unreported causes on April 17, 1864. After his discharge, John returned home to the Clemmonsville area of the county and was still living there in 1870. No further records.

1075. Loman, John Henderson

Private, Company A, 42nd Regiment N.C. Troops

John was born in 1836. He worked as a farmer in the Clemmonsville area prior to volunteering for service on November 26, 1861. John was reported present until he deserted on December 14, 1863. He was returned to service "in arrest" and was court-martialed on February 16, 1864. The summary judgment returned him to service as of October 31, 1864. No further records.

1076. Loman, Julian E.

Second Lieutenant, 65th Regiment N.C. Militia (1861 organization)

Julian lived in the Cotton Grove area of Davidson County. He was given a commission as a second lieutenant in the Cotton Grove District company on November 26, 1861. No further records.

1077. Lomax, Ira

Private, Company I, 10th Regiment N.C. State Troops (1st N.C. Artillery)

Ira was born on July 28, 1844, to William and Mary Lomax. Ira worked on his family's farm until he was conscripted into service prior to October 21, 1864. After the war, Ira returned home to the Allegheny township, where on October 18, 1868, he married Annie J. Hopkins. Ira and Annie would have only one child: Ebenezer (1869). Ira continued farming and also did some blacksmithing until his death on March 7, 1919. He is buried in the Lomax Family Cemetery.

1078. Lomax, John F.

Private, Chatam Light Infantry Company G, 48th Regiment N.C. Troops

John was born on April 26, 1842, to William and Nancy Lomax. John worked as a farmer, and on November 5, 1861, he married Susan Swicegood. John was conscripted into service on August 14, 1862,

and was captured at Sharpsburg, Maryland, only a month later. He was confined at Point Lookout, Maryland, until November 3, 1862, when he was paroled and transferred to Aiken's Landing, Virginia, for exchange. John was declared exchanged on November 10, 1862. He returned to service to be wounded twice: in the left thigh at Bristoe Station, Virginia, (October 14, 1863) and at Wilderness, Virginia (May 5, 1864). Service records indicate that he was captured on an unspecified date and was held in confinement until he was "paroled in North Carolina in October 1864." After the war John returned home to his wife in the Allegheny township. John and Susan would have eight children: Millie (1865), America (1866), Luther (1868), John (1869), Martha (1871), Henry (1873), William (1874), and Mary (1876). John passed away on December 26, 1926. He is buried at Pine Hill United Methodist Church.

1079. Lomax, Pinkney Ashbury

Private, Holtsburg Guards Company A, 54th Regiment N.C. Troops

Pinkney was born in 1830 to H. K. and Rebecca Lomax. He worked as a farmer, and, on March 19, 1859, he married Margaret Gobble. Pinkney and Margaret would have one child, Loman (1860), before Pinkney was conscripted into service on May 1, 1862. He was reported present until he died of unreported causes at Fredericksburg, Virginia, on January 2, 1863.

1080. Long, Adam

Private, Company A, 42nd Regiment N.C. Troops

Adam was born on August 29, 1828, to Jonathan and Mary Clodfelter Long. He worked as a farmer and a miller, and, on September 1, 1851, he married Eliza Perryman. Adam and Eliza would have two children, Mary (1853) and Phoebe (1858), before Adam was conscripted into service in Rowan County on July 29, 1862. He was reported present through October 1864. No record exists of his parole. After the war, Adam returned to the Midway township where he lived until his death on January 20, 1885. He is buried at Midway United Methodist Church.

1081. Long, George Washington

Private, Company A, 42nd Regiment N.C. Troops

George was born on November 24, 1841, to Jonathan and Mary Clodfelter Long. George worked as a farmer prior to volunteering for service on November 26, 1861. He was reported present until captured at Battery Anderson, Fort Fisher, North Carolina, on December 25, 1864. George was confined at Point Lookout, Maryland, via Fort Monroe, Virginia, until June 28, 1865, when he was released after taking the oath of allegiance. After the war, George returned home to the Midway township, where, on December 28, 1865, he married Mary Brinkley. George and Mary would have two children: John (1867) and Mary (1869). George operated a successful farm until his death on March 28, 1904. He is buried at Midway United Methodist Church.

1082. Long, Jacob

Private, Harnett Light Infantry Company F, 15th Regiment N.C. Troops (5th N.C. Volunteers)

Jacob was born on January 13, 1831. Jacob worked as a farmer, and, on April 6, 1858, he married Eliza Jane Mock. Jacob and Eliza would have one child, Franklin (1859), before Jacob was conscripted into service in Wake County on July 15, 1862. He was reported present until he was captured at LaGrange, Georgia, on April 20, 1865, and paroled the same day. Jacob died sometime prior to 1900. He is buried at Old Vernon Methodist Church.

1083. Long, James

Private, Company C, 70th Regiment N.C. Troops (1st N.C. Junior Reserves)

James was born on November 1, 1846, to Solomon and Mary M. Long. James worked as an apprentice gunsmith prior to enlisting in the Junior Reserves on May 24, 1864. After the war, James returned to the Midway township where he took over his father's gunsmithing business. James died on March 15, 1907. He is buried at Midway United Methodist Church.

1084. Long, Jesse

Private, Company A, 42nd Regiment N.C. Troops

Jesse was born on April 27, 1837, to Jonathan and Mary Clodfelter Long. Jesse worked as a farmer prior to volunteering for service on November 26, 1861. He was reported present until he was captured at Battery Anderson, Fort Fisher, North Carolina, on December 25, 1864. Jesse was imprisoned at Point Lookout, Maryland, via Fort Monroe, Virginia, until June 3, 1865, when he was released after taking the oath of allegiance. After the war, Jesse returned home to the Midway area. He remained single, and upon his father's death, he inherited the majority of the family farm, which he worked until his death on October 16, 1894. He is buried at Midway United Methodist Church.

1085. Long, John L.

Private, Thomasville Rifles
Company B, 14th Regiment N.C.
Troops (4th N.C. Volunteers)

John was born in 1842 to Charles and Catharine Long. John worked as a farmer prior to being conscripted into service in Wake County on July 16, 1862. He was reported present until he died of "acute diarrhea" at Staunton, Virginia, on November 10, 1863.

1086. Long, John M.

Private, Holtsburg Guards
Company A, 54th Regiment N.C.
Troops

John was born on February 27, 1826, to Mathias and Barbara Long. John worked as a farmer in the Cotton Grove area, and, in 1852, he married Sarah Miller Newsom. John and Sarah would have one child, David (1855), before John was conscripted into service on December 20, 1862. He was reported present until captured at Rappahannock Station, Virginia, on November 7, 1863. John was confined at Point Lookout, Maryland, until March 15, 1864, when he was paroled and transferred to City Point, Virginia, for exchange. He was declared exchanged on an unspecified date. John returned to service and was reported present until he was captured at Fort Stedman, Virginia, on March 28, 1865. He was once again confined at Point Lookout until June 28, 1865, when he was released after taking the oath of allegiance. Once paroled, John returned home to his wife Sarah, David, and his two-year-old son, John, who was born in mid–1863 when John was away. John and Sarah would have two more children: Charles (1866) and Edward (1868). John lived in the Cotton Grove area until his death on February 25, 1881, just two days shy of his 55th birthday. He is buried at Jersey Baptist Church.

1087. Long, John Peter

Private, Company C, 70th Regiment
N.C. Troops (1st N.C. Junior
Reserves)
Company H, 48th Regiment N.C.
Troops

John was born on September 10, 1845, to Israel and Catharine Sink Long. He worked as a farmer and was reported as one of Union (Bethany) Academy's best students prior to enlisting in the Junior Reserves. On May 19, 1864, he was placed into regular service in Company H, 48th North Carolina. John was reported present until he was captured at Hatcher's Run, Virginia, on March 31, 1865. John was confined at Point Lookout, Maryland, until June 28, 1865, when he was released after taking the oath of allegiance. After the war, John returned to the Bethany area, where on February 25, 1868, he married Caroline Hedrick. John and Caroline would have five children: Mary (1869), Mariah (1873), Cora (1876), Arementia (1880), and Alberta (1886). John died on October 6, 1922. He is buried at Bethany United Church of Christ.

1088. Long, Joseph

Second Lieutenant, 65th Regiment
N.C. Militia (1861 organization)
Corporal, Holtsburg Guards
Company A, 54th Regiment N.C.
Troops

Joseph was born in 1828 to Mathias and Barbara Long. He worked as an overseer on his father's plantation and was commissioned as a second lieutenant in the Cotton Grove District Company on November 25, 1861. Joseph served as a militia man until he was conscripted into service on May 14, 1862. Joseph was promoted to corporal in May 1863 and was captured at Rappahannock Station, Virginia, on November 7, 1863. He was confined at Point Lookout, Maryland, until March 9, 1864, when he was paroled and transferred to City Point, Virginia, for exchange. No further records.

1089. Long, Shuman Henry

Private, Company A, 42nd Regiment
N.C. Troops

Shuman was born in 1843 to Jonathan and Mary Clodfelter Long. He worked as a farmer prior to volunteering for service on November 26, 1861. Shuman was reported present until he was killed in action at Petersburg, Virginia, on July 20, 1864. He is buried in the mass grave at Blanford Cemetery in Petersburg.

1090. Long, Solomon

Private, Company A, 42nd Regiment
N.C. Troops

Solomon was born on September 10, 1839, to Jonathan and Mary Clodfelter Long. Solomon worked as a carpenter prior to volunteering on November 26, 1861. He was reported present until captured at Battery Anderson, Fort Fisher, North Carolina, on December 25, 1864. Solomon was confined at Point Lookout, Maryland, via Fort Monroe, Virginia, until June 28, 1865, when he was released after taking the oath of allegiance. After the war, Solomon returned home to the Midway area where, on April 12, 1866, he married Susan Everhart. Solomon and Susan would have three children: Charles (1867), Minnie (1871), and Hiram (1874). Solomon worked as a house carpenter until his death on November 16, 1923. He is buried at Midway United Methodist Church.

1091. Long, William D.

Private, Company B, 48th Regiment
N.C. Troops

William was born in 1832 to Jacob and Matilda Long. William worked as a farmer, and, on December 24, 1858, he married Barbara Miller. He was conscripted into service on August 8, 1862. William deserted on September 15, 1862, and returned to service subsequent to June 30, 1863. He was reported present until captured at Bristoe Station, Virginia, on October 14, 1863. William was confined at Point Lookout, Maryland, via Old Capital Prison, Washington, D.C., until March 4, 1865, when he was received for exchange. No further records.

1092. Long, William J.

Private, Harnett Light Infantry
Company F, 15th Regiment N.C. Troops
(5th N.C. Volunteers)

Will was born in 1839 to the Reverend Thomas and Amanda Long. Will worked as a farmer, and, in 1860, he married Susanna Livengood. Will and Susanna would have one child, George (1862), before Will was conscripted into service in Wake County on July 15, 1862. He was reported present until he deserted from service on July 1, 1863. No further records.

1093. Lookabill, Barney

Private, Thomasville Rifles
Company B, 14th Regiment N.C. Troops
(4th N.C. Volunteers)

Barney was born in 1840 and lived with his uncle Franklin in the Emmons township of Davidson County. Barney worked as a miner prior to volunteering for service on April 23, 1861. He was wounded in the right hand at Malvern Hill, Virginia, on July 1, 1862. Barney was reported absent, wounded, until November 24, 1862, when he was discharged because of his wounds. Barney was paroled at Greensboro, North Carolina, on May 10, 1865. After the war, Barney continued to work in the mines until at least 1880. No further records.

1094. Lookabill, David

Private, Company B, 37th Regiment
N.C. Troops

David was born in 1812. He worked as a farmer in the southern district of Davidson County, and, in 1833, he married Polly. David and Polly would have eight children, Jacob (1835), Elizabeth (1837), Martha (1844), Franklin (1845), Joel (1848), John (1851), Rebecca (1852), and Mary (1855), before the family began to move west. On the trip out, the family's wagon broke down in the vicinity of Council's Store, Watauga County, and the family settled in the Meat Camp area of Watauga County. David volunteered for service at the old muster grounds on September 14, 1861, and was mustered in as a sergeant. On March 1, 1862, he was reduced in rank to private. David died of pneumonia in Richmond, Virginia, on December 24, 1862.

1095. Lookabill, Franklin D.

First Lieutenant, 65th Regiment N.C.
Militia (1861 organization)

Franklin was born on December 25, 1827. He worked as a farmer and operated a small grist mill in the Emmons township. Franklin married Miranda in 1857. They would have three children: Franklin (1859), Bathsheba (1866), and Walter (1868). Franklin was commissioned as first lieutenant in the Conrad Hill District Company on November 26, 1861. After his term of service, Franklin devoted his time to his farm and served for a brief time as postmaster for Emmons. Franklin died on September 25, 1880. He is buried at Tom's Creek Primitive Baptist Church.

1096. Lopp, Jacob

Private, Lexington Wildcats
Company I, 14th Regiment N.C. Troops
(4th N.C. Volunteers)

Jacob was born on May 16, 1842, to John Jacob and Molly Younts Lopp. Jacob worked as a farmer prior to being conscripted into service in Wake County on July 16, 1862. He was reported present until wounded in the left arm at Gettysburg, Pennsylvania, on July 1, 1863. Jacob was confined at Point Lookout, Maryland, via Fort Delaware, Delaware, until February 18, 1865, when he was paroled and transferred to Cox's Wharf, Virginia, for exchange. Jacob was reported present with a detachment of paroled prisoners at Camp Lee, Virginia, on February 28, 1865. After the war, Jacob returned to his home in the Conrad Hill township. On October 6, 1872, Jacob married Mary Jane Boggs. Jacob and Mary Jane would have two children, Robert Lee (1872) and Kathleen (1878), before Mary Jane died in 1879. Jacob married Loucreitia Berrier on April 15, 1883. Jacob and Loucreitia would have six children: Furman (1884), William Avery (1885), John (1887), Henry Grady (1890), George (1894), and Elizabeth (1896). Jacob became a successful farmer and operated a small sawmill. In 1884, Jacob donated the lumber to build Holly Grove Academy. Jacob died on June 19, 1904. He is buried at Mount Tabor United Church of Christ.

1097. Lopp, Peter

Private, Company C, 76th Regiment N.C.
Troops (6th N.C. Senior Reserves)

Peter Lopp, planter and benefactor of Pilgrim Reformed Church (Gracy McCrary Lopp, *The Heritage of Davidson County*).

Mary G. Lopp and her son Thoyas (Grace McCrary Lopp, *The Heritage of Davidson County*).

Peter was born on February 20, 1823, the son of Jacob Lopp, who was one of the county's founders, commissioners, and foremost planters. Peter worked as an overseer on his father's plantation, and, on June 23, 1847, he married Mary Green. Peter and Mary would have ten children: Laurinda (1848), Jacob (1849), William (1852), Charles (1854), Louise (1856), Benjamin and Eliza (1858), John (1860), Peter (1862), and Thomas (1866).

In 1862, Peter's father died, leaving Peter with a large plantation with over a hundred slaves. Peter enlisted in the Senior Reserves in January 1865. After his term of service, Peter worked on his farm and was an active member of the Pilgrim congregation. Peter died on August 27, 1885. He is buried at Pilgrim United Church of Christ.

1098. Lopp, Phillip

Private, Company C, 76th Regiment N.C. Troops (6th N.C. Senior Reserves)

Phillip was born on November 21, 1824. He worked as a farmer in the northern district of Davidson County prior to 1860. Phillip enlisted in the Senior Reserves in January 1865. After his term of service, Phillip married Eliza Jane Hiatt. Phillip and Eliza would not have any children. Phillip lived in the North Thomasville township until his death on October 4, 1895. He is buried at Pilgrim United Church of Christ.

1099. Lore, Elkannah

Private, Carolina Rangers Company B, 10th Virginia Cavalry Regiment

"Kane" was born in 1838 to David and Sarah Sullivan Lore (Lohr). He worked as a farmer prior to volunteering for service in Davie County on October 29, 1861. Kane was reported present with the 10th Virginia Cavalry; the final records state that he drew a clothing ration on December 31, 1864. After the war, Kane returned to the Pilgrim area, where, in 1866, he married Mary Melinda Everhart. Kane and Mary would have two children: Charles (1869) and Martha (1872). Kane died of a heart attack sometime before 1880. He is buried in an unmarked grave at Pilgrim United Church of Christ.

1100. Lore, Solomon B.

Second Lieutenant, Company F, 76th Regiment N.C. Troops (6th N.C. Senior Reserves)

Solomon was born on January 23, 1818, to John and Charlotte Lore (Lohr). Solomon worked as a farmer and was a justice of the peace in the Pilgrim area. In 1852, Solomon married Isabella Darr. Solomon and Isabella would have three

Senior Reserve lieutenant and long time justice of the peace Solomon B. Lore (Richard L. Conrad, *The Heritage of Davidson County*).

children: William (1854), John (1860), and Frances (1866). Solomon enlisted in the Senior Reserves in January 1865. According to his obituary, he served as the company's second lieutenant. Solomon died on May 30, 1895. He is buried at Pilgrim United Church of Christ.

1101. Lowe, John W.

Private, Company H, 48th Regiment N.C. Troops

John was born in Davidson County and worked as a farmer prior to being conscripted into service on August 8, 1862. He was wounded at Sharpsburg, Maryland, on September 17, 1862. John was reported absent, wounded, through February 1863. He was hospitalized at Wilmington, North Carolina, on May 3, 1863, with "acute rheumatism." John was issued an extended furlough until he was detailed for light duty at Lexington, North Carolina, from January 19 through April 30, 1864. He rejoined the 48th N.C. sometime prior to September 1864 and was reported present until he was paroled at Appomattox Court House, Virginia, on April 9, 1865. No further records.

1102. Luay, Wesley

Private, Company B, 48th Regiment N.C. Troops

Wesley was born in 1859 to George and Mary Luay. He worked as a farmer, and, on July 5, 1859, he married Mary Shuler. Wesley volunteered for service on March 3, 1862. He was killed in action at King's School House, Virginia, on June 25, 1862.

1103. Mabry, John H.

Captain, Company B, 48th Regiment N.C. Troops

John was born on May 30, 1835, to John P. and Elizabeth J. Mabry. John's father operated the Lexington Inn. John was listed as a student in 1850, and by 1860, he was employed as a station agent for the North Carolina Railroad. John volunteered for service on February 22, 1862, and was promoted to second lieutenant one month later. On May 1, 1862, John was promoted to first lieutenant, and with A. A. Hill's promotion to major, John was appointed captain on October 20, 1862. John served the entire war at the head of his company and was paroled at Greensboro, North Carolina, on May 1, 1865. After the war, John returned to the his work as a railroad employee. He worked as a station hand, a demotion from his old job. In 1879, John caught pneumonia and died on September 6 of that year. He is buried in the Lexington City Cemetery.

1104. McBride, Thomas P.

Private, Holtsburg Guards Company A, 54th Regiment N.C. Troops

Thomas was born on October 28, 1838, to William and Ellnice McBride. Thomas worked as a farmer, and, on April 6, 1855, he married Cynthia Walser. Thomas and Cynthia would have three children, William (1857), Charles (1859), and Henry (1862), before Thomas volunteered for service on March 27, 1862. Thomas was reported present until he was captured at Rappahannock Station, Virginia, on November 7, 1863. He was confined at Point Lookout, Maryland, until March 15, 1864, when he was paroled and transferred to City Point, Virginia, for exchange. Thomas was declared exchanged on an unspecified date and was reported present until he was paroled at Appomattox Court House, Virginia, on April 9, 1865. After the war, Thomas returned to his family and his Boone township farm. Thomas and

Cynthia would have five more children: Ella (1866), Samuel (1869), Hiram (1872), Stephen (1874), and Frank (1876). Thomas died on January 27, 1884. He is buried at Pine Primitive Baptist Church.

1105. McBride, William A.

Sergeant, Company C, 70th Regiment N.C. Troops (1st N.C. Junior Reserves)

William was born on September 21, 1846, to A. J. and Polly McBride. He worked as a farmer prior to enlisting in the Junior Reserves on May 24, 1864. According to *Moore's Roster*, William served with the rank of sergeant. After the war, William returned home to the Boone township where, on July 20, 1871, he married Ellen Garrett. William and Ellen would have three children: Lou (1875), James (1879), and John (1881). William lived in the Boone township until his death on December 15, 1927. He is buried at Pine Primitive Baptist Church.

1106. McBurkehead, William

Second Lieutenant, 65th N.C. Militia Regiment (1861 organization)

William was a resident of the southern district of Davidson County in 1860. He was commissioned as a second lieutenant in the Rock Spring District Company on October 1, 1861. No further records.

1107. McCarn, Abraham

Private, Holtsburg Guards Company A, 54th Regiment N.C. Troops

"Abram" was born in 1839 to William and Mary McCarn. Abram worked as a farmer prior to volunteering for service on March 4, 1862. He was reported present until he was captured at Rappahannock Station, Virginia, on November 7, 1863. Abram was confined at Point Lookout, Maryland, until March 9, 1864, when he was paroled and transferred to City Point, Virginia, for exchange. He was hospitalized at Charlottesville, Virginia, on July 26, 1864, with a gunshot wound probably received at Stephenson's Depot, Virginia. Abram was transferred to a Lynchburg, Virginia, hospital and was detailed for light duty at Salisbury, North Carolina, in September and October 1864. He was called up from light duty

and rejoined his company sometime in February 1865. Abram was reported present until he was captured a second time: at Fort Stedman, Virginia, on March 25, 1865. He was once again confined at Point Lookout and was released on June 29, 1865, after taking the oath of allegiance. Abram made his way home to the Silver Hill township, where, on December 14, 1865, he married Mary E. Dickens. Abram and Mary would have five children: Joseph (1867), Henry (1869), Maria (1871), Pinkney (1873), and Fannie (1875). Abram became a fairly successful farmer in the Silver Hill area prior to his death sometime in the 1890s. He is buried at Holloways Baptist Church.

1108. McCarn, Alexander

Second Lieutenant, 65th N.C. Militia Regiment (1861 organization)

Alexander was born in 1835 to William and Mary McCarn. Alexander worked as a farmer, and, on August 23, 1855, he married Sarah A. Valentine. Alexander and Sarah would have eight children together: Missy (1856), Moses (1864), Sarah (1866), Daniel (1869), Martha (1871), Josephine (1874), Della (1876), and John (1879). Alexander was commissioned as second lieutenant in the Silver Hill District Company on December 26, 1861. After the war, Alexander assisted his younger brother, Abraham, in his farming and operated a small sawmill for a short time. Alexander died prior to 1900. He is buried at Holloways Baptist Church.

1109. McCarn, John H.

Corporal, Company C, 42nd Regiment N.C. Troops

John was born on August 28, 1844, to Michael and Nancy McCarn. John worked on his family's farm and as a miner prior to volunteering for service on February 2, 1862. John was mustered in as a corporal and served until he was discharged due to "double inguiral hernia" on December 15, 1862. After his service, John returned to the Silver Hill township where he found employment as a silver miner, and in 1869, John married Susan. John and Susan would have four children: Hillary (1871), Dinah (1875), John (1878), and Lindsay (1880). John and his family moved to the Cotton Grove township prior to 1880. John died

on February 25, 1924. He is buried at Stoner's Grove Baptist Church.

1110. McCrary, Alexander

Private, Company I, 10th Regiment N.C. State Troops (1st N.C. Artillery)

Alexander was born on March 3, 1830, to John and Sarah Baker McCrary. In 1850, he was working as an apprentice to bootmaker John Heitman. Alexander married Mary C. Hiatt on January 27, 1864. Alexander and Mary would have two children: Charles E. (1864) and Mary "Mamie" (1869). Alexander continued his work as a bootmaker until he was conscripted into service in New Hanover County on August 13, 1864. Alexander was reported present until he was paroled at Greensboro, North Carolina, on May 1, 1865. Alexander was listed as one of the Lexington township's finest bootmakers in 1870 and again in 1880. Alexander died on December 27, 1894. He is buried at Ebenezer United Methodist Church.

1111. McCrary, John Calhoun

Private, Harnett Light Infantry Company F, 15th Regiment N.C. Troops (5th N.C. Volunteers)

John was born in 1825 to Henry and Jane Cooper McCrary and was named for the current U.S. vice president, John C. Calhoun. He worked with his family as both a farmer and a small merchant. On December 10, 1853, John married Sarah Long. John and Sarah would have four children, Frances (1855), Mary (1856), William H. (1859), and Amanda (1861), before John was conscripted into service on July 15, 1862. He was reported present until wounded in the arm at Wilderness, Virginia, on May 5, 1864. John returned to duty prior to October 31, 1864. The Federal provost marshal's records indicate that he was paroled at Appomattox Court House, Virginia; however, both pension records and family history confirm that John died of disease, possibly resulting from his wound, at Richmond, Virginia, on April 6, 1865. He is buried in Hollywood Cemetery in Richmond.

1112. McCrary, John H.

Corporal, Company H, 48th Regiment N.C. Troops

John was born on January 7, 1838, the son of Michael McCrary. John worked as a cabinetmaker for Henry Heitman prior to volunteering for service at "Wagner's" on March 3, 1862. He was mustered in as a corporal and was reported present until he died of typhoid fever in a Petersburg, Virginia, hospital on July 15, 1862. John's body was sent home and buried at Ebenezer United Methodist Church.

1113. McCrary, Reuben

Private, Harnett Light Infantry
Company F, 15th Regiment N.C. Troops
(5th N.C. Volunteers)

Reuben was born in 1838 and lived with his grandparents Hugh and Nancy McCrary. Reuben worked as a farmer prior to being conscripted into service on July 15, 1862. He was wounded at Sharpsburg, Maryland, on September 17, 1862. Reuben died at an unreported location on October 3, 1862.

1114. McCrary, William

Private, Laurel Springs Guards
Company A, 34th Regiment N.C. Troops

William was born on August 8, 1822, to John and Sarah Raker McCrary. He worked as a farmer, and, on May 20, 1845, he married Mary Heitman. William and Mary would have five children, Isabel (1846), Sarah (1849), Tfirenia (1851), Nancy (1855), and Mary L. (1858), before Mary's death in 1862. William married Emmeline McCrary on September 25, 1863, just prior to William's conscription into service, although the exact date was not reported. He was reported present until he was captured at Fort Stedman, Virginia, on March 25, 1865. William was confined at Point Lookout, Maryland, until June 29, 1865, when he was released after taking the oath of allegiance. Emmeline died around 1865. William then married Nancy Hedrick. William and Nancy would go on to have five children: Hiram (1867), John (1868), Lula (1870), Notie Ella (1872), and Victoria (1876). William died on November 28, 1891. He is buried at Ebenezer United Methodist Church.

1115. McCrary, William

Private, Edgecombe Rifles
Company G, 13th Regiment N.C. Troops
(3rd N.C. Volunteers)

William was born in 1832 to Hugh and Nancy McCrary. He worked as a farmer prior to being conscripted into service in Wake County on February 28, 1864. William was reported present through February 1865. No further records.

1116. McCrary, William F.

Private, Thomasville Rifles
Company B, 14th Regiment N.C. Troops
(4th N.C. Volunteers)

William was born in 1839 to Hugh and Nancy McCrary. Shortly before the war, William had purchased land in Wilkes County and had lived there since December 1860. William volunteered for service on May 10, 1861. He was reported present until wounded in the shoulder at Gettysburg, Pennsylvania, on July 1, 1863. William recovered and rejoined his company on September 1, 1863. He was reported absent, wounded, between December 1863 and August 31, 1864. No further records.

1117. McCrary, William Franklin

Private, Company H, 48th Regiment N.C. Troops

William was born in 1841. William worked as a clerk until he was conscripted into service in Wayne County on May 8, 1862. He was reported present until, having suffered some kind of wound, he was assigned to light duty in Charlotte, North Carolina. He was reported as an overseer of hands in Salisbury, North Carolina, from January 1863 to February 10, 1865. William was paroled at Greensboro, North Carolina, on May 3, 1865. No further records.

1118. McCriston, Walter R.

First Lieutenant, 65th North Carolina Militia Regiment (1861 organization)

Walter was born in 1829. He worked as a farmer in the Cotton Grove area of Davidson County. On November 25, 1861, he accepted a commission as first lieutenant in the Cotton Grove District Company. Walter married Elizabeth C. in 1860. Walter and Elizabeth would have eight children: John (1861), William Tecumseh (1867), Mary (1870), Josiah (1872), Walter (1873), Catharine (1875), Charles (1877), and Nannie (1878). Wal-

ter lived in the Cotton Grove township until his death prior to 1890. No further records.

1119. McCutchan, Robert M.

Private, Thomasville Rifles
Company B, 14th Regiment N.C. Troops
(4th N.C. Volunteers)

Robert was born in 1842 in the state of Massachusetts. He moved to the Thomasville area to work in the Lines Shoe Factory in the 1850s, and in 1860, he was one of Rev. Miller's boarders. Robert volunteered for service on April 23, 1861, and was mustered in as a sergeant. He was promoted to first sergeant on September 26, 1861, but was court-martialed on unreported charges and reduced to private on April 9, 1863. Robert was reported present until he was wounded in the vicinity of Spotsylvania Court House, Virginia, on May 8, 1864. Robert died of his wounds on June 1, 1864.

1120. McEwing, Edward A.

Private, Thomasville Rifles
Company B, 14th Regiment N.C. Troops
(4th N.C. Volunteers)

Edward was born in Paisley, Scotland, in 1837. He came to Davidson County to work in the Lines Shoe Factory in Thomasville. Edward volunteered for service on April 23, 1861, but after fighting in the Peninsula campaign, he was discharged "by reason of being a foreigner" on July 22, 1862. No further records.

1121. McGuire, Hamilton J.

Private, Thomasville Rifles
Company B, 14th Regiment N.C. Troops
(4th N.C. Volunteers)
Private, Carolina Rangers
Company B, 10th Virginia Cavalry Regiment

Hamilton was born in 1843 outside of the county. In 1850, he was living with Peter and Sally Mock. Hamilton entered Yadkin College in the fall of 1860. When the war commenced, Hamilton left his classes and volunteered for service on April 23, 1861. He was reported present until discharged from the Thomasville Rifles because of disability on August 30, 1861. Hamilton volunteered for service as a cavalry trooper in Davie County on October 29, 1861. Company records state

First Sergeant James D. McIver died of wounds he received at the battle of Chancellorsville (Clark's Regiments).

that he was present through December 31, 1864, when he last received a clothing ration. He is mentioned in the letter from Hugh Clodfelter above. Apparently, Hamilton, Hugh, and William Hedrick were good friends during their time in service. After the war, Hamilton returned to the county and in 1870 was still living in the home of Sally Mock. Hamilton apparently left the county in the 1880s for land outside of North Carolina.

1122. McIver, Henry Evander

Private, Company C, 70th Regiment N.C. Troops (1st N.C. Junior Reserves)
Private, Davidson Guards Company A, 21st Regiment N.C. Troops (11th N.C. Volunteers)

Henry was born in 1847 to Dr. Evander and Eliza McIver. Henry worked as a carpenter's apprentice prior to enlisting in the Junior Reserves on May 24, 1864. He was transferred to the 21st N.C. Regiment on December 8, 1864. Henry was reported present until he was captured at Sayler's Creek, Virginia, on April 6, 1865. He was confined at Newport News, Virginia, until June 14, 1865, when he was released after taking the oath of allegiance. After the war, Henry returned home, and in 1870 he was listed as a house carpenter. On June 12, 1879, Henry married N. V. Thomas. Census records show the couple living in Forsyth County in 1880. No further records.

1123. McIver, James Daniel

First Sergeant, Davidson Guards Company A, 21st Regiment N.C. Troops (11th N.C. Volunteers)

James was born in 1841 to Dr. Evander and Eliza McIver. James worked as a carpenter prior to volunteering for service on May 8, 1861. He was mustered in as a sergeant and was promoted to first sergeant on August 22, 1862. Six days later, James was wounded at Second Manassas, Virginia, on August 28, 1862. He recovered from his wounds and returned to service prior to May 3, 1863, when he was wounded at Chancellorsville, Virginia. James died of his wounds near Fredericksburg, Virginia, on May 5, 1863.

1124. McMahon, Barney

Private, Holtsburg Guards Company A, 54th Regiment N.C. Troops

Barney was born in 1841 in Wadford County, Ireland. Like many Irishmen, he emigrated to America to find employment and a better life. Barney came to Davidson County in the late 1850s and worked as a miner in the Silver Hill area. Barney enlisted as a paid substitute for Adderton Stokes on June 17, 1862. He was detailed to serve as a lead miner on September 10, 1862, and served in that role through October 1864. After the war, Barney continued west and stopped briefly in Greene County, Tennessee, where the heritage book offers a few lines about him.

1125. Mahala, James Knox Polk

Private, Company H, 10th Regiment N.C. State Troops (1st N.C. Artillery)

James was born on July 11, 1832, to John and Elizabeth Mahala. James worked on his father's struggling plantation in the Cotton Grove township. In 1859, James married Crissie. James and Crissie would have two children, Sarah (1861) and James (1863), before James was conscripted into service in Wayne County on February 10, 1863. James was reported present through February 1865. After the war, James and Crissie would have six more children: Mary (1866), William (1867), John (1870), George (1873), Louisa (1875), and Ada (1879). Apparently, the plantation failed shortly after the war in the early days of Federal occupation, and James found employment as a foreman at the Silver Hill mine. James worked as a mine supervisor until his death on January 28, 1918. He is buried at Stoner's Grove Baptist Church.

Plantation home of Cotton Grove's Mahala family (Touart, *Building the Backcountry*).

1126. Maley, Jesse H.

Musician, Company A, 42nd Regiment N.C. Troops

Jesse was born in 1841. He worked as a laborer in the city of Lexington prior to volunteering for service on November 26, 1861. Jesse was promoted to corporal in January 1863. He was reported present until November of the same year when he was assigned to the regimental band as a musician. Jesse was reported present with the band until he was paroled at Greensboro, North Carolina, on May 5, 1865. After the war, Jesse returned to Lexington where, on March 29, 1866, he married Jane C. "Irene" Owens. Jesse lived in Lexington until his death on July 29, 1897. He is buried in the Lexington City Cemetery.

1127. Maley, John A.

Corporal, Holtsburg Guards Company A, 54th Regiment N.C. Troops

John was born in 1838. He worked as a farmer prior to volunteering for service on March 4, 1862. John was mustered in as a corporal and was reported present until he was killed in action at Williamsport, Maryland, on July 6, 1863.

1128. March, John A.

Captain (AQM), Quartermaster's Department, Richmond, Virginia

John was born on October 8, 1825. He received some formal education at Trinity College before becoming a businessman. John married Susanna Henly on June 27, 1859; they would not have any children. In 1860, John was working as a mercantilist and a stock trader in the city of Lexington. With the outbreak of war, his organizational and management skills were employed in the Quartermaster's Department of the Confederate Army. John worked as a clerk in the Richmond Depot, assigning supplies and materials to different units. After his service, John returned home and decided to construct a hotel. The March Hotel was fully operational by 1880 and was one of the city's leading businesses. Today, the hotel stands as a monument to Davidson County architecture. John died on August 2, 1897. He is buried in the Lexington City Cemetery.

1129. Martin, Samuel Alexander

Private, Davidson Guards Company A, 21st Regiment N.C. Troops (11th N.C. Volunteers)

Alex was born in 1831 to James and Nancy Martin. Alex worked as an apprentice hatter prior to volunteering for service on May 8, 1861. He was reported present until wounded at Winchester, Virginia, on May 25, 1862. Alex returned to duty on an unspecified date and was reported present until paroled at Appomattox Court House, Virginia, on April 9, 1865. No further records.

1130. May, Joseph J.

Private, Company D, 48th Regiment N.C. Troops

Joseph was born in 1843 to Benjamin and Mary May. He worked as a farmer prior to being conscripted into service on August 8, 1862. Joseph was last reported present in June 1863. No further records.

1131. May, Joshua B.

Private, Thomasville Rifles Company B, 14th Regiment N.C. Troops (4th N.C. Volunteers)

Joshua was born in 1843 to Benjamin and Mary May. He was the fraternal twin of Joseph. Joshua worked as a farmer prior to volunteering for service on April 27, 1861. Joshua was reported present until he died of "fever or dysenteria" at Richmond, Virginia, on June 17, 1862.

1132. May, Robert C.

Snead's Company, Local Defense

Robert was born on September 16, 1844, to Reuben and Eliza May. In 1860, he was working in the town of Thomasville as a clerk. Robert served in Snead's Local Defense Company, according to Barefoot's Roster as well as family history. After his service, Robert returned home, and, on December 2, 1869, he married Elizabeth Bodenheimer. Robert and Elizabeth moved in with Elizabeth's parents in 1870. Robert and Elizabeth would have six children: Ella (1872), Hattie (1874), Eliza (1876), John (1878), Philo (1884), and Frank (1884). Robert lived in the Midway township until his death on April 4, 1898. He is buried in his family's plot at Fair Grove United Methodist Church.

1133. May, Thomas A.

Sergeant, Company D, 48th Regiment N.C. Troops

Thomas was born in 1832 to Benjamin and Mary May. He worked as a farmer in the Conrad Hill township, and, in 1857, he married Polly Pope. Thomas was conscripted into service on August 8, 1862. He was captured at Sharpsburg, Maryland, on September 17, 1862, and was confined at Fort McHenry, Maryland, until he was paroled and transferred to Aiken's Landing, Virginia, for exchange on October 19, 1862. Thomas was declared exchanged on November 10, 1862. Two months later, he contracted "incipient phtisis" and was hospitalized at Danville, Virginia, on January 8, 1863. After nearly five months in the hospital, Thomas was granted a furlough on May 26, 1863, and he returned to service on June 26, 1863. Thomas was promoted to sergeant prior to October 31, 1864, and served in that capacity until he was captured at Hatcher's Run, Virginia, on April 2, 1865. He was confined at Point Lookout, Maryland, until June 29, 1865, when he was released after taking the oath of allegiance. After the war, Thomas returned briefly to Davidson County. Census records indicate that Thomas was living in Randolph County in 1870. No further records.

1134. Mayabb, William

Private, Company H, 48th Regiment N.C. Troops

William was born in 1842 to Jeremiah and Barbara Mayabb. William worked as a hireling for Haley Myers prior to volunteering for service on March 5, 1862. He died of typhoid fever at Richmond, Virginia, on December 6, 1862.

1135. Medlin, Henry

Private, Company A, 42nd Regiment N.C. Troops

Henry was born in 1844. Henry worked as a farmer in the Lexington township until he volunteered for service on February 14, 1862. He was reported present until wounded in the left arm at Cold Harbor, Virginia, on June 5, 1864. Henry recovered from his wound and returned to service in September 1864. He was reported present through January 24, 1865. After the war, Henry returned to the Lexington township, where, on May 14, 1865, he married Sofronia Shuler. Henry and Sofie would have six children: George (1866), Samuel (1869), Jefferson (1870), Phillip (1872), Eugenia (1877), and Smith (1879). Henry worked as a sawmill operator and a machinist in the Lexington township until his death prior to 1900. He is buried in an unmarked grave in the Lexington City Cemetery.

1136. Medlin, Jesse

Private, Company I, 42nd Regiment N.C. Troops

Jesse was born in Wake County, North Carolina, in 1825. Jesse worked as a farmer in the southern district of Davidson County, and, in 1854, he married Mary Farebee. Jesse and Mary would have two children, Elizabeth (1856) and Eliza Jane (1862), before Jesse volunteered for service on February 14, 1862. Jesse was reported present until March 16, 1865, when he was "brought home by his wife and died in Davidson County of unspecified wounds." No further records.

1137. Medlin, Nathan

Private, Company I, 42nd Regiment N.C. Troops

Nathan was born in 1840. He worked as a farmer in the Lexington township prior to volunteering for service on February 14, 1862. Nathan was reported present until he was imprisoned on unspecified charges at Petersburg, Virginia, on August 7, 1864. He was reported in confinement through October 1864. He was apparently released sometime in December 1864 and was wounded at Petersburg, Virginia, in 1865. Nathan was paroled at Greensboro, North Carolina, on May 5, 1865. After the war, Nathan returned home, where, on November 1, 1869, he married Sarah E. Bryant. Nathan and Sarah would have two children: Amanda (1870) and Wesley (1876). Nathan was working in the Lexington township in 1900. No further records.

1138. Mendenhall, Columbus Alfred

Private, Company I, 42nd Regiment N.C. Troops

Columbus was born in 1838 to Jemina Mendenhall. He worked as a farmer prior to being conscripted into service in

Rowan County on July 14, 1862. Columbus deserted on December 17, 1862. He returned to service on December 21, 1863, and was reported present through February 1864. No further records.

1139. Mendenhall, James F.

Private, Company H, 33rd Regiment N.C. Troops

James was born on March 15, 1831, to John J. and Susan Mendenhall. He worked as a farmer in the Abbott's Creek area and was married to Sarah prior to enlisting on an unspecified date. James was captured at Fort Stedman, Virginia, on March 25, 1865. He was confined at Point Lookout, Maryland, until June 27, 1865, when he was released after taking the oath of allegiance. After the war, James and Sarah moved to the Clemmonsville township in 1870. James lived in the area until his death on December 9, 1917. He is buried at New Friendship Baptist Church, Forsyth County.

1140. Mendenhall, James Newell

Private, Company C, 3rd Alabama Cavalry Regiment

James was born on October 2, 1844. He worked as a carpenter in the North Thomasville township prior to enlisting in North Carolina in February 1865 in the 3rd Alabama Cavalry, which was a part of the rear guard protecting the Army of Tennessee's retreat through North Carolina. After the war, James married Miriam Thomas in 1872. Around the same time, he began to work for Westmoreland's Chair Factory and then worked for the Standard Chair Company. James and Miriam would have two children: Ottis (1875) and Walter (1877). In 1900, James was working as a furniture manufacturer in the city of Lexington. James lived in Lexington until his death on August 13, 1917. He is buried in the Lexington City Cemetery.

1141. Mendenhall, John J., Jr.

Sergeant, Confederate Guards Company K, 48th Regiment N.C. Troops

John was born on October 15, 1826, to John J. and Susan Mendenhall. He worked as an apprentice blacksmith in the North Thomasville township, and, on April 25, 1851, John married Eliza Hilton. John and Eliza would have five

children, James (1852), Nancy (1854), Cyrus (1857), John (1859), and Mary (1861), before John enlisted into service at Camp Magnum, Wake County, on April 9, 1862. John was wounded in the wrist at Sharpsburg, Maryland, on September 17, 1862. He recovered from his wounds, returned to service on an unspecified date, and was promoted to corporal in March 1863. John was promoted to sergeant prior to October 31, 1864, and was reported present until captured at Hatcher's Run, Virginia, on April 2, 1865. He was confined at Hart's Island, New York, until June 18, 1865, when he was released after taking the oath of allegiance. After the war, John returned home where he began his own blacksmithing business. John and Eliza would have two more children: Joseph (1869) and Martha (1872). John continued his work as a blacksmith until his death on February 28, 1890. He is buried at Pleasant Grove United Methodist Church.

1142. Merrell, Ebenezer

Private, Company C, 76th Regiment N.C. Troops (6th N.C. Senior Reserves)

Ebenezer was born on March 9, 1816. He worked as a farmer in the southern district of Davidson County, and, on November 22, 1834, he married Ann Tavner. Ebenezer and Ann would have eight children: Samuel (1840), Paul (1842), Rebecca (1843), Barbara (1845), John (1848), William (1852), Sarah (1860), and William (1862). Ebenezer enlisted in Hill's Senior Reserves, which became Company C of the 6th N.C. Senior Reserves, in January 1865. After his service, Ebenezer continued his work as a farmer in the Jersey area until his death on May 30, 1884. He is buried at Jersey Baptist Church.

1143. Merrell, Paul W.

Private, Company B, 48th Regiment N.C. Troops

Paul was born in 1842 to Ebenezer and Ann Tavner Merrell. He worked as a farmer prior to volunteering for service in Forsyth County on March 4, 1862. Paul was wounded at King's School House, Virginia, on June 25, 1862. Paul died of his wounds at Richmond, Virginia, on June 26, 1862.

1144. Merrell, Samuel

Private, Company B, 48th Regiment N.C. Troops

Samuel was born in 1840 to Ebenezer and Ann Tavner Merrell. He worked as a farmer prior to volunteering for service on March 3, 1862. Samuel was killed in action at Sharpsburg, Maryland, on September 17, 1862.

1145. Messer, Henry

Private, Harnett Light Infantry Company F, 15th Regiment N.C. Troops (5th N.C. Volunteers)

Henry was born in 1828 to Deborah Messer. He worked as a farmer in the Clemmonsville area prior to being conscripted into service in Wake County on July 15, 1862. Henry was reported present until he was discharged because of disability on December 3, 1862. No further records.

1146. Michael, Austin

Private, Davidson Guards Company A, 21st Regiment N.C. Troops (11th N.C. Volunteers)

Austin was born in 1842. He worked as a farmer prior to volunteering for service on May 8, 1861. Austin was killed in action at Winchester, Virginia, on May 25, 1862.

1147. Michael, Barney

Private, Company H, 48th Regiment N.C. Troops

Barney was born in 1839 to Valentine and Cynthia Michael. He worked as a farmer prior to being conscripted into service on August 8, 1862. Barney was reported present until he died of pneumonia at Gordonsville, Virginia, on November 24, 1863.

1148. Michael, Henry

Private, Edgecombe Rifles Company G, 13th Regiment N.C. Troops (3rd N.C. Volunteers)

Henry was born on November 14, 1820, to Jacob and Susannah Koontz Michael. Henry worked as a farmer, and, on February 22, 1848, he married Louisa Myers. Henry and Louisa would have six children, Martha (1850), John Hiram (1852), Mary (1854), Margaret (1857),

Junius (1860), and Tullia (1861), before Henry volunteered for service in Davie County on June 3, 1861. After the war, Henry returned to the Beulah area where he and Louisa would have three more children: Clara (1867), Henry Clay (1872), and Bessie Ann (1883). Henry died on January 23, 1925, at the age of 104 years old (the second oldest man in Davidson County). He is buried at Beulah United Church of Christ.

1149. Michael, John H.

Private, Company C, 70th Regiment N.C. Troops (1st N.C. Junior Reserves)

John was born in 1846 to Jacob and Margaret Michael. John worked as a farmer prior to enlisting in the Junior Reserves on May 24, 1864. He was reported in a Wilmington, North Carolina, hospital in 1865. No further records.

1150. Michael, John Henry

Captain, Company H, 48th Regiment N.C. Troops

John was born on March 16, 1822, to John and Christina Leonard Michael. John was employed on his plantation and owned 58 slaves himself. He served as the sheriff of Davidson County for a period of time, and, on January 17, 1851, he married Margaret M. Lambeth. John and Margaret would have six children, Robert (1851), Mary A. (1853), John D. (1856–62), Merrill Shockley (1857), Charles (1860), and William Payne (1862), before John volunteered for service on March 13, 1862. John was elected captain the same day and served at the head of his company until his right arm was fractured by a Federal bullet at the battle of King's School House, Virginia, on June 25, 1862. He was reported absent, wounded, in September and October 1862. John remained in service until December 8, 1862, when he resigned due to his disability. His resignation was accepted on February 10, 1863. John returned home, and he and Margaret would have five more children: James (1865), Margaret Eldora (1867), Frederick (1869), Ida L. (1872), and Emma Victoria (1875). John lived in the Shiloh area of Davidson County, where he was a successful farmer as well as a life member in the church. John died on July 2, 1907. He is buried at Shiloh United Methodist Church.

1151. Michael, William

Private, Company H, 48th Regiment N.C. Troops

William was born in 1838. William worked as a farmer in the Beulah area prior to being conscripted into service at Petersburg, Virginia, on August 8, 1862. He was wounded and captured at Sharpsburg, Maryland, on September 17, 1862. William was confined in a hospital at Fort McHenry, Maryland, until October 17, 1862, when he was paroled and transferred to Aiken's Landing, Virginia, for exchange. William was declared exchanged on November 10, 1862, and was reported present until he deserted in March 1863. He was arrested and returned to duty on August 6, 1863. William deserted again on September 26, 1863, and returned to duty prior to March 1864. William was reported present until he was killed in action at Ream's Station, Virginia, on August 25, 1864.

1152. Michael, William Rankin

Private, Company A, 42nd Regiment N.C. Troops
Howard's Company N.C. Prison Guards, Salisbury Prison
Company A, 57th Regiment N.C. Troops

William was born on June 9, 1843, to Polly Michael. William worked as a farmer prior to volunteering for service in Rowan County on January 25, 1862. He was transferred to Captain Howard's Prison Guards on May 1, 1862. William served only a short time at Salisbury, North Carolina, as he enlisted in the 57th Regiment on July 4, 1862. William was reported present until he was wounded above the knee at Chancellorsville, Virginia, on May 4, 1863. He recovered from his wound and was reported present until he was captured near Silver Springs, Maryland, on July 12, 1864. William was confined at Elmira, New York, until March 14, 1865, when he was paroled and transferred to Boulware's Wharf, Virginia, for exchange. He was paroled at Greensboro, North Carolina, on May 5, 1865. After the war, William returned home where, on August 13, 1865, he married Pernina Jane Hedrick. William and Nina would have seven children: Calvin Luther (1866), Emma (1868), Mary (1871), Addie (1878), John (1881), Oscar (1884), and Zana P. (1888). William worked as a farmer and was a member of the A. A. Hill Camp, United Confederate Veterans. Upon his death on April 9, 1932, only five more Confederates were still living in the county. He is buried at Bethel Cemetery.

1153. Miller, Alexander R.

*Private, Company H, 48th Regiment
    N.C. Troops*

Alexander was born in 1827 to Nicholas and Eliza Livengood Miller. He worked as a farmer, and, on December 19, 1850, he married Elizabeth Leonard. Alexander and Elizabeth would not have any children. Alexander was conscripted into service in Lenoir County on May 20, 1863. He was reported present until hospitalized on August 23, 1863. Alexander would spend a large amount of time in a Richmond, Virginia, hospital. He died of "chronic diarrhea" on May 2, 1864.

1154. Miller, Allison A.

*Private, Company H, 48th Regiment
    N.C. Troops*

Allison was born in 1834 to Nicholas and Eliza Livengood Miller. Allison worked as a farmer, and, on December 15, 1855, he married Mary A. Walser. Allison and Mary would have one child, Richard (1859), before Allison was conscripted into service at Petersburg, Virginia, on August 8, 1862. He was captured at Sharpsburg, Maryland, on September 17, 1862. Allison was released on September 21, 1862, or on October 4, 1862. Apparently, he became very ill and was sent home on furlough. While at home, Allison died of unreported causes on January 20, 1863.

1155. Miller, Amos

*Private, Harnett Light Infantry
Company F, 15th Regiment N.C. Troops
    (5th N.C. Volunteers)*

Amos was born in 1836 to Jesse and Lucy Miller. Amos worked as a farmer prior to being conscripted into service in Wake County on July 16, 1862. He was wounded in a skirmish at Gum Swamp, Virginia, on May 22, 1863. Amos returned to duty prior to July 1, 1863, and was reported present until wounded and captured at Bristoe Station, Virginia, on October 14, 1863. He was confined at Point Lookout, Maryland, via Old Capital Prison, until March 13, 1864, when he died of disease. He is buried at Point Lookout National Cemetery.

1156. Miller, Benjamin F.

*Private, Company D, 48th Regiment
    N.C. Troops*

Benjamin was born in 1837 to Stephen and Mary Miller. Benjamin worked as a carpenter prior to being conscripted into service on August 8, 1862. He died of disease at Upperville, Virginia, on October 31, 1862.

1157. Miller, Benjamin Franklin

*Private, Harnett Light Infantry
Company F, 15th Regiment N.C. Troops
    (5th N.C. Volunteers)*

Benjamin was born in 1835 to Rebecca Miller. Benjamin worked as a day laborer prior to being conscripted into service in Wake County on July 15, 1862. He was captured at Crampton's Pass, Maryland, on September 14, 1862. Benjamin was confined at Fort Delaware, Delaware, until October 2, 1862, when he was paroled and transferred to Aiken's Landing, Virginia, for exchange. He was declared exchanged on November 10, 1862. Amos returned to service prior to January 1, 1863, and was reported present until October 16, 1863, when he was listed as absent without leave. No further records.

1158. Miller, Constantine V.

*Private, Company K, 15th Regiment
    N.C. Troops (5th N.C. Volunteers)
Company K, 48th Regiment N.C. Troops*

C. V. was born on March 29, 1834, to Jesse and Lucy Miller. C. V. worked as a farmer in the Friedburg area prior to being conscripted into service on August 8, 1862. He deserted one week later and was not listed as present until February 3, 1863, when he was transferred to the 48th N.C. Regiment. C. V. was reported present until wounded in action at Bristoe Station, Virginia, on October 14, 1863. He was absent, wounded, through May 11, 1864, when he was discharged due to disability. C. V. returned home to the Arcadia township where he died of complications from his wounds in June 1865. He is buried at Friedburg Moravian Church.

1159. Miller, David A.

*Private, Company A, 57th Regiment
    N.C. Troops*

David was born on September 10, 1844. David worked as a farmer prior to enlisting into service in Rowan County on July 21, 1862. He was reported present until "lost on the march" from Hagerstown, Maryland, and captured by the enemy on July 10, 1863. David was confined at Fort Delaware, Delaware, via Fort Mifflin, Pennsylvania, until June 19, 1865, when he was released after taking the oath of allegiance. After the war, David returned home where, on September 23, 1866, he married Mary Jane Burke. David and Mary would have eight children: Samuel (1867), Christian (1870), Mary (1873), David (1876), Delilah (1878), James (1883), Cora (1887), and Julius (1890). A Moravian, David worked as a modest farmer in the Arcadia township until his death on February 21, 1932. He is buried at Enterprise Moravian Church.

1160. Miller, Edwin

*Private, Harnett Light Infantry
Company F, 15th Regiment N.C. Troops
    (5th N.C. Volunteers)*

Edwin was born in 1839 to John and Rebecca Miller. Edwin worked as a farmer prior to being conscripted into service in Wake County on July 15, 1862. He died of disease at Liberty, Virginia, on October 23, 1862.

1161. Miller, Elias

*Private, Tuckahoe Braves
Company D, 27th Regiment N.C. Troops*

Elias was born in 1831 to Nicholas and Eliza Livengood Miller. Elias worked as a farmer in the Yadkin area, and, on April 7, 1852, he married Amelia Livengood. Elias and Amelia would have six children, John (1853), Martha (1856), Eliza (1857), Ellen Frances (1858), Henry (1859), and Cornelia (1861), before Elias was conscripted into service at Camp Holmes, North Carolina, on March 1, 1864. Elias was reported present until he was captured at Fort Stedman, Virginia, on March 25, 1865. He was confined at Point Lookout, Maryland, until June 29, 1865, when he was released after taking the oath of allegiance. After the war, Elias returned home to the Yadkin township where he and his family were living in 1870. No further records.

1162. Miller, Emanuel

*Private, Company G, 6th Regiment
N.C. State Troops*

Emanuel was born on February 18, 1835, to John and Sarah Miller. Emanuel worked as a farmer prior to volunteering for service in Mecklenburg County on May 29, 1861. He was reported present until he was captured at Rappahannock Station, Virginia, on November 7, 1863. Emanuel was confined at Point Lookout, Maryland, until March 16, 1865, when he was paroled and transferred to Boulware's Wharf, Virginia, for exchange. Emanuel survived the war and returned home to the Cotton Grove area where, in 1865, he married Sarah Reed. Emanuel died on January 11, 1904. He is buried in the Reed Family Cemetery.

1163. Miller, Felix

*Private, Company H, 48th Regiment
N.C. Troops*

Felix was born on October 24, 1824, to Nicholas and Eliza Livengood Miller. He worked as a farmer in the northern district of Davidson County, and, on June 30, 1844, he married Elizabeth Temple. Felix and Elizabeth would have nine children, Levi (1845), Christina (1850), Isaiah (1852), Amelia (1853), Sarah (1854), Ellen (1856), Delilah (1857), William (1858), and George W. (1861), before Felix was conscripted into service in Wake County on October 14, 1863. Felix was reported present until he died of "chronic diarrhea" at Gordonsville, Virginia, on May 29, 1864. Felix's letters are available in the Lexington Library.

1164. Miller, Franklin

*Private, Company H, 48th Regiment
N.C. Troops*

Franklin was born on September 21, 1843, to Daniel and Mary Miller. Franklin worked as a hireling for Mathias Everhart prior to volunteering for service on March 8, 1862. He was wounded in the left hip at Fredericksburg, Virginia, on December 13, 1862, and returned to service on May 23, 1863. Except for a brief stay in the hospital, Franklin was listed as present until September 22, 1864, when he was hospitalized with "debilities."

Franklin would spend the rest of the war in a hospital bed and was captured by Federal armies during the fall of Richmond, Virginia, on April 3, 1865. He was transferred to Newport News, Virginia, where he was confined until June 30, 1865, when he was released after taking the oath of allegiance. After the war, Franklin returned to the Pilgrim area where, on December 28, 1865, he married Mary Everhart. Franklin and Mary would have four children: Ellen (1866), Caroline (1869), Jasper Lee (1872), and Julian H. (1875). Franklin worked as a farmer in the Pilgrim area until his death on March 30, 1926. He is buried at Pilgrim United Church of Christ.

1165. Miller, George Washington

*Corporal, Holtsburg Guards
Company A, 54th Regiment N.C. Troops*

George was born on June 3, 1839, to George and Susanna Darr Miller. George worked as a farmer prior to enlisting on May 24, 1862. He was promoted to corporal in July 1862 and was reported present until wounded in the neck at Fredericksburg, Virginia, on December 13, 1862. George recovered from his wound and returned to duty on January 20, 1863. He was reported present until wounded and captured at Rappahannock Station, Virginia, on November 7, 1863. George was confined at Point Lookout, Maryland, until March 15, 1864, when he was paroled and transferred to City Point, Virginia, for exchange. He was declared exchanged on an unreported date and was listed as present until he died of unreported causes at Winchester, Virginia, on August 30, 1864.

1166. Miller, George Washington

*Private, Company F, 7th Regiment
N.C. State Troops*

George was born on March 24, 1843, to Isaac and Mary Miller. George worked as a farmer and a mule driver in the Conrad Hill township. In December 1862, he and Jane were married in Randolph County. George and Jane would have one child, John (1864), before George was conscripted into service in January 1864. He was reported present until paroled at Greensboro, North Carolina, on May 30, 1865. After the war, George returned home, where he and Jane would have seven more children: Alfred (1867), Bax-

ter (1869), Mary (1871), George (1873), Eliza (1875), Samuel (1877), and James (1880). George continued his farming and also began to breed and raise mules as a business. He served as a deacon for ten years at Liberty Baptist Church. George passed away on February 14, 1904. He is buried at Liberty Baptist Church.

1167. Miller, Henderson V.

*Private, Company C, 70th Regiment
N.C. Troops (1st N.C. Junior
Reserves)
Company A, 42nd Regiment N.C.
Troops*

Henderson was born in 1845. He worked as a farmer prior to enlisting in the Junior Reserves on May 24, 1864. Henderson was transferred to the 42nd Regiment sometime subsequent to October 31, 1864. Henderson was reported present until captured at Battery Anderson, Fort Fisher, North Carolina, on December 25, 1864. He was confined at Point Lookout, Maryland, until February 20, 1865, when he was paroled and transferred to Boulware's Wharf, Virginia, for exchange. Henderson was granted a furlough on February 26, 1865, and did not return to service. After the war, Henderson returned to the Cotton Grove township where, on August 14, 1873, he married Margaret Weaver. Henderson and Margaret would have three children: James (1875), Sophia (1877), and Benjamin (1879). Henderson died of disease on November 8, 1888. He is buried at Jersey Baptist Church. His stone was crafted by Henry J. Hege and bears the inscription: "Death is certain, the hour is unseen."

1168. Miller, Henry J.

*Private, Company H, 48th Regiment
N.C. Troops*

Henry was born in 1842 to Nicholas and Eliza Livengood Miller. Henry worked as a farmer prior to being conscripted into service on August 8, 1862. He was reported present through August 1864. Henry died of unreported causes on August 7, 1864.

1169. Miller, Jacob

*Private, Company H, 48th Regiment
N.C. Troops*

Jacob was born in 1839 to Joseph and Sarah Miller. Jacob worked as a farmer, and, on June 22, 1859, he married Selma Weir. Jacob was conscripted into service at Petersburg, Virginia, on August 8, 1862, and was wounded at Sharpsburg, Maryland, on September 17, 1862. He died of typhoid fever at Richmond, Virginia, on November 20, 1862.

1170. Miller, James P.

*Private, Company I, 27th Regiment
    N.C. Troops*

James was born in 1828. He worked as a miller in the southern district of Davidson County, and in 1847, he married Catharine. James and Catharine would have five children, Sarah J. (1849), William (1851), Jacob (1854), Robert (1857), and John Allison (1860), before James was conscripted into service at Camp Stokes, North Carolina, on October 23, 1864. He was reported present until he surrendered at Appomattox Court House, Virginia, on April 9, 1865. After the war, James returned home to the Silver Hill township where he continued working on his farm. James died on December 29, 1905. He is buried at Beck's United Church of Christ.

1171. Miller, John A.

*Private, Davidson Guards
Company A, 21st Regiment N.C. Troops*

John was born in 1837 to Nicholas and Elizabeth Miller. John worked as a farmer prior to volunteering for service on May 8, 1861. He was reported present until his death near Manassas Junction, Virginia, on August 1, 1861.

1172. Miller, John B.

*Captain, 65th Regiment N.C. Militia
    (1861 organization)*

John was born in 1818. He operated a grist mill in the northern district of Davidson County, and, in 1843, he married Eliza. John and Eliza would have nine children: Sarah (1845), Henrietta (1847), John W. (1850), Martha (1852), William (1854), Mary (1856), Alphonse (1859), Laura (1863), and Dora (1867). William was commissioned as captain in the Four Mile Branch District Company on November 26, 1861. After his service, John lived with his family in the Clemmonsville township. In 1880, the family moved to Salem, Forsyth County. No further records.

1173. Miller, John B.

*Private, Company B, 48th Regiment
    N.C. Troops*

John was born in 1832 to Jacob and Mary Miller. John worked as a farmer prior to volunteering on March 3, 1862. He was mustered in as a sergeant, however, he was reduced in rank in July 1863. John was reported present, then was dispatched to act as a nurse and ward master for a Raleigh, North Carolina, hospital from March 1864 through December 20, 1864. John was captured in Raleigh while in the hospital with typhoid fever, which he had contracted from treating ill soldiers. John died of typhoid fever at Raleigh on April 18, 1865.

1174. Miller, John F.

*Private, Company C, 70th Regiment
    N.C. Troops (1st N.C. Junior
    Reserves)*

John was born in 1847 to Thomas and Louvina Miller. John worked as an apprentice carpenter prior to enlisting in the Junior Reserves on May 24, 1864. No further records.

1175. Miller, John F.

*Private, Company I, 42nd Regiment
    N.C. Troops*

John was born in 1839 to the Reverend Joseph and Sarah Miller. John worked as a farmer prior to volunteering for service on March 11, 1862. He was reported present until wounded in the right arm at Petersburg, Virginia, on

July 9, 1864. John's right arm was amputated, and he was retired from service on February 3, 1865. John died of complications in Richmond, Virginia, on March 1, 1865.

1176. Miller, John H.

*Captain, Davidson Guards
Company A, 21st Regiment N.C. Troops
    (11th N.C. Volunteers)*

John was born in 1838 to Major John and Anne Owens Miller. He worked on

John H. Miller commanded three regiments at the surrender at Appomatox Court House (Clark's Regiments).

This two-story brick house was built four years after John H. Miller's return (Touart, ***Building the Backcountry***).

his father's modest plantation prior to receiving a four-year education at Trinity College. According to family history, John wished to become an attorney, but after a failing year on the plantation, funds were not available to continue his education. John worked as a farmer until he volunteered for service on May 8, 1861. He was promoted to first sergeant on September 1, 1861, and was elected second lieutenant on April 27, 1862. With the promotion of Captain Beall to major, John was elected by the company as first lieutenant and commanding officer on May 25, 1862. John's official commission as captain was not received until March 1, 1865. From May 1862 to April 1865, John led the company in every engagement. During the final days of the war, John was in command of the 21st Regiment. At Appomattox Court House, Virginia, on April 9, 1865, he was listed as the commanding officer for the 21st North Carolina, 54th North Carolina, and the 57th North Carolina. After the war, John returned to his family's home outside of Lexington. John continued to work on the farm and added 15 acres of orchard land as well as converting some of the wooded land into a pasture for horses. John never married and was active in the A. A. Hill Camp, United Confederate Veterans, until his death on March 10, 1890. He is buried in the Miller Family Cemetery, which was on his property.

1177. Miller, John Quincy

Private, Lexington Wildcats
Company I, 14th Regiment N.C. Troops
(4th N.C. Volunteers)

John was born in 1834 to Benjamin and Margaret Miller. John worked in his father's grist mill, and in 1856, he married Sarah. John and Sarah would have one child together, Victoria (1857), before John was conscripted into service in Wake County on July 16, 1862. He was killed in action at Spotsylvania Court House, Virginia, on May 12, 1864.

1178. Miller, Joseph H.

Second Lieutenant, 66th Regiment
N.C. Militia (1861 organization)

Joseph was born on June 15, 1831, to Joseph and Sarah Miller. Joseph worked as a farmer, and, in 1855, he married Rosina Delapp. Joseph and Rosina would have nine children: Augusta (1856), Franklin (1858), Joseph (1860), Sarah (1862), Solomon (1866), Mary (1868), Lenora (1871), Martha (1873), and Robert (1879). Joseph was commissioned as second lieutenant in the Midway District Company on November 26, 1861. After his service, Joseph began a small manufacturing operation building threshers from mail-order kits and selling them, as well as repairing other agricultural implements. Joseph worked at his business and became fairly successful. Joseph lived in the Midway-Arcadia area until his death on December 22, 1886. He is buried at Midway United Methodist Church.

1179. Miller, Josiah C.

Private, Harnett Light Infantry
Company F, 15th Regiment N.C. Troops
(5th N.C. Volunteers)

Josiah was born in 1839. Josiah worked as a farmer in the Arcadia area prior to being conscripted into service in Wake County on July 15, 1862. He was reported present until wounded in the arm at Bristoe Station, Virginia, on October 14, 1863. Josiah was reported absent, wounded, until he deserted on December 6, 1863. Josiah returned home and avoided the Home Guard until the end of the war. In 1867, he married Sarah. Josiah and Sarah would have one child, Charles (1869), prior to moving to Forsyth County in 1873. While in Forsyth County, Sarah died, and Josiah married Mary Hanes in 1890. Josiah and Mary lived in Forsyth County until his death on April 20, 1922. He is buried at Friedburg Moravian Church.

1180. Miller, Levi Franklin

Private, Company H, 48th Regiment
N.C. Troops

Levi was born on November 10, 1845, to Felix and Elizabeth Temple Miller. Levi worked as a farmer prior to enlisting into service at Orange Court House, Virginia, on January 18, 1864. Levi was reported present until he was wounded in both arms at Petersburg, Virginia, in June or July 1864. His left arm was amputated, and he was furloughed from a Richmond, Virginia, hospital on August 22, 1864. Levi survived his wounds and returned to the Yadkin township, where, on August 14, 1867, he married Phoebe Wilson. Levi and Phoebe would have eight children: Nannie (1868), Jennie (1870), Thomas (1872), Mary (1876), Nora (1878), Lillie Ethel (1883), Henry (1887), and David King (1889). Levi worked as a farmer until his death on January 6, 1906. He is buried at Friendship Methodist Church.

1181. Miller, Martin J.

Private, Davidson Guards
Company A, 21st Regiment N.C. Troops
(11th N.C. Volunteers)

Martin was born on June 5, 1845. Martin enlisted in Yadkin County on October 1, 1863, and was reported present until he was captured at Cedar Creek, Virginia, on October 19, 1864. He was confined at Point Lookout, Maryland, until March 30, 1865, when he was paroled and transferred to Boulware's Wharf, Virginia, for exchange. After the war, Martin moved to Forsyth County, where he married Nancy Melvina Rothrock. Martin died on November 5, 1921. He is buried at Friedburg Moravian Church.

1182. Miller, Michael A.

Second Lieutenant, 66th Regiment
N.C. Militia (1861 organization)

Michael was born in 1830 to Joseph and Sarah Miller. Michael worked as a blacksmith in the Midway township. In 1854, he married Eliza, and they would have nine children: John (1856), George (1858), Jacob (1861), Franklin (1865), Mary (1869), Andrew (1871), Charlie (1873), Julius (1877), and Felix (1879). Michael was commissioned as second lieutenant in the Midway District Company on November 26, 1861. Eliza died in 1880, and four years later, Michael married Rosa Miller. Michael and Rosa would have two children: Augusta (1885) and Amanda (1888). Michael and his three youngest children were listed as living in the Midway township in 1900. No further records.

1183. Miller, Nicholas Franklin

Private, Company H, 48th Regiment
N.C. Troops

Nicholas was born in 1840 to Nicholas and Eliza Livengood Miller. Nicholas worked as a farmer prior to being conscripted into service at Petersburg, Virginia, on August 8, 1862. Nicholas was reported present until he was killed in action at Bristoe Station, Virginia, on October 14, 1863.

1184. Miller, Obediah C.

Third Lieutenant, Thomasville Rifles
Company B, 14th Regiment N.C. Troops
(4th N.C. Volunteers)

Obediah was born in 1836 to Benjamin and Margaret Miller. Obediah worked as a miller prior to volunteering for service on May 14, 1861. He was promoted to third lieutenant on October 20, 1862, and served in that capacity until he was last reported present, in October 1864. After the war, Obediah returned home to the Silver Hill township, where on December 9, 1868, he married Frances Smith. Obediah and Frances would have one child: Frank (1872). Obediah constructed his own flour mill in the Conrad Hill area, which he operated from 1870 to 1880. Obediah was last reported as living in the Silver Hill township in 1900. No further records.

1185. Miller, Thomas Jefferson

Private, Davidson Guards
Company A, 21st Regiment N.C. Troops
(11th N.C. Volunteers)

Thomas was born on February 18, 1832, to John and Anne Miller. Thomas worked as a farmer and as an amateur bridle maker. On November 9, 1852, Thomas married Nancy H. Smith. Thomas and Nancy would have three children, Robert (1854), Thomas (1860), and John (1862), before Thomas was conscripted into service on November 3, 1864. He was reported present through February 1865. After the war, Thomas returned to his Cotton Grove home where he and Nancy would have another child: Hubert (1870). Thomas worked as a farmer until his death on November 16, 1873. He is buried at Jersey Baptist Church.

1186. Miller, William Franklin

Corporal, Company I, 42nd Regiment
N.C. Troops

William was born in 1844 to George and Susanna Darr Miller. William worked as a farmer prior to being conscripted into service at Petersburg, Virginia, on October 15, 1862. He was mustered in as a private and was promoted to

William F. and Barbara Crouse Miller (Mabel Miller Mabry, *The Heritage of Davidson County*).

corporal in March 1864. William was present at every engagement of which the 42nd Regiment was a part. Thomas was paroled at Greensboro, North Carolina, on May 9, 1865. After the war, Thomas returned to the Cotton Grove township where, on April 9, 1868, he married Barbara E. Crouse. William and Barbara would have nine children: George W. (1869), Susan (1872), William (1875), James Wiley (1878), Charles H. (1883), Amanda (1886), Luther (1888), Annie (1890), and Hugh Lindsay (1893). William worked as a farmer until his death in 1925. He is buried at Jersey Baptist Church.

1187. Miller, William Madison

Private, Company A, 42nd Regiment
N.C. Troops

William was born in 1842. He worked as a farmer prior to volunteering for service in Rowan County on March 20, 1862. William died of "purpura" in a Richmond, Virginia, hospital on December 23, 1862.

1188. Miller, Willis L.

Captain, Thomasville Rifles
Company B, 14th Regiment N.C. Troops
(4th N.C. Volunteers)

Willis was born in 1831 in Wake County. Willis was educated at the Raleigh Presbyterian Seminary, and in 1851, he married Sarah Ann Shackleford of Company Shops, North Carolina.

Willis was sent to the fledgling town of Thomasville by the church to pastor a newly established Presbyterian congregation. Willis and Sarah had two children, Mary (1852) and Anne (1854), before they arrived in Thomasville in December 1854. By February 1855, Willis was ministering to the citizens of the small railroad town. Willis and Sarah would have three more children, Henry (1856), Charles (1857), and William L. (1860), before Willis volunteered for service on April 23, 1861. He was mustered in as captain and served as commander of the Thomasville Rifles until he was not reelected by the men of his company. Willis resigned and returned home. According to North Carolina Presbytery records, he was sent to another church in Stokes County. No further records.

1189. Miller, Wisdom

Private, Company H, 48th Regiment
N.C. Troops
Company C, 76th Regiment N.C. Troops
(6th N.C. Senior Reserves)

Wisdom was born in 1819 to Isaac and Mary Miller. He worked as a farmer, and on August 20, 1854, he married Elizabeth Hughes. Wisdom and Elizabeth would have three children, Dovey (1857), William (1859), and Alfred (1860), before Wisdom volunteered for service on March 6, 1862. Wisdom was excused from service four days later after providing Leason Clodfelter as a substitute. Another son, John, was born in 1863. Wisdom enlisted in the Senior Reserves in January 1865 and served until the end of the war. After his service, Wisdom returned home to the Conrad Hill township where he and Elizabeth would have five more children: Eliza (1866), Mary Anne (1869), Benjamin (1871), Julia (1874), and Minta (1876). Wisdom served as a Sunday school teacher at Liberty Baptist Church until his death in February 1895. He is buried at Liberty Baptist Church.

1190. Milligan, Elijah

Second Lieutenant, 66th Regiment
N.C. Militia (1861 organization)

Eli was living alone and working as a farmer in the Lexington area in 1860. He was commissioned as a second lieutenant in the Ebenezer District Company on November 26, 1861. No further records.

1191. Millner, John Preston

Private, Company K, 38th Virginia Infantry Regiment

John was born in Davidson County in 1841. He moved to Rockingham County, North Carolina, where, according to the *Virginia Regimental History* series, he volunteered for service on an unspecified date. No further records.

1192. Mills, William

Private, Company E, 5th Regiment N.C. State Troops

William was born in 1826 to Jane Mills. In 1860, he was employed as a hireling and living with his mother. He volunteered for service in Rowan County on July 1, 1861. William was reported present until he died of pneumonia at Richmond, Virginia, on April 8, 1862. He is buried in the Hollywood Cemetery in Richmond.

1193. Mills, Woodward

Private, Company F, 7th Regiment N.C. State Troops

Wood was born in 1820 to Jane Mills. He worked as a farmer prior to volunteering for service in Rowan County on June 3, 1861. Wood was reported present until wounded at Ox Hill, Virginia, on September 1, 1862. Wood died of his wounds at Middleburg, Virginia, on September 30, 1862.

1194. Mitchell, Henry C.

Private, Company H, 15th Regiment N.C. Troops
Corporal, Company F, 53rd Regiment N.C. Troops

Henry was born in 1845. He worked as a farmer in the Clarksbury area prior to being conscripted into service in Wake County on July 16, 1862. Henry was transferred to the 53rd N.C. Regiment on January 12, 1863, and was promoted to corporal on August 1, 1863. He was reported present until killed in action near Charlestown, [West] Virginia, on August 21, 1864.

1195. Mize, Burgess Henry

Private, Lexington Wildcats
Company I, 14th Regiment N.C. Troops (4th N.C. Volunteers)

Burgess was born in 1838 to John and Elizabeth Mize. He worked as a farmer prior to volunteering for service on May 14, 1861. Burgess was wounded at Malvern Hill, Virginia, on July 1, 1862, and was absent, wounded, until he rejoined the company in May 1863. He was reported present until supposedly captured on May 19, 1864. After the war, Burgess returned home to the Reedy Creek area, where, in 1888, he married Jane. Burgess and Jane would have four children, Mattie (1891), Betty (1893), Sidney (1894), and Albert (1895), before moving out of the county in 1905. No further records.

1196. Mize, John

Private, Lexington Wildcats
Company I, 14th Regiment N.C. Troops (4th N.C. Volunteers)

John was born in 1843 to John and Elizabeth Mize. He worked as a farmer prior to volunteering for service on May 14, 1861. John was reported present until wounded in the hand and fingers on June 1, 1864. He was treated in a Richmond, Virginia, hospital and returned to duty on June 14, 1864. John was reported present until he was captured at Petersburg, Virginia, on April 3, 1865. He was confined at Hart's Island, New York, until June 17, 1865, when he was released after taking the oath of allegiance. After the war, John returned home to the Reedy Creek area, where, in 1869, he married Caroline. John and Caroline moved to the Boone township in 1870, and would have three children: Henry Clay (1871), Hidora (1874), and John (1878). John died in the 1880s and was buried in an unmarked grave at Shiloh United Methodist Church.

1197. Mock, Alexander B.

Private, Company H, 48th Regiment N.C. Troops

Alexander was born in 1841 to Adam and Nancy Mock. Alexander worked as a miller, and, on February 6, 1860, he married Louisa J. Rominger. He continued his work as a miller until he was conscripted into service at Petersburg, Virginia, on August 8, 1862. Alexander deserted from service on September 8, 1862, returned home, and managed to ellude capture for the rest of the war. After the war, Alex and Louisa would

have two children: Levi (1866) and Jacob (1869). Alex continued to operate his mill until he and his family moved out of the county in 1873. No further records.

1198. Mock, Christian S.

Private, Company E, 21st Regiment N.C. Troops (11th N.C. Volunteers)
Company B, 1st Battalion, N.C. Sharpshooters

Christian was born on April 12, 1841, to Peter and Phoebe Mock. He was baptized as a member of the Moravian church. Christian volunteered for service in Forsyth County on May 24, 1861, and was reported present until transferred to the 1st Battalion, N.C. Sharpshooters. Christian served as a sharpshooter for Hoke's-Kirkland's Brigade until he was paroled at Appomattox Court House, Virginia, on April 9, 1865. Christian returned home to the Arcadia township where he lived until September 29, 1866, when he died of pneumonia. He is buried at Freidburg Moravian Church.

1199. Mock, George Washington

Private, Harnett Light Infantry
Company F, 15th Regiment N.C. Troops (5th N.C. Volunteers)

George was born in 1844 to Adam and Nancy Mock. George worked as a farmer in the Reedy Creek area prior to being conscripted into service in Wake County on July 15, 1862. He was reported present until killed in action at Reams' Station, Virginia, on August 25, 1864.

1200. Mock, Henry Clay

Private, Company A, 42nd Regiment N.C. Troops

Henry was born in 1836 to Adam and Nancy Mock. He worked as a miller's apprentice prior to enlisting in Rowan County on July 29, 1862. Henry was reported present until he was hospitalized with "phthisis pulmonalis" on August 1, 1864. Two weeks later, Henry died at Goldsboro, North Carolina, of this disease. His body was returned and buried at Midway United Methodist Church.

1201. Mock, James A.

Private, Company C, 70th Regiment N.C. Troops (1st N.C. Junior Reserves)

James was born in 1847 to Adam and Nancy Mock. He worked as a farmer prior to enlisting in the Junior Reserves on May 24, 1864. No further records.

1202. Mock, James Augustus

Private, Harnett Light Infantry Company F, 15th Regiment N.C. Troops (5th N.C. Volunteers)

"Gus" was born in 1846 to Peter and Phoebe Mock. He had begun training as a blacksmith prior to enlisting in Wake County as a substitute for his father. Gus was reported present until wounded in the right hand at Spotsylvania Court House, Virginia, on May 7, 1864. Gus recovered from his wound, returned to service, and was reported present through October 31, 1864. Gus returned home to the Reedy Creek area where, on August 17, 1871, he married Amanda Frank. Gus and Amanda would have four children: John (1874), Mary (1876), Lelia (1877), and Bertie (1880). Gus continued his trade as a blacksmith and was in demand for his ability to "fix anything." Gus died on October 2, 1918. He is buried at Good Hope United Methodist Church.

1203. Mock, John Ayers

Private, Carolina Rangers Company B, 10th Virginia Cavalry Regiment

John was born on March 5, 1827. He operated a small general store in the North Thomasville township prior to volunteering for service in Davie County on October 29, 1861. John was reported present until sent on a horse procurement detail for the months of August and September 1863. He returned to service and rode along with the regiment until he was last recorded on December 31, 1864, as receiving a clothing ration. John survived the war and moved into the town of Thomasville. In 1867, John opened a general store on what is now Salem Street. John's store was fairly successful, but it was limited due to competition from the Thomas Store and the company shops of Lambeth, Lines, and Leach. John married Minnie Wagner on May 13, 1873, and they would have two children: John Herman (1875) and Essie Leigh (1878). In 1879, John bought an old house across

The Mock Hotel, Thomasville's finest accomodations, in 1900 (Pathfinders Past and Present).

from the railroad depot and constructed the Mock Hotel, which at the time was the largest building in Thomasville, three stories tall with an attic, cellar, and a "modern" kitchen and dining room. The Mock Hotel was prosperous right from the start. John made a habit of helping passengers off the train and welcoming his guests on the platform. John was killed in an accident while helping a lady with her baggage. The train moved slightly forward, John was thrown, and his legs were crushed. John died three days later, on September 12, 1882. His business carried on after his passing. He is buried in the Thomasville City Cemetery.

1204. Mock, Leander N.

Private, Harnett Light Infantry Company F, 15th Regiment N.C. Troops (5th N.C. Volunteers)

Leander was born in September 1842 to Adam and Nancy Mock. Leander worked as a farmer in the Arcadia area prior to being conscripted into service in Wake County on July 15, 1862. He was reported present until hospitalized at Richmond, Virginia, with "a serious wound of the right arm and/or left hand" on May 7, 1864. Leander was reported absent, wounded, until he was retired from service on January 6, 1865. He returned to the Arcadia township where he continued his farming as best he could. On November 14, 1872, Leander married Jane Knouse. He and Jane would have five children: John (1874), William

(1878), Carrie (1885), Robert Hoke (1887), and Emory (1894). Leander worked as a farmer until his death in the 1910s. He is buried at Mount Olivet United Methodist Church.

1205. Mock, Peter W.

Private, Harnett Light Infantry Company F, 15th Regiment N.C. Troops (5th N.C. Volunteers)

Peter was born on November 19, 1834, to Peter and Phoebe Mock. Peter worked as a farmer in the Arcadia area and, on January 9, 1862, he married Mariah M. Knouse. Peter was conscripted into service in Wake County on July 15, 1862. He was reported present until wounded in the right thigh at Bristoe Station, Virginia, on October 14, 1863. Peter recovered from his wound and returned to service on January 16, 1864. He was reported present through October 1864. Peter survived the war and returned home to his wife. They would have only one child, George (1867), who died of pneumonia at the age of 25 on January 31, 1892. Peter grieved for the loss of his son until his death on January 8, 1899. They are both buried at Mount Olivet United Methodist Church.

1206. Moore, Elijah

Private, North State Boys Company K, 45th Regiment N.C. Troops

Eli was born on April 12, 1832, to Nathan and Matilda Hammer Moore. Eli worked as a farmer, and, at the age of 21

Abbott's Creek home of Eli Moore (Touart, *Building the Backcountry*).

he married Keziah Hayworth. Eli and Keziah would have three children, John (1855), Lydia (1858), and Alfred (1861), before Eli was conscripted into service on October 24, 1864. He was reported present until he deserted to the enemy on January 29, 1865. Eli was confined at Washington, D.C., until February 24, 1865, when he was released after taking the oath of allegiance. Eli was provided coach transportation to Winchester, Virginia, on March 13, 1865. He made his way home from the upper Shenandoah Valley on his own. Eli continued his work as a farmer in the Abbott's Creek area, and he and Keziah would have four more children: Matilda (1866), Mary B. (1869), Alphonse (1870), and Lou Ella (1873). Eli worked as a small farmer until his death on September 15, 1887. He is buried at Abbott's Creek Primitive Baptist Church.

1207. Moore, George Washington

Private, Thomasville Rifles
Company B, 14th Regiment N.C. Troops
(4th N.C. Volunteers)

George was born in 1842 to Isaac and Mary Moore. He worked as a house carpenter in the North Thomasville area prior to volunteering for service on April 23, 1861. George was reported present until he was killed in action at Spotsylvania Court House, Virginia, on May 12, 1864.

1208. Moore, Walter Jones

Corporal, Lexington Wildcats
Company I, 14th Regiment N.C. Troops
(4th N.C. Volunteers)

Walter was born in 1844 to Isaac and Mary Moore. Walter lived in the Thomasville area and was employed as an artist prior to volunteering for service on May 21, 1861. He was mustered in as a private and was promoted to corporal on October 6, 1862. Walter was reported present until he was captured on the retreat from Gettysburg, Pennsylvania, above Hagerstown, Maryland, on July 5, 1863. He was sent to Fort Delaware, Delaware, and was transferred to Point Lookout, Maryland, shortly thereafter. Walter was confined at Point Lookout until he died of unreported causes on June 13, 1864. He is buried in the Point Lookout National Cemetery.

1209. Morgan, Jabez F.

Private, Thomasville Rifles
Company B, 14th Regiment N.C. Troops
(4th N.C. Volunteers)

Jabez was born in 1839. He lived in the town of Thomasville and worked as a laborer before he went to work as a carpenter for Samuel Dorsett. Jabez volunteered for service on April 27, 1861, and was known as a kind of "good-for-nothing" in the company. Despite this reputation, Colonel Bennett (in Clark's *His-*

tories of the Several Regiments) remarked: "The man was known as a rough man; however, he bravely stepped forward to volunteer to deliver an urgent dispatch to the 4th Regiment among a flurry of bullets at the battle of South Mountain, Maryland." Jabez survived his dangerous mission only to be mortally wounded in hand-to-hand combat with several members of the 61st New York Infantry at Sharpsburg, Maryland, on September 17, 1862. Jabez died on November 15, 1862.

1210. Morgan, James H.

First Sergeant, Company D, 46th Regiment N.C. Troops

James was born in Richmond County on August 23, 1840. He moved to the southern district of Davidson County in the late 1850s. James worked as a farmer prior to volunteering for service in Montgomery County on March 4, 1862. He was promoted to sergeant on September 1, 1862, and then to first sergeant on January 1, 1863. James served as first sergeant until he was wounded at Reams' Station, Virginia, on August 25, 1864. He was listed as absent, wounded, through October 1864. James received his parole at Greensboro, North Carolina, on May 1, 1865. James returned home to the Allegheny township, where, in 1870, he married Mary. James and Mary would have five children: Thomas (1871), Alfred (1875), Charles (1877), John D. (1878), and Howard (1883). James worked as a farmer until his death on February 3, 1915. He is buried at Lineberry United Methodist Church.

1211. Morris, Aaron Shepherd

Private, Company C, 70th Regiment N.C. Troops (1st N.C. Junior Reserves)

"Shep" was born on August 24, 1846, to John and Eunice Morris. Shep worked as a farmer prior to enlisting in the Junior Reserves on May 24, 1864. After the war, Shep returned home to the North Thomasville township, where, in 1873, he married Sarah A. Hilton. Shep and Sarah would have two children: John (1875) and Zeb Vance (1877). Sarah died in 1897, and Shep married Emma D. Hilton only a year later. Shep and Emma would have only one surviving child: Virgil (1899). Shep passed away on May 18, 1925. He is buried at Pleasant Grove United Methodist Church.

1212. Morris, James Murphy

*Private, Company C, 70th Regiment
  N.C. Troops (1st N.C. Junior
  Reserves)*

James was born in 1847 to Christopher and Sarah Murphy Morris. James worked as a farmer in the Jackson Hill area prior to enlisting in the Junior Reserves on May 24, 1864. After the war, James returned home, where, in 1871, he married Nancy. James and Nancy would have four children, Dora (1873), Lafayette (1874), Caroline (1875), and Ellen (1878), before the family moved out of the county in the mid–1880s. No further records.

1213. Morris, James T.

*Private, Company F, 7th Regiment
  N.C. State Troops*

James was born in 1843 to William and Anne Morris. He worked as a farmer in the Jackson Hill area prior to volunteering for service on February 22, 1862. James was reported present until wounded in the head and captured at Hanover Court House, Virginia, in May 1864. James was confined in a U.S. Army hospital in Washington, D.C., where he died on May 30, 1864.

1214. Morris, Jesse R.

*Private, Company A, 10th Battalion,
  N.C. Heavy Artillery*

Jesse was born in 1837 to John and Eunice Morris. He worked as a farmer in the Thomasville area prior to volunteering for service on March 15, 1862. Jesse was assigned to the artillery corps and was reported present until he was paroled at Greensboro, North Carolina, on May 6, 1865. Family history recalls Jesse serving as a driver on one of the 10th Battalion's horse-drawn limbers. After the war, Jesse returned to farming in the North Thomasville township, where he remained single until 1880, when he married Jane. Jesse and Jane would have two surviving children: Walter (1884) and May (1892). Jesse lived with his wife and children until his death in the 1910s. He is buried at Zion United Church of Christ.

1215. Morris, Jesse W.

*Private, Chatam Light Infantry
  Company G, 48th Regiment N.C. Troops
  Company B, 48th Regiment N.C. Troops*

Jesse was born on May 17, 1844, to Jesse and Mary Morris. Jesse worked as a farmer prior to being conscripted into service on August 14, 1862. He was reported present until hospitalized at Wilmington, North Carolina, on May 4, 1863, with acute dysentery. Jesse recovered from his illness and returned to service on June 10, 1863. He was reported present until he was transferred to Company B on July 1, 1863. Jesse was reported present with his new company until wounded in action at Hatcher's Run, Virginia, on April 2, 1865. Jesse survived the war and returned home to the Emmons township where he worked with his brother as sharecroppers. Jesse was married in 1892 to Elizabeth Morris. Jesse died on October 5, 1920. He is buried at Tom's Creek Primitive Baptist Church.

1216. Morris, John

*Private, Chatam Light Infantry
  Company G, 48th Regiment N.C.
  Troops*

John was born in 1844 and was a student at Kennedy's School House in Thomasville prior to being conscripted into service on August 14, 1862. John was killed in action at Sharpsburg, Maryland, on September 17, 1862.

1217. Morris, John Randall

*Private, Company B, 48th Regiment
  N.C. Troops*

John was born on January 18, 1842, to Jesse and Nancy Morris. John worked as a farmer prior to being conscripted into service on August 8, 1862. He was reported present until wounded in the right shoulder at Wilderness, Virginia, on May 5, 1864. John was sent to a hospital where he was reported as absent, wounded, through December 22, 1864, when he was retired to the Invalid Corps. John returned home and worked on a new farm. His farm struggled, and when his brother returned from the war, they began sharecropping. John worked as a farmer in Emmons and, in 1885, he married Nancy. John and Nancy would have one child: Jubal Early (1887). John died on October 23, 1913. He is buried at Tom's Creek Primitive Baptist Church. The inscription on his stone reads: "A tender father and a faithful friend."

1218. Morris, John W.

*Private, Company A, 10th Battalion,
  N.C. Heavy Artillery*

John was born on April 10, 1840, to John and Eunice Morris. John worked as a farmer prior to being conscripted into service on October 26, 1862. He was reported present until paroled at Greensboro, North Carolina, on May 6, 1865. After the war, John returned to the North Thomasville township, where, in 1867, he married Angelica Hilton. John and Angelica would have three children: Oscar (1869), Nettie (1875), and Wilson (1878). John lived as a farmer north of Thomasville until his death on July 18, 1893. He is buried at Pine Woods Methodist Church.

1219. Morris, John W.

*Private, Thomasville Rifles
  Company B, 14th Regiment N.C. Troops
  (4th N.C. Volunteers)*

John was born in 1839. He worked as a farmer prior to being conscripted into service in Wake County on July 16, 1862. John deserted at Hanover Junction, Virginia, on August 26, 1862. No further records.

1220. Morris, Murphy

*Private, Lexington Wildcats
  Company I, 14th Regiment N.C. Troops
  (4th N.C. Volunteers)*

Murphy was born in 1838 to John and Mary Morris. Murphy worked as a farmer prior to volunteering for service on May 14, 1861. He was reported present until he died of unreported causes at Richmond, Virginia, on August 30, 1862.

1221. Morris, Nathan James

*Private, Trojan Regulators
  Company F, 44th Regiment N.C. Troops
  Private, Stanley Marksmen
  Company H, 14th Regiment N.C. Troops
  (4th N.C. Volunteers)*

Nathan was born on March 20, 1834, to Jesse and Nancy Morris. He worked as a farmer prior to volunteering for service in Montgomery County on March 1, 1862. Nathan was reported present until August 20, 1863, when he was transferred to the 14th N.C. Regiment. He served in the 14th until paroled at Farmville, Virginia, on April 11, 1865. After the war,

Nathan returned to the Emmons township, where, in 1880 he married Anne C. Nathan died on September 30, 1924. He is buried in the Denton Town Cemetery.

1222. Morris, Nelson

Private, Company H, 7th Confederate Cavalry Regiment
Company F, 16th Battalion, N.C. Cavalry

Nelson was born on February 6, 1833. He worked as a farmer in the Jackson Hill area prior to enlisting in the 7th Confederate Cavalry subsequent to June 1864. Nelson was transferred to the 16th Battalion on July 11, 1864. He was reported absent, sick, at Goldsboro, North Carolina, through August 1864. Nelson was paroled at Goldsboro in 1865. After the war, Nelson returned home, where, in 1870, he married W. Adeline. Nelson and Adeline would have two children: William (1871) and Hattie (1877). Nelson died on May 6, 1923. He is buried at Siloam United Methodist Church.

1223. Morris, Thomas

Private, Company I, 42nd Regiment N.C. Troops

Thomas was born in 1843 to Christopher and Sarah Morris. He worked as an apprentice wagonmaker prior to volunteering for service on March 6, 1862. Thomas was listed as present until reported absent, wounded, in September 1864. Thomas survived the war and returned home, where, on August 25, 1865, he married Phoebe Cameron. Thomas and Phoebe would have one child, Emily (1868), before Thomas moved his business and family out of the county in the 1870s. No further records.

1224. Morris, William

Private, Company B, 48th Regiment N.C. Troops

William was born on February 18, 1840, to Jesse and Nancy Morris. He worked as a farmer prior to being conscripted into service on August 8, 1862. William was reported present through December 1864. William survived the war and returned home to the Emmons/Cotton Grove area, where, in 1878, he married Anna Newsom. William and Anna would have four children: Victoria (1879), John (1881), Grover Cleveland (1883), and Dowdy C. (1886). William died on June 20, 1906. He is buried at Macedonia United Methodist Church.

1225. Morrison, Kenneth M.

Second Lieutenant, 65th Regiment, N.C. Militia (1861 organization)

Kenneth was born in 1825. He worked as a schoolteacher in the Thomasville area and was commissioned as second lieutenant in the Thomasville District Company on November 26, 1861. After his service, Kenneth married Martha. Ken and Martha would have three children: Effie (1864), Luther (1866), and William (1869). In 1870 and 1880, Ken was listed as working as a carpenter, however, in 1900, he returned to teaching. Ken was living with John Fritts at the turn of the century as a widower with no surviving children. No further records.

1226. Morton, Hezekiah

Private, Company G, 66th Regiment N.C. Troops

Hezekiah was born on August 8, 1846. He was a student prior to being conscripted into service on September 8, 1862. Hezekiah was assigned to the 66th N.C. Regiment. After the war, Hezekiah returned home to the Boone township. He married Margaret A. Jordan in 1875 and was ordained as a Baptist minister the same year. Hezekiah and Margaret would have four children: Cora (1877), DeWitt (1879), Anna (1881), and Hattie (1886). Hezekiah pastored two churches, Churchland Baptist and First Baptist of Thomasville. He was also appointed by the association as an interim minister for Liberty in 1914. Hezekiah died on June 25, 1922. He is buried in the Thomasville City Cemetery.

1227. Mosely, John M.

Private, Holtsburg Guards
Company A, 54th Regiment N.C. Troops

John was born in 1835 in Yadkin County, North Carolina. John worked as a tobacconist in the city of Lexington prior to volunteering for service on March 14, 1862. He was reported present until he provided Reuben Johnson as a substitute. John was excused from service and operated a tobacco warehouse during the war, shipping Davidson County tobacco to Wilmington, North Carolina, and Savannah, Georgia, for export to Great Britain. On November 28, 1866, he married Mary Emeline Holder. John and Mary would have eight children: John (1867), Alice (1868), Dora (1869), Ida (1871), Eulale (1873), Margaret (1875), Charlie (1876), and Tilden (1877). John was in competition with the tobacco warehouses of both Pinnix and Moffitt prior to selling his interest in 1883 to Marshall Pinnix and moving to Forsyth County. No further records.

1228. Moss, Adolphus A.

First Lieutenant, Davidson Guards
Company A, 21st Regiment N.C. Troops (11th N.C. Volunteers)
Lieutenant Colonel, Moss's Senior Reserves
Colonel, 76th Regiment N.C. Troops (6th N.C. Senior Reserves)

Adolphus was born in Rowan County in 1820. He moved to Davidson County and settled in the Clemmonsville area before moving outside of Lexington. Adolphus operated a general store, provided capital, and speculated on both land and crops. On October 30, 1841, Adolphus married Louisa Eccles. Adolphus and Louisa would have five children: Henry (1847), Augusta (1850), Mary (1854), Lelia (1857), and Walter (1860). Adolphus volunteered for service on May 8, 1861, and was elected to the post of first lieutenant on July 8, 1861. He was reported present until he declined to run for reelection when the regiment was reorganized on April 26, 1862. Several years after he returned home, Adolphus raised a company of volunteer reserves over the age of 50. This group was separated into two companies and was designated as Moss's Battalion, N.C. Senior Reserves. In January 1865, the battalion was merged into the 6th N.C. Senior Reserves, and Moss was appointed as its lieutenant colonel. No further records.

1229. Moss, Columbus W.

Lieutenant Colonel, 66th Regiment N.C. Militia (1861 organization)

Columbus was born in 1833 in Rowan County. Columbus followed his cousin into the northern section of Davidson County. Columbus was living in the Clemmonsville township in 1860, and, unlike his brother, had begun a plantation. The Moss plantation contained 23 slaves in 1860. On September 23, 1858, Columbus married Mary E. Douthit. The two would have only one child: William (1859). Columbus was commissioned to serve as the lieutenant colonel for the 66th Militia from northern Davidson County on January 4, 1862, and he served in that capacity for the duration of the conflict. No further records.

1230. Motherly, Henry

Private, Davidson Guards
Company A, 21st Regiment N.C. Troops
   (11th N.C. Volunteers)

Henry was born in 1823. Henry worked as a miner, and, on May 14, 1852, he married Elizabeth Huffman. He and Elizabeth lived in the Lexington township until he was conscripted into service on June 6, 1863. Henry was reported present until wounded in the head at Gettysburg, Pennsylvania, on July 1, 1863. Henry died of "diarrhea chronic," or of his head wound, in Richmond, Virginia, on July 31, 1863.

1231. Motsinger, Charles Wesley

Surgeon, 71st Regiment N.C. Militia
   (1861 organization)

Charles was born on September 4, 1837, to Joseph and Louisa Motsinger. Charles attended medical college in Philadelphia, Pennsylvania, and took the Hippocratic oath in 1861. The new Dr. Motsinger returned to his Abbott's Creek home, where he was commissioned as the surgeon for one of Forsyth County's militia regiments on November 26, 1861. Charles served in that capacity until he was transferred to Raleigh in 1863. He returned after a four-month stay. The doctor was taken ill immediately after returning from treating diseased soldiers and died on August 5, 1864. He is buried at Abbott's Creek Primitive Baptist Church.

1232. Motsinger, David Noah

Private, Company F, 16th Missouri
   Infantry Regiment

David was born in 1830. He worked as a farmer and was living alone in 1860. David was one of a group of young men who traveled to Missouri shortly before the war. At the outbreak of hostilities, David volunteered for service at Cen-

trailia, Missouri, with Company F of the 16th Missouri Infantry Regiment. David served with the 16th at such battles as Lexington and Dry Wood, Missouri; Perryville, Kentucky; and Murfeesboro, Tennessee. After the war, David returned home, where, in 1869, he married Clata Anne. David and Clata would have four children: Maggie (1876), Joseph (1879), Eura Jane (1881), and Mary (1885). David lived in the Abbott's Creek township until his death on July 9, 1919. He is buried at Wallburg Baptist Church.

1233. Motsinger, Franklin Abram

Sergeant, Confederate Guards
Company K, 48th Regiment N.C. Troops

Frank was born on March 7, 1832. He worked as a single farmer prior to being conscripted into service on August 8, 1862. Frank was wounded in the shoulder at Fredericksburg, Virginia, on December 13, 1862. He recovered from his shoulder wound and returned to duty; he was promoted to corporal on March 1, 1863, and to sergeant in April 1863. Frank was wounded in action twice more, both times in the hand, at Bristoe Station, Virginia (October 14, 1863) and at Petersburg, Virginia (June 15, 1864). Frank recovered but was captured at Petersburg on October 31, 1864. He was confined at Point Lookout, Maryland, until March 5, 1865, when he died of pneumonia. He is buried in the Point Lookout National Cemetery.

1234. Motsinger, Jacob Lindsey

First Lieutenant, 66th Regiment N.C.
   Militia (1861 organization)

Jacob was born in 1831 to Adam and Mary Motsinger. He worked as a farmer in the Abbott's Creek area, and, in 1852, he married Edith Lane. Jacob and Edith would have three children: Robert (1855), Lucretia (1859), and John (1863). Jacob was commissioned as first lieutenant in the Bethany District Company on December 4, 1861. Records indicate that he "left the county" in 1864. No further records.

1235. Motsinger, Moses M.

Private, Company A, 42nd Regiment
   N.C. Troops
Howard's Company, Gibbs' Battalion,
   N.C. Prison Guards

Moses was born on March 7, 1834, to Adam and Mary Motsinger. Moses worked as a farmer prior to volunteering for service in Rowan County on January 30, 1862. He was reported present until he elected to serve as a prison guard at Salisbury, North Carolina, and was transferred to that duty on May 1, 1862. He served as a prison guard throughout the war. Moses was paroled at Salisbury and returned to the Abbott's Creek township, where, on July 18, 1865, he married Mary Jane Hedgecock. Moses worked as a farmer until his death on January 24, 1912. He is buried at Abbott's Creek Primitive Baptist Church.

1236. Murphy, John Randall

Private, Company C, 70th Regiment
   N.C. Troops (1st N.C. Junior
   Reserves)

John was born on August 22, 1846. He worked as a farmer prior to enlisting in the Junior Reserves on May 24, 1864. After the war, John returned home to the Midway township, where, on July 23, 1872, he married Mary Jane Swicegood. John and Mary would have five children: John (1874), Louise (1876), Hester (1883), Minnie (1887), and Flettie (1890). John worked as farmer in the Midway township until his death on September 23, 1912. He is buried at Mount Pleasant United Methodist Church.

1237. Murphy, Joseph

Private, Thomasville Rifles
Company B, 14th Regiment N.C. Troops
   (4th N.C. Volunteers)

Joseph was born in 1836 to Joseph and Mary Murphy. He worked as a farmer prior to being conscripted into service on July 15, 1862. Joseph deserted prior to September 15, 1862, when he was reported under arrest. The next time his name is mentioned in the record is on March 10, 1863, when he died of pneumonia.

1238. Murphy, Pleasant

Private, Company H, 48th Regiment
   N.C. Troops

Pleasant was born in 1827 to Joseph and Mary Murphy. Pleasant worked as a farmer, and, on July 25, 1853, he married Barbara Long. They would have three children, Mary (1854), Joseph R. (1859), and Julia (1862), before Pleasant was conscripted into service on August 8, 1862. Pleasant was reported present until he was captured at Hatcher's Run, Virginia, on March 31, 1865. He was confined at Point Lookout, Maryland, until June 29, 1865, when he was released after taking the oath of allegiance. After the war, Pleasant returned to his home southwest of Thomasville. He and Barbara would have seven more children: Jesse (1866), Robert Lee (1867), Dora Bell (1868), Lula (1871), Pleasant (1872), John (1875), and Clara (1878). Pleasant lived in the Bethany area until his death in the 1890s. He is buried at Bethany United Church of Christ.

1239. Murphy, Robert M.

Private, Company H, 48th Regiment N.C. Troops

Robert was born in 1823 to Sarah Murphy. In 1850, his mother married Farabee Butler, and Robert and his sister moved in with him. Robert worked on his stepfather's farm until he moved out in 1853; he married Susanna in 1857. Robert and Susanna would have three children, John (1858), Martin (1861), and Susan (1863), before Robert was conscripted into service prior to October 31, 1864. Robert was reported present until he was wounded and captured at Hatcher's Run, Virginia, on March 31, 1865. He was

confined at Point Lookout, Maryland, until June 29, 1865, when he was released after taking the oath of allegiance. After the war, Robert returned home to the North Thomasville township, and he and Susanna would have another son, Preston (1872). Robert's wife died and his children went their separate ways as he lived as a single man in 1900. No further records.

1240. Musgrave, George

Private, Company I, 61st Regiment N.C. Troops

George was born on July 6, 1838, to George and Anne Musgrave of Warksworth, Great Britain. George was raised in England but traveled to this country with his family, arriving in Davidson County as a single, young man in the late 1850s. George was employed as a silver miner and was living in the Carter Boardinghouse in 1860. He was conscripted into service on September 10, 1862, and was reported present through August 1864. After the war, George returned to Davidson County, where, on February 24, 1866, he married Matilda Isadore Cox. George and Matilda would have seven children: Christopher (1866), Martha (1869), Frank (1871–88), Charlotte (1873), Minnie (1876–87), Robert Lee (1880–81), and Addie Erma (1885). George retired from mine work and operated a small farm and

A Confederate contractor and later veteran of the 61st N.C. Troops, George Musgrave and wife (Susan Musgrave, *The Heritage of Davidson County*).

worked at a distillery that manufactured peneroil until his death on January 3, 1926. He is buried at Mount Tabor United Church of Christ.

1241. Myers, Albert Lindsey

Private, Company K, 31st Regiment N.C. Troops

Albert was born on February 9, 1843, to Benjamin and Elizabeth Wommack Myers. Albert worked on his father's farm prior to being conscripted into service at Camp Holmes, North Carolina, on May 23, 1863. He was reported present through December 1864. After the war, Albert returned home to the Tyro area, where, on April 22, 1867, he married Sarah Beck. Albert and Sarah would have nine children: Lenora (1868), Daniel (1870), Julia (1873), Arcus (1875), Jesse L. (1878), Clara (1883), Bertha (1886), Minnie (1888), and Isaac (1891). Albert became both a successful farmer and a businessman after the war. On his farm, he raised wheat, corn, and cotton, and he harvested timber from other sections of his land, which was the beginning of his lumber mill business. Albert ran both operations until his death on May 24, 1929. He is buried at Reeds Baptist Church.

1242. Myers, Alfred

Private, Company A, 57th Regiment N.C. Troops

Alfred was born in 1838 to Peter and Martha Meredith Myers. Alfred worked as a farmer prior to enlisting in

Albert Myers, along with three of his veteran brothers (Marie Hinson, *The Heritage of Davidson County*).

Rowan County on July 4, 1862. He was reported present until captured at Rappahannock Station, Virginia, on November 7, 1863. Alfred was confined at Point Lookout, Maryland, until June 10, 1865, when he was released after taking the oath of allegiance. After the war, Alfred returned to the Thomasville area, where, on December 18, 1866, he married Lovina Rothrock. Alfred and Lovina would have a family of ten children: John (1868), Martha (1869), Jonathan (1870), Henrietta (1873), Samuel (1875), Henry (1877), Ernest (1879), Alice (1882), Stimson (1885), and Edward (1888). Alfred worked as a modest farmer in the Thomasville township and was employed for five years at the Leach & Lambeth Tobacco Factory. Alfred died on February 20, 1900. He is buried at Fair Grove United Methodist Church.

1243. Myers, Ambrose

Private, Thomasville Rifles
Company B, 14th Regiment N.C. Troops
(4th N.C. Volunteers)

Ambrose was born in 1824 to Peter Myers and his first wife, whose name is unknown. Ambrose worked as a farmer south of Emanuel Church. On June 13, 1854, he married Elizabeth Shuler. Ambrose and Elizabeth would have two children, Susan (1856) and Thomas (1858), before Ambrose was conscripted into service on November 4, 1863. He was reported present until wounded and captured at Winchester, Virginia, on September 19, 1864. Ambrose was confined at Point Lookout, Maryland, until November 15, 1864, when he was paroled and transferred to Venus Point, Georgia, for exchange. After the war, Ambrose returned home to the Conrad Hill township, where he and Elizabeth would have one more child, Florence (1867). Ambrose worked as a small farmer until his death in the early 1900s. He is buried at Emanuel United Church of Christ.

1244. Myers, Benjamin D.

Private, Company C, 70th Regiment
N.C. Troops (1st N.C. Junior
Reserves)

Benjamin was born in 1846 to Andrew and Mary Myers. He worked as a farmer prior to enlisting in the Junior Reserves on May 24, 1864. After the war, Benjamin returned home to the Tyro

township, where, on March 25, 1866, he married Sarah E. Michael. Benjamin and Sarah would have eight children: Mary (1867), John (1870), Catharine (1875), Margaret (1877), Sarah (1879), Ben (1882), Joseph (1887), and William (1891). No further records.

1245. Myers, Benjamin F.

Corporal, Davidson Guards
Company A, 21st Regiment N.C. Troops
(11th N.C. Volunteers)

Benjamin was born in 1837 to Jacob and Abigail Myers. Benjamin worked as a farmer prior to volunteering for service on May 8, 1861; he was mustered in as a corporal. He was mortally wounded and died the same day at Winchester, Virginia, on May 25, 1862.

1246. Myers, Clarkson

Corporal, Thomasville Rifles
Company B, 14th Regiment N.C. Troops
(4th N.C. Volunteers)

Clark was born in 1841 to Andrew Myers and his first wife, whose name is unknown. Clark worked as a farmer prior to volunteering for service on April 27, 1861. He was promoted to corporal on April 28, 1862. Clark was wounded and captured at Sharpsburg, Maryland, on September 17, 1862. Clark was hospitalized at Frederick, Maryland, until he died of his wounds on October 18, 1862.

1247. Myers, Daniel G.

Private, Company B, 57th Regiment
N.C. Troops

Daniel was born in 1836 to Benjamin and Elizabeth Wommack Myers. He worked as a farmer prior to enlisting in Rowan County on July 4, 1862. No further records.

1248. Myers, David Giles

Second Lieutenant, 66th Regiment
N.C. Militia (1861 organization)

David was born on February 22, 1838, to Benjamin and Elizabeth Wommack Myers. He worked as a miller, and, in 1860, he married Sarah Byerly. David was commissioned as second lieutenant in the Tyro District Company on November 26, 1861. He died of unreported causes on December 10, 1861. He is buried at Reeds Baptist Church.

1249. Myers, David Henderson

Private, Company B, 57th Regiment
N.C. Troops

David was born on August 8, 1835, to Benjamin and Elizabeth Wommack Myers. David worked as a farmer, and, in 1859, he married Mahalia Hedrick. David enlisted into service in Rowan County on July 4, 1862. He was hospitalized at Richmond, Virginia, on November 1, 1862, with typhoid. David died of typhoid fever nine days later on November 10, 1862.

1250. Myers, Felix

Private, Company C, 70th Regiment
N.C. Troops (1st N.C. Junior
Reserves)

Felix was born in 1847 to Felix and Sarah Hunt Myers. He worked as a farmer prior to enlisting in the Junior Reserves on May 24, 1864. After the war, Felix returned home to the Emmons township, where, on September 10, 1868, he married Elizabeth O'Daniel. No further records.

1251. Myers, Felix

Private, Thomasville Rifles
Company B, 14th Regiment N.C. Troops
(4th N.C. Volunteers)

Felix was born in 1829 to Jacob and Catharine Hepler Myers. He worked as a farmer in the Fair Grove area, and, on December 29, 1853, he married Mary Sink. Felix and Mary would have three children, John (1855), Sarah (1857), and Esther (1859), before Felix was conscripted into service in Wake County on July 16, 1862. Felix was killed in action at Chancellorsville, Virginia, on May 3, 1863.

1252. Myers, George Washington

Private, Davidson Guards
Company A, 21st Regiment N.C. Troops
(11th N.C. Volunteers)

George was born in 1837 to Andrew and Mary Myers. He worked as a farmer prior to volunteering for service on May 8, 1861. George was listed as absent or on detail for most of the period between May 8, 1861, and February 1865. No further records.

1253. Myers, Hamilton Franklin

Private, Company C, 70th Regiment N.C.
Troops (1st N.C. Junior Reserves)

Hamilton was born on February 24, 1847, to Jacob and Caroline Wagner Myers. He worked as a carpenter prior to enlisting in the Junior Reserves on May 24, 1864. After the war, Hamilton returned home, where he continued his trade in the Thomasville township. In 1870, Hamilton married Mary L. Reddick. Hamilton bought some land in the Emanuel area and built a home for his family where the modern Kendall Mill and Johnsontown roads meet. Hamilton and Mary would have two children: Robert L. (1871) and Elizabeth (1876). Mary died in the 1880s. Hamilton married Virginia Mallard in 1894; the two would not have any children. Hamilton continued his work as a carpenter and served Emanuel Church by helping with many building projects. Hamilton died on September 6, 1911. He is buried at Emanuel United Church of Christ.

1254. Myers, Haley

Private, Company H, 48th Regiment N.C. Troops

Haley was born on February 27, 1829. Haley worked as a farmer in the Emanuel area, and, on April 13, 1857, he married Mary Ann Bowers. He and Mary would have one child, John (1860), before Haley was conscripted into service at Petersburg, Virginia, on August 8, 1862. Haley served as a private until he was granted a discharge on December 20, 1862, because of "chronic rheumatism with ulcus of the leg." Haley returned home where he remained for the duration of the war. He probably served in one of the various Home Guard units from the area. Haley and Mary would only have one more child: Mary (1868). However, even as financially limited as the family was, over the course of ten years Haley and Mary would adopt eight children, many of them war orphans. Haley worked as a farmer until his death on December 12, 1911. He is buried at Emanuel United Church of Christ.

1255. Myers, Henry

Private, Lexington Wildcats Company I, 14th Regiment N.C. Troops (4th N.C. Volunteers)

Henry was born in 1836 to John and Barbara Myers. Henry worked as a farmer in the Boone township prior to volunteering for service on May 14, 1861. He was reported present for duty, surviving all of the regiment's great battles, until he was captured at Petersburg, Virginia, on April 3, 1865. Henry was confined at Hart's Island, New York, until he was released after taking the oath of allegiance on June 17, 1865. Henry returned home to the Boone township, where, in 1875, he married Naomi. Henry and Naomi would have two children, Bettie (1877) and Charles (1880), before moving out of the county in the 1890s. No further records.

1256. Myers, Jacob

Private, Company H, 48th Regiment N.C. Troops

Jacob was born in 1843 to Thomas and Catharine Myers. He worked as a farmer prior to volunteering for service on March 3, 1862. Jacob was killed in action at Fredericksburg, Virginia, on December 13, 1862.

1257. Myers, James Addison

Private, Watauga Marksmen Company B, 37th Regiment N.C. Troops

James was born on August 30, 1845, to Benjamin and Elizabeth Wommack Myers. He worked on his family's farm, and on September 6, 1863, he married Susan Michael. James and Susan were married for less than one month before

Lee Snyder helped James A. Myers to build this Reeds home shortly after the end of hostilities (Touart, *Building the Backcountry*).

James A. Myers was conscripted late into the war (Marie Hinson and Mrs. Robbie Massey, *The Heritage of Davidson County*).

Family of James A. Myers. James and his wife are in the center (Marie Hinson and Mrs. Robbie Massey, *The Heritage of Davidson County*).

James was called away to service at Camp Holmes, Wake County, in October 1864. He was reported present through February 1865. James survived the war, and returned home to his wife and one-year-old daughter, Bessie. James immediately returned to farming to make a living for his family. James and Susan would have eight more children: Laura (1866), Cornelia (1868), Sallie (1870), Mary (1872), Robert Lee (1876), Martha (1880), James (1884), and Edna (1892). Susan died in 1903. James married a second time on February 4, 1909, to Sarah Elizabeth Sowers. They would not have any children. James continued work as a farmer and trained mules as a side job until his death on April 23, 1923. He is buried at Reeds Baptist Church.

1258. Myers, Jefferson C.

Private, Thomasville Rifles
Company B, 14th Regiment N.C. Troops
(4th N.C. Volunteers)
Company D, 48th Regiment N.C. Troops
Company G, 7th Confederate Cavalry
Regiment
Company D, 16th Battalion, N.C. Cavalry

Jeff was born in 1841. He worked as a farmer prior to volunteering for service

on April 23, 1861. Jeff was reported present until he was discharged at Fort Bee, Virginia, on December 12, 1861, due to "severe and protracted typhoid fever." Jeff came home, where he recovered from his disease and married Susan Kanoy on August 3, 1862. Jeff was conscripted into service five days later and served in the 48th Regiment; he was wounded severely at Sharpsburg, Maryland, on September 17, 1862. He was sent home on furlough; however, he did not return, and on May 1, 1864, he was dropped from the rolls upon his enlistment in the 7th Confederate Cavalry. Jeff was transferred to the 16th N.C. Cavalry in November 1864 and was reported present through December 1864. No further records.

1259. Myers, Jesse A.

Private, Thomasville Rifles
Company B, 14th Regiment N.C. Troops
(4th N.C. Volunteers)

Jesse was born on May 10, 1828, to Peter and Elizabeth Myers. Jesse worked as a farmer in the southern district of Davidson County, and, in 1850, he married Barbara Sechrist Hepler. Jesse and Barbara would have four children, Catharine (1851), Franklin (1854), Delphina (1855), and Polly (1859), before he

was conscripted into service on November 6, 1863. Jesse was listed as present for duty or was detailed for light service at Raleigh, North Carolina, and Gordonsville, Virginia, through August 1864. Jesse returned to the Conrad Hill township where he continued farming until his death on May 24, 1911. He is buried at Emanuel United Church of Christ.

1260. Myers, John W.

Private, Company C, 70th
Regiment N.C. Troops (1st
N.C. Junior Reserves)

John was born in 1848. He worked as an apprentice blacksmith in the Tyro area prior to enlisting in the Junior Reserves on May 24, 1864. John was reported present until paroled at Gordonsville, Virginia, on April 12, 1865. After the war, John returned home, where, in 1869, he married Cornelia. John and Cornelia would have four children: Ludella (1870), Charlie (1872), Daniel (1875), and Henry (1879). The family moved out of the county prior to 1900. No further records.

1261. Myers, Junius L.

Private, Davidson Guards
Company A, 21st Regiment N.C. Troops
(11th N.C. Volunteers)

Junius was born on February 27, 1841, to John and Jane Hammond Myers. He worked as a farmer prior to volunteering for service on May 8, 1861. Junius died of pneumonia at Richmond, Virginia, on May 24, 1862. A stone at Shiloh United Methodist Church was erected in his honor.

1262. Myers, Kenneth G.

Unknown rank, 14th Battalion, N.C.
Home Guard

Kenneth was born in 1830 to Daniel and Sarah Myers. He worked as a farmer in the Thomasville township, where, on November 13, 1869, he married Sarah Kennedy. Kenneth and Sarah would not have any children. The information about his service is from a 1909 short obituary in the *Lexington Dispatch*, which stated: "He was a member of Hargrave's

Home Guards." Kenneth died in 1909. He is buried at Emanuel United Church of Christ.

1263. Myers, Lemuel Jasper

Sergeant, Thomasville Rifles
Company B, 14th Regiment N.C. Troops
(4th N.C. Volunteers)

Lemuel was born on December 18, 1832, to Ambrose and Susanna Carroll Myers. He worked as a farmer prior to being conscripted into service in Wake County on July 16, 1862. Lemuel was wounded at Sharpsburg, Maryland, on September 17, 1862. Lemuel was granted a furlough and returned home. In December 1862, he married Melinda Myers, and he returned to service in January 1863. Lemuel was wounded by sharpshooter fire at Gettysburg, Pennsylvania, on July 2, 1863. He recovered from his hip wound and returned to service in September 1863. Lemuel was reported present and was promoted to corporal on April 26, 1864, then to sergeant on August 1, 1864. Lemuel was captured at Winchester, Virginia, on September 19, 1864. He was confined at Point Lookout, Maryland, until March 18, 1865, when he was paroled and transferred to Venus Point, Georgia, for exchange. After the war, Lemuel returned home to his wife and two-year-old daughter, Frances. Lemuel and Melinda would have two more children, Drucilla (1866) and William (1867), before Melinda died. Lemuel married Mary Louvina Pope in the 1880s. Lemuel and his family moved out west in the mid–1880s, eventually arriving in Utah. Lemuel claimed a homestead and lived in Utah until his death on September 10, 1904.

1264. Myers, Lorenzo Wood

Private, Company C, 70th Regiment
N.C. Troops (1st N.C. Junior
Reserves)

Wood was born in 1848 to Peter and Martha Meredith Myers. He was a student prior to enlisting in the Junior Reserves on May 24, 1864. Wood survived the war and returned home to begin a farm and a family in the Thomasville area. In 1867, he married Lenora C. Fouts. Wood and Lenora would have six children: Thomas (1870), Mattie (1874), Lou (1876), Peter (1879), Martha (1882), and Alice (1885). Wood, who was referred to

as "Doc," was an active member of the Emanuel congregation, while no documentation exists on his training in medicine, he was known for delivering many children in the Thomasville and Conrad Hill township. Wood contracted pneumonia and died on February 4, 1915. He is buried at Emanuel United Church of Christ.

1265. Myers, Malcolm

Private, Chatam Light Infantry
Company G, 48th Regiment N.C. Troops

Malcolm was born in 1837 to Daniel and Sarah Morrison Myers. He worked as a farmer prior to being conscripted into service at Petersburg, Virginia, on August 14, 1861. Malcolm was reported present until he was killed in action at Reams' Station, Virginia, on August 25, 1864.

1266. Myers, McKinley

Second Lieutenant, 65th Regiment
N.C. Militia (1861 organization)

McKinley was born on March 22, 1842. He worked as a farmer and mechanic in the Thomasville area and was living as a boarder with Burrell C. Lambeth in 1860. McKinley was commissioned as a second lieutenant in the 65th N.C. Militia on November 25, 1861. He served in this capacity until he died of natural causes on May 19, 1862. He is buried at Emanuel United Church of Christ.

1267. Myers, Mathias

Private, Company C, 70th Regiment
N.C. Troops (1st N.C. Junior
Reserves)

Mathias was born in 1847 to Thomas and Catharine Myers. He worked as a farmer prior to enlisting in the Junior Reserves on May 24, 1864. No further records.

1268. Myers, Peter

Private, Company C, 76th Regiment
N.C. Troops (6th N.C. Senior
Reserves)

Peter was born in 1816. He worked as a farmer in the northern district of Davidson County, and, on September 17, 1836, he married Martha Meredith. Peter and Martha would have six children who survived infancy: Lorenzo W.

(1848), Sarah (1857), John (1861), Samuel (1864), Martha (1866), and Peter (1869). Peter served as a private in Hill's Senior Reserves until it became the 6th N.C. Senior Reserves in January 1865. Peter worked as a modest farmer until his death on August 29, 1886. He is buried at Emanuel United Church of Christ.

1269. Myers, Richard Barton

Private, Company B, 57th Regiment
N.C. Troops

Barton was born on August 16, 1840, to Benjamin and Elizabeth Wommack Myers. He worked as a farmer in the Tyro area, and in 1861, he married Laura Ann Michael. Barton was conscripted into service in Rowan County on July 4, 1862. He was reported present until wounded shortly before the 57th Regiment's charge at Fredericksburg, Virginia, on December 13, 1862, which was said by General Longstreet to be "very efficient." In Barton's own words (and his original spelling):

The cannon ball struck our ranks for then we were in four ranks. The ball struck a young man nocking off the back of his head and that this same ball struck my gun against my head is the way I got wonded. Mr. Walser and others says that I and this other man fell forward on our faces and that we both kicked like hogs ding after being hit with a nife. We were the first wonded from our regment. It shoked the men and our Colonel seeing this, said Study men, Study, and gave the command to make the charge, which they did and run the yankys back but lost about one hun-

21-year-old Barton Myers, and his bride Laura Michael, on their wedding day in 1861 (Pace, *A History of Reeds Baptist Church*).

dred kiled of the regiment. Mr. James Craver was kiled in this charge. He had not bin married very long.

Barton rested in a hospital for an extended period of time. The wound that he had suffered was a serious skull fracture, which induced a week-long coma. He returned to service in November 1863 and was reported present until captured at Farmville, Virginia, on April 6, 1865. Barton was confined at Newport News, Virginia, until June 26, 1865, when he was released after taking the oath of allegiance. Barton lived in the Tyro area as a farmer and member of Reeds Baptist Church. He and Laura would have four children: Mary Etta (1878), Jennie (1881), Henry Cleveland (1884), and Benjamin (1887). Barton hosted many family gatherings, and even after his death, members of his family and their descendants continued to gather at Barton's home. Barton died on January 19, 1926. He is buried at Reeds Baptist Church.

1270. Myers, Samuel L.

Private, Carolina Rangers
Company B, 10th Virginia Cavalry
Regiment

Sam was born on June 26, 1833, to Daniel and Sarah Myers. He was employed as a carpenter, and, in 1856, he married Margaret Adelia. Sam and Margaret would have two children, Harper (1857) and Foster (1860), before Sam volunteered for service in Davie County on October 29, 1861. He was reported present until listed as absent on a horse detail in June–July 1863. Sam returned to service in August and was listed as present through December 31, 1864, when he received a clothing ration. Sam and Margaret's third child, Maggie, was born in 1864. Sam survived the war and returned home to the Thomasville area where he and Margaret would have four more children: Mattie (1866), John (1869), Smith (1875), and Elizabeth (1879). Sam worked as a successful farmer until his death on June 27, 1910. He is buried at Emanuel United Church of Christ.

1271. Myers, Silas Franklin

Private, Company H, 48th Regiment
N.C. Troops

Silas was born in 1842 to Peter and Martha Meredith Myers. He worked as a farmer prior to volunteering for service

The Richard Barton Myers family ca. 1890. Barton's youngest son, Ben, is seated in his lap (Mrs. Willie Veigh Myers Mitchum, *The Heritage of Davidson County*).

Barton and his family outside of their Reeds area home, built in 1866 (Marie Hinson, *The Heritage of Davidson County*).

on March 3, 1862. Silas was hospitalized with "rheumatism" at Richmond, Virginia, on November 15, 1862. He returned to duty on March 6, 1863. Silas was reported present until he was killed in action at Reams' Station, Virginia, on August 25, 1864.

1272. Myers, William A.

Private, Company H, 48th Regiment N.C. Troops

William was born in 1836. He worked as a farmer prior to being conscripted into service at Petersburg, Virginia, on August 8, 1862. William was reported present until he was furloughed from duty on August 22, 1864. William returned to service prior to December 8, 1864, when he was hospitalized in Richmond, Virginia. William recovered, returned to duty, and was reported present until captured at Hatcher's Run, Virginia, on March 31, 1865. William was confined at Point Lookout, Maryland, until June 16, 1865, when he was released after taking the oath of allegiance. No further records.

1273. Myers, William Addison

Private, Lexington Wildcats Company I, 14th Regiment N.C. Troops (4th N.C. Volunteers)

William was born on December 11, 1840, to David and Ellen Sullivan Myers. He worked as a farmer, and, in 1859, he married Eleanor Sullivan. William and Eleanor would have two children, Alexander (1859) and Jane (1860), before William volunteered for service on May 14, 1861. While William was away, William Jr. was born in March 1862. William was reported present until he was captured at Petersburg, Virginia, on April 3, 1865. He was confined at Hart's Island, New York, until June 17, 1865, when he was released after taking the oath of allegiance. William returned home to the Thomasville township, where he and Eleanor would have two more children: Lucinda (1865) and Franklin (1868). William was a member of the church and a loving father, according to family records. William died on July 11, 1915. He is buried at Emanuel United Church of Christ.

1274. Myers, William Henry

Private, Lexington Wildcats Company I, 14th Regiment N.C. Troops (4th N.C. Volunteers)

William was born on March 10, 1834. He worked as a farmer prior to being conscripted into service in Wake County on July 16, 1862. William was reported present until hospitalized with an unspecified wound on December 24, 1864; he returned to service three days later. William was captured prior to May 1, 1865. He was confined at Hart's Island, New York, until June 17, 1865, when he was released after taking the oath of allegiance. William returned home, where he lived until his death on May 15, 1926. He is buried at Macedonia United Methodist Church.

1275. Myers, William J.

Private, Carolina Rangers Company B, 10th Virginia Cavalry Regiment

William was born on April 19, 1844, to Jacob and Catharine Hepler Myers. William was a student and a good friend of Hugh Clodfelter's prior to volunteering for service in Davie County on October 29, 1861. He was reported present through August 1864, when he was listed as absent on detail. William returned to duty the next month and was reported present through December 31, 1864, when he was issued a clothing ration. William survived the war and returned home to the Thomasville area, where, on September 24, 1865, he married Cynthia L. Byerly. William and Cynthia would have six children: James (1867), Eli (1871), Julian (1875), Mary (1879), Edward (1885), and Belle (1889). William worked as a farmer until his death on June 2, 1898. He is buried at Emanuel United Church of Christ.

1276. Myers, William Lindsey

Corporal, Company H, 48th Regiment N.C. Troops

William was born on May 31, 1831, to Peter and Martha Meredith Myers. He worked as a farmer, and, in 1860, he married Susan B. Fouts. William and Susan would have one child, Mollie (1862), before William was conscripted into service at Petersburg, Virginia, on August 8, 1862. William was promoted to corporal on October 31, 1864, and served in that capacity until he was captured at Hatcher's Run, Virginia, on March 31, 1865. He was confined at Point Lookout, Maryland, until June 29, 1865, when he was released after taking the oath of allegiance. William returned home and moved his family into the town of Thomasville. William and Susan would have three more children, Fannie (1867), Magdalena (1871), and John (1875), before her death in 1879. William would marry twice more, to Maggie Saintsing and Mary F. Hiatt; he would have no children with either wife. William became a successful businessman in the town, owning two mercantile stores and stock in both Westmoreland and Standard Chair companies. He also was a speculator in tobacco futures. William died on November 10, 1930. He is buried in the Thomasville City Cemetery.

1277. Myers, William M.

Private, Company K, 31st Regiment N.C. Troops

William was born on November 7, 1844, to Andrew and Eleanor Bowers Myers. He worked as a farmer prior to being conscripted into service at Camp Holmes, North Carolina, on May 27, 1863. He was reported present until captured at Fort Harrison, Virginia, on September 30, 1864. William was confined at Point Lookout, Maryland, until June 12, 1865, when he was released after taking the oath of allegiance. After the war, William returned home to the Thomasville area where, in 1866, he married Helena Rickard. William and Helena would have only one child: Harrison (1868). William lived in the town of Thomasville and was employed at the Standard Chair Company until his death on June 9, 1924. He is buried at Emanuel United Church of Christ.

1278. Myers, William Romulus

Private, Company H, 48th Regiment N.C. Troops

William was born in 1837 to Thomas and Catharine Sink Myers. William worked as a farmer prior to marrying Martha Sechrist on November 3, 1860. William volunteered for service on March 3, 1862. He died of typhoid fever at Petersburg, Virginia, on June 20, 1862.

1279. Myrick, Jesse A.

Private, Lexington Wildcats Company I, 14th Regiment N.C. Troops (4th N.C. Volunteers)

Jesse was born in 1841 to John B. and Angeline Myrick. Jesse worked as a farmer prior to volunteering for service on May 14, 1861. He was reported present until he was captured at Strasburg, Virginia, on September 23, 1864. Jesse was confined at Point Lookout, Maryland, until June 3, 1865, when he was released after taking the oath of allegiance. After the war, Jesse returned to the Boone area, where, on March 24, 1867, he married Sarah Leonard. Jesse and Sarah would have six children: Florence (1868), James (1869), Dora (1871), Henry (1874), William (1877), and Lettie (1879). No further records.

1280. Myrick, John S.

*Private, Lexington Wildcats
Company I, 14th Regiment N.C. Troops
(4th N.C. Volunteers)*

John was born in 1843 to John B. and Angeline Myrick. John worked as a farmer prior to volunteering for service on May 14, 1861. He was killed in action at Sharpsburg, Maryland, on September 17, 1862. He is buried at Shepherdstown, [West] Virginia.

1281. Myrick, Lawson

*Private, Company A, 42nd Regiment
N.C. Troops
Howard's Company, Gibbs' Battalion,
N.C. Prison Guards, Salisbury
Company I, 14th Regiment N.C.
Troops*

Lawson was born in 1833 to John B. and Angeline Myrick. Lawson worked as a farmer, and on September 11, 1856, he married Mary Grubb. Lawson and Mary would have four children, George (1859), Henry (1860), Frank (1861), and Katy Anne (1862), before Lawson volunteered for service on January 22, 1862. Lawson was transferred from the 42nd Regiment to serve as a Prison Guard on May 1, 1862. Lawson guarded the Salisbury Prison until he was assigned to the 14th Regiment on October 14, 1863. Lawson was reported present until he was discharged in April 1864 of unreported circumstances. Lawson returned to the Tryo area where he and Mary would have one more child: Samuel James (1866). Lawson worked as a farmer in the Tyro township until his death in 1904. He is buried at Wesley's Chapel.

1282. Nading, Francis

*Private, Company A, 57th Regiment
N.C. Troops*

Francis was born on July 31, 1841. Francis worked as a farmhand in the Boone township in 1850, then as a farmer in the Clemmonsville area in 1860. Francis was conscripted into service in Forsyth County on March 12, 1864. He was hospitalized at Petersburg, Virginia, with gonorrhea on March 21, 1864. Francis recovered from his disease and returned to duty in September 1864. He was reported present until captured at Fort Stedman, Virginia, on March 25, 1865. Francis was confined at Point Lookout, Maryland, until June 15, 1865, when he was released after taking the oath of allegiance. After the war, Francis returned to the Clemmonsville area, where in 1872, he married Mary Orrender. Francis and Mary would not have any children together. Francis lived in the area until his death on January 11, 1877. He is buried at Old Vernon Methodist Church.

1283. Nance, Henry A.

*Private, Company K, 5th Regiment
N.C. State Troops*

Henry was born on October 5, 1837, in Randolph County to Jesse and Mary Nance. Henry moved with his family to the Jackson Hill area in the late 1850s, and in 1859, he married Sarah G. Miller. Henry and Sarah would have two children, Martha (1860) and Isham (1861), before Henry was conscripted into service in Wake County, North Carolina, on July 15, 1862. He deserted from camp on August 12, 1862. He returned home and went back to his farm. As a side business, Henry was one of Jackson Hill's finest distillers of corn liquor. Henry and Sarah would go on to have six more children: William (1865), James (1868), Wesley (1870), Oscar (1872), Allison (1874), and Lindsay (1875). Henry lived in the Jackson Hill area until his death on December 27, 1914. He is buried at Tom's Creek Primitive Baptist Church.

1284. Neal, Ephraim A.

*Private, Company F, 7th Regiment
N.C. State Troops*

Ephraim was born in 1835 in Cleveland County, North Carolina. Ephraim worked as a millwright in the Lexington township prior to volunteering for service in Rowan County on July 22, 1861. He was reported present until he died of pneumonia in a Richmond, Virginia, hospital on June 27, 1863.

1285. Nelson, Richard M.

*Private, Harnett Light Infantry
Company F, 15th Regiment N.C. Troops
(5th N.C. Volunteers)*

Richard was born in 1843 to Milton and Sarah Nelson. Richard worked as a farmer prior to being conscripted into service in Wake County on July 15, 1862. He was killed in action at Fredericksburg, Virginia, on December 13, 1862.

1286. Newby, Henry B.

*Artificer, Company A, 10th Battalion,
N.C. Heavy Artillery*

Henry was born on June 21, 1839. Henry worked as a bootmaker for the Shelly Shoe Company prior to being conscripted into service in New Hanover County on August 1, 1862. Henry served as an artificer and was wounded in action at Fort Caswell, Brunswick County, in February 1863. Henry returned to service for a year, then deserted from his post at Fort Campbell, boarding a Federal gunboat off the coast of Wilmington, North Carolina, on February 18, 1864, seeking asylum. Henry was paroled at Fort Monroe, Virginia, and, after taking the oath of allegiance, he was furnished transportation to Philadelphia, Pennsylvania. Henry rode out the rest of the war at Philadelphia and at Fort Mifflin, Pennsylvania, then returned to the town of Thomasville. Once home, Henry went into business for himself, starting a shoe repair and sales shop. On January 28, 1866, Henry married Delphina Kennedy. Henry and Delphina would have 11 children: Henry (1867), Emaline (1869), Nancy (1871), Sarah (1873), Robert (1875), Maggie (1876), John (1878), William (1880), Edward (1882), Rosa (1884), and Carl (1886). Henry lived in the Thomasville area until his death. He is buried at Pleasant Grove United Methodist Church.

1287. Newsome, Absalom Abram

*Private, Company A, 42nd Regiment
N.C. Troops*

Absalom was born in 1829. He worked as a farmer in the southern district of Davidson County, and, in 1849, he married Annie McCarn. Absalom and Annie would have four children, Mary (1852), James (1855), Anna (1859), and William (1862), before Absalom was conscripted into service on an unspecified date. He was reported present until captured at Battery Anderson, Fort Fisher, North Carolina, on December 25, 1864. Absalom was confined at Point Lookout, Maryland, via Fort Monroe, Virginia, until May 14, 1865, when he was released after taking the oath of allegiance. Absalom returned home to the Cotton Grove area where he and Annie would have three more children: Lewis (1866), Linda (1870), and Delphi (1874). No further records.

1288. Newsome, J. Franklin

Private, Rowan Artillery
Company D, 10th Regiment N.C. State
Troops (1st N.C. Artillery)

Franklin was born in 1840 to Lewis and Sarah Newsome. Franklin worked as a laborer in the Emmons area prior to volunteering for service in Alamance County on January 20, 1862. He was reported present through December 1864. Franklin deserted to the enemy in March 1865. No further records.

1289. Newsome, Jehu Franklin

Sergeant, Company F, 7th Regiment
N.C. Troops

Jehu was born in 1838 to Lewis and Sarah Newsome. Jehu worked as a teacher in the southern part of Davidson County prior to volunteering for service on June 30, 1861. He was mustered in as a sergeant but was reduced to corporal in March 1862. Jehu was wounded in the left arm at Gaines' Mill, Virginia, on June 27, 1862. He recovered from his wounds and returned to service in January 1863. Jehu was wounded in the cheek and neck at Chancellorsville, Virginia, in May 1863 and was promoted back to sergeant on December 1, 1863. Jehu served as sergeant until he was killed in action at Reams Station, Virginia, on August 25, 1864. His body was returned and buried in the Sampson Newsom Family Cemetery.

1290. Newsome, John

Private, Chatam Light Infantry
Company G, 48th Regiment N.C. Troops

John was born in 1844 to Sampson and Bathsheba Newsome. John worked as a farmer prior to being conscripted into service on August 14, 1862. He was captured at Sharpsburg, Maryland, on September 17, 1862. John was confined at Point Lookout, Maryland, until October 2, 1862, when he was paroled and transferred to Aiken's Landing, Virginia, for exchange. John was declared exchanged on November 10, 1862, and returned to duty on an unspecified date. He was reported present until hospitalized with a gunshot wound of the right hand at Danville, Virginia, on June 16, 1864. Two days later, John was transferred to Raleigh, North Carolina, where he remained in a hospital until listed as absent without leave on December 20, 1864. No further records.

1291. Newsome, Nixon Haywood

Sergeant, Company C, 61st Regiment
N.C. Troops

Nixon was born on May 21, 1844, to Lewis and Sarah Newsome. He worked as a farmer prior to being conscripted into service in Wake County on August 27, 1862. Nixon was promoted to corporal on March 1, 1864, and to sergeant on October 1, 1864. Nixon served as a sergeant until captured at Kinston, North Carolina, on March 10, 1865. He was confined at Point Lookout, Maryland, until June 29, 1865, when he was released after taking the oath of allegiance. After the war, Nixon returned home to the Allegheny township, where, on September 2, 1869, he married Mattie J. Thayer. Nixon and Mattie would have four surviving children: Walter (1870), Louetta (1872), Idola (1878), and Robert (1885). Nixon worked as a farmer until his death on January 24, 1921. He is buried in the Sampson Newsome Family Cemetery.

1292. Newsome, William

Private, Company F, 7th Regiment
N.C. State Troops

William was born in 1840 to Sampson and Bathsheba Newsome. William worked as a farmer in the Allegheny area prior to volunteering for service in Alamance County on June 29, 1861. William

was reported present until he died of unreported causes at Carolina City, North Carolina, on February 15, 1862.

1293. Nifong, Robert Alexander

Private, Company H, 48th Regiment
N.C. Troops

Robert was born on July 24, 1835, to Adam and Catharine Nifong. Robert worked as a farmer in the Arcadia area prior to being conscripted into service on August 8, 1862. One month later, Robert deserted from service only to return under arrest in March 1863. Robert remained in confinement as a deserter until he was returned to service in July 1863. He was sent to the hospital on July 20, 1863, then was transferred to Castle Thunder Prison, Richmond, Virginia, on August 5, 1863. The rest of the story is not known, however, Robert survived the war, and his widow was granted a pension after his death. After the war, Robert returned home where he married Anna in 1866. Robert and Anna would have six children: Amanda (1867), Sarah (1871), Fannie (1873), Mary (1875), Carrie (1877), and Edward (1880). Robert lived in the Arcadia area until his death on November 12, 1910. He is buried at Hebron United Church of Christ.

1294. Nifong, Samuel O.

Private, Company H, 48th Regiment
N.C. Troops

Samuel was born in 1839 to Alexander and Mary Nifong. Samuel worked as a farmer prior to being conscripted into service at Petersburg, Virginia, on August 8, 1862. He deserted on September 8, 1862. Samuel returned from his desertion on February 18, 1863. Samuel was reported present until he was killed in action at Reams' Station, Virginia, on August 25, 1864.

1295. Nifong, Solomon

Private, Company H, 48th Regiment
N.C. Troops

Solomon was born in 1840 to Adam and Catharine Nifong. Solomon worked as a farmer prior to being conscripted into service in Petersburg, Virginia, on August 8, 1862. He was reported present until he deserted from service with his brother Robert on September 8, 1862. Solomon returned on March 9, 1863, and was reported present until May 10, 1863, when he deserted once again. Solomon returned from his absence and was reported as present until he was hospitalized at Richmond, Virginia, on April 21, 1864. Solomon died of "chronic diarrhea" on May 5, 1864. He is buried at Hollywood Cemetery in Richmond.

1296. Nifong, Wiley A.

Private, Company C, 49th Regiment N.C. Troops

Wiley was born on May 1, 1836, to Adam and Susan Clodfelter Nifong. Wiley worked as a farmer, and, on February 22, 1858, he married Catharine Amanda Miller. Wiley and Amanda would have two sons, William (1860) and Julius (1862), before Wiley was conscripted into service on March 15, 1864. He was reported present until wounded in the left shoulder at Petersburg, Virginia, on March 25, 1865. Wiley was hospitalized at Danville, Virginia, until granted a 60-day furlough on April 9, 1865. After the war, Wiley returned home to the Midway township where he and Amanda would have four more children: Samuel (1866), Sarah (1870), George (1872), and Edwin (1875). Wiley worked as a farmer and a repairman of farm equipment until his death on March 6, 1919. He is buried at Midway United Methodist Church.

1297. Noah (Nooe), Bennett

Adjutant (First Lieutenant), 65th Regiment N.C. Militia (1861 organization)

Bennett was born on February 25, 1822. He worked as a merchant in the town of Lexington and served as a justice of the peace for three terms from 1851 to 1859. On November 17, 1857, Bennett married Mary A. Watson. Bennett and Mary would have six children: John (1858), Bennett (1860), Jessie (1864), Sallie (1867), Mary (1871), and Fred (1874). Bennett was commissioned as the adjutant of the 65th N.C. Militia on February 25, 1862, and served in that capacity until he resigned in 1863. After his service, Bennett continued in his mercantile business and sold some of the first automatic threshing machines. Bennett served as a city councilman in the 1880s and early 1890s. Bennett died on July 31, 1901. He is buried in the Lexington City Cemetery.

1298. Noah (Nooe), Thomas

Private, Company B, 48th Regiment N.C. Troops

Thomas was born in 1833 to Louvina Noah. Thomas worked as a farmer, and, on October 24, 1859, he married Sarah Ward. Thomas and Sarah would have a child, William (1860), before Thomas was conscripted into service on August 8, 1862. He was wounded in action at Sharpsburg, Maryland, on September 17, 1862. Thomas recovered from his wounds, but on November 15, 1862, he died of typhoid fever.

1299. Noah (Nooe), William

Private, Company F, 7th Regiment N.C. State Troops

William was born in 1836 to Louvina Noah. William worked as a farmer for William Carrick prior to volunteering for service on March 6, 1862. William was killed in action at Ox Hill, Virginia, on September 1, 1862.

1300. Nowell, Jackson

Private, Thomasville Rifles Company B, 14th Regiment N.C. Troops (4th N.C. Volunteers)

Jackson was born in 1823. He was a native of Massachusetts prior to coming to the town of Thomasville in the 1850s to work in the Lines Shoe Factory. Jackson worked as a shoe cutter and was a member of the Presbyterian church prior to volunteering for service on April 23, 1861. He was reported present until he deserted on April 27, 1862. No further records.

1301. Oakes, John Alexander

Private, Davidson Guards Company A, 21st Regiment N.C. Troops (11th N.C. Volunteers)

John was born in Rockbridge County, Virginia, on March 11, 1835, to John and Lucy Oakes. John was an exceptional student at the University of Virginia, excelling in the areas of religion, history, and Latin. In 1857, he was brought to Davidson County to serve as a tutor for the children of a state representative, Henry Walser. In 1859, he married Henry's youngest daughter, Lucy J. Walser. With the founding of Yadkin College, John was offered a professorship teaching natural

sciences. John and Lucy would have three children: Lucy (1860), and Peter (1863), and Sarah Jane (1865). As a son-in-law of a Confederate congressman, John was exempt from service until, in December 1864, he was pressed into service by an empty college and zealous Home Guardsmen. John enlisted at Camp Godwin, Virginia, on February 9, 1865. He was reported present for the duration of the war and was paroled at Appomattox Court House, Virginia, on April 9, 1865. John returned home to the Yadkin College area, but just as life began to return to normal, he contracted a disease that killed him on May 25, 1866. He is buried in the Walser-Warner Family Cemetery.

1302. Obsesca, Thomas H.

Private, Company H, 57th Regiment N.C. Troops Company C, 1st Regiment U.S. Volunteer Infantry

Thomas was born in 1846, the son of Polish immigrants. He was employed as a laborer prior to enlisting as a substitute in Rowan County on July 4, 1862. He was reported present until captured at Rappahannock Station, Virginia, on November 7, 1863. Thomas was confined at Point Lookout, Maryland, and was admitted to the smallpox hospital on December 5, 1863. He remained at Point Lookout until January 25, 1864, when he was released after taking the oath of allegiance and joining the Union Army. No further records.

1303. Olszewski, Anthony W.

Private, Confederate Guards Company K, 48th Regiment N.C. Troops

Anthony was born in 1844 to Polish immigrants Anthony and Susan Olszewski. He worked as a street peddler in Lexington prior to enlisting on May 1, 1862. Anthony was reported present until captured at Hatcher's Run, Virginia, on March 25, 1865. He was confined at Point Lookout, Maryland, until June 27, 1865, when he was released after taking the oath of allegiance. Anthony returned home and took his business out of the county to Salem in the 1880s. No further records.

1304. O'Neal, David T.

Private, Davidson Guards Company A, 21st Regiment N.C. Troops (11th N.C. Volunteers)

David was born in 1828 in Wadford County, Ireland. He came to Davidson County in the late 1840s and was working as a miner prior to being conscripted into service on June 6, 1863. He deserted sometime prior to September 19, 1864. David was arrested and returned to service; he stood trial on January 17, 1865. He was sentenced to one year of hard labor. David began to serve his term but was hospitalized at Salisbury, North Carolina, on February 12, 1865. He was captured in the hospital during Stoneman's raid on April 12, 1865, and was sent to Louisville, Kentucky. Part of a prison convoy, David and six others escaped while en route to prison on April 29, 1865. No further records.

1305. Orrell, Napoleon Bonaparte

Captain, 66th Regiment N.C. Militia
(1861 organization)
Corporal, Company A, 42nd Regiment
N.C. Troops
Howard's Company, Gibbs' Battalion,
N.C. Prison Guards, Salisbury

Nap was born in 1831. He lived on the small plantation of his grandfather Daniel Orrell, who was a veteran of the War of 1812, having served in the 3rd N.C. Militia. Nap worked as a manager for the plantation, and, on April 28, 1856, he married Christina Motsinger. Nap and Christina would have five children: Leadre (1859), Elizabeth (1862), Hilda

(1866), Daniel (1869), and Emily (1872). On November 26, 1861, Nap accepted a commission as a captain in the Abbott's Creek District Company of the 66th N.C. Militia. He served in this capacity until he volunteered for service in the 42nd Regiment on January 30, 1862. Nap was mustered in as a corporal and served in that post before he was transferred to Howard's Company on May 1, 1862. Nap served as a prison guard for the duration of the war. Nap worked as a merchant in the Browntown/Abbott's Creek township until his death in 1904. He is buried at Abbott's Creek Missionary Baptist Church.

1306. Osborne, Jesse

Private, Company B, 48th Regiment
N.C. Troops

Jesse was born in 1840. He was adopted in the early 1850s by Braswell Burton and lived as a hireling in the vicinity of Thomasville prior to volunteering for service on March 12, 1862. Jesse was reported present throughout his term of service with the 48th Regiment; the last entry that mentions him is dated December 24, 1864. No further records.

1307. Osborne, Zachias

Private, Lexington Wildcats
Company I, 14th Regiment N.C. Troops
(4th N.C. Volunteers)

Zachias was born in 1836. He was adopted in the early 1850s by Anderson Gobble and worked as a farmer in the Tyro area prior to volunteering for service on May 14, 1861. He was reported present until captured at Boonsboro, Maryland, on September 15, 1862. Zachias was confined at Fort Delaware, Delaware, until October 2, 1862, when he was paroled and transferred to Aiken's Landing, Virginia. Zachias was declared exchanged on November 10, 1862, and was returned to service the next day. He died near Fredericksburg, Virginia, on November 24, 1862, of unrecorded causes.

1308. Owen, Alfred

Private, Cabarrus Rangers
Company F, 9th Regiment N.C. Troops
(1st N.C. Cavalry)

Alfred was born on February 18, 1817, to Peter and Margaret Smith Owen. Alfred worked as a small planter in the Cotton Grove area, and, on July 25, 1854, he married Amanda Rowe. Alfred volunteered for service in Cabarrus County, North Carolina, on June 15, 1861. He was reported present in every engagement through December 1864. After the war, Alfred returned home, where he and Amanda would have four surviving children: William and John (1877), George (1879), and Peter (1880). Alfred remained a fairly successful farmer and sharecrop-

Napoleon B. Orrell moved this structure to its present location in the 1890s (Touart, ***Building the Backcountry***).

Alfred Owen in 1862, wearing a six-button sack coat with a roll-down collar and kepi (Barabra Jekins Thompson, *The Heritage of Davidson County*).

ping manager until his death in 1887. He is buried in the Owen Cemetery at the Junior Order Home.

1309. Owen, Alfred

*Private, Chatam Light Infantry
Company G, 48th Regiment N.C. Troops*

Alfred was born in 1832 to James and Barbara Owen. Alfred worked as a farmer, and, on April 1, 1856, he married Rachael Cross. Alfred and Rachael would have two sons, Peter (1857) and James (1860), before Alfred was conscripted into service on August 14, 1862. He was hospitalized at Culpepper, Virginia, on November 4, 1862. Alfred remained in the hospital at Culpepper until he died of unreported causes on December 1, 1862.

1310. Owen, C. Armistead

*Private, Company A, 42nd Regiment
N.C. Troops
Howard's Company, N.C. Prison
Guards, Salisbury*

C. A. was born in 1832. He worked as a farmer in the Cotton Grove area, and, in 1854, he married Charlotte Jarrett. C. A. and Charlotte would have two children, Sylvester (1856) and Walter (1859), before C. A. volunteered for service on November 26, 1861. He was mustered in as a private and served in that capacity until transferred to Howard's Company of prison guards on May 1, 1862. C. A. served the duration of the war as a prison guard at Salisbury, North Carolina. After the war, he returned home where he and Charlotte would have two more surviving children: Robert Lee (1873) and Henry Clay (1878). C. A. worked as a farmer in the Healing Springs township through 1900. No further records.

1311. Owen, Jacob

*Private, Company A, 10th Battalion,
N.C. Heavy Artillery
Company D, 10th Battalion, N.C.
Heavy Artillery*

Jacob was born in 1830 to James and Barbara Owen. Jacob worked as a farmer and a teamster, and, in 1855, he married Eveline. Jacob and Eveline would have two children, Rebecca (1856) and Ellen (1859), before Jacob was conscripted into service on March 19, 1863. Jacob served as a driver for one of the battalion's horse teams. He was transferred to Company D

of the same battalion and served through February 1865. No further records.

1312. Owen, Jesse

*Second Lieutenant, 66th Regiment
N.C. Militia (1861 organization)*

Jesse was born on April 11, 1829, to Mary Owen. Jesse worked as a schoolteacher, and was living in the home of Alex Craver in 1860. He married Mary in 1861 and was commissioned as second lieutenant in the Reeds Cross Roads District Company on February 25, 1862. After his service, Jesse returned to his life and was granted a headmastership in 1870. Jesse served as a teacher in the Tyro township until his death on June 24, 1879. He is buried at Reeds Baptist Church.

1313. Owen, William F.

First Sergeant, Company A, 42nd Regiment N.C. Troops

William was born in 1840 to Mary Owen. William worked as a farmer prior to volunteering for service in Rowan County on March 6, 1862. He was mustered in as a corporal and was promoted to first sergeant in January 1863. William served in this capacity until he was paroled at Greensboro, North Carolina, on May 16, 1865. After the war, William returned home to the Boone township, where, in 1866, he married Mary. William and Mary would have seven children: James (1867), Alfred (1869), William (1871), Minnie (1873), Thomas (1876), Charles (1879), and Mary (1880). No further records.

1314. Owens, Anderson J.

*Second Lieutenant, 65th
Regiment N.C. Militia
(1861 organization)*

Anderson was born in 1827. He worked as a planter in the Cotton Grove area, where, in 1843, he married Nancy. Anderson and Nancy would have nine children: Sarah (1845), Burgess L. (1847), Peter (1850), Susan (1852), Margaret (1857), Robert (1859), James (1861), Mary (1865), and Loveless (1869). Anderson was considered exempt from service due to his age and amount of

personal property; however, it is apparent that he served in the militia, according to an insert in the officer's roster dated May 10, 1862. After the war, Anderson leased some of his land for sharecropping and to other tenant farmers. Anderson died on February 4, 1905. He is buried at Jersey Baptist Church.

1315. Owens, Burgess

*Private, Company C, 70th Regiment
N.C. Troops (1st N.C. Junior
Reserves)*

Burgess was born on September 30, 1846, to Anderson and Nancy Owens. Burgess worked on his father's small plantation prior to enlisting in the Junior Reserves on May 24, 1864. After his term of service, Burgess returned home to the Cotton Grove area, where, on September 17, 1872, he married Fannie Johnson. Burgess and Fannie would move to the Fair Grove area where they lived until Burgess' death on February 18, 1928. He is buried at Fair Grove United Methodist Church.

1316. Owens, Burgess Lindsay

*Private, Holtsburg Guards
Company A, 54th Regiment N.C.
Troops*

Burgess was born in 1844 to Henry and Lourena Owens. Burgess worked as a farmer prior to enlisting in Davidson County on May 14, 1862. He was hospitalized with "remittent fever" in Richmond, Virginia, from December 19, 1862, to February 14, 1863. Burgess returned to service and was reported present until he

Cotton Grove home of Anderson Owens, photographed in 1880 (Touart, *Building the Backcountry*).

was hospitalized again on April 9, 1863, with bronchitis. Burgess died of the disease on April 22, 1863. He is buried at Hollywood Cemetery, Richmond, Virginia.

1317. Owens, Drewry David

Private, Company C, 70th Regiment N.C. Troops (1st N.C. Junior Reserves)

Drewry was born in 1846 to Henry and Lourena Owens. Drewry worked as a farmer prior to enlisting in the Junior Reserves on May 24, 1864. He was paroled at Lynchburg, Virginia, on April 19, 1865. After the war, Drewry returned to the Cotton Grove township where he lived at home, nursing his ailing mother. Drewry married Effie in 1884, and the two would have seven children: Henry (1884), James (1887), Bessie (1891), Emma (1892), Chloe (1893), Walter (1894), and Bertha (1897). No further records.

1318. Owens, George F.

Private, Holtsburg Guards Company A, 54th Regiment N.C. Troops

George was born in 1836 to William and Jane Owens. George worked as a farmer and, prior to 1860, he married Mary. He enlisted for service on May 14, 1862, and was wounded in the face at Fredericksburg, Virginia, on December 13, 1862. George returned to duty on January 20, 1863, and was present for duty until captured at Rappahannock Station, Virginia, on November 7, 1863. George was confined at Point Lookout, Maryland, until he died of disease on February 15, 1864. He is buried at Point Lookout National Cemetery.

1319. Owens, James L.

Private, Company C, 70th Regiment N.C. Troops (1st N.C. Junior Reserves)

James was born in 1846. He worked as a farmer in the Healing Springs area prior to enlisting in the Junior Reserves. After the war, James returned home, where, in 1879, he married Barbara. James and Barbara would have three children: Robert (1882), Lindsay (1885), and Daisy (1889). The family was living in the Healing Springs township in 1900. No further records.

1320. Owens, Martin Van Buren

Private, Company B, 48th Regiment N.C. Troops

Martin was born in 1847, the son of Martin Owens. He was named after the eighth president of the United States. Martin worked as a blacksmith prior to volunteering for service on March 7, 1862. He was reported present until wounded in an unspecified battle, possibly King's School House, Virginia. Martin recovered quickly and was present for duty until he died of disease in a Richmond, Virginia, hospital on October 10, 1864.

1321. Owens, Ralph

Private, Company B, 48th Regiment N.C. Troops

Ralph was born in 1830 to James and Barbara Owens. He worked as a farmer, and, in 1854, he married Elizabeth. Ralph and Elizabeth would have three children, Alfred (1856), Effie (1858), and Margaret (1860), before Ralph was conscripted into service on August 8, 1862. He was reported present through December 1864. In his service records, Major Hill remarked: "Displayed great coolness and courage in the battle of Fredericksburg, Virginia." After the war, Ralph returned home to the Cotton Grove township, where he and Elizabeth would have three more children: Nancy (1865), John (1867), and Eliza (1872). Ralph is buried in the Owens Family Cemetery.

1322. Owens, Richard A.

Private, Davidson Guards Company A, 21st Regiment N.C. Troops (11th N.C. Volunteers)

Richard was born in 1842 to Henry and Lourena Owens. Richard worked as a farmer prior to volunteering for service on May 8, 1861. He died of "enteric fever" in a Front Royal, Virginia, hospital on October 7, 1861.

1323. Pack, Charles

Private, Davidson Guards Company A, 21st Regiment N.C. Troops (11th N.C. Volunteers)

Charles was born in 1843 to Resin and Mary Pack. Charles worked as a mason in the Freidburg area prior to volunteering for service on May 8, 1861. He

died of typhoid fever at Thoroughfare, Virginia, on September 15, 1861.

1324. Pack, David

Musician, Davidson Guards Company A, 21st Regiment N.C. Troops (11th N.C. Volunteers)

David was born in 1832 to Resin and Mary Pack. David worked as a stone mason and was married to Sarah prior to 1860. He volunteered for service on May 8, 1861. David was promoted to musician and served in that position until February 1865. No further records.

1325. Painter, Hiram

Private, Confederate Guards Company K, 48th Regiment N.C. Troops Company H, 15th Regiment N.C. Troops (5th N.C. Volunteers)

Hiram was born in 1834, the son of Jacob Painter. Hiram worked as a farmer in the Clemmonsville area, and in 1859, he married Nancy Jane. Hiram and Nancy would have a child, Sarah (1861), before Hiram was conscripted into service on August 8, 1862. He deserted from service on August 15, 1862. Hiram returned in February 1863. Not surprisingly, a child, Belle (1863), was born as a result of his unauthorized furlough. Hiram was reported present until he was transferred to the 15th Regiment on April 14, 1863, in exchange for William E. Payne. Hiram was captured at Bristoe Station, Virginia, on October 14, 1863, and was confined at Washington, D.C.. He was transferred to Point Lookout, Maryland, on October 27, 1863, where he was confined until February 24, 1865, when he was transferred to Aiken's Landing, Virginia, for exchange. After the war, Hiram returned home to the Clemmonsville area where he and Nancy would have seven more children: Rhonda (1866), Lydia (1867), Jehu (1870), Charles (1872), Mary (1876), Alice (1877), and Lawson (1879). He is buried at New Mount Vernon Baptist Church, Forsyth County, North Carolina.

1326. Painter, Phillip

Private, Davidson Guards Company A, 21st Regiment N.C. Troops (11th N.C. Volunteers)

Phillip was born in 1823 to John and Catharine Painter. Phillip worked as a single farmer and inherited his father's land in the Freidburg area prior to being conscripted into service in Wake County on June 6, 1863. He was reported present until dropped from the rolls of the company prior to March 1, 1865. Apparently, Phillip contracted a serious illness and was given a furlough home, where he died in November 1865. He is buried at Freidburg Moravian Church.

1327. Palmer, George Washington

Lieutenant Colonel, 65th Regiment
    N.C. Militia (1861 organization)
First Sergeant, Holtsburg Guards
Company A, 54th Regiment N.C. Troops

George was born on July 14, 1833, to Abram and Crissie Palmer. George worked as a planter, and, on December 22, 1857, he married Amanda G. Holmes. George and Amanda would have one child, Robert (1859), before George was commissioned to serve as lieutenant colonel of one of Davidson County's two militia units on February 25, 1862. George served in this post until he volunteered for service on May 6, 1862. He was mustered in as a sergeant and was promoted to first sergeant in July 1862. A second child, Anna, was born in 1863. George was wounded severely in the left hand near Fredericksburg, Virginia, on May 4, 1863. He was discharged from service on April 1, 1864, because of disabil-

Colonial-style home of four generations of the Hammet J. Palmer family (Touart, ***Building the Backcountry***).

ity resulting from his wounds. George returned home to the Boone township where he and Amanda would have four more children: John (1867), Laura (1872), Alice (1874), and Hugh (1878). George remained a prominent member of his community, serving as postmaster and as

a county commissioner. George died on December 20, 1915. He is buried at Jersey Baptist Church.

1328. Palmer, Hammet J.

Corporal, Holtsburg Guards
Company A, 54th Regiment N.C. Troops

Hammet was born in 1844 to Abram and Crissie Palmer. He worked as a planter prior to enlisting in Davidson County on September 17, 1862. Hammet was promoted to corporal in May 1863 and was captured at Rappahannock Station, Virginia, on November 7, 1863. Hammet was confined at Point Lookout, Maryland, until March 9, 1864, when he was paroled and transferred to City Point, Virginia, for exchange. Hammet was exchanged on March 15, 1864, and returned to duty the next day. He was wounded at Cedar Creek, Virginia, on October 19, 1864, and was reported present until paroled at Appomattox Court House, Virginia, on April 9, 1865. After the war, Hammet moved to the Silver Hill area, farmed, and worked as a business agent for the Silver Hill mining company. Hammet married Martha Ann in 1867, and they would have three children: Charles (1870), Franklin (1872), and James (1874). Hammet died in 1924. He is buried at Holloways Baptist Church.

George Washington Palmer bought this log house in 1890 and converted it into his home in later life (Touart, ***Building the Backcountry***).

1329. Parks, Albert N.

Private, Company B, 48th Regiment
N.C. Troops

Albert was born in 1839 to Nathan and Elizabeth Parks. He worked for his father, first as a cabinetmaker, then as an undertaker. Albert resided in the Lexington area prior to being conscripted into service on August 8, 1862. Albert was discharged due to "surditas" on November 6, 1862. Albert returned home to Lexington and may have been a member of Hargrave's Home Guards; however, that is not confirmed. Albert married Ellen Lashmit on February 6, 1866. Albert and Ellen would have three children, Mary (1867), Eugene (1868), and Turner (1870), before Albert died in the 1870s. He is buried in the Lexington City Cemetery.

1330. Parks, James A.

First Lieutenant, Company C, 70th
Regiment N.C. Troops (1st N.C.
Junior Reserves)

James was born in 1847 to Isaac and Elizabeth Parks. James worked as a clerk in the Thomasville area and attended the Kennedy School prior to enlisting in the Junior Reserves on May 24, 1864. He was mustered in as first lieutenant and served in that capacity through the rest of the war. After the war, James returned home where he served as a manager for Standard Chair until 1874, then as a salesman for J. H. Lambeth. In 1876, Albert married Victoria Hilton. James and Victoria would have a child, Besse (1886), before moving to Guilford County in the 1890s. No further records.

1331. Parks, John Preston

Private, Chatam Light Infantry
Company G, 48th Regiment N.C. Troops

John was born in 1839 to Isaac and Elizabeth Parks. John was employed as a carpenter prior to being conscripted into service on August 14, 1862. John was killed in action only a month later at Sharpsburg, Maryland, on September 17, 1862. He is buried in Shepherdstown, [West] Virginia.

1332. Parnell, Benjamin

First Lieutenant, Company A, 57th
Regiment N.C. Troops

Benjamin was born in 1828. He worked as a blacksmith in both Davie and Davidson counties during the 1850s and early 1860s. Benjamin enlisted in Rowan County on July 4, 1862, and was appointed to the rank of second lieutenant the same day. Benjamin was placed in charge of the company in September 1862 and served as its commander until February 1863. Benjamin was promoted to first lieutenant on January 9, 1863. He served as first lieutenant until he resigned due to "ill health" on April 10, 1863. Benjamin returned to Lexington for a brief time, then moved to Mocksville where he died in 1867.

1333. Parrish, Ansel

First Lieutenant, 65th Regiment N.C.
Militia (1861 organization)

Ansel was born in 1826. Ansel worked as a farmer in the Conrad Hill area, and, in 1856, he married Melinda Pope. Ansel and Melinda would have five children: Lindsay (1857), Wiley (1859), Ensley (1861), Mary (1866), and James (1871). He was commissioned as first lieutenant in the Hannersville District Company on November 26, 1861. Ansel worked as a farmer in the Conrad Hill/Emmons area through 1880. No further records.

1334. Parrish, Benjamin Franklin

Corporal, Company I, 42nd Regiment
N.C. Troops

Frank was born on November 19, 1843. He worked as a farmer prior to volunteering for service in Rowan County on March 17, 1862. Frank was reported present through August 1862, when he was promoted to sergeant. He was reduced in rank for an unspecified reason in May 1863. Frank earned a promotion to corporal on February 24, 1864, and served through October 1864. After the war, Frank returned home to the Conrad Hill area, where, in 1881, he married Frances Miller. Frank and Frances would have one child, Charlie (1883). Frank moved to the Emmons township in 1900. He would live there until his death on November 23, 1909. He is buried at Pleasant Grove United Methodist Church.

1335. Parrish, James A.

First Lieutenant, 65th Regiment N.C.
Militia (1861 organization)

James was born in 1838 to William and Mary Parrish. James worked as a blacksmith in the Conrad Hill area and was commissioned as first lieutenant in the Conrad Hill District Company on November 25, 1861. After his service, James married Mary E. in 1880. James and Mary would have four children: Grover (1882), Thomas (1885), Margaret (1886), and Endora (1888). The family was last living in the Conrad Hill township in 1900. No further records.

1336. Patterson, William M.

Private, Holtsburg Guards
Company A, 54th Regiment N.C. Troops

William was born in 1839 in Edgefield, South Carolina. He moved in the 1850s to Davidson County where he worked as a farmer in the Cotton Grove area. In 1858, William married Elizabeth. William and Elizabeth would have two children, Mary (1859) and James (1860), before William enlisted into service on May 14, 1862. He was reported present until hospitalized at Charlottesville, Virginia, on July 26, 1864, with "chronic diarrhea." William was transferred to Lynchburg, Virginia, then to Staunton, Virginia, where he rested in a hospital bed. While in the hospital, William contracted typhoid fever; he died of typhoid on October 3, 1864.

1337. Payne, Alfred

Private, Company G, 2nd Battalion,
N.C. Infantry

Alfred was born on February 18, 1835, to Barnabus and Temperance Payne. Alfred worked as a farmer in the North Thomasville township, and, on November 21, 1857, he married Elizabeth Clinard. Alfred and Elizabeth would have two sons, Arthur (1859) and John (1861), before Alfred was conscripted into service in Wake County on June 14, 1864. Alfred was reported present until he was captured at or near Petersburg, Virginia, on March 24, 1865. He was confined at Point Lookout, Maryland, until June 16, 1865, when he was released after taking the oath of allegiance. After the war, Alfred returned home, where he and Elizabeth would have five more children: Barnabus (1867), Alfred (1870), Glendora (1876), William (1878), and Eliza (1879). Alfred lived in the North Thomasville township until his death on March 12, 1915. He is buried at Abbott's Creek Missionary Baptist Church.

1338. Payne, Charles

Private, Company G, 2nd Battalion, N.C. Infantry

Charles was born in 1840 to Barnabus and Temperance Payne. Charles worked as a farmer prior to volunteering for service in Forsyth County on September 19, 1861. He was captured at Roanoke Island, North Carolina, on February 8, 1862. Charles was paroled at Elizabeth City, North Carolina, and returned to service on February 21, 1862. Charles was reported present through December 1862. He died of pneumonia in a Raleigh, North Carolina, hospital on February 11, 1863. He is buried at Abbott's Creek Primitive Baptist Church.

1339. Payne, James C.

Private, Confederate Guards Company K, 48th Regiment N.C. Troops

James was born in 1815. James owned a plantation in northwestern Davidson County, and, in 1841, he married Elizabeth. James and Elizabeth had two sons, Jonathan (1842) and Thomas (1845), who worked as plantation overseers and financial managers. James' plantation was fairly successful prior to his volunteer enlistment on March 26, 1862. James was reported present until he was detailed for service as a provost guard at divisional headquarters for January–April 1864. James was returned to regular duty and was reported present until captured at Appomattox River, Virginia, on April 4, 1865. He was confined at Point Lookout, Maryland, until June 19, 1865, when he was released after taking the oath of allegiance. No further records.

1340. Payne, John Wesley

First Lieutenant, Company G, 2nd Battalion, N.C. Infantry

John was born in 1840 to Barnabus and Keziah Hayworth Payne. John worked as a farmer prior to volunteering for service in Forsyth County, North Carolina, on September 19, 1861. He was appointed first lieutenant on October 1, 1861. John was captured at Roanoke Island, North Carolina, on February 8, 1862. He was confined at Elizabeth City, North Carolina, until paroled on February 21, 1862. John returned to his company but was defeated for reelection when the battalion reorganized on September

Ambrotype of Lt. John Wesley Payne. John returned home when he was defeated for reelection to his post in September 1862 (Mike Gordon).

25, 1862. After his defeat, John returned home to the Abbott's Creek township, where, in 1866, he married Mary. John and Mary would have four children: George W. Denny (1869), Lindsey (1872), John Calhoun (1875), and Alice (1879). John and his family moved a couple of miles north, to Salem, where he continued farming. No further records.

1341. Payne, Jonathan T.

Private, Confederate Guards Company K, 48th Regiment N.C. Troops

John was born in 1842 to James and Elizabeth Payne. John worked as an overseer on his father's plantation prior to being conscripted into service on August 8, 1862. John was reported present for duty until he died of unreported causes at Goldsboro, North Carolina, on June 15, 1863.

1342. Payne, Robert Lee

Surgeon, 65th Regiment N.C. Militia (1861 organization)

Robert was born on December 29, 1831, to Dr. C. L. and Mary A. Payne. Robert graduated from medical school in Philadelphia, Pennsylvania, and began a practice in Lexington upon his return in 1855. Robert worked as a general physician and, in 1856, he married Winnifred T. Robert and Winnifred would have four children: Robert Lee (1857), Mary (1859),

Bessie (1863), and Fannie (1866). Robert was appointed to the position of surgeon of the 65th N.C. Militia on November 26, 1861. Robert served in this capacity and assisted Confederate medical personnel in the Thomasville hospital in the late days of the war after the battles of Averasborough and Bentonville, North Carolina. Robert continued his medical practice in and around the city of Lexington until he was murdered on February 25, 1895. He is buried in the Lexington City Cemetery.

1343. Payne, Solomon

First Sergeant, Company G, 2nd Battalion, N.C. Infantry

Solomon was born on April 15, 1834, to Barnabus and Temperance Payne. Solomon worked as a carpenter prior to volunteering for service in Forsyth County on September 19, 1861. Solomon was mustered in as a sergeant and was reported present until captured at Roanoke Island, North Carolina, on February 8, 1862. He was confined there until paroled at Elizabeth City, North Carolina, on February 21, 1862. Solomon returned to service and was promoted to first sergeant in May 1863. Solomon was captured at Richmond, Virginia, on April 3, 1865. He was confined at Libby Prison, Richmond, Virginia, until April 23, 1865, when he was paroled and released at Newport News, Virginia, after taking the oath of allegiance. After the war, Solomon returned home to the Thomasville township, where, in 1867, he married Phoebe. Solomon and Phoebe would have five children: William (1867), Temperance (1871), Mary (1873), Martha (1875), and John (1879). Solomon worked as a carpenter until his death on July 9, 1916. He is buried at Abbott's Creek Missionary Baptist Church.

1344. Payne, Thomas

Private, Company G, 2nd Battalion, N.C. Infantry

Thomas was born in 1845 to James and Elizabeth Payne. Thomas worked as an overseer on his father's plantation prior to volunteering for service on September 19, 1861. He was captured at Roanoke Island, North Carolina, on February 8, 1862, and was confined until paroled at Elizabeth City, North Carolina, on February 21, 1862, and returned to service. Eight months later, he was discharged due to the age provision of the Conscript Law on November 11, 1862. No further records.

1345. Payne, William E.

Private, Company H, 15th Regiment
N.C. Troops
Private, Confederate Guards
Company K, 48th Regiment N.C.
Troops

William was born in 1843 to James and Elizabeth Payne. William worked as an overseer on his father's plantation, and, on February 20, 1862, he married Parthenia Porter. William and Parthenia were not married long before William was conscripted into service in Wake County on July 15, 1862. William was reported present until he was transferred to the 48th Regiment in exchange for Hiram Painter on April 14, 1863. William deserted on September 10, 1863, returned prior to January 1864, and was reported present until he was captured at Hatcher's Run, Virginia, on April 2, 1865. He was confined at Hart's Island, New York, until June 18, 1865, when he was released after taking the oath of allegiance. After the war, William returned home to his wife. He lived in the area of Davidson that was given to Forsyth County. William died in 1935. He is buried at Old Vernon Methodist Church.

1346. Peace, Lorenzo Edward

Sergeant, Company A, 10th Battalion,
N.C. Heavy Artillery

Lorenzo was born on June 24, 1830, to Joseph and Sarah Peace. Lorenzo worked as a carpenter prior to volunteering for service on April 26, 1862. He was mustered into the artillery as a private and was promoted to sergeant in September 1862. Lorenzo served as a sergeant until he was paroled at Greensboro, North Carolina, on May 9, 1865. After the war, Lorenzo returned to the Thomasville area, where, on July 10, 1879, he married Emma F. Hamner. Lorenzo and Emma would have nine children: William (1880), Joseph (1881–86), James (1883), Walter (1884–86), Nellie (1886), Lenore (1887), Arthur (1890), Cleveland (1892), and Robert Lee (1895). Lorenzo worked as a carpenter until his death on April 26, 1909. He is buried at Pine Woods United Methodist Church.

1347. Peace, William M.

Private, Company A, 10th Battalion,
N.C. Heavy Artillery

William was born in 1844 to Joseph and Sarah Peace. William was employed as an engineer's assistant with the N.C. Railroad prior to volunteering for service on April 26, 1862. William was reported present for service until he died of disease at Fort Campbell, Brunswick County, on February 13, 1864.

1348. Peacock, John Ashley

Private, Company D, 62nd Battalion,
Georgia Cavalry
Company H, 16th Battalion, N.C.
Cavalry

John was born on October 17, 1831, to the Reverend Ansel and Nancy Peacock. John helped his father in the ministry, and, in 1857, he married Mary Ann. John and Mary would have three children, Julian (1858), Branson (1860), and Joel (1862), before he was conscripted into service in October 1864. He was reported present until he was transferred to the 16th N.C. Cavalry in January 1864. John served with the battalion until he was paroled at Greensboro, North Carolina, on May 10, 1865. After the war, John returned home to his farm and family. John and Mary would have three more children: James (1866), Ulysess (1871), and Cecilia (1878). John lived in the Emmons township until his death on August 17, 1893. He is buried at Tom's Creek Primitive Baptist Church.

1349. Peacock, John Leonard

Private, Company F, 56th Georgia
Infantry Regiment

John was born in 1836 in Davidson County. Records of the 56th Georgia indicate that he enlisted or was conscripted into service in February 1865. He is buried in the Lexington City Cemetery. No further records.

1350. Peacock, William

Private, McMillian Artillery
Company C, 36th Regiment N.C. Troops
(3rd N.C. Artillery)

William was born on December 31, 1824. William worked as a horse trainer and farmer in the Emmons township. In 1850, he married Margaret Smith.

William and Margaret would have five children, Frances (1852), Moses S. (1854), Nancy (1857), Barbara (1860), and Sarah (1863), before William was conscripted into service on August 21, 1864. He was hospitalized at Wilmington, North Carolina, between October 24, 1864, and December 2, 1864. William returned to active service, and, a few weeks later, he was captured by Sherman's army during the fall of Savannah on December 21, 1864. William was confined at Hilton Head Island, South Carolina, until transferred to the Federal provost marshal general in New York on January 25, 1865. After the war, William returned home, where he and Margaret would have two more children: John (1867) and Mary Anne (1868). William worked with mules and horses until his death on July 25, 1884. He is buried in the Clear Springs Cemetery.

1351. Peacock, William George

Private, Company E, 5th Regiment
N.C. State Troops

William was born on June 6, 1843, to Betsy Peacock. He worked as a farmer prior to volunteering for service in Rowan County on June 29, 1861. William was reported present until wounded in the left buttock and captured at Cedar Creek, Virginia, on October 19, 1864. He was confined at Point Lookout, Maryland, until November 15, 1864, when he was paroled and transferred to Venus Point, Georgia, for exchange. After the war, William returned home to the Healing Springs township, where, in 1866, he married Martha. William and Martha would have five children: Albert (1867), Samuel (1869), James (1873), Sarah (1878), and Mary (1880). William worked as a farmer until his death on March 28, 1912. He is buried at Macedonia United Methodist Church.

1352. Peacock, William R.

Private, Company F, 7th Regiment
N.C. State Troops

William was born on January 26, 1840, to the Reverend Ansel and Nancy Peacock. William worked as a farmer prior to being conscripted into service in Wake County on November 26, 1863. He was reported present until wounded near Richmond, Virginia, in June 1864. William recovered, rejoined the company in July 1864, and was reported present until he was paroled at Salisbury, North Carolina, on May 16, 1865. After the war, William returned home to the Emmons township, where, on June 1, 1877, he married Martha Avery. William and Martha would have one child, Nancy (1878). William died of pneumonia on September 8, 1896. He is buried at Tom's Creek Primitive Baptist Church.

1353. Pearson, Charles W.

Sergeant, Carolina Rangers
Company B, 10th Virginia Cavalry
*   Regiment*

Charles was born in 1839 to John and Anne Pearson. Charles worked as an engineer for the North Carolina Railroad prior to volunteering for service in Davie County on October 29, 1861. Charles was mustered in as a sergeant, however, in a year and a half, he requested a transfer to the Confederate States Engineer Corps. Charles' request was denied, and he served with the 10th Virginia in all its campaigns. He was last reported present on December 31, 1864, when he received a clothing ration. Charles was paroled at Salisbury, North Carolina, where he moved shortly after the end of the war. No further records.

1354. Peeler, Caleb

Captain, 66th Regiment N.C. Militia
*   (1861 organization)*

Caleb was born on June 5, 1814. Caleb worked as a miller in the northern district of Davidson County, and, in 1840, he married Soloma Rothrock. Caleb and Soloma would have three daughters: Esther (1842), Rosina (1844), and Harriet (1850). Caleb was given a commission as a captain in the Chestnut Grove District Company on December 13, 1861, and served in that capacity until he resigned on January 9, 1865. Caleb operated his farm and mill after the war and converted to the Moravian faith. Caleb died on May 1, 1897. He is buried at Hopewell Moravian Church.

1355. Penaluna, George W.

Private, Davidson Guards
Company A, 21st Regiment N.C.
*   Troops (11th N.C. Volunteers)*

George was born in 1829 in Warwickshire, England. He came to David-

David C. Perrell left this Reedy Creek home in 1862 to serve as a Confederate officer (Touart, *Building the Backcountry*).

son County in the late 1850s with his wife, Mariah, and their daughter, Mary. George worked as a carpenter prior to volunteering for service on May 8, 1861. He died of disease in a Richmond, Virginia, hospital on December 29, 1861. His widow married Jackson Feezor shortly after the end of the war.

1356. Penninger, Monroe

Private, Lexington Wildcats
Company I, 14th Regiment N.C. Troops
*   (4th N.C. Volunteers)*

Monroe was born in 1843. He worked as a farmer in the Lexington area prior to volunteering for service on May 14, 1861. Monroe was reported present until he died of unreported causes on August 20, 1862.

1357. Penry, Richard A.

Private, Lexington Wildcats
Company I, 14th Regiment N.C. Troops
*   (4th N.C. Volunteers)*

Richard was born in 1846 to Eli and Sarah Penry. Richard worked as a farmer prior to volunteering for service at age 15 in Northampton County on May 28, 1861. Richard was assigned to the Lexington Wildcats and served until he was killed in action at Williamsburg, Virginia, on

May 5, 1862. Once news reached the county about its first war casualty being a 16 year old, the citizens gathered at the courthouse to approve a resolution to memorialize this young man.

1358. Perrell, David Crook

Second Lieutenant, Company H, 48th
*   Regiment N.C. Troops*

David was born on May 5, 1839, to Joseph and Elizabeth Hanes Perrell. David worked as a farmer prior to volunteering for service on March 23, 1862. He was mustered in as a sergeant and was reported present until furloughed in December 1862. On January 10, 1863, David married Eliza Hege. David left his wife and returned to service, where he was elected third lieutenant on March 17, 1863. David was promoted to second lieutenant on June 3, 1863. David was wounded when a bullet fractured his left arm at Reams Station, Virginia, on August 25, 1864. He was reported absent, wounded. And then was retired to the Invalid Corps on March 31, 1865. David returned home to the Reeds area, where he and Eliza would have seven children, Jackson (1865), Walter L. (1870), Thomas (1871), Mattie V. (1873), David C. (1875), Flavis L. (1879), and Joshua (1881), before Eliza died in 1912. David married for a second time in 1918, to Mary Huffman. David and Mary would not have any children together. David died on May 26, 1926. He is buried in the Maple Grove Cemetery.

1359. Perrell, Henry James

Private, Company H, 48th Regiment N.C. Troops

Henry was born in 1845 to Joseph and Elizabeth Hanes Perrell. Henry worked as a farmer prior to being conscripted into service at Orange Court House, Virginia, on December 23, 1863. Henry was reported present until captured at Hatcher's Run, Virginia, on April 2, 1865. He was confined at Point Lookout, Maryland, until June 16, 1865, when he was released after taking the oath of allegiance. No further records.

1360. Perry, Alfred M.

Private, Company F, 76th Regiment N.C. Troops (6th N.C. Senior Reserves)

Alfred was born on April 4, 1816, to Temperance Perry. Alfred worked as a farmer in the southern district of Davidson County, and, in 1838, he married Geminah. Alfred and Geminah would have four children: Hezekiah (1839), James M. (1841), Hannah (1842), and Mary (1845). Alfred enlisted in Moss' Senior Reserves and served in the 6th N.C. Senior Reserves in January 1865. After the war, Alfred returned to his family and worked as a farmer until his death on November 27, 1886. He is buried at Fair Grove United Methodist Church.

1361. Perry, James Madison

Private, Company E, 10th Regiment N.C. State Troops (1st N.C. Artillery)

James was born in 1841 to Alfred and Geminah Perry. James worked as a farmer, and, in 1861, he married Louisa Elizabeth. James and Elizabeth would have a daughter, Emma (1862), before James was conscripted into service in Wake County on September 1, 1862. He was reported present through June 1864 and was paroled at Greensboro, North Carolina, on May 10, 1865. After the war, James returned to the Thomasville area where he worked as a farmer, laborer, and carpenter. James and Elizabeth would

have only one more child, Thomas (1875). James died in 1928. He is buried at Fair Grove Methodist Church.

1362. Perryman, Hamilton

Private, Company A, 42nd Regiment N.C. Troops
Howard's Company, Gibbs' Battalion, N.C. Prison Guards, Salisbury
Company B, 10th Virginia Cavalry Regiment

Hamilton was born in 1829 to Jesse and Margaret Perryman. He worked as a farmer prior to volunteering for service on November 26, 1861. Hamilton was transferred to Howard's Company on May 1, 1862. He served as a prison guard at Salisbury until enlisting in Davie County, North Carolina, on February 2, 1864. Hamilton was reported present through December 31, 1864, when he received a clothing ration. He was paroled at Greensboro, North Carolina, on May 9, 1865. After the war, Hamilton returned home to the Arcadia township, where, on March 28, 1865, he married Louisa Wilson. He and Louisa were still living in Davidson County in 1870. No further records.

1363. Perryman, Jesse F.

Private, Company A, 42nd Regiment N.C. Troops

Jesse was born in 1839 to Jesse and Margaret Perryman. Jesse worked as a farmer prior to volunteering for service on November 22, 1861. He was reported present until he died of typhoid fever and bronchitis in Petersburg, Virginia, on November 24, 1862.

1364. Perryman, John

Private, Davidson Guards
Company A, 21st Regiment N.C. Troops (11th N.C. Volunteers)

John was born on October 15, 1834, the son of John Perryman. John worked as a farmer prior to being conscripted into service in Wake County on June 6, 1863. He was reported present until he deserted on October 5, 1864. John made it home, where he was able to evade the Home Guard patrols until the end of the war. After the war, John continued farming in the Midway area, and, on November 12, 1865, he married Rebecca Smith. John and Rebecca would have two chil-

dren living in 1900: Lessie (1883) and John (1889). John died on November 13, 1917. He is buried at Midway United Methodist Church.

1365. Perryman, William F.

Private, Company C, 70th Regiment N.C. Troops (1st N.C. Junior Reserves)

William was born on March 1, 1847, to Jesse and Margaret Perryman. William worked as a farmer prior to enlisting in the Junior Reserves on May 24, 1864. After the war, William returned home, where, in 1865, he married Elizabeth. William and Elizabeth would have two children: Mary (1868) and William (1867). William worked as a farmer until his death on December 8, 1895. He is buried at Mount Olivet United Methodist Church.

1366. Peterson, John M.

Private, Company I, 42nd Regiment N.C. Troops

John was born in 1840 to Ollin and Martha Peterson. John worked as a farmer prior to volunteering for service on March 6, 1862. He was reported present until he died of disease at Weldon, North Carolina, on April 6, 1863.

1367. Peterson, Redding

Private, Company I, 42nd Regiment N.C. Troops

Redding was born in 1845 to Ollin and Martha Peterson. Redding worked as a farmer prior to volunteering for service on March 6, 1862. He died of disease in Salisbury, North Carolina, on May 23, 1862. He is buried in the Old Lutheran Cemetery in Salisbury.

1368. Phelps, Alvin

Private, Company H, 48th Regiment N.C. Troops

Alvin was born in 1836 to Samuel and Catharine Phelps. Alvin worked as a farmer prior to being conscripted into service at Petersburg, Virginia, on August 8, 1862. Alvin was wounded in both thighs at Fredericksburg, Virginia, on December 13, 1862. He recovered from his wounds and returned to duty prior to January 1, 1864. Alvin was reported present until he deserted to the enemy on

March 24, 1865. He was confined at Washington, D.C., until released on an unspecified date after taking the oath of allegiance. Alvin stayed in Washington after the end of the war and was then furnished transportation to Greensboro, North Carolina. Alvin returned home to Clemmonsville, where, on September 9, 1869, he married Mary L. Hauser. Alvin and Mary would have four children: Jane (1871), Ida (1873), John S. (1875), and Mildred (1878). No further records.

1369. Phelps, Erasmus

Private, Company H, 48th Regiment N.C. Troops

Erasmus was born in 1832 to Samuel and Catharine Phelps. Erasmus worked as an overseer for the Davidson County holdings of absentee planter Peter W. Hairston. In 1854, Erasmus married Sarah. Erasmus and Sarah would have three sons, Samuel (1855), Uriah (1856), and George (1860), before Erasmus was conscripted into service at Petersburg, Virginia, on August 8, 1862. He was captured at Sharpsburg, Maryland, on September 17, 1862, and was sent to a U.S. hospital with "intermittent fever" on October 12, 1862. Erasmus was paroled from Fort McHenry, Maryland, six days later and sent to Aiken's Landing, Virginia, for exchange. Erasmus was declared exchanged on November 10, 1862. He was still sick and was sent to a hospital in Washington, North Carolina, shortly after his exchange. Erasmus died of disease at Washington on January 27, 1863.

1370. Phelps, George Washington

Private, Company H, 48th Regiment N.C. Troops

George was born in 1841 to Samuel and Catharine Phelps. George worked as a farmer prior to being conscripted into service at Petersburg, Virginia, on August 8, 1862. He was reported present until captured at Sharpsburg, Maryland, on September 17, 1862. George was confined at Point Lookout, Maryland, until October 16, 1862, when he was paroled and transferred to Aiken's Landing, Virginia, for exchange. He was declared exchanged on November 10, 1862. George returned to service and was reported present until he deserted on December 15, 1864. George returned home, where he died on

May 31, 1869. He is buried at Mount Pleasant Methodist Church in Forsyth County, North Carolina.

1371. Phelps, Spencer

Private, Company H, 48th Regiment N.C. Troops

Spencer was born in 1828 to Samuel and Barbara Phelps. Spencer worked as a single hireling in the northern district of Davidson County prior to volunteering for service at Wagner's on March 3, 1862. He died of disease at Harpers Ferry, [West] Virginia, on September 20, 1862.

1372. Phelps, Thomas

Private, Company H, 48th Regiment N.C. Troops

Thomas was born in 1840 to John and Lucy Phelps. Thomas worked as a hireling prior to volunteering for service at Wagner's on March 3, 1862. He was wounded at King's School House, Virginia, on June 25, 1862. Thomas was taken to a Richmond, Virginia, hospital where he died of his wounds on July 4, 1862. He is buried in the Hollywood Cemetery in Richmond.

1373. Phillips, Henry T.

Corporal, Company C, 70th Regiment N.C. Troops (1st N.C. Junior Reserves)

Henry was born in 1847 to John S. and Margaret Phillips. Henry was a student at Yadkin College prior to enlisting in the Junior Reserves on May 24, 1864. He served as a corporal in the 70th Regiment. After the war, Henry did not complete his education. He began a small mercantile store and then a business in the Yadkin College area. Henry married Louvina Walser in 1876. Henry and Louvina would have two children, Pearl (1877) and Wade Hampton (1880). Henry served as the postmaster for the Yadkin College township in 1880–1902, until mail service was discontinued in the township. Henry died in 1919. He is buried at Yadkin College Methodist Church.

1374. Phillips, McKinney

Private, Company H, 48th Regiment N.C. Troops

McKinney was born in 1836. He worked as a hatter in Lexington prior to

volunteering for service on March 6, 1862. McKinney died of disease in Raleigh, North Carolina, on May 20, 1862.

1375. Phillips, Wesley A.

Private, Company F, 28th Regiment N.C. Troops

Wesley was born on June 28, 1845, to John S. and Margaret Phillips. Wesley worked as a clerk prior to enlisting in Yadkin County as a substitute on April 24, 1862. He was reported present until discharged from service on June 23, 1862, because of "general debility." Afterward, Wesley returned to the Yadkin College township, where, in 1866, he married Mary C. Wesley and Mary would have six children: Delilah (1868), Emmitt (1872), Thomas (1874), Roy (1880), Cora (1886), and William (1888). Wesley was a respected member of the community and a member of Friendship Church. Wesley died on December 30, 1923. He is buried at Friendship United Methodist Church.

1376. Pickard, Aaron

Sergeant, Company G, 2nd Battalion, N.C. Infantry

Aaron was born in 1842. Aaron worked as a hireling in the northern part of Davidson County prior to volunteering for service in Forsyth County on September 19, 1861. He was captured at Roanoke Island, North Carolina, on February 8, 1862. Aaron was confined until February 21, 1862, when he was paroled at Elizabeth City, North Carolina. Aaron returned to service and was appointed sergeant on January 14, 1863. He was admitted to a Richmond, Virginia, hospital with a gunshot wound of the neck on July 14, 1863, and was transferred to Raleigh, North Carolina, the next day. Aaron was granted a furlough from Raleigh in September and October 1863. Aaron recovered and returned to service, but he died of wounds received on July 19, 1864.

1377. Pickett, Alexander

Private, Thomasville Rifles Company B, 14th Regiment N.C. Troops (4th N.C. Volunteers)

Alexander was born on May 20, 1839, to Theophilus and Susan Hege Pickett. Alexander worked as a farmer prior to volunteering for service on May 13, 1861.

He was reported present until he died of typhoid fever in Richmond, Virginia, on June 17, 1862.

1378. Pickett, Alfred Franklin

Private, Company C, 76th Regiment N.C. Troops (6th N.C. Senior Reserves)

Alfred was born on February 2, 1818, to James and Elizabeth Eller Pickett. Alfred worked as a farmer in the Lexington area, and, on November 29, 1843, he married Nancy Koontz. Alfred and Nancy would have five children: Cranford (1847), David (1850), Sarah (1852), Irene (1854), and Yancey (1859). Alfred enlisted in Hill's Senior Reserve Battalion, which became part of the 6th N.C. Senior Reserves in January 1865. After the war, Alfred returned home to his wife and family. Alfred lived in the Lexington township until his death on March 21, 1909. He is buried at Beulah United Church of Christ.

1379. Pickett, David Alexander

Private, Company B, 48th Regiment N.C. Troops

David was born in 1845 to David and Sarah Koontz Pickett. He worked as a farmer prior to volunteering for service in Richmond, Virginia, on September 17, 1862. David was reported present until wounded at Bristoe Station, Virginia, on October 14, 1863. He was taken to a hospital where he died of his wounds on November 7, 1863. A memorial stone was placed in his honor at Beulah United Church of Christ.

1380. Pickett, Eli Thomas

Private, Company B, 48th Regiment N.C. Troops

Eli was born on February 4, 1841, to Theophilus and Susan Hege Pickett. He worked as a farmer prior to volunteering for service on April 3, 1862. Eli was captured at Frederick, Maryland, on September 12, 1862. He was confined at Fort Delaware, Delaware, until he died of smallpox on September 30, 1862.

1381. Pickle, Franklin Alexander

Private, Harnett Light Infantry Company F, 15th Regiment N.C. Troops (5th N.C. Volunteers)

Franklin was born on October 2, 1841, to Joseph and Mary Snider Pickle. Franklin worked as a farmer prior to being conscripted into service in Wake County on July 15, 1862. He was reported present until captured at Bristoe Station, Virginia, on October 14, 1863. Franklin was confined at Point Lookout, Maryland, until March 4, 1865, when he was paroled and transferred to Aiken's Landing, Virginia, for exchange. Apparently, Frank was not exchanged and did not return to service. After the war, Franklin returned home to the Arcadia township, where, on January 17, 1867, he married Elizabeth Hill Spaugh. Franklin and Elizabeth would have four children: Ada (1869), Emory (1872), Joseph (1875), and Frances (1877). Franklin died on January 17, 1923. He is buried at Good Hope United Methodist Church.

1382. Pierce, Strickland

Corporal, Company H, 48th Regiment N.C. Troops

Strickland was born in 1822. He worked as a farmer in the Conrad Hill area prior to volunteering for service on March 6, 1862. Strickland was reported present until he was killed in action at White Oak Swamp, Virginia, on June 15, 1864.

1383. Pitts, George I.

Private, Company F, Colonel Mallet's Battalion (Camp Guards)

George was born on September 28, 1838. He worked as a farmer in the Browntown area prior to serving in Mallet's Battalion. According to cemetery records, George died while in service on December 2, 1863. He is buried at Abbott's Creek Primitive Baptist Church.

1384. Pitts, Harrison

Private, Confederate Guards Company K, 48th Regiment N.C. Troops Company H, 15th Regiment N.C. Troops (5th N.C. Volunteers)

Harrison was born in 1828. Harrison worked as a carpenter in the Abbott's Creek area, and, in 1855, he married Sarah. Harrison and Sarah would have two children, William (1857) and Frances (1860), before Harrison volunteered for service in Forsyth County on March 26, 1862. He was reported present until June 17, 1863, when he was transferred to the 15th Regiment in exchange for James McRae. After the war, Harrison was reported present with the 15th North Carolina until August 18, 1863, when he deserted from a hospital in Richmond, Virginia. Harrison and his family lived in the Abbott's Creek township, and in 1870, Harrison was one of the finest cabinet-makers in the county. Harrison and his family moved to Winston, North Carolina, in the early 1900s. No further records.

1385. Pope, George Washington

Sergeant, Company B, 48th Regiment N.C. Troops

George was born in 1821 to John and Sarah Pope. George worked as a carpenter and blacksmith in the Conrad Hill area, and, on August 21, 1849, he married Catharine Johnson. George volunteered for service on March 7, 1862, and was mustered in as a private. He was promoted to sergeant on January 1, 1863, and served in that capacity through April 1864. On May 17, 1864, he was admitted to a Staunton, Virginia, hospital with a gunshot wound. George died of his wound three days later.

1386. Pope, John A.

Private, Company C, 70th Regiment N.C. Troops (1st N.C. Junior Reserves)

John was born in 1846 to Elijah and Nancy Pope. John worked in a Thomasville shoe shop prior to enlisting in the Junior Reserves on May 24, 1864. After the war, John returned home to the town of Thomasville where, in 1868, he married Martha. John and Martha would have three children die in early infancy in the 1870s and 1880s. In 1880, John was working as a carpenter; he was employed by Standard Chair in 1900. John and Martha had one son in 1890, William. The family moved to High Point in the 1910s. No further records.

1387. Pope, Sherman

First Lieutenant, 66th Regiment N.C. Militia (1861 organization)

Sherman was born in 1827 to John and Sarah Pope. Sherman worked as a farmer in the Midway area, and in 1849, he married Sarah. Sherman and Sarah would have three children: William Preston (1850), Sarah (1853), and Belinda (1864). Sherman was commissioned as first lieutenant in the Bethany District Company on an unspecified date. After the war, Sherman continued farming and was listed as a teacher at Bethany Reform Sunday school. Sherman died sometime after 1880. No further records.

1388. Porter, Gillam

Private, Confederate Guards
Company K, 48th Regiment N.C. Troops

Gillam was born in 1842 to Lawrence and Matilda Porter. He worked as a farmer in the northern district of the county prior to being conscripted into service on August 8, 1862. Gillam was shot through the foot and captured at Sharpsburg, Maryland, on September 17, 1862. He was confined at Frederick, Maryland, until October 23, 1862, when he was paroled and transferred to Aiken's Landing, Virginia, for exchange. Gillam was declared exchanged on November 10, 1862. He was detailed as a driver and a litter bearer for the ambulance corps of the 2nd Army Corps in January–April 1864. From July through October 1864, Gillam served in the corps hospital as an attendant. Gillam returned to regular service in January 1865 and was reported present until captured at Amelia Court House, Virginia, on April 5, 1865. He was confined at Point Lookout, Maryland, until June 16, 1865, when he was released after taking the oath of allegiance. No further records.

1389. Porter, Thomas A.

Private, Confederate Guards
Company K, 48th Regiment N.C. Troops

Thomas was born in 1834 to Lawrence and Matilda Porter. Thomas worked as a farmer, and, on September 20, 1859, he married Elmira Shuler. Thomas and Elmira had a daughter, Cynthia (1860), before Thomas was conscripted into service on August 8, 1862. He was reported present until captured at Petersburg, Virginia, on October 27, 1864. Thomas was confined at Point Lookout, Maryland, until May 14, 1865, when he was released after taking the oath of allegiance. After the war, Thomas and his wife moved to Forsyth County. No further records.

1390. Powell, Daniel

Second Lieutenant, 65th Regiment
N.C. Militia (1861 organization)

Daniel was born in 1835. He was given a commission to serve as a second lieutenant in the Reedy Creek District Company on October 1, 1861. No further records.

1391. Powers, Lewis Edward

Third Lieutenant, Davidson Guards
Company A, 21st Regiment N.C. Troops
(11th N.C. Volunteers)

Lewis was born in 1842 and was living with H. C. Walser before he attended Yadkin College in 1860. Lewis volunteered for service on May 8, 1861, and was mustered in as a private. Lewis was elected as third lieutenant on May 25, 1862. He was wounded in the fingers and thumb of the left hand at Sharpsburg, Maryland, on September 17, 1862. Lewis returned in October and served until wounded once again at Fredericksburg, Virginia, on December 13, 1862. Lewis recovered from his wounds and returned to duty in February 1863. He would be wounded once more, at Liberty, Virginia, prior to being paroled at Appomattox Court House, Virginia, on April 9, 1865. No further records.

1392. Primm, John M.

Private, Holtsburg Guards
Company A, 54th Regiment N.C. Troops

John was born in 1834. John worked as a miner at Silver Hill, and, on August 22, 1854, he married Celia A. Gallimore. John and Celia would have three children, Albert (1857), Maria (1860), and Maggie (1862), before John enlisted on April 23, 1862. He was reported present until September 10, 1862, when he was detailed to serve as a lead miner in Davidson County. John worked as a miner for the Confederate Army for the duration of the war. Although John was able to stay at home, the work in the mines was still dangerous. After the war, John and Celia would have three more children: Nancy (1866), John (1869), and Nannie (1870). John worked as a miner and lived in the Silver Hill area until his death on September 11, 1914. He is buried at Holloways Baptist Church.

1393. Proctor, Andrew Jackson

Private, Company H, 15th Regiment
N.C. Troops (5th N.C. Volunteers)

Andrew was born in 1835 to John and Mary Proctor. Andrew worked as a blacksmith in the Midway area, and in 1861, he married Bessie Susan. Andrew and Bessie would have a daughter, Jane (1862), before Andrew was conscripted into service in Wake County on July 15, 1862. He was reported present for every engagement fought by the 15th Regiment through October 1864. Andrew was paroled at Greensboro, North Carolina, on May 4, 1865. After the war, Andrew returned to the Midway township where he continued his blacksmithing trade. He and Bessie would have four more children: Mary (1866), Randolph (1868), Sophia (1873), and James (1874). Andrew died in 1917. He is buried at Bethany United Church of Christ.

1394. Proctor, Britton

Private, Confederate Guards
Company K, 48th Regiment N.C. Troops
Company K, 1st Regiment U.S. Volunteer Infantry

Britton was born in 1836 to William and Lanie Proctor. Britton worked as a farmer and laborer in the Abbott's Creek area, and, on August 19, 1855, he married Margaret James. He volunteered for service in Forsyth County on March 18, 1862, and was reported present until wounded in the shoulder at Fredericksburg, Virginia, on December 13, 1862. Britton recovered from his wound by January 1863 and was reported present until captured at Cold Harbor, Virginia, on June 3, 1864. He was confined at Point Lookout, Maryland, until June 14, 1864, when he took the oath of allegiance and joined the Union Army. Britton was mustered into Company K, 1st U.S. Volunteers, a unit of southerners who volunteered to fight for the Union, on the same day. No further records.

1395. Proctor, Joseph S.

Private, Company A, 42nd Regiment
N.C. Troops

Joseph was born in 1842 to Britton and Ruth Proctor. Joseph worked as a farmer prior to volunteering for service in Rowan County on March 15, 1862. He died of "typhoid pneumonia" at Petersburg, Virginia, on December 25, 1862.

1396. Proctor, Wyatt Randall

Private, Company A, 42nd Regiment N.C. Troops

Wyatt was born in 1845 to William and Lanie Proctor. He worked as a carpenter prior to volunteering for service in Rowan County on March 17, 1862. Wyatt was reported present until captured at Battery Anderson, Fort Fisher, North Carolina, on December 25, 1864. He was confined at Point Lookout, Maryland, via Fort Monroe, Virginia, until June 3, 1865, when he was released after taking the oath of allegiance. After the war, Wyatt returned home, where he began making furniture and cabinets. In 1878, Wyatt married Louisa. Wyatt and Louisa would have four children, Minnie (1879), Jane (1880), Caroline (1884), and Franklin (1886), before moving out of the county in the early 1900s. No further records.

1397. Pugh, James A.

Private, Company C, 70th Regiment N.C. Troops (1st N.C. Junior Reserves)

James was born in 1846 to James Edward and Lydia Pugh. Like his father, James worked as a blacksmith before he enlisted in the Junior Reserves on May 24, 1864. After the war, James returned to the town of Lexington, where, on March 24, 1867, he married Caroline J. Hall. James and Caroline would have four children: John (1869), Sirona (1871), and Minnie and Mary (1877). James continued his trade through the early 1900s. No further records.

1398. Pugh, John B.

Captain, 65th Regiment N.C. Militia (1861 organization)

John was born in 1832 to James Edward and Lydia Pugh. He worked as a brick mason in the town of Thomasville prior to being commissioned as a lieutenant in the Thomasville District Company on November 25, 1861. Sometime after the war and prior to 1870, he moved to Randolph County. No further records.

1399. Rachel, Eli Alexander

Private, Company F, 7th Regiment N.C. State Troops

Eli was born in 1836 to Alexander and Mary Rachel. His father was a veteran of the War of 1812. Eli worked as a farmer, and, on April 4, 1858, he married Temperance Russell. Eli and Tempy would have two children, James (1858) and Mary (1862), before Eli volunteered for service on March 1, 1862. He was reported present until hospitalized at Richmond, Virginia, with a serious gunshot wound of the left arm on May 9, 1863. Eli had received this wound at Chancellorsville, Virginia, and was reported absent, wounded, until he was discharged from service on December 14, 1863. Eli returned home where he and Tempy would have another child, William (1867), before he moved his family to Arkansas in 1877. While in Arkansas, Tempy died in 1886, and Eli married Nancy Martin in 1888. Eli and Nancy would have a child, Sallie Mae (1889). Eli died on an unspecified date in Polk County, Arkansas.

1400. Raker, David

Private, Thomasville Rifles
Company B, 14th Regiment N.C. Troops (4th N.C. Volunteers)

David was born in 1841. He worked as a farmer prior to volunteering for service on April 27, 1861. David was reported present until he was apparently furloughed where he died of disease at home on November 14–15, 1862.

1401. Raper, Elisha

Sergeant Major, Staff, 48th Regiment N.C. Troops

Elisha was born on December 25, 1822, to William and Anne Raper. Elisha was educated at Trinity College, and on February 24, 1857, he married Paulina B. Tesh. They had one child, Charles (1859), while Elisha worked as an overseer for Peter Hairston's plantation prior to being conscripted into service at Camp Holmes, Wake County, on August 21, 1863. Another child, Emsley, was born in 1864. Elisha was reported present until promoted to sergeant major of the regiment prior to October 31, 1864. Elisha served in this capacity through the end of the war. After the war, Elisha and Paulina would have four more children: Julius (1866), Albert (1869), Edward (1873), and Samuel (1877). In the decades of the 1870s and 1880s, Elisha was con-spicuous in public life. He served as the county examiner for two terms and was a county commissioner from the Enterprise area of the county. Elisha died on December 27, 1910. He is buried at Mount Olivet United Methodist Church.

1402. Raper, Joseph Madison

Private, Company D, 62nd Battalion, Georgia Cavalry
Company H, 16th Battalion, N.C. Cavalry

Joseph was born on April 23, 1827, to William and Anne Raper. Joseph worked as a successful merchant, and in 1853, he married Sarah Jane Spurgeon. Joseph and Sarah would have one child, William (1855), before Joseph was conscripted into service in January 1864. He rode in the 62nd Georgia Cavalry prior to being transferred to the 16th N.C. Cavalry on June 11, 1864. Joseph was reported present until he was paroled at Greensboro, North Carolina, on May 20, 1865. After the war, Joseph returned to his business, which had been run by his wife in his absence. In 1879, Sarah died, and Joseph married Eliza J. Teague in 1880. Joseph and Eliza would have two children: Minnie (1881) and Sidney (1885). Joseph died on December 23, 1891. He is buried at Abbott's Creek Missionary Baptist Church.

1403. Raper, Peter William

Private, North State Boys
Company K, 45th Regiment N.C. Troops

Peter was born in 1832 to William and Anne Raper. Peter worked as a farmer prior to being conscripted into service on October 24, 1864. He was reported present through February 1865. No further records.

1404. Raper, Samuel A.

Sergeant, North State Boys
Company K, 45th Regiment N.C. Troops

Samuel was born in 1839 to William and Anne Raper. Samuel worked as a farmer in the Abbott's Creek area, and in 1861, he married Louisa Swaim. He enlisted into service on May 16, 1862, and was promoted to corporal on November 1, 1862. Samuel was wounded in the left elbow and captured at Gettysburg, Pennsylvania, on July 3, 1863. He was confined at David's Island, New York, until September 8, 1863, when he was paroled and transferred to City Point, Virginia, for exchange. Samuel was declared exchanged, and sometime prior to October 31, 1864, he was promoted to sergeant. Samuel was captured at Petersburg, Virginia, on April 2, 1865. He was confined at Point Lookout, Maryland, until June 19, 1865, when he was released after taking the oath of allegiance. Samuel and Louisa would only have one child, George (1867), who died tragically from a fall at the age of 22. Samuel lived in the Abbott's Creek township until his death in 1913. He is buried at Abbott's Creek Primitive Baptist Church.

1405. Raper, William D.

Private, Company D, 62nd Battalion, Georgia Cavalry
Company H, 16th Battalion, N.C. Cavalry

William was born on January 9, 1825, to William and Anne Raper. William worked as a merchant, and on September 28, 1853, he married Mary E. Motsinger. William and Mary would have three children, Marticia (1856), David (1859), and Mary Belle (1862), before William was conscripted into service in January 1864. He rode in the 62nd Georgia Cavalry prior to being transferred to the 16th N.C. Cavalry on June 11, 1864. William was reported present until he was paroled at Greensboro, North Carolina, on May 20, 1865. After the war, William returned

home to the Arcadia township, where he and Mary would have four more children: William (1865), Sarah (1867), Martha (1870), and Endora (1875). William lived in the Arcadia township until his death on February 2, 1887. He is buried at Mount Olivet United Methodist Church.

1406. Ratts, Thomas O.

Corporal, Company A, 42nd Regiment N.C. Troops

Thomas was born on January 21, 1839, to Obediah and Catharine Sink Ratts. Thomas worked as a farmer in the Tyro area prior to volunteering for service on November 26, 1861. He was mustered in as a private and was promoted to corporal prior to July 1, 1862. Thomas was reported present until captured at Battery Anderson, Fort Fisher, North Carolina, on December 25, 1864. He was confined at Fort Delaware, Delaware, via Fort Macon, North Carolina, until June 19, 1865, when he was released after taking the oath of allegiance. After the war, Thomas returned home, where, on February 11, 1867, he married Cornelia Koontz. Thomas and Cornelia would have four children, Henry (1870), Catharine (1874), Walter (1878), and Myrtle (1884), before Cornelia died in 1885. Thomas married Lou C., and they would have five children: Gray (1889), Addie (1893), Jessie (1894), Minnie (1896), and Maude (1899). Thomas lived in the Tyro

township until his death on June 1, 1917. He is buried at Wesley's Chapel Methodist Church.

1407. Redman, John T.

Private, Carolina Rangers
Company B, 10th Virginia Cavalry Regiment

John was born in 1840 to William and Catharine Redman. John was a student prior to volunteering for service in Davie County, North Carolina, on October 29, 1861. He was present until reported absent, sick, from May through August 1863. John returned to service and was reported present until assigned to a horse detail on August 25–31, 1864. John was reported present through January 29, 1865. He was paroled at Mocksville, North Carolina, on June 9, 1865. No further records.

1408. Redwine, Green David

Third Lieutenant, Company F, 7th Regiment N.C. State Troops
Company I, 42nd Regiment N.C. Troops

Green was born on October 27, 1832, to David and Frances Redwine. Green worked as a carpenter prior to volunteering for service in Rowan County on June 29, 1861. He was mustered in as a private and was reported present until wounded in action on June 27, 1862.

Arcadia home of cavalryman, William D. Raper (Touart, *Building the Backcountry*).

Green D. Redwine served in Company F of the 7th N.C. State Troops before becoming an officer in the 42nd N.C. Troops (Nelson, *John, Sarah, and Other Redwines*).

Abagail Kearns, wife of Green D. Redwine (Nelson, *John, Sarah, and Other Redwines*).

Healing Springs planter and justice of the peace, William P. Redwine (Nelson, *John, Sarah, and Other Redwines*).

Clarinda, wife of William P. Redwine (Nelson, *John, Sarah, and Other Redwines*).

Green was reported absent, wounded, and then promoted to third lieutenant and transferred to the 42nd Regiment on December 23, 1862. Green was reported present with the 42nd N.C. through October 1864. After the war, Green returned home, where, on January 4, 1866, he married Abagail Kearns. Green and Abagail would have a daughter, Sallie (1866), before they moved to Arkansas. Green and his family settled in Cavanaugh, Arkansas, where Green began his own furniture-making company. Green and Abagail would have five more children: Lillian (1869), Robert Lee (1871), John (1874), Laura (1878), and Emma (1881). Green remained in Arkansas until his death on October 11, 1902. He is buried in the Fort Smith Cemetery in Cavanaugh.

1409. Redwine, James Madison

*Private, Company F, 7th Regiment
N.C. State Troops*

James was born in 1843 to David and Frances Redwine. James worked as a farmer prior to volunteering for service in Alamance County on August 19, 1861. He was reported present until he died while at home on sick furlough on September 23, 1862. James was buried at Lane's Chapel United Methodist Church in Montgomery County, North Carolina.

1410. Redwine, Jesse T.

*Private, Company C, 70th Regiment
N.C. Troops (1st N.C. Volunteers)*

Jesse was born in 1847 to William A. and Sarah Redwine. Jesse worked as a manager on his father's plantation prior to enlisting in the Junior Reserves on May 24, 1864. After the war, Jesse returned home to the Allegheny township, where, in 1875, he married Isabella Reeves. Jesse and Isabella would have one son: James Albert (1878). Jesse worked as a farmer until his death in 1881. He is buried at Lane's Chapel United Methodist Church in Montgomery County, North Carolina.

1411. Redwine, William Anderson

*Captain, 65th Regiment N.C. Militia
(1861 organization)*

William was born in 1825 to Jesse and Mary Noah (Nooe) Redwine. William married Sarah in 1843 and began work on his plantation. By 1860, the Redwine plantation was producing tobacco with the labor of 22 slaves and also contained a water-powered grist mill and horse stables. William and Sarah would have nine children, including two sets of twins: Jesse T. (1847), Nancy (1850), Sarah (1853), Mary (1856), Rebecca (1861), Vance and Polly (1865), and John and Adeline (1868). William was commissioned to serve as the captain of the

Rock Spring District Company on November 25, 1861. After the war, William converted half of his plantation into sharecropping lands. William lived in the Allegheny township until his death on July 4, 1875.

1412. Redwine, William Pinkney

*Second Lieutenant, 65th Regiment
N.C. Militia (1861 organization)
Private, Company F, 7th Regiment
N.C. State Troops*

William was born on March 29, 1836, to Michael and Nancy Redwine. William worked as a planter, and, on November 24, 1852, he married Clarinda Margaret. His plantation was fairly successful, and he was able to obtain a commission as a second lieutenant in the Lick Creek District Company on November 26, 1861. On June 29, 1862, William enlisted in Alamance County, North Carolina. He was reported present with the 7th N.C. State Troops until wounded in the left foot at Gettysburg, Pennsylvania, on July 1, 1863. William recovered from his wounds and returned to service in January 1864. He was reported present through October 1864. William and Clarinda would only have two children who survived infancy: Anne (1856) and James (1867). William lived in the Healing Springs township until his death on February 28, 1905. He is buried at Lick Creek Baptist Church.

1880s photograph of the Redwine homeplace. Seated is William P. Redwine (Nelson, *John, Sarah, and Other Redwines*).

1413. Reece, Enoch W.

*Private, Confederate Guards
Company K, 48th Regiment N.C. Troops
Company K, 1st Regiment U.S. Volunteer Infantry*

Enoch was born in 1833 to John W. and Susan Reece. Enoch worked as a farmer in the Browntown area prior to being conscripted into service on August 8, 1862. He deserted on September 2, 1862, and he returned to service in June 1863. Enoch was reported present until captured at Cold Harbor, Virginia, on June 3, 1864. He was confined at Point Lookout, Maryland, until June 14, 1864, when he was released after taking the oath of allegiance and joining the Union Army. Enoch was assigned to Company K, 1st U.S. Volunteer Infantry. No further records.

1414. Reeves, Elisha M.

*Private, Montgomery Boys
Company K, 34th Regiment N.C. Troops*

Elisha was born on July 1, 1841. He worked as a farmer prior to volunteering for service in Montgomery County, North Carolina, on September 9, 1861. Elisha was reported present until he was captured at Petersburg, Virginia, in March 1865. He was paroled at Farmville, Virginia, on April 11, 1865. After the war,

Elisha returned to the Allegheny township, where, in 1867, he married Delphina Morris. Elisha and Delphina would have four children: William (1867), Erasmus (1869), Edgar (1873), and Minnie (1876). In 1880, Elisha was a sharecropper, renting land and a house from Henry Turner. It is unclear if Elisha remained in this line of work; however, he lived in the Allegheny township until his death on February 7, 1923. He is buried at Clear Springs Baptist Church.

1415. Reid, Calvin Henry

Sergeant, Company F, 7th Regiment N.C. State Troops

Calvin was born in 1841 to Richmond and Eliza Reid. Calvin worked as an overseer on his father's plantation prior to volunteering for service in Rowan County on June 27, 1861. He was mustered in as a private and was promoted to sergeant on June 30, 1863. Calvin only served for a brief period as a sergeant as he was wounded in the leg during Pickett's charge at Gettysburg, Pennsylvania, on July 3, 1863. He was shot down and captured by members of a Vermont regiment and was taken to a field hospital. Calvin's left leg was amputated, but he died of infection on August 13, 1863. His body now lies in Oakwood Cemetery in Raleigh, North Carolina.

1416. Reid, David H.

Second Lieutenant, Company I, 42nd Regiment N.C. Troops

David was born on December 20, 1838, to George and Mary Eller Reid. David worked as a carpenter prior to volunteering for service in Rowan County on March 18, 1862. He was appointed second lieutenant on May 23, 1862, and was reported present until he offered his resignation on August 4, 1862, due to "suffering of chronic bronchitis." His resignation was accepted on August 11, 1862. David returned to the Beulah area where, on January 1, 1867, he married Drusilla Shoaf. David and Drusilla would have 11 children: Virginia (1869), Jennie (1871), William (1872), George (1874), John (1877), Hattie (1879), Marshall (1882), Etta (1885), Fred (1889), Glenn (1891), and Holland (1895). David lived in the Lexington township until his death on May 8, 1904. He is buried at Beulah United Church of Christ.

1417. Reid, George Washington

*Private, Lexington Wildcats
Company I, 14th Regiment N.C. Troops
(4th N.C. Volunteers)*

George was born in 1836 to George and Mary Eller Reid. George worked as a farmer prior to volunteering for service on May 14, 1861. He was reported present until wounded in the right leg at Spotsylvania Court House, Virginia, on May 12, 1864. George was sent to a Richmond, Virginia, hospital where he recovered from his serious wound; he was captured on April 3, 1865. George was taken from his hospital bed to Libby Prison in Richmond, where he was confined until he was released on June 30, 1865, after taking the oath of allegiance. No further records.

1418. Reid, Jesse

Sergeant, Company F, 7th Regiment N.C. State Troops

Jesse was born in 1835 to Richmond and Eliza Reid. Jesse was employed as a merchant in the Allegheny township prior to being conscripted into service in Iredell County, North Carolina, on August 20, 1862. He was promoted to sergeant on September 1, 1864. Jesse served as a sergeant until he died of disease at Farmville, Virginia, on April 4,

1865, just five days before the end of the war. His body was transported to Lexington and he was buried at Lick Creek Baptist Church.

1419. Reid, John H.

Private, Company F, 7th Regiment N.C. State Troops

John was born in 1838 to Richmond and Eliza Reid. John worked as an overseer on his father's plantation prior to volunteering for service in Rowan County on July 5, 1861. He was reported present until wounded in a skirmish on September 20, 1864. John died of his wounds on October 5, 1864. A stone was placed in his honor at Lick Creek Baptist Church.

1420. Rhidenhour, Anderson J.

*Private, Davie Greys
Company F, 13th Regiment N.C. Troops (3rd N.C. Volunteers)*

Anderson was born in 1830. Anderson worked as a farmer prior to being conscripted into service in Davie County on July 16, 1862. He was reported present until wounded at Gettysburg, Pennsylvania, on July 1, 1863. Anderson was captured and was confined at Chester, Pennsylvania, for a short time before dying of dysentery.

1421. Rhidenhour, John W.

Private, Company F, 13th Regiment N.C. Troops (3rd N.C. Volunteers)

John was born in 1833. John worked as a farmer prior to being conscripted into service on January 20, 1863. He was wounded and captured at Gettysburg, Pennsylvania, on July 1, 1863. John was hospitalized at Chester, Pennsylvania, until he died of "traumatic shock" on August 12, 1863.

1422. Rhodes, Jesse Franklin

Private, Company B, 48th Regiment N.C. Troops

Jesse was born in 1839 to Levi and Sophia Rhodes. Jesse worked as a farmer, and, on August 6, 1859, he married Susan Beck. Jesse was conscripted into service on August 8, 1862. He died of "diarrhea chronic" at Staunton, Virginia, on November 5, 1862.

1423. Rhodes, John A.

Private, Company B, 48th Regiment N.C. Troops

John was born in 1843 to Levi and Sophia Rhodes. John worked as a farmer prior to volunteering for service on March 6, 1862. He deserted from service in September 1862. John returned to service on March 1, 1863. He was reported present until killed in action at Bristoe Station, Virginia, on October 14, 1863.

1424. Rice, Robert

Private, Company D, 48th Regiment N.C. Troops

Robert was born in 1822. Robert lived in the Conrad Hill area prior to enlisting into service as a substitute on August 8, 1862. He deserted from camp on August 13, 1862. No further records.

1425. Rick, William

First Lieutenant, 65th Regiment N.C. Militia (1861 organization)

William was born in 1813. He worked as a single farmer in the southern district of Davidson County. William was commissioned to serve as first lieutenant in the Lick Creek District Company on November 25, 1861. Prior to 1870, William moved to Randolph County. No further records.

1426. Rickard, Emanuel

Private, Company B, 48th Regiment N.C. Troops

Emanuel was born in 1841 to George and Mary M. Rickard. Emanuel worked as a miller in the Lexington area prior to volunteering for service on March 7, 1862. He was reported as missing in action at Sharpsburg, Maryland, on September 17, 1862. He was later placed on the rolls as a deserter until he returned to duty prior to October 31, 1864. Emanuel was present until he was paroled at Appomattox Court House, Virginia, on April 9, 1865. No further records.

1427. Rickard, Israel J. E.

First Lieutenant, 65th Regiment N.C. Militia (1861 organization)

Israel was born on November 19, 1830, to John and Esther Rickard. Israel worked as a farmer in the Thomasville area, and on November 26, 1861, he accepted a commission to serve as first lieutenant in the Thomasville District Company. On April 21, 1864, Israel married Anna E. Lambeth. Israel and Anna would have five children: Jesse (1864), Annie (1866), Sarah (1874), and Julie and Esther (1877). Israel continued farming in the Thomasville township and operated a sawmill as a side business. Israel died on September 6, 1896. He is buried at Emanuel United Church of Christ.

1428. Rickard, James B.

Private, Company B, 57th Regiment N.C. Troops

James was born in 1837 to George and Mary M. Rickard. James worked as a miller in the Lexington area, and, in 1860, he married Rebecca Amanda. He enlisted for service in Rowan County on July 4, 1862. James was reported present on detail as a teamster through October 31, 1864. James returned to regular service and was reported present until wounded in the abdomen at Fort Stedman, Virginia, on March 25, 1865. He was transported to Richmond, Virginia, where he was captured after the city's fall on April 3, 1865. James was confined at Point Lookout, Maryland, until June 26, 1865, when he was released after taking the oath of allegiance. After the war, James returned to the Lexington area and moved to Cotton Grove in 1867. James lived in the Cotton Grove township until his death in 1922. He is buried at Center Hill Baptist Church.

1429. Rickard, Lewis

Private, Company B, 48th Regiment N.C. Troops

Lewis was born in 1840 to George and Mary M. Rickard. Lewis worked as a farmer in the Lexington area prior to volunteering for service on March 6, 1862. He was reported present through April 1864. The rosters contain no further information after that period; however, a muster found in a private collection indicates that Lewis was killed in action at Wilderness, Virginia, on May 5 or 6, 1864.

1430. Rickard, Peter S.

Private, Company B, 48th Regiment N.C. Troops

Peter was born in 1840 to Leonard and Barbara Rickard. Peter worked as a miller prior to volunteering for service on March 3, 1862. He was reported present until he was discharged due to "epilepsy" on February 16, 1863. Peter returned home to the Silver Hill area, where, on March 8, 1868, he married Rebecca Whitaker. Peter and Rebecca would have four children, Louisa (1869), Laura (1874), Barbara (1876), and John Edgar (1878), before the family moved out of the county in the 1890s. No further records.

1431. Riggins, James Madison

Private, Confederate Guards
Company K, 48th Regiment N.C. Troops

James was born in 1843 to Lucy Riggins. James worked as a farmer prior to being conscripted into service on August 8, 1862. He was wounded in the left shoulder at Fredericksburg, Virginia, on December 13, 1862. James was reported absent, wounded, through April 1864. No further records.

1432. Riggins, John Isham

Second Lieutenant, 66th Regiment
*   N.C. Militia (1861 organization)*

John was born in 1828. John worked as a blacksmith in the northern district of Davidson County. In 1852, John married Emily Leonard. John and Emily would have three children: Florence (1853), Augusta (1855), and John (1857). He became a successful blacksmith, and as a result of his ability, he was commissioned as second lieutenant in the Reedy Creek District Company on February 26, 1862. No further records.

1433. Riley, Cecil

Second Lieutenant, 66th Regiment
*   N.C. Militia (1861 organization)*

Cecil was living in Lexington in 1850. He was commissioned as second lieutenant in the Rich Fork District Company on December 13, 1861. No further records.

1434. Riley, James F.

Private, Company F, 7th Regiment
*   N.C. State Troops*

James was born in 1845 to Peter and Rebecca Riley. James worked as a farmer in the Jackson Hill area prior to being conscripted into service in Wake County on November 26, 1863. He was reported present until November 5, 1864, when he deserted to the enemy. James was released on November 13, 1864, after taking the oath of allegiance. After his release James made his way home, returning in May 1865. On July 26, 1866, James married Martha Kearns. James and Martha would have seven children: Melinda (1868), Frances (1872), Albert (1875), Eunice (1877), William (1879), James (1884), and Effie (1888). James lived in the Silver Hill area through 1900. No further records.

1435. Ripley, Peter O.

Second Lieutenant, 65th Regiment
*   N.C. Militia (1861 organization)*

Peter was born in 1810. Peter worked as a farmer in the southern district of Davidson County, and, in 1840, he married Rebecca Smith. Peter and Rebecca would only have one child: Cornelia (1846). He was commissioned to serve as second lieutenant in the Conrad Hill District Company on November 26, 1861. Peter and his family lived in the Conrad Hill township through 1870. No further records.

1436. Roberts, Romulus

Private, Company C, 70th Regiment
*   N.C. Troops (1st N.C. Junior*
*   Reserves)*

Romulus was born on June 6, 1847, to Granderson and Eliza Roberts. He worked as a farmer prior to enlisting in the Junior Reserves on May 24, 1864. Romulus died of disease at Richmond, Virginia, on November 10, 1864. His body was retrieved and was buried at Wesley's Chapel Methodist Church.

1437. Roberts, Solomon

Private, Confederate Guards
Company K, 48th Regiment N.C.
*   Troops*

Solomon was born in 1843 to Lucy Roberts. Solomon worked as a farmer prior to being conscripted into service on August 8, 1862. He was killed in action at Fredericksburg, Virginia, on December 13, 1862.

1438. Rodman, John F.

First Sergeant, Company E, 5th Regi-
*   ment N.C. State Troops*

Company K, 5th Regiment N.C. State
*   Troops*

John was born in 1845 to John and Mary Rodman. John was a student prior to volunteering in Rowan County on June 29, 1861. John served in Company E until ordered discharged by the secretary of war, personally, on August 25, 1862. John reenlisted, into company K, on April 1, 1864, and was mustered in as a first sergeant. John was captured at Leesburg, Virginia, on July 16, 1864. He was confined at Elmira, New York, until September 16, 1864, when he was released. No further records.

1439. Roland, John W.

Private, Lexington Wildcats
Company I, 14th Regiment N.C. Troops
*   (4th N.C. Volunteers)*

John was born in 1837. John worked as a farmer in the Lexington area prior to volunteering for service on May 14, 1861. He was reported present until he deserted from service near Hamilton's Crossing, Virginia, on April 6, 1863. No further records.

1440. Rominger, Franklin J.

Private, Ellis Guards
Company C, 15th Regiment N.C. Troops
*   (5th N.C. Volunteers)*

Franklin was born in 1844 to the Reverend Jordan and Catharine Kimel Rominger. Franklin worked as a farmer prior to being conscripted into service in Wake County on July 15, 1862. He was captured at Crampton's Pass, Maryland, on September 14, 1862. Franklin was confined at Fort Delaware, Delaware, until paroled and transferred to Aiken's Landing, Virginia, for exchange on October 2, 1862. He was declared exchanged on November 10, 1862. Franklin returned to service and was wounded at Fredericksburg, Virginia, on December 13, 1862. Franklin recovered and was reported present until captured at Bristoe Station, Virginia, on October 14, 1863. He was confined at Point Lookout, Maryland, until paroled and transferred once again to Aiken's Landing for exchange on March 4, 1865. After the war, Franklin returned home to the Arcadia township where, in 1867, he married Vidora. Franklin and Vidora lived in the Arcadia area before moving to Forsyth

County in the 1880s. He is buried in the Salem Moravian Cemetery in Forsyth County.

1441. Rominger, Jacob E.

*Private, Harnett Light Infantry
Company F, 15th Regiment N.C. Troops
(5th N.C. Volunteers)*

Jacob was born on November 16, 1843, to the Reverend Jordan and Catharine Kimel Rominger. Jacob worked as a farmer prior to being conscripted into service in Wake County on July 15, 1862. He was reported present until wounded in the right leg at Bristoe Station, Virginia, on October 14, 1863. Jacob was hospitalized until he was retired to the Invalid Corps on December 22, 1864. Jacob returned home where his parents took care of him until his death on May 3, 1870. He is buried in the Kimel Family Cemetery.

1442. Rominger, William

*Private, Company C, 70th Regiment
N.C. Troops (1st N.C. Junior
Reserves)*

William was born in 1847 to the Reverend Jordan and Catharine Kimel Rominger. He worked as a farmer prior to enlisting in the Junior Reserves on May 24, 1864. Apparently, William died in service, but the exact date and place of his death were not reported.

1443. Rothrock, Henry Tippet

*Private, Confederate Guards
Company K, 48th Regiment N.C. Troops*

Henry was born on May 3, 1840, to Jonathan and Eleanor Hanes Rothrock. He worked as an assistant in his father's carriage-making business. Henry married Mary Green on December 26, 1861. He was conscripted into service on August 8, 1862. Henry was reported present until he "abused" his furlough, which had been issued for September and October 1862. He returned to service and was wounded at Wilderness, Virginia, and Turkey Ridge, Virginia, before deserting to the enemy on August 20, 1864. Henry was confined at Washington, D.C., until he was released on an unspecified date after taking the oath of allegiance. After the war, Henry was furnished transportation home, where he met his daughter Christen (1863) for the

first time. Henry moved his family to the Thomasville township where he became a manufacturer of coaches. Henry and Mary would raise four more children: William (1866), Martha (1870), Laura (1875), and Ella (1879). Henry lived in the Thomasville area until his death on October 14, 1929. He is buried at Fair Grove United Methodist Church.

1444. Row, Henry

*Private, Company B, 48th Regiment
N.C. Troops*

Henry was born in 1823. Henry worked as a hireling in northern Davidson County, and, in 1844, he married Susanna. He and Susanna would have three children, Mary (1847), Martha (1850), and Jason (1858), before Henry volunteered for service on March 6, 1862. He was wounded at King's School House, Virginia, on June 25, 1862. Henry recovered from his wound and returned to service on November 1, 1862. He was reported present for the duration of the war with the 48th Regiment and was paroled at Appomattox Court House, Virginia, on April 9, 1865. Henry returned home, and he and his family moved to Randolph County prior to 1870. No further records.

1445. Rush, Abner E.

*Private, Lexington Wildcats
Company I, 14th Regiment N.C. Troops
(4th N.C. Volunteers)*

Abner was born in 1837 in Randolph County, North Carolina. He was living with Jackson Hill carpenter Jesse Cody in 1850 and prior to volunteering for service on May 14, 1861. Abner was wounded in action at Malvern Hill, Virginia, on July 1, 1862. He recovered and returned to the unit prior to January 1, 1863. He was reported present until wounded in the thorax at Chancellorsville, Virginia, on May 3, 1863. After a brief stay in a field hospital, Abner returned, only to be captured at Gettysburg, Pennsylvania, on July 5, 1863. He was confined at Fort Delaware, Delaware, until May 4, 1865, when he was released after taking the oath of allegiance. No further records.

1446. Russell, Alexander

*Private, Chatam Light Infantry
Company G, 48th Regiment N.C. Troops*

Alexander was born on October 6, 1832. He worked as a farmer, and, on February 14, 1858, he married Miranda Fry. Alex and Miranda would have two children, Julie (1860) and Mabry (1862–66), before Alexander was conscripted into service on August 14, 1862. He was reported present until he deserted to the enemy at Petersburg, Virginia, on October 9, 1864. Alexander was confined at Washington, D.C., until he was released on an unspecified date after taking the oath of allegiance. After the war, Alexander returned home to the Jackson Hill township, where he and Miranda would have three more children: James (1874), Art (1877), and Travis (1881). Upon his death on January 13, 1906, he had been a member of the Methodist church for 30 years. He is buried at Chapel Hill United Methodist Church.

1447. Russell, Elias

*Private, Company F, 7th Regiment
N.C. State Troops*

Elias was born in Montgomery County on March 5, 1828. Elias worked as a farmer in the Allegheny area, and, in 1850, he married Elizabeth Newsome. Elias and Elizabeth would have three children, Mary (1851), William (1856), and Linda (1860), before Elias was conscripted into service in Wake County on November 26, 1863. He was reported present until he deserted from service on February 22, 1864. After a short time of seeking refuge in the Uwharrie Mountains, he returned home. Elias traveled to Salisbury, North Carolina, where he took the oath of allegiance on June 10, 1865. Elias and his family lived in the Healing Springs township until his death on June 20, 1903. He is buried at Lick Creek Baptist Church.

1448. Saintsing, George Washington

*Private, Harnett Light Infantry
Company F, 15th Regiment N.C. Troops
(5th N.C. Volunteers)*

George was born in 1832 to Benjamin and Sarah Saintsing. George worked as a teacher in the Thomasville area, and, in 1852, he married Nancy Thomas. George and Nancy would have five children; Mary (1853), Julia (1855), George (1857), Daniel (1859), and Sallie (1861), before George was conscripted into service in

George W. Saintsing's home currently stands on Old Greensboro Road in the Ledford area (Touart, *Building the Backcountry*).

Wake County on July 16, 1862. He was wounded in the left hip and captured at Sharpsburg, Maryland, on September 17, 1862. George was confined at Fort McHenry, Maryland, until December 4, 1862, when he was paroled and transferred to City Point, Virginia, for exchange. George was reported absent, wounded, until detailed as a shoemaker on August 15, 1863, and returned to Davidson County. George served the duration of the war on this detail, and was paroled at Greensboro, North Carolina, on May 6, 1865. After the war, George continued his teaching in the Thomasville area but held on to his other trade and became a part-time shoe repairman. George and Nancy would have five more children: Benjamin (1867), William (1869), Sarah (1873), Mattie (1875), and John (1878). George died on November 3, 1904. He is buried at Bethesda United Methodist Church.

1449. Sapenfield, Andrew

Musician, Company H, 48th Regiment N.C. Troops

Andrew was born in 1842 to Elizabeth Sapenfield. In 1860, Andrew was working as a live-in hireling for David Everhart. Andrew volunteered for service on March 21, 1862. He was reported present in the ranks until promoted to musician in May 1863. Andrew served as a drummer until he died of typhoid fever at Richmond, Virginia, on September 18, 1864.

1450. Sapenfield, David

Private, Company H, 48th Regiment N.C. Troops

David was born in 1843 to Elizabeth Sapenfield. David worked as a hireling prior to volunteering for service on March 8, 1862. He was reported present until he died of disease at Richmond, Virginia, on August 1, 1864.

1451. Scarlett, George W.

Private, Chatam Light Infantry Company G, 48th Regiment N.C. Troops

George was born in 1840 to Robert and Mary Elizabeth Scarlett. George worked as a farmer prior to being conscripted into service on August 14, 1862. He deserted to the enemy at Sharpsburg, Maryland, on September 17, 1862. George was paroled on September 27, 1862, after taking the oath of allegiance. Apparently, he waited sometime before returning home to the Conrad Hill area. The first mention of his name appears in the voter records for 1875. In 1876, George married Margaret. George and Margaret would have two children, Amanda (1877) and Cynthia (1883), before moving out of the county in the 1900s. No further records.

1452. Scarlett, Samuel H.

Private, Chatam Light Infantry Company G, 48th Regiment N.C. Troops

Samuel was born in 1844 to Robert and Mary Elizabeth Scarlett. Samuel worked as a farmer prior to being conscripted into service on August 14, 1862. He was wounded at Sharpsburg, Maryland, on September 17, 1862. Samuel recovered from his wounds and returned to service in June 1863. He was reported present until he was captured at Bristoe Station, Virginia, on October 14, 1863. Samuel was confined at Point Lookout, Maryland, until he died of disease on August 23, 1864. He is buried in the Point Lookout National Cemetery.

1453. Scarlett, Stephen

Private, Company C, 70th Regiment N.C. Troops (1st N.C. Junior Reserves)

Stephen was born in 1847 to Robert and Mary Elizabeth Scarlett. Stephen worked as a farmer prior to enlisting in the Junior Reserves on May 24, 1864. Apparently, he died while in service. The exact date and place of death were not reported.

1454. Scott, Alexander

Private, Harnett Light Infantry Company F, 15th Regiment N.C. Troops (5th N.C. Volunteers)

Alexander was born in 1830. Alexander worked as a farmer, and, on April 20, 1859, he married Nancy Weaver. Alexander and Nancy would have one son, George (1860), before Alexander was conscripted into service in Wake County on July 15, 1862. He was hospitalized at Richmond, Virginia, with typhoid fever on December 23, 1862. Alexander died of his disease on Christmas Day, 1862.

1455. Scott, Alexander H.

Surgeon, North Carolina Conscript Bureau, Asheboro

This surgeon was listed as serving in the Asheboro office of the Bureau of Conscription with the remark: "previously practiced as physician in Davidson County." No further records.

1456. Scott, Elijah

*Private, Company H, 48th Regiment
N.C. Troops*

Elijah was born in 1833 to Margaret Scott. Elijah worked as a farmer, and in 1860, he was a live-in farmer for widow Jane Brinkley. He was conscripted into service at Petersburg, Virginia, on August 8, 1862. Elijah died of disease at Madison Court House, Virginia, on November 5, 1862.

1457. Scott, George Washington

*Private, Davidson Guards
Company A, 21st Regiment N.C. Troops
(11th N.C. Volunteers)*

George was born in 1842 to Jarrett and Parmelia Scott. George worked as a farmer prior to volunteering for service on May 8, 1861. He was reported present until wounded in the thigh at Chancellorsville, Virginia, on May 3, 1863. George recovered from his injury and returned to service on an unspecified date. He was reported present until paroled at Appomattox Court House, Virginia, on April 9, 1865. After the war, George returned home to the Reedy Creek area where, in 1874, he married Louisa Jane Mock. George and Louisa would have five children: Carrie (1877), Mattie (1878), William (1882), Robert Lee (1884), and John (1887). George was living in the Reedy Creek township in 1900. No further records.

1458. Scott, John Franklin

*Private, Davidson Guards
Company A, 21st Regiment N.C. Troops
(11th N.C. Volunteers)*

John was born on March 4, 1840, to William and Mary Scott. John worked as a farmer prior to volunteering for service on May 8, 1861. He was reported present until wounded in the shoulder, breast, and left arm at the second battle of Manassas on August 28, 1862. Immediately afterward, John was paralyzed in his left arm for 18 months. He recovered partial use of the arm and was retired from service on February 17, 1865. John returned home, where he began to slowly recover from his debilitating wounds. In 1867, he married Sarah Cornelia Foltz. John and Sarah would have eight children: Samuel (1868), Lafayette (1869), Henry (1871), Linnie (1873), Ella (1874), Mary (1876), Mack (1883), and Sidney (1887). John worked as a farmer in the Arcadia township until his death on January 12, 1920. He is buried at Arcadia United Methodist Church.

1459. Scott, Robert W.

*Private, Davidson Guards
Company A, 21st Regiment N.C. Troops
(11th N.C. Volunteers)*

Robert was born on September 4, 1841, to William and Mary Scott. He was conscripted into service sometime prior to March 16, 1864, when his name appears in a company record. No further records exist of his service. Robert moved out of the county before 1870 and returned shortly before he died on August 27, 1926. He is buried at Mount Olivet United Methodist Church.

1460. Scott, Thomas Jefferson

*Sergeant, Guilford Men
Company E, 22nd Regiment N.C. Troops
(12th N.C. Volunteers)*

Thomas was born on July 8, 1838. Thomas worked as a mechanic prior to volunteering for service on June 23, 1861. He was reported present until wounded in three places at Seven Pines, Virginia, on May 31, 1862. Thomas recovered from his wounds and was promoted to sergeant in August 1862. He served as a sergeant until captured at Petersburg, Virginia, on April 3, 1865. Thomas was confined at Petersburg until April 25, 1865, when he was released after taking the oath of allegiance. After the war, Thomas returned to the Lexington area where he worked as a repairman of carriages and houses. In 1889, Thomas married Sarah Jane Grimes. Thomas and Sarah would have two children: Arthur (1892) and Pearl (1894). Thomas worked as a repairman for the many businesses of H. H. Hartley beginning in 1885 until Thomas' death on March 23, 1906. He is buried in the Lexington City Cemetery.

1461. Sears, Clem

*Private, Holtsburg Guards
Company A, 54th Regiment N.C. Troops*

Clem was born in 1821 and was a free black man living in Boone township in 1850 and 1860. He was the only Sears listed in Davidson County. Clem married a mulatto by the name of Ellen. As was the custom, the date of marriage was not recorded nor was a bond issued for it. Clem and Ellen would have at least two children, Margaret (1847) and Henry (1859), before Clem enlisted in Davidson County on February 1, 1863. He was reported present until he died in camp at Fredericksburg, Virginia, on May 16, 1863.

1462. Sechrist, Ambrose

*Private, Company H, 48th Regiment
N.C. Troops*

Ambrose was born in 1837 to Solomon and Catharine Sechrist. Ambrose worked as a farmer prior to volunteering for service on March 3, 1862. He was reported present for duty until wounded in a skirmish on April 30, 1864. Ambrose was sent home to recover and had his furlough extended through February 19, 1865. No further records.

1463. Sechrist, Amos L.

*Private, Lexington Wildcats
Company I, 14th Regiment N.C. Troops
(4th N.C. Volunteers)*

Amos was born in 1837 to Jonathan and Rachael Sechrist. Amos worked as a farmer prior to volunteering for service on May 14, 1861. He was reported present until captured at Boonsboro, Maryland, on September 17, 1862. After a brief stay with the Federal provost marshal he was sent to Aiken's Landing, Virginia, for exchange without imprisonment on October 6, 1862. Amos was exchanged on November 10, 1862. He returned to service on January 1, 1863, and was reported present until he deserted while on campaign in Maryland on July 11, 1864. Amos was confined at Elmira, New York, until May 29, 1865, when he was released after taking the oath of allegiance. After the war, Amos returned home to the Tyro area, where, in 1866, he married Miranda. Amos and Miranda would have two children, Maria (1867) and Eliza (1868), before moving out of the county in the 1870s. No further records.

1464. Sechrist, Andrew

*Private, Thomasville Rifles
Company B, 14th Regiment N.C. Troops
(4th N.C. Volunteers)*

Andrew was born in 1838 to Lawrence and Asenith Sechrist. Andrew worked as a laborer for A. E. Gursh prior to being conscripted into service in Wake County on July 16, 1862. He was captured at Boonsboro, Maryland, on September 17, 1862. Andrew was confined at Point Lookout, Maryland, until October 2, 1862, when he was paroled and transferred to Aiken's Landing, Virginia, for exchange. He was declared exchanged on November 10, 1862. Andrew returned to service and was reported present until he was captured at Winchester, Virginia, on September 19, 1864. He was confined at Point Lookout again until March 15, 1865, when he was exchanged. After the war, Andrew returned home to the Thomasville area where, in 1865, he married Mary Ann. Andrew and Mary would have three children: Nancy (1866), Charles (1868), and Flora (1871). Andrew worked as a farmer until his death on April 10, 1916. He is buried at Emanuel United Church of Christ.

1465. Sechrist, Conrad

Private, Thomasville Rifles
Company B, 14th Regiment N.C. Troops
(4th N.C. Volunteers)

Conrad was born in 1846 to Lawrence and Asenith Sechrist. Conrad worked as a laborer for A. E. Gursh prior to volunteering for service in Davidson County on March 20, 1862. Conrad served in every engagement of the 14th Regiment until he was drummed out of service by order of a general court-martial on November 13, 1863. No further records.

1466. Sechrist, Daniel

Private, Lexington Wildcats
Company I, 14th Regiment N.C. Troops
(4th N.C. Volunteers)

Daniel was born on June 17, 1840. Daniel worked as a farmer in the Conrad Hill area prior to volunteering for service on May 14, 1861. He was reported present, serving in every engagement of the 14th Regiment, until paroled at Appomattox Court House, Virginia, on April 9, 1865. After the war, Daniel returned home and began working as a miner in 1870. Daniel married Jane in 1871. Daniel and Jane would have five children: Julie (1874), James (1877), Lunda (1882), Sarah (1883), and Charles (1887). Daniel lived in the Conrad Hill area until his death on December 14, 1924. He is buried at Clarksbury Methodist Church.

1467. Sechrist, David

Private, Company A, 1st Regiment
Confederate Engineers

David was born in 1831 to Solomon and Catharine Sechrist. David worked as a farmer, and in 1854, he married Neety. David and Neety would have three children, William (1856), Elizabeth (1858), and Franny (1861), before Neety's death in 1865. After the war, David raised his three children by himself as a sharecropper in the Conrad Hill area. By 1880, his children had grown, and David was employed by Pleasant Hoover. By 1900, David was in the county home, where he resided in one of the dormitory rooms until his death on April 23, 1915. He is buried in the cemetery adjacent to the home, now behind the Davidson County schools' maintenance garage.

1468. Sechrist, Eli Kingsberry

Private, Company H, 48th Regiment
N.C. Troops

Eli was born on October 22, 1842, to Jesse Sepe and Mary Owens Sechrist. Eli worked as a hireling prior to volunteering for service on March 7, 1862. He was wounded in the right hand at Sharpsburg, Maryland, on September 17, 1862. Eli was reported absent, wounded, until he failed to return from furlough and was declared absent without leave through December 1863. Eli returned to service in February 1864 and was reported present until he was captured at Hanover Junction, Virginia, on May 24, 1864. He was confined at Point Lookout, Maryland, until May 14, 1865, when he was released after taking the oath of allegiance. After the war, Eli returned home to the Conrad Hill area, where, in 1865, he married Angeline. Eli and Angeline would have six children: Robert Lee (1866), Louella (1871), William (1874), Minnie (1878), Mary (1879), and Rilla (1883). Eli worked as a farmer until his death on March 15, 1924. He is buried in Old Embler Cemetery, formerly Embler's Grove.

1469. Sechrist, Henry

Private, Company H, 48th Regiment
N.C. Troops

Henry was born in 1842 to Jonathan and Rachael Sechrist. Henry worked as a hireling prior to volunteering for service on March 7, 1862. He was wounded at Sharpsburg, Maryland, on September 17, 1862. Henry was reported absent, sick, until he was listed as a deserter on June 22, 1863. Henry returned to the company on October 14, 1864. He was reported present until captured in a hospital in Richmond, Virginia, on April 3, 1865. Henry was paroled at Newport News, Virginia, on June 30, 1865, after taking the oath of allegiance. No further records.

1470. Sechrist, James

Private, Lexington Wildcats
Company I, 14th Regiment N.C. Troops
(4th N.C. Volunteers)

James was born in 1842. James worked as a farmer prior to volunteering for service on May 14, 1861. He was wounded at Sharpsburg, Maryland, on September 17, 1862. James recovered from his wounds and rejoined the company prior to January 1, 1863. He was reported present until he deserted while on campaign in Maryland on July 11, 1864. James was confined at Elmira, New York, until May 10, 1865, when he died of "chronic diarrhea." He is buried in the Elmira National Cemetery.

1471. Sechrist, Lindsey

Private, Company I, 42nd Regiment
N.C. Troops

Lindsey was born in 1839 to Jesse Sepe and Mary Owens Sechrist. Lindsey worked as a farmer prior to volunteering for service on March 6, 1862. He was reported present until captured "in front of Petersburg, Virginia, on the night of June 17, 1864." Lindsey was confined at Point Lookout, Maryland, until May 9, 1865, when he died of scurvy. He is buried in the Point Lookout National Cemetery.

1472. Sechrist, Noah

Private, Stanley Marksmen
Company H, 14th Regiment N.C. Troops
(4th N.C. Volunteers)

Noah was born in 1833 to Lawrence and Asenith Sechrist. Noah worked as a carpenter, and, on January 4, 1855, he married Rebecca A. Wilson. Noah and Rebecca would have a daughter, Polly (1859), before Noah was conscripted into service in Wake County on July 15, 1862. He died of disease on October 20, 1862.

1473. Sechrist, Robert Franklin

Private, Company C, 70th Regiment N.C. Troops (1st N.C. Junior Reserves)

Robert was born in 1847 to Felix and Elizabeth Sechrist. Robert worked as a farmer prior to enlisting in the Junior Reserves on May 24, 1864. After the war, Robert returned to the Conrad Hill area, where, in 1868, he married Sarah Clinard. Robert and Sarah would have three children: Catharine (1870), Luella (1871), and Minnie (1874). The family was reported as living in the Rich Fork area in the 1900 Census. No further records.

1474. Sechrist, William F.

Private, Company H, 48th Regiment N.C. Troops

William was born in 1840 to Solomon and Catharine Sechrist. He worked as a farmer prior to being conscripted into service on August 8, 1862. William was wounded and captured at Sharpsburg, Maryland, on September 17, 1862. He died in the hands of the enemy on October 17, 1862.

1475. Semone, James

Private, Lexington Wildcats Company I, 14th Regiment N.C. Troops (4th N.C. Volunteers)

James was born in 1839. James worked as a farmer in the Lexington area prior to volunteering for service on May 14, 1861. He was reported present until captured at Gettysburg, Pennsylvania, on July 4, 1863. James was confined at Point Lookout, Maryland, until February 18, 1865, when he was paroled and transferred to Boulware's Wharf, Virginia, for exchange. James arrived two days later. No record of his exchange is listed, but he is reported present on a detail of exchanged prisoners at Camp Lee, Virginia, on February 28, 1865. No further records.

1476. Sexton, Corneilius Charles

First Lieutenant, 65th Regiment N.C. Militia (1861 organization)

Corneilius was born in 1825. Corneilius worked as a carpenter in the southern district of Davidson County, and, in 1853, he married Elizabeth, a native of Darlington, South Carolina. Corneilius and Elizabeth would have six children: Monroe (1854), Jeremiah (1861), Mary (1864), Martha (1866), Martitia (1868), and Ulysses (1871). Corneilius was operating a mill in 1860, and, as a result, was commissioned to serve as first lieutenant in the Jackson Hill District Company on February 11, 1862. Corneilius continued milling into the 1870s, operating both a grist mill and a saw mill. He was last living in the Jackson Hill township in 1880. No further records.

1477. Sexton, Daniel

Private, Company F, 2nd Battalion, N.C. Infantry

Daniel was born on December 13, 1839, to William and Mary Morris Sexton. Daniel worked as a farmer, and, in 1859, he married Bathsheba Newsome. Daniel and Bashy would have two children, Elizabeth (1860) and John (1862), before he volunteered for service on October 18, 1861. He was reported present until captured at Roanoke Island, North Carolina, on February 8, 1862. Daniel was confined at Elizabeth City, North Carolina, until he was paroled and released on February 21, 1862. He did not return to service. After the war, Daniel returned home to the Emmons township, where he and Bashy would have five more children: James (1865), Cicero (1867), William (1869), Willis (1871), and Nancy (1873). Daniel worked as a farmer until his death on August 8, 1909. He is buried at Mount Ebal United Methodist Church.

1478. Sexton, James B.

Private, Men of Yadkin Company B, 38th Regiment N.C. Troops

James was born on September 10, 1844, to William and Mary Morris Sexton. James worked as a carpenter prior to being conscripted into service at Camp Vance, North Carolina, on August 14, 1864. He was reported present until he deserted to the enemy on January 27, 1865. James was confined at Washington, D.C., until an unspecified date when he took the oath of allegiance. James remained in Washington for a couple of months before being furnished transportation to City Point, Virginia. After the war, James returned home to the Emmons township, where, on November 24, 1870, he married Martha E. Hopkins. The only children Martha gave birth to were twins, Louvina and Eula, in 1884; however, within a year, both girls would die. James helped to found Mount Ebal Methodist Church and served as a deacon and community leader until his death on January 21, 1908. He is buried at Mount Ebal Methodist Church.

1479. Sexton, John

Private, Company F, 2nd Battalion, N.C. Infantry

John was born on September 14, 1842, to William and Mary Morris Sexton. John worked as a farmer prior to volunteering for service on October 18, 1861. He was reported present until captured at Roanoke Island, North Carolina, on February 8, 1862. John was confined at Elizabeth City, North Carolina, until he was paroled and released on February 21, 1862. He did not return to service. After the war, John returned home to the Emmons township, where, on May 16, 1872, he married Elizabeth Garner. John and Elizabeth would have three children, Ulysses (1873), William (1875), and Alexander (1879), before Elizabeth died in 1887. John married Caroline in 1892. The two would not have any children. John worked as a farmer until his death on April 27, 1920. He is buried at Mount Ebal Methodist Church. The inscription on his stone reads: "Friend to his country and a believer in Christ."

1480. Shackleford, Terry D.

Sergeant, Holtsburg Guards Company A, 54th Regiment N.C. Troops

Terry was born in 1831. Terry worked as an overseer for absentee plantation owner Peter W. Hairston. Terry married Camille shortly before he volunteered for service on March 4, 1862, and was mustered in as a sergeant. Terry was reported present until hospitalized at Richmond, Virginia, on May 1, 1863, with hepatitis. Terry died of his disease at Richmond on May 22, 1863.

1481. Shaddox, Wilson

Private, Company A, 10th Battalion, N.C. Heavy Artillery

Wilson was born in Davidson County. Wilson worked as a farmer prior to volunteering for service on April 3, 1862. He was reported present through September 1864. No further records.

1482. Sharpe, Alexander

*Second Lieutenant, 66th Regiment
N.C. Militia (1861 organization)*

Alexander was born on April 2, 1823. Alexander worked as a farmer in the western section of Davidson County, and on December 27, 1846, he married Sarah Williams. Alexander and Sarah would have five children: Susan (1848), Zachariah (1849), John (1853), Sarah (1861), and Daniel (1864). Alexander was commissioned to serve as second lieutenant in the Reeds Cross Roads District Company on November 26, 1861. Alexander worked as a successful farmer in the Churchland area until his death on February 10, 1892. He is buried at Churchland Baptist Church.

1483. Sharpe, Robert L

*Private, Carolina Rangers
Company B, 10th Virginia Cavalry
Regiment*

Robert was born on March 16, 1846, to Richmond and Mary Sharpe. Robert worked as a farmer prior to enlisting into service on March 12, 1864. He was reported present and received two clothing and pay rations prior to being sent on detached service on January 27, 1865. He was paroled at Salisbury, North Carolina, on May 18, 1865. After the war, Robert returned home to the Boone township, where, on August 1, 1867, he married Sophie Swicegood. Robert and Sophie would have seven children: Mary (1868), Minnie (1871), George (1873), Amanda (1875), Lilly (1878), Garner (1880), and Ida (1884). Robert worked as a farmer in the Boone township until his death on August 27, 1923. He is buried at St. Luke's Lutheran Church.

1484. Sharpe, Wilson A.

*Private, Holtsburg Guards
Company A, 54th Regiment N.C.
Troops*

Wilson was born on June 9, 1840, to Matthias and Mary Sharpe. Wilson worked as a farmer prior to volunteering for service on March 6, 1862. He was reported present until captured at Rappahannock Station, Virginia, on November 7, 1863. Wilson was confined at Point Lookout, Maryland, until March 9, 1864, when he was paroled and transferred to City Point, Virginia, for exchange. Wilson was declared exchanged sometime in April 1864, returned to service, and was captured at Stephenson's Depot, Virginia, on July 20, 1864. He was confined at Camp Chase, Ohio, until March 2, 1865, when he was paroled and transferred to Boulware's Wharf, Virginia, for exchange. After the war, Wilson returned home to the Boone township, where, on March 5, 1868, he married Sarah E. Koontz, widow of Ezekiel Koontz. Wilson and Sarah would have two surviving children, Melinda (1869) and John (1871), before Sarah died in the 1880s. Wilson married Barbara in 1894. The two would not have any children. Wilson worked as a farmer until his death on September 19, 1928. He is buried at Churchland Baptist Church.

1485. Shaw, Henry

*Private, Lexington Wildcats
Company I, 14th Regiment N.C. Troops
(4th N.C. Volunteers)*

Henry was born in 1836 to Rachael Shaw. Henry worked as a carpenter prior to volunteering for service on May 14, 1861. He was reported present during every engagement of the 14th Regiment until paroled at Appomattox Court House, Virginia, on April 9, 1865. After the war, Henry returned to the Tyro township, where, in 1865, he married Jane. Henry and Jane would have seven children: Ellen (1866), Lenora (1869), John (1871), George (1872), Gregory (1875), Henry (1878), and Elizabeth (1880). The family was last reported as living in the Tyro township in 1880. No further records.

1486. Shaw, Jacob

*Private, Company B, 48th Regiment
N.C. Troops*

Jacob was born in 1820. Jacob worked as a farmer in the southern district of Davidson County, and, on March 21, 1847, he married Margaret A. Owen. Jacob and Margaret would have three children, John (1850), Jacob (1855), and Mary (1860), before Jacob volunteered for service on March 6, 1862. He was wounded at King's School House, Virginia, on June 25, 1862. Jacob was taken to Richmond, Virginia, where he died of his wounds on July 8, 1862.

1487. Shaw, John H.

*Private, Company B, 48th Regiment
N.C. Troops*

John was born in 1841 to Rachael Shaw. John worked as an apprentice blacksmith, and in 1862, he married Netie. John was married for only a couple of months prior to volunteering for service on March 3, 1862. He was reported present until captured when "left sick" in Frederick, Maryland. John was confined at Fort Delaware, Delaware, until October 2, 1862, when he was paroled and transferred to Aiken's Landing, Virginia, for exchange. John was declared exchanged on November 10, 1862. He returned to the company on February 18, 1863. John was reported present for the duration of the war, suffering slight head wounds at Wilderness, Virginia, and Petersburg, Virginia, and a shoulder wound at Cold Harbor, Virginia, on June 3, 1864. John was paroled at Greensboro, North Carolina, on May 3, 1865. After the war, John returned home to Netie and his two-year-old daughter, Eliza, who was born while he was away. John and Netie moved to the Mount Tabor area, where they would have six more children: Franklin (1866), Crissila (1868), Avanella (1872), Atta (1873), Druscilla (1874), and Robert Lee (1880). John was living in the Silver Hill area in 1900. He is buried at Mount Tabor United Church of Christ.

1488. Shaw, Obediah

*Private, Company B, 48th Regiment
N.C. Troops*

Obed was born in 1841 to Rachael Shaw. Obed worked as a hireling prior to volunteering for service on March 3, 1862. He was wounded in the left arm at Fredericksburg, Virginia, on December 13, 1862. Obed recovered from his wound and returned to service on March 1, 1863. Obed was reported present until paroled at Greensboro, North Carolina, on May 3, 1865. After the war, Obediah returned home, and moved to the Mount Tabor area with his brother John. Obediah married Malinda Shrilock on May 7, 1878. Obed and Malinda would have three children: Arthur (1882), Henry (1885), and Maude (1889). Obed and his family were last reported in the Silver Hill township in 1900. No further records.

The Reverend Henry S. Sheets, a leader and historian of the North Carolina Baptist Church (Sheets, *A History of the Liberty Baptist Association*).

1489. Sheets, Henry S.

Private, Laurel Springs Guard
Company A, 34th Regiment N.C. Troops

Henry was born on December 15, 1841, to Simeon and Rebecca Sheets. Henry worked as a farmer prior to volunteering for service in Yadkin County on August 10, 1861. He was reported present until wounded in the right hip at Chancellorsville, Virginia, between May 1 and 4, 1863. Henry recovered from his hip wound and returned to service prior to August 25, 1864, when he was captured at Reams Station, Virginia. Henry was confined at Old Capital Prison in Washington, D.C., until December 5, 1864, when he was released after taking the oath of allegiance. After the war, Henry returned home to the Emmons township where, on September 15, 1865, he married Martha Garner. Henry and Martha would only have one child: Roxanne (1866). Henry was ordained as a minister at Liberty Baptist Church in 1870, beginning a career which would last nearly 50 years. Henry served as pastor for four Davidson County churches: Reeds Crossroads, Liberty, Summerville,

and Holloways. Henry's ministry took him to the upper levels of the Baptist hierarchy: he served as a state representative and was nationally recognized for service. In 1903, Henry's *A History of the Liberty Baptist Association* was published by Edwards & Broughton of Raleigh, North Carolina. His work is a scholarly record of the Baptist church's influence and impact on the central Piedmont. In 1915, he gave the commencement address at Murfreesboro, North Carolina's Chowan College. Henry remained in the service of the church until his death on September 30, 1917. He is buried in the Lexington City Cemetery.

1490. Sheets, John W.

Private, Davidson Guards
Company A, 21st Regiment N.C. Troops
(11th N.C. Volunteers)

John was born in 1839 to William Jesse and Tabitha Sheets. John worked as a farmer in the Clemmonsville area prior to volunteering for service on May 8, 1861. He was reported present until wounded in the left hand at Winchester, Virginia, on May 25, 1862. John was reported absent, wounded, through April 11, 1865. After the war, John married Charlotte in 1867. John and Charlotte would have eight children: John and Margaret (1868), Mary (1869), George (1872), William (1873), Martha (1874), Charles (1876), and Raymond (1879). No further records.

1491. Shelly, John M.

Private, Charlotte Artillery
Company C, 10th Regiment N.C. State
Troops (1st N.C. Artillery)

John was born in 1840 to Jesse and Tabitha Edwards Shelly. John moved with his family to Thomasville, where he was a partner in his father's shoe-manufacturing operation. John enlisted into service in Mecklenburg County on August 8, 1862. He was reported present until detailed to serve as a teamster in the Confederate Ordnance Department on August 22, 1863. John served in that capacity until February 1865 when he was returned to regular service. John was paroled at Greensboro, North Carolina, on May 20, 1865. After the war, John continued in the family business, even buying out his brother William in 1870. John took over the factory upon his father's

death in 1887 and guided it through a tough period of transition, when the old industry was giving way to the new furniture trade. John was a citizen of Thomasville and, at one time, was president of the shooting club. John died in 1911. He is buried in the Thomasville City Cemetery.

1492. Shelly, Romulus W.

First Lieutenant, Thomasville Rifles
Company B, 14th Regiment N.C. Troops
(4th N.C. Volunteers)

Romulus was born in 1836 to Jesse and Tabitha Edwards Shelly. Romulus moved to the Thomasville area with his family upon the opening of the Shelly Shoe Factory in the 1850s. Romulus worked as a manager prior to volunteering for service on April 23, 1861, when he was mustered in as first lieutenant. Romulus was reported present until he resigned his commission on May 27, 1861. After his resignation, Romulus moved to the Trinity area; however, he did retain his shares in his father's company.

1493. Shelly, William W.

Sergeant, Thomasville Rifles
Company B, 14th Regiment N.C. Troops
(4th N.C. Volunteers)

William was born in 1843 to Jesse and Tabitha Edwards Shelly. William moved with his family to Thomasville, where he was a partner in his father's shoe-manufacturing operation. William volunteered for service on April 23, 1861. He was promoted to sergeant on July 29, 1861. William served as a sergeant until he was discharged on January 1, 1862, after providing a substitute. William returned home and helped manage the factory through the pressing economic times of the war. In 1870, William sold his shares to his brother John and moved out of state. No further records.

1494. Shelton, John H.

Surgeon, 66th Regiment N.C. Militia
(1861 organization)

John was born in 1832. He received his medical training from the state university in Chapel Hill, where he also excelled in Latin. John began practicing in the Arcadia area in 1861 and was commissioned to serve as surgeon (major) of the 66th Regiment N.C. Militia on February 24, 1862.

In 1869, John married Nellie. John and Nellie would have four children, Carrie (1872), Charles (1874), Henry (1877), and Martha (1879), before moving out of the county in the 1880s. No further records.

1495. Shemwell, Lorenzo D.

*Sergeant, Company F, 7th Regiment
N.C. Troops*

Lorenzo was born in 1839 to Nancy Shemwell. Lorenzo worked as a teacher in the Jackson Hill area prior to volunteering for service in Rowan County on June 29, 1861. He was promoted to sergeant on September 15, 1861, and served in that capacity until he was discharged on September 27, 1862, because of "pulmonary phthisis." Lorenzo returned home and continued his teaching career. In 1870, Lorenzo opened a dry goods and mercantile store. He operated this store into the 1880s, before moving to the Randolph County community of Farmer. No further records.

1496. Shemwell, Obediah M.

*Surgeon, 66th Regiment N.C. Militia
(1861 organization)*

Obediah was born on February 27, 1830, to Nancy Shemwell. Obediah completed his medical training at the University of Virginia in 1856. He returned to Davidson County immediately after-

ward and married Sarah E. Thompson on April 7, 1857. Obediah and Sarah would have six surviving children: Baxter (1858), Cora (1864), Delilah (1868), Alice (1874), Harold (1876), and Mary (1878). Tragically, the couple would also have five children who would not live to see their second birthday. Obediah was commissioned to serve as a surgeon (captain) for the 66th Regiment N.C. Militia on February 24, 1862. After his service, Obediah continued his practice and also served as part-time physician for the Silver Hill mining company up until his death on October 25, 1880. He is buried in the Shemwell Family Cemetery.

1497. Shemwell, Thomas Franklin

*Private, Company B, 48th Regiment
N.C. Troops*

Thomas was born in 1838 to Nancy Shemwell. Thomas worked as a clerk prior to being conscripted into service at Petersburg, Virginia, on August 8, 1862. He died of pneumonia at Charlottesville, Virginia, on December 11, 1862.

1498. Shepherd, John B.

*Private, Company C, 70th Regiment
N.C. Troops (1st N.C. Junior
Reserves)*

John was born in 1847 to John and Hannah Shepherd. John worked as a

farmer prior to enlisting in the Junior Reserves on May 24, 1864. After the war, John went to work as a paid farmhand for Nancy Booker and was living with her in 1870. No further records.

1499. Shepherd, Thaddeus

*Private, Company A, 53rd Regiment
N.C. Troops*

Thad was born in 1844. Thad worked as a farmer prior to being conscripted into service on March 24, 1864. He was severely wounded in the right thigh at Spotsylvania Court House, Virginia, on May 12, 1864. Thad recovered from his wound after several months, finally returning to service in November 1864. He was reported present until captured at a Richmond, Virginia, hospital during the city's fall on April 3, 1865, Thad was confined at Newport News, Virginia, until June 30, 1865, when he was released after taking the oath of allegiance. After the war, Thad married Molly Johnson in 1867. Thad lived in the Thomasville area until his death in 1922. He is buried at Prospect United Methodist Church in Guilford County, North Carolina.

1500. Shields, John D.

*Private, Company D, 62nd Battalion,
Georgia Cavalry
Company H, 16th Battalion, N.C.
Cavalry*

John was born in Surry County, North Carolina, on August 6, 1812. John moved to Davidson County in the 1850s. He worked as a farmer in the Abbott's Creek area, and, in 1856 he married Roseanne Brown; they had no children. John enlisted in the 62nd Georgia Cavalry in January 1864 and rode with that unit until transferred to the 16th N.C. Cavalry on July 11, 1864. John was reported present until paroled at Appomattox Court House, Virginia, on April 9, 1865. After the war, John returned home to the Abbott's Creek area. John died on April 7, 1880. He is buried at Abbott's Creek Missionary Baptist Church.

1501. Shields, Joseph M.

*Second Lieutenant, 66th Regiment
N.C. Militia (1861 organization)*

Joseph was born in 1836 to William and Phoebe Shields. Joseph worked as a

Dr. Obediah Shemwell bought this Tyro home five years before his death (Touart, ***Building the Backcountry***).

Survivors of Eli B. Shoaf: Susan Smith Shoaf (wife) and children Robert and Mary, stand outside their father's home (Touart, *Building the Backcountry*).

miller prior to being commissioned as a second lieutenant in the Browntown District Company on November 26, 1861. No further records.

1502. Shipton, George

Private, Company A, 10th Battalion, N.C. Heavy Artillery

George was born in 1829. He worked as a farmhand for Bazil Floyd during the 1850s. In 1851, George married Elizabeth. George and Elizabeth would have four children, Roby (1852), Dow (1854), Mary (1857), and Alice (1863), before George was conscripted into service on March 9, 1863. He deserted from service on May 10, 1863. George returned home to his family and avoided capture for the duration of the war. George and Elizabeth would have two more children: Andrew (1864) and Rachael (1871). George lived in the Healing Springs township until his death on March 30, 1917. He is buried at Floyd Baptist Church.

1503. Shoaf, Addison

Private, Company H, 48th Regiment N.C. Troops

Addison was born in 1842 to David and Susanna Shoaf. Addison worked as a farmer in the Lexington area, and, in January 1862, he married Fanny Chamberlain. Addison and Fanny would have three children before her death in 1870: Eddie (1864), Bettie (1866), and Robert (1870). Addison was conscripted into service on August 8, 1862. He deserted on September 19, 1862. While at home he helped his wife with the harvest, and he returned to duty in May 1863. Addison was reported present until wounded on an unspecified date; he deserted again on December 16, 1864. Addison married Mary Shuler Everhart, widow of Lewis Everhart, on March 15, 1877. The two would not have any children. Addison lived in the Lexington township until his death on May 8, 1896.

1504. Shoaf, David

Private, Company H, 48th Regiment N.C. Troops

David was born in 1846 to Jesse and Ellen Shoaf. David worked as a farmer prior to being conscripted into service on October 18, 1863. He was reported present until he deserted from service on August 2, 1864. No further records.

1505. Shoaf, David Africa

Private, Company A, 42nd Regiment N.C. Troops

David was born in 1842 to Jacob and Elizabeth Brinkley Shoaf. David worked as a farmer prior to volunteering for service on March 3, 1862. He was reported present until wounded in a minor skirmish on July 26, 1864. David was taken to Richmond, Virginia, where he was hospitalized. David died from his wounds in Richmond on October 2, 1864. He is buried in the Hollywood Cemetery in Richmond.

1506. Shoaf, Eli B.

Private, Company B, 48th Regiment N.C. Troops

Eli was born in 1834 to Henry and Elizabeth Berrier Shoaf. Eli worked as a farmer, and, on December 6, 1859, he married Susan Smith. Eli and Susan would have two children, Robert (1860) and Mary Elizabeth (1862), before Eli was conscripted into service on August 8, 1862. He was reported present for duty through March 1864. On April 18, 1864, Eli was detailed to serve as a teamster for the division's quartermaster department. Eli served in this capacity through September 30, 1864, when he returned to his company. He was hospitalized at Richmond, Virginia, on December 29, 1864. Eli died of unreported causes on January 8, 1865.

1507. Shoaf, Emanuel

Private, Company I, 42nd Regiment N.C. Troops

Emanuel was born in 1830 to David and Susanna Leonard Shoaf. Emanuel worked as a farmer, and, in 1850, he married Rebecca. Emanuel and Rebecca would have six children, Louisa (1851), William L. (1853), David and John H. (1855), Mary (1857), and Charlie (1861), before Emanuel volunteered for service in Rowan County on April 15, 1862. He was reported present until captured at Wise's Forks, Virginia, on March 10, 1865. Emanuel was confined at Point Lookout, Maryland, until June 19, 1865, when he was released after taking the oath of allegiance. After the war, Emanuel made his way back to the Beulah area and to his family. Emanuel worked as a farmer in the Lexington township until his death in the 1890s. He is buried at Beulah United Church of Christ.

1508. Shoaf, Henderson

Private, Holtsburg Guards Company A, 54th Regiment N.C. Troops

Henderson was born on December 10, 1833, to John and Frances Brinkley

Shoaf. Henderson worked as a farmer prior to volunteering for service on March 4, 1862. He was hospitalized on November 10, 1862, with "general debility." Henderson deserted from the hospital but returned in February 1863. He was reported present until he deserted again on December 5, 1863. Henderson returned to duty prior to September 1864 and was reported present until captured at Fort Stedman, Virginia, on March 25, 1865. Henderson was confined at Point Lookout, Maryland, until June 20, 1865, when he was released after taking the oath of allegiance. After the war, Henderson returned home to the Boone area, where, on September 9, 1865, he married Caroline Bruff. Henderson and Caroline would have five children: Charles (1867), Columbus and Alfred (1868), Henry (1872), and Sarah (1875). Henderson worked as a farmer until he died in 1906. He is buried at Churchland Baptist Church.

1509. Shoaf, Henry Ellis

Private, Company A, 42nd Regiment
N.C. Troops

Henry was born on October 27, 1836, to Henry and Catharine Koontz Shoaf. Henry worked as a farmer prior to volunteering for service on November 26, 1861. He was mustered in as a sergeant; however, he was reduced in rank for unreported reasons on July 28, 1863. Henry was reported present through October 1864. He was paroled at Greensboro, North Carolina, on May 3, 1865. After the war, Henry returned home where, on January 8, 1867, he married Margaret Farabee. Henry and Margaret would raise eight children in their Boone township home: Mary (1868), Cicero (1870), Sallie (1872), Charles (1875), Lemuel (1877), Currie (1882), Beulah (1885), and Maude (1892). Henry worked as a farmer in the Boone/Tyro area until his death on October 15, 1899. He is buried at Bethel Cemetery.

1510. Shoaf, Henry Washington

Private, Harnett Light Infantry
Company F, 15th Regiment N.C. Troops
(5th N.C. Volunteers)

Henry was born on April 24, 1834, to Jacob and Elizabeth Brinkley Shoaf. Henry worked as a farmer, and, in 1857, he married Christina Livengood. Henry

and Crissie would have three sons: Jacob (1858), Franklin (1861), and Lorenzo (1862), before Henry was conscripted into service in Wake County on July 15, 1862. He was wounded in the foot at Fredericksburg, Virginia, on December 13, 1862. After a long stay at home, Henry returned to duty on June 12, 1863. He was reported present until wounded in the head at Bristoe Station, Virginia, on October 14, 1863. Henry recovered from his wound, returned to his company in December 1863, and was reported present through October 1864. After the war, Henry returned home to his family and newborn son, Corneilius (1864), who was born while he was away. Henry and Crissie would have one more son, Roswell (1867). Henry worked as a farmer with the help of his sons until his death on August 4, 1894. He is buried at Bethany United Church of Christ.

1511. Shoaf, Jacob A.

Private, Company A, 42nd Regiment
N.C. Troops

Jacob was born in 1846 to Henry and Catharine Koontz Shoaf. Jacob worked as a farmer prior to volunteering for service in Rowan County on March 10, 1862. He was reported present until wounded at Petersburg, Virginia, on August 26, 1864. Jacob was reported absent, wounded, through October 1864 and was paroled at Greensboro, North Carolina, on May 3, 1865. After the war, Jacob returned to the Tyro township, where, on December 19, 1867, he married Priscilla Koontz. Jacob and Priscilla were living in the Tyro township in 1870. No further records.

1512. Shoaf, Jacob Roswell

Private, Company A, 42nd Regiment
N.C. Troops

Jacob was born on December 16, 1846, to Jacob and Elizabeth Brinkley Shoaf. Jacob worked as a farmer prior to volunteering for service in Rowan County on March 3, 1862. He was reported present until wounded in action in June 1864. Jacob was hospitalized at Richmond, Virginia, until July 25, 1864, when he died of his wounds.

1513. Shoaf, Jesse

Private, Watauga Marksmen
Company B, 37th Regiment N.C. Troops

Jesse was born in 1825. Jesse worked as a farmer, and, on July 10, 1858, he married Sarah Sowers. Jesse was conscripted into service at Camp Holmes, North Carolina, on October 1, 1864. He was reported present until captured at Hatcher's Run, Virginia, on April 2, 1865. Jesse was confined at Point Lookout, Maryland, until June 19, 1865, when he was released after taking the oath of allegiance. No further records.

1514. Shoaf, John F.

Private, Company A, 42nd Regiment
N.C. Troops

John was born in 1846 to William and Mary Shoaf. John worked as a farmer in the Boone township prior to being conscripted into service on March 20, 1864. He was reported present until captured at Battery Anderson, Fort Fisher, North Carolina, on December 25, 1864. John was confined at Point Lookout, Maryland, via Fort Monroe, Virginia, until May 13, 1865, when he was released. After the war, John made his way home to the Boone township, where, in 1867, he married Mary. John and Mary would have seven children: Martha (1869), Cornelia (1871), Mary (1872), William (1874), Washington (1876), Margaret (1879), and Laura (1880). John and his family lived in the Boone area through 1880. No further records.

1515. Shoaf, John F.

Private, Carolina Rangers
Company B, 10th Virginia Cavalry
Regiment

John was born in 1826 to Jacob and Susan Hinkle Shoaf. John worked as a farmer and a miller in the northern district of Davidson County, and, in 1845 he married Catharine Leonard. John and Catharine would have three children: Richmond (1848), Hambrick (1857), and Robert (1861), before John volunteered for service in Davie County on October 29, 1861. He was sent to a Danville, Virginia, hospital to recover from a bout of rheumatism on January 1, 1863. John returned to service in February 1863 and was reported present until sent to the hospital with another complaint at Scotsville, Virginia, on April 10, 1863. He returned to service in June 1863 and was reported present through August 1864. John was paroled at Greensboro, North

Carolina, on May 1, 1865. After the war, John lived as a successful farmer in the Macedonia area until his death on October 6, 1901. He is buried at Macedonia United Methodist Church.

1516. Shoaf, John Travis

Private, Company A, 42nd Regiment N.C. Troops

John was born on April 2, 1846, to Jacob and Eliza Grubb Shoaf. John worked as a farmer in the Boone area prior to being conscripted into service in Davidson County on March 24, 1864. He was reported present until captured at Battery Anderson, Fort Fisher, North Carolina, on December 25, 1864. John was confined at Point Lookout, Maryland, via Fort Monroe, Virginia, until May 13, 1865, when he was released. John made his way home, where, on February 4, 1868, he married Mary F. Sharpe. John and Mary would have seven children: Martha (1868), William (1874), Doc (1876), Margaret Eunna (1879), Hoyt (1883), Curtis (1886), and Della (1889). John worked as a farmer in the Boone township until his death on May 29, 1931. He is buried at Pine Primitive Baptist Church.

1517. Shoaf, Madison Riley

Private, Harnett Light Infantry Company F, 15th Regiment N.C. Troops (5th N.C. Volunteers)

Madison was born on October 27, 1844, to Jacob and Elizabeth Brinkley Shoaf. Madison worked as a miller prior to being conscripted into service in Wake County on July 15, 1862. He was reported present until hospitalized at Danville, Virginia, on June 4, 1864, with a gunshot wound of the leg, which was probably received at Cold Harbor, Virginia. Madison recovered from his wound and was reported present through October 1864. After the war, Madison returned to milling but also began trading with various mercantile stores, as well as operating a farm. In 1866, Madison married Martha C. Sink. Madison and Martha would have ten children: Mary (1867), David (1869), Lilla (1871), Sallie (1874), Minnie (1877), Cornia (1879), Ida (1882), Mattie Sue (1884), Holland (1887), and Sadie (1891). Madison lived in the Midway area until his death on June 17, 1924. He is buried at Midway United Methodist Church.

1518. Shoaf, William H.

Private, Company A, 10th Battalion, N.C. Heavy Artillery

William was born in 1843 to Elizabeth Shoaf. William worked as a shoemaker in the Shelly Shoe Factory prior to volunteering for service on April 23, 1862. He died of disease in Georgia on June 16, 1864.

1519. Shoup, Daniel

Sergeant, Company C, 70th Regiment N.C. Troops (1st N.C. Junior Reserves)

Daniel was born in 1845 to Johann Frederick and Amanda Lambeth Shoup. Daniel worked as a farmer prior to enlisting in the Junior Reserves on May 24, 1864. No further records.

1520. Shoup (Schaub), Julius Lafayette

First Sergeant, Thomasville Rifles Company B, 14th Regiment N.C. Troops (4th N.C. Volunteers)

Julius was born in 1842 to Johann Frederick and Amanda Lambeth Shoup. He was a student at Yadkin College prior to volunteering for service on April 27, 1861. Julius was promoted to corporal on January 11, 1862, and was promoted to second sergeant on November 2, 1862. Julius served as second sergeant until promoted to first sergeant on August 1, 1864. Julius was present at every engagement of the 14th Regiment. He was paroled at Appomattox Court House, Virginia, on April 9, 1865. In 1873, he married Ida Lee Wooten, and they would have three children: Baxter Lindsay, Ida, and Martha. Julius moved around Georgia, finally settling in LaGrange, Georgia, in 1881. Julius opened a photography studio in LaGrange at 110 Church Street, where he photographed such celebrities as Jefferson Davis and William Jennings Bryan. Julius was an active member of the United Confederate Veterans Chapter 405 and served as its commander for seven years. Along with being a civic leader, Julius wrote a small book about his experiences during the war and two major articles for *Confederate Veteran*. In 1874, he officially changed his name to Schaub, although the motivation behind the change is unknown. Around the turn of the century, many of Julius' photo-

graphs became popular because of their availability on postcards. Julius lived in LaGrange, Georgia, until his death on December 31, 1911.

1521. Shoup, Leonard

Private, Company C, 70th Regiment N.C. Troops (1st N.C. Junior Reserves)

Leonard was born in 1847 to Johann and Mary Kepler Shoup. He was the fraternal twin of Samuel Shoup. Leonard worked as a farmer prior to enlisting in the Junior Reserves on May 24, 1864. No further records.

1522. Shoup, Samuel

Private, Company C, 70th Regiment N.C. Troops (1st N.C. Junior Reserves)

Samuel was born in 1847 to Johann and Mary Kepler Shoup. He was the fraternal twin of Leonard Shoup. Samuel worked as a farmer prior to enlisting in the Junior Reserves on May 24, 1864. No further records.

1523. Shuler, David

Private, Randolph Rangers Company G, 46th Regiment N.C. Troops

David was born in 1834 to Andrew and Barbara Fouts Shuler. David worked as a farmer in the Thomasville area, and in 1854, he married Sarah Gorday. David and Sarah would have one surviving child, Andrew (1858), before David enlisted as a substitute in Randolph County on March 19, 1862. He was reported present until killed in a skirmish in the vicinity of Spotsylvania Court House, Virginia, on May 10, 1864.

1524. Shuler, Emsley

Private, Guilford Greys Company B, 27th Regiment N.C. Troops

Emsley was born in 1830 to Andrew and Barbara Fouts Shuler. Emsley worked as a clerk in the town of Thomasville, and in 1859, he married Margaret Edwards. He and Margaret would not have any children . Emsley volunteered for service in Guilford County on May 6, 1862. He was reported present until wounded in the left hip at Bristoe Station, Virginia, on October 14, 1863. Emsley was reported absent, wounded and disabled, through

February 1865. After the war, Emsley and Margaret moved to the Summerfield area of Guilford County. After Margaret's death, Emsley married Mary Hunt. Emsley lived in Guilford County until his death.

1525. Shuler, Franklin H. R.

Private, Company C, 70th Regiment N.C. Troops (1st N.C. Junior Reserves)

Franklin was born on June 12, 1847, to Andrew and Barbara Fouts Shuler. Franklin worked as a farmer prior to enlisting in the Junior Reserves on May 24, 1864. After the war, Franklin returned home, where, on April 14, 1870, he married Caroline Rickard. Franklin and Caroline would have only one surviving child: Mary Magdelena (1878). Franklin lived in the Thomasville township until his death on February 2, 1928. He is buried at Emanuel United Church of Christ.

1526. Shuler, John

Private, Company I, 42nd Regiment N.C. Troops

John was born in 1828. John worked as a farmer in the northern district of Davidson County, and, on March 11, 1858, he married Eliza Jane Byerly. John and Eliza would have a child, Robert (1860), before John volunteered for service on March 1, 1862. He was reported present for duty until paroled at Greensboro, North Carolina, on May 3, 1865. No further records.

1527. Shuler, Nicholas

Private, Company C, 76th Regiment N.C. Troops (6th N.C. Senior Reserves)

Nicholas was born in 1827. Nicholas worked as a farmer in the northern district of Davidson County, and, on February 2, 1848, he married Polly Everhart. Nicholas and Polly would have three children: Catharine (1849), David (1851), and Sophia (1853). He enlisted in Hill's Senior Reserve Battalion, which became part of the 6th N.C. Senior Reserves in January 1865. After the war, Nicholas returned to the Lexington township where he continued working on his farm. Nicholas lived in the Lexington township until his death in the 1880s. He is buried at Beulah United Church of Christ.

1528. Shutt, James C.

Private, Harnett Light Infantry Company F, 15th Regiment N.C. Troops (5th N.C. Volunteers)

James was born in 1844. James worked as a farmhand for Daniel Kimel in the Friedburg area prior to being conscripted into service in Wake County on July 15, 1862. He was captured at Crampton's Pass, Maryland, on September 14, 1862. James was confined at Fort Delaware, Delaware, until October 2, 1862, when he was paroled and transferred to Aiken's Landing, Virginia, for exchange. He was declared exchanged on November 10, 1862. James returned to service where he was reported present until wounded in the leg at Bristoe Station, Virginia, on October 14, 1863. He was reported absent, wounded, through April 1864. James returned to duty prior to October 1864. After the war, James returned home, where, in 1869, he married Mary Henrietta. James died in the 1890s. He is buried at Friedburg Moravian Church.

1529. Siceloff, Lumas P.

Musician, Company D, 42nd Regiment N.C. Troops

Lumas was born in 1843 to Andrew and Sarah A. Siceloff. Lumas worked as a farmer in the vicinity of "Wagner's" prior to being conscripted into service on October 1, 1863. He served as a private until appointed musician in March 1864. Lumas was reported present with the regimental band through August 1864. After the war, Lumas returned to the Midway area, where, in 1867, he married Martha C. Lumas and Martha would have five children: Mary (1868), Ellen (1870), James (1872), Caroline (1878), and David (1880). Lumas died sometime after 1890.

1530. Sills, Leonard T.

Private, Company F, 7th Regiment N.C. State Troops

Leonard was born in 1837. Leonard worked as a farmhand for Spencer Surratt in the Allegheny township. He volunteered for service on July 7, 1861. Leonard was wounded at Hanover Court House, Virginia, on May 27, 1862, and was taken out of action until he recovered in January 1863. Leonard was reported present until wounded in the right thigh and captured at Gettysburg, Pennsylvania, on July 3, 1863. He was confined at Point Lookout, Maryland, until October 2, 1863, when he was paroled and transferred to City Point, Virginia, for exchange. Leonard was exchanged on March 16, 1864, and was reported present until retired to the Invalid Corps on December 28, 1864. Leonard returned home and moved in with relatives in Montgomery County. He is buried at Lanes Chapel Methodist Church in Montgomery County.

1531. Sills, William H.

Corporal, Company F, 7th Regiment N.C. State Troops

William was born in 1841. William worked as a farmer in the Allegheny township prior to volunteering for service on March 3, 1862. He was wounded in the jaw at Fredericksburg, Virginia, on December 13, 1862. William recovered from his wounds and returned to service in March 1863. He was promoted to corporal on September 1, 1864, and was reported present through October 1864. William was paroled at Greensboro, North Carolina, on May 1, 1865. After the war, William returned to the Allegheny township, where, on March 29, 1866, he married Margaret Taylor. William and Margaret would have one child, John (1869), before moving to Montgomery County in the early 1900s. He is buried at Chandler's Grove United Methodist Church.

1532. Simerson, Burrell

Private, Holtsburg Guards Company A, 54th Regiment N.C. Troops

Burrell was born in 1843 to Robert and Rebecca Simerson. Burrell worked as a laborer prior to volunteering for service on March 4, 1862. He was reported present until captured at Rappahannock Station, Virginia, on November 7, 1863. Burrell was confined at Point Lookout, Maryland, until March 9, 1864, when he was paroled and transferred to City Point, Virginia, for exchange. No further records.

1533. Simerson, John H.

Private, Company M, 7th Confederate Cavalry Regiment Company H, 16th Battalion, N.C. Cavalry

John was born in 1845 to Robert and Rebecca Simerson. John worked as a farmer prior to enlisting in the 7th Confederate Cavalry in January 1862. The unit was disbanded, and he was transferred to the 16th N.C. Cavalry on July 11, 1864. John was reported present through October 1864. After the war, John returned home to the Boone township, where, on January 10, 1867, he married Mary A. Wood. John and Mary would have seven children: Martha (1869), Sarah (1871), Margaret (1873), Curtis (1875), James (1877), Mary (1878), and John (1880). John worked as a farmer until his death in the late 1880s. He is buried at Smith Grove Baptist Church.

1534. Simerson, Samuel Elijah

Private, Holtsburg Guards
Company A, 54th Regiment N.C. Troops

Samuel was born on April 20, 1846, to William and Fannie Nunally Simerson. Samuel worked as a farmer in the Boone township prior to volunteering for service when he turned 18 years old on April 20, 1864. He was wounded in the left elbow at Drewery's Bluff, Virginia, on May 16, 1864. Samuel was absent, wounded, in a Richmond, Virginia, hospital until furloughed on June 8, 1864. He was retired from service on December 30, 1864. After his retirement, Samuel returned home, where, in 1866, he married Louisa Wilson. Samuel and Louisa would have seven children: Sarah (1869), Tom (1872), Dora (1876), William Bud (1878), Ellen (1881), Roy (1882), and Farris (1885). Louisa died in 1891, and Samuel married Allie Walser Towe five years later. Samuel and Allie would not have any children. Samuel brandished an ugly scar on his left arm as a result of his wound until his death on August 15, 1927. He is buried at Churchland Baptist Church.

1535. Sink, Alexander Reid

Private, Company A, 42nd Regiment N.C. Troops

Alexander was born on November 27, 1845, to Peter and Mary Sink. Alexander worked as a farmer prior to being conscripted into service in New Hanover County on December 15, 1863. He was reported present until wounded in the vicinity of Petersburg, Virginia, on July 21, 1864. Alexander was reported absent,

The children of Andrew H. Sink and Gazelle Sink ca. 1900. Lee and Alfred are not pictured (Margaret F. Sink, *The Heritage of Davidson County*).

wounded, through October 1864. After the war, Alexander returned home to the Tyro township, where, on July 22, 1870, he married Susan Swicegood. Alexander and Susan would have one child, John H. (1871), before moving to the Salisbury area in 1875. Alexander later worked as a mill supervisor, and he and Susan would have four more children: Alex, William P., Nannie, and Essie. Alexander lived in what is now the China Grove area until his death on March 20, 1919. He is buried in the Union Lutheran Cemetery in Rowan County, North Carolina.

1536. Sink, Andrew

Corporal, Company C, 76th Regiment N.C. Troops (6th N.C. Senior Reserves)

Andrew was born on February 5, 1824, to Adam and Barbara Clodfelter Sink. Andrew worked as a farmer, and, in 1864, he married Mary Jane. He enlisted in Hill's Senior Reserves, which became a part of the 6th N.C. Senior Reserves in January 1865. After the war, Andrew and Mary would have nine children in their Pilgrim area home: Henry (1866), Lucy (1868), William (1870), Luther (1872), Laura (1875), Mary (1878), J. Franklin (1881), Lettie Pearl (1883), and Maude Olivia (1886). Andrew raised his family

on a modest farmer's income and was an active member of the church. Andrew lived in the Lexington township until his death on November 11, 1930. He is buried at Pilgrim Lutheran Church.

1537. Sink, Andrew Hege

Sergeant, Company A, 42nd Regiment N.C. Troops

Andrew was born on November 27, 1834, to Henry and Elizabeth Hege Sink. Andrew worked as a farmer prior to volunteering for service on November 26, 1861. He was mustered in with the rank of sergeant. Andrew was reported present until captured at Battery Anderson, Fort Fisher, North Carolina, on December 25, 1864. He was confined at Point Lookout, Maryland, until June 20, 1865, when he was released after taking the oath of allegiance. After the war, Andrew returned home to the Lexington township, where, on August 14, 1866, he married Gazelle Shoaf. Andrew and Gazelle would have a family of 11 children: Lee (1868), Alfred (1870), Susan Augusta (1872), John Cicero (1874), Mittie (1877), Martha (1879), Mary (1880), Robert Frank (1883), Washington (1885), David (1887), and Dedie M. (1891). Andrew made his farm a success and was respected as one of the finest men of the community. Andrew lived in the Lexington area until his death on January 18, 1893. He is buried at Shiloh United Methodist Church.

1538. Sink, Andrew Yokely

Private, Thomasville Rifles
Company B, 14th Regiment N.C. Troops
(4th N.C. Volunteers)

Andrew was born on March 16, 1838, to Daniel and Elizabeth Yokely Sink. Andrew worked as a farmer and considered the ministry prior to marrying Mary J. Delapp on March 8, 1859. Andrew and Mary had just begun their life together when Andrew volunteered for service on August 29, 1861. He was reported present until wounded in the neck on July 1, 1863, and was captured when left at Gettysburg, Pennsylvania, on July 5, 1863. Andrew was confined at David's Island, New York, until August 28, 1863, when he was paroled and transferred to City Point, Virginia, for exchange. He rejoined the company in January 1864 and was reported present until wounded in the right arm at Spotsylvania Court House, Virginia, on May 12, 1864. Andrew was retired to the Invalid Corps on December 12, 1864. After his return home, Andrew and Mary would have four children: Geneva (1867), Charles (1869), George (1874), and Sarah (1879). Mary died in 1898, and on December 3, 1899, Andrew married Caroline Hege. Caroline died of pneumonia four years later. Andrew married for a third time in 1910 and moved to Forsyth County with his bride, Elizabeth Charles. Andrew lived in the Forsyth/Midway area until his death on June 12, 1916. He is buried at Friendship Baptist Church.

1539. Sink, David

Private, Company B, 48th Regiment
N.C. Troops

David was born on August 25, 1843, to Andrew and Elizabeth Byerly Sink. David worked as a farmer in the Lexington township prior to volunteering for service on March 12, 1862. He was reported present in the company records through October 1864. David was paroled at Greensboro, North Carolina, on May 3, 1865. After the war, David returned home, where, on September 21, 1865, he married Amanda Yarbrough. David and Amanda would have eight children: Fannie (1867), Ada (1870), Marshall (1873),

Martha (1875), Amelia (1877), John (1879), Mary Daisy (1881), and Charles Oscar (1882). David worked as a farmer and, later, as a supervisor at C. A. Hunt's mill in Lexington. David lived in Lexington until his death on March 13, 1918. He is buried in the Lexington City Cemetery.

1540. Sink, Gashem

Private, Lexington Wildcats
Company I, 14th Regiment N.C. Troops
(4th N.C. Volunteers)

Gashem was born in 1842 to Absalom and Mary Everhart Sink. Gashem worked as a blacksmith prior to volunteering for service on May 14, 1861. He was reported present until he died of typhoid fever at Richmond, Virginia, on June 8, 1862.

1541. Sink, George

Private, Cleveland Rangers
Company G, 33rd Regiment N.C. Troops

George was born in 1839 to Michael and Christina Tesh Sink. George worked as a farmer in the Midway area, and, on July 27, 1859, he married Sarah E. Kelly. George was conscripted into service in Forsyth County on July 15, 1862. He died of disease at Richmond, Virginia, on December 16, 1862. A stone was placed in his honor at Old Vernon Methodist Church.

1542. Sink, George Mero

Private, Harnett Light Infantry
Company F, 15th Regiment N.C. Troops
(5th N.C. Volunteers)

George was born on February 24, 1831, to George and Eva Long Sink. George worked as a farmer, and, on March 5, 1859, he married Amanda Yokely. George and Amanda would live north of Thomasville before George was conscripted into service in Wake County on July 15, 1862. He was wounded in the hip at Fredericksburg, Virginia, on December 13, 1862. George died of his wounds at Richmond, Virginia, on December 28, 1862.

1543. Sink, Gideon

Private, Company A, 42nd Regiment
N.C. Troops

Gideon was born on October 18, 1827, to Michael and Mary Nifong Sink.

Gideon married Albertine Sink in 1851. Gideon and Albertine would have four children, Mary (1852), Lucy (1857), Joseph (1859), and Caroline (1862), before Gideon was conscripted into service in New Hanover County on January 10, 1863. He was reported present until killed in action at Cold Harbor, Virginia, on June 3, 1864. A stone was placed in his honor at Pilgrim Lutheran Church.

1544. Sink, Henry L.

Private, Company C, 76th Regiment
N.C. Troops (6th N.C. Senior
Reserves)

Henry was born on August 14, 1815, to Christian and Mary Leonard Sink. Henry worked as a farmer in the southern district of Davidson County, and, in 1858, he married Malinda B. Clodfelter. Henry and Malinda would not have any children. Henry enlisted in Hill's Senior Reserves, which became part of the 6th N.C. Senior Reserves in January 1865. After the war, Henry continued farming in the Cotton Grove area. Henry died on July 19, 1873. He is buried at Jersey Baptist Church.

1545. Sink, Henry Luther

Private, Company A, 42nd Regiment
N.C. Troops

Henry was born on January 21, 1842, to Henry and Mary Shoaf Sink. Henry worked as a farmer in the Boone area prior to volunteering for service on November 26, 1861. He was reported present until captured at Battery Anderson, Fort Fisher, North Carolina, on December 25, 1864. Henry was confined at Point Lookout, Maryland, via Fort Monroe, Virginia, until June 20, 1865, when he was released after taking the oath of allegiance. After the war, Henry returned home to the Boone township where he lived as a single farmer until marrying Sarah Hedrick on June 28, 1888. Henry and Sarah would have two children: William (1894) and Zella Mae (1900). Henry died on November 8, 1929. He is buried at St. Luke's Lutheran Church.

1546. Sink, Jacob

Private, Cleveland Rangers
Company G, 33rd Regiment N.C. Troops

Jacob was born on July 15, 1820, to Jacob and Magdalena Clodfelter Sink.

Jacob worked as a farmer, and, on August 9, 1841, he married Sarah Leonard. Jacob and Sarah would have five children, George (1842), Albertine (1844), Druscilla (1849), Sarah (1853), and John Frank (1857), before Jacob was conscripted into service on August 20, 1863. He was present until he died of unreported causes in Virginia on February 21, 1864. A stone was placed in his honor at Old Vernon Methodist Church.

1547. Sink, Jacob

Private, Harnett Light Infantry
Company F, 15th Regiment N.C. Troops
(5th N.C. Volunteers)

Jacob was born on October 15, 1840, to Adam and Barbara Clodfelter Sink. Jacob worked as a farmer prior to being conscripted into service in Wake County on July 15, 1862. He was reported present until wounded in the leg at Bristoe Station, Virginia, on October 14, 1863. He lost his leg to the wound and then died at Richmond, Virginia, on October 28, 1863. His body was brought home and interred at Hebron United Church of Christ.

1548. Sink, Jacob L.

Private, Company A, 42nd Regiment
N.C. Troops

Jacob was born in 1847 to Henry and Mary Shoaf Sink. Jacob worked as a farmer prior to volunteering for service on March 4, 1862. He died of disease in a Richmond, Virginia, hospital on September 16, 1862.

1549. Sink, Jesse

Private, Company A, 42nd Regiment
N.C. Troops

Jesse was born on January 28, 1825, to Jacob and Magdalena Clodfelter Sink. Jesse worked as a farmer in the Midway area, and, in 1846, he married Susan Clodfelter. Jesse and Susan would have eight children, Sarah (1847), Jacob (1850), Henry (1852), Hamilton (1854), Joseph (1856), Regina (1858), Louretta (1860), and Eliza (1862), before Jacob was conscripted into service in New Hanover County on January 10, 1863. He was reported present until he died of "gastritis" at a Raleigh, North Carolina, hospital on August 4, 1864. His body was brought home and buried at Midway United Methodist Church.

Lt. John F. Sink and family, in front of their mill, ca. 1895 (Edward Hill, *The Heritage of Davidson County*).

1550. Sink, John

Private, Company H, 15th Regiment
N.C. Troops (5th N.C. Volunteers)

John was born in 1835 to Andrew and Elizabeth Livengood Sink. John worked as a farmer, and, in 1861, he married Lucy Brinkley. John and Lucy would have a son, Eli (1862), before John was conscripted into service in Wake County on July 15, 1862. He was wounded in the arm at Fredericksburg, Virginia, on December 13, 1862. John returned home on a furlough and then returned to duty in May 1863. While he was away, his second son, Samuel, was born in December 1863. John was present until he died of unreported causes at Orange Court House, Virginia, on March 20, 1864.

1551. Sink, John D.

Private, Harnett Light Infantry
Company F, 15th Regiment N.C. Troops
(5th N.C. Volunteers)

John was born in 1838 to Adam and Barbara Clodfelter Sink. John worked as a farmer prior to enlisting in Wake County as a substitute on July 15, 1862. He was hospitalized at Richmond, Virginia, on December 11, 1862, with a gunshot wound. John died of his wounds or infection two days later, on December 13, 1862.

1552. Sink, John Franklin

Third Lieutenant, Company A, 42nd
Regiment N.C. Troops

John was born on August 18, 1842, to Michael and Lucy Tussey Sink. John lived in the Tyro area prior to volunteering for service on November 26, 1861. He was mustered in as a sergeant and was promoted to first sergeant on July 1, 1862. John was appointed to serve as third lieutenant on November 20, 1862. He was reported present until wounded in the right elbow and right forearm near Petersburg, Virginia, on June 18, 1864. John was reported absent, wounded, until discharged from service on February 6, 1865, because of "disabling wounds received." After his discharge, John returned home, where, on December 16, 1866, he married Callie Smith. John and Callie would have six children: Mary Elizabeth (1868), William (1872), Lee David (1873), George (1874), Walter (1879), and Ora Lucy (1881). John moved in the 1870s to the city of Lexington where he became a respected citizen and a master carpenter. John died on April 14, 1885. He is buried in the Lexington City Cemetery.

1553. Sink, John Travis

*Sergeant, Company A, 42nd Regiment
N.C. Troops*

John was born on February 23, 1839, to Peter and Mary Sink. John worked as a carpenter prior to volunteering for service on November 26, 1861. He was mustered in as a private and was promoted to sergeant on July 28, 1863. John served as a sergeant until captured at Battery Anderson, Fort Fisher, North Carolina, on December 25, 1864. He was confined at Fort Delaware, Delaware, via Fort Macon, North Carolina, until June 19, 1865, when he was released after taking the oath of allegiance. After the war, John returned home to the Tyro township, where, on April 26, 1866, he married Alice F. Koontz. John and Alice would not have any children. John continued his work as a carpenter until his death on April 25, 1906. He is buried at St. Luke's Lutheran Church.

1554. Sink, Joseph A.

*Private, Yanceyville Greys
Company A, 13th Regiment N.C. Troops
(3rd N.C. Volunteers)*

Joseph was born in 1827 to Adam and Barbara Clodfelter Sink. Joseph worked as a farmer in the northern district of Davidson County, and, in 1851, he married Mary A. Hedrick. Joseph and Mary would have three children, Cornelia (1855), John (1859), and Mary Anne (1861), before Joseph was conscripted into service at Camp Holmes, North Carolina, on February 28, 1864. He was reported present until wounded at Wilderness, Virginia, on May 5, 1864. Joseph was reported absent, wounded, until he returned to service that July. He died of unreported causes at Richmond, Virginia, on December 11, 1864.

1555. Sink, Joseph D.

*Private, Company A, 42nd Regiment
N.C. Troops*

Joseph was born on June 6, 1828, to Jacob and Magdalena Clodfelter Sink. Joseph worked as a farmer, and, in 1850, he married Wilhelmina Sink. Joseph and Wilhelmina would have five children, Gideon (1851), Jacob (1853), Amanda (1855), Mary (1858), and David (1860), before Joseph was conscripted into service in Northampton County on Janu-

ary 10, 1863. He was reported present until captured at Battery Anderson, Fort Fisher, North Carolina, on December 25, 1864. Joseph was confined at Point Lookout, Maryland, until June 20, 1865, when he was released after taking the oath of allegiance. After the war, Joseph returned home to the Lexington township and to a new son, John, who was born while he was away. Joseph and Wilhelmina would have one more child: Robert Lee (1867). Joseph lived in the Lexington township until his death on May 17, 1892. He is buried at Pilgrim United Church of Christ.

1556. Sink, Matthias

*Private, Company H, 15th Regiment
N.C. Troops (5th N.C. Volunteers)*

Matthias was born on October 12, 1838, to Andrew and Elizabeth Livengood Sink. Matthias worked as a farmer, and on January 12, 1862, he married Chrissie Bowers. Matthias and Chrissie were married for only six months when Matthias was conscripted into service in Wake County on July 15, 1862. He was reported present for duty through October 1864 and was paroled at Greensboro, North Carolina, on May 8, 1865. After the war, Matthias returned home to the Thomasville area, where he met his daughter, Agnes, who was born in 1863. Matthias and Chrissie would go on to have seven more children: Mollie (1866), William (1867), David Lee (1869), Charles (1871), Sally (1873), Margaret (1875), and John (1877). Matthias worked as a farmer until his death on August 15, 1920. He is buried at Pilgrim United Church of Christ.

1557. Sink, Obediah

*Private, Company A, 42nd Regiment
N.C. Troops*

Obed was born on July 17, 1844, to Michael and Lucy Tussey Sink. Obed worked as a farmer prior to being conscripted into service in Rowan County on October 31, 1862. He was reported present until captured at Battery Anderson, Fort Fisher, North Carolina, on December 25, 1864. Obed was confined at Point Lookout, Maryland, until June 20, 1865, when he was released after taking the oath of allegiance. After the war, Obed returned home to the northern part of the Cotton Grove township, where, on January 16, 1866, he married Sarah Long.

Sarah died only two years later. Obed married Sarah Thompson Miller on November 14, 1869. Tragically, after having one child, Cora (1871), Sarah died also, in 1872. Six years passed before Obed married for a third and final time, to Sallie Yokely Mock on January 8, 1878. Obed and Sallie lived together until his death on February 10, 1919. He is buried at Pilgrim United Church of Christ.

1558. Sink, Ransom

*Private, Company K, 21st Regiment
N.C. Troops (11th N.C. Volunteers)*

Ransom was born on July 27, 1828, to Daniel and Belinda Leonard Sink. Ransom worked as a farmer prior to being conscripted into service in Forsyth County on July 8, 1862. He was reported present until captured at Chancellorsville, Virginia, on May 3 or 4, 1863. He was confined at Old Capital Prison, Washington, D.C., until June 18, 1865, when he was released upon taking the oath of allegiance. After the war, Ransom returned home to the Lexington area, where, on September 2, 1866, he married Mary Ann Nifong. Ransom and Mary would have seven children together: Melinda (1867), Albert (1868), Dora Belle (1871), James Alex (1873), Emma Jane (1875), Clarinda (1878), and Mary (1880). Ransom worked as a farmer in the Hebron area until his death on March 12, 1864. He is buried at Hebron United Church of Christ.

1559. Sink, Samuel A.

*Private, Thomasville Rifles
Company B, 14th Regiment N.C. Troops
(4th N.C. Volunteers)*

Samuel was born on December 16, 1828, to Andrew and Elizabeth Livengood Sink. Samuel worked as a farmer in the Thomasville area prior to volunteering for service on April 23, 1861. He was reported present until hospitalized at Richmond, Virginia, on September 1, 1862. Samuel died of typhoid fever on September 8, 1862.

1560. Sink, Solomon

*Private, Company H, 15th Regiment
N.C. Troops (5th N.C. Volunteers)*

Solomon was born in 1833 to Andrew and Elizabeth Livengood Sink. Solomon worked as a farmer, and, in 1853, he married Elizabeth Clodfelter. Solomon and Elizabeth would have three sons, William (1854), Samuel (1857), and Colburn (1859), before Solomon was conscripted into service in Wake County on July 15, 1862. He died of pneumonia at Richmond, Virginia, on November 26, 1862.

1561. Sink, Valentine

Private, Company H, 48th Regiment N.C. Troops

Valentine was born on November 24, 1823, to Jacob and Magdalena Clodfelter Sink. Valentine worked as a farmer in the northern district of Davidson County, and, on January 15, 1847, he married Elizabeth Clodfelter. Valentine and Elizabeth would have two children: Henry (1848) and Susannah (1851). He lived with his family until conscripted into service in Wake County on October 18, 1863. Valentine was reported present until sent to a Lynchburg, Virginia, hospital for an unreported illness. He was in the hospital for about three months until dying of "chronic diarrhea" on March 21, 1864. His body was brought home and buried at Bethany United Church of Christ.

1562. Sink, William

Private, Harnett Light Infantry Company F, 15th Regiment N.C. Troops (5th N.C. Volunteers)

William was born on August 27, 1829, to Adam and Barbara Clodfelter Sink. William worked as a farmer, and, on July 4, 1858, he married Alunda Darr. William and Alunda would have three children, Molly (1859), Julie Ann (1860), and Isabella (1862), before William enlisted into service as a substitute in Wake County on July 15, 1862. He was reported present through October 1864. After the war, William returned home to the Lexington township. William and Alunda would have another three children: Adam (1866), Thomas Jackson (1867), and Charles Edgar (1871). William worked as a farmer until his death on May 4, 1892. He is buried at Pilgrim United Church of Christ.

1563. Sink, William

Private, Company H, 48th Regiment N.C. Troops

William was born in 1835 to Absa-lom and Mary Everhart Sink. William worked as a farmer, and, on February 28, 1854, he married Frances Everhart. William and Frances would have three children; Charles (1857), Mary (1858), and Julia (1862), before he was conscripted into service at Petersburg, Virginia, on August 8, 1862. He was reported present until hospitalized at Richmond, Virginia, on September 30, 1864. William spent the last three months of his life in the hospital; he died prior to January 1865.

1564. Sink, William Adam

Private, Harnett Light Infantry Company F, 15th Regiment N.C. Troops (5th N.C. Volunteers)

William was born on October 31, 1834, to John and Elizabeth Sink. William worked as a farmer in the Thomasville area, and, on August 19, 1857, he married Mahalia Yokely. William was conscripted into service in Wake County on July 15, 1862. He was captured at Crampton's Pass, Maryland, on September 14, 1862. William was confined at Fort Delaware, Delaware, until October 2, 1862, when he was paroled and transferred to Aiken's Landing, Virginia, for exchange. He was declared exchanged on November 10, 1862. William returned to service and was reported present until he was captured at Bristoe Station, Virginia, on October 14, 1863. He was confined at Old Capital Prison in Washington, D.C., until he died of dysentery on February 19, 1864.

1565. Sink, Zeno Nathaniel

Private, Company K, 21st Regiment N.C. Troops (11th N.C. Volunteers)

Zeno was born on October 11, 1843, to Solomon and Elizabeth Schneider Sink. Zeno worked as a farmer prior to being conscripted into service in Wake County on November 13, 1863. He was reported present until captured at Sayler's Creek, Virginia, on April 6, 1865. Zeno was confined at Newport News, Virginia, until June 27, 1865, when he was released after taking the oath of allegiance. After the war, Zeno moved to the Waughtown area of Forsyth County, where, in 1867, he married Sarah Norman. Zeno and Sarah would have four children: Henry (1868), Thomas (1869), Joseph (1871), and Walter (1874). Zeno worked as a farmer in Forsyth County, North Carolina, until his death on Feb-ruary 21, 1939. He is buried at Waughtown Baptist Church in Forsyth County.

1566. Skeen, James L.

Private, Company B, 48th Regiment N.C. Troops

James was born in 1837 to Osborne and Temperance Skeen. James worked as a farmer prior to being conscripted into service on August 8, 1862. He was reported present until captured at Bristoe Station, Virginia, on October 14, 1863. James was confined at Point Lookout, Maryland, until November 6, 1864, when he died of "an inflammation of the kidneys." He is buried in the Point Lookout National Cemetery.

1567. Skeen, James S.

Second Lieutenant, 65th Regiment N.C. Militia (1861 organization)

James was born in 1827 to Matthew and Rutha Lanier Skeen. James worked as a farmer in the southern district of Davidson County, and, in 1854, he married Mary E. James and Mary would have two children; Ivy (1856) and Dicy (1860), before James accepted a commission to serve as second lieutenant in the Jackson Hill District Company on February 11, 1862. No further records.

1568. Skeen, Joseph C.

Captain, 65th Regiment N.C. Militia (1861 organization)

Joseph was born on November 15, 1830, to Osborne and Temperance Skeen. Joseph worked as a miller in the Jackson Hill area prior to accepting a commission to serve as a captain in the Jackson Hill District Company on February 11, 1862. After his service, Joseph married Minerva Morris in 1865. Joseph and Minerva would have seven children: Temperance (1867), Newton (1870), Jane (1874), William (1876), Homer (1879), and Grover and Hendrix (1884). Joseph worked as a farmer and a miller until his death on July 18, 1909. He is buried at Canaan United Methodist Church. The inscription on his stone reads: "His trials are past/ His work is done/ He fought the fight/ The Victory won."

1569. Skeen, Milton D.

Company D, 5th Battalion, N.C. Home Guard

Milton was born on April 15, 1843. Milton worked as a laborer in the Allegheny township prior to joining the Home Guard in 1863. Church records from Pleasant Hill and family history report that he joined Rush's Home Guards, commanded by Noah E. Rush of Randolph County. After his service, Milton returned to the Allegheny area, where, in 1872, he married Julia Ann. Milton and Julia would only have one child, Allen (1874), who would die before his third birthday. Milton died of pneumonia on February 6, 1877. He is buried at Pleasant Hill United Methodist Church.

1570. Slater, Christian

Private, Company G, 2nd Battalion, N.C. Infantry

Christian was born in 1839 to William and Mary Slater. Christian was living with Solomon Payne before he volunteered for service in Forsyth County on September 19, 1861. He was reported present until captured at Roanoke Island, North Carolina, on February 8, 1862. Christian was confined at Elizabeth City, North Carolina, until paroled and released on February 21, 1862. He returned to duty and was reported present until deserting at Greenscastle, Pennsylvania, on June 25, 1863. No further records.

1571. Slater, William

Private, Company G, 2nd Battalion, N.C. Infantry

William was born in 1838 to William and Mary Slater. William worked as a farmer prior to volunteering in Forsyth County on September 19, 1861. He was never mustered in and was sent home. William reenlisted on March 25, 1863, and was reported present until captured at Gettysburg, Pennsylvania, on July 4, 1863. He was confined at Fort Delaware, Delaware, until July 30, 1863, when he was paroled and transferred to City Point, Virginia, for exchange. William was declared exchanged on August 1, 1863, and was reported present until he died of "acute dysentery" at Richmond, Virginia, on June 15, 1864.

1572. Sledge, Milton M.

Private, North State Boys Company K, 45th Regiment N.C. Troops

Milton was born in 1825 to Parrot and Lourena Allison Pate Sledge. Milton worked as a farmer in the Lexington township, and, in 1850, he married Elizabeth Regan Porter. Milton and Elizabeth would have four daughters, Louretta (1851), Roxanne (1854), Susan (1856), and Jane (1859), before Milton enlisted at Camp Magnum, Wake County on March 27, 1862. He died of unreported causes at Goldsboro, North Carolina, on May 20, 1862. He is buried in Goldsboro.

1573. Sledge, Moses S.

Private, Company I, 42nd Regiment N.C. Troops

Moses was born in 1827 to Parrot and Lourena Allison Pate Sledge. Moses worked as a teamster and a farmer, and, on February 24, 1852, he married Sarah Whirlow. Moses and Sarah would have three children, Paulina (1855), Henry (1859), and Robert (1862), before Moses volunteered for service on March 3, 1862. He was reported present for duty in every engagement of the 42nd North Carolina through October 1864. Moses was paroled at Greensboro, North Carolina, on May 1, 1865. After the war, Milton returned home where he and Sarah would have two more children: George (1867) and Peter (1870). Moses was contracted to carry the mail for the Lexington township in 1873 and did so until his death in 1887. Moses is possibly buried at Beulah United Church of Christ.

1574. Smith, Alfred A.

Private, Company A, 42nd Regiment N.C. Troops
Company G, 7th Confederate Cavalry

Alfred was born on April 5, 1837, to Solomon and Deborah Sapp Smith. Alfred worked as a farmer in the Jersey area prior to volunteering for service on November 26, 1861. He was reported present with the 42nd North Carolina until transferred to the 7th Cavalry on August 13, 1863, in exchange for Jacob C. Doty. After the war, Alfred returned home, where, on December 21, 1866, he married Phoebe Elmina Hedgecock. Alfred and Phoebe would have 11 children in their Cotton Grove home: Henry (1867), Flora (1869), Charlie (1870), Lillie (1873), Etta (1876), Martha (1878), Emma (1881), Lenora (1883), William (1886), Connie (1889), and Amanda (1890). Alfred

worked as a farmer until his death on October 28, 1925. He is buried at Jersey Baptist Church.

1575. Smith, Alfred H.

Private, Thomasville Rifles Company B, 14th Regiment N.C. Troops (4th N.C. Volunteers)

Alfred was born in 1843 to Henry and Susannah McCrary Smith. Alfred worked as a farmer prior to volunteering for service on April 23, 1861. He was reported present until captured at Mechanicsville, Virginia, on May 30, 1864. Alfred was confined at Elmira, New York, until June 19, 1865, when he was released after taking the oath of allegiance. After the war, Alfred returned home, where, in 1866, he married Phoebe. Alfred and Phoebe would have two children; Henry (1868) and Flora (1869), prior to moving out of the Midway township in the late 1870s. No further records.

1576. Smith, Andrew H.

Private, Confederate Guards Company K, 48th Regiment N.C. Troops

Andrew was born in 1841 to David and Caroline Smith. Andrew worked as a farmer prior to being conscripted into service on August 8, 1862. He was reported present until killed in action at Wilderness, Virginia, on May 5, 1864.

1577. Smith, Benjamin Franklin

Second Lieutenant, Davidson Guards Company A, 21st Regiment N.C. Troops (11th N.C. Volunteers)

Benjamin was born in 1834 to Benjamin and Christina Smith. Benjamin worked as a manager for his father's small plantation in the southern district of Davidson County, and, on February 10, 1855, he married Cynthia Walser. In 1856, the couple had a child, Lucy, who died after only three weeks. Ben volunteered for service on May 8, 1861, and was elected as third lieutenant. He was elected as second lieutenant on July 3, 1861, and served in that rank until he died of typhoid fever at Charlottesville, Virginia, on August 9, 1861.

1578. Smith, Calhoun M.

Corporal, Lexington Wildcats

Company I, 14th Regiment N.C. Troops (4th N.C. Volunteers)

Calhoun was born in 1841. Calhoun worked as a wheelwright in the town of Lexington prior to volunteering for service on May 14, 1861. He was mustered in as a private and was promoted to corporal on April 25, 1862. While serving as corporal, Calhoun was nominated for the Badge of Distinction for his actions during the battle of Chancellorsville, Virginia, on May 3, 1863. Calhoun was reported present throughout the war and was paroled at Appomattox Court House, Virginia, on April 9, 1865. No further records.

1579. Smith, Casper M.

Private, Company I, 42nd Regiment N.C. Troops

Casper was born in 1833 to Henry and Susannah McCrary Smith. Casper was named after his prominent grandfather, who was a large landowner in the Cotton Grove area. On November 19, 1856, Casper married Mary E. Smith. Casper and Mary would have one child, Susan (1858), before Casper enlisted in Rowan County on July 10, 1862. He was reported present until captured at Wise's Forks, Virginia, on March 10, 1865. Casper was confined at Point Lookout, Maryland, until May 14, 1865, when he was released after taking the oath of allegiance. No further records.

1580. Smith, Charles W.

Captain, 65th Regiment N.C. Militia (1861 organization)

Charles was born in 1844 to John and Susan Smith. Charles worked as a miller in the Lexington township prior to accepting a commission to serve as captain of the Lexington District Company on November 26, 1861. After his service, he returned to milling and also leased some of his land to sharecropping enterprises. In 1869, Charles married Clarinda Adams. Charles and Clarinda would have three children, John (1871), Mary (1877), and Nancy (1880), before moving out of the county in the 1880s. No further records.

1581. Smith, David

Major, 65th Regiment N.C. Militia (1861 organization)

David was born on February 21, 1822. David worked as a farmer in the southern district of Davidson County, and, in 1855, he married Alunda. David and Alunda would have four children: Lucinda (1856), Martha (1859), Sarah (1861), and Adam (1864). David was involved in the prewar militia, and when the 1861 organization took place, David was commissioned to serve as major of the 65th Militia. After his service, David continued his successful farm in the Healing Springs township until his death on December 29, 1919. He is buried at Clear Springs Cemetery. The inscription on his stone reads: "Nearly a century of faithfulness to God's duty."

1582. Smith, David

Corporal, Holtsburg Guards Company A, 54th Regiment N.C. Troops

David was born on February 5, 1830, to John and Susan Smith. David worked as a farmer in the Cotton Grove area, and, in 1855, he married Crissie Palmer. David and Crissie would have three children, Lindsay (1856), James (1858), and Nancy (1861), before David was mustered in as a corporal on May 6, 1862. He was reported present until June 13, 1862, when he was discharged after providing John Hotchedler as a substitute. After his return, David served as a Confederate justice of the peace until he was replaced during Reconstruction. David and Crissie would have seven more children: Mary (1863), Frances (1866), Zeb Vance (1869), Julius (1872), William (1874), George (1876), and Henry (1879). David returned to his post as a justice of the peace in 1875 and served in that office until his death on November 17, 1884. He is buried at Jersey Baptist Church.

1583. Smith, David H.

Private, Company B, 48th Regiment N.C. Troops

David was born in 1841 to John and Susannah Smith. David worked as a farmer prior to volunteering for service on March 6, 1862. He was killed in action at Sharpsburg, Maryland, on September 17, 1862.

1584. Smith, Ebenezer

Sergeant, Company A, 42nd Regiment N.C. Troops

Company A, 54th Regiment N.C. Troops

Ebenezer was born in 1839 to former N.C. Militia General George W. and Elizabeth Smith. Ebenezer worked as a farmer prior to volunteering for service on November 26, 1861. He was promoted to corporal prior to March 25, 1862, when he was transferred to the 54th North Carolina. Ebenezer was mustered into the 54th as a sergeant and served in that capacity until he died of disease in camp on November 6, 1862.

1585. Smith, Edward W.

Sergeant, Davidson Guards Company A, 21st Regiment N.C. Troops (11th N.C. Volunteers)

Edward was born in 1843 to William and Phoebe Hedgecock Smith. Edward worked as a farmer prior to volunteering for service on May 8, 1861. He was promoted to corporal on March 1, 1863, and to sergeant the following May. Edward was reported present until wounded in the hip and captured at Winchester, Virginia, on September 19, 1864. He was confined at Point Lookout, Maryland, until October 26, 1864, when he was released and transferred to Venus Point, Georgia, for exchange. Edward was exchanged on November 15, 1864, and was reported absent, wounded, through February 1865. After the war, Edward returned to the Cotton Grove township, where, on September 24, 1865, he married Betty A. Warford. No further records.

1586. Smith, Emanuel W.

Private, Harnett Light Infantry Company F, 15th Regiment N.C. Troops (5th N.C. Volunteers)

Emanuel was born in 1838 to James L. and Elizabeth Smith. Emanuel worked with his father in the blacksmith trade prior to being conscripted into service in Wake County on July 15, 1862. He was reported present until captured at Bristoe Station, Virginia, on October 14, 1863. Emanuel was confined at Point Lookout, Maryland, until April 24, 1864, when he was paroled and transferred to City Point, Virginia, for exchange. Emanuel returned to duty and was reported present through October 31, 1864. After the war, Emanuel returned to the Midway area, where, in 1867, he married Hazeltine. Emanuel lived in the Midway area until his death in the 1910s. He is buried at Macedonia United Methodist Church.

1587. Smith, Erasmus H.

Second Lieutenant, Company H, 48th Regiment N.C. Troops

Erasmus was born in 1842. Erasmus was a student prior to volunteering for service on March 3, 1862; he was mustered in as a sergeant. He was elected third lieutenant on August 30, 1862, and was reported present until wounded in the face at Fredericksburg, Virginia, on December 13, 1862. Erasmus recovered from his wounds and was elected second lieutenant on February 10, 1863. He was killed in action at Cold Harbor, Virginia, on June 3, 1864.

1588. Smith, Fielding S.

Private, Allen's Company, Gibb's Battalion, N.C. Prison Guards, Salisbury

Fielding was born on August 25, 1842, to former N.C. Militia General George W. and Elizabeth Smith. Fielding worked on his father's plantation prior to receiving an appointment to serve as a guard at the Salisbury Prison in Allen's Company. While serving in this capacity, Fielding contracted pneumonia and died on March 10, 1865. He is buried at Jersey Baptist Church.

1589. Smith, Francis Marion

Private, Confederate Guards Company K, 48th Regiment N.C. Troops

Francis was born on November 29, 1844, to George and Jane Smith. Francis worked as a clerk prior to being conscripted into service in Forsyth County on August 8, 1862. He was wounded at Fredericksburg, Virginia, on December 13, 1862. Francis was issued a 60-day furlough and returned to service in March 1863. He was reported present through October 1864. After the war, Francis returned to the Lexington township, where, in 1869, he married Mary Elizabeth Berrier. Francis bought several properties within the city before moving out to the Shiloh area in 1883. Francis lived in the Shiloh area until his death on December 13, 1888. He is buried at Shiloh United Methodist Church.

1590. Smith, George Franklin

Captain, Holtsburg Guards Company A, 54th Regiment N.C. Troops

George was born on September 27, 1825, to Casper and Elizabeth Smith. George worked as a small planter in the Cotton Grove area, and, on December 1, 1847, he married Nancy Miller. George and Nancy would have four sons; George (1849), Henry (1850), Elisha (1856), and Thomas (1859), before he volunteered for service on March 4, 1862. He was appointed first lieutenant on May 26, 1862, and was promoted to captain on September 7, 1862. George served as company commander until he was captured at Rappahannock Station, Virginia, on November 7, 1863. He was confined at Johnson's Island, Ohio, until June 13, 1865, when he was released after taking the oath of allegiance. After his return, George and Nancy would have three more children: Maria (1863), Nannie (1866), and William V. (1869). George served as a county commissioner for two terms and also leased land for sharecropping to a large number of freedmen. He contributed two articles to *Confederate Veteran* magazine. George lived in the Cotton Grove area until his death on September 13, 1893. He is buried at Jersey Baptist Church.

1591. Smith, George Washington

Private, Company B, 48th Regiment N.C. Troops

George was born in 1845 to John and Elizabeth Darr Smith. George worked as a farmer prior to volunteering for service on March 4, 1862. He was reported present until he became sick in September 1862. George returned in November and was reported present until wounded in the left shoulder at Bristoe Station, Virginia, on October 14, 1863. George was discharged from service on March 31, 1864, due to "anchylosis of his left arm," a condition resulting directly from his wound. After his return home, George married Elizabeth Huff on July 17, 1865. George and Elizabeth would have five surviving children: Daniel (1866), Mary (1871), Claude (1882), Frederick (1887), and Paul (1893). George lived in the Cotton Grove area through 1900. No further records.

1592. Smith, Green

Private, Company I, 42nd Regiment N.C. Troops

Green was born in 1825. Green worked as a farmer in the southern district of Davidson County, and, on November 9, 1851, he married Elizabeth Miller. Green and Elizabeth would have three children, Franklin (1852), George (1857), and Phoebe (1861), before Green volunteered for service on March 3, 1862. He was discharged for unreported reasons on May 28, 1862. No further records.

1593. Smith, Henry A.

Private, Company A, 10th Battalion, N.C. Heavy Artillery

Henry was born on March 15, 1813, to Solomon and Deborah Sapp Smith. Henry worked as a farmer in the area north of Thomasville, and, on March 25, 1843, he married Sophia Louvina Shields. Henry and Sophia would have one child, Amanda (1850), before Henry was conscripted into service on December 15, 1862. He was reported present for duty through September 1864. No further records.

1594. Smith, James

Laborer, Charlotte Ordinance Depot, Confederate States Navy

James was born in 1847 to Benjamin and Christina Smith. James worked as a clerk in his father's mercantile shop in Lexington, and, in 1861, he married Cornelia. James and Cornelia would have two children: William (1862) and Gracie (1868). According to *Moore's Roster*, James was detailed to work as a supply handler at the Confederate Navy Yard at Charlotte. His duties included supervising ordnance transport to different tracks and fulfilling requisitions from various Navy departments. After his return to Lexington, he opened his own general store and became a successful merchant. In 1880, he was the postmaster for the city of Lexington. James moved out of the county around the turn of the century. No further records.

1595. Smith, James

Private, Company B, 48th Regiment N.C. Troops

James was born on July 24, 1829. James worked as a merchant in the Boone area, and, in 1850, he married Margaret Sharpe. James and Margaret would have six children, William (1851), Francis (1854), James (1857), Alfred (1858), Dicy (1859), and Susan (1861), before James was conscripted into service on August 8, 1862. He was wounded when a bullet fractured his left leg and was captured at Sharpsburg, Maryland, on September 17, 1862. James was hospitalized at Philadelphia, Pennsylvania, until transferred to Fort Delaware, Delaware, on December 12, 1862. James stayed in Delaware only three days, as he was paroled and transferred on December 15, 1862. He was declared exchanged on December 18, 1862. James was reported absent, wounded, through November 19, 1864, when he was discharged because of "disabling wounds." After his return from the war, James and Margaret would have two more children: George (1865) and Mary (1867). James continued as a merchant in the Tyro community until his death on December 8, 1896. He is buried at Churchland Baptist Church.

1596. Smith, James L.

Private, Company C, 70th Regiment
N.C. Troops (1st N.C. Junior
Reserves)

James was born in 1847 to Joel and Judith Smith. James worked as a farmer prior to enlisting in the Junior Reserves on May 24, 1864. He was reported in a Lynchburg, Virginia, hospital in February 1865. No further records.

1597. Smith, James T.

Private, Company B, 48th Regiment
N.C. Troops

James was born in 1842 to Charles and Nancy Smith. James worked as a farmer, and in 1861, he married Catharine. He was conscripted into service on August 8, 1862, and was wounded at Sharpsburg, Maryland, on September 17, 1862. James died of his wounds the next day. A memorial stone was placed in his honor at the Lexington City Cemetery.

1598. Smith, James W. S.

Private, Company H, 48th Regiment
N.C. Troops

James was born in 1842 to George and Rebecca Smith. James worked as a farmer prior to enlisting in Wayne

County on May 8, 1862. He was reported present until wounded in the foot at Fredericksburg, Virginia, on December 13, 1862. James recovered and returned to duty on March 1, 1863. He was wounded in the right leg and captured at Sayler's Creek, Virginia, on April 6, 1865. James was sent to a Washington, D.C., hospital, where his right leg was amputated. James died a little over a month later of "pyaemia" in Washington on May 13, 1865.

1599. Smith, John F.

Private, Company F, 7th Regiment
N.C. State Troops

John was born in 1837 to Henry and Susannah McCrary Smith. John worked as a farmer prior to volunteering for service on June 29, 1861. He was mustered in as a sergeant but was reduced in rank on September 15, 1861. John served as a private until discharged at Camp Graham on December 17, 1861, because of "incipient consumption and typhoid fever." John returned home and was last reported as living in the Tyro township in 1870. No further records.

1600. Smith, John F.

Third Lieutenant, Company H, 48th
Regiment N.C. Troops

John was born in 1827. John worked as a small planter in the southern district of Davidson County, and, in 1854, he married Emily. John and Emily would have a daughter, Mary Jane (1857), before John enlisted, he was appointed third lieutenant on April 5, 1862. He was reported present until his commission was revoked on the basis that "the company did not have men enough." No further records.

1601. Smith, John H.

Private, Company B, 48th Regiment
N.C. Troops

John was born on August 24, 1846, to Alexander and Anne Conrad Smith. John worked as a farmer prior to being conscripted into service on an unreported date. He was reported present through October 31, 1864, and was paroled at Greensboro, North Carolina, on May 3, 1865. After the war, John returned to the Silver Hill township, where, in 1870, he married Mary Francis. John lived in the

Tabor area until his death on May 31, 1927. He is buried at Mount Tabor United Church of Christ.

1602. Smith, John H.

Private, Davidson Guards
Company A, 21st Regiment N.C. Troops
(11th N.C. Volunteers)

John was born in 1836 to Michael and Frances Smith. John worked as a farmer, and in 1860, he married Mary Hedrick. John lived in the Lexington area prior to enlisting in Wake County on April 27, 1862. He was reported present until captured at Gettysburg, Pennsylvania, on July 2, 1863. John was confined at Fort Delaware, Delaware, until June 19, 1865, when he was released after taking the oath of allegiance. No further records.

1603. Smith, Lindsay F.

Private, Company B, 48th Regiment
N.C. Troops

Lindsay was born in 1844 to Alexander and Anne Conrad Smith. Lindsay worked as a farmer prior to volunteering for service on March 6, 1862. He was wounded at King's School House, Virginia, on June 25, 1862. Lindsay recovered from his wounds and returned to service by March 1, 1863. He was reported present through October 1864 and was paroled at Greensboro, North Carolina, on May 3, 1865. After the war, Lindsay returned home to the Silver Hill area where, in 1870, he married Mary Edwards, a recent arrival from Illinois. Lindsay and Mary moved to Columbia, South Carolina, for a short time, where Edward (1876), was born. By 1880, the couple had moved back to Lexington where Lindsay found work in C. A. Hunt's mill. Lindsay lived in the town of Lexington until his death on August 4, 1916. He is buried in the Lexington City Cemetery.

1604. Smith, Martin V.

Private, Confederate Guards
Company K, 48th Regiment N.C. Troops

Martin was born on November 5, 1840, to Thompson and Lucinda Smith. Martin worked as a farmer, and, on January 9, 1862, he married Phoebe Ann Thomas. Martin and Phoebe would be married for only seven months before Martin was conscripted into service on August 8, 1862. He was severely wounded at Sharpsburg, Maryland, on September 17, 1862, and then was reported absent, wounded, through June 1863. While he was home on furlough, Martin's first son, Joseph (1863), was born. Martin was placed on light duty at Charlotte, North Carolina, from July 1863 to April 1864. Martin returned to regular service in May 1864 and was reported present until captured at Hatcher's Run, Virginia, on March 25, 1865. He was confined at Point Lookout, Maryland, until June 20, 1865, when he was released after taking the oath of allegiance. After the war, Martin returned to the North Thomasville township where he and Phoebe would have six more children: Belle (1866), Charles (1869), Thomas (1873), Robert (1879), Emma (1884), and Noah (1893). Martin worked as a small farmer until his death on October 12, 1909. He is buried at Abbott's Creek Primitive Baptist Church.

1605. Smith, Moses L.

Private, Company A, 42nd Regiment N.C. Troops

Moses was born in 1845 to Yarbrough and Rebecca Smith. Moses worked as a farmer prior to volunteering for service on November 26, 1861. He was reported present through October 1864. Moses was paroled at Greensboro, North Carolina, on May 10, 1865. No further records.

1606. Smith, Peter

Private, Company F, 76th Regiment N.C. Troops (6th N.C. Senior Reserves)

Peter was born on March 4, 1818. Peter worked as a small planter in the southern district of Davidson County, and, in 1853, he married Ellen Lenora. Peter and Ellen would have six children: Wesley (1855), Martin (1856), Elizabeth (1857), Ellen (1858), George (1859), and Thomas (1861). He served in Moss' Senior Reserves, which became Company F of the 6th N.C. Senior Reserves in January 1865. After the war, Peter returned home, where he and his family made a living on the land. Peter lived in the Conrad Hill township until his death on June 23, 1902. He is buried at Beck's United Church of Christ.

1607. Smith, Peter M.

Sergeant, Holtsburg Guards
Company A, 54th Regiment N.C. Troops

Peter was born on February 25, 1835, to Henry and Susannah McCrary Smith. Peter was working as an overseer in 1860 and employed a free black man named Lindsay Sears as his assistant. Peter volunteered for service on March 4, 1862, and was mustered in as a corporal. He was promoted to sergeant in July 1862 and served in that capacity until wounded in the back and head at Fredericksburg, Virginia, on December 13, 1862. Peter was reported absent, wounded, until he returned to duty prior to May 1, 1863. He was wounded again when a bullet fractured his left foot near Fredericksburg, Virginia, on May 4, 1863. Peter had two toes amputated and was reported as absent, sick, in November 1863. He was assigned to "conscription duty" in Lexington, North Carolina, from June 18, 1864, to October 31, 1864. As of April 6, 1865, Peter was reported as absent, disabled. After the war, Peter returned to his father's farm in the Cotton Grove area and, ten years later, on January 24, 1875, he married Margaret Broadway. Peter would marry twice more over his life: to Mary Koontz and then to Sally Ingram. Peter lived in the Cotton Grove township until his death on January 16, 1919. He is buried at Jersey Baptist Church.

1608. Smith, Robert A.

Private, Company A, 42nd Regiment N.C. Troops

Robert was born in 1844 to Thompson and Lucinda Smith. Robert worked as a blacksmith prior to volunteering for service on March 31, 1862. He was reported present until captured at Battery Anderson, Fort Fisher, North Carolina, on December 25, 1864. Robert was confined at Point Lookout, Maryland, via Fort Monroe, Virginia, until June 20, 1865, when he was released. No further records.

1609. Smith, Thomas

Private, Company D, 48th Regiment N.C. Troops

Thomas was born in 1832 to Casper and Elizabeth C. Smith. Thomas worked as a farmer in the Healing Springs area, and, in 1854, he married Nancy D.

Thomas and Nancy would have four children; Julian (1855), Louisa (1857), Anderson (1859), and David (1862), before Thomas was conscripted into service on August 8, 1862. He was wounded in the left shoulder at Sharpsburg, Maryland, on September 17, 1862. Thomas recovered and was reported present until wounded in the right arm at Wilderness, Virginia, on May 5 or 6, 1864. He was furloughed on June 18, 1864, and returned to service prior to September 1864. Thomas was reported present until paroled at Burkittsville, Virginia, between April 14 and 17, 1865. After the war, Thomas returned to the Allegheny township where he and Nancy would have four more children: Jeremiah (1866), James (1869), Eli (1873), and Andorra (1875). Thomas continued working as a farmer until his death on July 17, 1903. He is buried at Allegheny United Methodist Church.

1610. Smith, William

Private, Carolina Rangers
Company B, 10th Virginia Cavalry Regiment

William was born in 1831. William worked as a farmer in the northern district of Davidson County, and, in 1859, he married Sarah Mock. William and Sarah would have a son, Cicero (1860), before William volunteered for service in Davie County on October 29, 1861. He was reported present until detailed in May and June 1863. Once he returned from detail, William was reported present through December 31, 1864, when he was last issued clothing. After the war, William returned to the Tyro area where he continued to work on his farm, producing a high-yield corn. William and Sarah would have six more children: Robert (1866), Charlie (1868), Mack (1871), Samuel (1873), Etta (1877), and Julia (1879). William lived in the Bethel area until his death on December 5, 1896. He is buried at Bethel United Methodist Church.

1611. Smith, William

Private, Chatam Light Infantry
Company G, 48th Regiment N.C. Troops

William was born on December 18, 1833, to Michael and Nancy Smith. William worked as a wagonmaker in the Abbott's Creek area, and, in 1856, he married Eliza Ruth Yokely. Leason Clodfelter was working for him in 1860. William and Eliza would have three children, Madison (1857), Laura (1859), and Phoebe (1861), before William was conscripted into service on August 8, 1862. He was reported either captured or deserted to the enemy at Sharpsburg, Maryland, on September 17, 1862. William was released on September 27, 1862, after taking the oath of allegiance. William returned to the county after some time and returned to Abbott's Creek. William and Eliza would have three more children: Pleasant (1866), William (1867), and John (1870). Business rebounded fairly quickly after the war, and William was still listed as a wagonmaker in 1870. William continued in his trade until his death on September 21, 1876. He is buried at Abbott's Creek Primitive Baptist Church.

1612. Smith, William C.

Private, Confederate Guards
Company K, 48th Regiment N.C. Troops

William was born in 1843 to David and Catharine Smith. William worked as a farmer prior to being conscripted into service on August 8, 1862. He died of disease at Winchester, Virginia, on October 20, 1862.

1613. Smith, William W.

Private, Company B, 48th Regiment
N.C. Troops

William was born in 1817. William worked as a farmer in the southern district of Davidson County, and, on December 14, 1840, he married Phoebe Ann Hedgecock. William and Phoebe would have three surviving children, Edward (1843), Eliza (1852), and Elisha (1853), before William was conscripted into service on August 8, 1862. He was wounded in the head at Sharpsburg, Maryland, on September 17, 1862. William recovered from his wounds and returned to service on November 1, 1862. He was reported present through October 1864. No further records.

1614. Smith, Yarbrough H.

Private, Lexington Wildcats
Company I, 14th Regiment N.C. Troops
(4th N.C. Volunteers)
Company B, 48th Regiment N.C. Troops

Yarbrough was born in 1820. Yarbrough worked as a tailor in the southern district of Davidson County, and, in 1842, he married Rebecca Myers. Yarbrough and Rebecca would have three children, Moses (1845), Lovey (1847), and George (1849), before Yarbrough volunteered for service on May 14, 1861. He was reported present until discharged on August 14, 1862, because of being over age. For the next year, Yarbrough continued his work at home, and then he enlisted into service as a substitute on October 21, 1863. He was present until he was sent to a division hospital in September 1864. Yarbrough deserted to the enemy on an unreported date. He was later released after taking the oath of allegiance. Yarbrough returned home, where he died prior to 1870. He is buried at Holloways Baptist Church.

1615. Snider, Amos P.

Private, Company B, 57th Regiment
N.C. Troops

Amos was born in 1834 to Solomon and Elizabeth Byerly Snider. Amos worked as a farmer prior to enlisting in Rowan County on July 4, 1862. He was hospitalized at Richmond, Virginia, on November 1, 1862. Amos died of pneumonia eight days later on November 9, 1862. He is buried in the Hollywood Cemetery in Richmond.

1616. Snider, David Henderson

Private, Chatam Light Infantry
Company G, 48th Regiment N.C. Troops

David was born on March 11, 1835, to Lewis and Mary Workman Snider. David worked as a farmer, and, in 1856, he married Caroline Lomax. David and Caroline would have three children, Lewis (1858), Franklin (1859), and Frances (1861), before David was conscripted into service on August 14, 1862. He was wounded at Sharpsburg, Maryland, on September 17, 1862. David recovered and was reported present by January 1863. He was wounded at Fredericksburg, Virginia, on May 2, 1863, and again at Burgess' Mill, Virginia, when a "cannon shot struck a tree and caused a limb to fall on him." David was reported present until he was captured at Hatcher's Run, Virginia, on February 2, 1865. David deserted to the enemy on February 22, 1865. He was confined at

Washington, D.C., until he was released after taking the oath of allegiance. After the war, David returned home to the Boone township and his new daughter, Albertine (1863). David and Caroline would have three more children: Sarah (1866), Ulysses (1869), and Martha (1873). David and his family lived in the Boone area until his death on November 18, 1912. He is buried at Pine Primitive Baptist Church.

1617. Snider, Eli

Private, Davidson Guards
Company A, 21st Regiment N.C. Troops
(11th N.C. Volunteers)

Eli was born in 1836 to Solomon and Elizabeth Byerly Snider. Eli worked as a farmer prior to volunteering for service on May 8, 1861. He died of "enteric fever" in a Front Royal, Virginia, hospital on October 4, 1861.

1618. Snider, Franklin F.

Private, Company B, 48th Regiment
N.C. Troops

Franklin was born on May 15, 1828, to Solomon and Elizabeth Byerly Snider. Franklin worked as a farmer in the Shiloh area, and, in 1859, he married Martha Wilson. Franklin volunteered for service on March 6, 1862, and was hospitalized at Richmond, Virginia, on December 6, 1862. Apparently, his disease was so severe that he was allowed to return home, where, on March 7, 1863, he passed away. He is buried at Shiloh United Methodist Church.

1619. Snider, George Washington

Corporal, Company H, 48th Regiment
N.C. Troops

George was born on April 9, 1838, to Solomon and Elizabeth Byerly Snider. George worked as a farmer prior to volunteering for service on March 17, 1862. He was mustered in as a private and promoted to corporal before October 31, 1864. George was reported present for every campaign of the 48th North Carolina until, for reasons undisclosed, he deserted to the enemy at Petersburg, Virginia, on March 6, 1865. George was confined at Washington, D.C., four days later and was held until taking the oath of allegiance on an unreported date. After the war, George was furnished transportation by the U.S. government back to the Yadkin/Tyro area. George returned and grieved for the loss of several of his brothers. On January 2, 1866, George married Elizabeth Waitman. George and Elizabeth would have eight children: Clark (1867), Alexander (1868), Mary (1870), Clara (1871), Lizzie (1872), Thomas (1874), Zeb V. (1876), and Melinda (1880). Neither George nor his widow would be able to draw a pension from the state, despite George's three years of faithful service: his desertion disqualified him and his family from receiving compensation. George lived in the Tyro area until his death on January 28, 1906. He is buried at Shiloh United Methodist Church.

1620. Snider, John N.

Corporal, Company A, 42nd Regiment N.C. Troops

John was born on February 22, 1826, to Solomon and Elizabeth Byerly Snider. John worked as a farmer in western Davidson County, and, in 1850, he married Emeline Gobble. John and Emeline would have six children, Margaret (1851), Joseph (1852), Mary (1855), Franklin (1856), Fanny (1858), and Pretine (1859), before John enlisted in Rowan County on May 15, 1862. He was reported present and was promoted to corporal in January 1863. John was wounded in the forehead on June 18, 1864, at Petersburg, Virginia. As part of his treatment, "pieces were taken out of the broken skull." John died on June 20, 1864, and is buried at Shiloh United Methodist Church, although his service record continues. After a review of the information from the National Archives, it is the conclusion of the author that John N. Snider becomes confused in the records with a John Snider of Davie County.

1621. Snider, Jonathan H.

Private, Franklin Guides to Freedom Company K, 44th Regiment N.C. Troops

Jonathan was born in 1831. Jonathan worked as a farmer in the southern district of Davidson County, and, on March 15, 1856, he married Sarah Riley. Jonathan and Sarah would have three children, Rebecca Jane (1857), William C. (1859), and Elizabeth (1862), before Jonathan was conscripted into service on November 29, 1862. He was reported present until cap-tured at Burgess' Mill, Virginia, on October 27, 1864. Jonathan was confined at Point Lookout, Maryland, until May 2, 1865, when he died of "dropsy." He is buried in the Point Lookout National Cemetery.

1622. Snider, Keelion D.

Second Lieutenant, 66th Regiment N.C. Militia (1861 organization)

Keelion was born on November 10, 1820, to Jacob and Sarah Snider. Keelion worked as a farmer, and, in 1844, he married Elizabeth. Keelion and Elizabeth would have seven surviving children: Elizabeth (1846), Jacob (1850), Archibald (1854), Victoria (1856), Merido P. (1859), Ada (1874), and John (1877). Keelion was commissioned to serve as a second lieutenant in the Reedy Creek District Company on November 26, 1861. Keelion lived in the Arcadia area until his death on December 19, 1891. He is buried at Mt. Olivet United Methodist Church.

1623. Snider, Lewis Wesley

Private, Franklin Guides to Freedom Company K, 44th Regiment N.C. Troops

Lewis was born in 1829 to Jonathan and Elizabeth Stewart Snider. Lewis married Elizabeth P. Riley in 1849, and the two became the first Sniders to settle in southern Davidson County. Lewis and Elizabeth's home was one mile north of the present town of Denton, out of which grew the Snider Lumber Company, a thriving business. Lewis and Elizabeth would have five children, James (1850), Rocity (1852), Margaret (1855), Peter (1859), and Lewis W. Jr. (1862), before Lewis was conscripted into service on November 29, 1862. He was reported present until captured at Bristoe Station, Virginia, on October 14, 1863. Lewis was confined at Point Lookout, Maryland, via Washington, D.C., until June 25, 1864, when he died of unreported causes while a prisoner of war. He is buried in the Point Lookout National Cemetery.

1624. Snider, Peter

Private, Saulston Volunteers Company K, 27th Regiment N.C. Troops

Peter was born in 1825 to Solomon and Elizabeth Byerly Snider. Peter worked as a farmer in the Tyro area, and, in 1857, he married Mary Lanning. Peter and Mary would have two sons, Charles (1859) and John (1861), before Peter was conscripted into service at Camp Holmes, North Carolina, on May 23, 1863. He was reported present until wounded at Wilderness, Virginia, on May 5, 1864. Peter died of unreported causes on August 8, 1864.

1625. Snider, Romulus S.

Private, Thomasville Rifles Company B, 14th Regiment N.C. Troops (4th N.C. Volunteers)

Romulus was born on August 28, 1835, to Benjamin and Mary Snider. Romulus worked as a carpenter in the Midway area prior to volunteering for service on April 23, 1861. He was reported present until wounded in the right arm at Williamsburg, Virginia, on May 5, 1862. Romulus recovered from his wounds and rejoined the company in January 1863. He was reported present until wounded in the neck and captured at Winchester, Virginia, on September 19, 1864. Romulus was confined at Point Lookout, Maryland, until October 18, 1864, when he was paroled and transferred to Venus Point, Georgia, for exchange. Romulus was exchanged on November 15, 1864, and returned to service prior to April 3, 1865, when he was captured once again, at Petersburg, Virginia. He was confined at Hart's Island, New York, until he was released on June 21, 1865, after taking the oath of allegiance. After the war, Romulus returned to the Midway township, where, on February 2, 1869, he married Barbara S. Livengood. Romulus worked as a carpenter until his death on December 27, 1914. He is buried at New Friendship Baptist Church.

1626. Snider, Solomon

Private, Company E, 10th Regiment N.C. State Troops (1st N.C. Artillery)

Solomon was born on January 21, 1835, to the Reverend Phillip and Mahalia Snider. Solomon worked as a farmer, and on February 25, 1860, he married Mary A. Garner. Solomon was conscripted into service on September 12, 1862, and was assigned to artillery service. He was reported present through June 1864 and was paroled at Greensboro, North Carolina, on May 8, 1865. After the war, Solomon returned to the Emmons area where he and Mary would have nine children: John (1865), Sarah and Sabrina (1868), Martha (1870), Phillip Lee (1872), Ruth (1874), Mary (1876), Flora (1879), and Amanda (1881). Solomon would be remembered in later years for his exceptionally long, white beard. Solomon lived in the Emmons township until his death on June 14, 1910. He is buried at Tom's Creek Primitive Baptist Church.

1627. Snider, William Dobson

Private, Chatam Light Infantry
Company G, 48th Regiment N.C. Troops

William was born on January 1, 1829, to Lewis and Mary Workman Snider. William worked as a farmer in the western part of Davidson County, and, in 1850, he married Margaret Luticia Williams. William and Margaret would have five children, Mary (1851), Margaret (1853), John (1856), Cynthia (1858), and Sarah (1859), before William was conscripted into service on August 14, 1862. He was wounded at Sharpsburg, Maryland, on September 17, 1862. William was sent home and in May 1863, company records state that William is "now at home, trying to die." William survived, however, and was paroled at Salisbury, North Carolina, on May 20, 1865. After the war, William moved to Davie County and lived there until his death on December 15, 1896. He is buried at No Creek Baptist Church.

1628. Sowers, Ambrose

Private, Company F, 76th Regiment N.C. Troops (6th N.C. Senior Reserves)

Ambrose was born on August 29, 1819, to John and Margaret Sink Sowers. Ambrose worked as a farmer in the northern district of Davidson County, and, on March 4, 1842, he married Sarah Reagan. Ambrose and Sarah would have three daughters: Mariah (1844), Elizabeth (1848), and Frances (1850). Ambrose served in Moss' Senior Reserves, which became a part of the 6th N.C. Senior Reserves in January 1865. Sometime after the war, Ambrose moved to Forsyth County and settled in the Lewisville area. He would be married twice more, to Abigail Myers and Amanda Myers. Ambrose lived in the Lewisville area until his death sometime after 1883.

1629. Sowers, Christian

Private, Company I, 42nd Regiment N.C. Troops

Christian was born on August 29, 1846, to Michael and Elizabeth Sink Sowers. Christian worked as a farmer in the Beulah area until he was conscripted into service in Washington County on May 1, 1864. He was reported present through October 1864. After the war, Christian returned home, where, on August 6, 1867, he married Albertine L. Byerly. Christian and Albertine would have two children: Margaret (1869) and Walter Thomas (1874). Christian worked as a farmer in the Lexington township until his death on February 15, 1914. He is buried at Beulah United Church of Christ.

1630. Sowers, Edward Lafayette

Private, Company H, 48th Regiment N.C. Troops

Edward was born in 1831 to Michael and Elizabeth Sink Sowers. Edward worked as a farmer in the Beulah area, and, on June 13, 1855, he married Nancy A. Byerly. Edward and Nancy would have a daughter, Martha (1859), before Edward was conscripted into service on August 8 1862. He was reported present until he died of disease at Spotsylvania Court House, Virginia, on May 17, 1864.

1631. Sowers, Felix

Private, Company C, 76th Regiment N.C. Troops (6th N.C. Senior Reserves)

Felix was born on April 28, 1820, to Phillip and Magdalena Leonard Sowers. Felix lived as a single farmer prior to enlisting in Hill's Senior Reserves, which became a part of the 6th N.C. Senior Reserves in January 1865. He survived the war and returned to farming in the Lexington township. Felix died on April 28, 1879. He is buried at Beulah United Church of Christ.

1632. Sowers, Felix

Private, Company I, 42nd Regiment N.C. Troops

Felix was born on May 11, 1837, to Michael and Elizabeth Sink Sowers. Felix worked as a farmer prior to volunteering for service on March 3, 1862. He was reported present for every engagement of

the 42nd North Carolina through October 1864. After the war, Felix returned to the Lexington township, where, on July 31, 1865, he married Susannah Pickett. Felix and Susannah would have five children: Susan (1867), Eliza (1869), Sarah (1873), Michael L. (1875), and Annie (1879). Felix worked as a farmer until his death on November 10, 1896. He is buried at Beulah United Church of Christ.

1633. Sowers, George Sink

Private, Company H, 48th Regiment N.C. Troops

George was born on March 13, 1833, to John and Margaret Sink Sowers. George worked as a farmer in the Lexington area, and, on January 7, 1857, he married Jane Emily Sullivan. George and Jane would have a daughter, Sarah (1860), before George was conscripted into service on August 8, 1862. He was reported present until he died of dysentery in a Farmville, Virginia, hospital on May 26, 1864. He left behind his wife and two daughters, the second of whom, Mary, had been born in January 1863.

1634. Sowers, Hiram

Private, Company B, 48th Regiment N.C. Troops

Hiram was born in 1840 to John and Margaret Sink Sowers. Hiram worked as a farmer in the Beulah area prior to enlisting into service on May 16, 1862. He was killed in action at King's School House, Virginia, on June 25, 1862.

1635. Sowers, Humphrey

Private, Company B, 48th Regiment N.C. Troops

Humphrey was born on September 22, 1827, to John and Margaret Sink Sowers. Humphrey worked as a hireling in the Beulah area prior to enlisting into service on March 6, 1862. He died two months later of "fever" in a Raleigh, North Carolina, hospital on May 8, 1862. His body was interred at Emanuel United Church of Christ.

1636. Sowers, Jacob

Private, Company I, 42nd Regiment N.C. Troops

Jacob was born on February 24, 1834, to Michael and Elizabeth Sink Sowers.

Jacob Sowers and wife, Amanda Leonard Sowers, ca. 1900 (Betty Sowers).

Jacob worked as a farmer, and, on August 19, 1856, he married Amanda Leonard. Jacob and Amanda would have a daughter, Frances (1861), before Jacob volunteered for service on March 3, 1862. He was reported present for every action of the 42nd North Carolina through October 1864. After the war, Jacob returned to the Lexington township, where he continued his farming. Jacob and Amanda would have four more children: Betty (1866), Martin (1868), David (1872), and John R. (1875). Jacob lived in the Beulah area until his death on January 15, 1909. He is buried at Beulah United Church of Christ.

1637. Sowers, Jesse

Private, Carolina Rangers
Company B, 10th Virginia Cavalry
Regiment

Jesse was born on October 28, 1837, to George and Catharine Eller Sowers. Jesse worked as a farmer prior to volunteering for service in Davie County

on October 29, 1861. He was reported present until July 25, 1863, when he was commissioned to serve as a Confederate mail carrier. Jesse's contract and appointment was declared illegal, and he was ordered to return to service a week later. Jesse was reported present until he deserted in August 1864. After the war, Jesse returned to the Lexington township, where on December 20, 1866, he married Mary Swicegood. Jesse and Mary would have seven children: Charles (1868), Molly (1869), Delilah (1872), Fred (1874), William (1876), R. B. Hayes (1878), and Harry C. (1879). Sometime after 1880, Jesse moved with his wife and four youngest sons to Salisbury, North Carolina. Jesse lived in Salisbury until his death on December 5, 1904. He is buried in the Chestnut Hill Cemetery.

1638. Sowers, Joseph Stafford

Private, Company G, 7th Confederate
Cavalry Regiment

Joseph was born on January 15, 1830, to George and Catharine Eller Sowers. Joseph worked as a farmer and a storekeeper, and, on January 24, 1854, he married Amanda Berrier. Joseph and Amanda would have four daughters, Frances (1857), Mary (1858), Sarah (1861), and Catharine (1862), before Joseph volunteered for service in March 1862. Joseph was reported present with the 7th Cavalry until the unit was disbanded in July 1864. After the war, Joseph opened a hotel in the town of Lexington. Joseph and his wife were listed as the owners and operators in both 1870 and 1880. Joseph conducted business in Lexington and was a member of the Methodist church until his death on September 22, 1898. He is buried in the Lexington City Cemetery.

1639. Sowers, Michael

Private, Company I, 42nd Regiment
N.C. Troops

Michael was born in 1844 to Michael and Elizabeth Sink Sowers. Michael worked as a farmer prior to volunteering for service on March 4, 1862. He was present until he died of unreported causes in a Richmond, Virginia, hospital on August 20, 1864.

1640. Sowers, Michael

Private, Bridger's Artillery
Company C, 40th Regiment N.C. Troops
(3rd N.C. Artillery)

Michael was born on March 30, 1823, to Jacob and Mary B. Sink Sowers. Michael worked as a farmer in the Midway area, and, on December 5, 1845, he married Elizabeth Burke. Michael and Elizabeth would have six children, Phillip (1849), Mary (1852), Pleasant (1853), Lelia (1858), Isabella (1860), and Albert (1863), before Michael was conscripted into service on March 4, 1864. He was reported present through October 1864. After the war, Michael returned home, where he and Elizabeth would have another child: John (1868). Michael worked as a farmer in the Midway area until his death on February 27, 1915. He is buried at Midway United Methodist Church.

1641. Sowers, Nathaniel James

Private, Adams' Battery
Company D, 13th Battalion, N.C. Light
Artillery

Nathan was born in 1840 to Jacob and Mary B. Sink Sowers. Nathan worked as a farmer prior to being conscripted into service on November 4, 1863. He was reported present with Adam's Battery through February 1865. It is probable that Nathan died prior to May 1865. No further records.

1642. Sowers, Valentine

Private, Company H, 48th Regiment
N.C. Troops

Val was born in 1825 to Phillip and Magdalena Leonard Sowers. Val worked as a farmer, and, on September 8, 1859, he married Emeline Walser. Val and Emeline would have a daughter, Sarah (1860), before he was conscripted into service in

Lenoir County on May 20, 1862. Val died of unreported causes near Richmond, Virginia, in March 1863.

1643. Sowers, William Augustus

Private, Thomasville Rifles
Company B, 14th Regiment N.C. Troops
(4th N.C. Volunteers)

William was born on March 18, 1842, to Samuel and Amelia Michael Sowers. William worked as a farmer, and, in 1860, he married Susan Livengood. William and Susan would have a son, Lafayette (1861), before William volunteered for service on May 13, 1861. He was reported present for every action of the 14th North Carolina through January 31, 1865. William was paroled at Greensboro, North Carolina, on May 1, 1865, and returned to the Lexington area. William and Susan would have two more children, Bettie (1865) and James (1869), before the couple moved to Missouri in 1870. William created a new life for his family, which eventually included six more children: Martha, Ida, William, Myrtle, Early, and Russell. William lived in Waverly, Missouri, until his death in 1917. No further records.

1644. Sparks, William R.

Private, Davie Greys
Company E, 13th Regiment N.C. Troops
(3rd N.C. Volunteers)

William was born on November 22, 1844. William worked as a farmer in the Bethany area prior to being conscripted into service at Bunker Hill, Virginia, on September 27, 1862. He was reported present until he deserted on May 10, 1863. William avoided arrest and was able to return to the county in 1870. William lived in the Midway-Thomasville area until his death on July 8, 1911. He is buried at Bethany United Church of Christ.

1645. Spaugh (Spach), Benjamin A.

Private, Company I, 33rd Regiment
N.C. Troops

Benjamin was born in 1830. Benjamin worked as a cobbler in the Friedburg area, and, on November 9, 1858, he married Elizabeth Hill. Benjamin continued his trade prior to being conscripted into service on July 8, 1862. He was reported present until he died of typhoid fever in a Lynchburg, Virginia, hospital on February 15, 1863. His body was brought home and buried at Friedburg Moravian Church.

1646. Spaugh (Spach), David A.

Private, Carolina Rangers
Company B, 10th Virginia Cavalry
Regiment

David was born on January 1, 1837, to Christian and Catharine Hege Spaugh. David worked as a farmer prior to enlisting in Davie County on June 13, 1863. He was reported present with the 10th Virginia until he was paroled at Appomattox Court House, Virginia, on April 9, 1865. After the war, David continued working on his father's land, which he inherited in 1872. David died on May 1, 1900. He is buried at Friedburg Moravian Church.

1647. Spaugh (Spach), Emanuel James

Private, Harnett Light Infantry
Company F, 15th Regiment N.C. Troops
(5th N.C. Volunteers)

Emanuel was born on May 26, 1839, to Christian and Catharine Hege Spaugh. Emanuel worked as a teacher in the Friedburg community prior to being conscripted into service in Wake County on July 15, 1862. He was reported present until wounded in the leg and captured at Bristoe Station, Virginia, on October 14, 1863. Emanuel was confined at Point Lookout, Maryland, until May 3, 1864, when he was paroled and transferred to Aiken's Landing, Virginia, for exchange. He was declared exchanged, returned to service, and was reported present through October 1864. After the war, Emanuel returned to the classroom, and, on December 22, 1870, he married Adeline Douthit. Emanuel and Adeline lived a comfortable life in the Arcadia township until Emanuel's death on May 5, 1925. He is buried at Friedburg Moravian Church.

1648. Spaugh (Spach), George Gottlieb

Private, Davie Greys
Company E, 13th Regiment N.C. Troops
(3rd N.C. Volunteers)

George was born on March 11, 1844. George worked as a farmer in the Friedburg community prior to being conscripted into service at Camp Holmes, North Carolina, on February 27, 1864. He was reported present until wounded in the right arm at Malvern Hill, Virginia, on June 13, 1864. George was reported absent, wounded, until he was retired from service on November 30, 1864. George returned home, where he was taken in by his cousin Emanuel. George died on February 4, 1874. He is buried at Friedburg Moravian Church.

1649. Spaugh (Spach), James A.

Private, Company H, 33rd Regiment
N.C. Troops

James was born in 1830. James worked as a farmer in the Arcadia township, and, on September 5, 1859, he married Mary Elizabeth Berrier. James and Mary lived in the Friedburg community prior to James being conscripted into service in Forsyth County on July 15, 1862. He was reported present until hospitalized in Richmond, Virginia, on March 8, 1863. James died of typhoid fever at Richmond on March 17, 1863. James' body was retrieved and buried at Friedburg Moravian Church.

1650. Spaugh (Spach), James L.

Private, Company K, 57th Regiment
N.C. Troops

James was born on February 10, 1838. James worked as a carpenter in the Arcadia township prior to being conscripted into service in Wake County on March 8, 1864. He was reported present until he deserted on October 28, 1864. James avoided arrest and remained in Salem, Forsyth County, for a time; he was listed as living in Friedburg in 1880. James lived as a single carpenter until his death on September 26, 1905. He is buried at Friedburg Moravian Church.

1651. Spaugh (Spach), Lewis

Private, Harnett Light Infantry
Company F, 15th Regiment N.C. Troops
(5th N.C. Volunteers)

Lewis was born in 1832. Lewis worked as a farmer in the Arcadia township prior to being conscripted into service in Wake County on July 15, 1862. He was killed in action at Crampton's Pass, Maryland, on September 14, 1862.

Freidburg home of Theophilus and Maria Beckel Spaugh, built in 1872 (Touart, *Building the Backcountry*).

1652. Spaugh (Spach), Martin

Private, Confederate Guards Company K, 48th Regiment N.C. Troops

Martin was born on October 14, 1840, to George and Anna Spaugh. Martin owned a small plantation, which stretched his ties to the Moravian faith, and also helped to manage his father's farm prior to volunteering for service on March 21, 1862. Martin died of disease at Goldsboro, North Carolina, on May 13, 1862. His father retrieved his body and had him buried at Friedburg Moravian Church.

1653. Spaugh (Spach), Solomon Augustus

Private, Thomasville Rifles Company B, 14th Regiment N.C. Troops (4th N.C. Volunteers)

Solomon was born on February 7, 1835, to Christian and Catharine Hege Spaugh. Solomon worked as a merchant, and in 1860 he was renting a room from Clemmonsville doctor J. H. Shelton. Solomon was conscripted into service in Wake County on July 15, 1862, and died of unreported causes near Culpeper Court House, Virginia, on September 16, 1862.

1654. Spaugh (Spach), Theophilus T.

Private, Harnett Light Infantry Company F, 15th Regiment N.C. Troops (5th N.C. Volunteers)

Theo was born on September 13, 1843, to Solomon and Catharine Hege Spaugh. Theo worked as a farmer prior to being conscripted into service in Wake County on July 15, 1862. He deserted on June 29, 1863. Theo avoided arrest and remained in the Friedburg area for the rest of the war. In 1869, he married Maria Beckel. Theo and Maria would go on to raise four children: Caroline (1870), Mary C. (1871), Ada Louisa (1875), and Arthur (1878). Theo worked as a farmer in the Arcadia township until his death on October 24, 1913. He is buried at Friedburg Moravian Church.

1655. Spaugh (Spach), Timothy Samuel

Private, Carolina Rangers Company B, 10th Virginia Cavalry Regiment

Timothy was born on May 28, 1841, to Daniel and Anna Fishel Spaugh. Timothy worked as a farmer prior to being conscripted into service on August 1, 1864. He was wounded in action on October 1, 1864, and was reported absent, wounded, through January 27, 1865.

After the war, Timothy returned to the Arcadia township, where, on November 9, 1865, he married Sarah Hill. Timothy and Sarah would have five children: Mary (1866), Elizabeth (1868), James (1869), Caroline (1871), and Sarah Jane (1876). Timothy worked as a farmer in the Arcadia township until his death on January 21, 1900. He is buried at Friedburg Moravian Church.

1656. Spaugh (Spach), Traugott Henry

Private, Company K, 21st Regiment N.C. Troops (11th N.C. Volunteers)

Traugott was born on December 13, 1825. Traugott worked as a farmer in both Davidson and Forsyth counties prior to being conscripted into service in Wake County on October 15, 1864. He was reported present until paroled at Appomattox Court House, Virginia, on April 9, 1865. After the war, Traugott returned to the Friedburg community, where he worked as a small farmer and as caretaker of the church cemetery. Traugott remained single until his death on April 3, 1891. He is buried at Friedburg Moravian Church.

1657. Spencer, David

Private, Company H, 15th Regiment N.C. Troops (5th N.C. Volunteers)

David was born in 1832 in Rowan County. David moved to the Lexington area to work as a mason, and, on November 16, 1857, he married Elizabeth Sink. David was conscripted into service in Wake County on July 15, 1862, and was killed in action at Fredericksburg, Virginia, on December 13, 1862.

1658. Springs, A. Alexander

Private, Company B, 53rd Regiment N.C. Troops

Alex was born on February 10, 1847. Alex worked as a blacksmith in the Clemmonsville area prior to volunteering for service in Mecklenburg County on February 26, 1864. He was hospitalized at Richmond, Virginia, on May 31, 1864. Alex remained in the hospital until June 7, 1864, when he returned to service. He was reported present until paroled at Appomattox Court House, Virginia, on April 9, 1865. After the war, Alex returned to the Clemmonsville area, where, on February 2, 1870, he married Sarah E. Holland. Alex and Sarah moved in the 1920s to Lexington, where Alex lived the last years of his life. He died on November 15, 1925, and is buried in the Lexington City Cemetery.

1659. Spurgeon, Austin R.

Second Lieutenant, 66th Regiment
N.C. Militia (1861 organization)

Austin was born in 1833 to John and Sarah Spurgeon. Austin worked as a carpenter prior to receiving a commission to serve as a second lieutenant in the Browntown District Company on November 26, 1861. No further records.

1660. Spurgeon, John Stanford

Private, Company A, 42nd Regiment
N.C. Troops
Howard's Company, Gibbs' Battalion,
N.C. Prison Guards, Salisbury

John was born on May 7, 1840, to John and Sarah Spurgeon. John was studying at Yadkin College before he volunteered for service on January 30, 1862. He was reported present until assigned to duty as a prison guard on May 1, 1862. For the duration of the war, John served as a prison guard at the Salisbury Prison. After the war, John returned to the Abbott's Creek area, where he became a teacher, and, in 1867, he married Emma G. Payne. John and Emma would have four children: Charlie (1869), William (1874), Delilah (1877), and Charlotte (1880). John worked as a teacher until his death on January 14, 1928. He is buried at Abbott's Creek Missionary Baptist Church.

1661. Stafford, George W.

Private, Company F, 7th Regiment
N.C. State Troops

George was born in 1836 to Charity Stafford. George worked as a farmer in the southern district of Davidson County, and, in 1854, he married Nancy Newsome. George and Nancy would have four children; Doctor (1856), Frank (1857), Jane (1860), and Ellard (1864), before George was conscripted into service in Wake County on February 24, 1864. He was reported present until wounded in the head and left wrist on September 20, 1864. George was granted a sixty-day furlough from a Danville, Virginia, hos-

pital on December 1, 1864. George stayed at home and was paroled at Salisbury, North Carolina, on May 20, 1865. After the war, George and Nancy would have two more children: Esther (1877) and Reid (1879). George lived in the Jackson Hill township through 1880. No further records.

1662. Stafford, John Henry

Private, Company A, 42nd Regiment
N.C. Troops

John was born in 1833 to Charity Stafford. John worked as a farmer prior to being conscripted into service on an unreported date. He was reported present until captured at Battery Anderson, Fort Fisher, North Carolina, on December 25, 1864. John was confined at Point Lookout, Maryland, until June 9, 1865, when he died of pneumonia. He is buried in the Point Lookout National Cemetery.

1663. Stafford, William Pinkney

Private, Company A, 42nd Regiment
N.C. Troops

William was born on March 3, 1830, to Charity Stafford. William worked as a miller, and, in 1856, he married Annie Surratt. William and Annie would have a son, James (1860), before he was conscripted into service on an unreported date. He was reported present until captured at Battery Anderson, Fort Fisher, North Carolina, on December 25, 1864. William was confined at Point Lookout, Maryland, until May 15, 1865, when he was released after taking the oath of allegiance. After the war, William returned home to the Healing Springs area where he and Annie would have another son, Mack in 1872. William continued his work as a miller until his death on June 20, 1904. He is buried at Lick Creek Baptist Church.

1664. Staley, Joseph

Private, Holtsburg Guards
Company A, 54th Regiment N.C.
Troops

Joseph was born in 1835 and worked as a silver miner in the Silver Hill area. Joseph married Crissy in 1853, and they would have three children, Obediah (1854), Mary (1857), and Sarah (1861), before Joseph volunteered for service on

March 20, 1862. He was reported present until detailed to serve as a lead miner back in Davidson County on September 10, 1862. Joseph served in this capacity throughout the war. After the war, Joseph returned to the silver mines. Joseph and Crissy would have four more children: William (1866), Margaret (1867), John (1869), and Alice (1871). Joseph moved around the county and was last listed as living in the Boone township in 1900. No further records.

1665. Starr, John B.

Private, Holtsburg Guards
Company A, 54th Regiment N.C.
Troops

John was born on November 4, 1840, to Solomon and Catharine Starr. John worked as a silver miner prior to volunteering for service on March 4, 1862. He was reported present until detailed to serve as a lead miner back in Davidson County on September 10, 1862. John served in this capacity throughout the war. John married Elizabeth Trexler on February 14, 1864. John and Elizabeth would have two children, Thomas (1865) and Catharine (1867), before her death in 1868. John married Sarah J. Workman on December 11, 1870, and would have four children with her: William (1872), Mary (1874), Sarah (1878), and James (1882). John worked in the silver mines and lived in the Cotton Grove township until his death on December 10, 1920. He is buried at Holloways Baptist Church.

1666. Stewart (Stuart), Andrew Madison

Musician, North State Boys
Company K, 45th Regiment N.C.
Troops

Andrew was born in 1845 to James and Elizabeth Stewart. Andrew worked as a carpenter prior to enlisting as a substitute on March 22, 1862. He was assigned to temporary service as a musician in July 1862, and as a result of his ability, he was promoted to full musician in March 1864. Andrew served for the duration of the war with the regimental band and was paroled at Greensboro, North Carolina, on May 11, 1865. After the war, Andrew returned home to the Midway township where he continued his work as a house carpenter. In 1878, Andrew married Annie Elizabeth Delapp. Andrew and

Annie would have five children: Loulie (1879), Edward (1880), Luther (1885), Dorsett (1890), and Ethel (1896). Andrew lived in the Midway township until his death on May 20, 1907. He is buried at Hebron United Church of Christ.

1667. Stewart (Stuart), Franklin

Private, Company H, 15th Regiment N.C. Troops (5th N.C. Volunteers) Company G, 48th Regiment N.C. Troops

Franklin was born in 1837. Franklin worked as a farmer in northern Davidson County, and, in 1856, he married Hannah. Franklin and Hannah would have four children, Amanda (1857), Charles and Alfred (1858), and Frank (1861), before Franklin was conscripted into service in Wake County on July 15, 1862. He was transferred to the 48th Regiment on August 14, 1862, and was wounded at Sharpsburg, Maryland, on September 17, 1862. He was hospitalized until he deserted on November 22, 1862. No further records.

1668. Stewart (Stuart), Henry

Private, Company H, 15th Regiment N.C. Troops (5th N.C. Volunteers)

Henry was born on March 11, 1844, to James and Elizabeth Stewart. Henry worked as a farmer prior to being conscripted into service on July 15, 1862. He was reported present until he died of dysentery on September 7, 1863.

1669. Stewart (Stuart), Lewis Fountain

Private, Company G, 2nd Battalion, N.C. Infantry

Lewis was born on August 13, 1843. Lewis worked as a farmer and was employed by Andrew Sink before being conscripted into service on September 10, 1864. He was reported present until captured at Strasburg, Virginia, on October 19, 1864. Lewis was confined at Point Lookout, Maryland, until June 20, 1865, when he was released after taking the oath of allegiance. After the war, Lewis returned to the Midway township, where, in 1872, he married Ellen Reid. Lewis and Ellen would have only one child: Sarah (1874). Lewis lived in the Midway township until his death on October 1, 1932. He is buried at Bethlehem United Church of Christ.

1670. Stewart (Stuart), Madison F.

Private, Company H, 15th Regiment N.C. Troops (5th N.C. Volunteers) Company G, 48th Regiment N.C. Troops

Madison was born in 1842. Madison worked as a farmer in the northern district of Davidson County prior to being conscripted into service in Wake County on July 15, 1862. He was transferred to the 48th Regiment on August 14, 1862, and was wounded at Sharpsburg, Maryland, on September 17, 1862. Madison was reported absent, sick, through November 22, 1862, when he deserted. He returned to service in July 1863 and was admitted to a hospital on July 12, 1863. Madison was taken by Confederate authorities and confined at Castle Thunder Prison in Richmond, Virginia, through April 1864. Madison was discharged from service on March 4, 1865, because of "general debility." No further records.

1671. Stewart (Stuart), Michael M.

Private, Ellis Guards Company C, 15th Regiment N.C. Troops (5th N.C. Volunteers)

Michael was born in 1842 to James and Elizabeth Stewart. Michael worked as a farmer prior to being conscripted into service in Wake County on July 15, 1862. He was captured at Crampton's Pass, Maryland, on September 14, 1862. Michael was confined at Fort Delaware, Delaware, until October 2, 1862, when he was paroled and transferred to Aiken's Landing, Virginia, for exchange. He was declared exchanged on November 10, 1862. Michael returned to service and was reported present until he was captured at Hatcher's Run, Virginia, on April 2, 1865. He was confined at Point Lookout again until June 20, 1865, when he was released after taking the oath of allegiance. No further records.

1672. Stewart (Stuart), S. A.

Private, Company H, 15th Regiment N.C. Troops (5th N.C. Volunteers)

S. A. was born in 1841. He worked as a farmer prior to being conscripted into service in Wake County on July 15, 1862. S. A. was reported present until captured at Bristoe Station, Virginia, on October 14, 1863. He was confined at Old Capital Prison in Washington, D.C., until he was transferred to Point Lookout, Maryland, on October 27, 1863. S. A. was confined at Point Lookout until he died of unreported causes on February 23, 1864. He is buried in the Point Lookout National Cemetery.

1673. Stewart (Stuart), William Nelson

Private, Davidson Guards Company A, 21st Regiment N.C. Troops (11th N.C. Volunteers)

William was born in 1842 to Daniel and Nancy Stewart. William worked as a farmer prior to being conscripted into service in Wake County on July 25, 1862. He was reported present until hospitalized at Richmond, Virginia, on March 27, 1865, with a gunshot wound of the leg. William was captured in the hospital during the city's fall on April 3, 1865. After the war, William returned to the Arcadia township, where, on August 4, 1867, he married Christina Bodenheimer. William and Christina lived in the area around Old Vernon Church. William worked as a farmer until his death on December 11, 1898. He is buried at Old Vernon Methodist Church.

1674. Stinson, Edwin David

Private, Company M, 7th Confederate Cavalry

Edwin was born in 1845 to James P. and Elizabeth Stinson. Edwin was a student at Yadkin College before he enlisted in the 7th Confederate Cavalry in January 1862. After the war, Edwin returned to the town of Lexington, where, on July 26, 1866, he married Laura F. Hargrave. Edwin operated a hotel in the area directly south of Lexington and was a member of the Presbyterian church. He lived in Lexington until his death in 1895. He is buried in the Lexington City Cemetery.

1675. Stinson, James P.

Private, Company C, 70th Regiment N.C. Troops (1st N.C. Junior Reserves)

James was born in 1847 to James P. and Elizabeth Stinson. James lived with his parents prior to enlisting in the Junior Reserves on May 24, 1864. No further records.

1676. Stokes, Pleasant G.

Private, Franklin Guides to Freedom Company G, 44th Regiment N.C. Troops

Pleasant was born in 1834 to William and Jemina Stokes. Pleasant worked as a farmer in the Allegheny township prior to being conscripted into service in Montgomery County on October 8, 1862. He was reported present until hospitalized at Richmond, Virginia, on May 5, 1863 with a gunshot wound. Pleasant returned to service on January 1, 1864, and was reported present until captured at Five Forks, Virginia, on April 1, 1865. He was confined at Point Lookout, Maryland, until June 20, 1865, when he was released after taking the oath of allegiance. After the war, Pleasant moved to Montgomery County, where, in 1870, he married Rebecca. Pleasant lived out his days in Montgomery County until his death on February 13, 1908. He is buried at Lane's Chapel United Methodist Church.

1677. Stokes, Thomas B.

Private, Company I, 42nd Regiment N.C. Troops

Thomas was born in 1843 to Kinchen and Mary Stokes. Thomas worked as a farmer in the Allegheny township prior to being conscripted into service on March 4, 1864. He was reported present through October 1864. After the war, Thomas returned home, where, on March 3, 1870, he married Margaret C. Turner. Thomas and Margaret would have nine children: Curtis (1872), Esten (1873), Rosseau (1875), Eula (1880), Thomas (1882), Stella (1884), Charles (1886), Bernard (1889), and Maggie (1893). Thomas worked as a farmer in the Allegheny township until his death on November 12, 1926. He is buried at Allegheny Methodist Church.

1678. Stone, Bloomfield F.

First Lieutenant, 66th Regiment N.C. Militia (1861 organization)

Bloom was born on October 2, 1824, to Quakers John and Mary Carter Stone. Bloom worked as a farmer in the area north of Thomasville, and, in 1849, he married Frances Leonard. Bloom and Frances would have six children: Roswell (1850), Marcus (1853), Sarah (1855), Mary (1858), John B. (1862), and Robert Lee (1866). Bloom was appointed to serve as first lieutenant in the Thomasville District

A wartime portrayal of William Stoner. The light edges of the photograph were touched up with pencil (Ruth B. Stoner, *The Heritage of Davidson County*).

Company on November 26, 1861. After his service, Bloom continued farming in the North Thomasville township until his death on March 27, 1898. He is buried at Pine Woods United Methodist Church.

1679. Stoner, John A.

Private, Davidson Guards Company A, 21st Regiment N.C. Troops (11th N.C. Volunteers) Corporal, Lexington Wildcats Company I, 14th Regiment N.C. Troops (4th N.C. Volunteers)

John was born in 1835 to Henry and Rachael Stoner. John worked as a farmer prior to volunteering for service on May 8, 1861. He was reported present until he was discharged on January 1, 1862, because of "medical concerns." John remained at home for six months until he was conscripted into service in Wake County on July 16, 1862. He was promoted to corporal in the 14th Regiment on October 1, 1862. John died of pneumonia at White Sulphur Springs, Virginia, on November 23, 1862.

1680. Stoner, William Franklin

First Sergeant, Holtsburg Guards Company A, 54th Regiment N.C. Troops

William was born on December 31, 1831, to Mary Stoner. William worked as a farmer in the Cotton Grove area, and, in 1853, he married Fannie Irvin. William and Fannie would have three children, James (1855), John (1858), and Mary (1860), before William enlisted on May 14, 1862. He was promoted to sergeant in July 1862 and served in that capacity until captured at Rappahannock Station, Virginia, on November 7, 1863. William was confined at Point Lookout, Maryland, until March 9, 1864, when he was paroled and transferred to City Point, Virginia, for exchange. William stayed in several hospitals before returning to duty on November 1, 1864, when he was promoted to first sergeant. William was reported present until he was captured at Fort Stedman, Virginia, on March 25, 1865. He was again confined at Point Lookout until May 14, 1865, when he was released after taking the oath of allegiance. After the war, William returned home to the Cotton Grove area, where he and Fannie would raise another three children: William (1866), Luke (1867), and Charles (1870). William became recognized as a distinguished veteran and member of the church. William lived in the Cotton Grove area until his death on March 13, 1878. He is buried at Holloways Baptist Church.

1681. Stout, Joseph A.

Private, Washington Greys
Company K, 10th Regiment N.C. State
Troops (1st N.C. Artillery)

Joseph was born in 1829 to Samuel and Osea Stout. Joseph was a small slaveholder, owning six slaves in 1860. In 1850, Joseph had married Rowena Smith. Joseph and Rowena would have three children, Sophia (1851), Samuel (1855), and Columbus (1858), before Joseph was conscripted into service in Randolph County on March 23, 1863. He was reported present through October 1864. After the war, Joseph and his family moved to the area around Columbus, Ohio. No further records.

1682. Stout, William Lewis

Private, Company E, 42nd Regiment
N.C. Troops

William was born in 1835 to Samuel and Osea Stout. William worked as a merchant prior to volunteering for service on March 18, 1862. He was reported present until he was discharged on June 17, 1863, due to "general debility and chronic neuralgia." It is believed that William died of his neuralgia sometime in 1864. No further records.

1683. Strange, Burgess Seth

Private, Lexington Wildcats
Company I, 14th Regiment N.C. Troops
(4th N.C. Volunteers)

Burgess was born on December 17, 1840, to Julius and Anna Billings Strange. Burgess worked as a farmer prior to volunteering for service on May 14, 1861. He was promoted to corporal on September 12, 1861, and to sergeant on April 23, 1862. Burgess was wounded in action at Malvern Hill, Virginia, on July 1, 1862, recovered from his wounds, and returned to service in January 1863. He was reduced in rank prior to April 1863 but would soldier on until he was paroled at Appomattox Court House, Virginia, on April 9, 1865. A story about Burgess is recalled by his granddaughter, Virginia Smith Young of Lexington:

> Burgess was waiting to be surrendered to the Yankees at Appomattox on April 9, 1865. He rested in the shade of an elm tree, and took one of the branches from it, since he expected this was a historic occasion. When he returned home, he planted it at the church. Thelm tree is gone now, but it stood in the corner of the cemetery of Beck's into the 1930s.

Burgess returned home to the Cotton Grove–Silver Hill area where, on May 25, 1865, he married Sarah Crouse. Burgess and Sarah would raise five children in their modest home: Robert (1868), Walter (1869), Minnie (1872), Thomas (1876), and Sarah (1878). Burgess worked as a farmer until his death on July 10, 1879. He is buried at Beck's United Church of Christ.

1684. Strayhorn, Hillary

Private, Company B, 14th Regiment
N.C. Troops (4th N.C. Volunteers)
Company A, 10th Battalion, N.C.
Heavy Artillery

Hillary worked as a shoemaker at the Shelly Shoe Factory prior to volunteering for service on August 26, 1861. Hillary was reported present until he deserted on February 22, 1863. Only a month later, he assumed the name of Thomas Strayhorn and volunteered for service in Randolph County on March 30, 1863. He was reported present until his identity was discovered, and he was arrested and removed from the 10th Battalion and returned to the 14th Regiment as a deserter in January 1864. Hillary deserted again on June 28, 1864. No further records.

1685. Styers, Jesse Samuel

Private, Company H, 33rd Regiment
N.C. Troops

Jesse was born on June 15, 1829. Jesse worked as a farmer in the southern district of Davidson County, and, on September 19, 1849, he married Mary Harrison. Jesse and Mary would have three children, Elizabeth (1850), Rosita (1855), and Jane (1859), before Jesse was conscripted into service in Forsyth County on July 15, 1862. He was reported present until listed as absent, sick, in November 1863. Jesse was dropped from the rolls in January 1864 because he was "supposed to be dead." Obviously, Jesse did not die as he returned to the Jackson Hill township, where he and Mary would raise their children on their modest farm. In 1890, Mary died, and Jesse married Elizabeth in 1898. Jesse and Elizabeth lived together until Jesse died on May 7, 1904. He is buried at Tom's Creek Primitive Baptist Church.

1686. Styers, John A.

Private, Davidson Guards
Company A, 21st Regiment N.C. Troops
(11th N.C. Volunteers)

John was born in 1838. John worked as a carpenter in the Lexington area prior to volunteering for service on May 8, 1861. He was mustered in as a corporal and was promoted to sergeant on August 8, 1861. For unreported reasons, John was broken to private in November 1861. John served as a private and was reported present until wounded in the foot at Chancellorsville, Virginia, between May 1 and 4, 1863. He returned to duty shortly after but then deserted on October 1, 1863. John returned to service on March 1, 1864, and was reported present until captured at Sayler's Creek, Virginia, on April 6, 1865. He was confined at Newport News, Virginia, until June 25, 1865, when he was released after taking the oath of allegiance. No further records.

1687. Styers, John P.

Private, Allen's Company, Gibbs' Battalion, N.C. Prison Guards, Salisbury

John was born in 1847 to Daniel and Mary Styers. John worked as a farmer prior to being mustered into service as a prison guard at Salisbury, North Carolina, on May 1, 1862. The remainder of his service is unknown, and the only trace of this soldier after his enlistment is a tombstone, with no date, placed for him at Jersey Baptist Church.

1688. Styers, Joseph

*Private, Chatam Light Infantry
Company G, 48th Regiment N.C. Troops
Company A, 46th Regiment N.C. Troops*

Joseph was born in 1834 to Samuel and Isabella Styers. Joseph worked as a farmer in the southern district of Davidson County, and, on December 6, 1858, he married Elizabeth Farris. Joseph and Elizabeth would have a son, William (1860), before Joseph was conscripted into service on August 14, 1862. In June 1863, he was transferred to Company A of the 46th Regiment. Joseph deserted from service on July 18, 1863. No further records.

1689. Styers, Milbrey

*Second Lieutenant, 65th Regiment
N.C. Militia (1861 organization)*

Milbrey was born in 1830 to Samuel and Isabella Styers. Milbrey worked as a miller in the southern district of Davidson County, and, in 1858, he married Eliza Hannah. Milbrey and Eliza would raise eight children in their Jackson Hill home: Nancy (1859), Sarah (1861), Elizabeth (1863), Sam (1865), Corneilius (1867), Mary (1869), John (1871), and Cicero (1873). Milbrey was commissioned to serve as a second lieutenant in the Jackson Hill District Company on February 11, 1862. After the war, Milbrey and Eliza lived in the Jackson Hill area before moving to the Farmer area of Randolph County in the 1890s. No further records.

1690. Suggs, John C.

*Private, Company C, 47th Regiment
N.C. Troops*

John was born in August 1845 to Charles and Avazilla Parrish Suggs. John was employed as a worker at the Shelly Shoe Factory prior to being conscripted into service in Wake County on April 15, 1864. He was reported present until paroled at Appomattox Court House, Virginia, on April 9, 1865. After the war, John returned home to the Thomasville area where he was working for Shelly in 1870 and for Leach & Lambeth Tobacco in 1880. On September 24, 1871, John married Nancy Jane Veach. John and Nancy would raise four children in their Thomasville home: Numa (1872), Theodore (1874), Annie (1876), and Belvin (1880). John lived in the town of Thomasville until his death on November 5, 1902. He is buried in the Thomasville City Cemetery.

1691. Sullivan, Franklin

*Private, Company D, 48th Regiment
N.C. Troops*

Franklin was born in 1843 to George and Mary Sullivan. Franklin worked as a farmer prior to being conscripted into service on August 8, 1862. He was killed in action at Sharpsburg, Maryland, on September 17, 1862.

1692. Sullivan, James Clarkson

*Private, Company A, 10th Battalion,
N.C. Heavy Artillery*

James was born in 1844 to James J. and Bathsheba Sullivan. James worked as a farmhand for John R. Eddinger, Sr., prior to enlisting into service on March 30, 1863. He was reported present through September 1864 and was paroled at Greensboro, North Carolina, on May 5, 1865. After the war, James stayed with his uncle. By 1880, James had moved out of the county. No further records.

1693. Sullivan, Pleasant M.

*Private, Carolina Rangers
Company B, 10th Virginia Cavalry
Regiment*

Pleasant was born in 1840 to John and Eleanor Sullivan. Pleasant worked as a farmer in the Holly Grove area prior to volunteering for service in Davie County on October 29, 1861. He was reported present until he died of typhoid fever in a Richmond, Virginia, hospital on June 24, 1862.

1694. Sullivan, Wesley E.

*Private, Lexington Wildcats
Company I, 14th Regiment N.C. Troops
(4th N.C. Volunteers)
Company G, 3rd Maryland Cavalry
Regiment*

Wesley was born in 1839 to John and Eleanor Sullivan. Wesley worked as a farmer in the Holly Grove area prior to volunteering for service on May 14, 1861. He was reported present until he deserted to the enemy on the retreat from Gettysburg, Pennsylvania, at Williamsport, Maryland, on July 10, 1863. Wesley was confined at Point Lookout, Maryland, until September 22, 1863, when he was released after joining the U.S. Army. He was assigned to the 3rd Maryland Cavalry, which saw action in the Valley campaign of 1864 and served as part of the cavalry patrol which apprehended John Wilkes Booth. Wesley did not return home, and the Montgomery County, Maryland, 1870 Census lists a Wes Sullivan as age 30, single, and working as a farmer. No further records.

1695. Sullivan, William Alexander

*Private, Lexington Wildcats
Company I, 14th Regiment N.C. Troops
(4th N.C. Volunteers)*

William was born on January 1, 1844, to Daniel and Sarah Grimes Sullivan. William was a student living in the home of Daniel Burkhart prior to volunteering for service on May 14, 1861. He was reported present until wounded at Sharpsburg, Maryland, on September 17, 1862. William was sent home to recover in November 1862. While at home, William married Mary Alunda Conrad on January 8, 1863. William was married for a month before he returned to service in February 1863. He was reported present until paroled at Appomattox Court House, Virginia, on April 9, 1865. After the war, William returned home, where he first saw his baby girl, Lucretia, who had been born in December 1863. William and Mary would raise eight more children in their Holly Grove home: Charles (1866), Martha (1868), John David (1870), Edward (1872), Andrew (1874), Miriam (1876), Daisy C. (1881), and Flavis I. (1886). William worked as a farmer and was contracted to serve as the mail carrier for the Holly Grove post

William A. Sullivan and wife Mary Alunda Conrad ca 1900 (Ruth M. Sullivan, *The Heritage of Davidson County*).

office. William lived in the Conrad Hill/Thomasville area until his death on November 19, 1911. He is buried at Emanuel United Church of Christ.

1696. Sumner, Asa

Private, Thomasville Rifles Company B, 14th Regiment N.C. Troops (4th N.C. Volunteers)

Asa volunteered for service in Davidson County on April 28, 1861. He was reported present until he died of typhoid fever in Richmond, Virginia, on August 28, 1862.

1697. Sumner, Julian Everard

First Lieutenant, 65th Regiment N.C. Militia (1861 organization)

Julian was born in 1833. Julian worked as a carpenter in Thomasville prior to being commissioned as first lieutenant in the Thomasville District Company on May 10, 1862. After his service, Julian married Martha J. Loflin on March 14, 1866. Julian and Martha would have four children: Laura (1868), Daisy (1870), Thomas (1872), and Ernest (1876–98). Julian acquired several properties in the town, including some he had built, and became one of the first landlords in the town of Thomasville. Several of his properties once stood in the East Main Street/College Street area. Julian lived in the city of Thomasville until his death in 1901. He is buried in the Thomasville City Cemetery.

1698. Surratt, Beverly A.

Private, Company B, 48th Regiment N.C. Troops

Beverly was born in 1836 to Spencer and Catharine Smith Surratt. Beverly worked as a farmer in southern Davidson County, and, on December 12, 1860, he married Elizabeth Angelina Delk. Beverly and Elizabeth would have a son, William (1862), before Beverly was conscripted into service on August 8, 1862. He was "wounded in the back by a shell fragment" at Sharpsburg, Maryland, on September 17, 1862. Beverly recovered from his wound and was present until reported absent without leave on December 6, 1862. He returned to service in January 1863 and was reported present through October 1864. After the war, Beverly returned to the Jackson Hill township where he and Elizabeth would have a daughter, Amanda (1866), before moving to the Concord township in Randolph County in 1867. Beverly and Elizabeth would have five more children: Mary Jane (1868), Charity (1870), Spencer (1872), Lewellen (1875), and John (1877). No further records.

1699. Surratt, George Washington

Musician, Company B, 48th Regiment N.C. Troops

George was born on February 23, 1835, to Spencer and Catharine Smith Surratt. George worked as a farmer in the southern district of Davidson County, and, in 1859, he married Martha B. Coggins. George and Martha would have two sons, John (1860) and Watson

George W. Surratt, drummer, in a shell jacket and impressive beard (1912 *Methodist-Protestant Herald*).

(1862), before George was conscripted into service on August 8, 1862. He was reported present until, upon hearing news of his wife's illness, he deserted on December 6, 1862. Martha died one week later. George trusted the care of his two young sons to their grandparents and returned to duty in February 1863. No charges were filed and he returned to service where he was appointed to the regimental band as a drummer in June 1863. George served as a musician and, according to an article in a 1912 Methodist denominational magazine, his duties included: "Not only beating the drum, but functioning as a litter bearer during a battle to assist the regimental surgeons. Many men were taken out of danger and some owe their life to his brave execution of his duty." George was reported present through October 1864. After the war, George returned to the Jackson Hill township where, on October 15, 1865, he married Martha J. Badgett. George and Martha would have three children, Rebecca (1868), William (1871), and Telithia (1873), before Martha died in childbirth. George then married Sarah Nance on February 5, 1874, and they would have three children together: Ellen (1875), Martha (1877), and Daisy (1882). George served as a representative of Pleasant Grove Church in the Methodist Conference for over 30 years and was a member of the A. A. Hill Camp, United Confederate Veterans. George lived in the Jackson Hill township until his death on September 27, 1912. He is buried at Pleasant Grove United Methodist Church.

1700. Surratt, Ivy

Private, Company B, 48th Regiment N.C. Troops

Ivy was born in 1844 to William and Judith Surratt. Ivy worked as a farmer in the Jackson Hill area prior to being conscripted into service on August 8, 1862. He was captured at Sharpsburg, Maryland, on September 17, 1862. Apparently, he was released on September 20, 1862, but Ivy failed to return to duty and was arrested as a deserter in May 1863. Ivy returned to service in July 1863 and was reported present until he was mortally wounded at Bristoe Station, Virginia, on October 14, 1863. He died of his wounds six days later, on October 20, 1863.

1701. Surratt, John G.

*Private, Company F, 7th Regiment
N.C. State Troops*

John was born on February 6, 1832, to Spencer and Catharine Smith Surratt. John worked as a farmer and a blacksmith in the Jackson Hill area, and, in 1855, he married Rebecca Elliot. John and Rebecca moved to the Allegheny township where they would have three children, Martha (1856), Margaret (1858), and Frances (1860), before John volunteered for service on August 9, 1861. He was reported present until wounded in the right leg during vicious hand-to-hand combat behind Federal lines at Gettysburg, Pennsylvania, on July 3, 1863. John was carried back to safety, and his leg was amputated shortly afterward. John was taken by wagon along with other field amputees to Richmond, Virginia, where he was retired to the Invalid Corps on October 10, 1864. Apparently, John stayed in Richmond until after the war, when he and other paroled Confederates were put on a train with Federal soldiers who were on their way south to serve as occupational troops. When the train passed through the county, John was thrown out, and he lay on the railroad tracks for a couple of hours before John Badgett saw him there and took him home. After the war, John and Rebecca would have three more children: Mary (1866) and Pegram and Hugh (1870). John secured a wooden leg and was referred to as "Peg Leg John" for years afterward. John was a member of the Farmer's Alliance and was elected to the state House of Representatives for two terms in the 1890s. John lived in the Allegheny township until his death on July 26, 1916. He is buried at Allegheny Methodist Church.

1702. Surratt, Peyton G.

*Private, Company F, 7th Regiment
N.C. State Troops*

Peyton was born in 1837 to Spencer and Catharine Smith Surratt. Peyton worked as a farmer in the southern district of Davidson County prior to volunteering for service on March 1, 1862. Peyton was reported present for the major campaigns of the 7th Regiment until he deserted from service on May 3, 1863. Upon his return, Peyton married Elizabeth Myers on June 5, 1863. He remained at home, helping his brothers' families with the September harvest and taking care of some of the family's personal business. Peyton returned to service with amnesty on December 10, 1863, and was reported present through October 1864. After the war, Peyton returned home to his wife and their one-year-old daughter, Ellen. Peyton and Elizabeth would go on to raise six more surviving children in their Allegheny township home: Laura (1867), Nancy (1872), George (1874), Jasper (1875), Ivey Mitchell (1879), and Branson (1906). Peyton worked as a small farmer until his death on August 6, 1906. He is buried at Chapel Hill United Methodist Church. The inscription on his tombstone reads "He was a member of the 7th Infantry Regiment."

1703. Surratt, Travis T.

*Private, Company B, 48th Regiment
N.C. Troops*

Travis was born in 1840 to Spencer and Catharine Smith Surratt. Travis worked as a farmer prior to being conscripted into service on August 8, 1862. He was killed in action at Sharpsburg, Maryland, on September 17, 1862.

1704. Swaim, Columbus

*Second Lieutenant, Company E, 21st
Regiment N.C. Troops (11th N.C.
Volunteers)*
*Company B, 1st Battalion, N.C. Sharp-
shooters*
*Company G, 2nd Battalion, N.C.
Infantry*

Columbus was born in 1843 to Joseph S. and Mary Teague Swaim. Columbus worked as a clerk in the Abbott's Creek area prior to volunteering for service on May 11, 1861. He was transferred to the 1st N.C. Sharpshooters on April 26, 1862, and was appointed corporal on February 1, 1863. He was appointed second lieutenant and transferred to the 2nd N.C. Battalion in June 1863. Columbus was wounded and captured at Fisher's Hill, Virginia, on September 22, 1864. He was confined at Fort Delaware, Delaware, until June 17, 1865, when he was released after taking the oath of allegiance. After the war, Columbus returned home, where, in 1867, he married Temperance Moss. Columbus and Temperance would have one child, Victor (1869), before their Clemmonsville township home was given to Forsyth and became part of that county. No further records.

1705. Swaim, Joseph S.

*First Lieutenant, Company G, 2nd
Battalion, N.C. Infantry*

Joseph was born on August 12, 1820. Joseph worked as a small planter in the Abbott's Creek area, and, in 1840, he married Mary Teague. Joseph and Mary would have nine children, Amanda (1842), Columbus (1843), Mary (1847), Alverson (1848), Laura (1850), Sarah (1852), Eliza (1854), Cicero (1858), and Rufus (1861), before Joseph volunteered for service in Forsyth County on September 19, 1861. He was appointed second lieutenant on October 1, 1861, and was captured at Roanoke Island, North Carolina, on February 8, 1862. He was confined at Elizabeth City, North Carolina, until paroled and exchanged on February 21, 1862. Joseph returned to his post and was elected first lieutenant on September 25, 1862. He served as first lieutenant until he offered his resignation due to "ill health" on April 23, 1863. Shortly after the end of the war, Joseph died on June 19, 1865. He is buried at Abbott's Creek Missionary Baptist Church.

1706. Swaim, Michael

*Private, Ellis Guards
Company C, 15th Regiment N.C. Troops
(5th N.C. Volunteers)*

Michael was born in 1835. Michael worked as a farmer in the Abbott's Creek area, and, in 1855, he married Sarah Hayworth. Michael and Sarah would have two children, Jacob (1856) and Jane (1859), before Michael was conscripted into service in Wake County on July 15, 1862. He was captured at Crampton's Pass, Maryland, on September 14, 1862. Michael was confined at Fort Delaware, Delaware, until October 2, 1862, when he was paroled and transferred to Aiken's Landing, Virginia, for exchange. He was declared exchanged on November 10, 1862. Michael returned to service and was reported present until he deserted on December 1, 1863. He was arrested and sentenced to imprisonment at Richmond's Castle Thunder Prison. Michael was imprisoned for only two weeks before he died of typhoid fever at Castle Thunder, Virginia, on December 13, 1863.

1707. Swaney, Alfred

Private, Company B, 48th Regiment N.C. Troops

Alfred was born in Randolph County in 1841. Alfred worked as a farmer in Conrad Hill prior to volunteering for service on March 18, 1862. He was reported present until he was hospitalized with pneumonia at Charlottesville, Virginia, on December 2, 1863. Alfred returned to duty on January 13, 1863. He was reported present through October 1864 and was paroled at Greensboro, North Carolina, on May 1, 1865. No further records, although he probably returned to Randolph County. The 1870 Census lists Alfred and Hiram Swaney in that county.

1708. Swaney, Hiram M.

Private, Company B, 48th Regiment N.C. Troops

Hiram was born in Randolph County in 1845. Hiram worked as a farmer in the Conrad Hill area prior to enlisting into service at Poctaglico, South Carolina, on April 4, 1863. He was reported present through October 1864 and was paroled at Greensboro, North Carolina, on May 11, 1865. After the war, Hiram and his brother Alfred probably returned to Randolph County prior to 1870. No further records.

1709. Swaney, James

Private, Company B, 48th Regiment N.C. Troops

James was born in Randolph County in 1828. James worked as a farmer in the Conrad Hill area prior to volunteering for service on March 18, 1862. He was reported present until wounded in the arm at Reams' Station, Virginia, on August 25, 1864. James was reported absent until assigned to light duty as a hospital guard in Charlotte, North Carolina, from November 8, 1864, through December 31, 1864. He was paroled at Greensboro, North Carolina, on May 11, 1865. After the war, James returned to the Conrad Hill township where he lived as a single farmer until his death in 1891. He is buried in an unmarked grave at Liberty Baptist Church.

1710. Swaney, Rueben

Corporal, Company B, 48th Regiment N.C. Troops

Rueben was born in Randolph County in 1841. Rueben worked as a farmer in the Conrad Hill area, and, on January 11, 1857, he married Cynthia Jarrett. He volunteered for service on March 12, 1862, was reported present, and was promoted to corporal on January 6, 1863. He served his company as a corporal through October 1864 and was paroled at Greensboro, North Carolina, on May 11, 1865. No further records.

1711. Swicegood, Alexander

Captain, 66th Regiment N.C. Militia (1861 organization)

Alexander was born on May 6, 1824, to Andrew Madison and Susanna Swicegood. Alexander worked as a miller, and in 1856, he married Lemma Caroline. Alexander and Lemma would have a daughter, Alice (1857). Alexander was commissioned to serve as the captain of the Tyro Creek District Company on November 26, 1861. Alexander continued to operate his family's mill, along with his brother George, until his death on November 18, 1912. He is buried at St. Luke's Lutheran Church.

1712. Swicegood, Alfred

Private, Company B, 48th Regiment N.C. Troops

Alfred was born in 1846 to George and Catharine Swicegood. Alfred worked as a farmer in the Boone area prior to enlisting on May 31, 1862. He died of meningitis at Petersburg, Virginia, on July 31, 1862. His body was recovered and was buried at St. Luke's Lutheran Church.

1713. Swicegood, Daniel J.

Private, Company C, 70th Regiment N.C. Troops (1st N.C. Junior Reserves)

Daniel was born in 1847 to the Reverend John C. and Sarah Sharpe Swicegood. Daniel worked as a farmer prior to enlisting in the Junior Reserves on May 24, 1864. After the war, Daniel returned home, where, in 1866, he married Mary A. Daniel and Mary would have two children while living with his parents in the Boone township: Ellen (1867) and Robert Lee (1870). Daniel and Mary would move out of the county sometime in the 1880s or 1890s. No further records.

1714. Swicegood, George W.

Captain, 65th Regiment N.C. Militia (1861 organization)

George was born on December 29, 1815, to Andrew Madison and Susanna Swicegood. George worked in his family's mill in the Boone/Tyro area, and on January 23, 1844, he married Catharine Taylor. George and Catharine would have four children: Alfred (1846), William (1848), Mary L. (1849), and Amanda (1856). George served as postmaster for the Confederate postal service in the Boone township while holding his captain's commission (dated February 11, 1862). George returned to milling in the 1870s and sold fertilizers as a side business. George was a member of the Masonic order and the A. A. Hill Camp, United Confederate Veterans. George lived in the Boone township until his death on March 5, 1886. He is buried at St. Luke's Lutheran Church.

1715. Swicegood, George W.

Corporal, Lexington Wildcats Company I, 14th Regiment N.C. Troops (4th N.C. Volunteers)

George was born in 1837. George worked as a farmer in the Tyro township prior to volunteering for service on May 14, 1861. He was promoted to corporal on November 18, 1861. George was reduced in rank to private on April 25, 1862, however, he was again promoted to corporal in September 1864. He was captured at Strasburg, Virginia, on September 23, 1864. George was confined at Point Lookout, Maryland, until May 13, 1865, when he was released after taking the oath of allegiance. No further records.

1716. Swicegood, Henry Franklin

Private, Company D, 48th Regiment N.C. Troops

Henry was born on January 14, 1834, to Adam and Sophia Davis Swicegood. Henry worked as a farmer in the western section of Davidson County, and, on March 11, 1858, he married Susan Sink. Henry and Susan would have a son, Robert (1862), before Henry was conscripted into service on August 8, 1862. He was discharged due to "phthisis" on November 14, 1862. After his discharge, Henry returned to the Boone township where he and Susan would have five more

Built in 1869, this was the home to Holtsburg Guard and Justice of the Peace John H. Swicegood (Touart, *Building the Backcountry*).

children: Frances (1866), Henry (1867), Adam (1871), John (1872), and William (1874). Henry worked as a farmer in the Boone area and was a respected member of the Lutheran congregation there. Henry died on April 17, 1908. He is buried at St. Luke's Lutheran Church.

1717. Swicegood, Henry Hiram

Private, Company K, 15th Regiment
N.C. Troops (5th N.C. Volunteers)

Henry was born in 1839 to Phillip and Eliza Swicegood. Henry worked as a farmer, and, in 1860, he married Ellen. Henry and Ellen would have a son, Charles (1861), before he was conscripted into service in Wake County on July 15, 1862. He was captured at Crampton's Pass, Maryland, on September 14, 1862. Henry was confined at Fort Delaware, Delaware, until October 2, 1862, when he was paroled and transferred to Aiken's Landing, Virginia, for exchange. He was declared exchanged on November 10, 1862. Henry returned to service and was reported present until he was captured or deserted to the enemy at Bristoe Station, Virginia, on October 14, 1863. He was confined at Old Capital Prison, Washington, D.C., until March 15, 1865, when he was released after taking the oath of allegiance. Henry returned home to the

Tyro township where he saw his second child, Cornelia, for the first time. Henry and Ellen would have one more child, Roberta (1867), before moving out of the county in the 1880s. No further records.

1718. Swicegood, Jackson H.

Private, Company K, 57th Regiment
N.C. Troops

Jackson was born in 1837. Jackson was conscripted into service on July 17, 1862. He was reported absent, sick, from November 1862 through February 1863. After he recovered, Jackson was reported present until captured at Rappahannock Station, Virginia, on November 7, 1863. He was confined at Point Lookout, Maryland, until April 27, 1864, when he was transferred to City Point, Virginia, for exchange. Jackson was exchanged and was reported present until he was captured at Winchester, Virginia, on September 19, 1864. Jackson worked as a nurse at a Federal hospital in Baltimore's Fort McHenry until he was released on February 20, 1865. No further records.

1719. Swicegood, James A.

Private, Lexington Wildcats
Company I, 14th Regiment N.C. Troops
(4th N.C. Volunteers)

James was born in 1835. James worked as a farmer in the Boone township prior to volunteering for service on May 14, 1861. He was reported present until captured at Petersburg, Virginia, on April 3, 1865. James was confined at Hart's Island, New York, until June 17, 1865, when he was released after taking the oath of allegiance. No further records.

1720. Swicegood, James Hamilton

Private, Company A, 42nd Regiment
N.C. Troops

James was born in 1839 to Adam and Sophia Swicegood. James worked as a farmer prior to enlisting in Rowan County on May 7, 1862. He was reported present until captured at Battery Anderson, Fort Fisher, North Carolina, on December 25, 1864. James was confined at Point Lookout, Maryland, via Fort Monroe, Virginia, until May 13, 1865, when he was released. After the war, John made his way home to the Tyro township, where, in 1867, he married Franny. James and Franny would have seven children: Cora (1868), Charles (1869), Ellen (1873), Margaret (1875), James L. (1877), Lola (1883), and Jesse (1885). James worked as a farmer in the Tyro township through 1900. No furthre records.

1721. Swicegood, John H.

Private, Holtsburg Guards
Company A, 54th Regiment N.C. Troops

John was born on August 27, 1837, to Richmond and Mary Swicegood. John worked as a farmer in the Boone area, and, in 1859, he married Mary E. Simerson. John and Mary would have two children, Ella (1860) and William (1862), before John enlisted on May 2, 1862. He was hospitalized at Richmond, Virginia, with an unspecified complaint in September 1862. John recovered from his illness, returned to service, and was wounded in the left thigh at Turkey Ridge, near Cold Harbor, Virginia, on June 7, 1864. John was taken to a hospital where his left leg was amputated. John survived the operation and was retired from service on March 23, 1865. After he returned home, John and Mary would have eight more children: John (1865), Noah (1867), Lindsay (1868), Francis (1870), Lemuel (1871), Walter (1875), Ida (1877), and Jesse (1879). John often joked around, calling himself "Old One Leg" or

"One-legged John." John lived in the Boone township until his death on March 23, 1908. He is buried at St. Luke's Lutheran Church.

1722. Swicegood, Romulus S.

Private, Company A, 42nd Regiment N.C. Troops

Romulus was born in 1840 to Richmond and Mary Swicegood. Romulus was a student prior to volunteering for service on November 26, 1861. He was reported present until wounded in the hip at Gaines' Mill, Virginia, on June 7, 1864. Romulus returned to service that July and was reported present until he was admitted to a Raleigh, North Carolina, hospital with a gunshot wound of the left hip on February 23, 1865. Romulus was transferred to Thomasville on March 8, 1865, and was paroled on May 1, 1865. After the war, Romulus returned to the Tyro township, where, in 1867, he married Melinda Snider. Romulus and Melinda would have six children: Cicero (1870), Mary (1872), David (1874), Maggie (1876), Thomas (1879), and Willard (1882). Romulus lived in the Tyro township through 1900. No further records.

1723. Swift, Benton T.

Private, Carolina Rangers Company B, 10th Virginia Cavalry Regiment

Benton was born on December 16, 1824. Benton worked as a farmer in the northern district of Davidson County, and, in 1851, he married Matilda. Benton and Matilda would have three children, Albertine (1852), John (1855), and Joseph (1859), before Benton enlisted in Davie County on December 26, 1862. He was detailed to serve as a teamster in July and August 1863. Benton returned from his detail and was reported present until wounded in action on May 1, 1864. Benton died in Salisbury, North Carolina, on July 16, 1864. He is buried in the Old Lutheran Cemetery.

1724. Swing, Alfred R.

Private, Company B, 48th Regiment N.C. Troops

Alfred was born in 1840 to David and Mary Swing. Alfred worked as a farmer prior to volunteering for service on March 4, 1862. He was reported present through October 1864 and was paroled at Greensboro, North Carolina, on May 8, 1865. After the war, Alfred returned home to the Conrad Hill township, where, on October 26, 1865, he married Mary Kepley. Alfred and Mary would raise five children in their Holly Grove home: Charles (1867), David (1870), Matthias (1873), George (1875), and Robert Lee (1881). Alfred lived in the Conrad Hill township and helped Hiram Lafayette Conrad ("Big Fayte") construct the Holly Grove Academy. Alfred died on March 15, 1905. He is buried at Holly Grove Lutheran Church.

1725. Swing, Anderson

Private, Company B, 48th Regiment N.C. Troops

Anderson was born in 1845 to William and Hannah Swing. Anderson worked as a farmer prior to volunteering for service on March 4, 1862. He died of typhoid fever at Petersburg, Virginia, on July 15, 1862.

1726. Swing, Daniel

Private, Company I, 42nd Regiment N.C. Troops

Daniel was born in 1825 to Catharine Swing. Daniel worked as a farmer and then as a miner in the Silver Hill area, and, in 1856, he married Temperance. Daniel and Temperance would have two children, Amanda (1857) and Frances (1860), before Daniel was conscripted into service on an unreported date. He was reported present until captured at Battery Anderson, Fort Fisher, North Carolina, on December 25, 1864. Daniel was confined at Point Lookout, Maryland, via Fort Monroe, Virginia, until June 20, 1865, when he was released. After the war, Daniel returned to the Silver Hill township where he was living as a farmer in 1870. No further records.

1727. Swing, John D.

Private, Company B, 48th Regiment N.C. Troops

John was born in 1841 to David and Mary Swing. John worked as a farmer prior to volunteering for service on March 5, 1862. He was left sick at Frederick, Maryland, on September 19, 1862. Federal authorities at Frederick released John on September 20, 1862. John returned to service in January 1863 and was reported present through December 24, 1864. After the war, John returned to the Conrad Hill area, before moving to Cotton Grove in 1870. By 1880, John had moved again, this time to work as a railroad laborer in Salisbury, North Carolina. No further records.

1728. Swing, John H.

Private, Lexington Wildcats Company I, 14th Regiment N.C. Troops (4th N.C. Volunteers)

John was born in 1837 to John and Elizabeth Swing. John worked as a carpenter prior to volunteering for service on May 14, 1861. He was reported present until captured at Sharpsburg, Maryland, on September 17, 1862. John was confined at Fort McHenry, Maryland, until he was transferred to City Point, Virginia, for exchange on November 21, 1862. John returned to service in January 1863 and soldiered on for the duration of the war until paroled at Appomattox Court House, Virginia, on April 9, 1865. After the war, John returned home to the Cotton Grove area where, in 1866, he married Margaret. John and Margaret lived in the Cotton Grove/Silver Hill area until his death on March 13, 1926. He is buried at Cotton Grove United Methodist Church.

1729. Swing, John H. Calhoun

Private, Rocky Face Rangers Company G, 38th Regiment N.C. Troops

John was born on January 15, 1837. He was named after South Carolinian John H. C. Calhoun, former vice president and secession advocate. John was employed as a silver miner, and, on May 1, 1858, he married Martha J. Workman. John and Martha would have two children, Margaret (1859) and Mary Ann (1862), before John was conscripted into service at Camp Holmes, North Carolina, on August 14, 1864. He was reported present until he deserted to the enemy on March 5, 1865. John was confined at Washington, D.C., until April 1865 when he was released after taking the oath of allegiance. After the war, John returned to the Silver Hill township where he and Martha would have four more children: Clarissa (1866), James (1869), Susan (1872), and Martha (1874). John lived in the Silver Hill township until his death on May 27, 1915. He is buried at Holloways Baptist Church.

Silver Hill home of Company B, 57th N.C. Troops' Lemuel R. Tate (Touart, *Building the Backcountry*).

1730. Swing, Obediah

Private, Company G, 18th Regiment N.C. Troops (8th N.C. Volunteers)

Obed was born on January 1, 1822, to Barnhart and Christina Swing. Obed worked as a farmer, and, on October 12, 1854, he married Dolly A. Swing. Obed and Dolly would have a son, Albert (1859), before Obed was conscripted into service at Camp Holmes, North Carolina, on September 5, 1864. He was reported present through February 1865 and was paroled at Greensboro, North Carolina, on May 8, 1865. His wife had died in 1864, and his son was left in the care of his paternal grandfather. After the war, Obed returned home to the Silver Hill township, where, on April 27, 1868, he married Mariah Hedrick. Obed and Mariah would not have any children together, however, she brought five children into the marriage: Tempy, Burgess, Delilah, Sara, and John. Obed helped to found Hedrick's Grove Church in the 1890s and lived in the Silver Hill township until his death on July 30, 1909. He is buried at Hedrick's Grove United Church of Christ.

1731. Swing, Wiley D.

Private, Company B, 48th Regiment N.C. Troops

Wiley was born in 1843 to John and Elizabeth Swing. Wiley worked as a farmer prior to volunteering for service on March 5, 1862. He died of disease at Madison Court House, Virginia, on November 19, 1862.

1732. Swink, Adam W.

Private, Company A, 42nd Regiment N.C. Troops

Adam was born in Rowan County in 1825 to Henry and Elizabeth Jacobs Swink. Adam moved to Davidson County in the early 1850s with his new wife, Elizabeth. Adam and Elizabeth would have seven children: Martha (1852), Thomas (1854), Millard (1856), Luzena (1858), Mary (1860), John (1863), and George (1871). Adam worked as a tanner and was originally exempt from conscription and service. However, as the war progressed, Adam's supply of leather and tanning goods became more scarce by the day. Once Adam's production dropped completely off, he was notified by the Home Guard in January 1864 that he would no longer be exempt from the Conscript Act. Adam was conscripted into service in January 1864 and was reported present until captured at Battery Anderson, Fort Fisher, North Carolina, on December 24, 1864. He was confined at Point Lookout, Maryland, until June 20, 1865, when released after taking the oath of allegiance. After the war, Adam returned to the Cotton Grove township and to his tanning business in the Jersey community until his death on February 12, 1900. He is buried at Jersey Baptist Church.

1733. Tackett, Thomas H.

Private, Company H, 48th Regiment N.C. Troops

Thomas was born in 1841. Thomas worked as a hireling prior to volunteering on an unreported date. His "name was cancelled" on April 23, 1862, and he was dropped from the rolls. No further records.

1734. Tate, Lemuel R.

Private, Company B, 57th Regiment N.C. Troops

Lemuel was born on March 7, 1829. Lemuel worked as a farmer and as a part-time miner, and, in 1854, he married Sarah Smith. Lemuel built on to the small house in which he had been living to make room for his family. Lemuel and Sarah would have three children, Sarah (1856), James (1858), and Robert (1861), before Lemuel enlisted in Rowan County on July 4, 1862. He was hospitalized at Danville, Virginia, on February 3, 1863, due to "otterheoa." Lemuel returned to service on March 16, 1863, and was reported present until captured at Fort Stedman, Virginia, on March 25, 1865. He was confined at Washington, D.C., until June 14, 1865, when he was released after taking the oath of allegiance. After the war, Lemuel returned home and went to work in the mines as a career. Lemuel and Susanna would go on to have four more children: Jacob (1869), William (1875), Lee (1878), and Nancy (1880). Lemuel lived in the Cotton Grove township until his death on June 17, 1889. He is buried at Jersey Baptist Church.

1735. Taylor, Christian C.

Corporal, Company B, 48th Regiment N.C. Troops

Christian was born in 1831 to William A. and Mary Taylor. Christian worked as a farmer, and, on July 17, 1855, he married Mary Lucy Sink. Christian volunteered for service on March 6, 1862, and was mustered in as a corporal. He was wounded at King's School House, Virginia, on June 25, 1862. Christian died of his wounds at Richmond, Virginia, on June 26, 1862.

1736. Taylor, Clemmons T.

*Private, Company D, 48th Regiment
N.C. Troops*

Clem was born in 1839 to William A. and Mary Taylor. Clem worked as a farmer, and, in 1858, he married Mary. Clem and Mary would have a daughter, Margaret (1860), before Clem was conscripted into service on August 8, 1862. He was wounded in action at Sharpsburg, Maryland, on September 17, 1862. Clem died as a result of either his wounds or disease at Staunton, Virginia, on December 6, 1862.

1737. Taylor, David W.

*Private, Company D, 48th Regiment
N.C. Troops*

David was born in 1837 to William A. and Mary Taylor. David worked as a farmer prior to being conscripted into service on August 8, 1862. He was wounded and captured at Sharpsburg, Maryland, on September 17, 1862. David was paroled on September 29, 1862, and was sent home to recover. David died of disease while at home on November 30, 1862.

1738. Taylor, Franklin

*Private, Company B, 48th Regiment
N.C. Troops*

Franklin was born in 1836 to William A. and Mary Taylor. Franklin worked as a farmer, and, on June 10, 1860, he married Barbara Strange. Franklin volunteered for service on March 17, 1862. He was wounded at King's School House, Virginia, on June 25, 1862. Franklin was absent, wounded, until he died of "typhoid pneumonia" at Petersburg, Virginia, on January 24, 1863.

1739. Taylor, Travis

*Private, Company A, 42nd Regiment
N.C. Troops*

Travis was born in 1829 to William A. and Mary Taylor. Travis worked as a farmer, and, on August 30, 1852, he married Catharine Koontz. Travis volunteered for service on March 6, 1862. He died of pneumonia at Petersburg, Virginia, on December 14, 1862. He is buried in the mass North Carolina grave in the Blanford Cemetery in Petersburg.

1740. Teague, Isaac B. H.

*Private, Company A, 10th Battalion,
N.C. Heavy Artillery
Company D, 10th Battalion, N.C.
Heavy Artillery*

Isaac was born in 1837. Isaac worked as a shoemaker in the Abbott's Creek area, and, on February 21, 1856, he married Esther Roberts. Isaac and Esther would have three children, John and Edward (1859) and Isaac II (1862), before Isaac was conscripted into service on December 15, 1862. He was transferred to Company D on May 23, 1863. Isaac was present until he died of unreported causes at Fort Campbell, Brunswick County, on February 17, 1864. There is a stone placed in his honor at Abbott's Creek Primitive Baptist Church.

1741. Teague, Jacob M.

*Private, Company H, 15th Regiment
N.C. Troops (5th N.C. Volunteers)*

Jacob was born in 1843 to John and Keziah Teague. Jacob worked as a farmer in the Abbott's Creek area prior to being conscripted into service in Wake County on July 15, 1862. Jacob was listed as "missing and supposed to be dead" at Sharpsburg, Maryland, on September 17, 1862. No further records.

1742. Teague, Jacob R.

*Private, Company G, 2nd Battalion,
N.C. Infantry*

Jacob was born in 1845 to James and Susanna Teague. Jacob worked as a farmer prior to volunteering for service shortly after his 18th birthday on July 16, 1863. He was reported present until wounded at Alsop's Farm, Virginia, near Cold Harbor on May 29, 1864. Jacob died of his wounds on July 10, 1864.

1743. Teague, Joseph Columbus

*Private, Confederate Guards
Company K, 48th Regiment N.C. Troops*

Joseph was born in 1831 to Moses and Martha Teague. Joseph worked as a mechanic, and, in 1853, he married Jane. Joseph and Jane would have two children, George (1855) and Calvin (1858), before Joseph was conscripted into service on August 8, 1862. He was killed in action at Sharpsburg, Maryland, on September 17, 1862.

1744. Teague, Joseph F.

*Private, Company G, 2nd Battalion,
N.C. Infantry*

Joseph was born in 1827. Joseph worked as a farmer in the northern district of Davidson County, and, in 1851, he married Emily Hayden. Joseph and Emily would have five children, David (1852), Moses (1853), Charles (1855), John C. (1857), and William (1859), before Joseph was conscripted into service on January 20, 1863. He was present until reported missing and captured on August 25, 1864. Joseph was never heard from again, leaving his wife and five young sons to care for the family home. No further records.

1745. Teague, Romulus

*Private, Company G, 2nd Battalion,
N.C. Infantry*

Romulus was born in 1843 to James and Susanna Teague. Romulus worked as a farmer prior to volunteering for service in Forsyth County on September 19, 1861. He was reported present until captured at Roanoke Island, North Carolina, on February 8, 1862. Romulus was confined at Elizabeth City, North Carolina, until he was paroled on February 21, 1862. Romulus returned to service but died of unreported causes at High Point, North Carolina, on March 8, 1862.

1746. Terry, James

*Private, Company B, 48th Regiment
N.C. Troops*

James was born in 1815 in Great Britain. James immigrated with his parents to Davidson County in the 1830s. James worked as a hireling in the Conrad Hill area, and, in 1841, he married Charity Myers. James and Charity would have five children, Emily (1842), Lemuel (1846), Susan (1851), Farley (1854), and Edwin (1859), before James volunteered for service on March 6, 1862. He was discharged because of "phthisis" on September 24, 1862. No further records.

1747. Tesh, George W.

*Private, Company H, 15th Regiment
N.C. Troops (5th N.C. Volunteers)*

George was born on September 29, 1840, to George and Sarah Beckel Tesh. George worked as a carpenter prior to being conscripted into service in Wake County on July 15, 1862. He was reported present until wounded in the right hip and foot at Bristoe Station, Virginia, on October 14, 1863. George recovered from his wounds and returned to service in January 1864. He was reported present until wounded again, this time in the cheek, at Ream's Station, Virginia, on August 25, 1864. George was reported in a Richmond, Virginia, hospital on March 11, 1865, and was well enough to assist in the evacuation of the city on April 2, 1865. George was paroled at Appomattox Court House, Virginia, on April 9, 1865. After the war, George returned to the Arcadia township, where, in 1867, he married Elvira Miller. George and Elvira would have a daughter, Frannie (1870). George lived in the Arcadia township until his death on December 17, 1913. He is buried at Friedburg Moravian Church.

1748. Tesh, Jacob A.

Private, Davidson Guards
Company A, 21st Regiment N.C. Troops
(11th N.C. Volunteers)

Jacob was born on August 23, 1841, to Charles and Christina Tesh. Jacob worked as a farmer prior to volunteering for service on May 8, 1861. He was reported present until captured at Charles Town, West Virginia, on August 22, 1864. Jacob was confined at Elmira, New York, until June 21, 1865, when he was released after taking the oath of allegiance. After the war, Jacob made his way home to the Arcadia township, where, in 1866, he married Louvina C. Jacob and Louvina would have seven children: Edward (1869), Robert (1870), Bertha (1872), Franklin (1873), Sophia (1874), Charles (1877), and Claudia (1879). Jacob worked as a farmer in the Arcadia area until his death on July 15, 1927. He is buried at Mount Olivet United Methodist Church.

1749. Tesh, John D.

Captain, 66th Regiment N.C. Militia
(1861 organization)

John was born in 1811. John worked as a farmer in the northern district of Davidson County, and, on August 27, 1837, he married Elizabeth Charles. John was commissioned to serve as the commander of the Sandy Ridge District Company on December 13, 1861. No further records.

1750. Tesh, Levi

Private, Confederate Guards
Company K, 48th Regiment N.C. Troops

Levi was born in 1819. Levi worked as a blacksmith in the Abbott's Creek area, and, on November 17, 1846, he married Mary Teague. Levi and Mary would have four children, James (1848), Sarah (1850), Jane (1852), and Crissie (1860), before Levi was conscripted into service on August 8, 1862. He was reported missing at Harpers Ferry, West Virginia, in September 1862. The exact nature of the rest of his service is unknown, but he may have also served in the Senior Reserves. Levi and Mary would have two more children: Mary (1873) and Jenette (1879). Levi worked as a blacksmith in the Abbott's Creek township until his death on December 15, 1891. He is buried at Bethany United Church of Christ.

1751. Tesh, Romulus B.

Private, Confederate Guards
Company K, 48th Regiment N.C. Troops

Romulus was born in 1840 to David and Rachael Tesh. Romulus worked as a farmer in the Arcadia township prior to being conscripted into service on August 8, 1862. He was wounded in the arm and left shoulder at Fredericksburg, Virginia, on December 13, 1862. Romulus recovered and was reported present through January 1864, when he was listed as absent without leave. While absent, Rom married Christine Green on August 21, 1864. Rom received his parole at Greensboro, North Carolina, on May 5, 1865. After the war, Rom and Christine would have six children, Joseph (1865), William (1867), David (1872), Hugh (1875), John (1877), and Regina (1879), before moving to Forsyth County in the 1890s. No further records.

1752. Tesh, Solomon

Corporal, Company H, 15th Regiment
N.C. Troops (5th N.C. Volunteers)

Solomon was born in 1831 to George and Sarah Beckel Tesh. Solomon worked as a farmer, and, in 1851, he married Phoebe Perryman. Solomon and Phoebe would have four children, Lutetia (1852), Laura (1854), Robert (1857), and Benjamin (1860), before Solomon was conscripted into service on July 15, 1862. He was wounded at Crampton's Pass,

Maryland, on September 14, 1862. Solomon returned to service in January 1863 and was promoted to corporal on April 8, 1863. Solomon served as a corporal until he died of typhoid fever at Richmond, Virginia, on December 18, 1864.

1753. Thomas, Autian Addison

First Lieutenant, 66th Regiment N.C.
Militia (1861 organization)

Autian was born in 1825 to Mary W. Thomas. Autian worked as a miller's assistant prior to being commissioned as first lieutenant in the Bulow District Company on May 3, 1862. No further records.

1754. Thomas, Francis E.

Second Lieutenant, Company C, 70th
Regiment N.C. Troops (1st N.C.
Junior Reserves)

Francis was born in 1847 to Lewis and Martha Thomas. Francis was a student prior to enlisting in the Junior Reserves on May 24, 1864, and being elected as second lieutenant. After the war, Francis returned home to the Thomasville township, where, in 1874, he married Nettie Lambeth. Francis and Nettie would have four children, Irene (1879), Arthur (1882), Robert (1886), and Hattie (1896), before moving out of the county in the 1890s. No further records.

1755. Thomas, Henry Clay

Private, Thomasville Rifles
Company B, 14th Regiment N.C. Troops
(4th N.C. Volunteers)
Company A, 10th Battalion, N.C. Heavy
Artillery

Henry was born on March 14, 1844, to Senator John W. and Mary Thomas. Henry worked as a clerk at Thomas' Depot prior to volunteering for service on April 23, 1861. He was promoted to sergeant on November 17, 1861, but was reduced in rank on April 29, 1862. Henry was discharged from service because of being under age on July 22, 1862. Henry returned to "Cedar Lodge" and helped to run his father's home while he was away at the Confederate Congress. Henry enlisted again, this time into the artillery, on January 16, 1864. He was reported present until paroled in Randolph County on April 29, 1865. After the war, Henry returned home to Thomasville, and, in

This Midway home, built in 1845, belonged to James K. Polk Thomas (Touart, *Building the Backcountry*).

1871 he completed his medical training at the state university at Chapel Hill, North Carolina. Trained to serve as a cancer doctor, Henry specialized in the treatment of visible tumors, as well as handling a general practice. Henry married Caroline Bowers in 1872, and they would have four children: Mamie (1872), Bessie (1874), Hattie (1876), and Lawrence (1880). Henry continued his work as a doctor in the town of Thomasville until his death on March 10, 1917. He is buried in the Thomasville City Cemetery.

1756. Thomas, James K. Polk

Private, Company H, 15th Regiment N.C. Troops (5th N.C. Volunteers)

James was born on April 27, 1825 to William and Catharine Leonard Thomas. James worked as a farmer in the Midway area prior to being conscripted into service in Wake County on July 15, 1862. He was reported present until wounded at Reams' Station, Virginia, on August 25, 1864. James recovered from his wounds and was captured sometime between October 13, 1864, and March 25, 1865. He was confined at Point Lookout, Maryland, until June 21, 1865, when he was released after taking the oath of allegiance. After the war, James made his way home to the Midway township, where, on

January 12, 1867, he married Ellen Hammer. James and Ellen would have eight children: Martha (1868), George (1870), Eliza (1872), Laura (1874), Henry (1879), William (1885), James (1889), and Robert (1892). James lived in the Midway township until his death on May 1, 1930. He is buried at Midway United Methodist Church.

1757. Thomas, Pleasant C.

First Lieutenant, Thomasville Rifles Company B, 14th Regiment N.C. Troops (4th N.C. Volunteers)

Pleasant was born on May 12, 1838, to Senator John W. and Mary Thomas. Pleasant worked as a clerk at Thomas' Depot prior to volunteering for service on April 23, 1861, and being elected to the post of second lieutenant. He was promoted to first lieutenant on May 26, 1861. Pleasant served as lieutenant until he was defeated for reelection when the regiment was reorganized on April 25, 1862. Pleasant returned home and was exempted from further service. He wrote two letters to his father in Raleigh, trying to obtain another commission, but his father could not obtain his appointment. Pleasant married Annie in 1864. Pleasant and Annie would have eight children: David (1866), Charles (1868), Mary (1872),

Edward (1874), John W. (1876), Sally Jesse (1879), Robert Lee (1885), and Minnie (1889). Pleasant inherited several thousand dollars in property when his father died in 1873. He became a successful landlord and helped to further the development of industry in the young town. Pleasant lived in Thomasville until his death on February 1, 1921. He is buried in the Thomasville City Cemetery.

1758. Thomason, Andrew

Private, Company I, 42nd Regiment N.C. Troops

Andrew was born in 1839 to George and Nancy Wilson Thomason. Andrew worked as a farmer in the Shiloh area prior to volunteering for service on March 4, 1862. He died "at home" of unreported causes on May 30, 1862.

1759. Thomason, David

Private, Company I, 42nd Regiment N.C. Troops

David was born in 1841 to George and Nancy Wilson Thomason. David worked as a farmer in the Shiloh area prior to volunteering for service on March 4, 1862. He died of unreported causes "at home" on June 6, 1862.

1760. Thomason, George Arnold

Sergeant, Company I, 42nd Regiment N.C. Troops

George was born on December 31, 1839, to John W. and Adeline Thomason. George worked as a merchant in Lexington prior to volunteering for service on March 4, 1862, and being mustered in as a sergeant. George served as a sergeant throughout the war and was reported present through October 1864. He was paroled at Greensboro, North Carolina, on May 1, 1865. After the war, George returned to Lexington, where, on December 20, 1868, he married Sarah Elizabeth McCrary. George and Sarah would have ten children: Claudia (1867), Arnold (1873), Gustan (1876), James (1878), William (1881), Daisy (1883), Mary (1886), James (1888), Bradley (1891), and George (1894). George became an insurance agent and a Lexington businessman, insuring both the rebuilt courthouse and the March Hotel. George lived in the city of Lexington and was a member of the Methodist church until his death on

May 26, 1926. He is buried in the Lexington City Cemetery.

1761. Thomason, Jesse

Private, Company I, 42nd Regiment N.C. Troops

Jesse was born in 1842 to George and Nancy Wilson Thomason. Jesse worked as a carpenter prior to volunteering for service on March 4, 1862. He was reported present until confined and court-martialed on October 15, 1862. His punishment was hard labor at Fort Fisher, North Carolina, at which he served until April 1863. Jesse returned to service in May 1863 and was reported present until October 1864. After the war, Jesse moved to Lexington, where, on March 28, 1867, he married Susan Essick. Jesse and Susan would have four children: Lee (1868), Lewis (1869), Gaither (1880), and Minnie (1885). Jesse and his family were living in Lexington through 1900. No further records.

1762. Thomason, John

Private, Cleveland Mountain Boys Company D, 15th Regiment N.C. Troops (5th N.C. Volunteers) 2nd Company B, 49th Regiment N.C. Troops

John was born in 1836 to George and Nancy Wilson Thomason. John worked as a farmer in the Shiloh area prior to being conscripted into service on July 15, 1862. He was transferred to the 49th Regiment on January 9, 1863. John was reported present until he died of pneumonia in a Petersburg, Virginia, hospital on January 20, 1864. He is buried in the mass North Carolina grave in the Blanford Cemetery at Petersburg.

1763. Thomason, Richmond D.

Corporal, Company I, 42nd Regiment N.C. Troops

Richmond was born on November 30, 1834, to John W. and Adeline Thomason. Richmond worked as a farmer prior to being conscripted into service on October 23, 1863. He was promoted to corporal in March 1864 and was reported present through February 27, 1865. He was paroled at Greensboro, North Carolina, on May 1, 1865. After the war, Richmond returned home to the Lexington area, where, on August 2, 1898, he married Susan Wagner. By 1900, Susan had died, and Richmond was living with his nephew Albert Beck. Richmond died on June 24, 1908. He is buried at Ebenezer United Methodist Church.

1764. Thompson, Charles M.

Private, Lexington Wildcats Company I, 14th Regiment N.C. Troops (4th N.C. Volunteers)

Charles was born on August 20, 1845, to Hiram and Cynthia Ratts Thompson. Charles was a student in the Tyro area prior to volunteering for service on May 14, 1861. He was reported present until wounded in the right arm at Spotsylvania Court House, Virginia, on May 12, 1864. Charles lost his arm to the surgeon's saw but survived the amputation. He was reported absent, wounded, in Richmond, Virginia, until discharged from service on March 18, 1865. Charles returned home to the Tyro township, where he married Mary Peebles in 1867. Charles and Mary would have six children, Lizzie (1870), Minnie (1873), Joseph (1875), Jessie (1877), Lloyd (1879), and Clifton (1884), before they moved to Lexington in the 1880s. Charles opened a cabinetry shop, which grew into a factory that produced window sashes and blinds for distribution throughout the entire nation. Charles contributed an article to *Confederate Veteran* magazine and served as a commander and member of the A. A. Hill Camp, United Confederate Veterans. Charles joked with his friend Frank Robbins that, since Frank had lost his left arm and he had lost his right, the two could split a pair of gloves. In the interest of saving money, they did exactly that. Charles became a well-known and respected member of the Piedmont business community. Charles died on January 25, 1927. He is buried in the Lexington City Cemetery.

1765. Thompson, James Giles

Private, Company H, 15th Regiment N.C. Troops (5th N.C. Volunteers)

James was born in 1828 to Elizabeth Thompson. James worked as a farmer prior to being conscripted into service in Wake County on July 15, 1862. He was reported present until he died of "apoplexia" in a Lynchburg, Virginia, hospital on January 22, 1863.

1766. Thompson, John F.

Third Lieutenant, Holtsburg Guards Company A, 54th Regiment N.C. Troops

John was born on October 17, 1836, to Hiram and Cynthia Ratts Thompson. John managed the Tyro tavern for a short period before going into the mercantile business. John married Susan Miller in 1861, volunteered for service on March 3, 1862, and was appointed third lieutenant on May 26, 1862. He died of disease at the home of Dr. William P. Darricute at Petersburg, Virginia, on October 6, 1862. A stone was placed in his honor at St. Luke's Lutheran Church. An article which ran in the *Spirit of the Age* states: "He was a warm and generous friend, a good officer, and an honorable gentleman."

1767. Thompson, Phillip

Private, Company H, 15th Regiment N.C. Troops (5th N.C. Volunteers)

Phillip was born in 1845. Phillip worked as a farmer before volunteering for service in Johnston County on May 22, 1863. He was captured at Bristoe Station, Virginia, on October 14, 1863. Phillip was confined at Washington, D.C., until November 15, 1864, when he was paroled and transferred to Venus Point, Georgia, for exchange. Phillip was exchanged but was captured again while serving with another unit at Bentonville, North Carolina, on March 19, 1865. He was confined at Hart's Island, New York, until June 20, 1865, when he was released after taking the oath of allegiance. No further records.

1768. Thompson, William Lewis

Corporal, Lexington Wildcats Company I, 14th Regiment N.C. Troops (4th N.C. Volunteers)

William was born on December 14, 1841, to Hiram and Cynthia Ratts Thompson. William was a student at Yadkin College prior to volunteering for service on May 14, 1861. He was promoted to corporal on November 1, 1862. William was reported present through February 25, 1865, but was on detached service as a courier for the brigade staff. After the war, William returned home, where, on November 6, 1866, he married Mary Penry. William and Mary settled down in the Yadkin College village where they would raise three children: John (1869), Lillian (1873), and Sarah Grayson (1878). William lived in the Yadkin College area until his death on December 17, 1892. He is buried at Yadkin College Methodist Church.

1769. Tice, Constatine

Private, Company A, 42nd Regiment N.C. Troops

"Costen" was born in 1828. Costen worked as a farmer in the northern district of Davidson County, and, on September 15, 1852, he married Katharine Hayworth. Costen and Katharine would have five children: Louisa (1853), Houke (1855), Martha (1857), Samuel (1861), and Sarah (1863). In 1860, Costen was working as an assistant for Dr. F. W. Stinson. Costen volunteered for service on February 4, 1862, and was reported present until captured at Battery Anderson, Fort Fisher, North Carolina, on December 25, 1864. Costen was confined at Point Lookout, Maryland, via Fort Monroe, Virginia, until June 3, 1865, when he was released after taking the oath of allegiance. After the war, Costen moved his family to Bartholomew County, Illinois, but he died in October 1865. He is buried in Bartholomew County.

1770. Tice, Hamilton

Private, Company A, 42nd Regiment N.C. Troops

Hamilton was born in 1826. Hamilton worked as a farmer in the northern district of Davidson County, and, on September 13, 1848, he married Barbara Weir. Hamilton and Barbara would have four children, Louisa (1849), Lawrence (1851), Gannetta (1855), and Media (1859), before Hamilton volunteered for service on March 25, 1862. He was reported present until captured at Battery Anderson, Fort Fisher, North Carolina, on December 25, 1864. Records of the Federal provost marshal conclude that Hamilton never arrived at the prison. However, these records also speculate that Hamilton assumed a false name, probably that of one of the men who were to be released, paroled, or exchanged, and therefore escaped a long imprisonment. Hamilton returned home to the Abbott's Creek area. He died on April 7, 1884, and is buried at Bethany United Church of Christ.

1771. Timms, John

Private, Company G, 2nd Battalion, N.C. Infantry
Company A, 10th Battalion, N.C. Heavy Artillery

John was born in 1839. John worked as a farmhand for Bennett Hedgecock prior to volunteering for service in Forsyth County on September 19, 1861. He was reported present until captured at Roanoke Island, North Carolina, on February 8, 1862. John was paroled at Elizabeth City, North Carolina, on February 21, 1862, and was transferred to the 10th Heavy Artillery on August 1, 1862. John was reported present with the 10th Battalion until he died of disease on August 24, 1864.

1772. Tippett, John Wilson

Private, Company D, 62nd Battalion, Georgia Cavalry
Company H, 16th Battalion, N.C. Cavalry

John was born in 1836 to Luke and Elizabeth Tippett. John enlisted in the 62nd Georgia Cavalry and was present at Plymouth, North Carolina, before being transferred to the 16th N.C. Cavalry on July 11, 1864. The last records of his company state that he was "captured by the enemy in July 1864." No further records.

1773. Tippett, Travis T.

Private, Company B, 48th Regiment N.C. Troops

Travis was born in 1830 to Martha Tippett. Travis worked as a farmer, and, in 1862, he married Elizabeth. Travis was conscripted into service on August 8, 1862. He was reported present through October 1864 and was paroled at Salisbury, North Carolina, on May 13, 1865. After the war, Travis returned home to the Cotton Grove area to see his son, John, who had been born in 1863. Travis and Elizabeth would have three more children, Burwell (1867), James (1874), and Elizabeth (1880), before moving out of the county in the 1890s. No further records.

1774. Todd, Milo G.

Private, Lexington Wildcats
Company I, 14th Regiment N.C. Troops (4th N.C. Volunteers)

Milo was born in 1834. Milo was working as a carpenter prior to volunteering for service on May 14, 1861. He was reported present until he died of unreported causes at his parents' home in Rowan County on January 3, 1863.

1775. Tonkins, John W.

Private, Holtsburg Guards
Company A, 54th Regiment N.C. Troops

John was born in 1841. John worked as a miner prior to volunteering for service on March 4, 1862. He was reported present until captured at Rappahannock Station, Virginia, on November 7 1863. John was confined at Old Capital Prison, Washington, D.C., until admitted to a hospital on December 26, 1863, with "variola." John was exchanged on an unreported date. After the war, John continued to work as a silver miner and built a new home for himself in the Emmons township. John remained single until his death on February 4, 1897. He is buried at New Jerusalem United Church of Christ.

1776. Tranthum, Alexander J.

Private, Company F, 76th Regiment N.C. Troops (6th N.C. Senior Reserves)

Alex was born in 1821 to Martin and Mary Younts Tranthum. Alex worked as a farmer in the Lexington area, and, on October 12, 1841, he married Christina Shoaf. Alex and Christina would have eight children: Francis H. (1843), Daniel J. (1845), Henry A. (1847), John T. (1849), Mary (1852–61), Andrew (1855), Julius (1858), and Cicero Lee (1862). Alex was part of A. A. Hill's Senior Reserves, which became part of the 6th N.C. Senior Reserves in January 1865. After his service, Alex continued to live in the Lexington area and grieved for the loss of two of his sons. Alex died on May 20, 1891. He is buried at Shiloh United Methodist Church.

1777. Tranthum, Daniel James

Private, Company A, 42nd Regiment N.C. Troops

Daniel was born on November 23, 1845, to Alexander and Christina Shoaf Tranthum. Daniel worked as a farmer prior to enlisting in Davidson County on March 1, 1863. He was reported present until he died of "the effects of disease" at Richmond, Virginia, on September 20, 1864. He is buried in the Hollywood Cemetery, in Richmond.

1778. Tranthum (Transom), Francis A.

Private, Company D, 21st Regiment N.C. Troops (11th N.C. Volunteers)

Francis was born in 1844 to William and Mary Tranthum. Francis volunteered for service in Forsyth County on June 11, 1861. He died of disease at Front Royal, Virginia, on September 19, 1861.

1779. Tranthum, Francis Hamilton

Sergeant, Holtsburg Guards Company A, 54th Regiment N.C. Troops

Francis was born on January 2, 1843, to Alexander and Christina Shoaf Tranthum. Francis worked as a farmer prior to enlisting in Davidson County on April 27, 1862. He was promoted to corporal on June 13, 1862, and promoted to sergeant in July 1862. Francis was reported present until he was captured at Rappahannock Station, Virginia, on November 7, 1863. He was confined at Point Lookout, Maryland, until March 9, 1864, when he was paroled and transferred to City Point, Virginia, for exchange. Francis was reported missing and presumed dead at Stephenson's Depot, Virginia, on July 20, 1864.

1780. Tranthum, Henry Alexander

Private, Company C, 70th Regiment N.C. Troops (1st N.C. Junior Reserves)

Henry was born on April 2, 1847, to Alexander and Christina Shoaf Tranthum. Henry worked as a farmer prior to enlisting in the Junior Reserves on May 24, 1864. After the war, Henry returned home to the Cotton Grove township, where, on April 14, 1870, he married Mary F. Gobble. Henry and Mary would have six children: John (1871), Charles (1872), Annie V. (1874), Crissie (1883), Margaret (1887), and Henry C. (1888). Mary died in 1911, and, four years later, Henry married Sarah Jane Money. Sarah would die of the flu in 1924, leaving Henry a widower again. Three years later, Henry married for the last time, to Lucy A. Michael Wilson. A descendant of Henry's, Ken Walker of Central Davidson

High School, has in his possession the powder horn which Henry carried to his muster on May 24, 1864. Family history states that this horn was carried for the length of Henry's service. Henry lived in the Cotton Grove area until his death on December 19, 1929. He is buried at Jersey Baptist Church.

1781. Trexler, David L.

Private, Lexington Wildcats Company I, 14th Regiment N.C. Troops (4th N.C. Volunteers)

David was born in 1832. David worked as a blacksmith in the town of Lexington, and, in 1858, he married Susan Jane. David and Susan would have two children, Lucy (1859) and Jefferson (1862), before David was conscripted into service on January 27, 1863. He was reported present through October 1864. After the war, David returned to Lexington where he and Susan would have two more children: Charles (1867) and Edward (1871). David lived in the Lexington area through 1880. No further records.

1782. Trexler, John H.

Private, Davidson Guards Company A, 21st Regiment N.C. Troops (11th N.C. Volunteers)

John was born in 1838. John lived with and worked for Jacob Myers prior to volunteering for service on May 8, 1861. He died of typhoid fever at Camp Rhett, Virginia, on August 20, 1861.

1783. Turner, Edmund D.

Private, Davie Sweep Stakes Company G, 4th Regiment N.C. State Troops

Edmund was born on February 29, 1841. Edmund volunteered for service in Davie County on June 4, 1861. He was reported present until wounded in the right thigh and arm at Seven Pines, Virginia, on May 31, 1862. He was sent to a hospital and then home to recover and was reported absent, wounded, through August 1864. He was paroled at Greensboro, North Carolina, on May 9, 1865. Edmund returned to the town of Lexington, where he worked as a carpenter, and, in 1870, he married Connie Poplin. Edmund and Connie would have five children: William (1871), Mittie (1875),

Dorothy (1880), John (1886), and Rena (1890). Edmund worked as a carpenter in the city of Lexington and helped with the rebuilding of the courthouse after it burned in 1865. Edmund died on November 20, 1904. He is buried in the Lexington City Cemetery.

1784. Turner, John Spencer

Private, Company B, 68th Regiment N.C. Troops

John was born on February 19, 1847. John worked as a carpenter in the town of Thomasville prior to being conscripted into service on July 7, 1863. After the war, John returned home where there was plenty of carpentry work available. John married Martha in 1867, and the couple would have two children: Zeb Vance (1871) and Edney (1880). John worked as a carpenter in Thomasville and was a founding member of Unity Church. John died on May 9, 1926. He is buried at Unity Methodist Church.

1785. Turner, William F.

Private, Company F, 7th Regiment N.C. State Troops

William was born in 1843 to James and Nancy Turner. William worked as a farmhand for A. C. Redwine prior to volunteering for service on March 2, 1862. He was reported present until retired to the Invalid Corps on October 12, 1864. After the war, William returned home to the Allegheny township, where, on September 20, 1866, he married Nancy Skeen. William and Nancy would have six children: Cicero (1867), Cora (1869), Lucy (1873), John (1876), and Mary and Catharine (1880). William lived in the Allegheny township until his death in 1893. He is buried in an unmarked grave at Pleasant Grove United Methodist Church.

1786. Turner, William L.

Private, Company F, 7th Regiment N.C. State Troops

William was born in 1834 to Eli and Mary Turner. William worked as a farmer in the Lexington township, and, in 1859, he married Elizabeth Beck. William and Elizabeth would have a daughter, Alice (1860), before William volunteered for service on June 30, 1861. He was wounded at Frayser's Farm,

Virginia, on June 30, 1862, and was captured at Frederick, Maryland, on September 12, 1862. William was confined at Point Lookout, Maryland, until October 30, 1862, when he was paroled and transferred to Aiken's Landing, Virginia, for exchange. He was exchanged on November 10, 1862, and returned to service in January 1863. William was wounded in the left leg and captured again at Gettysburg, Pennsylvania, on July 3, 1863. He was received at City Point, Virginia, for exchange on September 23, 1863. William returned to service and was wounded for a third time in September 1864. He was discharged from service due to disability on February 1, 1865. After the war, he and Elizabeth would have four more surviving children: John (1865), Lillie (1867), Lucy (1876), and Albert (1887). William later lived in the state Confederates' home with Isaiah Younts. No further records.

1787. Tussey, David Allison

Private, Company H, 48th Regiment N.C. Troops

David was born on April 7, 1825, to Gersham and Sarah Byerly Tussey. David worked as a farmer, and, in 1850, he married Susan Kanoy. David and Susan would have one child, Teritha (1851), before Susan died in 1855. Later that year, David married Eliza Clodfelter on October 23, 1855. David and Eliza would have two sons, Julian (1857) and William (1860), before David was conscripted into service on August 8, 1862. He died of disease at Warrenton, Virginia, on October 3, 1862.

1788. Tussey, Franklin H.

Sergeant, Company H, 48th Regiment N.C. Troops

Franklin was born on February 28, 1837, to Gersham and Sarah Byerly Tussey. Franklin worked as a farmer, and, on September 17, 1853, he married Elizabeth Sink. Franklin and Elizabeth would have three children, Arlena (1854), Sarah (1857), and Gersham (1860), before Franklin was conscripted into service at Petersburg, Virginia, on August 8, 1862. He was promoted to corporal on November 1, 1862, and to sergeant on February 21, 1863. Franklin was reported present until he died at home of unreported causes on February 25, 1863. He is buried at Pilgrim United Church of Christ.

Zeno Tussey and his wife were married for three years before moving into this Lexington home (Touart, *Building the Backcountry*).

1789. Tussey, Zeno Benton

Private, Company B, 48th Regiment N.C. Troops

Zeno was born on December 18, 1845, to Mary Tussey. Zeno was a student prior to volunteering for service on March 3, 1862. He was reported present until wounded in the head and left wrist at Cold Harbor, Virginia, on June 3, 1864. Zeno was dropped from the rolls, perhaps due to disability, on November 1, 1864. After his service, Zeno returned to the Lexington area but left to finish his studies at Trinity College. On September 10, 1869, Zeno married Barbara Swing, and they moved to the Silver Hill township. Zeno and Barbara would have six children: Mary (1871), Jacob (1873), Zeno M. (1875), David (1878), Jesse (1883), and Bessie (1889). Zeno served as a justice of the peace, an attorney, and a probate judge for the county from 1879 to 1926. Zeno had been retired for four years before his death on November 9, 1930. He is buried at Beck's United Church of Christ.

1790. Tysinger, Alexander

Private, Thomasville Rifles Company B, 14th Regiment N.C. Troops (4th N.C. Volunteers)

Alex was born in 1845 to John and Elizabeth Tysinger. Alex worked as a

blacksmith prior to volunteering for service on May 15, 1861. He was reported present until wounded in the right arm at Malvern Hill, Virginia, on July 1, 1862. Alex was reported absent, wounded, until he rejoined the company in January 1863. He was discharged due to unreported reasons on January 25, 1864. After he returned to the Emmons township, Alex married Delphina Surratt in 1865. Alex and Delphina would have three children, Catharine (1866), Charles (1869), and Robert (1874), before her death in 1876. Alex remarried in 1883, to Louisa. Alex and Louisa would have five children: Marvin (1886), Margaret (1889), Joseph (1891), William (1895), and Farley (1898). Alex moved to Randolph County sometime in the early 1900s. No further records.

1791. Tysinger, Alexander

Private, Davidson Guards Company A, 21st Regiment N.C. Troops (11th N.C. Volunteers)

Alex was born in 1840. Alex worked as a farmer prior to volunteering for service on May 8, 1861. He was reported present until wounded in the right leg and foot at Cedar Mountain, Virginia, on August 9, 1862. Alex's right leg was amputated, and he was granted a furlough until officially retired to the Invalid Corps on November 21, 1864. Alex

Home of famous Denton blacksmith Robert B. Tysinger (Touart, *Building the Back-country*).

returned home and lived with his cousins. He was last reported as living in the Healing Springs township in 1900. No further records.

1792. Tysinger, Daniel

Private, Rough and Ready Guard
Company F, 14th Regiment N.C. Troops
(4th N.C. Volunteers)
Company D, 4th Regiment U.S. Volunteer Infantry

Daniel was born on August 13, 1842, to David and Elizabeth Newsome Tysinger. Daniel worked as a miner prior to being conscripted into service on November 26, 1863. He was reported present until captured at Port Republic, Virginia, on September 28, 1864. Daniel was confined at Point Lookout, Maryland, until October 14, 1864, when he volunteered to serve in the Union Army. Daniel was assigned to Company D, 4th U.S. Volunteer Infantry, which held a post at Alexandria, Virginia, until the end of the war. After the war, Daniel returned to his work in the mines and, on December 14, 1879, he married Tryphenia Hedrick. Daniel and Tryphenia would have four children: Margaret (1883), John (1885), Charles (1888), and Eliza (1890). Daniel lived in the Emmons township until his death on February 28, 1918. He is buried at Old Bethany/Tysinger Methodist Church.

1793. Tysinger, Farley

Private, Thomasville Rifles
Company B, 14th Regiment N.C. Troops
(4th N.C. Volunteers)

Farley was born in 1840. Farley worked as a farmer prior to volunteering for service on August 26, 1861. He was reported present until killed in action at Sharpsburg, Maryland, on September 17, 1862.

1794. Tysinger, Peter N.

First Sergeant, Lexington Wildcats
Company I, 14th Regiment N.C. Troops
(4th N.C. Volunteers)

Peter was born in 1831 to David and Elizabeth Tysinger. Peter worked as a teacher in the Silver Hill area prior to volunteering for service on May 14, 1861, when he was mustered in as a sergeant. Peter was promoted to first sergeant on September 12, 1861. Peter was reported present until wounded in the left leg in a skirmish at Bethesda Church, Virginia, on May 30, 1864. He was reported absent, wounded, until he returned to service in August 1864. Peter would continue to serve as first sergeant until he was paroled at Appomattox Court House, Virginia, on April 9, 1865. After the war, Peter returned home to the Silver Hill area, where in 1870, he left the teaching profession to be a clerk in a dry goods store.

Ten years later, Peter would open his own store and become one of the foremost merchants in Davidson County. Peter married Martha Hedrick in 1874, and they would have only one child: Frank (1876). Peter was last reported as living in the Silver Hill township in 1900. No further records.

1795. Tysinger, Robert

Private, Company I, 42nd Regiment N.C. Troops

Robert was born in September 15, 1835, to Michael and Dovey Tysinger. Robert worked as a blacksmith in the southern district of Davidson County, and, in 1858, he married Margaret Andrews. Robert and Margaret would have two children, Lee (1861) and Thomas (1862), before Robert was conscripted into service at Camp Holmes, North Carolina, on October 1, 1863. He was reported present through October 1864. After the war, Robert returned to the Healing Springs area where he and Margaret would have eight more children: Luella and Rocity (1866), Sarah (1872), Rena (1874), Priscilla (1876), Clay (1879), Eli (1881), and Essie (1894). Robert worked as a blacksmith in the Healing Springs township until his death on December 30, 1913. He is buried at First Baptist Church in Denton, North Carolina. The inscription on his stone reads: "He died as he lived, a pure, upright man."

1796. Tysinger, Solomon

Private, Confederate Guards
Company K, 48th Regiment N.C. Troops

Solomon was born in 1844. Solomon worked as an overseer prior to volunteering for service on March 18, 1862. He was reported present until captured at Hatcher's Run, Virginia, on April 2, 1865. Solomon was confined at Point Lookout, Maryland, until June 19, 1865, when he was released after taking the oath of allegiance. No further records.

1797. Tysinger, William B.

Private, Company B, 48th Regiment N.C. Troops

William was born in 1841. William worked as a blacksmith prior to volunteering for service on March 4, 1862. He was wounded in the head and leg at Fredericksburg, Virginia, on December 13, 1862. William was listed as absent, wounded, until he was retired to the Invalid Corps on April 18, 1864. He was paroled at Raleigh, North Carolina, on May 6, 1865. After his service, William returned to his trade in the Emmons township, and, in 1867, he married Eleanor. William and Eleanor would have six children: John A. (1869), Phillip (1876), Robert Lee (1879), Mary (1882), Crissie (1884), and Jenny (1887). William lived in the Emmons township until his death on February 16, 1928. He is buried at Fairview United Methodist Church.

1798. Underwood, Christopher Columbus

Corporal, Company C, 70th Regiment N.C. Troops (1st N.C. Junior Reserves)

Christopher was born in 1847 to Asa and Priscilla Underwood. Christopher was a student prior to enlisting in the Junior Reserves on May 24, 1864. After the war, Christopher bought a train ticket to Illinois to start a new life there or perhaps to travel farther west. No further records.

1799. Usry, William D.

Private, Company H, 48th Regiment N.C. Troops

William was born in 1838. William worked as a porter in the town of Lexington prior to being conscripted into service before October 21, 1864. He was reported present until captured at Richmond, Virginia, on April 3, 1865. William was confined at Newport News, Virginia, on April 24, 1865. No further records.

1800. Varner, James

Private, Holtsburg Guards Company A, 54th Regiment N.C. Troops

James was born in 1843 to Mary A. Varner. James worked as a miner prior to volunteering for service on March 4, 1862. He was reported present until detailed to serve as a lead miner in Davidson County on September 10, 1862. James served in this capacity for the duration of the war and was paroled at Greensboro, North Carolina, on May 5, 1865. No further records.

1801. Varner, William E.

Private, Wilmington Light Artillery Company E, 10th Regiment N.C. State Troops (1st N.C. Artillery)

William was born in 1836 to Eli and Elizabeth Varner. William worked as a farmer in the Thomasville area, and, in 1856, he married Harriet A. Kennedy. William and Harriet would have two children, Louisa (1857) and Franklin (1860), before William was conscripted into service in Wake County on September 12, 1862. He was reported present through June 1864. No further records.

1802. Vaughn, Azariah

Private, Thomasville Rifles Company B, 14th Regiment N.C. Troops (4th N.C. Volunteers) Company D, 45th Regiment N.C. Troops

Azariah was born in Rockingham County in 1838 and came to Thomasville in the 1850s to serve as a mechanic for the Lines Shoe Factory. Azariah volunteered for service on April 23, 1861. He was reported present until he was discharged due to "severe and protracted effects of typhoid" on December 18, 1861. Azariah returned to his home in Wentworth and later served in the 45th Regiment N.C. Troops. No further records.

1803. Veach, Joseph P. K.

Private, Company A, 10th Battalion, N.C. Heavy Artillery

Joseph was born in 1837 to Zadock and Margaret Veach. Joseph worked as a farmer prior to enlisting into service on April 26, 1862. He died of disease on May 15, 1862.

1804. Veach, McKendrie L.

Private, Company A, 10th Battalion, N.C. Heavy Artillery

McKendrie was born in 1840 to Zadock and Margaret Veach. McKendrie worked as a farmer prior to enlisting on April 26, 1862. He died of disease at Wilmington, North Carolina, on August 28, 1862.

1805. Veach, Samuel Jones

Private, Company A, 10th Battalion, N.C. Heavy Artillery

Samuel was born in 1843 to Zadock and Margaret Veach. Samuel worked as a farmer prior to enlisting on April 2, 1862. He was promoted to sergeant on July 1, 1862, but he was reduced in rank in September 1862. Samuel was reported present through September 1864. He was paroled at Salisbury, North Carolina, on May 23, 1865. No further records.

1806. Veach, William D.

Private, Thomasville Rifles Company B, 14th Regiment N.C. Troops (4th N.C. Volunteers)

William was born in 1839 to Zadock and Margaret Veach. William worked as a farmer and a mechanic, and, in 1858, he married Rosena Gray. William and Rosena would have two children, Irene (1859) and John (1861), before William was conscripted into service in Wake County on July 16, 1862. He was reported present until paroled at Appomattox Court House, Virginia, on April 9, 1865. In a postwar history (*Histories of the Several Regiments*) of the 14th North Carolina, Colonel R. T. Bennett notes: "Particularly conspicuous at every engagement was the courage and bravery of Private Will Veach of Company B." After the war, William returned home to the North Thomasville area where he would become a repairman for Leach & Lambeth as well as the head of machine maintenance for Standard Chair in 1879. William worked as a mechanic until his death on December 6, 1896. He is buried in the Thomasville City Cemetery.

1807. Vestal, Adolphus Gustavus

Private, Company A, 10th Battalion, N.C. Heavy Artillery

Adolphus was born in 1847 to Solomon and Esther Vestal. Adolphus worked as a farmer prior to being conscripted into service in New Hanover County on March 14, 1864. He was captured at Savannah, Georgia, on December 7, 1864. Adolphus was confined at Fort Delaware, Delaware, until June 19, 1865, when he was released after taking the oath of allegiance. No further records.

1808. Wagner, Daniel W.

Captain, 66th Regiment N.C. Militia (1861 organization) Private, Company B, 68th Regiment N.C. Troops

Militia officer and late-war volunteer Daniel Wagner (Leonard, *Jacob Wagner of "Old" Rowan*).

Daniel was born on December 6, 1827, to Daniel and Christina Eller Wagner. Daniel worked as a farmer, and, on June 26, 1851, he married Barbara Grimes. Daniel and Barbara would have seven children: Hilliard (1852), William (1853), Victoria (1855), Shocky (1857), Susan (1860), Sarah (1862), and Daniel (1865). Daniel was commissioned to serve as commander of the Farmer's Creek District Company on October 1, 1861. He served in that capacity until he enlisted in the 68th North Carolina in January 1865. After the war, Daniel worked as a farmer in the Lexington township until his death on February 5, 1907. He is buried at Bethany United Church of Christ.

1809. Wagner, Emanuel

Private, Thomasville Rifles
Company B, 14th Regiment N.C. Troops
(4th N.C. Volunteers)

Emanuel was born in 1843 to Daniel and Sarah Leonard Wagner. Emanuel was working with his brother Jacob as a farmer prior to volunteering for service on May 13, 1861. He was reported present until he was discharged from service in April 1863 due to disability. No further records.

1810. Wagner, Jacob

Private, Thomasville Rifles
Company B, 14th Regiment N.C. Troops
(4th N.C. Volunteers)

Jacob was born on March 13, 1837, to Daniel and Sarah Leonard Wagner. Jacob

worked as a farmer, and, on February 25, 1859, he married Louisa Wagner Dobson. Jacob and Louisa took in his brother Emanuel in 1860. Jacob volunteered for service in Alamance County on February 8, 1862, but, on April 30, 1862, his name was cancelled. Two months later, Jacob was conscripted into service in Wake County on July 15, 1862. He was reported present until captured at Winchester, Virginia, on September 19, 1864. Jacob was confined at Point Lookout, Maryland, until May 12, 1865, when he was released after taking the oath of allegiance. After the war, Jacob returned home to the Lexington township, where he and Louisa would have seven children: Betty (1865), Jenny (1867), Emma (1868), William (1871), Christina (1874), Joseph (1878), and Bessie (1882). Jacob worked as a farmer in the Lexington area until his death on January 2, 1907. He is buried at Bethesda United Methodist Church.

John Peter Wagner, far removed from the battlefield (Leonard, *Jacob Wagner of "Old" Rowan*).

John and his sister, Sarah Emiline Wagner, ca. 1858 (Leonard, *Jacob Wagner of "Old" Rowan*).

1811. Wagner, John Peter

Private, Carolina Rangers
Company B, 10th Virginia Cavalry
Regiment

John was born on April 10, 1845, to Matthias and Molly Hedrick Wagner. John worked as a farmer prior to volunteering for service in Davie County on October 29, 1861. He was reported present until sent on a horse detail in August and September 1863. John returned from his detail and was reported present through January 27, 1865, when he was issued a clothing ration. After the war, John returned home to the Lexington township, where, on July 30, 1865, he married Martha Jane Michael. John and Martha would have seven children together: Irene (1866), Mary (1868), Robert (1872), Franklin (1874), Henry (1879), Myrtle (1881), and Hessie (1888). John worked as a farmer in the Lexington township until his death on July 17, 1911. He is buried at Beulah United Church of Christ.

1812. Wagner, John W.

Private, Thomasville Rifles
Company B, 14th Regiment N.C. Troops
(4th N.C. Volunteers)

John was born in 1837 to Joseph and Polly Eddinger Wagner. John married

Martha May in 1852, and they would have two children, Joseph (1853) and Mary (1856), before Martha died in 1857. In 1860 John married Gazelle Wray. John was married for a little over two years when he was conscripted into service in Wake County on July 16, 1862. He was killed in action at Sharpsburg, Maryland, on September 17, 1862.

1813. Wagner, John Wesley, Jr.

Private, Carolina Rangers
Company B, 10th Virginia Cavalry
*   Regiment*

John was born in 1841 to Joseph and Bathsheba Sink Wagner. John worked as a single farmer prior to volunteering for service in Davie County on October 29, 1861. He was reported present until he died of typhoid fever in a Richmond, Virginia, hospital on August 7, 1862.

1814. Wagner, John Wesley, Sr.

Private, Carolina Rangers
Company B, 10th Virginia Cavalry
*   Regiment*
Company A, 10th Battalion, N.C.
*   Heavy Artillery*

John was born on September 9, 1841, to David S. and Elizabeth Yokely Wagner. John worked as a farmer, and in 1858, he married Christina Shoaf. John and Christina were living with Susan Shoaf before he volunteered for service on December 19, 1861. He was reported present until sent to a Richmond, Virginia, hospital with syphilis on June 26, 1864. John was transferred to Lynchburg, Virginia, on July 9, 1864. He recovered in Lynchburg and was transferred to the 10th Heavy Artillery on August 22, 1864. No records of the 10th Battalion confirm this. After the war, John returned to the Lexington area before venturing to South Carolina to start a new life. John lived in Rock Hill, South Carolina, and Charlotte, North Carolina, until his death on April 19, 1919. He is buried in Fort Mill, South Carolina.

1815. Wagner, Joseph D. W.

Private, Confederate Guards
Company K, 48th Regiment N.C. Troops

Joseph was born in 1845 to Alveron and Mary Wagner. Joseph worked as an overseer on his father's modest plantation prior to volunteering for service on

Robert J. Wagner enlisted at age 17 in 1864 (Leonard, *Jacob Wagner of "Old" Rowan*).

March 1, 1862. He was wounded at Fredericksburg, Virginia, on December 13, 1862. Joseph returned to service in March 1863 and was reported present until wounded at Bristoe Station, Virginia, on October 14, 1863. Joseph returned on an unspecified date and was reported present until wounded in the hand at Petersburg, Virginia, on June 15, 1864. No further records.

1816. Wagner, Robert Julian

Private, Company C, 70th Regiment
*   N.C. Troops (1st N.C. Junior*
*   Reserves)*

Robert was born on April 11, 1847, to George and Gazel Watson Wagner. Robert worked as a farmer prior to enlisting into the Junior Reserves on May 24, 1864. After the war, Robert returned to the Lexington area and built a one-room cabin in the middle of 85 acres. On January 1, 1871, Robert married Crissie Leonard. Robert and Crissie would have six children, Joseph (1872), Mary (1875), Julian Ellis (1877), Samuel (1879), Thomas (1880), and Roby Lee (1882), before Crissie died in 1887. Robert remarried a year later, to Sarah E. Kanoy. Robert and Sarah would have seven children: Charles (1888), George (1891), Minnie (1894), Nova (1896), Jesse Henry (1897), Roy D. (1899), and Lorenzo (1902). Robert was an active member of the A. A. Hill Camp, United Confederate Veterans, and was said to have never missed a reunion. He would dress in his uniform as a show of respect for his fallen comrades. Robert lived until May 17, 1933, and was one of the last Confederate veterans from the county to pass on. He is buried in uniform at Bethesda United Methodist Church.

1817. Wagner, Samuel J.

Private, Carolina Rangers
Company B, 10th Virginia Cavalry
Regiment

Samuel was born in 1843 to David S. and Elizabeth Yokely Wagner. Samuel worked as a farmer prior to volunteering for service in Davie County on October 29, 1861. He was reported present until he died of typhoid fever in Richmond, Virginia, on August 7, 1862.

1818. Wagner, William

Private, Company H, 15th Regiment
N.C. Troops (5th N.C. Volunteers)

William was born in 1824 to Joseph and Polly Eddinger Wagner. William worked as a farmer, and, prior to 1850, he married Mary F. Clinard. He was conscripted into service in Wake County on July 15, 1862. He was reported present until captured at Bristoe Station, Virginia, on October 14, 1863. William was confined at Old Capital Prison, Washington, D.C., until transferred to Point Lookout, Maryland, on October 27, 1863. William was confined at Point Lookout until he died of unreported causes on December 24, 1863. He is buried in the Point Lookout National Cemetery.

1819. Waitman, Jacob Lindsay

Private, Company C, 70th Regiment N.C.
Troops (1st N.C. Junior Reserves)

Jacob was born on July 10, 1847, to David and Elizabeth Waitman. Jacob was a student and helped on his father's plantation in the Mount Carmel area prior to enlisting in the Junior Reserves on May 24, 1864. After the war, Jacob returned home, where, in 1870, he married Sarah C. Swicegood. Jacob and Sarah would raise six children: Mary (1873), Phillip (1876), Delilah (1879), Walter (1881), Lula (1885), and Olivia (1891). Jacob retained the family's 500-acre tract upon his father's death and made a good income from farming, selling lumber, and leasing to sharecroppers. Jacob lived in the Tyro township until his death on December 10, 1915. He is buried at Shiloh United Methodist Church.

1820. Walk, Joseph

Second Lieutenant, 66th Regiment
N.C. Militia (1861 organization)

Joseph was born in 1814. Joseph owned a flour mill in the northern district of Davidson County, and, on October 30, 1841, he married Mary Ann Berrier. Joseph and Mary would have six daughters: Elizabeth (1843), Mary (1846), Emily (1848), Sarah (1850), Harriett (1852), and Susan (1856). Joseph was commissioned to serve as a second lieutenant in the Muddy Creek District Company on November 9, 1861. Joseph served in that capacity for the duration of the war. His flour mill in Arcadia remained in operation through the tough years of occupation, and in 1870 he began to hire more workers. By 1880, Joseph and his wife had left Davidson County, but his oldest daughter was still living in the county and working as a schoolteacher. No further records.

1821. Walker, John N.

Private, Company C, 70th Regiment
N.C. Troops (1st N.C. Junior
Reserves)

John was born in 1846 to John N. and Charlotte Walker. John worked as an assistant millwright prior to enlisting in the Junior Reserves on May 24, 1864. He did not survive the war. No further records.

1822. Walker, William

Private, Company F, 7th Regiment
N.C. State Troops

William was born on December 25, 1842, to Susanna Walker. William worked as a farmer in the Jackson Hill area prior to being conscripted into service in Wake County on November 26, 1863. He was reported present through October 1864 and was paroled at Salisbury, North Carolina, on May 20, 1865. After the war, William returned home, where, on August 16, 1866, he married Sarah Stokes. William and Sarah would have four children: Adora (1867), William (1869), Blanch (1877), and Edward (1880). William worked as a farmer in the Jackson Hill township and in the Allegheny area until his death on February 21, 1925. He is buried at Chandler's Grove United Methodist Church.

1823. Wall, Samuel B.

First Lieutenant, 66th Regiment N.C.
Militia (1861 organization)

Samuel was born in 1835 to George and Catharine Wall. Samuel worked as a farmer, and, in 1858, he married Christina Leonard. Samuel and Christina would have five children: Jane (1859), John (1861), George (1865), Charles (1867), and Emma (1869). Samuel was commissioned to serve as first lieutenant in the Piney Grove District Company on December 13, 1861. After the war, Samuel continued farming in the area just north of Thomasville until his death in 1903. He is buried in an unmarked grave at Pine Woods United Methodist Church.

1824. Wall, Thomas

Private, Company H, 48th Regiment
N.C. Troops

Thomas was born in 1839 to Grandison P. and Sarah Beck Wall. Thomas worked as a hireling prior to volunteering for service on March 6, 1862. He was wounded at Fredericksburg, Virginia, on December 13, 1862. Thomas recovered from his wounds and was detailed to serve as a guard at Gordonsville, Virginia, from October 9, 1863, to March 1864. After the war, Thomas returned home to the Conrad Hill township, where, in 1872, he married Nancy Miller. Thomas and Nancy would have three children: James (1873), Jones (1881), and Charles (1890). Thomas was last reported as living in the Conrad Hill township in 1900. No further records.

1825. Wall, William

Private, Chatam Light Infantry
Company G, 48th Regiment N.C. Troops

William was born in 1835 to Grandison P. and Sarah Beck Wall. William lived as a single farmer prior to being conscripted into service on August 14, 1862. He was reported present until wounded at Bristoe Station, Virginia, on October 14, 1863. William returned to service in January 1864 and was reported present until listed as absent without leave on December 28, 1864. No further records.

1826. Walser, Albert

Private, Rockingham Guards
Company H, 13th Regiment N.C. Troops
(3rd N.C. Volunteers)

Albert was born in 1845 to William and Mary Wood Walser. Albert was a student under the care of John Oakes prior to being conscripted into service at Camp Holmes, North Carolina, on January 29, 1864. He was reported present until captured at Petersburg, Virginia, on April 3, 1865. Albert was confined at Hart's Island, New York, until June 20, 1865, when he was released after taking the oath of allegiance. After the war, Albert returned to the Yadkin/Tyro township, where, on December 14, 1869, he married Mary Augusta Snider. Albert and Mary would have 11 children: Martha (1870), Sarah (1872), Mary (1876), James (1880), Delilah (1882), Henry (1884), Jesse (1887), Ella (1890), Adam (1892), Eva (1896), and Robert (1898). Albert lived in the Tyro township until his death in 1907. He is buried at Shiloh United Methodist Church.

1827. Walser, Burton

Private, Company B, 57th Regiment
N.C. Troops

Burton was born on March 18, 1841, to Casper and Priscilla Michael Walser. Burton operated a small section of his father's plantation, and, on February 18, 1860, he married Louisa Margaret Lomax. Burton and Louisa would have a son, Cicero (1861), before Burton enlisted in Rowan County on July 4, 1862. He was reported present until listed as sick in September 1863. Burton recovered from his illness and returned to service on May 1, 1864. He was captured at Fisher's Hill, Virginia, on September 22, 1864. Burton was confined at Point Lookout, Maryland, until he was paroled and transferred to Boulware's Wharf, Virginia, on March 19, 1865, for exchange. After the war, Burton returned home to the Churchland area where he continued to operate a farm with many of his former slaves working as sharecroppers. Burton and Louisa would have another son: John (1868). Burton lived and worked in the Tyro township until his death on February 13, 1890. He is buried at Churchland Baptist Church.

1828. Walser, Gaither

Private, Davidson Guards
Company A, 21st Regiment N.C. Troops
(11th N.C. Volunteers)

Gaither was born on November 1, 1837, to the Honorable Henry C. and Elizabeth Warner Walser. Gaither was a student at Yadkin College prior to volunteering for service on May 8, 1861. He was reported present until, by request of his father, a member of the Confederate Congress, he was discharged at Danville, Virginia, on July 1, 1861. Gaither returned home, where, on January 23, 1862, he married Frances Byerly. Gaither and Frances would have two sons: Zeb Vance (1865) and Joseph C. (1869). Gaither was employed as a trading agent for the North Carolina Railroad and was later a banker and stock trader with offices in Lexington and Greensboro, North Carolina. Gaither lived in the Yadkin College area until his death on November 19, 1905. He is buried at Yadkin College United Methodist Church.

1829. Walser, Henderson

Private, Company H, 48th Regiment
N.C. Troops

Henderson was born in 1830 to William and Mary Wood Walser. Henderson worked as a carpenter in the western district of the county, and, on July 26, 1858, he married Elizabeth Wood. Henderson and Elizabeth would have two sons, Andrew (1859) and Charles (1861), before Henderson was conscripted into service at Petersburg, Virginia, on August 8, 1862. He was reported present until he deserted to the enemy on March 24, 1865. Henderson was confined at Washington, D.C., until April 1865, when he was released after taking the oath of allegiance. After a brief stay in the nation's capital, Henderson was furnished transportation home. After his return, Henderson and Elizabeth would have six more children: Flora (1866), John (1868), Curran (1870), William W. (1873), Henry S. (1876), and Albert Sidney Johnston (1878). Henderson worked as a master carpenter and at one time had ten men working for him. Henderson lived in the Boone/Tyro area until his death on April 19, 1881. He is buried at Shiloh United Methodist Church.

1830. Walser, Henry Clay II

Private, Davidson Guards
Company A, 21st Regiment N.C. Troops
(11th N.C. Volunteers)

Henry was born on July 11, 1844, to the Honorable Henry C. and Elizabeth Warner Walser. Henry was a student at Yadkin College prior to volunteering for service on May 8, 1861. He was reported present until discharged because of being under age on July 10, 1862. After his return, Henry studied for a brief period at Trinity College and after the end of the war, he attended the state university in Chapel Hill, North Carolina. Henry graduated with a law degree in 1867. Henry returned to Davidson County where he began a successful law practice, and, in 1868, he married Nancy Taylor. Henry and Nancy would have three children: Ella (1869), Anna (1871), and Lena (1873). In 1872, Henry served as a grant elector and began to serve as the district attorney for Davidson County. Henry served as a county commissioner and would have surely followed in his father's footsteps and begun a career in politics, but he died of pneumonia on January 29, 1879. He is buried at Yadkin College United Methodist Church. The inscription on his stone reads: "Lawyer, Grant Elector of 1872. One of nature's noblemen with heart brave, true, and tender."

1831. Walser, Hiram

Private, Company H, 48th Regiment
N.C. Troops

Hiram was born in 1831 to William and Mary Wood Walser. Hiram worked as a carpenter, and, on June 9, 1861, he married Adeline Michael. Hiram and Adeline were married for just over a year when Hiram was conscripted into service in Petersburg, Virginia, on August 8,

This Yadkin College home of Henry C. Walser II, Esq., at one time rested on seven hundred acres (Touart, *Building the Backcountry*).

1862. He died of "variola" at Liberty, Virginia, on December 20, 1862.

1832. Walser, Jacob S.

Private, Company H, 48th Regiment N.C. Troops

Jacob was born in 1837 to William and Salome Snider Walser. Jacob worked as a farmer prior to volunteering for service on March 17, 1862. He was mustered in as a sergeant and served in that capacity until he was sent to a hospital with the complaint "finger shot off" on July 7, 1862. Jacob recovered and returned to duty in August 1862. He was reduced in rank to private in the winter of 1863 and was reported present until he died of pneumonia at Richmond, Virginia, on April 17, 1864.

1833. Walser, John Hubbard

Private, Company B, 57th Regiment N.C. Troops

John was born on May 24, 1839, to William and Salome Snider Walser. John worked as a farmer, and, in 1859, he married Eliza Jane Myers. John and Eliza would have a daughter, Melinda (1861), before John enlisted in Rowan County on July 4, 1862. He was reported present until captured at Rappahannock Station, Virginia, on November 7, 1863. John was confined at Point Lookout, Maryland, until March 16, 1864, when he was paroled and transferred to City Point, Virginia, for exchange. John was hospi-

talized with "reubola" at Richmond, Virginia, on June 27, 1864, and was restricted to the hospital until October 1864. John was captured at Hatcher's Run, Virginia, on February 9, 1865. He was confined again at Point Lookout until June 21, 1865, when he was released after taking the oath of allegiance. After the war, John returned home to the Tyro township, where he and Eliza would have three more children: William (1865), Susan (1867), and Mary (1869). Tragically, Eliza died during her last childbirth. John remarried three years later, to Sarah Myers Fry. John and Sarah would have two children: Laura (1873) and Mittie (1875). John continued to work as a farmer in the fertile land along the banks of the Yadkin River until his death on April 28, 1910. He is buried at Reeds Baptist Church.

1834. Walser, Rollin

Corporal, Company B, 57th Regiment N.C. Troops

Rollin was born on August 14, 1839, to Casper and Priscilla Michael Walser. Rollin worked as a small slaveholding farmer prior to enlisting in Rowan County on July 4, 1862. He was captured during "the raid on Lee's rear" on May 23, 1863, and was released the same day. Rollin was promoted to corporal in July 1863 and served in that capacity until captured at Rappahannock Station, Virginia, on November 7, 1863. He was confined at Point Lookout, Maryland, until

February 24, 1865, when he was paroled and transferred to Aiken's Landing, Virginia, for exchange. After the war, Rollin returned to the Tyro/Yadkin township, where, on November 21, 1865, he married Sarah Myers. Rollin and Sarah would have eight children: Peter (1866), Joseph (1868), John (1871), Roswell C. (1873), Levi (1875), William (1876), Sarah (1878), and Fienna (1882). Rollin began a small mercantile business, selling agricultural implements and supplies. He was an active member of the A. A. Hill Camp, United Confederate Veterans. Rollin lived in the Reeds area until his death on December 12, 1928. He is buried at Reeds Baptist Church.

1835. Walser, Spurgeon

Private, Company I, 42nd Regiment N.C. Troops

Spurgeon was born in 1831 to William and Mary Wood Walser. Spurgeon worked as a farmer, and, on August 20, 1858, he married Mary Hainey. Mary died in childbirth on January 6, 1862. Spurgeon grieved for two months before volunteering for service on March 4, 1862. He was reported present until captured at Wise's Forks, Virginia, on March 8, 1865. Spurgeon was confined at Point Lookout, Maryland, until June 21, 1865, when he was released after taking the oath of allegiance. No further records.

1836. Ward, Franklin

Private, Company B, 48th Regiment N.C. Troops

Franklin was born in 1832 to Joseph M. and Nancy Ward. Franklin worked as a farmer, and, on February 17, 1859, he married Eva Hedrick. Franklin was conscripted into service at Petersburg, Virginia, on August 8, 1862. He died of pneumonia in a Charlottesville, Virginia, hospital on November 18, 1862.

1837. Ward, John A.

Private, Holtsburg Guards Company A, 54th Regiment N.C. Troops

John was born in 1832 to Joseph M. and Nancy Ward. John worked as a farmer, and on January 11, 1856, he married Sarah Jane Warford. John and Sarah would have three children: Mary (1857), Nancy (1860), and Sarah (1862), before John enlisted on May 14, 1862. He was reported present until captured at Rappahannock Station, Virginia, on November 7, 1863. John was confined at Point Lookout, Maryland, until March 19, 1864, when he was paroled and transferred to City Point, Virginia, for exchange. John returned to service in August 1864 and was reported present until he was paroled at Appomattox Court House, Virginia, on April 9, 1865. After the war, John returned to the Cotton Grove township, where, he and Sarah would have three more children: William (1865), Amanda (1867), and Stokes (1868). Sarah died in 1869, and John married Mary in 1871. John and Mary would have four children: Herbert (1872), Alice (1874), Fannie (1874), and Cornelia (1876). John was last listed as living in the Cotton Grove township in 1880. No further records.

1838. Ward, Peter D.

Private, Company B, 48th Regiment N.C. Troops

Peter was born in 1839 to Rachael Ward. Peter worked as a farmer, and, in 1857, he married Elizabeth Kanoy. Peter and Elizabeth would have a daughter, Sarah Ann (1860), before Peter was conscripted into service on August 8, 1862. He was wounded at Fredericksburg, Virginia, on December 13, 1862. Peter was taken to a Lynchburg, Virginia, hospital where he died of his wounds on January 1, 1863.

1839. Ward, Seth W.

Private, Franklin Guides to Freedom Company K, 44th Regiment N.C. Troops

Seth was born in 1844 to Commodore and Barbara Ward. Seth worked as a farmhand for Daniel Fine prior to being conscripted into service on November 29, 1862. He was reported present until he deserted on January 16, 1863. Seth returned home and married Caroline Hughes on August 30, 1863, in Randolph County. Seth avoided capture, did not return to service, and he and Caroline would have two children, James (1866) and Ella (1868), before her death in 1872. Thirteen years later, Seth married Emily F. Myers in 1885. Seth and Emily would have five children: John (1888), Charles (1890), Julia (1891), William (1893), and Enos (1897). Seth lived in the Conrad Hill area until his death in the 1910s. He is buried at Liberty Baptist Church.

1840. Ward, Thomas G.

Private, Company B, 48th Regiment N.C. Troops

Thomas was born in 1841 to Rachael Ward. Thomas worked as a farmer, and, on September 4, 1860, he married Ellen Leonard. Thomas and Ellen were married for just under two years when Thomas was conscripted into service on August 8, 1862. He died of disease at Sharpsburg, Maryland, on September 17, 1862.

1841. Ward, William

Private, Company B, 48th Regiment N.C. Troops

William was born on July 26, 1827, to Hiram and Esther Ward. William worked as a farmer in the Allegheny area, and, in 1847, he married Rebecca Smith. William and Rebecca would have five children, Martha (1848), Joyce (1849), Sarah (1851), Daniel Clay (1857), and Harriet (1860), before William was conscripted into service on August 8, 1862. He was reported present through April 1864 and, according to family history, was killed at Reams' Station, Virginia, on August 25, 1864.

1842. Ward, William Stout

Private, Company D, 48th Regiment N.C. Troops

William Stout Ward, two years before his death in a Charlottesville, Virginia, hospital (Nancy Kearnes Crouse Jeffries, *The Heritage of Davidson County*).

William was born on April 8, 1832, to Lewis and Elizabeth Ward. William worked as a farmer, and, in March 1862, he married Susan B. Hedrick. Only married six months, William was forced to leave his pregnant wife for service on August 8, 1862. He died of pneumonia at Charlottesville, Virginia, on November 24, 1862. Roxanne, his daughter, was born in January 1863. Susan, his widow, would marry Jacob R. Beck of Company B, 48th Regiment N.C. Troops, in 1865.

1843. Ward, Willis Webster

Private, Company D, 48th Regiment N.C. Troops

Willis was born on July 8, 1836, to Lewis and Elizabeth Ward. Willis worked as a farmer prior to being conscripted into service on August 8, 1862. He was left sick at a hospital at Rapidan Station, Virginia, in September 1862. Willis was reported absent, sick, until listed as a deserter and dropped from the rolls on May 1, 1864. After the war, Willis returned to the Emmons township, where, in 1867, he married Margaret Ann Harris. Willis and Margaret would have four children: Sarah (1868), Cora (1870), Martha (1873), and Walter (1877). Willis worked as a farmer in the Emmons township until his death on April 23, 1919. He is buried at Clear Springs United Methodist Church.

1844. Warford, Alexander

Private, Holtsburg Guards Company A, 54th Regiment N.C. Troops

Alexander was born in 1827 to William and Hannah Cross Warford. Alexander worked as a farmer in the Cotton Grove area, and, on September 4, 1851, he married Patience Cox. Alexander and Patience would have three children, William (1854), Hannah (1856), and David (1859), before Alexander was conscripted into service on December 23, 1862. He was reported present until hospitalized at Richmond, Virginia, on June 12, 1864, with a gunshot wound. His wounds were probably received at Cold Harbor, Virginia. Alexander died of his wounds at Richmond on June 30, 1864.

1845. Warford, Henry I.

Private, Holtsburg Guards Company A, 54th Regiment N.C. Troops

Henry was born in 1843 to William and Hannah Cross Warford. Henry worked as a farmer prior to enlisting on May 14, 1862. He was hospitalized on November 12, 1862, but was returned to service on November 27, 1862. Henry was reported present until he was sent to a Goldsboro, North Carolina, hospital with an unreported complaint on May 10, 1864. He returned to duty on May 30, 1864, and was reported present until he was paroled at Appomattox Court House, Virginia, on April 9, 1865. No further records.

1846. Warford, Jonathan

Private, Holtsburg Guards
Company A, 54th Regiment N.C. Troops

Jonathan was born in 1830 to James and Charity Warford. Jonathan worked as a farm laborer prior to enlisting on May 14, 1862. He was reported present until hospitalized at Richmond, Virginia, on February 25, 1863, with "erysipelas and debilitas." Jonathan died of his ailments in Richmond on March 23, 1863.

1847. Warford, Joseph E.

Private, Holtsburg Guards
Company A, 54th Regiment N.C. Troops

Joseph was born in 1844 to Rueben and Hannah Warford. Joseph worked as a farmer in the Cotton Grove area, and, on December 21, 1861, he married Susan H. Joseph and Susan would have a daughter, Mary (1862), before Joseph was conscripted into service on August 20, 1862. He was reported present until he was paroled at Appomattox Court House, Virginia, on April 9, 1865. After the war, Joseph returned to the Cotton Grove township, where he and Susan would have three more children: Florence (1866), Thomas (1867), and Nancy (1870). Joseph and his family were last reported as living in Cotton Grove in 1880. No further records.

1848. Warford, William A.

Private, Holtsburg Guards
Company A, 54th Regiment N.C. Troops

William was born in 1837 to Rueben and Hannah Warford. William worked as a farmer, and, on February 12, 1857, he married Margaret E. Wood. William and Margaret would have two children, George (1859) and Lindsay (1861), before

William enlisted into service on April 20, 1862. He was hospitalized at Richmond, Virginia, on December 23, 1862. William died of "variola" on January 1, 1863.

1849. Warner, Britton

Private, Company H, 48th Regiment N.C. Troops

Britton was born in 1832 to Vincent and Sarah Warner. Britton worked as a farmer prior to being conscripted into service in Wake County on July 15, 1862. He was captured at Crampton's Pass, Maryland, on September 14, 1862. Britton was sent to a Baltimore, Maryland, hospital where he died of "chronic diarrhea" on September 30, 1862.

1850. Warner, Henry

Private, Davidson Guards
Company A, 21st Regiment N.C. Troops (11th N.C. Volunteers)

Henry was born in 1828 to Vincent and Sarah Warner. Henry worked as a farmer, and, on August 21, 1845, he married Rebecca Smith. Henry and Rebecca would have six children, Christina (1846), Sarah (1849), Eliza (1851), Henry (1854), John (1857), and Parthenia (1860), before Henry volunteered for service on May 8, 1861. He was reported present until he died of unreported causes at Petersburg, Virginia, on February 21, 1865.

1851. Warner, Hubbard

Corporal, Chatam Light Infantry
Company G, 48th Regiment N.C. Troops

Hubbard was born in 1839 to Britton Warner and his first wife, whose name is unknown. Hubbard worked as a farmer prior to being conscripted into service on August 14, 1862. He was reported present until wounded in the left hand at Bristoe Station, Virginia, on October 14, 1863. Hubbard recovered and was promoted to corporal in January 1864. He was reported present until wounded in the right thigh at Wilderness, Virginia, on May 5, 1864. Hubbard would be wounded again at Reams' Station, Virginia, on August 25, 1864. He recovered from his third set of wounds and was reported present until captured at Farmville, Virginia, on April 14, 1865. Hubbard was confined at Newport News, Virginia, until June 26, 1865, when he was released after taking the

oath of allegiance. After the war, Hubbard returned to the Thomasville township, where, on July 10, 1866, he married Emily Lambeth. By 1870, Emily had died, and Hubbard married Alice Hepler in 1872. He is buried at Fair Grove Methodist Church.

1852. Watford, Elijah Franklin

Private, Company D, 48th Regiment N.C. Troops

Eli was born in 1842 to Josiah and Frances Wiggins Watford. Eli worked as a farmer with his father prior to being conscripted into service on August 8, 1862. He was captured at Sharpsburg, Maryland, on September 17, 1862. Eli was confined at Fort Delaware, Delaware, until October 2, 1862, when he was paroled and transferred to Aiken's Landing, Virginia, for exchange. He was declared exchanged on November 10, 1862. Eli returned to service and was reported present until he died of pneumonia at Richmond, Virginia, on February 26, 1864. He is buried in the Hollywood Cemetery in Richmond.

1853. Watford, Green Daniel

Private, Thomasville Rifles
Company B, 14th Regiment N.C. Troops (4th N.C. Volunteers)

Green was born in 1839 in Randolph County, North Carolina, to Josiah and Frances Wiggins Watford. Green worked as a carpenter in the town of Thomasville and was a member of its militia company prior to volunteering for service on April 23, 1861. He was reported present for service until mortally wounded by a bayonet while attempting to save the colors of the 14th Regiment at Sharpsburg, Maryland, on September 17, 1862. Green died of his wounds while in enemy hands on October 31, 1862. He is buried at Mount Olivet Cemetery, Sharpsburg.

1854. Watford, Joseph Alfred

Private, Company C, 70th Regiment N.C. Troops (1st N.C. Junior Reserves)

Joseph was born in 1846 to Josiah and Frances Wiggins Watford. Joseph was a student prior to enlisting in the Junior Reserves on May 24, 1864. He died of disease at Raleigh, North Carolina, on March 1, 1865.

1855. Watford, Sidney Corneilius

Second Lieutenant, 14th Battalion,
*   N.C. Home Guard*

Neil was born in Franklin County, North Carolina, on September 18, 1837, to Josiah and Frances Wiggins Watford. Neil worked as a farmer and helped his father with financial matters prior to volunteering for service on March 4, 1862. Before he was assigned to a unit, he was rejected from service due to the weak condition of his back and legs. Neil obtained a position as a constable for the Conrad Hill township and served as a peace officer for the county before he is first reported in the state's Home Guard on March 14, 1864. He was appointed to the rank of lieutenant by Colonel Jesse Hargrave. The next reference to his record is a letter from Confederate Congressman J. M. Leach thanking him for the "apprehension of several of the incendiaries who attempted to burn a bridge on the N.C. Rail Road." Neil's service was honorable, and, after the war, he married Celia Ann Lassiter on December 2, 1869. Neil and Celia would have seven children: Emma G. (1870), Margaret Eldora (1872), Madia L. (1874), Mary Louvina (1877), Arthur Edward (1879), John Raymond (1883), and Jesse Benjamin (1886). Neil was still listed as a constable in the 1870 voter registration records, and he also had begun a side business, a dry goods store. Neil served as a court caller from 1872 to 1904 and, on occasion, as an assistant to Henry C. Walser II, Esq. His dry goods store became a success, and, from 1885 to 1910, he worked as a postmaster, receiving mail at his store in Light. After Celia's death in 1889, Neil hired Margaret Beck as a live-in housekeeper but relied heavily on Ben Adams, a free black man before the war, to help look after his children when he was on official business in Lexington. Grandchild Lee Roy Watford remembers a story which brings up his funny side: "One time when Grandpa Watford had lost his eyesight, he was sitting at the table eating molasses and a piece of bread with flies buzzing around. I said, 'Papaw, you're going to end up with flies in that molasses.' He said loudly, 'If the flies can stand this stuff, so can I.'" Neil lived in the Conrad Hill township until his death on December 2, 1925. He is buried at Liberty Baptist Church.

1856. Watkins, Franklin M.

Sergeant, Davidson Guards
Company A, 21st Regiment N.C. Troops
*   (11th N.C. Volunteers)*

Franklin was born in 1839 to Mary Watkins. Franklin worked as a farmhand for Henry Harris prior to volunteering for service on May 8, 1861. He was promoted to sergeant on April 26, 1862, and was wounded in the hand at Gaines' Mill, Virginia, on June 27, 1862. Henry was reported absent, wounded, and he returned to the Clemmonsville township in February 1864. While at home, Franklin married Sarah Bullard on October 30, 1864. Franklin did not return to service, and he and Sarah would have seven children: Lee (1865), Carrie (1867), William (1868), Ollin (1871), Harriet (1872), Emma (1877), and Charles (1879). Franklin was living in the Clemmonsville township when it was given to Forsyth County. No further records.

1857. Watkins, William Henry

Private, Company E, 42nd Regiment
*   N.C. Troops*

William was born in 1834 to Mary Watkins. William was working as a farmhand for Emanuel Houser in 1850. On March 10, 1858, he married Sarah A. Hoover, and by 1860, William had found a job working on the railroad. William and Sarah would have a daughter, Martha (1859), before William volunteered for service on March 15, 1862. He was reported present through October 1864 and was paroled at Salisbury, North Carolina, on May 22, 1865. After the war, William and Sarah would have three more children, Bettie (1865), Laura (1866), and Permelia (1870), before William and his family moved to Company Shops (now Burlington) in Alamance County, North Carolina. No further records.

1858. Watson, Albert B.

Private, Company B, 48th Regiment
*   N.C. Troops*

Albert was born on April 6, 1836, to Allison and Elizabeth Yarbrough Watson. Albert worked for his father prior to being conscripted into service on August 8, 1862. He was killed in action at Sharpsburg, Maryland, on September 17, 1862.

1859. Watson, Alexander Archibald

Private, Company B, 48th Regiment
*   N.C. Troops*

Alex was born on July 15, 1844, to Allison and Elizabeth Yarbrough Watson. Alex lived with his parents prior to being conscripted into service on August 8, 1862. He was reported present until wounded at Cold Harbor, Virginia, on June 3, 1864. Alex was hospitalized with his wound at Richmond, Virginia, four days later and died on June 21, 1864. His body was retrieved and buried in the Lexington City Cemetery.

1860. Watson, Haywood P.

Private, Company C, 70th Regiment
*   N.C. Troops (1st N.C. Junior*
*   Reserves)*
Company A, 10th Battalion, N.C.
*   Heavy Artillery*

Haywood was born on September 10, 1846, to Allison and Elizabeth Yarbrough Watson. Haywood was a student prior to enlisting in the Junior Reserves on May 24, 1864. In August 1864, Haywood was transferred to the 10th Heavy Artillery Battalion, which was posted in the vicinity of Fort Pulaski, Georgia. Haywood was paroled at Greensboro, North Carolina, on May 9, 1865. After the war, Haywood returned to Lexington where he worked for his father and married Amelia Lindsay, the daughter of Dr. William Dillion Lindsay, late surgeon of the 48th North Carolina. Haywood lived in Lexington until his death on November 17, 1892. He is buried in the Lexington City Cemetery.

1861. Watson, James G.

Private, Company B, 48th Regiment
*   N.C. Troops*

James was born on July 1, 1844, to Allison and Elizabeth Yarbrough Watson. James worked for his father prior to being conscripted into service on August 8, 1862. He was reported present until he died of unreported causes at Orange Court House, Virginia, on January 26, 1864. A stone is placed in his honor in the Lexington City Cemetery.

1862. Weatherington, James W.

Private, Company C, 70th Regiment N.C.
*   Troops (1st N.C. Junior Reserves)*

Preston Weaver while serving as a corporal. He would return to live with his parents in Wilkes County (John F. Weaver, Mast, *State Troops and Volunteers, Vol. 1*).

James was born in 1847 to Alston R. and Margaret Weatherington. James worked as a shoemaker prior to enlisting in the Junior Reserves on May 24, 1864. After the war, James returned, and, in 1870, he was employed by the Leach & Lambeth Company. James was last reported as living in Thomasville in 1875. No further records.

1863. Weaver, Andrew A.

Private, Ellis Guards
Company C, 15th Regiment N.C. Troops
(5th N.C. Volunteers)

Andrew was born in 1838. Andrew worked as a farmer in the Freidburg com- munity, and, in 1861, he mar- ried Sarah Zimmerman. An- drew and Sarah would have a child, Louis (1862), before Andrew was conscripted into service in Wake County on July 15, 1862. He was reported present until wounded in action at Bristoe Station, Vir- ginia, on October 14, 1863. Andrew died of his wounds the next day on October 15, 1863.

1864. Weaver, Elias

Private, Company H, 48th Regiment N.C. Troops

Elias was born in 1834 to John and Hannah Weaver. Elias worked as a farmer, and, on March 5, 1858, he married Elizabeth Younts. Elias and Elizabeth would have two chil- dren, John (1859) and George (1862), before Elias was con- scripted into service at Peters- burg, Virginia, on August 8, 1862. He was wounded at Sharpsburg, Maryland, on September 17, 1862. Elias re- covered and returned to ser- vice in February 1863. He was listed as absent without leave in September 1864. Elias was sent to a Richmond, Virginia, hospital on December 26, 1864, with a gunshot wound. He was issued a 60-day fur- lough on February 24, 1865, and did not return to service. Upon his arrival home, he saw his daughter Margaret (1863) for only the second time. Elias and Elizabeth would have five more chil- dren: May (1866), Barbara (1868), Mary (1870), Eliza (1871), and Elias M. (1876). Elias continued farming in the Reedy Creek/Yadkin area until at least 1880. No further records.

1865. Weaver, Henry C.

Private, Lexington Wildcats
Company I, 14th Regiment N.C. Troops
(4th N.C. Volunteers)

Henry was born in 1841. By 1850, he was living with the Mabry family of Lex- ington. Henry worked as a carpenter prior to being conscripted into service on an unreported date in 1863. He was reported present until captured at Spot- sylvania Court House, Virginia, on May 12, 1864. Henry was confined at Elmira, New York, until February 9, 1865, when he was transferred to Cox's Wharf, Vir- ginia, for exchange. Henry was declared exchanged on February 20, 1865. He was granted a furlough from a hospital in Richmond, Virginia, on February 25, 1865, but he did not return to Davidson County. No further records.

1866. Weaver, Henry F.

Private, Ellis Guards
Company C, 15th Regiment N.C. Troops
(5th N.C. Volunteers)

Henry was born on January 18, 1837. Henry worked as a farmhand for Edward Fishel prior to being conscripted into ser- vice in Wake County on September 15, 1862. He was reported present until he was captured while in a Richmond, Virginia, hospital on April 3, 1865. Henry was paroled at Richmond on April 18, 1865. After the war, Henry returned to the Freidburg area, where, on September 18, 1866, he married Teresa Weisner. Henry worked as a cooper in the Arcadia town- ship until his death on April 29, 1888. He is buried at Freidburg Moravian Church.

1867. Weaver, Horace N.

First Lieutenant, Lexington Wildcats
Company I, 14th Regiment N.C. Troops
(4th N.C. Volunteers)

Horace was born in 1845. Horace came to Lexington in the late 1850s to work as a landscape artist. Horace worked as an artist prior to volunteering for ser- vice on May 14, 1861. He was elected as first lieutenant on the same day. Horace served as a lieutenant until he resigned or was defeated for reelection on April 25, 1862. No further records.

1868. Weaver, Preston D.

Sergeant, Lexington Wildcats
Company I, 14th Regiment N.C. Troops
(4th N.C. Volunteers)

Preston was born in 1842 in Wilkes County, North Carolina. Preston came to Davidson County in 1859 to work as a har- ness maker in Lexington. Preston was one of two harness makers in the area prior to volunteering for service on May 14, 1861. He was mustered in as a corporal but was reduced in rank to private on April 25,

1862. Preston was wounded at Malvern Hill, Virginia, on July 1, 1862. He recovered from his wounds and returned to service by November 1, 1862, when he was promoted to sergeant. Preston was reported present until wounded in a skirmish along the Weldon Railroad at Petersburg, Virginia, on August 21, 1864. Preston returned to service and was paroled at Appomattox Court House, Virginia, on April 9, 1865. After the war, Preston returned to Wilkesboro, North Carolina, and operated a shop there into the 1900s. No further records.

1869. Weaver, William, Jr.

*Private, Company H, 48th Regiment
N.C. Troops*

William was born in 1843. William worked as a hireling in the Clemmonsville area prior to volunteering for service on March 7, 1862. He was reported present until hospitalized at Richmond, Virginia, on December 12, 1864. William was granted a 60-day furlough on January 3, 1865, and did not return to service. He was paroled at Greensboro, North Carolina, on May 4, 1865. After the war, William returned to the Clemmonsville area where, in 1869, he married Ellen. William and Ellen would have four children: Louisa (1871), Sarah (1873), Bessie (1876), and Henry E. (1878). William was listed as living in the Clemmonsville township when it was given to Forsyth County. No further records.

1870. Weaver, William, Sr.

*Private, Company H, 48th Regiment
N.C. Troops*

William was born in 1832 to Henry and Susanna Weaver. William worked as a farmer, and, in 1856, he married Charlotte Ann. William and Charlotte would have two children, Sarah (1857) and Fanny (1860), before William was conscripted into service at Petersburg, Virginia, on August 8, 1862. He was reported present until hospitalized with "dropsy" in January 1863. William was listed as absent, sick, until he was listed as a deserter on April 30, 1864. William and Charlotte would have three more children: Nancy (1864), William (1865), and Mary (1868). William lived in the Clemmonsville township until his death in 1886. He is buried at Old Vernon United Methodist Church.

1871. Weavil, David

*Private, Company H, 15th Regiment
N.C. Troops (5th N.C. Volunteers)*

David was born in 1834 to Eve Weavil. David worked as a farmer in the Arcadia township prior to being conscripted into service in Wake County on July 15, 1862. He died of disease in camp on September 1, 1862.

1872. Weavil, Henry

*Private, Company H, 15th Regiment
N.C. Troops (5th N.C. Volunteers)*

Henry was born in 1836 to Eve Weavil. Henry worked as a farmer in the Arcadia township until he was conscripted into service in Wake County on July 15, 1862. He was reported present until he died of disease "at home" on February 22, 1864.

1873. Webster, John H.

*Private, Company I, 42nd Regiment
N.C. Troops*

John was born in 1844. John worked as a farmer in the western part of the county prior to volunteering for service on March 6, 1862. He was reported present until wounded in August 1864. John was issued a 60-day furlough on September 22, 1864, and was retired to the Invalid Corps on March 3, 1865. After the war, John married D.E. Snider on November 23, 1865. John and D. E. were last reported as living in the Tyro township in 1870. No further records.

1874. Weisner, Andrew M.

*First Lieutenant, 66th Regiment N.C.
Militia (1861 organization)*

Andrew was born in 1817. Andrew worked as a schoolteacher and in 1860 was living with his brother in the area north of Thomasville. Andrew was commissioned to serve as first lieutenant in the 66th Militia on February 13, 1862. No further records.

1875. Weisner, Ephraim M.

*Private, Company H, 15th Regiment
N.C. Troops (5th N.C. Volunteer)*

Ephraim was born in 1832 to David and Anne M. Weisner. Ephraim worked as a teacher in the Arcadia area prior to being conscripted into service in Wake County on July 15, 1862. He was wounded in the neck at Fredericksburg, Virginia, on December 13, 1862. Ephraim returned to service in January 1863 and was reported present until captured at Hatcher's Run, Virginia, on April 2, 1865. He was confined at Hart's Island, New York, until June 18, 1865, when he was released after taking the oath of allegiance. After the war, Ephraim returned to Arcadia, where, in 1866, he married Matilda. Ephraim and Matilda would have two children: Joseph (1867) and David (1870). Ephraim moved to the city of Lexington in 1900 and served as director of "colored education." No further records.

1876. Weisner, Joshua

*First Lieutenant, 66th Regiment N.C.
Militia (1861 organization)*

Joshua was born in 1827. Joshua worked as a miller in the Arcadia township, and, in 1848, he married Parthena Knauss. Joshua and Parthena would have two children: Adeline (1850) and Sarah (1858). Joshua was commissioned to serve as first lieutenant in the Piney Grove Schoolhouse District Company on February 13, 1862. Joshua returned to milling after his service and made a substantial profit. Joshua and his family moved to the growing city of Winston in 1899. No further records.

1877. Welborn, James M.

*Private, Company A, 10th Battalion,
N.C. Heavy Artillery*

James was born in 1842 to Evan and Chloe Welborn. James worked as a farmer in the Thomasville area prior to enlisting in the artillery on April 21, 1862. He was reported present through September 1864. He did not survive the war.

1878. Welborn, John Henry

*Private, Thomasville Rifles
Company B, 14th Regiment N.C. Troops
(4th N.C. Volunteers)*

John was born in 1843 to Evan and Chloe Welborn. John was a student at Trinity College prior to volunteering for service on April 27, 1861. He was reported present through August 1864. While on some form of leave, John married Sarah Mary Wier on October 13, 1864. John was paroled at Greensboro, North Carolina,

Lexington home of politician and land owner John Welborn (Touart, *Building the Backcountry*).

on May 5, 1865. After the war, John moved to Orange County, where, in 1867, he completed his law degree at the state university. John moved to Lexington where he opened a successful practice and became immediately involved in civic affairs. Sarah died in 1874, and John married Anna Fowle that same year. John and Anna would have only one child, William F. (1878). John served as the first mayor of Lexington in 1872 and was active in church, business, and political affairs until his death in 1887. On the day of his death, John was the second largest landowner in Davidson County. He is buried in the Lexington City Cemetery.

1879. Welborn, Lamma C.

First Lieutenant, Thomasville Rifles Company B, 14th Regiment N.C. Troops (4th N.C. Volunteers)

Lamma was born in 1837 to Evan and Chloe Welborn. Lamma was a student at Trinity College prior to volunteering for service on April 23, 1861; he was mustered in as a private. He was promoted to corporal on December 19, 1861, and to sergeant on January 11, 1862. Lamma was elected as first lieutenant on April 25, 1862, and served as an officer until he died of typhoid fever in Richmond, Virginia, on June 26, 1862.

1880. Welborn, Phillip Henry

Private, Confederate Guards Company K, 48th Regiment N.C. Troops

Phillip was born in 1834 to James M. and Sarah Horney Welborn. Phillip worked as a small planter, and, in 1861, he married Sarah Snider. He operated his plantation in the Browntown area prior to being conscripted into service in Guilford County on October 24, 1864. He was reported present until captured at Petersburg, Virginia, on April 2, 1865. Phillip was confined at Point Lookout, Maryland, until June 26, 1865, when he was released after taking the oath of allegiance. After the war, Phillip and Sarah would have six children: Henry (1866), Jane (1867), Sarah (1869), Louisa (1872), John F. (1875), and Charles B. (1880). Phillip leased some of his land for sharecropping, operated a sawmill, and harvested lumber from his land to offset the effects of the war. He was a member of the A. A. Hill Camp, United Confederate Veterans. Phillip lived in the Abbott's Creek area until his death on May 18, 1922. He is buried at Abbott's Creek Primitive Baptist Church.

1881. Welborn, William M.

Private, Company C, 70th Regiment N.C. Troops (1st N.C. Junior Reserves)

William was born in 1847 to John and Mary Welborn. William worked as a shoemaker in the Lexington area prior to enlisting in the Junior Reserves on May 24, 1864. After the war, William returned to the Lexington township where he continued to work as a shoemaker. William married Martha Everhart in 1873, and they would have six children: Daisy (1873), Mollie (1875), Lindsay (1877), Clay (1878), John (1881), and Charlie (1891). William lived in the city of Lexington until his death in 1914. He is buried in the Lexington City Cemetery.

1882. Welborn, Wisdom P.

Corporal, Company G, 2nd Battalion, N.C. Infantry

Wisdom was born in 1842 to Barnabus and Smirett Welborn. Wisdom worked as a farmer prior to volunteering for service on September 19, 1861. He was reported present until captured at Roanoke Island, North Carolina, on February 8, 1862. Wisdom was confined at Elizabeth City, North Carolina, until February 21, 1862, when he was paroled and released. He was appointed corporal on December 17, 1862, and served in that capacity until wounded and captured at Gettysburg, Pennsylvania, on July 3, 1863. Wisdom was confined at Fort Delaware, Delaware, until he died on October 12, 1863. He is buried in the Fort Delaware National Cemetery.

1883. Welch, Albert H.

Private, Company D, 62nd Battalion, Georgia Cavalry Company H, 16th Battalion, N.C. Cavalry

Albert was born on October 3, 1822. Albert worked as a farmer in the Abbott's Creek area, and, on May 14, 1851, he married Elizabeth Bodenheimer. Albert and Elizabeth would have three children, Hazeltine (1852), Martha (1854), and Rachael (1858), before Albert enlisted in the 62nd Georgia Cavalry at New Bern, North Carolina, in March 1863. He was transferred to the 16th N.C. Cavalry on July 11, 1864. Albert was reported present through October 1864. After the war, Albert returned to his family, and he and Elizabeth would have three more children: Ida (1865), William (1867), and Randolph (1869). Albert worked as a farmer in the Abbott's Creek township until his death on March 21, 1898. He is buried at New Friendship Baptist Church.

1884. Welch, Alfred A.

Private, Company D, 62nd Battalion, Georgia Cavalry

Alfred was born on March 26, 1835, to William and Elizabeth Welch. Alfred worked as a farmer prior to enlisting in the 62nd Georgia Cavalry at New Bern, North Carolina, in March 1863. He was reported present until he died of disease "at home" on June 1, 1863. He is buried at Abbott's Creek Primitive Baptist Church.

1885. Welch, Cyrus

Private, Company F, 2nd Battalion, N.C. Infantry

Cyrus was born on September 28, 1843. Cyrus worked as a farmer prior to volunteering for service on September 19, 1861. Cyrus was reported present until he deserted to the enemy on February 17, 1865. Records of the Federal provost marshal list him as a "rebel deserter" who took the oath of allegiance in Washington, D.C., on February 21, 1865, and was furnished transportation to Indianapolis, Indiana. Cyrus remained in the city of Indianapolis until the war was over. He then returned to the Arcadia area, where, in 1876, he married Lydia P. Cyrus and Lydia would not have any children together. Cyrus operated a sawmill on his property and was the proprietor of this business until his death on February 3, 1918. He is buried at Spring Hill United Methodist Church.

1886. Welch, Henry N.

Corporal, Company B, 1st Battalion, N.C. Sharpshooters

Henry was born on October 7, 1842, to William and Elizabeth Welch. Henry worked as a farmer until he joined the 1st N.C. Sharpshooters on April 26, 1862. He was appointed corporal on August 31, 1863, and served in that capacity until he was killed in a skirmish at Batchelor's Creek, New Bern, North Carolina, on February 1, 1864. His body was retrieved and buried at Abbott's Creek Primitive Baptist Church.

1887. Welch, John A.

Private, Holtsburg Guards Company A, 54th Regiment N.C. Troops

John was born in 1830 to William and Elizabeth Welch. John enlisted into service as a substitute for former captain Jesse Hargrave on June 17, 1862. He was detailed to serve as a lead miner in Davidson County on September 10, 1862. John was reported on detail through October 1864. No further records.

1888. Welch, William A.

Private, North State Boys Company K, 45th Regiment N.C. Troops

William was born on April 22, 1836. William worked as a farmer prior to being conscripted into service in Guilford County on October 24, 1864. He was reported present until captured at Farmville, Virginia, on April 6, 1865. William was confined at Point Lookout, Maryland, until he died of disease on April 28, 1865. He is buried in the Point Lookout National Cemetery.

1889. Welch, William H.

Private, North State Boys Company K, 45th Regiment N.C. Troops

William was born on May 13, 1820, to William and Rachael Welch. William worked as a farmer prior to being conscripted into service on February 28, 1863. His service records are incomplete except for his enlistment and the remark "wounded by accident." After the war, William returned to the Thomasville area where he continued farming until he sought employment at Standard Chair Company in Thomasville. In 1871, William married Rachael Craven. William and Rachael would only have one son: Charles Banner (1875). William lived in the Thomasville township until his death on April 20, 1892. He is buried at Spring Hill United Methodist Church.

1890. Welfare, Edward A.

Private, Davidson Guards Company A, 21st Regiment N.C. Troops (11th N.C. Volunteers)

Edward was born in 1839 to Rueben and Eliza Welfare. Edward was preparing for the ministry under the Reverend Jordan Rominger prior to volunteering for service on May 8, 1861. He was reported present until wounded in September 1864. Edward was listed as absent, wounded, through February 1865 and was paroled at Greensboro, North Car-

olina, on May 1, 1865. After the war, Edward married Susan A. Rominger on February 3, 1867. The couple would have a daughter, Cora Lee (1868), before Edward left the county for his ministry in the 1870s. Edward was last reported as living in Lincoln County in 1880. No further records.

1891. West, Alexander

Private, Company D, 48th Regiment N.C. Troops

Alexander was born in 1836 to John and Mary West. Alexander worked as a farmer prior to being conscripted into service on August 8, 1862. He deserted on August 29, 1862, and was reported absent without leave until he returned under amnesty in June 1863. Alexander was reported present until sent to a Raleigh, North Carolina, hospital on January 12, 1864. Alexander was transferred to Charlotte, North Carolina, where he died of "chronic diarrhea" on May 27, 1864. He is buried in the Confederate section of the Elmwood Cemetery in Charlotte.

1892. West, Augustus

Private, Company B, 14th Regiment N.C. Troops (4th N.C. Volunteers) Company K, 14th Regiment N.C. Troops (4th N.C. Volunteers)

Augustus was born in 1838 to John and Mary West. Augustus worked as a farmer prior to volunteering for service on April 23, 1861. He was reported present until he deserted on December 6, 1862. Augustus remained at home in the Conrad Hill area until he returned under arrest in March 1863. The charges against Augustus were cleared, and he was returned to service by September 1, 1863. He was transferred to Company K on September 8, 1863. Augustus was captured at Cedar Creek, Virginia, on October 19, 1864. He was confined at Point Lookout, Maryland, until he died of "cerebritis" on February 4, 1865. He is buried in the Point Lookout National Cemetery.

1893. Westmoreland, David S.

14th Battalion, N.C. Home Guard

David was born on December 13, 1827, to William and Charity Morris Westmoreland. David worked as a carpenter, and, in 1846, he married Julia

Sullivan. David and Julia would have eight children, William J. (1847), Stephen (1849), Rueben (1852), John F. (1853), Sally (1856), Martha (1857), Rozelle (1861), and Robert (1863), before Julia died in 1864. David was declared "nonexempted" from Home Guard service in a letter to Colonel Jesse Hargrave on January 4, 1864. On December 16, 1865, David married Nancy Southern. David and Nancy would have three children: Nancy (1869), Clarnedon (1872), and Roy (1875). By 1866, he was one of two furniture and cabinet makers in Thomasville. By 1870, David's chairs, cabinetry, and furniture were among the best in the state. David's business grew into the Standard Chair Company, which was the forerunner of the multibillion-dollar business of Thomasville's furniture industries. David lived in the town of Thomasville and continued crafting furniture until his death on December 2, 1891. He is buried in the Thomasville City Cemetery.

1894. Westmoreland, John Frank

Private, Company C, 3rd Regiment
N.C. State Troops

John was born on April 27, 1847, to William and Charity Morris Westmoreland. John worked as a printer prior to serving in Company C, 3rd N.C. State Troops, according to a pension request filed by Nancy McGee, his widow. After the war, John returned to work as a printer and ran a bustling shop on Randolph Street. In 1871, John married Nancy McGee. John and Nancy would have two children: William (1876) and David (1883). John made a successful venture into the publishing business in 1905 but never had a chance to expand his business due to his death on May 13, 1913. He is buried in the Thomasville City Cemetery.

1895. Westmoreland, William J.

Private, Company C, 70th Regiment N.C.
Troops (1st N.C. Junior Reserves
Company I, 35th Regiment N.C. Troops

William was born in 1847 to David S. and Julia Southern Westmoreland. William worked as a carpenter prior to enlisting in the Junior Reserves on May 24, 1864. William was transferred to the 35th North Carolina on September 7, 1864. He was reported present until captured at Five Forks, Virginia, on April 1, 1865. William was confined at Hart's Island,

New York, until June 21, 1865, when he was released after taking the oath of allegiance. After the war, William returned home to Thomasville where he helped his father build Westmoreland Furniture ,which eventually became the Standard Chair Company. William married Mary C. Fouts on March 29, 1868, and they would have six children: David (1869), Bertha (1876), Maggie (1879), Nancy (1880), William (1883), and Victor (1887). William worked as the supervisor of cabinetmaking in his family's business and helped to expand production to finer furniture, and he worked closely with J. E. Lambeth to expand the business further after David Westmoreland's death in 1891. William was married twice more between 1900 and 1910. William retained a controlling interest in Standard Chair until 1912, when he was outbid by his friend Lambeth. William was a benefactor to Fair Grove Methodist Church and a friend to the Thomasville community until his death in 1929. He is buried at Fair Grove United Methodist Church.

1896. Whirlow, Alexander W.

Private, Company I, 42nd Regiment
N.C. Troops

Alex was born in 1828 to Henry and Catharine Whirlow. Alex worked as a farmer, and, on May 29, 1851, he married Elizabeth Crotts. Alex and Elizabeth would have five children, David (1852), Hiram (1854), John A. (1855), Mary A. (1858), and Martha (1861), before Alex volunteered for service on March 3, 1862. He was reported present through November 24, 1864, and was paroled in Raleigh, North Carolina, on April 20, 1865. Alexander returned home, and in the 1870 Census he was listed as living in the Lexington township. No further records.

1897. Whisenhunt, John W.

Private, Davidson Guards
Company A, 21st Regiment N.C. Troops
(11th N.C. Volunteers)

John was born in 1845 to Thomas and Martha Whisenhunt. John worked as a farmer in the Clemmonsville area prior to enlisting in Wake County on June 6, 1863. He was reported present until he deserted from service on October 5, 1864. After his desertion, John returned to Clemmonsville, where, in 1866, he married Lucy. John and Lucy would have two

children: Betty (1868) and Elizabeth (1869). John was last reported as living in the Clemmonsville township in 1870. No further records.

1898. White, Anderson

Private, Company I, 42nd Regiment
N.C. Troops

Anderson was born in 1827. Anderson worked as a farmer in the western part of the county, and, in 1853, he married Elizabeth Shoaf. Anderson and Elizabeth would have three children, Nancy and William (1855) and Mary (1859), before Anderson volunteered for service on March 4, 1862. He died of unreported causes on May 18, 1862.

1899. White, Theophilus

Private, North State Boys
Company K, 45th Regiment N.C. Troops

Theo was born on March 11, 1830. Theo worked as a farmer in the Thomasville area, and, in 1852, he married Nellie, who died in 1861. Theo was conscripted into service in Guilford County on October 24, 1864. He was reported present until captured at Farmville, Virginia, on April 6, 1865. Theo was confined at Point Lookout, Maryland, until June 21, 1865, when he was released after taking the oath of allegiance. After the war, Theo returned to the Thomasville township, where he married Hannah in 1887. Theo lived in the Spring Hill area until his death on March 20, 1914. He is buried at Spring Hill United Methodist Church.

1900. White, William

Private, Davidson Guards
Company A, 21st Regiment N.C. Troops
(11th N.C. Volunteers)

William was born in 1842. William worked as a farmer prior to volunteering for service on May 8, 1861. He was reported present until he was discharged due to "an irreducible hernia" on February 17, 1862. No further records.

1901. Whiteheart, Willis

Laborer, Ordnance Depot, Confederate
Navy, Charlotte

Willis was born in 1837 to William and Elizabeth Whiteheart, natives of Savannah, Georgia. Willis worked as a chair maker prior to being pressed into naval service at Wilmington, North Carolina, on December 3, 1863. He was assigned to the Charlotte Ordnance Depot and served in that capacity until the end of the war. After the war, Willis married Mahalia in 1865. Willis and Mahalia would have one son: Wiley F (1867). Willis worked as a chairmaker in Thomasville, and his designs where bought out by David S. Westmoreland. Willis soon became a supervisor for Standard Chair until his death in the 1910s. He is buried at Pine Woods United Methodist Church.

1902. Whitlow, Jesse

Private, Company H, 8th Georgia
*   Cavalry*
Company D, 62nd Battalion, Georgia
*   Cavalry*
Company H, 16th Battalion, N.C.
*   Cavalry*

Jesse was born on February 4, 1832, to Phoebe Whitlow. Jesse worked as a tailor, and, in 1854, he married Elizabeth Burke. Jesse and Elizabeth would have one child, Barbara (1857), before Elizabeth's death in January 1862. Jesse was conscripted into service on July 15, 1862, and was assigned as an ambulance driver with the 8th Georgia Cavalry. Jesse was transferred to the 62nd Georgia Cavalry in March 1863 and was transferred to the 16th N.C. Cavalry on July 11, 1864. He was reported present through August 1864. After the war, Jesse returned to the Lexington township, where on December 22, 1865, he married Amanda Y. Sink. Jesse and Amanda would have five children: John (1868), Mary Lou (1871), Moses (1873), Gazeal (1877), and May (1880). Jesse lived in the Lexington township, worked as a tailor, and operated a sawmill until his death on July 2, 1901. He is buried at Bethesda United Methodist Church.

1903. Wicks, William H.

Private, Company E, 43rd Regiment
*   N.C. Troops*

William was born on June 6, 1825, in Hertfordshire, England. William came to Davidson County in the 1850s to work as a miner. William married Sarah Wallace in 1861, and they would have a daughter, Emma (1861), before William volunteered for service on February 24, 1862. He was reported present until wounded at Winchester, Virginia, on September 19, 1864. William recovered from his wounds and returned to service in November 1864 and was reported present through February 1865. After the war, William returned to the Silver Hill township where he and Sarah would have six more children: John (1865), Alfred (1867), Mary A. (1871), Cora (1873), Patty (1876), and William (1879). William worked in the mines at Silver Hill until his death on June 5, 1881. He is buried at Holloways Baptist Church.

1904. Wier (Weir), Adam

Private, Company H, 15th Regiment
*   N.C. Troops (5th N.C. Volunteers)*

Adam was born in 1829 to Adam and Catharine Wier. Adam worked as a farmer in the Midway township, and, on June 1, 1853, he married Margaret J. Sink. Adam and Margaret would have four children, Fidela (1854), Emanuel (1856), Mary (1858), and Elizabeth (1860), before Adam was conscripted into service in Wake County on July 15, 1862. He was captured at Crampton's Pass, Maryland, on September 14, 1862. Adam was confined at Fort Delaware, Delaware, until October 2, 1862, when he was paroled and transferred to Aiken's Landing, Virginia, for exchange. He was declared exchanged on November 10, 1862. Adam returned to service and was reported present through October 1864. After the war, Adam returned to the Midway township where he and Margaret would have two more children: Eliza (1866) and David (1869). Adam was last reported as living in Midway in 1870. No further records.

1905. Wier (Weir), Henry Phillip

Captain, 66th Regiment N.C. Militia
*   (1861 organization)*

Henry was born in 1823 to Adam and Catharine Wier. Henry worked as a carpenter, and, in 1846, he married Margaret. Henry and Margaret would have six children: William (1848), David (1849), Jane and Andrew (1851), Adam (1854), and Phoebe (1857). Henry was commissioned to serve as a captain in the Piney Grove District Company on December 13, 1861. Henry was last reported as living in Davidson County in the 1880s. No further records.

1906. Wier (Weir), Henry W.

Private, Company H, 15th Regiment
*   N.C. Troops (5th N.C. Volunteers)*

Henry was born in 1844 to Aaron Houke and Susan Wier. Henry worked as a farmer prior to being conscripted into service in Wake County on July 15, 1862. He was present until he was reported absent without leave on May 1, 1863. No further records.

1907. Wier (Weir), Jacob

Private, Confederate Guards
Company K, 48th Regiment N.C.
*   Troops*

Jacob was born in 1842 to Aaron Houke and Susan Wier. Jacob worked as a carpenter prior to being conscripted into service in Wake County on July 15, 1862. He was killed in action at Sharpsburg, Maryland, on September 17, 1862.

1908. Wier (Weir), Jacob

Captain, 66th Regiment N.C. Militia
*   (1861 organization)*

Jacob was born in 1821 to Adam and Catharine Wier. Jacob worked as a teacher, and, in 1851, he married Barbara Shuler. Jacob and Barbara would have seven children: Elizabeth (1852), Louisa (1853), David (1859), Phillip (1861), John (1864), Andrew (1867), and William (1870). Jacob was commissioned to serve as a captain of the Bethany District Company on December 13, 1861. After the war, Jacob worked in the Midway township before moving with his wife to Salem in the 1880s. No further records.

1909. Wier (Weir), James

Private, Company K, 21st Regiment
*   N.C. Troops (11th N.C. Volunteers)*

James was born in 1842 to Aaron Houke and Susan Wier. James worked as an apprentice to Michael Miller prior to being conscripted into service in Wake County on November 13, 1863. He deserted to the enemy on December 28, 1863. James took the oath of allegiance at Washington, D.C., on March 14, 1864. No further records.

1910. Wier (Weir), Wiley

Private, Company H, 15th Regiment
*   N.C. Troops (5th N.C. Volunteers)*

Wiley was born in 1840 to Aaron Houke and Susan Wier. Wiley worked as a farmer, and, in 1857, he married Elizabeth. Wiley and Elizabeth would have two children, Mary (1858) and Robert (1860), before Wiley was conscripted into service in Wake County on July 15, 1862. He was reported present until he died of disease at Lynchburg, Virginia, on January 1, 1863.

1911. Wilkerson, Allen

Private, Company B, 48th Regiment N.C. Troops
Company A, 46th Regiment N.C. Troops

Allen was born in 1815. Allen worked as a farmer in the southern district of Davidson County, and, on February 24, 1840, he married Elizabeth Sarah. Allen and Elizabeth would have only one child who survived infancy, Sarah Laura (1860), before Allen volunteered for service on March 5, 1862. He was wounded at King's School House, Virginia, on June 25, 1862, and was reported absent, wounded, until January 1863. Allen was transferred to the 46th Regiment in July 1863. Allen was reported present until he died of spinal meningitis on January 24, 1865. He is buried in the Hollywood Cemetery, Richmond, Virginia.

1912. Williams, Alexander James

Private, Company B, 48th Regiment N.C. Troops

Alex was born in 1821 to William and Mary Williams. Alex worked as a farmer, and, on October 4, 1850, he married Catharine Cooper. Alex and Catharine would have five children, Martha (1851), John H. (1855), William (1856), Edwin (1857), and Sarah (1860), before Alex enlisted as a substitute on March 17, 1862. He was wounded at King's School House, Virginia, on June 25, 1862. Alex died of his wounds in a Richmond, Virginia, hospital on June 28, 1862.

1913. Williams, Anderson B.

Private, Holtsburg Guards
Company A, 54th Regiment N.C. Troops

Anderson was born in 1840 to Susan Williams. Anderson worked as a farmer prior to volunteering for service on March 6, 1862. He was reported present until captured at Rappahannock Station, Virginia, on November 7, 1863. Anderson

was confined at Point Lookout, Maryland, until transferred to City Point, Virginia, on March 15, 1864, for exchange. He returned to duty in July 1864 and was reported present until captured at Fort Stedman, Virginia, on March 25, 1865. Anderson was confined again at Point Lookout until June 21, 1865, when he was released after taking the oath of allegiance. After the war, Anderson returned home to the Churchland area, where, in 1866, he married Lucy C. Anderson and Lucy would have five children: Nancy (1868), John (1872), Henry (1874), Andrew (1877), and Calvin (1878). Anderson lived in the Tyro township until his death on November 22, 1879. He is buried at Pine Primitive Baptist Church.

1914. Williams, Andrew Madison

Private, Company B, 57th Regiment N.C. Troops

Andrew was born on December 8, 1836, to William and Mary Williams. Andrew worked as a farmer, and, on October 20, 1858, he married Mary Wilson. Andrew and Mary would have two sons, Hiram (1859) and James (1861), before Andrew was conscripted into service in Rowan County on October 10, 1862. Andrew was wounded in the left hand at Fredericksburg, Virginia, on December 13, 1862. Andrew returned to service after a short time and was reported present until captured at Winchester, Virginia, on September 19, 1864. He was confined at Point Lookout, Maryland, until May 14, 1865, when he was released after taking the oath of allegiance. According to family history, while Andrew would never admit he had killed anyone, he always told a story: "I drew my sights on a Yankee once, and not knowing I was there, he began to pray silently. After that, I could not kill him." After the war, Andrew returned to the Tyro/Boone area, where he and Mary would have four more children: Amanda (1865), William (1867), Cynthia (1868), and Henry (1872). Andrew worked as a farmer in the Tyro township until his death on January 28, 1922. He is buried at Pine Primitive Baptist Church.

1915. Williams, George W.

Private, Thomasville Rifles
Company B, 14th Regiment N.C. Troops (4th N.C. Volunteers)

George was born on November 7, 1840, to James and Catharine Williams. George worked as a farmer prior to volunteering for service on August 13, 1861. He was reported present until wounded at Sharpsburg, Maryland, on September 17, 1862. George recovered and returned to service in January 1863. He was reported present until he deserted on June 28, 1864. George remained at home for the rest of the war, and, on September 3, 1867, he married Nancy Garner. George and Nancy would have five children: Elizabeth (1868), Dulcinea (1872), Sarah (1875), R. B. Hayes (1877), and Bessie (1886). George worked as a farmer in the Emmons township until his death on November 1, 1934. He is buried at Tom's Creek Primitive Baptist Church. The inscription on his stone reads: "A tender father and a faithful friend."

1916. Williams, Hiram

Private, Company B, 57th Regiment N.C. Troops

Hiram was born in 1831 to William and Mary Williams. Hiram worked as a farmer in the Lexington area prior to enlisting in Rowan County on July 4, 1862. He was wounded at Fredericksburg, Virginia, on December 13, 1862. Hiram recovered from his injury and returned to service on February 28, 1863. He was reported present until captured at Fort Stedman, Virginia, on March 25, 1865. Hiram was confined at Point Lookout, Maryland, until June 21, 1865, when he was released after taking the oath of allegiance. After the war, Hiram returned to Lexington, and in 1880, he was living as a boarder at his sister Albertine's home. No further records.

1917. Williams, Hiram F.

Private, Company H, 15th Regiment N.C. Troops (5th N.C. Volunteers)

Hiram was born on October 15, 1843, to Azariah and Mary Wagner Williams. Hiram worked as a farmer prior to being conscripted into service in Wake County on July 15, 1862. He was reported present until wounded in the right shoulder at Wilderness, Virginia, on May 5, 1864. Hiram recovered and returned to service prior to October 31, 1864. He was reported present until captured at Hatcher's Run, Virginia, on April 2, 1865. Hiram was confined at Hart's Island, New

York, until June 18, 1865, when he was released after taking the oath of allegiance. After the war, Hiram returned to the Midway area where he resided as a single farmer until his death on June 13, 1920. He is buried at Midway United Methodist Church.

1918. Williams, James W.

Private, Holtsburg Guards
Company A, 54th Regiment N.C. Troops

James was born in 1847 to Azariah and Mary Wagner Williams. James worked as a farmer prior to volunteering for service on his 16th birthday on October 4, 1863. He was reported present until November 7, 1863. No further records.

1919. Williams, John Patrick

Private, Company D, 48th Regiment
N.C. Troops

John was born in 1832 to Susan Williams. John was a student in the Yadkin area, and, on November 9, 1857, he married Elizabeth Williams. John continued his studies until he was conscripted into service on August 8, 1862. He was reported present until hospitalized on November 25, 1863. John was reported absent, sick, until assigned to light duty at Salisbury, North Carolina, on October 24, 1864. He was paroled at Salisbury on May 23, 1865. After the war, John returned home to his wife. By 1870, John had become a practicing physician and had built a home in the Clemmonsville area. John served the county as a man of medicine until his death on February 11, 1898. He is buried at Pine Primitive Baptist Church.

1920. Williams, Jonathan J.

Private, Company D, 48th Regiment
N.C. Troops

Jonathan was born in 1830 to William and Mary Williams. Jonathan worked as a farmer, and, in 1852, he married Albertine. Jonathan and Albertine would have four children, Joseph (1853), John (1856), Sarah (1857), and David (1862), before Jonathan was conscripted into service on August 8, 1862. He was reported present until captured while in a hospital at Richmond, Virginia, on April 3, 1865. Jonathan was confined at Newport News, Virginia, until June 30, 1865, when he was released after taking the oath of allegiance. After the war, Jonathan returned to the Boone/Tyro area where he and Albertine would have three more children: Rufus (1866), James (1869), and William (1872). Jonathan was last reported working as a farmer in the Boone township in 1880. No further records.

1921. Williams, Lewis H.

Private, Company C, 70th Regiment
N.C. Troops (1st N.C. Junior
Reserves)

Lewis was born on March 3, 1846, to James and Catharine Williams. Lewis worked as a brick mason prior to enlisting in the Junior Reserves on May 24, 1864. After the war, Lewis returned to his trade, and, on December 22, 1872, he married Nancy Bedford. Lewis and Nancy would have three children, Minnie (1875), James (1877), and Bertha (1880), before Nancy's death in 1883. Lewis married a second time in 1888, to Louisa Jane. Lewis and Louisa would have four children in their Thomasville home: Daniel (1889), Eva (1893), Rosa (1894), and Nathaniel (1900). Lewis worked as a brick mason and was a member of the Masonic order. Lewis died on July 27, 1924. He is buried at Pine Woods United Methodist Church.

1922. Williams, Richard Albert

Private, Holtsburg Guards
Company A, 54th Regiment N.C. Troops

Richard was born in 1843 to William and Mary Williams. Richard worked as a farmer prior to enlisting in Rowan County on July 4, 1862. He was wounded in the left thigh at Fredericksburg, Virginia, on December 13, 1862, and was reported absent until he returned on May 1, 1863. Richard was captured at Rappahannock Station, Virginia, on November 7, 1863. Richard was confined at Point Lookout, Maryland, until March 19, 1864, when he was paroled and transferred to City Point, Virginia, for exchange. He returned to service in August 1864 and was hospitalized on September 19, 1864. Richard died of "enteritis" in a Winchester, Virginia, hospital on September 25, 1864.

1923. Williams, Thomas H.

Private, Company B, 48th Regiment
N.C. Troops

Thomas was born in 1844 to Susan Williams. Thomas worked as a farmer prior to volunteering for service on March 3, 1862. He was killed in action at King's School House, Virginia, on June 25, 1862.

1924. Williams, William A.

Private, Company B, 57th Regiment
N.C. Troops

William was born in 1831 to William and Mary Williams. William worked as a farmer, and, in 1849, he married Mary Swicegood. William and Mary would have four children, Mary (1851), John H. (1855), Joel C. (1859), and Obediah (1861), before William enlisted into service in Rowan County on July 4, 1862, and was reported present through August 1864. After the war, William returned to the Boone township, where he was last reported living in 1880. No further records.

1925. Williams, William M.

Private, Company C, 70th Regiment N.C.
Troops (1st N.C. Junior Reserves

William was born in 1847. William worked as a farmer in southern Davidson County prior to enlisting in the Junior Reserves on May 24, 1864. He did not survive the war. An article by Wade Phillips in a 1971 issue of the *Lexington Dispatch* listed W. M. Williams as being one of the reserves who died of disease while in service.

1926. Williamson, Emmett R.

Private, Company G, 2nd Virginia Volunteer Infantry

Emmett was born on June 2, 1845, to John and Lucy Williamson. Emmett's father was a native of Virginia and a professor at Yadkin College. While a student in Richmond, Virginia, Emmett volunteered for service in Henrico County, Virginia, on April 15, 1861. He was discharged from service on May 18, 1861, because of "general disability for service." After his discharge, Emmett returned home and attended Yadkin for two years before it was shut down temporarily. Emmett received a professorship at Yadkin and taught religious science for five years. Emmett lived in the Yadkin College township until his death on October 5, 1892. He is buried at Yadkin College United Methodist Church.

Daniel Wilson would not return to this home, built in the 1850s, after July 10, 1862 (Touart, *Building the Backcountry*).

1927. Willis, Burgess

Private, Company I, 42nd Regiment N.C. Troops

Burgess was born in 1841 to John and Nancy Willis. Burgess worked as an apprentice to Louis Craver prior to volunteering for service on March 3, 1862. He was reported present until captured at Wise's Forks, Virginia, on March 10, 1865. Burgess was confined at Point Lookout, Maryland, until May 15, 1865, when he was released after taking the oath of allegiance. After the war Burgess returned to the Tyro township, where, on November 30, 1865, he married Mary Ellen Wilson. Burgess and Mary lived in the Tyro township through 1900. No further records.

1928. Wilson, Daniel

Private, Company H, 15th Regiment N.C. Troops

Daniel was born in 1840 to Sarah Wilson. Daniel worked as a farmer prior to being conscripted into service in Wake County on July 15, 1862. He was captured at Crampton's Pass, Maryland, on September 14, 1862. Daniel was confined at Fort Delaware, Delaware, until October 2, 1862, when he was paroled and transferred to Aiken's Landing, Virginia, for exchange. He was declared exchanged on November 10, 1862. Daniel died of scurvy in Richmond, Virginia, the day after his exchange, on November 11, 1862.

1929. Wilson, George Washington

Private, Company C, 70th Regiment N.C. Troops (1st N.C. Junior Reserves)

George was born in 1847 to Dennis and Jemina Wilson. George worked as a farmer prior to enlisting in the Junior Reserves on May 24, 1864. After the war, George returned home to the Emmons township, where, in 1871, he married Elizabeth Morris. George and Elizabeth would have four children: Cicero (1873), Leonard (1876), Jones (1877), and John H. (1883). George worked as a farmer in the Emmons township through 1900. No further records.

1930. Wilson, Giles

Private, Lexington Wildcats Company I, 14th Regiment N.C. Troops (4th N.C. Volunteers)

Giles was born in 1827. Giles worked as a miller in the Tyro area, and, in 1854 he married Cynthia Ratts. Giles and Cynthia would have three children, Abram (1856), William (1858), and Maggie (1860), before he was conscripted into service in Wake County on July 15, 1862. He was captured at Crampton's Pass, Mary-

land, on September 14, 1862. Giles was confined at Fort Delaware, Delaware, until October 2, 1862, when he was paroled and transferred to Aiken's Landing, Virginia, for exchange. He was declared exchanged on November 10, 1862. Giles returned to service by January 1, 1863, and was reported present until captured at Strasburg, Virginia, on September 23, 1864. Giles was confined at Point Lookout, Maryland, until June 21, 1865, when he was released after taking the oath of allegiance. After the war, Giles returned to his mill in Tyro. He and Cynthia would have four more children: Henry (1866), Julian (1869), George (1872), and Martha (1875). Giles was last reported as living in the Tyro township in 1880. No further records.

1931. Wilson, Henry F.

Private, Company H, 15th Regiment N.C. Troops (5th N.C. Volunteers)

Henry was born in 1839 to Joshua and Frances Wilson. Henry worked as a farmer in the Reedy Creek area prior to being conscripted into service in Wake County on July 15, 1862. He was reported present until wounded in the face at Wilderness, Virginia, on May 5, 1864. Henry recovered from his wounds and returned to service on October 22, 1864. He was reported present until captured at Hatcher's Run, Virginia, on April 2, 1865. Henry was confined at Hart's Island, New York, until July 11, 1865, when he was released after taking the oath of allegiance. After the war, Henry returned home, where, in 1866, he married Jane. Henry and Jane would have seven children: Lou (1867), Nancy (1869), Mary L. (1871), Charles (1873), Joseph (1875), Edward (1878), and Leona (1881). Henry worked as a farmer until his death on December 15, 1914. He is buried at Mount Olivet United Methodist Church.

1932. Wilson, James Wiseman

Private, Booe's Partisan Rangers Company H, 63rd Regiment N.C. Troops (5th N.C. Cavalry)

James was born in 1832 to John and Catharine Ratts Wilson. James worked as a farmer prior to enlisting in Davie County in July 15, 1862. He was reported present until captured at Madison County Court House, Virginia, on September 22, 1863. James was confined at Point Lookout, Maryland, until March

15, 1864, when he was paroled and transferred to City Point, Virginia, for exchange in April 1864. James was reported present through August 1864. He was paroled at Salisbury, North Carolina, on May 16, 1865. After the war, James returned to the Pine area, where, in 1872, he married Caroline Deadman. James worked as a farmer in the Tyro township until his death in 1893. He is buried at Pine Primitive Baptist Church.

1933. Wilson, John Henderson

Private, Lexington Wildcats
Company I, 14th Regiment N.C. Troops
(4th N.C. Volunteers)

John was born on September 16, 1835, to John and Catharine Ratts Wilson. John worked as an artist in Lexington prior to volunteering for service on May 8, 1861. He was reported present until wounded in the left arm at Malvern Hill, Virginia, on July 1, 1862. John was discharged from service due to his severe wounds on August 10, 1862. The veteran in later life recalled:

> The Federals attacked us leaving about ten of us lost in the shuffle of the retreat. I had been wounded in the arm and had fallen down. I watched several of the men from my regiment being ran down and shot before they could surrender. A Yankee asked his sergeant if they should shoot me as well. The sergeant replied, "Aw, you don't need to shoot him, he'll die sooner or later."

The Confederates counterattacked and took the forward position, where John was lying, and he was rushed to a field hospital. John would never be able to move his left arm again. John returned to his parent's home in the Boone township after his discharge. In 1867, he married Jane Beck. John and Jane would have five children, Martha (1868), Margaret (1869), Sarah (1871), James (1873), and John (1875), before Jane died in 1879. John remarried on May 9, 1880, to Mary Susan Broadway. The two would not have any children. John lived in the Boone township until his death on February 6, 1917. He is buried at Pine Primitive Baptist Church.

1934. Wilson, John L.

Private, Carolina Rangers
Company B, 10th Virginia Cavalry
Regiment

John was born in 1823 to Isaac and Catharine Hartley Wilson. John worked as a miller in the Boone area, and, in 1847, he married Susan Catharine Gobble. John and Susan would have four children, Harriet (1849), Mary (1854), Louisa (1855), and Martha (1858), before John enlisted in Davie County on December 19, 1861. He was reported present until sent on a horse detail from May through December 1863. John returned to service and was reported present through December 31, 1864, when he was issued a clothing ration. After the war, John returned home to his farm and small mill. John lived in the Boone/ Tyro area until his death in 1902. He is buried at St. Luke's Lutheran Church.

1935. Wilson, Joseph

Private, Company C, 70th Regiment
N.C. Troops (1st N.C. Junior
Reserves)

Joseph was born in 1847 to Joshua and Frances Wilson. Joseph worked as a farmer in the Tyro township prior to enlisting in the Junior Reserves on May 24, 1864. No further records.

1936. Wilson, Lewis

Private, Company H, 15th Regiment
N.C. Troops (5th N.C. Volunteers)

Lewis was born on January 3, 1842, to Hamilton and Catharine Wilson. Lewis worked as a farmer in the Midway area, and, in 1861, he married Susan Payne. Lewis and Susan had been married less than a year when Lewis was conscripted into service in Wake County on July 15, 1862. He was reported present until captured at Hatcher's Run, Virginia, on April 2, 1865. Lewis was confined at Hart's Island, New York, until June 18, 1865, when he was released after taking the oath of allegiance. After the war, Lewis returned to the Midway township where he met his two-year-old son, Lewis Jr., born in 1863. Lewis and Susan would have two more children: Phoebe (1867) and Mary (1869). Lewis worked as a farmer in the Midway township until his death on May 28, 1902. He is buried at New Friendship Baptist Church.

1937. Wilson, Madison

Private, Company H, 15th Regiment
N.C. Troops (5th N.C. Volunteers)

Madison was born in 1829. Madison worked as a farmer in the northern district of Davidson County, and, in 1853, he married Rebecca Smith. Madison and Rebecca would have two children, Crissila (1855) and David (1858), before Madison was conscripted into service in Wake County on July 15, 1862. He died of typhoid fever at Richmond, Virginia, on December 21, 1862.

1938. Wilson, Robert Franklin

Private, Company B, 57th Regiment
N.C. Troops

Robert was born on January 23, 1829, to John and Catharine Ratts Wilson. Robert worked as a farmer, and, on February 5, 1850, he married Mary J. Greene. Robert and Mary would have four children, John (1851), Laura Ann (1854), Charles (1859), and Robert (1862), before Robert enlisted in Rowan County on July 4, 1862. He was wounded in the finger at Fredericksburg, Virginia, on December 13, 1862. Robert was issued a furlough in January 1863, but when he did not return, he was listed as absent without leave. Robert returned in January 1864 and was reported present until captured at Fort Stedman, Virginia, on March 25, 1865. He was confined at Point Lookout, Maryland, until June 21, 1865, when he was released after taking the oath of allegiance. After the war, Robert returned to the Boone township where he and Mary would have three more children: Marion (1866), Mary (1869), and Flora (1872). Robert worked as a farmer in the Boone township until his death on May 16, 1898. He is buried at Wesley's Chapel United Methodist Church.

1939. Wilson, Solomon

Private, Company H, 48th Regiment
N.C. Troops

Solomon was born in 1842 to Sarah Wilson. Solomon worked as a farmer, and, in 1860, he was living with John and Elizabeth Raker. Solomon was conscripted into service on August 8, 1862. He was captured at Sharpsburg, Maryland, on September 17, 1862. Solomon was exchanged on October 4, 1862, and was reported present until he deserted to the enemy on March 6, 1865. He was confined at Washington, D.C., until he was released in April 1865 after taking the oath of allegiance. No further records.

1940. Wilson, William

Private, Company D, 62nd Battalion,
Georgia Cavalry
Company H, 16th Battalion, N.C. Cavalry

William was born on July 20, 1846, to Dennis and Minnie Wilson. William worked as a farmer in the eastern part of the Conrad Hill township prior to enlisting in the 62nd Georgia in January 1863. He was transferred to the 16th North Carolina on July 11, 1864. William was reported present through August 1864. After the war, William returned home to the Conrad Hill township, where in 1872, he married Elizabeth Hughes. William and Elizabeth helped to found Hughes' Grove Baptist, which now lies in Noahtown. William lived in the Conrad Hill area until his death on November 5, 1913. He is buried at Hughes' Grove Baptist Church.

1941. Wilson, William B.

Private, Holtsburg Guards
Company A, 54th Regiment N.C. Troops

William was born in 1838 to Abram and Mary Wilson. William worked as a farmer prior to volunteering for service on March 6, 1862. He was reported present until hospitalized at Richmond, Virginia, on January 13, 1863, with typhoid pneumonia. William died of "variola confluent" on February 19, 1865.

1942. Witt, Henderson

Laborer, Ordnance Depot, Confederate
Navy, Charlotte

Henderson was born in 1844. Henderson worked as a farmer prior to enlisting in the Confederate Navy at Wilmington, North Carolina, on June 14, 1863. He was assigned to the Ordnance Depot at Charlotte, according to family history. After the war, Henderson returned home to the Clemmonsville area where, in 1872, he married Elizabeth Grover, who brought two children, Ida and John W., from a previous marriage. Henderson and Elizabeth would have two children together: Sarah (1874) and William (1878). Henderson was last reported as living in the Clemmonsville township in 1880. No further records.

1943. Wommack, James C.

Private, Davidson Guards
Company A, 21st Regiment N.C. Troops
(11th N.C. Volunteers)

James was born in 1842. James worked as a clerk in Clemmonsville prior to volunteering for service on May 8, 1861. He was reported present through February 1865. After the war, James returned home, where, in 1866, he married Elizabeth Douthit. James and Elizabeth would have six children: Roswell (1867), Lucy (1869), Georgia (1871), Sarah (1873), Mary (1876), and James (1878). James was last listed as living in the Clemmonsville township in 1880. No further records.

1944. Wommack, Roswell A.

Private, Davidson Guards
Company A, 21st Regiment N.C. Troops
(11th N.C. Volunteers)

Roswell was born in 1838. Roswell worked as a silversmith prior to volunteering for service on May 8, 1861. He was mustered in as a sergeant and was promoted to first sergeant on July 8, 1861. Roswell was elected second lieutenant on September 3, 1861. He served as a lieutenant until defeated for reelection on April 26, 1862. Roswell, unlike most defeated officers, chose to stay on with his unit and fought as a private with the company through February 1865. No further records.

1945. Wood, Casper E.

Private, Davidson Guards
Company A, 21st Regiment N.C. Troops
(11th N.C. Volunteers)

Casper was born in 1834 to Mary A. Wood. Casper worked as a farmer, and, on January 26, 1856, he married Catharine Ward. Casper and Catharine would have two daughters, Mary (1857) and Sarah (1860), before Casper volunteered for service on May 8, 1861. He was reported present until he died of unreported causes at Charlottesville, Virginia, on April 27, 1862.

1946. Wood, John E.

Private, Holtsburg Guards
Company A, 54th Regiment N.C. Troops

John was born in 1842. John worked as a farmer prior to being conscripted into service on May 1, 1863. He was reported present until captured at Fort Stedman, Virginia, on March 25, 1865. John was confined at Point Lookout, Maryland, until June 21, 1865, when he was released after taking the oath of allegiance. After the war, John returned home to the Boone township, where, on December 27, 1866, he married Sarah Spaugh. John and Sarah would have at least one child, Sylvester (1874), before the couple moved out of the county in the 1870s. The 1900 Census for Anson County, North Carolina, lists the family of 57-year-old J. E. Wood. No further records.

1947. Wood, Joseph W.

Private, Chatam Light Infantry
Company G, 48th Regiment N.C. Troops

Joseph was born in 1832. Joseph worked as a farmer prior to being conscripted into service on August 14, 1862. He was wounded at Sharpsburg, Maryland, on September 17, 1862. Joseph recovered from his wounds in November 1862 and was reported present until wounded in the thigh at Payne's Farm, Virginia, on November 27, 1863. He was sent to a Gordonsville, Virginia, hospital on December 21, 1863. Joseph died of pneumonia at Gordonsville on December 27, 1863.

1948. Wood, Richard W.

Private, Lexington Wildcats
Company I, 14th Regiment N.C. Troops
(4th N.C. Volunteers)

Richard was born in 1841. Richard worked as a farmer prior to volunteering for service on May 14, 1861. He was reported present until he died "at home" on September 16, 1862.

1949. Wood, William A.

Private, Holtsburg Guards
Company A, 54th Regiment N.C. Troops

William was born in 1842. William worked as a farmer for Henry Beck prior to volunteering for service on March 4, 1862. He was reported present until sent to a Richmond, Virginia, hospital on June 11, 1864, with a gunshot wound. William returned to service on July 29, 1864, and was wounded and captured at Cedar Creek, Virginia, on October 19, 1864. He was confined at Point Lookout, Maryland, until February 14, 1865, when he was paroled and transferred to Cox's Wharf, Virginia, for exchange. William was issued a 60-day furlough on March 1, 1865. He was paroled at

Salisbury, North Carolina, on May 22, 1865. No further records.

1950. Woosley, Franklin

Private, Company G, 2nd Battalion, N.C. Infantry

Franklin was born in 1841 to David and Dulcinea Woosley. Franklin enlisted on March 2, 1863, and was captured during Pickett's charge at Gettysburg, Pennsylvania, on July 3, 1863. He was confined at Fort Delaware, Delaware, until July 30, 1863, when he was paroled and transferred to City Point, Virginia, for exchange. Franklin was exchanged in August 1863. He was wounded during the Mine Run campaign between November 27 and December 3, 1863. Franklin was captured at Winchester, Virginia, on September 19, 1864. He was confined at Point Lookout, Maryland, until March 15, 1865, when he was paroled and transferred to Aiken's Landing, Virginia, for exchange. Franklin was declared exchanged on March 18, 1865. After the war, Franklin returned to the Freidburg community where he worked as a carpenter and served as an elder of the Moravian Church in 1871, when his brother Samuel was installed as its minister. Franklin was an active member of the community and the church until his death in January 1898. He is buried at Freidburg Moravian Church.

1951. Woosley, John

Private, Company H, 15th Regiment N.C. Troops (5th N.C. Volunteers)

John was born in 1824 to William and Mary Woosley. John worked as a single farmer in the northern district of Davidson County prior to being conscripted into service in Wake County on July 15, 1862. He was wounded at Sharpsburg, Maryland, on September 17, 1862. John was reported absent, wounded, until he died on November 16, 1862, of a disease he had contracted while in the hospital at Farmville, Virginia.

1952. Woosley, Samuel Augustus

Private, Company C, 70th Regiment N.C. Troops (1st N.C. Junior Reserves)

Samuel was born on May 10, 1846, to David and Dulcinea Woosley. Samuel was a student prior to enlisting in the Junior

Reserves on May 24, 1864. After the war, Samuel was confirmed in the ministry of the Moravian church and worked as a temporary minister at Bethabra before being assigned to his home church of Freidburg in 1871. Samuel married Jane in that same year, and the couple would have four children: David (1872), William (1875), Alice (1877), and Elizabeth (1880). Samuel served as the spiritual leader of the Freidburg community and the Arcadia township until his death on September 6, 1898. He is buried at Freidburg Moravian Church.

1953. Workman, David D.

Private, Company I, 42nd Regiment N.C. Troops

David was born in 1841 to William and Nancy Goss Workman. David worked as a farmer prior to volunteering for service on November 26, 1861. He was reported present until killed in action at Reams' Station, Virginia, on August 25, 1864. David's body was retrieved by his mother and was buried in the Goss Family Cemetery.

1954. Workman, James E.

Private, Lexington Wildcats Company I, 14th Regiment N.C. Troops (4th N.C. Volunteers)

James was born in 1840 to William and Nancy Goss Workman. James worked as a farmer prior to volunteering for service on May 14, 1861. He was reported present until captured at Boonsboro, Maryland, on September 15, 1862. James was confined at Fort Delaware, Delaware, until October 2, 1862, when he was paroled and transferred to Aiken's Landing, Virginia, for exchange. He was declared exchanged on November 10, 1862. James returned to service and was reported present until he was wounded at Spotsylvania Court House, Virginia, on May 12, 1864. He was reported absent, wounded, through August 1864. After the war, James returned to the Emmons township, where, on January 22, 1865, he married Martha A. Loflin. James and

Home of William and Nancy Goss Workman, where James was raised (Touart, *Building the Backcountry*).

Martha would have seven children: Nancy (1867), Amelia (1869), Alice (1871), David (1873), William (1875), Hosea (1878), and Mary (1879). James worked as a farmer in the Emmons township until his death in 1906. He is buried in the Workman Family Cemetery at Cedar Grove.

1955. Worley, John R.

Private, Company B, 57th Regiment N.C. Troops

John was born in 1830. John worked as a carpenter in the Lexington area, and, on January 21, 1851, he married Amanda J. Wiseman. John and Amanda would have two children; William (1854) and Elizabeth P. (1858), before John enlisted in Rowan County on July 4, 1862. He was reported present until captured at Rappahannock Station, Virginia, on November 7, 1863. John was confined at Point Lookout, Maryland, until March 14, 1864, when he was paroled and transferred to City Point, Virginia, for exchange. John was exchanged on March 20, 1864, and was reported present until wounded in the vicinity of Cedar Creek, Virginia, on October 21, 1864. He was reported absent, wounded, through February 28, 1865. After the war, John returned home, where he continued to work as a carpenter until his death in the early 1880s. According to a descendant of J. R. Worley, John is buried in an unmarked grave at Ebenezer United Methodist Church.

1956. Worrell, J. E.

Private, Company C, 70th Regiment N.C. Troops (1st N.C. Junior Reserves)

J. E. was born in 1847 to Thomas and Margaret Worrell. J. E. worked as a farmer prior to enlisting in the Junior Reserves on May 24, 1864. No further records.

1957. Wrenn, John

Private, Company B, 48th Regiment N.C. Troops

John was born in 1824 to John and Patience Wrenn. John worked as a farmer, and, in 1850, he married Delilah Jane Rickard. John and Delilah would have five children, Kilby (1851), Robert (1854), John (1856), Mary (1859), and George (1861), before John was conscripted into service on February 10, 1863. He was detailed to serve as a teamster for the brigade of J. R. Cooke from August 1, 1863, to October 31, 1863. John returned to regular service in February 1864 and was reported present until he died of pneumonia in Richmond, Virginia, on June 1, 1864. He is buried in the Hollywood Cemetery in Richmond.

1958. Wright, Ambrose

Private, Company A, 42nd Regiment N.C. Troops

Ambrose was born in 1845 to Micajah and Holly Wright. Ambrose worked as a farmer prior to being conscripted into service on October 20, 1863. He was wounded in the shoulder at Cold Harbor, Virginia, in May 1864 but was reported present until captured at Battery Anderson, Fort Fisher, North Carolina, on December 24, 1864. Ambrose was confined at Point Lookout, Maryland, via Fort Monroe, Virginia, until June 17, 1865, when he was released after taking the oath of allegiance. No further records.

1959. Wright, Joseph F.

Private, Company A, 42nd Regiment N.C. Troops

Joseph was born in 1843 to Silas and Susan Wright. Joseph worked as a farmer prior to volunteering for service on March 25, 1862. For unreported reasons, Joseph was arrested at Petersburg, Virginia, on August 28, 1864, and was jailed at Richmond, Virginia. Joseph was last reported in prison and awaiting trial in October 1864. No further records.

1960. Wright, Silas

Private, Company A, 42nd Regiment N.C. Troops

Silas was born in 1822. Silas worked as a farmer in the southern district of Davidson County, and, in 1841, he married Susanna Stout. Silas and Susanna would have four children, Joseph (1843), Margaret (1847), Alexander (1849), and Ruth (1853), before Silas volunteered for service in Rowan County on March 21, 1862. He was reported present until discharged due to "chronic rheumatism" on May 26, 1863. Silas returned home to the Emmons township where he was last reported as living in 1880. No further records.

1961. Yarbrough, Charles A.

Private, Company B, 48th Regiment N.C. Troops

Charles was born on March 3, 1844, to Charles and Polly Wommack Yarbrough. Charles worked as a farmer prior to enlisting into service on July 30, 1862. He was hospitalized at Richmond, Virginia, with "phthisis" on November 8, 1862. Charles was issued a 60-day furlough. Charles returned in February 1863 and was reported present until killed in action at Wilderness, Virginia, on May 5, 1864.

1962. Yarbrough, John Thomas

Private, Company B, 48th Regiment N.C. Troops

John was born on February 1, 1839, to Charles and Polly Wommack Yarbrough. John worked as a farmer, and, in 1861, he married Amanda Jane Sink. John enlisted into service on July 30, 1862, and was reported present through August 1864. The roll of honor states that John "displayed great courage at Fredericksburg, Virginia, on December 13, 1862." John often served as a blacksmith and as a teamster during his term of service. He was paroled at Greensboro, North Carolina, on May 3, 1865. After the war, John returned to his young wife in the Lexington area. John and Amanda would have seven children: Amelia (1866), George (1870), Ellen (1873), Mary (1876), John (1879), Della (1880), and Cora (1883). He was a citizen of Lexington and a member of the A. A. Hill Camp, United Confederate Veterans. John lived in the Lexington area until his death on July 20, 1925. He is buried in the Lexington City Cemetery.

1963. Yarbrough, Pleasant Addison

Private, Company B, 48th Regiment N.C. Troops

Pleasant was born in 1838 to the Reverend Aaron and Elizabeth Wommack Yarbrough. Pleasant worked as a farmer, and, in 1859, he married Ellen Owens. Pleasant and Ellen would have two children die in infancy prior to 1861, and in 1861 Ellen herself died. Pleasant volunteered for service on March 6, 1862, and was mortally wounded at King's School House, Virginia, on June 25, 1862. Pleasant died the next day. In the package sent home to his father, Captain A. A. Hill enclosed some Confederate script, a receipt for his last pay ration, and a gold ring. It is believed that the gold ring was Pleasant's wedding band, which he wore until his death.

1964. Yarbrough, Robert A.

Private, Company B, 48th Regiment N.C. Troops

Robert was born in 1837 to Charles and Polly Wommack Yarbrough. Robert worked as a farmer and was planning to take over his father's plantation. On January 18, 1856, Robert married Margaret Shemwell, daughter of Dr. Obediah Shemwell. Robert and Margaret would have two children, Whitson (1856) and Charles (1860), before Robert volunteered for service on March 4, 1862. He died of pneumonia in a Charlottesville, Virginia, hospital on November 19, 1862.

1965. Yarbrough, William G.

Private, Perquimans Beaureguards Company D, 27th Regiment N.C. Troops

William was born in 1825 to Zacariah and Hannah Stout Yarbrough. When his father died in 1857, his mother remarried and moved to Iowa. William chose to remain in the county and was a teacher prior to being conscripted into service at Camp Holmes, North Carolina, on March 21, 1864. He died of disease at the home of his maternal grandfather on August 20, 1864. He is buried at Reeds Baptist Church.

Plantation home of Joseph Yokely, built in 1857 (Touart, *Building the Backcountry*).

1970. Yokely, Joseph

Private, Confederate Guards
Company K, 48th Regiment N.C. Troops

Joseph was born on January 24, 1836, to David and Mary Yokely. Joseph worked as an overseer on his father's small plantation prior to being conscripted into service on August 8, 1862. He deserted one month later, on September 8, 1862. On August 16, 1864, Joseph married Cordelia Hines. After the war, Joseph returned home to the Abbott's Creek area where he and Cordelia would have three children: James (1866), Mary (1871), and John (1875). Joseph worked as a farmer in the Abbott's Creek township until his death on February 25, 1923. He is buried at Mount Vernon United Methodist Church.

1966. Yearby, Allen

Private, Company B, 48th Regiment
N.C. Troops

Allen was born in 1834. Allen worked as a farmer in the Lexington township, and, in 1859, he married Susan A. Smith. Allen and Susan would have a daughter, Ann (1860), before Allen volunteered for service on March 17, 1862. He was reported present until wounded in action at Reams' Station, Virginia, on August 25, 1864. Allen died of his wounds sometime shortly thereafter.

1967. Yokely, Charles Jefferson

Private, Confederate Guards
Company K, 48th Regiment N.C. Troops

Charles was born in 1840 to Samuel and Chloe Charles Yokely. Charles worked as a farmer prior to being conscripted into service on August 8, 1862. He deserted one month later, on September 8, 1862. Charles returned home to the Abbott's Creek area, where, in 1865, he married Polly Teague. Charles and Polly would have two children: Polly (1866) and Mary (1870). Charles lived in the Abbott's Creek area and helped to found Wallburg Baptist Church. Charles died on November 19, 1901, and is buried at Wallburg Baptist Church.

1968. Yokely, David Pinkney

Private, Confederate Guards
Company K, 48th Regiment N.C. Troops

David was born on April 9, 1843, to Samuel and Chloe Charles Yokely. David worked as a farmer prior to being conscripted into service on August 8, 1862. He deserted one month later, on September 8, 1862. David returned to the Abbott's Creek area where, on December 24, 1865, he married Emeline Louisa Clodfelter. David and Emeline would not have any children, and she died in 1887. David married Ellen M. in 1891. David and Ellen remained together until his death on August 6, 1926. He is buried at Wallburg Baptist Church.

1969. Yokely, Jacob Mock

Private, Company A, 42nd Regiment
N.C. Troops

Jacob was born in 1846 to Samuel and Mary Yokely. Jacob worked as a farmer prior to volunteering for service on November 26, 1861. He was reported present through October 1864 and, according to pension records, was wounded at Cold Harbor, Virginia, in May 1863. After the war, Jacob returned to the Thomasville area, where, on October 1, 1865, he married Sallie Yokely. Jacob and Sallie would have seven children: Mary (1873), John (1875), William (1876), Jeanette (1879), Annie (1881), Felix (1884), and David (1888). Jacob lived in the North Thomasville township until his death on April 15, 1927. He is buried at Fairview United Methodist Church.

1971. Yokely, Samuel

Private, Carolina Rangers
Company B, 10th Virginia Cavalry
Regiment

Samuel was born in 1847 to Samuel and Chloe Charles Yokely. Samuel worked as a farmer prior to volunteering at age 14 in Davie County on October 29, 1861. He was reported present until reported absent, sick with gonorrhea, at Charlottesville, Virginia, on April 24, 1864. Samuel recovered from his ailment and returned to duty four days later. Samuel was reported present through December 31, 1864, when he received a clothing ration. After the war, Samuel returned home to the Abbott's Creek township, where, on April 8, 1865, he married Emily Swaim. Samuel and Emily would have eight children, Andrew (1866), Callie (1867), Galveston (1869), Sam (1871), David (1874), Sarah (1876), John Lemuel (1879), and Robert Lee (1887), before Emily died in 1888. Samuel married Julia in 1894; the two would not have any children. He was a member of the A. A. Hill Camp, United Confederate Veterans. Samuel worked as a farmer in the Abbott's Creek township until his death in 1938; he had been the third oldest living veteran in the county. He is buried at Wallburg Baptist Church.

1972. York, Evander I.

Private, Holtsburg Guards
Company A, 54th Regiment N.C. Troops

The York homeplace, remodeled in 1910, was one of the more impressive homes in the Abbott's Creek township (Touart, *Building the Backcountry*).

Evander was born in 1842 in Davie County, North Carolina. Evander came to Davidson County in the early 1850s to work in the mines. Evander worked as a miner prior to enlisting on an unreported date. He was reported present until captured at Rappahannock Station, Virginia, on November 7, 1863. Evander was confined at Point Lookout, Maryland, until he died of typhoid fever on February 29, 1864. He is buried in the Point Lookout National Cemetery.

1973. Young, Adam

Private, Chatam Light Infantry Company G, 48th Regiment N.C. Troops

Adam was born in 1838 to Barnabus and Lucy Ann Young. Adam worked as a farmer and was married to Margaret prior to being conscripted into service on August 14, 1862. He was wounded in the foot at Fredericksburg, Virginia, on December 13, 1862. Adam was taken to a field hospital where his foot was probably taken off before he was transferred to Lynchburg, Virginia. Adam died of gangrene from his wounds at Lynchburg on January 1, 1863.

1974. Young, Andrew Jackson

Private, Holtsburg Guards Company A, 54th Regiment N.C. Troops

Andrew was born on May 5, 1840, to Andrew and Margaret Young. Andrew worked as a farmer prior to being conscripted into service on June 7, 1862. He was discharged on an unreported date, but he reenlisted on January 1, 1863. Andrew was reported sick for two short periods and was wounded at Cedar Run, Virginia, on September 1, 1864. Andrew was reported present until captured at Fort Stedman, Virginia, on March 25, 1865. He was confined at Point Lookout, Maryland, until June 22, 1865, when he was released after taking the oath of allegiance. After the war, Andrew returned home to the Boone township, where, in 1866, he married Mary. Andrew and Mary would have seven children: Jane (1867), Amanda (1870), Ida (1875), Maggie (1878), Noah (1883), John (1887), and Gracie (1889). Andrew worked as a farmer in the Boone area until his death on April 8, 1923. He is buried at Smith Grove Baptist Church.

1975. Young, Burrell B.

Second Lieutenant, 65th Regiment N.C. Militia (1861 organization)

Burrell was born on December 7, 1825, to Andrew and Margaret Young. Burrell worked as a farmer, and, in 1859, he married Isabella Ruth. Burrell and Isabella would have eight children: Joseph (1861), Julia (1863), Margaret (1866), Burrell (1869), William (1872), Wilmouth (1875), Robert Lee (1877), and Minnie (1879). Burrell was commissioned to serve as a second lieutenant in the Sand Hill District Company on December 16, 1861. After his service, Burrell returned to the Boone township, where he continued working on his farm and operated a sawmill as a side business. Burrell would be an active member of his church until his death on February 22, 1922. He is buried at Smith Grove Baptist Church.

1976. Young, Franklin

Private, Lexington Wildcats Company I, 14th Regiment N.C. Troops (4th N.C. Volunteers)

Franklin was born in 1838. Franklin worked as a farmer in the Lexington area prior to volunteering for service on May 14, 1861. He was reported present until he died of unreported causes on July 6, 1862.

1977. Young, George H.

Private, Lexington Wildcats Company I, 14th Regiment N.C. Troops (4th N.C. Volunteers)

George was born in 1835 to Frederick and Annie C. Young. George worked as a farmer prior to volunteering for service. He was wounded in the side during the Seven Days battles around Richmond, Virginia. George died of a gunshot wound to the side on July 6, 1862.

1978. Young, Hiram Stokes

Private, Company D, 48th Regiment N.C. Troops

Hiram was born in 1835 to John and Elizabeth Young. Hiram worked as a farmer, and, on April 7, 1853, he married Eliza Leonard. He was conscripted into service in Davidson County on August 8, 1862. Hiram was reported present until he died of "erysipelas" at a Richmond, Virginia, hospital on November 29, 1863.

1979. Young, J. John

Private, Lexington Wildcats Company I, 14th Regiment N.C. Troops (4th N.C. Volunteers) Company I, 1st Regiment U.S. Volunteer Infantry

John was born in 1838 to Barnabus and Lucy Ann Young. John worked as a farmer prior to volunteering for service on May 14, 1861. He was reported present until wounded in the left side at Malvern Hill, Virginia, on July 1, 1862. John recovered from his wounds and returned to service one week later, on July 9, 1862. He was reported present until captured in the vicinity of Spotsylvania Court House, Virginia, on May 19, 1864. John was confined at Point Lookout, Maryland, until he was released on May 28, 1864, after joining the Union Army. After he was mustered out of the Union Army, John returned home to the Boone township, where, in 1867, he married Elizabeth Shuler. John and Elizabeth would have six children: Lucy (1868), Dora (1870), Sarah (1872), Lula (1874), James (1876), and John (1880). John was last reported as living in the Tyro township in 1880. No further records.

1980. Young, James A.

*Private, Company K, 15th Regiment
    N.C. Troops (5th N.C. Volunteers)*

James was born on February 3, 1831, to Barnabus and Lucy Young. James worked as a farmer, and, on July 24, 1851, he married Elizabeth Hedrick. James and Elizabeth would have five children, Ellen (1851), George (1853), John (1856), America (1858), and Adam (1859), before James was conscripted into service in Wake County on July 15, 1862. James was reported present until wounded at Wilderness, Virginia, on May 6, 1864. James was sent to a Danville, Virginia, hospital on May 18, 1864, and was issued a furlough from that hospital in June 1864. James was reported absent on furlough through October 1864. After the war, James returned home to the Tyro township, where he and Elizabeth would have six more children: William (1865), Lucy (1866), Mary (1867), Benjamin (1869), James (1871), and Thaddeus (1873). James was called to the ministry in 1869 and served as the minister at Shiloh United Methodist Church for several years. James lived in the Tyro township until his death on December 13, 1910. He is buried at Shiloh United Methodist Church.

1981. Young, James Andrew

14th Battalion, N.C. Home Guard

James was born in 1844. James worked as a farmer and was denied exemption from the Home Guard on March 13, 1864. After his service, James remained at home in the Boone township. The race of this Guardsman is unknown. James was living as a 16-year-old boarder with a white family in 1860, and his race was not mentioned. In 1880, however, the only James A. Young with a birthdate of 1844 was noted as being "mulatto," and there is a James A. Young buried at New Jersey African Methodist Episcopal Zion Church. No further records.

1982. Young, John Henry

*Second Lieutenant, 66th Regiment
    N.C. Militia (1861 organization)*

John was born in 1830 to John and Elizabeth Young. John worked as a miller in the Boone area, and, in 1850, he married Eliza. John and Eliza would have seven children: John (1852), Mary (1855), Sarah (1858), Cynthia (1860), Eliza and Alice (1866), and Eugenia (1866). John was commissioned to serve as a second lieutenant in the Reeds District Company on December 16, 1861. He apparently left the militia and served in the Home Guard, as a March 16, 1864, letter to Lt. Colonel Jesse Hargrave reads: "Tell Mr. J. H. Young he is not exempt and must report for service in your Home Guard." John lived and worked as a farmer and as a small miller in the Boone township through 1900. No further records.

1983. Young, Lewis F.

*Private, Holtsburg Guards
Company A, 54th Regiment N.C. Troops*

Lewis was born in 1846 to Phillip and Catharine Young. Lewis worked as a farmer prior to volunteering on his 18th birthday on June 8, 1864. He was reported present until captured at Farmville, Virginia, on April 6, 1865. Lewis was confined at Newport News, Virginia, until June 26, 1865, when he was released after taking the oath of allegiance. No further records.

1984. Young, Thomas

*Second Lieutenant, 65th Regiment
    N.C. Militia (1861 organization)*

Thomas was born on July 25, 1827. Thomas worked as an operator of a flour mill, and on December 18, 1849, he married Catharine Beck. Thomas and Catharine would have three children: Clarinda (1851), Alfred (1854), and Delilah (1857). Thomas was commissioned to serve as a second lieutenant in the Silver Hill District Company on December 26, 1861. After his service, Thomas continued as a miller, operating one of the most profitable mills in the Silver Hill/Conrad Hill area. Thomas lived in the Silver Hill township until his death on January 9, 1908. He is buried at Beck's United Church of Christ.

1985. Young, William M.

*Private, Lexington Wildcats
Company I, 14th Regiment N.C. Troops
    (4th N.C. Volunteers)*

William was born in 1836 to Barnabus and Lucy Ann Young. William worked as a farmer prior to volunteering for service on May 14, 1861. He was reported present until he died of unreported causes in Richmond, Virginia, on July 17, 1862.

1986. Younts, Franklin

*Private, Carolina Rangers
Company B, 10th Virginia Cavalry
    Regiment*

Franklin was born on August 29, 1842, to Samuel and Anna Grimes Younts. Franklin was a student prior to volunteering for service in Davie County on October 29, 1861. He was reported present until captured at Rapidan Station, Virginia, on October 11, 1863. Franklin was confined at Point Lookout, Maryland, until August 31, 1864, when he was paroled and transferred to City Point, Virginia, for exchange. As soon as Franklin was exchanged on October 11, 1864, he was hospitalized in Richmond, Virginia. Franklin was last reported present when he drew a clothing ration while in the hospital on October 22, 1864. After the war, Franklin returned home to the Tyro township, where, on October 18, 1866, he married Delilah Palmer. Franklin and Delilah would have two children, Erastus (1869) and Mary (1874), before her death in 1878. Several years later, in 1895, Franklin married Melinda Sharpe. Franklin and Melinda would have two children: Annie (1895) and Sarah (1898). Franklin continued to work as a farmer into his advanced years. Franklin died on July 11, 1927. He is buried at Lebanon Lutheran Church.

Isaiah L. Younts and his wife, Susannah (Richard L. Conrad).

1987. Younts, Isaiah Lindsey

Private, Company B, 48th Regiment N.C. Troops

Isaiah was born on July 9, 1844, to Samuel and Anna Grimes Younts. Isaiah worked as a farmer and as a distiller, operating a liquor still, which eventually became his primary source of income. He was commissioned as a producer of liquor for the Confederate government but was conscripted anyway on August 8, 1862. Isaiah deserted from service at Sharpsburg, Maryland, on September 17, 1862, returning home in order to "check his business." Apparently his contract was renewed, and Isaiah was exempted from service again. After the war, Isaiah married Susannah Elizabeth Clodfelter. Isaiah and Susan would have six children: Charles (1871), Elenora (1874), Minnie (1877), Marvin (1878), Roscoe (1881), and Flavius (1884). Isaiah worked as a farmer, but he did continue to operate what his family called "the business" into the 1900s. Isaiah resided in the Old Soldiers' Home in Raleigh, North Carolina, in his later years and stayed there until his death on April 2, 1912. He is buried at Rich Fork Baptist Church.

1988. Younts, John F.

Private, Lexington Wildcats Company I, 14th Regiment N.C. Troops (4th N.C. Volunteers)

John was born in 1842. John worked as a farmhand for Dr. Obediah Shemwell prior to volunteering for service on May 14, 1861. He was reported present through August 1864. John was paroled at Greensboro, North Carolina, on May 16, 1865. After the war, John married Mary prior to 1880, when Laura, their daughter, was born. John was lasted reported as living in the Lexington township in 1900. No further records.

1989. Younts, Peter C.

Private, Company H, 48th Regiment N.C. Troops

Peter was born in 1842 to George and Mary Younts. Peter worked as a farmer prior to being conscripted into service on August 8, 1862. He was promoted to sergeant on November 1, 1862, and was reported present until furloughed for 60 days because of sickness in January 1863. Peter failed to return from his furlough, was listed as absent without leave, and was reported under arrest on October 9, 1863. He was reduced in rank to private in January 1864, and was killed in action at Reams' Station, Virginia, on August 25, 1864.

1990. Younts, Rufus A.

Private, Company C, 70th Regiment N.C. Troops (1st N.C. Junior Reserves)

Rufus was born in 1847 to John and Susannah Younts. Rufus worked as a farmer prior to enlisting in the Junior Reserves on May 24, 1864. After the war, Rufus returned home to the Conrad Hill township, where he was working as a carpenter in 1870. In 1875, Rufus married Minerva. Rufus and Minerva would have five children: Walker (1876), Columbus (1878), Dora (1879), John (1884), and Frank (1890). Rufus lived in the Conrad Hill township until his death in 1918. He is buried at Holly Grove Lutheran Church.

1991. Younts, William Clark

Private, Lexington Wildcats Company I, 14th Regiment N.C. Troops (4th N.C. Volunteers)

William was born in 1844. William worked as a farmer prior to volunteering for service on May 14, 1861. He was reported present until wounded in a skirmish in the vicinity of Bristoe Station, Virginia, on October 15, 1863. William rejoined the company in January 1864 and was reported present until paroled at Appomattox Court House, Virginia, on April 9, 1865. After the war, William returned home to the Lexington area, where, on September 20, 1866, he married Sarah Sharpe. William and Sarah moved out of the county prior to 1870. No further records.

1992. Younts, William I.

Private, Davidson Guards
Company A, 21st Regiment N.C. Troops
(11th N.C. Volunteers)

William was born in 1841 to Christian and Catharine Younts. William worked as a farmer, and, in 1859, he married Barbara. William and Barbara would have a daughter, Eliza (1860), before William volunteered for service on May 8, 1861. He was reported present until wounded at Winchester, Virginia, on May 25, 1862. William died from his wounds five days later.

1993. Zimmerman, David

Private, Company H, 15th Regiment
N.C. Troops (5th N.C. Volunteers)

David was born on December 7, 1840, to George and Elizabeth Zimmerman. David worked as a farmer, and, on November 20, 1860, he married Nancy Evans. David and Nancy would have a son, Joseph (1862), before David was conscripted into service in Wake County on July 15, 1862. He was reported present until discharged due to ill health on October 3, 1863. After he returned home, David continued to work on his farm and helped out with the needs of the Arcadia community. In 1865, three-year-old Joseph died of pneumonia. Sadly, he was the only child which the couple would have. David died in his sleep three years later, on April 21, 1868. He is buried at Mount Olivet United Methodist Church.

1994. Zimmerman, George Washington

Sergeant, Booe's Partisan Rangers
Company H, 63rd Regiment N.C. Troops
(5th N.C. Cavalry)

George was born on March 17, 1839. George worked as a farmer prior to enlisting in Davie County on July 8, 1862.

Emanuel, son of George W. Zimmerman, pauses with his family for this ca. 1900 photograph in front of the house his father built shortly before his death (Touart, *Building the Backcountry*).

He was mustered in as a corporal and was promoted to sergeant on August 1, 1863. George was reported present through February 1865. After the war, George married Martha Jane Teague in 1867. George and Martha would have only one child, Emanuel (1875), while living in the Abbott's Creek/Arcadia area. George worked as a farmer in the Arcadia township until his death on August 14, 1903. He is buried at New Friendship Baptist Church.

1995. Zimmerman, Jackson G.

Private, Carolina Rangers
Company B, 10th Virginia Cavalry
Regiment

Jackson was born on December 12, 1840. Jackson worked as a farmer in the northern district of Davidson County prior to enlisting in Davie County on May 13, 1862. He was reported present through December 31, 1864, when he was issued a clothing ration, and was paroled at Lexington, North Carolina, on June 9, 1865. After the war, Jackson returned home to the Arcadia township, where, on May 3, 1875, he married Sarah Sappenfield. Jackson and Sarah would move to the Shady Grove township in Davie County prior to 1878; they settled in the Elbaville area. Jackson worked as a farmer in Davie County until his death on March 24, 1894. He is buried at Elbaville United Methodist Church.

1996. Zimmerman, John

Private, Company H, 15th Regiment
N.C. Troops

John was born in 1843. John worked as a farmer in the northern district of Davidson County prior to being conscripted into service in Wake County on July 15, 1862. He died of pneumonia in a Richmond, Virginia, hospital on September 27, 1862.

Bibliography

Manuscripts and Collections

"The Civil War Recollections of Richard Barton Myers."
Davidson County Public Library, Lexington, NC.
Davidson County Genealogical Society.
Hargrave Collection. Davidson County Public Library,
Lexington, NC. Clement Hargrave.
Henry Reeves Papers. Davidson County Public Library, Lex-
ington, NC. Davidson County Genealogical Society.
Julius L. Schaub Collection (1861–1948). Troupe County,
Georgia Archives, LaGrange, GA. Troupe County
Historical Society.

Newspapers

Charlotte Western Democrat
Denton Orator
Greensboro Patriot and Flag
Lexington Dispatch
Spirit of the Age, Raleigh, NC
Thomasville Times

Periodicals

Confederate Veteran. 40 vols. 1893–1932.
Genealogical Journal. Vols. 15–18. 1995–1999.
Methodist Protestant Herald. 1912.

Public Documents

Federal Census of Caldwell County, NC: 1870
Federal Census of Catawba County, NC: 1870, 1880
Federal Census of Davidson County, NC: 1850, 1860,
1870, 1880, 1900, 1910
Federal Census of Davie County, NC: 1850, 1870, 1880
Federal Census of Forsyth County, NC: 1870, 1880,
1900
Federal Census of Guilford County, NC: 1850, 1870,
1900
Federal Census of Montgomery County, NC: 1870
Federal Census of North Carolina: 1820, 1840
Federal Census of Randolph County, NC: 1870, 1880, 1900
Federal Census of Rowan County, NC: 1850, 1870, 1880,
1900
Federal Census of South Carolina: 1840
Federal Census of Cocke County, TN: 1870
Federal Census of Greene County, TN: 1870
Federal Census of Carroll County, VA: 1870, 1880
Federal Census of Patrick County, VA: 1870, 1880
Federal Census of Virginia: 1840, 1850
Register of Deaths of Davidson County, NC
Register of Deaths, Forsyth County, NC
Register of Deaths, Montgomery County, NC
Register of Deaths, Rowan County, NC
Register of Deeds, Davidson County, NC
Register of Marriages, Davidson County, NC
Register of Marriages, Rowan County, NC

PUBLISHED WORKS

Anderson, Thelma. *The Workman Family History*. Salt Lake City, UT: Publisher's Press, 1962.

Bietzell, Edwin W. *Point Lookout Prison Camp for Confederates*. Baltimore: Gateway Press, 1982.

Bradley, Stephen A., ed. *North Carolina Confederate Militia Officers Roster*. Wilmington, NC: Broadfoot, 1992.

_____. *North Carolina Militia and Home Guards Records (Abstracts)*. Wilmington, NC: Broadfoot, 1994.

Byerly, Wesley G. *The Byerlys of Carolina*. 3 vols. Hickory, NC: Economy Printers, 1966–76.

Clark, Walter, ed. *Histories of the Several Regiments and Battalions from North Carolina in the Great War 1861–1865*. 5 vols., Raleigh, NC: E. M. Uzzell, 1901.

Davis, Eleanor. *Davis: A Quaker Family Genealogy*. Baltimore, MD: Gateway Press, 1895.

Driver, Robert J. *10th Virginia Cavalry*. Lynchburg, VA: H. E. Howard, 1982.

Easter, Louise E. *The Descendants of Michael Easter*. Bladensburg, MD: Genealogy Recorders, 1961.

Fritts, Gregory, and Patricia Fritts. *The Fritts Family Heritage, Vol. 1*. Gary, IN: Becker Impressions, 1979.

"Hargraves Since the Civil War." *Who's Who* series. New York: Family News, 1997.

Hartman, Donald, and Jeanine Hartman. *The Glattfelders in America*. Toole, UT: Family Heritage, 1993.

Hendricks, Garland. *Saints and Sinners in the Jersey Settlement*. Lexington: Jersey Historical, Inc., 1965.

Heuss, Lois I. Hotchkiss, ed. *Christian Bodenhamer of Rowan County, North Carolina, and His Descendants*. Marceline, MO: Eaton and Walsworth, 1979.

Ingersoll, Louise. *Lanier*. Washington, DC: Goetz, 1965.

Jordan, W. T., and Louis Manarin. *North Carolina Troops 1861–1865: A Roster*. Raleigh, NC: NC Department of Cultural Resources, Division of History and Archives.

Lomax, John B. *Samuel Lomax and His Descendants*. Menlo Park, CA: Sonoma, 1991.

_____. *Thomas Lomax and His Descendants*. Menlo Park, CA: Sonoma, 1995.

_____. *John Lomax and His Descendants*. Menlo Park, CA: Sonoma, 1997.

Mast, Greg. *State Troops and Volunteers: A Photographic History of North Carolina's Civil War Soldiers*. Raleigh, NC: NC Department of Cultural Resources, Division of History and Archives, 1995.

Moore, John W., ed. *Roster of N.C. Troops in the War Between the States*. 4 vols. Raleigh, NC: Edwards & Broughton, 1882.

Morris, Lewis. *Along the Way*. Marceline, MO: Eaton and Walsworth, 1996.

Neese, Edward H. *Kanoy–Canoy–Knoy Family History*. Baltimore, MD: Gateway Press, 1988.

Neese, Rev. James E. *The Dutch Settlement on Abbott's Creek: A History of Pilgrim Reformed*. Winston-Salem, NC: Hunter, 1979.

Nelson, Martha R. *John and Sarah and Other Redwines*. Baltimore, MD: Gateway Press, 1990.

Nine, W. G., and Ronald Wilson, eds. *The Appomattox Paroles*. Lynchburg, VA: H. E. Howard, 1989.

Sandrock, Marguerita, ed. *Our Family Tree: The Saga of Smith*. Winston-Salem, NC: Martin, 1998.

Sheets, Rev. Henry A. *A History of the Liberty Baptist Association*. Raleigh, NC: Edwards and Broughton, 1907.

Sink, M. Jewell, and Mary Green. *Wheels of Faith and Courage: A History of Thomasville, North Carolina*. High Point, NC: Hall, 1952.

_____. *Pathfinders Past and Present: A History of Davidson County*. High Point, NC: Hall, 1958.

Stanley, Hartman, and Sheck, compilers. *Forsyth County, North Carolina, Cemetery Records*. 5 vols. Winston-Salem, NC: Hunter, 1978.

Stokes, Violet M. *Sink Descendants*. Lexington, NC: Young Graphics, 1983.

Surratt, Laura, and Norman Surratt. *Surratt/Sarratt Families 1715–1980*. Fresno, CA: Pioneer, 1980.

The Heritage of Davidson County. Winston-Salem, NC: Hunter, 1982.

Touart, Paul. *Building the Backcountry: An Architectural History of Davidson County, North Carolina*. Charlotte, NC: Delmar, 1987.

Trotter, William R. *Silk Flags and Cold Steel: The Piedmont (The Civil War in North Carolina, v. I)*. Winston-Salem, NC: John F. Blair, 1991.

Tussey, W. Glenn. *Gersham Tussey and His Kin*. Earlysville, VA: Halcyon House, 1992.

UNPUBLISHED AND SELF-PUBLISHED WORKS

Beck, Kevin. "Beck Families of Davidson County, North Carolina." May 1993.

Burkhart, Marie C. "Descendants of George and Catharina Burkhart 1759–1987." 1987.

Cast, Marian Lopp. "The Laup-Lopp Genealogy." 1989.

Cook, Gerald W. "The Last Tarheel Militia, 1861–1865." 1987.

Cox, Eliza B. Ambrose N. Cox, Sr. Descendants 1772–1972. 1973.

Craver, Kathleen. "Family Tree Stories." 1986.

Crotts, Henry L. "The Crotts Trail." 1984.

Davis, Mynra C., and Carroll Clodfelter. "Descendants of George Clodfelter and Christina Grimes." 1984.

Delap, Fred. "Delap, Delapp, Dunlap Family Tree." July 1994.

Dinken, Pat S., and T. Walter Sneading, eds. "Descendants of David S. Westmoreland." December 1993.

DiRamio, Virginia E., ed. "Federal Census of Davidson County, North Carolina, 1850–1880, 1900–1910." 1986–91.

Elgin, J. Hoover. "Genealogy of George and Margaret Hoover and Their Descendants." 1979.

Elliot, Daniel. "The Descendants of Abraham Grubb." 1997.

Ellis, John A., and Margaret Hiatt. "The Ellis Family Record." July 1966.

Essick, Foil. "The Family of Noah and Dolly Leonard Essick." 1980.

Everhart, Doris G. "Christian Eberhard and Allied Families 1764–1994." 1994.

Farabee, Lewis T. "Genealogy of the Farabees in America." 1917.

Fogler, William W. "Family Records." 2 vols. 1966, 1976.

Freedle, Peggy M. "Freedle Family History." 1995.

Fritz, James D., comp. "Ancestors and Descendants of James H. Fritts." 1989.

Fulbright, Beverly. "The Levi Rhodes Family Tree." January 1997.

Gobble, Luther L. "The Gobbel Family of Rowan." 1976.

Goodman, Ruth, and Henry Goodman, eds. "The Ancestors of Walter Augustus Everhart." September 1997.

Hedrick, Rev. Aubry W. "The Hedrick Family." 2 vols. 1964, 1970.

Hege, Mike. "The Hege and Pugh Families." June 1997.

Heuss, Louis Hotchkiss. "Frederick Goss of Rowan County, North Carolina, and His Descendants." 1968.

High, Mary F. "A History of the Farabee Family." 1975.

Hinson, Marie L., comp. "Marriages of Davidson County, North Carolina." 2 vols. 1992, 1993.

Hoffman, Robert H. "Hoens/Hanes Family." November 1997.

Howard, Joshua. "Forgotten Heroes: Davidson County, North Carolina, in the War between the States." 1997.

Hughes, Joyce Flowers. "Cloninger: Our Heritage, Our Children." 1990.

Hunt, H. R., and James Sutphin. "The History and Genealogy of the George Michael Hunt Family." April 1993.

Leonard, C. Ronald, ed. "The Leonard Family." 1967.

Leonard, Frances Wagner, et al., eds. "'Old' Jacob Wagner of Davidson (Old Rowan) County and Some of His Descendants." 1984.

Link, Robert, comp. "The Joseph W. Link Collection of Private Papers." 1997.

McCrary, Nancy L. "The Kinney Family: Descendants of Ebenezer and Hannah Floyd Kinney." 1995.

Medlin, Claude V. "The History of the Family of Nathaniel Medlin." 1993.

Pace, John H. "Reeds X Roads Baptist Church: An Arm Which Became a Body." 1991.

Phillips, Margaret J. "The Descendants of John Watford 1639–1995." 1995.

Regan, Randy, comp. "Leonard and Related Families." 1992.

_____. "The Descendants of Henry Shoaf." 1993.

_____. "The Descendants of Adam Glattfelder (1547–)." May 1993.

_____. "The Descendants of George Miller, Sr. (?–1791)." 1994.

_____. "The Descendants of Jacob Zink/Sink." 1994.

_____. "The Descendants of Johann G. Meir, Sr." 2 vols. May 1994.

_____. "The Descendants of Henry Raper (1669–1735)." July 1994.

Rickard, Aileen B. "The Rickard Family History." January 1991.

Sheek, Ann Ellis. "A History of Twelve Generations of the Ellis Family 1636–1974." September 1984.

Sink, Loreta, and Randy Regan, comp. "The Descendants of John N. Michael (1696–)." 1994.

Sledge, Larry D. "Sledge Family History: 1608–1989." December 1991.

Sowers, Betty. "Koontz and Heitman Family History." 1996.

_____. "Davidson County Civil War Veterans." March 1997.

Swicegood, Frank, et al., eds. "Cemetery Records of Davidson County." 8 vols. 1985–1989.

Watford, Christopher M. "North Carolina's Infantry: Regiments, Battalions, and Companies." 1996.

_____. "The Lexington Wildcats: Company I, 14th North Carolina." 1998.

_____. "Roster of Confederate Soldiers from Davidson County." 1998.

FAMILY HISTORY FILE FOLDERS

(Courtesy of the Davidson County Public Library, Lexington Branch)

Badgett	Cecil #2	Essick
Beck	Charles #1, 2	Evans
Berrier	Clodfelter	Everhart
Black	Crouse	Farabee
Bodenheimer	Davis	Feezor
Briggs	Delapp	Ford
Brinkley	Disher	Foust
Carroll	Dorsett	Frank

Gallimore	Johnson	Leatherman	McCrary	Reeves	Tysinger
Grimes	Jones	Leonard #1–3	Martin	Roberts	Wagner
Grubb	Kennedy	Link/Linker	Miller #1, 2	Shemwell	Warner
Haden	Kesler	Livengood	Michael #2	Shipton	Warford
Hanes	Kepley	Loflin/Loftin	Myers #1, 2	Shoaf #1, 2	Williams
Hedrick #1, 2	Kimel	Lomax	Myrick	Smith #1, 2	Wilson
Hege	Kinney	Long	Payne	Snider	Yates
Heitman	Koontz #1–3	Lopp	Perryman	Stewart/Stuart	Yokely
Hill	Lambeth	Louya/Louja/	Phelps	Surratt	Young
Idol	Lanier	Louie	Phillips	Swicegood	Younts
Jackson	Lanning	McCarn	Raker	Thomas	Zimmerman

Index

Except as noted in italic type, references are to entry numbers.